PRACTICALS IN FINANCIAL ACCOUNTS

FOR B.COM. PART-II, C.A. INTER, ICWA,
BANKING EXAMINATION ETC.

VOLUME II

P.G. ITNAL

SECOND EDITION
REVISED AND ENLARGED

ATLANTIC PUBLISHERS AND DISTRIBUTORS

Published by
ATLANTIC PUBLISHERS AND DISTRIBUTORS
B-2, Vishal Enclave, Opp. Rajouri Garden, New Delhi-110 027
Phones : 5413460, 5429987

Sales Office
4215/1, Ansari Road, Darya Ganj, New Delhi-110 002
Phones : 3273880, 3285873, 3280451
Fax : 91-11-3285873
e-mail : info@atlanticbooks.com
web site : http://www.atlanticbooks.com

SECOND EDITION

Typeset at
APD Computer Graphics, Delhi

Printed in India at
Nice Printing Press, Delhi-51

Preface

There are many good books available dealing with theoretical aspects of the subject. The students studying the subject now-a-days attend classes for practical problems and their solutions rather than for theoretical aspects. Therefore, the main objective of this book is to provide solutions to the questions set at the university examinations. The solutions along with the Working Notes, calculations wherever necessary, help the students to understand the problems easily. In each of the topics covered, maximum possible number of problems of different varieties with satisfactory solutions have been made available. This will create greater confidence among the students in facing the examinations. Only on a few topics the important points and the relevant portion of theoretical aspect has been expressed in minimum words.

It is my sincere and honest effort to satisfy the students in the subject.

I hope that the students will welcome this book.

I welcome from my friends/colleagues, teaching the subject, the constructive suggestions and the honest expressions about the utility of the said book the purpose for which it is meant. This will help me to accommodate their valuable suggestions.

I am very much thankful to the Publishers, in particular Dr. K.R. Gupta, Managing Director of M/s Atlantic Publishers and Distributors, New Delhi.

P.G. ITNAL

Contents

Theory Questions

Answer in *One* or *Two* sentences each

1. What is interim dividend? Who declares it?
2. What is Capital Profits?
3. What is Divisible Profits?
4. What is Amalgamation of Companies?
5. Define Holding Company.
6. What is Profit prior to Incorporation? Why it is calculated?
7. Give two advantages of Self-Balancing System?
8. What is Contingent Liability? Give two examples of Banking Company Contingent Liabilities.
9. What is Liquidator's Final Statement of Account?
10. What is Dividend Equalisation Fund?
11. How do you treat excess provisions for taxation made in earlier years?
12. What do you mean by Absorption of a Company?

[K.U.D., April 1998(N)]

Answer any *ten* Questions in *One* or *Two* sentences each

1. What do you mean by Absorption of a Company?
2. How do you treat the following in the case of Amalgamation of Companies?
   (a) Worker's Savings Deposits.
   (b) Workmen's Compensation Fund.
3. What is Interim Dividend ? Who declares it?
4. How do you treat loss made by a company prior to Incorporation?
5. Mention any two examples of preferential creditors in case of liquidation of companies.
6. Define Holding Company.
7. How do you treat excess provisions for taxation made in earlier years?
8. What is meant by cost of control in Holding Company Account?

9. On what basis managerial remuneration is determined when a company has no profits or makes inadequate profits?
10. How do you treat a debt owed by an absorbing to an absorbed company?
11. What is Hire-Purchase system of sale?
12. What is Self-Balancing system of ledger keeping?

[K.U.D., April 1997(N)]

Answer any *ten* Questions of the following

1. What do you understand the term Purchase Consideration? How is it calculated?
2. What is consolidated Balance sheet? Is it a compulsory to prepare it?
3. What is a Liquidator's Statement of Account?
4. What is a contingent liability? Where do you show it in a Balance sheet?
5. What is Interest Suspense Account? When is it opened?
6. Give two objects of Self-Balancing system.
7. Why are profits prior to Incorporation ascertained separately?
8. Are capital profits available for payment of dividend? Give two examples of capital profits.
9. What is Dividend Equalisation Fund?
10. What do you mean by Preliminary Expenses? Give two examples.
11. What is Final Dividend? Who declares it?
12. How will you treat the Workmen's Compensation Fund on Amalgamation of Companies?

[K.U.D., October 1997(N)]

Answer any *ten* Questions

1. What is Capital Profit?
2. What is Final Dividend? Who declares it?
3. When will you recommend a company to undergo external Reconstruction?
4. What is Amalgamation of Companies?
5. How do you compute purchase consideration payable to selling company?
6. What is a Liquidator's Statement of Account?
7. What are the Rights of Debenture holders in respect of interest arrears in the event of liquidation of a company.

8. Why the consolidated Balance sheet of a Holding Company with its subsidiary company is prepared?
9. Why the shares held by a Holding Company in its Subsidiary Company are not shown in consolidated Balance sheet?
10. What is Interest Suspense Account?
11. What is General Ledger kept under Self-Balancing Ledger system?
12. Give two examples of Contingent Liabilities in a Banking Company.

[K.U.D., April 1996(N)]

Answer any *ten* Questions in *One* or *Two* sentences

1. What is Divisible Profit?
2. How are unclaimed dividend treated in company Account?
3. State two main bases on which expenses are bifurcated between periods before and after incorporation of a company.
4. What is Internal Reconstruction of a company?
5. How do you treat Absorption expenses paid by the purchasing company in the books of companies under merger?
6. Mention two advantages of Self-Balancing Ledger System.
7. What is Statutory Reserve created by a Banking Company?
8. How do you treat unrealised profits included in stocks of subsidiary company in preparing a consolidated Balance sheet of a Holding Co.?
9. How do you compute Liquidator's Remuneration on unsecured creditors in case of an Insolvent Company?
10. What is Instalment System of Selling?
11. Why Rebate on Bills is provided by a Banking Company?
12. What are the Self-Balancing Entries required to adjust transfer a Debtor's Balance to a Creditor's Account?

[K.U.D., October 1996(N)]

1

Joint Stock Company Accounts—I

(a) FINAL ACCOUNTS OF THE COMPANIES

The Joint Stock Companies Act specifies the prescribed form of prepairing Final Accounts of the Joint stock companies viz., preparation of (a) Profit & Loss A/c to indicate the business result i.e., the performance resulting in either Profit or Losses and also (b) Balance Sheet of the company existing its company capital and liabilities and the Assets position of the company. As per the provisions of the Joint Stock Companies Act, it is the responsibility of the Board of Directors to present. Profit and Loss A/c and Balance Sheet of the companies for the previous Accounting year, i.e. Financial year generally for the period of 12 months to the General Body of shareholders in the Annual General meeting.

The final Accounts i.e., (a) Profit & Loss A/c and (b) The Balance Sheet are to be prepared and duly certified by the qualified Auditor specified in the Act. Therefore the Chartered Accountant shall be an Auditor of the Joint Stock Company. The Auditor having examined in detail the Accounts of the Company, prepares Final Accounts : (a) Profit & Loss A/c and (b) The Balance Sheet for the year ending along with Audit Report. The provisions of the company Act specifies the functions of the Auditor responsibilities and the liabilities towards the Shareholders of the company and therefore the Final Accounts presented should disclose true and fair view of the state of affairs of the company at the end of the financial year and shall subject to the provisions of the companies Act in this regard.

From the above it is noticed that the Joint Stock Company may be carrying on business activities of trading and/or manufacturing, have to account the same, the items of expenditures and receipts pertaining to activities.

So, the Trading Account and/or manufacturing accounts are required to prepare along with Profit & Loss Account.

PRO-FORMA OF TRADING ACCOUNT AND/OR MANUFACTURING ACCOUNT

Manufacturing Account for the year ended....

Particulars		Particulars	
To Raw materials Opening stock	—	By Sales	—
Add : Purchase	—	By Purchase returns	—
To Manufacturing wages	—	By Closing stock	—

Particulars		Particulars	
To Carriage Inward	—		
To Gas	—		
To Fuel	—		
To Power	—		
To Gross Profit	—		
	—		—

Trading A/c for the year ended....

To Opening stock		By Sales	—
To Purchase		*Less* : Returns	—
Less : Returns	—	By Closing stock	—
To Carriage Inward	—		
To Gross Profit	—		
	—		—

Profit and Loss A/c for the year ended....

To Salaries	—	By Gross Profit	—
To Rent, Taxes etc.	—	By Incomes Received	—
To Postage telegram	—	(During the period)	
To Printing and stationery	—	By Incomes accrued	—
To Advertisement	—		
To General Expenses	—		
To Directors fee	—		
To Audit fees	—		
To Depreciation			
On Premises	—		
On Plant & Machinery	—		
On Furniture	—		
To Provision for doubtful debtors	—		
To Provision for Taxation	—		
To Net Profit	—		
	—		—

Profit and Loss Appropriation A/c for the year ended....

Particulars		Particulars	
To Provision for	—	By Net Profit	—
To Reserve Fund			
To Capital Redemption Reserve			
To Debenture Redemption fund	—		
To Income Tax Paid	—		
To Provision for Income Tax	—		

Particulars		Particulars	
To Proposed Dividend	—		
To Net Profit	—		
	—		—

Note : If interim dividend paid — appears in Trial Balance. It should be deducted from Final Dividend declared —
i.e. Proposed, Dividend —
Less : Interim Dividend paid —
Balance — Proposed dividend payable —

Balance Sheet as at 31-12-....

Liabilities	Amount	Assets	Amount
(1) *Share Capital*		(1) Fixed Assets	
Authorised		Goodwill	
No. of shares... of Rs.... each		Land & Building	
Issued Capital		Plant & Machinery	
No. of shares... of Rs.... each		Furnitures	
Subscribed and paidup		(2) Investments	
No. of shares... of Rs.... each		(3) *Current Assets*	
Less : Call in arrears		Stock	
Add : Forfeited shares		Debtors	
(2) *Reserves & Surplus*		Bills Receivable	
Capital Reserve		Bank Balance	
General Reserve		(4) *Miscellaneous Account*	
Share Premium		Preliminary Expenses	
Other specified Reserve		Discount on Issue of Debentures	
Sinking Fund		Prepaid Expenses	
Investment fluctuation Reserves		Interest Receivable	
Profit & Loss A/c			
(3) *Secured Loan*			
Debentures			
Interest on debentures			
(4) *Unsecured Loan*			
(5) *Current Liabilities & Provisions*			
(a) Sundry Creditors			
(b) Bills Payable			
Provisions			
Provision for taxation			
Outstanding Liabilities			
Dividend Payable :			
on Equity shares			
on Pref. shares			
	xxx		xxx

Problem No. 1

Ashok Co. Ltd. was incorporated on 1-7-1996, taking over the Business of Babu as from 1-4-1996. The following was the Profit and Loss Account for the year ended 31-3-1997.

Profit & Loss A/c for the year ended 31-3-1997

Particulars		Particulars	
To Salaries	1,44,000	By Gross Profit	2,80,000
To Rent and Rates	7,200	By Net Loss	12,000
To Office Expenses	48,000		
To Commission on Sales	32,000		
To Free Samples	8,000		
To Audit Fees	4,000		
To Depreciation	16,000		
To Interest on Debentures	12,000		
To Directors Fees	4,000		
To Formation Expenses	4,000		
To Printing and Stationery	8,000		
To Sundry Expenses	1,600		
To Bad Debts	3,200		
	2,92,000		2,92,000

Additional Information

(a) Sales upto 1-7-96 amounted to Rs. 3,20,000 and thereafter Rs. 4,80,000.

(b) Rent was paid Rs. 400 p.m.

(c) Bad Debt upto 30-6-1996 — Rs. 800.

Prepare, a Profit and Loss Account showing Profit or Loss prior to incorporation and after incorporation.

[K.U.D., April 1998 (N)]

Solution :

Profit & Loss A/c for the year ended 31-3-1997

Particulars	Basis	Total Rs.	Prior to Incorporation Rs.	After Incorporation Rs.	Particulars	Prior to Incorporation Rs.	After Incorporation Rs.	Total Rs.
To Salaries	Time 1:3	1,44,000	36,000	1,08,000	By Gross Profit Sales Ratio 2:3	1,12,000	1,68,000	2,80,000
To Rent and Rates		7,200			By Loss		50,000	
Ren – Rs.400 pm 400×12.40	actual 400pm	4,800	1,200	3,600	By Net Loss 50,000 −38,000			12,000
Rates	Time 1:3	2,400	600	1,800				

Particulars	Basis	Total Rs.	Prior to Incorpo-ration Rs.	After Incorpo-ration Rs.	Particulars	Prior to Incorpo-ration Rs.	After Incorpo-ration Rs.	Total Rs.
To Office Expenses	Time 1:3	48,000	12,000	36,000				
To Commission on Sales	Sales 2:3	32,000	12,800	19,200				
To Free Sample	Sales 2:3	8,000	3,200	4,800				
To Audit fees	Time 1:3	4,000	1,000	3,000				
To Depreci-ation	Time 1:3	16,000	4,000	12,000				
To Interest on Debentures	Co. Exp. after Co.	12,000	—	12,000				
To Directors fees	after	4,000	—	4,000				
To Formation Expenses	Co. Exp. after	4,000	—	4,000				
To Printing & Stationery	Time 1:3	8,000	2,000	6,000				
To Sundry Exp.	Time 1:3	1,600	400	1,200				
To Bad Debts	Actual	3,200	800	2,400				
To Net Profit		—	38,000	—				
Total		2,92,000	1,12,000	2,18,000		1,12,000	2,18,000	2,92,000

Note : Profit Prior to Incorporation Rs. 38,000
Loss after Incorporation Rs. 50,000
Net Loss Rs. 12,000

Basis for apportionments

Gross Profit Sales ratio — Sales upto 1-7-96 Rs. 3,20,000
after 1-7-96 Rs. 4,80,000
Sales Ratio 2:3

Time Basis : 1-4-96 to 1-7-96 3 months
1-7-96 to 31-3-97 9 months
Time Ratio 1:3

Problem No. 2

The following Profit and Loss Account by Praveen Ltd. Co. provided for the year ended 31-3-1997.

Profit & Loss A/c for the year ended 31-3-1997

Particulars	Rs.	Particulars	Rs.
To Salaries & Wages	4,90,000	By Gross Profit	22,90,000
To Directors fees	25,000	By Profit on Sales of	
To Repairs	1,50,000	Fixed Assets	1,00,000
To Depreciation	3,25,000	By Subsidy from Govt.	3,60,000
To General Charges	1,00,000		
To Scientific Research	87,500		
To Income tax	4,00,000		
To Interest on Debentures	1,25,000		
To Dev. Rebate Reserve	75,000		
To Proposed Dividend	3,00,000		
To Net Profit	6,72,500		
	27,50,000		27,50,000

The Depreciation as per section 350 works out to be Rs. 2,00,000 calculate the Remuneration payable to the Managing Director.

[K.U.D., April 1998(N)]

Solution :

Calculation of Net Profit

Net Profit			6,72,500
Add inadmissible deductions			
(1)	Depreciation	3,25,000	
(2)	Scientific Research	87,500	
(3)	Income Tax	4,00,000	
(4)	Dev. Rebate Reserve	75,000	
(5)	Propored Dividend	3,00,000	11,87,500
			18,60,000
Less Admissible deductions			
	Depreciation		2,00,000
Net Profit Adjusted			16,60,000

Managing Directors Remuneration

5% of Net Profit

Rs. 16,60,000 × 5% = Rs. 83,000

Managing Director's

Remunerations 5% on N.P. = Rs. 83,000

Alternatively

Gross Profit			22,90,000
Add Profit on sale of Fixed Assets		1,00,000	
Subsidy from Govt.			3,60,000
			27,50,000
Less Admissible deductions			
(1)	Salaries & Wages	4,90,000	
(2)	Directors fees	25,000	
(3)	Repairs	1,50,000	
(4)	Depreciation upto 350	2,00,000	
(5)	General Charges	1,00,000	
(6)	Int. on Debentures	1,25,000	10,90,000
	Net Profit Adjusted		16,60,000

Managing Director's Remuneration

5% on Net Profit

Rs. 16,60,000 × 5% = Rs. 83,000

Manag. Director's RemunerationRs. 83,000

Problem No. 3 (Extra 1)

Following is the Profit & Loss Account of AB Co. Ltd. for the year ending 31-3-1997. You are required to calcutate Managing Director's Remuneration as per the provisions of the Companies Act. Managing Director is entitled to a Commission of 5% on Net Profit of the Company.

Profit & Loss A/c for the year ended 31-3-1997

Particulars	Rs.	Particulars	Rs.
To Salaries & allowances	3,50,000	By Gross Profit	10,68,875
To Directors fees	7,875	By Profit on Sale of	
To Voluntary Compensation	10,500	Fixed Assets	1,40,000
To Rates and Taxes	17,500	By Premium on Issue	
To Insurance	6,563	of shares/debentures	30,625
To Sundry Expenses	40,687	By Interest on Investment	10,500
To Repairs	26,250	By Subsidy from Govt.	1,50,000
To Bad Debts	4,375		
To Interest on Bank O/D	23,887		
To Interest on Debentures	13,125		
To Loss on Sale of Invest.	21,875		
To Donations	52,500		
To Provisions for Doubtful Debts	12,500		
To Provisions for Income Tax	2,29,250		
To Scientific Research	45,000		
To Proposed Dividend	1,50,000		
To Net Profit	3,88,113		
	14,00,000		14,00,000

Note : (1) Donation allowed under the provisions of Income Tax

(2) Fixed Assets – Original Cost Rs. 1,75,000

Written down value of Fixed Assets 52,500

Sales Proceeds of Fixed Assets 1,92,500

Solution :

Calculations of Net Profit for the purpose of calculation of Managing Director's Remuneration

		Rs.	Rs.
Net Profit as per Profit & Loss A/c			3,88,113
Add inadmissible deductions :			
(1) Voluntary Compensation		10,500	
(2) Loss on sale of Investments		21,875	
(3) Donations	52,500		
Less admissible as per Income Tax	50,000		
Provisions Excess		2,500	
(4) Provision for Doubtful Debts		12,500	
(5) Scientific Research		45,000	
(6) Provision for Income Tax		2,29,250	
(7) Proposed Dividend		1,50,000	4,71,625
Total Profit			8,59,738
Less Admissible deductions :			
(1) Profit on Sales of Fixed Assets			
Sales price – Original Cost = Capital Profit			
(1,92,500 – 1,75,000) =		17,500	
(OR Written down value + Profit – Original Cost			
52,500 + 1,40,000 = 1,92,500 – 1,75,000 = 17,500)			
(2) Premium on Issue of Shares/Debentures		30,625	48,125
Adjusted Net Profit for Remuneration Payable to Managing Director			Rs. 8,11,613

Managerial Remuneration @ 5% on Net Profit

Adjusted N.P. 8,11,613 × 5/105 = Rs. 38,648

Adjusted Profit Rs. 8,11,613

Less 5% Commission 38,648

Net Profit after 5% Com. 7,72,965

Now 5% Com. on N.P. 7,72,965 × 5% = Rs. 38,648

Commission payable to Managing Director as Remuneration = Rs. 38,648

Problem No. 4

Dharwad Co. Ltd. was registered with a Nominal Capital of Rs. 15,00,000 divided into equity shares of Rs. 100 each on 31st March 1996. The following were the Ledger balances in the company's Books :

		Rs.
1.	Calls in arrears	18,750
2.	Stock on 1-4-1995	1,87,500
3.	Sundry Debtors	2,17,500
4.	Purchases	4,62,500
5.	Rent	12,000
6.	Debenture Interest	22,250
7.	General Reserve	62,500
8.	Equity shares fully paid	11,50,000
9.	Goodwill	62,500
10.	Cash in hand	6,125
11.	Directors fees	14,350
12.	Commission on sales	18,000
13.	Debentures	7,50,000
14.	Govt. Securities	1,50,000
15.	Sundry Creditors	1,25,000
16.	Plant and Machinery	9,00,000
17.	Fixtures	18,000
18.	Buildings	7,50,000
19.	Interim Dividend Paid	18,750
20.	General Expenses	12,250
21.	Bills Payable	95,000
22.	Profit and Loss Appropriation A/c (Cr.)	36,250
23.	Preliminary Expenses	12,500
24.	Freight	32,750
25.	Wages	2,12,000
26.	Cash at Bank	95,750
27.	Bad Debts	5,275
28.	Salaries	36,250
29.	Sales	1,03,750
30.	Provision for Bad Debts	8,750

The stocks on 31-3-1996 was estimated at Rs. 2,52,500. The following Adjustments have also to be made :

(1) Depreciate - Plant and Machinery by 10% p.a. and on Fixtures @ 5%.

(2) Wages include Rs. 25,000 paid for the construction of additional Rooms to the building.

(3) Final Dividend @ 5% to be provided.

(4) Preliminary expenses to be written off by 20%.

(5) Provision for bad debts to be maintained @ 5% on Sundry Debtors.

(6) Rs. 25,000 to be transferred to General Reserve.

(7) A provision for Income tax was to be made at Rs. 62,500.

Prepare Trading and Profit and Loss Account for the year ending 31-3-1996 and also Appropriation A/c and the Balance sheet as on that date.

[K.U.D., October 1997(N)]

Solution :

Trading A/c for the year ended 31-3-1996

Particulars		Rs.	Particulars	Rs.
To Stocks on 1-4-95		1,87,500	By Sales	10,37,500
To Purchases		4,62,500	By Stock on 31-3-96	2,52,500
To Freight Charges		32,750		
To Wages	2,12,000			
Less Wages paid for	25,000	1,87,000		
(Construction of room building capitalised)				
To Gross Profit (transferred) to Profit and Loss A/c		4,20,250		
		12,90,000		12,90,000

Profit and Loss A/c for the year ended 31-3-1996

Particulars		Rs.	Particulars	Rs.
To Salaries		36,250	By Gross Profit	4,20,250
To Rent		12,000		
To Debenture interest		22,250		
To Directors fees		14,350		
To Commission in sales		18,000		
To General Expenses		12,250		
To Preliminary Expenses (12,500 × 20%)		2,500		
To Bad Debt	5,275			
Add New Reserve	10,875			
On Drs. 217500 × 5%	16,150			
Less Old Reserve	8,750	7,400		

Particulars		Rs.	Particulars	Rs.
To Depreciation on Plant of Machinery				
9,00,000 × 10%	90000			
Fixtures 18,000 × 5%	900	90,900		
To Net Profit transferred to Profit & Loss Appropriation A/c		2,04,350		
		4,20,250		4,20,250

Profit and Loss Appropriation A/c

Particulars	Rs.	Particulars	Rs.
To General Reserve transferred	25,000	By Profit & Loss A/c Net Profit for the year	2,04,350
To Provision for Income Tax	62,500	*Add* Appropriation A/c Balance	36,250
To Proposed Dividend Final Dividend @5% On equity share capital Rs. 11,50,000	57,500		
To Net Profit transferred to B/s	95,600		
	2,40,600		2,40,600

Final Dividend @ 5% on equity share capital	11,50,000	57,500	*Note* : Final Dividend be calculated on Paidup Capital Subscribed Capital—	
Less Interim Dividend paid		18,750	fully paid	Rs. 11,50,000
			Less Calls in Arrears	18,750
To be paid shown in B/s on Liability side		38,750		Rs. 11,31,250
			Final Dividend @ 5% on 11,31,250	Rs. 56,562.50

Balance Sheet as at 31-03-1996

Liabilities	Rs.	Assets	Rs.	Rs.
Share Capital		Building	7,50,000	
Aurthorised		*Add* Wages for construct	25,000	7,75,000
15000 equity shares of Rs. 100 each	15,00,000	Plant of Machinery	9,00,000	
Subscribed capital		*Less* Depreciation 10%	90,000	8,10,000
11500 equity shares of		Fixtures	18,000	
Rs. 100 each		*Less* Depreciation @ 5%	900	17,100
fully called up	11,50,000	Stock on 31-3-96		2,52,500

Liabilities		Rs.	Assets	Rs.	Rs.
Less calls in arrears		18,750	Debtors	2,17,500	
		11,31,250	*Less* provision for		
Reserves & Surplus			D.D. @ 5%	10,875	2,06,625
General Reserve	62,500		Preliminary expenses	12,500	
Addition during the year	25,000	87,500	*Less* Written off 20%	2,500	10,000
Profit Appropriation A/c		95,600	Govt. Securities		1,50,000
Secued Loan :			Goodwill		62,500
Debentures		7,50,000	Cash in hand		6,125
Current Liabilities			Cash at Bank		95,750
Sundry creditors		1,25,000			
Bills payable		95,000			
Provisions					
Proposed Dividend	57,500				
Less Paid Dividend					
payable	18,750	38,750			
Provision for Income Tax		62,500			
		23,85,600			23,85,600

Problem No. 5

M. Company Ltd. was incorporated on 1-8-1995 to take over the Business of Basava as a going concern as from 1-4-1995. The Profit and Loss Account of the company for the year ending 31-3-1996 was as follows :

Profit and Loss A/c for the year ended 31-3-1996

Particulars	Rs.	Particulars	Rs.
To Salaries and Allowances	30,000	By Gross Profit	1,00,000
To Rent and Rates	11,500		
To Directors fees	1,500		
To Selling Expenses	2,000		
To Discount on Sales	500		
To Audit fees	2,250		
To Formation Expenses	900		
To Miscellaneous Expenses	750		
To Interest on Debentures	700		
To Interest to Vendors upto 30-9-95	3,000		
To Depreciation	1,200		
To Net Profit	45,700		
	1,00,000		1,00,000

The following is the further information :

(a) Rent was paid at Rs. 500 P.M. upto 1-8-95 and thereafter it was increased to Rs. 1,000 P.M.

(b) The average monthly sales for the first four months during the year was Rs. 30,000, whereas the average monthly sales for the subsequent period was Rs. 35,000.

Prepare the statement showing profit prior to Incorporation of the company.

[K.U.D., October 1997(N)]

Solution :

Note : Calculations of Basis for apportionment

(1) Sales — First four months — Monthly average 30,000 × 4 = 1,20,000

subsequent period 8 months — Monthly average 35,000 × 8 = 2,80,000

Total sales 4 month – 1,20,000 – 8 month 2,80,000

4 month 8 month ratio - 12 : 28

3 : 7

(2) Time Basis

1-4-95 1-8-95 31-3-96

4 : 8

1 : 2

Statement Showing Profit Prior to Incorporation
Profit and Loss A/c for the year ended 31-3-1996

Particulars	Total Rs.	Basis	Prior to Incorporation Rs.	After Incorporation Rs.	Particulars	Prior to Incorporation Rs.	After Incorporation Rs.
To Salaries & Allowances	30,000	Time 1:2	10,000	20,000	By Gross Profit Sales Ratio 3:7	30,000	70,000
To Rent Rs. 500 × 4 = 10,000 Rs. 1000 × 8	10,000	Time actual	2,000	8,000			
To Rates - 1500	1,500	Time 1:2	500	1,000			
To Directors fee	1,500	Co. exp.	—	1,500			
To Selling Exp.	2,000	Sales 3:7	600	1,400			
To Discount on sales	500	Sales 3:7	150	350			
To Audit fees	2,250	Time 1:2	750	1,500			
To Formation Exp.	900	Co. exp.	—	900			
To Miscellaneous Exp.	750	Time 1:2	250	500			

Particulars	Total Rs.	Basis	Prior to Incorporation Rs.	After Incorporation Rs.	Particulars	Prior to Incorporation Rs.	After Incorporation Rs.
To Interest on Debentures	700	Co. exp.	—	700			
To Interest to vendor upto 30-9-95	3,000	Period 4:2	2,000	1,000			
1-4-95 to 1-8-95 4:2		Time					
To Depreciation	1,200	1:2	400	800			
Net Profit	45,700	—	13,350	32,350			
			30,000	70,000		30,000	70,000

Problem No. 6

The Share capital of Shri Sar Ltd. consist of (a) 100000 Equity shares of Rs. 10 each Rs. 5 per share paid up. (b) 3000 10% Preference shares of Rs. 100 each fully paid up.

The company made a profit of Rs. 2,00,000 during the year ended 31-3-1995

The Directors have decided as follows :

(a) To transfer 20% to General Reserves

(b) To transfer Rs. 20,000 to Sinking Fund

(c) To pay dividend on preference shares and 15% on Equity share capital.

The tax Deduction at source is 20%.

Pass journal entries assuming that the unclaimed dividend after 42 days amounted to Rs. 10,000.

[K.U.D., April 1997(N)]

Solution :

Journal Entries		Dr. Rs.	Cr. Rs.
(1) Profit & Loss A/c	Dr	1,65,000	
To Genereal Reserve A/c			40,000
To Sinking Fund A/c			20,000
To Preference share Dividend Payable A/c			30,000
To Equity Share Dividend Payable A/c			75,000
[Being provisions made for			
(a) General Reserve Rs. 40,000 20% on 2,00,000			
(b) Transfer to Sinking Fund Rs. 20,000			
(e) Preference Share Dividend 10% on 3,00,000 and			
(d) Equity Share Dividend @ 15% on 5,00,000]			

Journal Entries		Dr. Rs.	Cr. Rs.
(2) Preference Share Dividend payable A/c	Dr	6,000	
Equity Share Dividend Payable A/c	Dr	15,000	
To Income Tax payable A/c			21,000
(being Income Tax deducted at source) 20% on 30,000 = 6,000; 20% on 75,000 = 15,000			
(3) Income Tax Payable A/c	Dr.	21,000	
To Bank A/c			21,000
(being Income Tax deducted at source deposited into Bank A/c for payment)			
(4) Dividend Banks (spl.) A/c	Dr	84,000	
To Bank A/c			84,000
[being Net dividend payable after deducting tax at sources - on (a) Preference Share Dividend = 30,000 – 20% = 30,000 – 6,000 = 24,000; (b) Equity Share Dividend = 75,000 – 20% = 75,000 – 15,000 = 60,000; deposited into Dividend Spl. Bank A/c for payment]			
(5) Preference Share Dividend payable A/c	Dr	24,000	
Equity Share Dividend payable A/c	Dr	50,000	
To Dividend Bank (spl.)			74,000
(being dividend disbursed within 42 days and the Balance of Rs. 10,000 treated as unclaimed dividend)			

Working Note

(a) Preference share Dividend payable		
3000 10% preference shares of Rs. 100 paid		
3,00,000 × 10% Dividend	30,000	
Less 20% Tax deducted at sources	6,000	
		24,000
(b) Equity shares of Rs. 10% each Rs. 5 paid		
1,00,000 × 5 = 5,00,000 × 15 dividend	75,000	
Less Tax deducted at source 20%	15,000	60,000
		84,000

(c) Tax deducted at source

(i) Preference Share Dividend — Tax thereon		6,000
(ii) Equity Share Dividend — Tax thereon		15,000
Income tax deducted at sources Tax payable		21,000
(d) Dividend Banks (Spl.) Deposited		84,000
Less Dividend paid within 42 days		
Pref. Share Dividend	24,000	
Equity Share Dividend	50,000	
Dividend paid		74,000
Balance unpaid is unclaimed Dividend		10,000
Profit and Loss A/c		Rs. 2,00,000
Less Appropriation :		
(a) General Reserve 20%	40,000	
(b) Sinking Fund A/c	20,000	
(c) Preference Share Dividend	30,000	
(d) Equity Share Dividend	75,000	
Total		1,65,000
Balance c/f		Rs. 35,000

Problem No. 7

R & Co. Ltd. was formed on 1-4-1995 to take over the Business of M/s Ross Traders w.e.f. 1-1-1995. The Profit and Loss Account of the Company for the year ending 31-12-1995 in given below :

Profit and Loss A/c for the year ended 31-12-1995

Particulars	Rs.	Particulars	Rs.
To Salaries and Alllowances	32,000	By Gross Profit	1,40,000
To Rent and Rates	7,000		
To Directors fees	3,600		
To Commission to Agents	11,200		
To General Expenses	9,600		
To Advertising	2,800		
To Audit fees	2,000		
To Debentures Interest	3,600		
To Depreciation	12,800		
To Interest to Vendor (upto 30-6-95)	2,000		
To Net Profit	53,400		
	1,40,000		1,40,000

Additional Information :

(a) The average monthly sales for the first three months of 1995 was Rs. 32,000 and for the rest of the year was Rs. 64,000.

(b) Rent paid was Rs. 400 P.M. upto 31-3-95 and thereafter it was increased to Rs. 600 P.M.

Ascertain Profit before and after incorporation.

[K.U.D., April 1997(N)]

Solution :

Note : Calculations of Basis for apportionment :

Sales — First 3 months average sales Rs. 32,000 × 3 = Rs. 96,000 for the rest of the year 9 months average sales Rs. 64,000 × 9 = 5,76,000

Total Sales — for 3 months Rs. 96,000 for 9 months Rs. 5,76,000

ratio 96 : 576

Sales ratio 1 : 6

Time Ratio 3 months 9 months

1-1-95 to 31-3-95 31-12-95

Ratio 3:9

Time ratio 1:3

Statement Showing Profit before and after Incorporation
Profit and Loss A/c for the year ended 31-12-1995

Particulars	Total Rs.	Basis	Prior to Incorporation Rs.	After Incorporation Rs.	Particulars	Prior to Incorporation Rs.	After Incorporation Rs.
To Salaries and Allowances	32,000	Time 1:3	8,000	24,000	By Gross Profit Sales ratio 1:6	20,000	1,20,000
To Rent = 7000 – 6600 Rs. 400 p.m. × 3 Rs. 600 p.m. × 9	6,600		1200	5400			
Rates (7,000 – 6,600)	400	Time 1:3	100	300			
To Directors fees	3,600	Co. Exp.	—	3,600			
To Commission to Agent	11,200	Sales 1:6	1,600	9,600			
To General Expenses	9,600	Time 1:3	2,400	7,200			
To Advertising	2,800	Sales 1:6	400	2,400			
To Audit fees	2,000	Time 1:3	300	1,500			
To Debenture Interest	3,600	Co exp.	—	3,600			
To Depreciation	12,800	Time 1:3	3,200	9,600			
To Interest to Vendor upto 30-6-95 from 1-1-95 to 1-4-93 3:3	2,000	Period 3:3	1,000	1,000			
To Net Profit	53,400		1,600	51,800			
	1,40,000		20,000	1,20,000		20,000	1,20,000

Problem No. 8

The Following Profit & Loss Account is prepared by X Co. Ltd. for the year ending 31-3-1996.

Profit & Loss A/c for the year ended 31-3-1996

Particulars	Rs.	Particulars	Rs.
To Salaries to staff	5,00,000	By Gross Profit	20,00,000
To Directors fees	30,000	By Profit on sale of Building	1,00,000
To Repairs & Maintenance	1,00,000	By Subsidy from Govt.	3,80,000
To Depreciation	3,00,000		
To General Expenses	80,000		
To Research & Development Expenses	50,000		
To Income Tax	4,00,000		
To Interest on Debentures	1,50,000		
To Development Rebate Reserve	50,000		
To Proposed Dividend	1,00,000		
To Net Profit	7,20,000		
	24,80,000		24,80,000

Additional Information :

(1) Depreciation allowable for Income tax purpose in Rs. 2,80,000.

(2) The Sale proceeds of the building sold were Rs. 3,00,000, the original cost of which is Rs. 2,60,000 and the written down value was Rs. 2,00,000.

(3) The Resarch and development expenses incurred were on the new Laboratory set up by the company.

Calculate the Maximum Remuneration payable to the Managing Director.

[K.U.D., April 1996(N)]

Solution :

	Rs.	Rs.		Rs.	Rs.
			Balance b/d		16,20,000
Net Profit		7,20,000	Less Admissible deductions :		
Add inadmissible deductions :			(1) Depreciation	2,80,000	
(1) Depreciation	3,00,000		(2) Profit on sale of Build.		
(2) R&D Expenses	50,000		2,00,000 + 1,00,000		
(3) Income Tax	4,00,000		− 2,60,000		
(4) Develop. Rebate Res.	50,000		(3,00,000 − 2,60,000)	40,000	3,20,000
(5) Proposed Dividend	1,00,000	9,00,000	Net Profit		13,00,000
			For calculation of Managing Director's Remuneration @ 5% on Net Profit		
			N.P. Rs. 13,00,000 × 5% = Rs. 65,000		
		16,20,000	Remuneration payable Rs. 65,000		

Problem No. 9

A Co. Ltd. was incorporated on 1-7-1995, taking over the business of Ahamad, as from 1-4-1995. The following was the Profit and Loss A/c for the year ended 31-3-1996

Profit & Loss A/c for the year and 31-3-1996

Particulars	Rs.	Particulars	Rs.
To Salaries and Wages	72,000	By Gross Profit	1,40,000
To Rent and Rates	3,600	By Net Loss	60,000
To Office Expenses	24,000		
To Commission on sales	16,000		
To Free Samples	4,000		
To Audit fees	2,000		
To Depreciation	8,000		
To Interest on Debentures	6,000		
To Directors fees	2,000		
To Formation Expenses	2,000		
To Printing & Stationery	4,000		
To Sundry Expenses	800		
To Bad Debts	1,600		
	1,46,000		1,46,000

Additional Information :

(a) Sales upto 1-7-95 amounted to Rs. 1,60,000
and thereafter Rs. 2,40,000

(b) Rent was paid Rs. 200 P.M.

(c) Bad Debts upto 30-6-1995 Rs. 400

Prepare a statement showing Profit or Loss prior to Incorporation.

[K.U.D., April 1996(N)]

Solution :

Sales — from 1-4-95 to 30-6-95 — Rs. 1,60,000 prior to incorporation
after Incorporation — 2,40,000
ratio — 1,60,000 — 2,40,000
Sales Ratio 2 : 3

Time Ratio — 1-4-95 to 30-6-95 prior to Incorporation 3 months
1-7-95 to 31-3-96 after incorporation 9 months
3 months — 9 months
3 : 9 = 1 : 3 ratio

Profit & Loss A/c for the year ended 31-3-1996

Particulars	Total Rs.	Basis	Prior to Incorporation Rs.	After Incorporation Rs.	Particulars	Prior to Incorporation Rs.	After Incorporation Rs.
					By Gross Profit		
To Salaries & Wages	72,000	Time 1 : 3	18,000	54,000	Sales Ratio 2 : 3	56,000	84,000
To Rent							
Rs. 200 P.M.	2,400	Time 1 : 3	600	1,800	Net Loss	—	24,760
Rates 3,600 – 2,400	1,200	Time 1 : 3	300	900			
To Office Expenses	24,000	Time 1 : 3	6,000	18,000	Net Loss after incorpora-		
To Commission on sales	16,000	Sales 2 : 3	6,400	9,600	tion – 24,760 Net Profit		
To Free Samples	4,000	2 : 3	1,600	2,400	prior to + Incorpora-		
To Audit fees	2,000	Time 1:3	500	1,500	tion 18,760 Net Loss for		
To Depreciation	8,000	1:3	2,000	6,000	the year 6,000		
To Interest on Debit	6,000	Co. Exp.	—	6,000			
To Directors feese	2,000	Co. Exp.	—	2,000			
To Printing and Stationery	4,000	Time 1:3	1,000	3,000			
To Sundry Exp.	800		200	600			
To Bad Debts	1,600	Sales 2:3	640	960			
Total Expenses			37,240	1,08,760			
Net Profit			18,760	—			
	1,46,000		56,000	1,08,760		56,000	1,08,760

(1) Sales ratio — 2 : 3

		2 : 3	
Commission on sales —	16,000	6,400	9,600
Free samples	4,000	1,600	2,400
Bad Debts	1,600	640	960

(2) Time Ratio 3 months – 9 months

3 : 9 = 1 : 3

1 : 3 = Salaries and wages

Rent & Rates – Rent – Rs. 200 P.M.	200 × 3 = 600	200 × 9 = 1,800
Office exp.	– 6,000	– 18,000
Audit fees	500	1,500
Depreciation	2,000	6,000
Printing & Stationery	1,000	3,000
Sundry Expenses	200	600

(3) Expenses : wholly Co. Expenses — Interest on Debentures, Formation Expenses, Directors fees } after Incorporation

Problem No. 10

The following accounts appear in the books of Zee Ltd. as on 1-4-94 :

Advance Income — Tax Account	60,000
Tax Deducted at Source Account	5,000
Provision for Income Tax Account (1993-94)	80,000

On 31 October 1994 the assessment was completed for the accounting year 1993-94 and the tax liability was fixed at Rs. 95,000. During the year 1994-95 the company had paid an advance tax (1994-95) Rs. 75,000 and has tax deducted at source on Rs. 10,000 on 31-3-1995 it made a Provision for tax Rs. 1,00,000.

Show the necessary accounts for the year ending 31 March 1995.

(October 1996)

Solution :

Advance Income Tax Account

Particulars	Rs.	Particulars	Rs.
1-4-94 To Balance b/d	60,000	By Income Tax A/c	60,000
To Bank A/c (94-95)	75,000	31-3-95 By Balance c/d	75,000
	1,35,000		1,35,000
1-4-95 To Balance b/d	75,000		

Tax Deducted at Source

1-4-94 To Balance b/d	5,000	By Income Tax A/c	5,000
To Income Tax A/c	10,000	By Balance c/d	10,000
	15,000		15,000
1-4-95 To Balance c/d	10,000		

Provision for Income Tax A/c

To Income Tax A/c (Tax Liability for 1993-94)	95,000	1-4-94 By Balance b/d	80,000
		By Profit & Loss A/c	15,000
To Balanee c/d	1,00,000	By Profit & Loss A/c (94-95)	1,00,000
	1,95,000		1,95,000
		1-4-95 By Balance b/d	1,00,000

Income Tax Account

Particulars	Rs.	Particulars	Rs.
To Advance Tax	60,000	By Provision for Income Tax A/c	95,000
To Tax deducted at Source A/c	5,000		
To Bank A/c	30,000		
	95,000		95,000

Problem No. 11

From the following Trial Balance as on 31st March 1996, prepare Financial Statement according to the provisions of Indian Company Law :

	Rs.	Rs.
Authorised and Subscribed Capital :		
1,500 10% Preference shares	—	1,50,000
2,000 Equity shares	—	2,00,000
Premises (at cost)	2,00,000	—
Machinery (at cost)	1,00,000	—
Provision for depreciation up to 31-3-1995		
On Premises	—	50,000
On Machinery	—	25,000
Gross Profit as per Trading Account (1995-96)	—	2,00,000
Administration Expenses	22,500	—
Rent, Rates, Taxes	5,000	—
Investment in shares	1,00,000	—
Dividend on shares (Gross)	—	5,000
General Reserve	—	12,500
Income-tax deducted on dividend	500	—
Dividend Equalisation Reserve	—	10,000
Stock on 31-3-1996	1,25,000	—
Cash on hand	4,000	—
Cash at Bank	60,000	—
Sundry Debtors and Creditors	58,000	18,000
Profit and Loss Appropriation Account (1-4-95)	—	14,500
Audit Fees	2,000	—
Managing Directors remuneration	5,000	—
Directors Meeting Fees	3,000	—
Sundry Expenses	2,500	—
Miscellaneous receipts	—	2,500
	6,87,500	6,87,500

Other Information :

(a) Provide depreciation on Premises and Machinery at 10% on WDV.
(b) Managing Director is entitled to remuneration at 5% of net Profit.
(c) Make provision for tax Rs. 57,000.
(d) The directors recommended dividend at 20% on equity shares.
(e) Transfer Rs. 17,500 to General reserve and Rs. 5,000 to Dividend Equalisation Reserve.

(October 1996)

Solution :

Profit and Loss Account for the year ended 31st March 1996

Particulars		Amount	Particulars	Amount
To Administration Exp.		22,500	By Gross Profit b/d	2,00,000
To Rent, Rates, Taxes		5,000	By Dividend equal. Reserve	5,000
To Audit Fees		2,000	By Misc. Receipts	2,500
To Directors meeting fee		3,000		
To Sundry Exp.		2,500		
To Depr. on Premises (10% on 1,50,000)		15,000		
To Provision for Tax		57,000		
To Mng. Directors remumeration :				
Paid	5,000			
Due	2,500	7,500		
To Net Profit		85,500		
		2,07,500		2,07,500

Note : Managing Directors Remuneration :

Profit (before tax provision and Managing Director Remuneration)
= 2,07,500 – 57,500 = 1,50,000
Managing Directors Remuneration = 1,50,000 × 5% = 7,500
Due = 7,500 – 5,000 = 2,500.

Profit and Loss Appropriation Account

Particulars	Amount	Particulars	Amount
To General Reserve	17,500	By Balance b/d	14,500
To Dividend equal. Reserve	5,000	By Profit & Loss A/c	85,500
To Pref. Shares Dividend (10% on Rs. 1,50,000)	15,000		
To Equity shares Dividend (20% on 2,00,000)	40,000		
To Balance c/d	22,500		
	1,00,000		1,00,000

Balance Sheet as on 31st March 1996

Liabilities		Rs.	Assets	Rs.
(I) *Share Capital :*			(I) *Fixed Assets :*	
10% Pref. Shares Rs. 100		1,50,000	Premises (at cost)	2,00,000
Equity Shares		2,00,000	Machinery (at cost)	1,00,000
(II) *Reserve & Surplus :*			(II) *Investments :*	
General Reserve	12,500		Shares	1,00,000
Addition	17,500	30,000	(III) *Current Assets, Loans and Advances :*	
Dividend equalisation			Sundry Debtors	58,000
Reserve	10,000		Stock	1,25,000
Addition	5,000	15,000	Cash	4,000
Profit & Loss			Bank	60,000
Appropriation (Surplus)		22,500	Tax deducted at source	500
(III) *Secured Loans*		—	(IV) *Misc. Exp.*	—
(IV) *Unsecured Loans*		—		
(V) *Current Liabilities and Provisions :*				
Sundry Creditors		18,000		
Mng. Directors Remuneration due		2,500		
Proposed Pref. Shares Dividend		15,000		
Proposed Equity Shares Dividend		40,000		
Depr. Fund :				
Premises	50,000			
Addition	15,000	65,000		
Machinery	25,000			
Addition	7,500	32,500		
Provision for Tax		57,000		
		6,47,500		6,47,500

Contingent Liabilities : Nil.

Problem No. 12

From the following Trial Balance of Vikas Cement Co. Ltd. as on 31-12-1989 prepare Final Accounts :

Trial Balance as on 31-12-1989

	Dr Rs.	Cr Rs.
1. Share Capital (8000 Equity share of Rs. 10)	—	80,000
2. Stock (1-1-1989)	51,000	
3. Purchases and Sales	2,20,000	
4. Returns	3,800	
5. Trade Expenses	1,800	
6. Wages	12,000	
7. Salaries	18,700	
8. Travelling Expenses	3,200	
9. Rent	4,900	
10. Discount Received		2,700
11. Advertisement	1,550	
12. Interest	850	
13. Bad Debts	2,500	
14. Building	95,000	
15. Machinery	98,000	
16. Debtors and Creditors	45,000	55,000
17. 6% on Loan		75,000
18. Cash	1,400	
19. Reserve Fund		23,000
20. Preliminary Expenses	11,000	
21. Profit & Loss Account (1-1-1989)		5,000
22. 5% Debentures		20,000
23. Investments (Tata Co. Shares)	10,000	
24. Goodwill	10,000	
	5,90,700	5,90,700

Adjustments :

1. Provision for taxation Rs. 25,000.
2. Provide dividend on shares capital at 15%.
3. Transfer Rs. 5,000 to Reserve Fund.
4. Stock in Trade on 31-12-1989 Rs. 32,000.
5. Write off 1/5 preliminary expenses.
6. Outstanding wages Rs. 500.

(K.U.D., March 1991)

Solution :

Final Accounts of the Vikas Cement Company Limited

Trading A/c for the year ended 31-12-1989

Particulars		Amount	Particulars		Amount
To Stock (on 1-1-1989)		51,000	By Sales	3,30,000	
			Less Returns	3,800	3,26,200
To Purchases		2,20,000			
To Wages	12,000		By Stock on 31-12-89		32,000
Add : Outstanding	500	12,500			
To Trade Expenses		1,800			
To Gross Profit (Transfer to Profit & Loss A/c)		72,900			
		3,58,200			3,58,200

Profit & Loss A/c for the year ended 31-12-1989

Particulars	Amount	Particulars	Amount
To Salaries	18,700	By Gross Profit	72,900
To Travelling Expenses	3,200	By Discount Received	2,700
To Rent	4,900		
To Advertisement	1,550		
To Interest	850		
To Bad Debts	2,500		
Preliminary Expenses Written off 1/5 × 11,000	2,200		
To Provision for Taxation	25,000		
To Net Profit (Transferred to Appropriation A/c)	16,700		
	75,600		75,600

Profit & Loss Appropriation A/c

Particulars	Amount	Particulars	Amount
To Proposed Dividend 15% on 80,000	12,000	By Profit & Loss A/c	16,700
		By Profit on 1-1-1989	5,000
To Transfer to Reserve fund	5,000		
To Balance of Profit	4,700		
	21,700		21,700

Balance Sheet as on 31-12-1989

Liabilities		Rs.	Assets		Rs.
Share Capital			*Fixed Assets*		
Authorised			Goodwill		10,000
Issued and paid up			Building		95,000
8,000 equity shares of			Machinery		98,000
Rs. 10 each		80,000			
			Investments		
Reserves & Surplus :			Tata Co. Shares		10,000
Reserve Fund	23,000		*Current Assets*		
Addition during			Stock on 31-12-89		32,000
the year	5,000	28,000	Debtors		45,000
Profit & Loss A/c		4,700	Cash		1,400
Secured Loan			*Miscellaneous Exp.*		
5% Debenture		20,000	Preliminary Exp.	11,000	
Unsecured Loan			*Less* : Written off	2,200	8,800
6% on Loan		75,000			
Current Liabilities					
and Provisions					
Creditors		55,000			
Provision for Taxation		25,000			
Proposed Dividend		12,000			
Outstanding Wages		500			
		3,00,200			3,00,200

Problem No. 13

Raj Laxmi Manufacturing Co. Ltd. has an authorised capital of Rs. 10,00,000 divided into 75,000 Equity shares of Rs. 10 each and 2500 9% preference shares of Rs. 100 each. The following is the Trial Balance of the Company as on 31-12-1989 :

Trial Balance as on 31-12-1989

Debit Balances	Rs.	Credite Balances	Rs.
Land and Building	4,50,000	*Share Capital*	
Plant & Machinery	6,75,000	45000 Equity shares of Rs. 10 each	4,50,000
Goodwill	2,10,000		
Purchases	4,80,000	9% Preference shares of Rs. 100	2,00,000
Opening Stock 1-1-89	90,000		
Wages	1,45,000	Profit & Loss A/c on 1-1-89	82,000

Debit Balances	Rs.	Credite Balances	Rs.
Manufacturing Expenses	42,5000	General Reserve	2,00,000
Power	22,500	Sundry Creditors	1,00,000
Carriage Inward	15,000	Sinking Fund	1,35,000
Carriage Outward	30,000	Sales	12,55,000
Salaries	90,000	Salaries and Allowance *Less* Paid	47,000
Insurance	15,000	Interest received on Investment	4,500
Sundry Debtors	1,45,000	In Govt. Securities 6% Debentures	3,00,000
Bank Balance	50,000		
Sinking fund Investment in 6% Govt. securities face value 1,50,000	1,35,000		
Debentures Interest	9,000		
Directors fees	15,000		
Audit fees	9,000		
Income Tax Paid	61,500		
Dividend paid on :			
(a) Pref. Shares	9,000		
(b) Interim on Equity shares	45,000		
(c) Preliminary Expenses	30,000		
	27,73,500		27,73,500

Adjustments :

(1) The Closing stock on 31-12-1989 was Rs. 1,16,000.

(2) A provision for Income Tax for 1989 be made Rs. 75,000.

(3) The Directors recommend that Rs. 50,000 be transferred to General Reserve and also a final dividend declared at 15% on Equity shares.

(4) Rs. 15,000 have to be added to the Sinking Fund and interest received also be transferred.

(5) Provision for Depreciation on Land and Building at 5%, Plant and Machinery @ 10%.

(6) Provision Reserve for Doubtful Debt on Debtors @ 5%.

(7) Write off Preliminary Expenses by 20%.

Prepare the Final Account of the Company for the year ending 31-12-1989 and also a Balance Sheet as on that date.

Solution :

Manufacturing and Trading A/c for the year ended 31-12-89

Particulars	Amount	Particulars	Amount
To Opening stock 1-1-89	90,000	By Sales	12,55,000
To Purchases	4,80,000	By Closing Stock	1,16,000
To Wages	1,45,000		
To Manufacturing Exp.	42,500		
To Power	22,500		
To Carriage Inward	15,000		
To Gross Profit	5,76,000		
	13,71,000		13,71,000

Profit & Loss A/c for the year ended 31-12-1989

To Salaries		90,000	By Gross Profit	5,76,000
To Carriage outward		30,000	By Interest on Sinking Fund Investment in Govt. Securities	4,500
To Insurance		15,000	By Interest on Investment receivable	4,500
To Directors Fees		15,000		
To Audit Fees		9,000		
To Debenture interest				
Paid	9,000			
Payable	9,000	18,000		
To Preliminary Exp.	30,000			
Less : Written off 20%	6,000			
	24,000	6,000		
To *Depreciation on*				
Land & Building @ 5%	22,500			
Plants Machinery	67,500	90,000		
To Provision for Doubtful debts		7,250		
To Net Profit		3,04,750		
		5,85,000		5,85,000

Profit & Loss Appropriation A/c for the year ended 31-12-1989

Particulars		Amount	Particulars	Amount
To Income Tax Paid		61,500	By Profit & Loss A/c (Net Profit)	3,04,750
To Provision for Income Tax		75,000	By Profit & Loss A/c Balance 1-1-1989	82,000
To Transfer to General Reserve		50,000		
To Sinking Fund A/c (15,000 + 9,000)		24,000		
To Dividend on Preference shares				
Paid	9,000			
Payable	9,000	18,000		
To Proposed Divid. on Equity shares @ 15% Final		67,500		
To Interim divid. paid	45,000			
To Dividend payable	22,500			
To Balance Profit & Loss		90,750		
		3,86,750		3,86,750

Balance Sheet as at 31-12-1989

Liabilities	Rs.	Rs.	Assets	Rs.	Rs.
Share Capital			*Fixed Assets*		
Authorised Capital			Goodwill		2,10,000
Equity Shares 75000 of Rs. 10		7,50,000	Land & Building	4,50,000	
9% Preference share 2500 of Rs. 1,000		2,50,000	*Less* : Depreciation @ Rs. 5%	22,500	4,27,500
		10,00,000	Plant & Machinery	6,75,000	
Issued & Paid up			*Less* Depreciation of Rs. 10%	67,500	6,07,500
45000 Equity shares of Rs. 10		4,50,000	*Investments*		
2500 6% preference share of Rs. 100		2,00,000	Sinking Fund in 6% Govt. Security (Face Value Rs. 1,50,000)		1,35,000
Reserve & Surplus			*Current Assets*		
General Reserve	2,00,000		Closing & stock		1,16,000
Addition during the year	50,000	2,50,000	Sundry Debtors	1,45,000	
			Less RDD 5%	7,250	1,37,750

Liabilities	Rs.	Rs.	Assets	Rs.	Rs.
Sinking Fund	1,35,000		Bank Balance		50,000
Addition			*Miscellaneous A/c*		
during the year			Interest on Sinking		
(15,000 + 9,000)	24,000	1,59,000	Fund investment		4,500
Surplus :			Preliminary Expenses		24,000
Profit & Loss A/c		90,750			
Secured Loan :					
6% Debenture	3,00,000				
Add interest	9,000	3,09,000			
Current Liabilities &					
Provision :					
Sundry Creditors		1,00,000			
Outstanding Liabilities :					
Salaries & Allow.	47,000				
Provision for					
income tax	75,000				
Dividend Payable :					
On Pref. shares	9,000				
On Equity shares	22,500	1,53,500			
		17,12,250			17,12,250

Problem No. 14

The following are the Balances extracted from the Books of Nirmal Co. Ltd., Bombay as on 31-12-1991 :

Debits	Rs.	Credits	Rs.
1. Premises	5,10,000	1. Share capital	12,00,000
2. Plant & Machinery	9,50,000	Equity shares of Rs. 10	
3. Fixtures	60,000	2. Reserve Fund	90,000
4. Furnitures	43,500	3. Profit & Loss A/c	53,100
5. Preliminary Expenses	30,000	(on 1-1-91)	
6. Cash in hand	20,000	4. Sundry Creditors	1,80,000
7. Cash at Bank	93,000	5. Purchases returns	30,000
8. Calls in arrears	9,000	6. Sales	18,45,000
9. 5% Govt. Bonds	54,000	7. 6% Debentures	6,00,000
(Face value Rs. 60,000)		8. Bank Over Draft	75,000
10. Goodwill	54,000		
11. Salaries	90,000		

Debits	Rs.	Credits	Rs.
12. Bills recoverable	57,000		
13. Sundry Debtors	1,24,500		
14. Interim Devidend paid	27,000		
15. Vehicles	2,20,000		
16. Postage & Telegram	4,500		
17. Purchases	12,20,000		
18. Sales returns	42,000		
19. Advertisement	15,000		
20. Carriage inward	22,500		
21. Wages paid	1,38,000		
22. Insurance	30,000		
23. Stock on 1-1-91	2,15,000		
24. General Expenses	25,500		
25. Debenture Interest (*Less* Tax @ 30%)	12,600		
26. Audit Fees	6,000		
	40,73,100		40,73,100

The following additional informations are provided :

1. Closing stock on 31-12-1991 was Rs. 2,70,000.
2. Write off preliminary expenses Rs. 6,000 only.
3. Provide Depreciation on :
   (a) Premises @ 5%
   (b) Plants & Machinery @ 10%
   (c) Fixtures @ 10%
   (d) Furnitures @ 10% and
   (e) Vehicles @ 20%.
4. Prepaid Insurance Rs. 3,000.
5. Provide for Doubtful debtors @ 5% on Sundry debtors.
6. Transfer to Reserve Fund Rs. 15,000.
7. Interim dividend for 6 months ending on 30-6-1991 @ 3%.
8. Wages accrued Rs. 5,000.
9. Debenture interest for 6 months.

Prepare Final accounts of the company and the Balance Sheet as on 31-12-1991.

Nirmal Co., Ltd.

Trading and Profit and Loss Account

Particulars		Amount	Particulars		Amount
To Opening stock (1-1-1991)		2,15,000	By Cash	18,45,000	
To Purchase	12,20,000		*Less* returns	42,000	18,03,000
Less returns	30,000	11,90,000	By Closing stock (31-12-1991)		2,70,000
To Wages	1,38,000				
Add : accrued	5,000	1,43,000			
To Carriage		22,500			
To Gross Profit		5,02,500			
		20,73,000			20,73,000
To Salaries		90,000	By Gross Profit		5,02,500
To Audit fees		6,000	By Interest on Govt. Bonds @ 5% on 60,000 receivable		3,000
To Advertisement		15,000			
To Postage & Telegram		4,500			
To Insurance	30,000				
Less : Prepaid	3,000	27,000			
To Preliminary Exp. written off		6,000			
To General Exp.		25,500			
To Depreciation :					
(a) Premises @ 10%	25,500				
(b) Plant & Machinery	95,000				
(c) Fixtures @ 10%	6,000				
(d) Furnitures @ 10%	4,350				
(e) Vehicles @ 20%	44,000	1,74,850			
R.D.D. @ 5% on 1,24,500		6,225			
To Debentures interest Gross Amount (12,600×100/70)	18,000				
Interest payable for 6 months	18,000	36,000			
To Net profit transfer to Appropriation A/c		1,14,425			
		5,05,500			5,05,500

Profit & Loss Appropriation A/c

Particulars	Amount	Particulars	Amount
To Reserve Fund transfer	15,000	By Balance b/d	53,100
To Interim Dividend		By Net Profit	1,14,425
@ 3% on 11,91,000	35,730		
To Balance of Profit c/d	1,16,795		
	1,67,525		1,67,525

Balance Sheet as at 31-12-1991

Liabilities	Rs.	Rs.	Assets	Rs.	Rs.
Share Capital			*Fixed Assets*		
Authorised			Goodwill		54,000
Subscribed & Paidup			Premises	5,10,000	
120000 Equity shares			*Less* Depreciation		
of Rs. 10 each	12,00,000		5%	25,500	4,84,500
Less : Calls in arrears	9,000	11,91,000	Plant & Machinery	9,50,000	
Reserves & Surplus			*Less* Depreciation		
Reserve Fund	90,000		@ 10%	95,000	8,55,000
Addition	15,000	1,05,000	Fixtures	60,000	
Profit & Loss A/c		1,16,795	*Less* Depreciation		
Secured Loan			@ 10%	6,000	54,000
6% Debentures			Furnitures	43,500	
of Rs. 100	6,00,000		*Less* Depreciation		
Interest on			@ 10%	4,350	39,150
Debenture	18,000	6,18,000	Vehicles	2,20,000	
Unsecured Loan			*Less* Depreciation		
Bank Over Draft		75,000	@ 10%	44,000	1,76,000
Current Liabilities			*Investments*		
& Provisions			5% Govt. Bond		
Sundry Creditors		1,80,000	(Face value 60,000)		54,000
Wages outstanding		5,000	*Current Assets*		
Tax on Debenture			Stock		2,70,000
interest @ 30%	18,000	5,400	Sundry Debtors	1,24,500	
Dividend payable	35,730		*Less* RDD	6,225	1,18,275
Less : Paid	27,000	8,730	Bills receivable		57,500
			Cash in hand		20,000
			Cash at Bank		93,000
			Miscellaneous		
			Prepaid Insurance	3,000	
			Preliminary Exp.	24,000	
			Interest Receivable	3,000	30,000
		23,04,925			23,04,925

Problem No. 15

X Y and Co. Ltd. had an authorised capital of Rs. 12,00,000 in equity shares of Rs. 10 each. The following is the Trial Balance of the company as on 31-12-1990 :

Debits	Rs.	Credits	Rs.
1. Premises	6,00,000	1. Share capital Auth. & Paidup 92000 equity share of Rs. 10 each.	9,20,000
2. Plant & Machinery	7,20,000	2. General Reserve	50,000
3. Interim Devidend paid	15,000	3. 6% Debentures	6,00,000
4. Calls in arrears	15,000	4. Profit & Loss A/c	29,000
5. Purchases	37,000	5. Sundry Creditors	1,00,000
6. Preliminary Exp.	10,000	6. Provisions for Doubtful Debts	7,000
7. Freight	26,200	7. Sales	8,30,000
8. Director Fee	11,480	8. Bills payable	76,000
9. Bad Debts	4,220		
10. 8% Govt. Securities	1,20,000		
11. Stock on 1-1-1990	1,50,000		
12. Fixtures	14,400		
13. Sundry Debtors	1,74,000		
14. Goodwill	50,000		
15. Wages	1,69,600		
16. Cash in hand	1,500		
17. Cash at Bank	79,800		
18. General Exp.	29,000		
19. Salaries	33,800		
20. Debenture Interest	18,000		
	26,12,000		26,12,000

Prepare the Final Accounts of the Co. and Balance Sheet as on 31-12-1990 after taking into consideration of the following :

(a) Write off preliminary expenses 20%.

(b) Provide depreciation on :

(1) Premises @ 5% (2) Plant & Machinery @ 10%

(3) Fixtures at 5%.

(c) Bad debt. provision shall be only @ 5% on debtors.

(d) Transfer Rs. 10,000 to General Reserves.

(e) Make provision for Taxation Rs. 25,000.

(f) Stock on 31-12-1990 was Rs. 2,50,000.

(g) Directors proposed 5% Dividend on equity share capital.

X Y Co. Ltd. Final Accounts

Trading Accounts year ending 31-12-1990

Particulars	Rs.	Particulars	Rs.
To Opening Stock	1,50,000	By Sales	8,30,000
To Purchases	3,70,000	By Stock on 31-12-90	2,50,000
To Freight charges	26,200		
To Wages	1,69,600		
To Gross profit	3,64,200		
	10,80,000		10,80,000

Profit and Loss A/c for the year ended 31-12-1990

To Salaries		33,800	By Gross profit	36,4200
To General Exp.		29,000		
To Directors Fee		11,480		
To Preliminary Exp. 20% of Rs. 10,000		2,000		
To Reserve for Doutful debt.				
RDD New	8,700			
Add Bad debt.	4,220			
	12,920			
Less Reserve (old)	7,000	5,920		
Debenture Interest	18,000			
Depreciation	18,000	36,000		
Premises @ 5%	30,000			
Plant & Machinery 10%	72,000			
Fixtures @ 5%	720	1,02,720		
To Provision for Taxation		25,000		
To Net profit		1,18,280		
		3,64,200		3,64,200

Profit and Loss Appropriation A/c

To General Reserve Transfer	10,000	By Net profit	1,18,280
To Proposed Dividend	45,250		
To Balance of Profit	63,030		
	1,18,280		1,18,280

Proposed Dividend A/c

To Interim Dividend paid	15,000	By Profit & Loss Appropriation A/c	45,250
To Balance c/d	30,250		
	45,250		45,250

Balance Sheet as at 31-12-1990

Liabilities	Rs.	Rs.	Assets	Rs.	Rs.
Share Capital			*Fixed Assets*		
Authorised Capital			Goodwill		50,000
120000 Equity shares of Rs. 10		12,00,000	Premises	6,00,000	
Subscribed & Paidup			*Less* Depreciation	30,000	5,70,000
92000 Equity shares of Rs. 10 each	9,20,000		Plant & Machinery	7,20,000	
Less Calls in arrear	15,000	9,05,000	*Less* Depreciation	72,000	6,48,000
Reserves & Surplus			Fixtures	14,400	
General Reserve			*Less* Depreciation	720	13,680
Balance	50,000		*Investments*		
Addition during year	10,000	60,000	8% Govt. Securities		1,20,000
Profit & Loss A/c			*Current Assets*		
Balance	29,000		Stock		2,50,000
Addition during the year	63,030	92,030	Sundry Debtors	1,74,000	
Secured Loan			*Less* RDD	8,700	1,65,300
6% Debentures	6,00,000		Cash in hand	1,500	
Interest Due	18,000	6,18,000	Cash at Bank	79,800	81,300
Unsecured Loan & provision	—	—	Preliminary Exp.		8,000
Current Liabilities & Provision					
Sundry Creditors		1,00,000			
Bills payable		76,000			
Dividend payable		30,250			
Provision for Taxation		25,000			
		19,06,280			19,06,280

Problem No. 16

From the following Trial Balance of Uma Shankar Co. Ltd., as on 31st December 1988 prepare the Profit and Loss Account relating to 1988 and the Balance Sheet as at the end of the year :

Debit Balance	Rs.	Credit Balance	Rs.
1. Opening stock	60,000	1. Sundry Creditors	45,000
2. Purchases	3,20,000	2. Provision for Income Tax	45,000
3. Wages	90,000	3. Profit & Loss A/c on 1-1-88	38,000
4. Power	15,000		

Debit Balance	Rs.	Credit Balance	Rs.
5. Manufacturing Exp.	35,000	4. General Reserve	1,00,000
6. Carriage Inward	10,000	5. Share Capital	
7. Carriage Outward	20,000	Equity Shares	3,00,000
8. Salaries	60,000	6% Redeemable pref. (Redeemable on 31-12-92)	2,00,000
9. Insurance	10,000		
10. Sundry Debtors	90,000	6% Debentures (Secured by mortgage on fixed assets)	2,00,000
11. Bank Balance	6,000		
12. Sinking Fund investment (4% Govt. securities face value of Rs. 1,00,000)	90,000	6. Sales	7,70,000
13. Debenture Interest	6,000	7. Interest received on Govt. Securities (Sinking Fund)	2,000
14. Land & Building	3,00,000		
15. Plant & Machinery	4,50,000	8. Sinking Fund	90,000
16. Directors fees	10,000		
17. Audit fees	6,000		
18. Income Tax paid	41,000		
19. Dividend paid on pref. shares	6,000		
Interim on equity shares	5,000		
20. Goodwill	1,40,000		
21. Preliminary Exp.	20,000		
	17,90,000		17,90,000

Adjustments :

(1) The Closing stock on 31st December 1988 was Rs. 58,000.

(2) There was no further liability for Income Tax for 1988 for which a provision for Rs. 50,000 should be made.

(3) The Directors recommend that Rs. 25,000 be transferred to General Reserve and that a final dividend of 10% on equity shares be paid.

(4) Rs. 10,000 have to be added to the sinking fund.

(5) Depreciation is to be provided @ 2% on Land and Building and @ 10% on plant and machinery.

(6) Write off Rs. 5,000 from preliminary expenses.

Solution :

Manufacturing & Trading A/c for the year ended 31-12-88

Particulars	Amount	Particulars	Amount
To Opening stock	60,000	By Sales	7,70,000
To Purchases	3,20,000	By Closing stock	58,000
To Wages	90,000		
To Power	15,000		
To Manufacturing exp.	35,000		
To Carriage inward	10,000		
To Gross profit transfer	2,98,000		
	8,28,000		8,28,000

Profit & Loss A/c for the year ended 31-12-1988

To Salaries		60,000	By Gross Profit		2,98,000
To Carriage outward		20,000	By Interest on Govt. securities received	2,000	
To Insurance		10,000	Interest on Govt. securities due but not received	2,000	4,000
To Debentures Interest paid	6,000				
Add : Int. outstanding	6,000	12,000			
To Directors Fees		10,000			
To Audit Fees		6,000			
To Preliminary Exp.	20,000				
Less : Written off	5,000				
Balance c/d	15,000	5,000			
To Depreciation :					
Land & Building @ 2%	6,000				
Plant & Machinery	45,000	51,000			
Net Profit		1,28,000			
		3,02,000			3,02,000

Profit & Loss Appropriation A/c

To General Reserve	25,000	By Net Profit	1,28,000
To Dividend on Pref. Share @ 6% on 2,00,000	12,000	By Net Profit on 1-1-1988	38,000
To Proposed Dividend on Equity Shares @ 10% on 3,00,000	30,000	By Provision for Income Tax (Transferred)	45,000

Particulars	Amount	Particulars	Amount
To Sinking fund (10,000 + 4,000)	14,000		
To Income Tax paid	41,000		
To Provision for income tax	50,000		
To Balance c/d	39,000		
	2,11,000		2,11,000

Proposed Dividend A/c

To Interim Dividend paid	5,000	By Profit & Loss	
To Balance c/d	25,000	Appropriation A/c	30,000
	30,000		30,000

Balance Sheet as at 31-12-1988

Liabilities	Rs.	Rs.	Assets	Rs.	Rs.
Share Capital			*Fixed Assets*		
Equity shares of Rs. 10 fully paid		3,00,000	Goodwill		1,40,000
6% redeemable pref. shares of Rs. 100 each (Redeemable on 1-1-92)		2,00,000	Land & Building	3,00,000	
			Less : Depr. @ 2%	6,000	2,94,000
Reserves & Surplus			Plant & Machinery	4,50,000	
General Reserve	1,00,000		*Less* : Depreciation		
Additions during the period	25,000	1,25,000	@ 10%	45,000	4,05,000
Sinking Fund	90,000		*Investments*		
Addition during the period (10,000 + 4,000)	14,000	1,04,000	Sinking Fund (4% Govt. securities face value 1,00,000)		90,000
Surplus Profit & Loss A/c		39,000	*Current Assets*		
Secured Loan			Closing Stock		58,000
6% Debenture secured			Sundry Debtors		90,000
by mortgage on			Interest Receivable		2,000
fixed assets	2,00,000		Bank Balance		6,000
Add : Interest paid	6,000	2,06,000	*Miscellaneous Exp.*		
Unsecured Loan			Preliminary Exp.	20,000	
Current Liabilities & Provision			*Less* : Written off	5,000	15,000
Sundry Creditors		45,000			
Provisions :					
Dividend on Pref. shares		6,000			
Provision for Income Tax		50,000			
Proposed Dividend		25,000			
		11,00,000			11,00,000

Problem No. 17

The following is the Trial Balance of Sunrise Co. Ltd. as at 31-12-1989. The Authorised Capital of the company is Rs. 50,00,000 divided into equity shares of Rs. 10 each :

Trial Balance as on 31-12-1989

Debits	Rs.	Credits	Rs.
Calls in arrear	64,000	Share Capital	10,00,000
Land	1,00,000	Provision for doubtful debts	14,000
Building	2,50,000	Sales	18,00,000
Plant & Machinery	1,50,000	Return outward	34,000
Furnitures & fixtures	32,000	Sundry Creditors	1,32,000
Carriage Inward	23,000	Discount Received	2,500
Wages	2,14,000	Share premium	60,000
Salaries	46,000	General Reserve	2,40,000
Rent, Rates, Taxes	5,000		
Purchases	15,00,000		
Return Inward	17,000		
General Exp.	36,500		
Sundry Debtors	4,40,000		
Stock on 1-1-89	2,50,000		
Cash at Bank	1,55,000		
	32,82,500		32,82,500

Adjustments :

1. Closing stock on 31-12-1989, Rs. 5,25,000.
2. Included in sales are goods on sale or return basis costing Rs. 9,000 sales price being with Profit at 25% on sales.
3. Goods worth Rs. 6,000 were destroyed by fire and the Insurance Company admitted a claim for Rs. 3,000 but the amount is yet to be received.
4. Transfer Rs. 20,000 to General Reserve.
5. Directors recommend a dividend of 10%.
6. Make provision for taxation Rs. 75,000.
7. General Expenses include Insurance prepaid Rs. 1,000.
8. Provide for the following outstanding expenses :
   (a) Salaries Rs. 4,000 (b) Rates & Taxes Rs. 2,000.
   (c) Auditors Remuneration Rs. 5,000.
9. Make provision of 5% on Sundry debtors and allow 3% discount on creditors.
10. Provide Depreciation : Building @ 5%, Machinery @ 15%, Furnitures & Fixtures @ 10%.

You are required to prepare final accounts of the company and the Balance Sheet as at 31-12-1989.

Solution :

Trading A/c for the year ended 31-12-1989

Particulars		Amount	Particulars		Amount
To Opening stock 1-1-1989		2,50,000	By Sales	18,00,000	
			Less : Return inward	17,000	
To Purchases	15,00,000			17,83,000	
Less : Returns outward	34,000	14,66,000	*Less* : profit on sale or return 25% on 9,000	2,250	17,80,750
To Wages		2,14,000	By Goods destroyed by fire		6,000
To Carriage Inward		23,000	By Insurance claim admitted	3,000	
To Gross Profit		3,58,750	Profit & Loss A/c (Loss)	–3,000	—
			By Closing stock		5,25,000
		23,11,750			23,11,750

Profit & Loss A/c for the year ended 31-12-89

Particulars		Amount	Particulars	Amount
To Salaries	46,000		By Gross Profit	3,58,750
Add : Outstanding	4,000	50,000	By Discount Received	2,500
To General Exp.	36,500		By Discount on Creditors 3% on Rs. 1,32,000	3,960
Less : Insurance prepaid	1,000	35,500		
To Rent, Rates, Taxes	5,000			
Add : Outstanding	2,000	7,000		
To Auditor remuneration		5,000		
To Loss by fire		3,000		
To Provision for doubtful debtors require on 5% on Rs. 4,40,000	22,000			
Existing old RDD	14,000	8,000		
To Depreciation :				
Building 5%	12,500			
Machinery 15%	22,500			
Furniture 10%	3,200	38,200		
To Provision for taxation		75,000		
To Net profit		1,43,510		
		3,65,210		3,65,210

Profit & Loss Appropriation A/c

Particulars	Amount	Particulars	Amount
To Proposed Dividend 10% of Rs. 9,36,000	93,600	By Net Profit	1,43,510
To Transfer General Reserve	20,000		
To Net Profit	29,910		
	1,43,510		1,43,510

Balance Sheet as at 31-12-1989

Liabilities		Rs.	Assets		Rs.
Share Capital			*Fixed Assets*		
Authorised Capital			Land		1,00,000
500000 equity shares of Rs. 10		50,00,000	Building	2,50,000	
Issued & Paidup capital			*Less* : Depr. @ 5%	12,500	2,37,500
100000 equity shares of Rs. 10 each	10,00,000		Machinery	1,50,000	
Less : Calls in Arrears	64,000	9,36,000	*Less* : Depr. @ 15%	22,500	1,27,500
Reserves & Surplus			Furnitures & Fixtures	32,000	
Share premium		60,000	*Less* Depr. @ 10%	3,200	28,800
General reserve	2,40,000		*Investments*		—
Add : during the year	20,000	2,60,000	*Current Assets*		
Surplus : Profit & Loss A/c		29,910	Closing Stock		5,25,000
Secured Loan		—	Debtors	4,40,000	
Unsecured Loan		—	*Less* : RDD	22,000	
Current Liabilities and Provisions				4,18,000	
Sundry Creditors	1,32,000		*Less* : Provision for sales or return 25% on 9,000	2,250	4,15,750
Less : 3% allowance provision	3,960	1,28,040	Cash at Bank		1,55,000
Outstanding Liabilities			*Miscellaneous*		
Salaries	4,000		Insurance prepaid		1,000
Rates & Taxes	2,000		Insurance Company amount received		3,000
Auditors Remuneration	5,000				
Provision for Taxation	75,000	86,000			
Proposed Dividend		93,600			
		15,93,550			15,93,550

Problem No. 18

Bharat Manufacturing Co. Ltd. had an Authorised capital of 150000 Equity share of Rs. 10 each and 5,000 6% pref. shares of Rs. 100 each.

Following is the Trial Balance of the Company :

Trial Balance as on 31-12-1990

Particulars	Dr Rs.	Cr Rs.
Share capital — issued and paidup :		
100000 Equity shares of Rs. 10 each		10,00,000
6% 2000 Pref. shares of Rs. 100 each		2,00,000
Land and Building 1-1-1990	4,50,000	
Plant & Machinery 1-1-1990	15,00,000	
Additions to Machinery	3,00,000	
General Reserve		3,00,000
Furnitures 1-1-1990	30,000	
7% Debentures		2,00,000
Surplus (Profit & Loss A/c Cr 1-1-90)		2,500
Profit for the year 1990 before charging Depreciation		4,35,000
Expenses of Debenture Issue	7,000	
Stock Closing on 3-12-90 :		
Raw materials	35,000	
Finished Goods	1,40,000	
Provision for taxes on 1-1-90		70,000
Sundry Creditors		83,000
Sundry Debtors	1,80,000	
Taxes paid	50,000	
Depreciation Reserves :		
Building 1-1-1990		30,000
Machinery 1-1-1990		4,50,000
Furniture 1-1-1990		2,000
Interest on Debentures accrued and due		7,000
Govt. Securities	1,25,000	
Bank Loan		2,10,000
Bills Receivable	28,000	
Loose Tools	3,500	
Prepaid Expenses	2,000	
Investments	55,500	
Bank Balance	51,500	
Advance Tax paid	32,000	
	29,89,500	29,89,500

Adjustments :

(1) Provide depreciation on : (a) Building Rs. 5,000, (b) Machinery 1,20,000, (c) Furnitures Rs. 1,500.

(2) The Board of Directors recommend the following appropriations :

(a) Transfer Rs. 25,000 to General Reserve.

(b) Rs. 1,00,000 to Development Reserve.

(c) Payment of 10% dividend on equity shares.

(3) Provide for taxation Rs. 60,000.

(4) Write off Rs. 2,500 Debenture Issue expenses.

Prepare the final accounts of the company for the year ended 31-12-1990 and the Balance Sheet as at 31-12-1990.

Solution :

Profit & Loss A/c for the year ended 31-12-1990

Particulars		Amount	Particulars	Amount
To Debenture Issue Expenses	7,000		By Net Profit before charging depreciation	4,35,000
Less : Written off	2,500	2,500		
Balance c/d	4,500			
To Depreciation Reserve				
Building	5,000			
Machinery	1,20,000			
Furniture	1,500	1,26,500		
To Taxes paid	50,000			
Add : Provision for Taxation	60,000			
	1,10,000			
Less : Existing Provision for taxation Amount required	70,000	40,000		
To Net Profit transferred to Appropriation A/c		2,66,000		
		4,35,000		4,35,000

Profit & Loss Appropriation A/c

Particulars	Amount	Particulars	Amount
To Transfer to General Reserve	25,000	By Net Profit	2,66,000
To Development Reserve	1,00,000	By Surplus 1-1-1990	2,500
To Proposed dividend on equity shares @ 10%	1,00,000		
To Dividend on Pref. shares @ 6%	12,000		
To Balance of Profit c/d	31,500		
	2,68,500		2,68,500

Balance Sheet as on 31-12-1990

Liabilities	Rs.	Rs.	Assets	Rs.	Rs.
Share Capital			*Fixed Assets*		
Authorised			Land & Building		4,50,000
150000 equity shares of Rs. 10		15,00,000	Plant & Machinery		15,00,000
2500 6% pref. shares of Rs. 100 each		2,50,000	Addition during the year		3,00,000
		17,50,000	Furnitures		30,000
			Loose tools		3,500
Issued & Paidup Capital			*Investments*		55,500
100000 equity shares of Rs. 10 each		10,00,000	In Govt. securities		1,25,000
2000 6% pref. shares of Rs. 100 each		2,00,000	*Current Assets*		
			Stock on 31-12-90		
			Raw material		35,000
Reserves & Surplus			Furnished Goods		1,40,000
General Reserves	3,00,000		Sundry Debtors		1,80,000
Add : during the year	25,000	3,25,000	Bills Receivable		28,000
Development Reserve		1,00,000	Bank Balance		51,500
Surplus for the year		31,500	*Miscellaneous*		
Secured Loan			Prepaid Expenses		2,000
7% Debentures	2,00,000		Advance Tax paid		32,000
Interest on Debentures	7,000	2,07,000	Expenses on debenture issue	7,000	
Unsecured Loan			*Less* : Written off	2,500	4,500
Bank Loan		2,10,000			
Current Liabilities & Provisions					
Sundry Creditors		83,000			
Provision for Tax		60,000			

Liabilities	Rs.	Rs.	Assets	Rs.
Depreciation Reserve				
Building	30,000			
Add :	5,000	35,000		
Machinery	4,50,000			
Add :	1,20,000	5,70,000		
Furnitures	2,000			
Add :	1,500	3,500		
Proposed dividend on Equity shares		1,00,000		
Dividend on Pref. Shares		12,000		
		29,37,000		29,37,000

Problem No. 19

Nirmal Industries Co. Ltd. had an Authorised capital of Rs. 10,00,000 divided into equity shares of Rs. 10 each. The company issued 40,000 equity shares of Rs. 10 each fully paid. The following is the Trial Balance as on 30th June 1987 :

Debits	Rs.	Credits	Rs.
Land & Building (cost Rs. 4,00,000)	3,10,000	Share capital (40,000 × 10) (fully paid)	4,00,000
Plant & Machinery (cost Rs. 4,50,000)	3,40,000	Share premium	40,000
		Profit & Loss Appropriation	25,000
Preliminary Exp.	15,000	General Reserve	1,00,000
Stock on 1st July 1986	65,000	Bank Loan @ 6% taken on 1st Jan. 1987	2,00,000
Purchases	3,30,000		
Salaries	50,000	Sundry Creditors	35,000
General Exp.	15,000	Sales	6,00,000
Directors Fee	3,000		
Audit Fee	2,000		
Wages	60,000		
Manufacturing wages	20,000		
Carriage inward	5,000		
Advertising	20,000		
Sundry Debtors	60,000		
Goodwill	90,000		
Bank Balance	15,000		
	14,00,000		14,00,000

Adjustments :

1. The Closing stock on 30th June 1987 was Rs. 55,000.
2. The Managing Director is entitled to a commission of 5% on Net Profit before charging income tax and his commission.
3. General expenses include Rs. 300 prepaid rates.
4. Provision of income tax to the extent of Rs. 15,000 is desired.
5. The Directors recommend a dividend of 5%.
6. Depreciation should be written off :

   Plant and Machinery @ 10% and on Land and Building @ 2% on cost.

Prepare Trading and Profit and Loss Account for the year ended 30th June 1987 and the Balance Sheet as at 30th June 1987.

Solution :

Trading Account for the year ended 31-12-1987

Particulars	Amount	Particulars	Amount
To Opening stock 1-7-1986	65,000	By Sales	6,00,000
To Purchases	3,30,000	By Closing stock	55,000
To Wages	60,000		
To Manufacturing Exp.	20,000		
To Carriage inward	5,000		
Gross profit transferred to Profit and Loss A/c	1,75,000		
	6,55,000		6,55,000

Profit and Loss Account for the year ended 30th Jan. 1987

To Sales		50,000	By Gross Profit	1,75,000
To General Exp.	15,000			
Less : Prepaid Tax	300	14,700		
To Directors Fee		3,000		
To Auditors Fee		2,000		
To Advertisement		20,000		
To Depreciation :				
On Land & Building 4,50,000 @ 2%	8,000			
On Plant & Machinery 4,50,000 @ 10%	45,000	53,000		
To Interest on Bank Loan @ 6% on 20,000	12,000			
for 6 months ½ × 12,000		6,000		

Particulars	Amount	Particulars	Amount
To Managing Directors Commission 5% on net profit before charging his commission & income tax 1,75,000			
Gross Profit (–) 1,48,700			
26,300			
× 5/105	1,252		
To Income Tax Provision	15,000		
To Net Profit	10,048		
	1,75,000		1,75,000

Profit and Loss Appropriation A/c

To Proposed Dividend @ 5% on Rs. 4,00,000	20,000	By Net Profit	10,048
To Net Profit c/f	15,048	By Profit & Loss A/c Balance	25,000
	35,048		35,048

Balance Sheet as at 30-6-1987

Liabilities	Rs.	Assets			Rs.
Share Capital		*Fixed Assets*			
Authorised Capital		Goodwill			90,000
100000 Equity share of Rs. 10 — Issued & Paidup	10,00,000	Land & Building cost	4,00,000		
40000 Equity share of Rs. 10 Fully paid	4,00,000	*Less* Depreciation upto the date 90,000			
Reserve & Surplus		For the year	8,000	98,000	3,02,000
Share Premium	40,000	Plant & Machinery			
General Reserve	1,00,000	Cost	4,50,000		
Surplus Profit & Loss A/c	15,048	*Less* Depreciation			
Secured Loan	—	upto date 1,10,000			
Unsecured Loan		For the year	45,000	1,55,000	2,95,000
Bank loan @ 6% taken on 1st Jan. 1987	2,00,000	*Investments*			
Add Interest Payable	6,000	Closing Stock			55,000

Liabilities	Rs.	Assets	Rs.
Current Liabilities & Provisions		Sundry Debtors	60,000
		Bank Balance	15,000
Sundry Creditors	35,000	*Miscellaneus Exp.*	
Provision for Income Tax	15,000	Prepaid Rates	300
Proposed Dividend	20,000	Preliminary Exp.	15,000
Managing Directors Commission	1,252		
	8,32,300		8,32,300

Problem No. 20

The Bangalore Trader Co. Ltd. had an Authorised Capital of Rs. 10,00,000 divided in Equity shares of Rs. 10. Following is the Trial Balance as on 31-12-1990 :

Trial Balance as on 31-12-1990

Particulars	Dr. Rs.	Cr. Rs.
Land and Building	3,40,000	
Plant & Machinery	6,60,000	
Furnitures	60,000	
Preliminary Expenses	20,000	
Cash in Hand	11,000	
Calls in Arrears	6,000	
Share Capital paid up 80000 equity share of Rs. 10 each		8,00,000
Reserve Fund		60,000
Profit and Loss Account 1-1-1990		35,400
5% Govt. Bonds (Tax Free value Rs. 40,000)	36,000	
Bills Receivable	58,000	
Goodwill	36,000	
Motor Vehicle	40,000	
Sundry Debtors & Sundry Creditors	83,000	1,20,000
Return inward & Return outward	28,000	20,000
Purchases and Sales	9,60,000	12,30,000
Interim Dividend	18,000	
Repairs	3,000	
Advertisement	10,000	
Audit fee	4,000	

Particulars	Dr. Rs.	Cr. Rs.
Carriage inward	15,000	
Wages	92,000	
Insurance	20,000	
Stock on 1-1-1990	1,90,000	
General Expenses	17,000	
Debenture interest (less tax @ 30%)	8,400	
6% Debentures of Rs. 100 each		4,00,000
Bank Over draft		50,000
	27,15,400	27,15,400

Adjustments :

(1) Stock on 31-12-1990 Rs. 1,80,000

(2) Provide Depreciation on (a) Land & Building @ 2%
(b) Machinery @ 15% and (c) Furniture @ 15%
(d) Motor vehicles @ 20%.

(3) Prepaid Insurance Rs. 2,000.

(4) Transfer to Reserve Fund Rs. 10,000.

(5) Director declared interim dividend @ 3% for six months ending 30-6-90.

(6) Wages outstanding Rs. 3,000.

(7) Interest on Debentures for 6 months.

Prepare final accounts of the company for the year ended 31-12-90 and the Balance Sheet as at that dated.

Solution :

Trading A/c for the year ended 31-12-1990

Particulars		Amount	Particulars		Amount
To Opening Stock on 1-1-1990		1,90,000	By Sales	12,30,000	
			Less : Return Inward	28,000	
To Purchases	9,60,000				12,02,000
Less : Return outward	20,000	9,40,000	By Closing stock 31-12-90		1,80,000
To Wages	92,000				
Add : Outstanding	3,000	95,000			
To Carriages Inward		15,000			
To Gross Profit		1,42,000			
		13,82,000			13,82,000

Profit & Loss A/c for the year ended 31-12-1990

Particulars		Amount	Particulars	Amount
To Repairs		3,000	By Gross Profit	1,42,000
To Advertisement		10,000	By Interest on Govt.	
To Audit Fees		4,000	Bonds receivable	2,000
To Insurance	20,000			
Less Prepaid	2,000	18,000		
To General Exp.		17,000		
To Debenture Interest				
Less Tax @ 30%	8,400			
Due for	12,000	20,400		
To Depreciation :				
Land & Building	6,800			
Machinery	33,000			
Furniture	9,000			
Motor Van	8,000	56,800		
To Net Profit		14,800		
		1,44,000		1,44,000

Profit & Loss Appropriation A/c for the year ended 31-12-1990

To General Reserve Transfer	10,000	By Net profit	14,800
To Interim dividend 3% on 7,94,000	23,820	*Add* : Profit & Loss A/c	35,400
To Balance of Profit c/d	16,380		
	50,200		50,200

Balance Sheet as at 31-12-1990

Liabilities		Rs.	Assets		Rs.
Share Capital			*Fixed Assets*		
Authorised Capital			Goodwill		36,000
100000 Equity shares			Land & Building	3,40,000	
of Rs. 10 each		10,00,000	*Less* : Depr. @ 2%	6,800	3,33,200
Issued & Paidup			Machinery	6,60,000	
80000 equity shares			*Less* : Depr. @ 5%	33,000	6,27,000
of Rs. 10	8,00,000		Furnitures	60,000	
Less : Sales in arrears	6,000	7,94,000	*Less* : Depr. @ 15%	9,000	51,000
Reserve & Surplus			Motor Vehicle	40,000	
General Reserve	60,000		*Less* : Depr. 20%	8,000	32,000
Additions	10,000	70,000			

Liabilities		Rs.	Assets	Rs.
Surplus			*Investments*	
Profit & Loss A/c		16,380	5% Govt. Bonds	
Secured Loan			face value Rs. 40,000	36,000
6% Debentures	4,00,000		*Current Assets*	
Add : Interest	12,000	4,12,000	Stock	1,80,000
Unsecured Loan			Debtors	83,000
Bank Loan		50,000	Bills Receivable	58,000
Current Liabilities & Provisions			Cash in Hand	11,000
			Miscellaneous	
Sundry Creditors		1,20,000	Prepaid Insurance	2,000
Interim Dividend	23,820		Preliminary exp.	20,000
Less : Paid	18,000	5,820	Interest Receivable	2,000
Wages Outstanding		3,000		
		14,71,200		14,71,200

Note : Tax deducted on debenture interest assumed have been paid.

Problem No. 21

Bharat Machine Tools Co. Ltd., has an Authorised Capital of Rs. 50,00,000 divided into 400000 equity shares of Rs. 10 each and 10000 9% preference shares of Rs. 100 each.

Following is the Trial Balance of the Company as on 31-12-1990

Debits	Rs.	Credits	Rs.
Goodwill	5,00,000	Share Capital	
Land & Building	19,00,000	300000 equity shares	
Plant & Machinery	20,00,000	of Rs. 10 each	30,00,000
Furnitures	90,000	6000 9% Preference shares	
Investment 8%		of Rs. 100 each	6,00,000
Development Bonds	9,10,000	General Reserve	5,25,000
6% Govt. Securities		Share premium	2,00,000
Face value Rs. 2,25,000	2,17,500	Capital Redemption Reserve	2,10,000
Opening Stock 1-1-90	1,75,000	Development Reserve	7,00,000
Purchases	11,50,000	Profit & Loss A/c 1-1-1990	25,000
Sales Returns	25,000	Sales	20,00,000
Wages paid	98,000	Purchased Returns	15,000
Carriage Inward	9,000	10% Debentures	4,00,000
Salaries	2,10,000	Sundry Creditors	1,80,000
Rent, Rates and Taxes	35,000	Reserve for Doubtful Debts	7,500

Debits	Rs.	Credits	Rs.
Preliminary Exp.	40,000	Provision for taxation	32,000
Advertisement	25,000		
Printing & Stationery	30,000		
Postage	25,000		
Audit Fees	12,000		
Directors Fees	18,000		
Interest on Debentures paidup to 30-6-1990	20,000		
Sundry Debtors	2,00,000		
Bank Balance	2,05,000		
	78,94,500		78,94,500

Adjustments :

(1) Closing Stock on 31-12-1990 was Rs. 3,50,000.

(2) Write off preliminary expenses by 20%.

(3) Provide Reserve for Doubtful debts on Sundry debtors @ 5%.

(4) Provide for depreciation on : (a) Land & Building @ 2%. (b) Plant & Machinery @ 5% (c) Furnitures @ 10%.

(5) Make provision for taxation upto Rs. 50,000.

(6) Managers Commission @ 5% on Net profit before providing for taxation.

(7) Directors recommend the appropriation of profit by transferring Rs. 20,000 to General Reserve and declare dividend on equity shares @ 10%.

Prepare the Final Account of the Company for the year ending 31-12-1990 and the Balance Sheet as at that date.

Solution :

Trading A/c for the year ending 31-12-1990

Particulars		Amount	Particulars		Amount
To Opening Stock 1-1-1990		1,75,000	By Sales	20,00,000	
To Purchases	11,50,000		*Less* : Sales Return	25,000	19,75,000
Less : Purchase Return	15,000	11,35,000	By Closing Stock		3,50,000
Wages		98,000			
Carriage Inward		9,000			
		14,17,000			
Gross Profit		9,08,000			
		23,25,000			23,25,000

Profit & Loss A/c for the year ended 31-12-1990

Particulars		Amount	Particulars	Amount
To Salaries		2,10,000	By Gross Profit	9,08,000
To Rent, Rates, Taxes		35,000	By Interest on Investment Receivable	
To Preliminary Exp.	40,000		8% Development Bonds	
Less : Written off 20%	8,000	8,000	9,10,000	72,800
To Advertisement		25,000	6% Govt. Securities	
To Printing & Stationery		30,000	Face value Rs. 2,25,000	13,500
To Postage		25,000		
To Audit fees		12,000		
To Director fees		18,000		
To Depreciations :				
Land & Building 2%	38,000			
Plant & Machinery	1,00,000			
Furniture @ 10%	9,000	1,47,000		
To Reserve for Doubtful Debts @ 5% on 2,00,000	10,000			
Less : Old Reserve	7,500	2,500		
To Interest on Debentures				
Paid up to 30-6-90	20,000			
Payable	20,000	40,000		
Total		5,52,500		
Manager Commission				
5% on Net Profit	4,41,800	22,090		
To Provision for taxation				
up to	50,000			
Less : existing old	32,000	18,000		
To Net Profit		4,01,710		
		9,94,300		9,94,300

Profit & Loss Appropriation A/c

Particulars	Amount	Particulars	Amount
To General Reserve	20,000	By Net Profit	4,01,710
To Pref. share dividend @ 9% on Rs. 6,00,000	54,000	By Profit & Loss balance b/d (1-1-90)	25,000
To Proposed Dividend on Equity shares @ 10%	3,00,000		
To Balance of Profit	52,710		
	4,26,710		4,26,710

Balance Sheet as at 31-12-1990

Liabilities		Rs.	Assets		Rs.
Shares Capital			*Fixed Assets*		
Authorised 400000 equity shares of Rs. 10		40,00,000	Goodwill		5,00,000
			Land & Building	19,00,000	
10000 9% Pref. shares of Rs. 100		10,00,000	*Less* : Depr. @ 2%	38,000	18,62,000
		50,00,000	Plant & Machinery	20,00,000	
Issued & Paidup			*Less* : Depr. @ 5%	1,00,000	19,00,000
			Furniture	90,000	
300000 Equity shares of Rs. 10		30,00,000	*Less* : Depr. @ 10%	9,000	81,000
			Investments :		
6000 9% Pref. shares of Rs. 100		6,00,000	8% Development Bonds	9,10,000	
Reserve & Surplus					
Share Premium		2,00,000	6% Govt. Securities	2,17,500	11,27,500
General Reserve	5,25,000		(face value 2,25,000)		
Addition during the year	20,000	5,45,000	*Current Assets*		
			Closing stock		3,50,000
Capital Redemption Reserve		2,10,000	Sundry Debtors	2,00,000	
Development Reserve		7,00,000	*Less* : RDD	10,000	1,90,000
Surplus			Bank Balance		2,05,000
Profit & Loss A/c		52,710	*Miscellaneous A/c*		
Secured Loan			Preliminary exp.	40,000	
10% Debentures	4,00,000		*Less* : Written off 20%	8,000	32,000
Add : Interest on Debentures	20,000	4,20,000	*Interest on Investment Receivable*		
Unsecured Loan		—	5% on 9,10,000	72,800	
Current Liabilities & Provisions			6% on 2,25,000	13,500	86,300
Sundry Creditors		1,80,000			
Manager Commission	22,090				
Provision for taxation	50,000				
Pref. shares dividend	54,000				
Provide Dividend on equity shares	3,00,000	4,26,090			
		63,33,800			63,33,800

Problem No. 22

Sri Mahadev Mills Co. Ltd. was registered with an authorised capital of Rs. 8,00,000 divided into 50000 equity shares of Rs. 10 each and 3000 9% preference shares of Rs. 100 each. Following is the Trial Balance of the company as on 31-12-1992.

Trial Balance as on 31-12-1992

Debtors	Rs.	Creditors	Rs.
Goodwill	1,00,000	Profit & Loss A/c 1-1-92	45,000
Purchases	12,15,000	Interest on Bank Balance	3,900
Stock on 1-1-1992	76,500	Share capital (equity shares)	2,16,000
Manufacturing expenses	2,70,000	9% Preference shares	1,50,000
Salaries & wages	39,600	Pension Fund	69,000
Directors fees	600	Dividend equalisation fund	30,000
General expenses	16,500	Tax provisions	25,500
Interim Dividend paid	27,000	Unclaimed dividend	3,000
Building	1,51,500	Deposits	4,800
Plant & Machinery	1,05,600	Sundry Creditors	3,72,000
Furnitures	15,300	Sales	16,65,000
Motor Vehicles	61,200		
Stores	45,000		
Bills Receivable	67,500		
Sundry Debtors	1,71,000		
Investment (8% Development Bonds, Face value)	62,000		
Cash at Bank	1,59,900		
	25,84,200		25,84,200

Adjustments :

(1) Closing stock on 31-12-1992 was Rs. 1,09,000.

(2) Provide Reserve for Doubtful debts on Sundry debt. @ 2%.

(3) Provide for depreciation on : (a) Building @ 2% (b) Plant & Machinery @ 10% (c) Furnitures @ 10% (d) Motor Vehicles @ 20%.

(4) There was no liabilities in respect of tax for previous year and therefore tax provision amount be written back. Further tax provision for the year be made @ 60% of the Net Profit.

(5) Directors propose final Dividend on Equity shares @ 20%.

(6) Outstanding Expenses : Manufacturing expenses Rs. 50,000, Salaries & wages Rs. 10,000, General Expenses Rs. 5,000.

(7) Interest on Bank Balance receivable Rs. 3,000.

Prepare the Final Accounts of the Company for the year ended 31-12-1992 and the Balance Sheet at that date.

Solution :

Manufacturing A/c for the year ended 31-12-92

Debtors		Rs.	Creditors	Rs.
To Opening Stock		76,500	By Sales	16,65,000
To Purchases		12,15,000	By Closing Stock	1,09,000
To Manufacturing Expenses	2,70,000			
Add : Outstanding	50,000	3,20,000		
To Gross Profit		1,62,500		
		17,74,000		17,74,000

Profit and Loss A/c for the year ended 31-12-1992

To Salaries & Wages	39,600		By Gross Profit		1,62,500
Add : Outstanding	10,000	49,600	By Interest on Bank Balance	3,900	
To Directors fee		600	*Add* : Recoverable	3,000	6,900
To General Exp.	16,500				
Add : Outstanding	5,000	21,500	By Interest on investment @ 8% on Rs. 62,000		4,960
To Reserve for Doubtful Debts @ 2% on 1,71,000		3,420	By Tax Provision transferred (Since no liability on it)		25,500
To Depreciation on					
Building @ 2%	3,030				
Plant & Machinery @ 10%	10,560				
Furniture 10%	1,530				
Motor vehicle 20%	12,240	27,360			
To Provision for Taxation 60% on Net profit	71,880				
(*i.e.* 1,74,360 – 1,02,480)		43,128			
To Net Profit (Transfer to Appropriation A/c)		54,252			
		1,99,860			1,99,860

Profit & Loss Appropriation A/c

Debtors	Rs.	Creditors	Rs.
To Dividend on Pref. shares @ 9% on Rs. 1,50,000	13,500	By Net Profit	54,252
To Proposed Dividend on equity @ 20% on Rs. 2,16,000	43,200	By Profit & Loss A/c (Balance b/d)	45,000
To Balance of Profit c/d	42,552		
	99,252		99,252

Balance Sheet as at 31-12-1992

Liabilities		Rs.	Assets		Rs.
Share Capital			*Fixed Assets*		
Authorised Capital			Goodwill		1,00,000
50000 Equity shares of Rs. 10 each	5,00,000		Building	1,51,500	
			Less : Depr. @ 2%	3,030	1,48,470
3000 9% Pref. share of Rs. 100	3,00,000	8,00,000	Plant & Machinery	1,05,600	
			Less : Depr. @ 10%	10,560	95,040
Issued & Paid			Furnitures	15,300	
			Less : Depr. @ 10%	1,530	13,770
21600 Equity shares of Rs. 10	2,16,000		Motor Vehicle	61,200	
			Less : Depr. @ 20%	12,240	48,960
15000 Pref. shares of Rs. 100	1,50,000	3,66,000	Stores		45,000
Reserves & Surplus			*Investment*		
Dividend Equilisation fund		30,000	8% Development Bonds		62,000
Profit & Loss A/c		42,552	*Current Assets*		
Secured Loan		—	Closing Stock		1,09,000
Usecured Loan		—	Sundry Debtors	1,71,000	
Deposits		4,800	*Less* : RDD 2%	3,420	1,67,580
Current Liabilities and Provision			Bills Reccivable		67,500
			Cash at Bank		1,59,900
Sundry Creditors		3,72,000	*Miscellaneous A/c*		
Unclaimed dividend	3,000		Interest on Bank Bonds	3,000	
Pension fund	69,000				
Provision for taxation	43,128		Interest on Investment	4,960	7,960
Dividend Payable					
Preference dividend	13,500				

Liabilities		Rs.	Assets	Rs.
Equity shares :				
Proposed				
Dividend	43,200			
Less : paid	27,000	16,200		
Outstanding Exp. :				
(a) Manufacturing Exp.	50,000			
(b) Salaries wages	10,000			
(c) General Exp.	5,000	2,09,828		
		10,25,180		10,25,180

(b) PROFIT PRIOR TO INCORPORATION

A joint stock company some times takes over a running business from a certain date, but the company comes into existence at a later date. The profit earned from the date of purchase to the date of Registration (Incorporation) is called Profit prior to incorporation.

Profit earned prior to incorporation is treated as Capital profit and is not made available for distribution of Dividend to shareholders. The profit earned after incorporation is a Revenue profit and is made available for dividend payment. Capital profit is transferred to Capital Reserve. It is used to writteoff capital expenses or losses such as preliminary expenses, discount on issue of shares & debentures etc.

Allocation of total profit into :

(a) Profit prior to incorporation and

(b) Profit after incorporation.

The total profit for the year of purchase of Business is to be divided into from the date of purchase to the date of Registration or incorporation of the company and the remaining period upto the date of preparing Final account, is the profit after incorporation or Registration.

Procedure and the Basis for Allocation

(1) Propose Trading Account for the entire period.

(2) The Gross profit so arrived be divided in the ratio of sales or turn over basis of two periods.

(3) Division of Profit and Loss Account into two parts :

(a) Prior to incorporation and (b) After incorporation.

Basis for Allocation of Expenses

Expenses	Details	Basis
1. Sales Expenses	Commission on sales, discount allowed, carriage outward, Advertisement Expenses, Travelling Expenses etc.	Sales Ratio
2. Fixed Expenses	Rent, Rates and Taxes, Insurance, Salaries and allowances, interest, postage, telegramme, printing and stationery, General expenses, Audit fee, Depreciation etc.	Time basis (Ratio)
3. Expenses that arise only after Company comes into existence.	Preliminary Expenses, discount on issue of shares and debentures, Directors fees, Interest of Debentures etc.	After incorporate.
	Interest paid to vendor (Proportionate to period)	From date of purchase to date of incorporate and after incorporate date of payment.

Problem No. 23

Karnataka Traders Co. Ltd. was incorporated on 1st April, 1986 to take over as from 1st January 1986 the existing business of Bangalore Traders. The terms of acquisition of Business was the purchase consideration being Rs. 7,00,000. The Bangalore Traders received half of it in cash on 1st January 1986 together with interest at 10% p.a. The other half of the purchase consideration was the allotment of 35000 fully paid equity shares of Rs. 10 each in the company under the take over agreement. All the profit made from 1st January 1986 are to being to company.

The following Balance appear in the company ledger as on 31st December 1986 :

(1)	Share Capital (45000 equity shares Rs. 10 each including shares issued to vendors)	4,50,000
(2)	Bank Overdraft (Security stock)	1,65,000
(3)	Fixed Deposit received (Unsecured)	35,000
(4)	Sundry Creditors	65,000
(5)	Freehold land at cost	50,000
(6)	Building at cost	1,30,000

(7)	Furniture & Fixtures at cost	15,000
(8)	Motor Vehicles at cost	35,000
(9)	Stock in trade on 1st January 1986	4,20,000
(10)	Book Debts	95,000
(11)	Cash in hand	12,000
(12)	Preliminary expenses (There are to be fully written off)	8,000
(13)	Salaries & wages	48,000
(14)	Rent Received	13,000
(15)	Rates & Taxes	7,000
(16)	Repairs to Building	3,000
(17)	Miscellaneous	22,000
(18)	Directors fees	2,400
(19)	Interest to vendors	17,500
(20)	Purchases	7,70,000
(21)	Sales	9,10,000
(22)	Goodwill	3,100

Adjustments :

(1) Stock in Trade on 31-12-1986 Rs. 4,80,000

(2) Bad debts amount to Rs. 1,000 out of which Rs. 500 related to Book Debts — taken over by the company have to be written off and a provision for doubtful debts Rs. 5,000 be made.

(3) Depreciation : on Building @ 5%

on Furnitures & Fixtures @ 10%.

on Motor Vehicles @ 20%.

You are required to :

(1) Prepare Profit & Loss A/c for the period from 1st January 1986 to 31st December 1986.

(2) Compute profit prior to incorporation and after incorporation.

(3) Prepare Company's Balance Sheet as at 31-12-1986. For the purpose of determining the profit prior to incorporation, you should assume the turnover to be spread evenly over the year.

Solution :

Trial Balance as on 31-12-1986 as follows :

Particulars	Dr. Rs.	Cr. Rs.
Share capital (45000 equity shares of Rs. 10 each including shares issued to vendor)		4,50,000
Bank Overdraft (Security-stock in trade)		1,65,000
Fixed Deposit		35,000
Sundry Creditors		65,000
Freehold Land at cost	50,000	
Building at cost	1,30,000	
Furnitures and Fixtures at cost	15,000	
Motor vehicles at cost	35,000	
Stock in trade (on 1st January 1986)	4,20,000	
Book Debts	95,000	
Cash in hand	12,000	
Preliminary expenses (they are to be written off fully)	8,000	
Salaries & wages	48,000	
Rent received		13,000
Rates and taxes	7,000	
Repairs to Building	3,000	
Miscellaneous expenses	22,000	
Directors fees	2,400	
Interest to vendors	17,500	
Purchases and sales	7,70,000	9,10,000
Goodwill	3,100	
	16,38,000	16,38,000

Karnataka Traders Co. Ltd.

Trading A/c for the year ended 31-12-1986

Particulars	Amount	Particulars	Amount
To Opening Stock	4,20,000	By Sales	9,10,000
To Purchases	7,70,000	By Closing Stock	4,80,000
To Gross Profit	2,00,000		
	13,90,000		13,90,000

Profit & Loss A/c for the year ended 31-12-1986

		Prior to incorporation	After incorporation		Prior to incorporation	After incorporation
To Salaries & wages (time 1:3)		12,000	36,000	By Gross Profit	50,000	1,50,000
To Repairs on Building (1:3)		750	2,250	By Rent Received	3,250	9,750
To Rent & Taxes (1:3)		1,750	5,250			
To Misc. Exp. (1:3)		5,500	16,500			
Interest to vendor 1/2 × 17,500		8,750	8,750			
To Directors fees		—	2,400			
To Bad debts (as given)		500	500			
Provision for Doubtful debts		—	5,000			
To Preliminary Exp.		—	8,000			
To Depreciation (1:3) :						
Building @ 5%	6,500					
Furnitures @ 10%	1,500					
Motor vehicle @ 20%	7,000	3,750	11,250			
To Balance Transferred to Capital Reserve		20,250	—			
To Net Profit			63,850			
		53,250	1,59,750		53,250	1,59,750

Notes : (1) Sales are evenly spread over for 12 months :
Date of incorporation – 1st April 1986
From 1-1-1986 to 1-4-1986, 3 months.
After incorporation 1-4-86 to 31-12-1986, 9 months, Ratio 1:3.
Gross Profit Basis dates 1:3 i.e., 50,000 : 1,50,000

(2) Directors fees & Preliminary Exp.- Co. exp. after incorporation.

(3) Other fixed business exp. time basis.

(4) Bad debts as given RDD as given.

(5) Interest to vendor from 1-1-1986 to 1-7-1986 6 months
Prior & After 1 : 1 6 months.

Balance Sheet as at 31-12-1986

Liabilities		Rs.	Assets		Rs.
Share Capital			*Fixed Assets*		
Authorised Capital			Goodwill	3,100	
Issued & Paidup Capital			Deducted from capital reserve		
45000 equity shares of Rs. 10 each		4,50,000	(per contra)	3,100	—
Reserves & Surplus			Freehold land at cost		50,000
Capital Reserves			Building cost	1,30,000	
Profit prior to			*Less* : Depreciation		
incorporation	20,250		@ 5%	6,500	1,23,500
Less : Goodwill	3,100	17,150	Furnitures & Fixtures	15,000	
Profit & Loss A/c		63,850	*Less* : Depr. @ 10%	1,500	13,500
Secured Loan			Motor vehicles	35,000	
Bank Overdraft		1,65,000	*Less* : Depr. @ 20%	7,000	28,000
(secured = stock)			*Current Assets*		
Unsecured Loan		—	Stock in Trade		4,80,000
Fixed deposit		35,000	Debtors	95,000	
Current Liabilities			*Less* : Bad debts	1,000	
Sundry Creditors		65,000		94,000	
			Less : RDD	5,000	89,000
			Cash in hand		12,000
		7,96,000			7,96,000

Problem No. 24

X Ltd. was incorporated on 1-5-1995 to take over a running business from 1-1-95. The Profit and Loss Account of the company for the year ending 31-12-1995 was as follows :

Debits	Rs.	Credits	Rs.
To Salaries	39,000	By Gross Profit	3,29,000
To General expenses	15,000		
To Carriage	30,000		
To Advertising	40,000		
To Interest on Debentures	12,000		
To Preliminary exp. written off	8,000		
To Audit fees	10,000		
To interest to vendors (up to 30th June)	15,000		

Debits	Rs.	Credits	Rs.
To Selling expenses	10,000		
To Depreciation	40,000		
To Net Profit	1,10,000		
Total	3,29,000	Total	3,29,000

Sales up to 1-5-1995 were Rs. 4,00,000 and thereafter Rs. 16,00,000.

Prepare a statement ascertaining Profit and Loss before and after incorporation.

(October 1996)

Solution :

Statement showing Profit or Loss prior to and after incorporation

Particulars	Total	Basis	Profit	
			Prior to incorporation	After incorporation
(I) Gross Profit	3,29,000	Sales (1:4)	65,800	2,63,200
(II) Expenses :				
Salaries	39,000	Time (1:2)	13,000	26,000
General expenses	15,000	-do-	5,000	10,000
Carriage	30,000	Sales (1:4)	6,000	24,000
Advertising	40,000	-do-	8,000	32,000
Interest on Debentures	12,000	Co. A/cs.	—	12,000
Preliminary exp. written off	8,000	-do-	—	8,000
Audit Fees	10,000	Time (1:2)	3,333	6,667
Interest to vendors up to 30th June	15,000	Time (2:1)	10,000	5,000
Selling expenses	10,000	Sales (1:4)	2,000	8,000
Depreciation	40,000	Time (1:2)	13,333	26,667
Total expenses	2,19,000		60,666	1,58,334
Total Profit	3,29,000		65,800	2,63,200
Less : Expenses	2,19,000		60,666	1,58,334
Net Profit	1,10,000		5,134	1,04,866

Problem No. 25

X Y Z Co. Ltd. was incorporated on 1st May 1990 to take over the business of Hind Co. Ltd. as a going concern from 1st January 1990. The Profit & Loss A/c for the year ending 31-12-1990 was as follows :

Profit & Loss A/c for the year ended 31-12-1990

Debtors	Rs.	Creditors	Rs.
To Salaries	48,000	By Gross Profit	1,50,000
To Rent & Rates	15,000		
To Insurance	6,000		
To Electricity	4,800		
To Directors fees	2,000		
To Commission	5,000		
To Audit fees	1,200		
To Advertisement	2,500		
To Office expenses	4,200		
To Carriage	5,000		
To Bank charges	1,500		
To Preliminary exp.	6,500		
To Bad debts	2,000		
To Interest on debentures	3,000		
To Net Profit	43,300		
	1,50,000		1,50,000

Total turnover for the year ending 31-12-1990 was Rs. 10,00,000. Divided into Rs. 4,00,000 for the period up to 1st May 1990 and Rs. 6,00,000 for the remaining period.

Ascertain the profit earned to and after incorporation of the company.

(K.U.D., April 1992)

Solution :

Basis for apportionment of expenses and Gross profit.

Note : Turnover basis – Total = 10,00,000

Prior to up to May = 4,00,000

After Incorporation = 6,00,000

Turnover basis = 4/10 = 2/5

Ratio 2:3 = 6/10 = 3/5

January to May — 4 months = 4/12 = 1/3

May to December = 8/12 = 2/3 Ratio : 1:2

Profit & Loss A/c for the year ended 31-12-1992

Particulars	Total	Basis Time	Prior to incorpo-ration	After incor-poration	Particular	Prior to incorpo-ration	After incor-pora-tion
To Salaries	48,000	1:2	16,000	32,000	By Gross profit	60,000	90,000
To Rent & Rates	15,000	1:2	5,000	10,000			
To Insurance	6,000	1:2	2,000	4,000			
To Electricity	4,800	1:2	16,000	32,000			
To Directors fees	2,000	after	—	2,000			
To Commission	5,000	2:3	2,000	3,000			
To Auditors	1,200	1:2	400	800			
To Advertisement	2,500	2:3	1,000	1,500			
To Office Exp.	4,200	1:2	1,400	2,800			
To Carriage	5,000	2:3	2,000	3,000			
To Bank charges	1,500	1:2	500	1,000			
To Preliminary	6,500	After	—	6,500			
To Bad Debts	2,000	2:3	800	1,200			
To Interest on Debtors	3,000	After	—	3,000			
			32,700	74,000		60,000	90,000
Net Profit after incorporation			—	16,000		—	—
Capital Profit prior to incorporation			27,300	—		—	—
			69,000	90,000		60,000	90,000

Problem No. 26

Sri Virupay & Co. Ltd. was incorporated on 1-5-87. It acquired a running business as from 1-1-1987. The Profit & Loss A/c for the year ending 31-12-1987 was as under :

Profit & Loss A/c for the year ended 31-12-1987

Debits	Rs.	Credits	Rs.
To Salaries	80,000	By Gross Profit	4,00,000
" General Expenses	20,000		
" Carriage Outward	30,000		
" Advertisement	40,000		
" Interest on Debentures	12,000		
" Directors fees	8,000		
" Audit fees	10,000		
To Interest to Vendors (upto 3-6-1987)	20,000		
To Depreciation	40,000		
To Net Profit	1,40,000		
	4,00,000		4,00,000

Additional Information :

(1) Sales upto 1-5-1987 were Rs. 4,00,000 and after 1-5-1987 to 31-12-1987 were Rs. 16,00,000.

Solution :

Profit and Loss Account for the year end 31-12-1987

Particulars	Prior to incorporation	After incorporation	Particulars	Prior to incorporation	After incorporation
To Salaries 1:2	26,667	53,333	By Gross Profit	80,000	3,20,000
To General Exp. 1:2	667	13,333	(Sales basis 1:4)		
To Carriage outward 1:4	6,000	24,000			
To Advertisement 1:4	8,000	32,000			
To Interest on Debtors	—	12,000			
To Directors fee		8,000			

Particulars	Prior to incorpo-ration	After incorpo-ration	Particulars	Prior to incor-poration	After incorpo-ration
To Audit fee 1:2	3,333	6,667			
To Interest to Vendor	13,333	6,667			
To Depreciation 1:2	13,333	26,667			
Total	77,333	1,82,667			
To Net Profit	—	1,37,333			
To Capital Profit	2,667	—			
	80,000	3,20,000		80,000	3,20,000

Problem No. 27

Rahav Traders Ltd. was formed on 1-4-1976 to take over the business of M/s Raghu Traders, with effect from 1-1-1976. The following was the position of Profit and Loss Account prepared for the year ending 31-12-1976 :

Profit and Loss Account for the year ended 31-12-1976

Debits	Rs.	Credits	Rs.
To Salaries and wages	1,60,000	By Gross Profit	7,00,000
To Rent and rates	35,000		
To Directors fees	18,000		
To Commission on sales	56,000		
To General Expenses	48,000		
To Advertising	14,000		
To Audit fees	10,000		
To Depreciation	64,000		
To Interest to Vendor (up to 30-6-76)	10,000		
To Interest on Debentures	18,000		
To Net Profit	2,67,000		
	7,00,000		7,00,000

The following further information is available :

(1) The average monthly sales for the first three (3) months during 1976, was Rs. 1,60,000 whereas the monthly average sales for the subsequent period was Rs. 3,20,000.

(2) Rent was paid Rs. 2,000 per month up to 31-3-1976 and thereafter it was increased to Rs. 3,000 per month.

Prepare the statement showing Profit prior to incorporation.

(KUD, 1978)

Solution :

Profit and Loss Account for the year ended 31-12-1976

Particulars		Prior to incorpo- ration	After incorpo- ration	Particulars	Prior to incor- poration	After incorpo- ration
To Salaries & Allowances 1:3		40,000	1,20,000	By Gross Profit Basis Sales 1:6	1,00,000	6,00,000
To Rent & Rate	35,000					
Rent 2000 × 3	6,000	6,000				
	29,000					
Rent 3000 × 9	27,000		27,000			
Taxes 1:3	2,000	500	1,500			
To Directors Fee			18,000			
To Commission sales 1:6		8,000	48,000			
General Exp. 1:3		12,000	36,000			
To Advertisement 1:6		2,000	12,000			
To Audit Fee 1:3		2,500	7,500			
To Depreciation 1:3		16,000	48,000			
To Interest to vendors. Up to 30-6-76 31-4-76 30-6-76 ½ 1:1		5,000	5,000			

Particulars	Prior to incorpo-ration	After incorpo-ration	Particulars	Prior to incor-poration	After incorpo-ration
To Interest on Debentures		18,000			
Total	92,000	3,41,000			
To Net profit	—	2,59,000			
To Capital profit	8,000	—			
	1,00,000	6,00,000		1,00,000	6,00,000

Note : Apportionment of Expenses Prior to incorporate and After corporate Period : 1-1-1976 to 31-3-1976, 1-4-1976 to 31-12-1976

	3 months	9 months		
Ratio	1	3		
		1:3		Rate
Sales : First 3 months		1,60,000 × 3 =	4,80,000	1 } 1 : 6
next 9 months		3,20,000 × 9 =	28,80,000	6

Problem No. 28

Ultra-Modern Company Limited was incorporated on 1st May 1986 to take over the running business of Modern Trader from 1st January 1986. The Profit & Loss Account for the year ending 31st December 1986 is as under :

Profit & Loss A/c for the year ending 31-12-1986

Debits	Rs.	Credits	Rs.
To Salaries	36,000	By Gross Profit	1,55,000
To Rent & Taxes	12,000		
To Insurance	3,000		
To Electricity Charges	2,400		
To Directors fees	3,000		
To Audit fees	1,600		

Debits	Rs.	Credits	Rs.
To Commission	6,000		
To Advertisement	4,000		
To Discount	3,500		
To Office Expenses	7,500		
To Carriage Outward	3,000		
To Bank Charges	1,500		
To Preliminary Expenses	6,500		
To Bad debts	2,000		
To Interest on Loan	3,000		
To Net Profit	60,000		
	1,55,000		1,55,000

The total turnover for the year ending 31st December 1986 was Rs. 5,00,000 dividing into 1,50,000 for the period up to 1st May 1986 and 3,50,000 for the remaining period.

Ascertain the profit prior to incorporation and obtain incorporation of the company.

(K.U.D., April 1987 & October 1994)

Solution :

Profit & Loss A/c for the year ended 31-12-1986

Particulars	Prior to incorpo-ration	After incorpo-ration	Particulars	Prior to incor-poration	After incor-poration
To Salaries 1:2	12,000	24,000	By Gross Profit	46,500	1,08,500
To Rent & Taxes 1:2	4,000	8,000			
To Insurance	1,000	2,000			
To Electricity Charge	800	1,600			
To Directors fees	—	3,000			
To Audit fees 1:2	533	1,067			

Particulars	Prior to incorporation	After incorporation	Particulars	Prior to incorporation	After incorporation
To Commission 3:7	1,800	4,200			
To Advertisement 3:7	1,200	2,800			
To Discount 3:7	1,050	2,450			
To Office Exp. 1:2	2,500	5,000			
To Carriage Outward	900	2,100			
To Bank Charges	500	1,100			
To Preliminary Exp.	—	6,500			
To Bad Debts	600	1,400			
To Interest on Loan	1,000	2,000			
	27,883	67,117			
To Net Profit	—	41,383			
To Capital Profit (Prior to incorporate transferred)	18,617	—			
	46,500	1,08,500		46,500	1,08,500

Note : Basis for apportionment of Expenses.

Prior to incorporation – After incorporation

Sales 1,50,000 3,50,000 = 3:7

(1) Commission (2) Advertisement (3) Bad Debts (4) Carriage Outward

Time – 4 Months 8 Months = 1:2 Other Expenses.

Expenses after incorporation :

(a) Directors fees (b) Preliminary Expenses.

Problem No. 29

Shobha Ltd. was incorporated on 1-5-1989 to take over the business of Parvati and Sarojani as a going concern from 1-1-1989. The Profit & Loss Account of the Company for the year ending 31-12-89 was as follows :

Profit & Loss A/c for the year ended 31-12-1989

Debits	Rs.	Credits	Rs.
To Salaries & Allowances	60,000	By Gross Profit	2,00,000
To Rent & Taxes	23,000		
To General Expenses	7,200		
To Directors Expenses	3,000		
To Selling Expenses	4,000		
To Discount on sales	1,000		
To Advertising	3,000		
To Audit fees	4,500		
To Formation Expenses	1,800		
To Miscellaneous Expenses	1,500		
To Interest on Debentures	1,400		
To Interest to Vendor up to 30-6-89	6,000		
To Repairs to Building	1,200		
To Depreciation	2,400		
To Net Profit	80,000		
	2,00,000		2,00,000

The following is further information :

(a) Rent was paid at Rs. 1,000 per month up to 1-5-89 and thereafter it was paid to Rs. 2,000 per month.

(b) Average monthly sales for the first four months during the year was Rs. 60,000 subsequent period was Rs. 70,000.

Prepare the Profit & Loss Account showing the Profit Prior to Incorporation of the Company.

(K.U.D., October 1990)

Profit & Loss A/c for the year ended 31-12-89

Particulars	Prior to incorporation	After incorporation	Particulars	Prior to incorporation	After incorporation
To Salaries & Wages (1:2)	20,000	40,000	By Gross Profit	60,000	1,40,000
To Rent & Taxes Rent = 1,000 × 4 = 4,000 2,000 × 8 = 16,000	4,000	16,000			
To Taxes 3,000 (1:2)	1,000	2,000			
To General Exp. (1:2)	2,400	4,800			
To Directors Exp.	—	3,000			
To Selling Exp. (3:7)	1,200	2,800			
To Discount on sales (3:7)	300	700			
To Advertising (3:7)	900	2,100			
To Audit fee (1:2)	1,500	3,000			
To Formation Fees (affer)		1,800			
To Miscellaneous Exp. (1:2)	500	1,000			
To Interest on Debentures (after)	—	1,400			
To Interest to Vendor up to 30-6-89 — 4 months 2 months (2:1)	4,000	2,000			
To Repairs to Building (1:2)	400	800			
To Depreciation (1:2)	800	1,600			
	37,000	83,000			
To Net Profit	—	57,000			
To Capital Profit	23,000	—			
	60,000	1,40,000		60,000	1,40,000

Note : Bases for apportionment of Expenses.

Prior to incorporation – After incorporation.

(1) Sales – 60,000 × 4 = 2,40,000 – 70,000 × 8 = 5,60,000

24 : 56

3 : 7 = 3 : 7

(2) Time – Upto 1-5-1989		from 1-5-98 to 31-12-89
4 Months		8 Months
1	:	2 = 1 : 2

Problem No. 30

Sunshina Co. Ltd. was incorporated on 1st May 1988 to take over the bussiness of M/s Ram Laxman as a going concern from 15th January 1988. The Profit and Loss Account for the year ending 31-12-1988 was as under :

Profit and Loss Account for the year ended 31-12-1988

Debits	Rs.	Credits	Rs.
To Salaries A/c	1,26,000	By Gross Profit	5,42,500
To Office Expenses	26,250		
To Rent & taxes	42,000		
To Insurance	10,500		
To Electrical Charge	8,400		
To Directors Fee	10,500		
To Audit Fee	5,600		
To Commission	21,000		
To Advertisement	14,250		
To Discount	12,250		
To Carriage	10,500		
To Bank Charges	5,250		
To Preliminary Exp.	22,750		
To Bad Debits	7,000		
To Interest on loan	10,500		
To Discount on issue of shares	21,000		
To Net profit	1,88,750		
	5,42,500		5,42,500

The total turnover for the priof upto 31-12-1988 was Rs. 15,00,000 divided into Rs. 4,50,000 for the period upto 1st May 1988 and Rs. 10,50,000 for the remaining 8 months period of 1988.

Ascertain profit earned prior to incorporation and after incorporation of the Company.

Solution :

Profit & Loss A/c for the year ended 31-12-1988

Particulars		Prior to incorporation	After incorporation	Particulars	Prior to incorporation	After incorporation
To Salaries	1:2	42,000	84,000	By Gross Profit (Sales ratio 3:7)	1,62,750	3,79,750
To Office Exp.	1:2	8,750	17,500			
To Rent & Taxes	1:2	14,000	28,000			
To Insurance	1:2	3,500	7,000			
To Electric Charge		2,800	5,600			
To Directors fee Co A/c		—	10,500			
To Audit fees	1:2	1,867	3,733			
To Commission	3:7	6,300	14,700			
To Advertising	3:7	4,275	9,975			
To Discount	3:7	3,675	8,575			
To Carriage	3:7	3,150	7,350			
To Bank Charge	1:2	1,750	3,500			
To Preliminary Exp. Co. A/c		—	22,750			
To Bad Debts	3:7	2,100	4,900			
To Interest on Loan	1:2	3,500	7,000			
To Discount on issue of shares		—	21,000			
To Net Profit		—	1,23,667			
To Capital Profit		65,083	—			
		1,62,750	3,79,750		1,62,750	3,79,750

Profit Prior to Incorporation		65,083	Capital Profit
Profit After Incorporation		1,23,667	
Total Profit	Profit and Loss A/c	1,88,750	

Note : Basis for allocation of expenses :

Prior to Incorporation – After Incorporation

(1) Gross Profit – Sales 4,50,000 : 10,50,000 = 3:7

(2) Time Basis = 4 Months : 8 Months = 4:8 = 1:2.

Problem No. 31

Vijay Trading Co. Ltd. was incorporated on 1st May 1989 to takeover the running Business of M/s Ashok & Sons from 1st January 1989. The Profit & Loss Account for year ended 31-12-1989 was as under :

Profit & Loss A/c for the year ended 31-12-1989

Debits	Rs.	Credits	Rs.
To Salaries	72,000	By Gross Profit	3,50,000
To General Expenses	9,000	By Discount	6,000
To Preliminary Exp.	8,500		
To Carriage Outward	26,250		
To Advertising	35,000		
To Debenture Interest	10,500		
To Directors fee	8,750		
To Audit fees	7,200		
To Depreciation	36,000		
To Rent, Rates & Taxes	21,000		
To Interest to Vendor (up to 30th June)	16,500		
To Commission on Sales	20,000		
To Net Profit	85,300		
	3,56,000		3,56,000

The sales up to 1st May 1989 were Rs. 3,50,000 and after 1st May 1989 till 31st December 1989 was Rs. 14,00,000. Ascertain profit Prior to incorporation and profit After incorporation.

Solution :

Profit and Loss A/c for the year ended 31-12-89

Particulars		Prior to incorpo-ration	After incorpo-ration	Particulars	Prior to incor-poration	After incor-poration
To Salaries	1:2	24,000	48,000	By Gross Profit (Sales 1:4)	70,000	2,80,000
To General Exp.	1:2	3,000	6,000	By Discount (Sales 1:4)	1,200	4,800
To Carriage Outward	1:4	5,250	21,000	By Capital Loss	4,450	—
To Advertising	1:4	7,000	28,000			
To Debenture Interest		—	10,500			

Particulars		Prior to incorporation	After incorporation	Particulars	Prior to incorporation	After incorporation
To Director fee		—	8,750			
To Audit fee	1:2	2,400	4,800			
To Depreciation	1:2	12,000	24,000			
To Rent, Rates & Taxes	1:2	7,000	14,000			
To Interest to Vendor (Upto 30th June)	2:1	11,000	5,500			
To Commission on Sales	1:4	4,000	16,000			
To Net Profit		—	89,750			
		75,650	2,84,800		75,650	2,84,800

Note 1 : Basis for allocation of expenses :

(a) Prior to Incorporation,

(b) After Incorporation.

(1) Gross Profit, – Sales 3,50,000 – 14,00,000 = 1:4

(2) Time Basis 1st Jan to 1st May – 1st May to 31-12-89

4 Months 8 Months = 1:2

(3) Interest to Vendor = Jan. 89 to 1st May 89 = 4 Months

1st May to 30th June 89 = 2 Months

Ratio = 2:1

Note 2 : Prior to Incorporation Gross Profit 71,200 – 75,650 (Expenses)

Net Loss = -4,450 Capital Loss.

(Treated as Goodwill)

Problem No. 32

Shri Krishna Co. Ltd. was incorporated on 1st May 1991 to take over the business of Shri Ram and Sons, as a going concern from 1st January 1991.

To Profit and Loss Account for the year ending 31-12-1991 was as follows :

Profit and Loss Account for the year ended 31-12-1991

Debits	Rs.	Credits	Rs.
To Salaries	1,20,000	By Gross Profit	3,75,000
To Electricity	12,000	By Interest Recieved	6,000
To Insurance	15,000	By Miscellaneous Income	3,000
To Rent, Rate & Taxes	37,500		
To Directors Fees	9,000		
To Audit Fees	4,500		
To Commission	12,500		
To Office Expenses	10,500		
To Carriage Outward	12,500		
To Bank Charges	3,750		
To Preliminary Exp.	16,000		
To Bad Debts	4,500		
To Interest on Debentures	7,500		
To Interest paid to vendor up to 31-7-91	7,000		
To Depreciation	24,000		
To Net Profit	87,750		
	3,84,000		3,84,000

The Total turnover for the year ending was Rs. 20,00,000 divided into Rs. 5,00,000 for the period upto 1st May 1995 and thereafter Rs. 15,00,000.

Ascertain profit prior to incorporation and profit after incorporation of the company.

Solution :

Profit & Loss Account for the year ended 31-12-91

Particulars		Prior to incorporation	After incorporation	Particulars	Prior to incorporation	After incorporation
To Salaries	1:2	40,000	80,000	By Gross Profit (Sales ratio 1:3)	93,750	2,81,250
To Electricity	1:2	4,000	8,000	By Interest (Time = 1:2)	2,000	4,000
To Insurance	1:2	5,000	10,000			
To Rent, Rate & Taxes	1:2	12,500	25,000	By Miscellaneous Income (Time 1:2)	1,000	2,000
To Direct. fee (After)		—	9,000			
To Audit fee	1:2	1,500	3,000			

Particulars	Prior to incorporation	After incorporation	Particulars	Prior to incorporation	After incorporation
To Commission 1:3	3,125	9,375			
To Office Exp. 1:2	3,500	7,000			
To Carriage Outward 1:3	3,125	9,375			
To Bank Charge1:2	1,250	2,500			
To Preliminary Exp. (After)	—	16,000			
To Bad Debts 1:3	1,125	3,375			
To Interest on Debentures	—	7,500			
To Interest paid to Vendor :					
Jan. to April 4:3 4 months	4,000	3,000			
May to July 3 months					
To Depreciation 1:2	8,000	16,000			
	87,125	2,09,125			
To Capital Profit	9,625	78,125			
	96,750	2,87,250		96,750	2,87,250
(Revenue – Profit After Incorporation)					

Note : Basis for allocation of Expenses and Incomes.

Gross Profit – Sales Basis upto 1st May Rs. 5,00,000

Or Turnover Basis from 1st May to 31st Dec. 15,00,000

Ratio : 5,00,000 : 15,00,000 = 1:3 Or 1/4:3/4

Time :

From Jan. 1991 to 1st May — 4 Months

From 1st May to 31st December — 8 Months

Ratio = 4:8 = 1:2

Problem No. 33

Electronics Appliances Co. Ltd. was inccorporated on 1st May 1992 to take over the running business of M/s Ganesh and Sons from 1st January 1992.

Following is the Profit & Loss A/c of the Company for the year ended 31-12-1992 :

Debits	Rs.	Credits	Rs.
To Salaries	1,08,000	By Gross Profit	5,34,000
To General Expenses	13,500		
To Preliminary Expenses	12,750		
To Carriage Outward	39,375		
To Advertising	52,500		
To Debenture Interest	15,750		
To Directors fee	12,000		
To Audit fees	10,800		
To Depreciation	54,000		
To Rent, Rates & Taxes	31,500		
To Interest to Vendor Up to 30th June	24,000		
To Commission on Sales	30,000		
	4,04,175		
New Profit	1,29,825		
	5,34,000		5,34,000

Total Sales for the year 1992 was Rs. 20,00,000 divided into sales up to 1st May Rs. 4,00,000 and for the remaining period, Rs. 16,00,000. Ascertain Profit or Loss Prior to incorporation and After incorporation.

Solution :

Profit & Loss A/c for the year ended 31-12-1992

Particulars	Basis	Prior to incorporation	After incorporation	Particulars	Prior to incorporation	After incorporation
To Salaries	1:2	36,000	72,000	By Gross Profit (Sales Basis)	1,06,800	4,27,200
To General Exp.	1:2	4,500	9,000			
To Preliminary Expenses		—	12,750	By Loss Being Capital Loss	6,175	—
To Carriage Outward	1:4	7,875	31,500			
To Advertise	1:4	10,500	42,000			

Particulars	Basis	Prior to incorporation	After incorporation	Particulars	Prior to incorporation	After incorporation
To Debentures interest			15,750			
To Directors fee			12,000			
To Audit fee	1:2	3,600	7,200			
To Depreciation	1:2	18,000	36,000			
To Rent, Rate & Taxes	1:2	10,500	21,000			
To Interest to Vendor up to 30-6-92	2:1	16,000	8,000			
To Commission on Sales	1:4	6,000	24,000			
Total		1,12,975	2,91,200			
Net Profit		—	1,36,000			
		1,12,975	4,27,200		1,12,975	4,27,200

Note 1 : Prior to Incorporation :

Total Expenses	1,12,975
Income	1,06,800
Loss	– 6,175 Capital Loss treated as Goodwill.

Note 2 : Basis for allocation of expenses & Gross Profit :

(1) Gross Profit – Sales Basis = Jan. 1992 to 1st May Rs. 4,00,000
1st May 1992 to 31st Dec. Rs. 16,00,000

Sales Ratio = 4,00,000 : 16,00,000
= 4:16 = 1:4

(2) Time Basis Jan. 1992 to 1st May 1992 – 4 Months
1st May 92 to 31st Dec. 1992 – 8 Months
Ratio = 4:8 = 1:2

(3) Interest to Vendor = Jan. 1992 to 1st May = 4 Months
1st May to 30th June 1992 = 2 Months
Ratio = 2:1.

2

Joint Stock Company Accounts—II

AMALGAMATION, ABSORPTION AND RECONSTRUCTION

(1) Amalgamation

It is the combination of two or more Cos. carrying on similar type of Business.

The existing Cos. amalgamated are liquidated and a new Co. is formed to take over their business.

The assets and the liabilities of the old Cos. amalgamated are generally taken over by the New Co.

The Shareholders of the old Cos. are issued Shares in the New Co.

Advantages :

(1) Elimination of Competition.

(2) Economics of Large-scale Production.

(3) Reduction in the Administrative Expenses.

Example :

Features :

(1) Two or more Cos. amalgamated are liquidated.

(2) Formation of New Co.

(2) Absorption

The one existing Co. takes over the business of another existing Co. and continues to function in its own name. The Co. takenover by the another existing Co., goes into liquidation. The Co. taking over the business of another Co. is called absorbing Co.

Features :

(1) Liquidation of one Co. (absorbing).

(2) Existing Co. continue to function.

(3) Reconstruction

Two Types :

(1) *Internal or Reduction of Share Capital :*

With a view to write off accumulated losses and the assets at their realisable value.

No liquidation of the Co.

(2) *External :*

The existing Co. facing financial difficulties and the business cannot be continued without losses may resort to reconstruction i.e. the existing Co. will be liquidated and a new Co. is formed to take over the business of old Co.

The same body of Shareholders and the Creditors, Debenture holders if desire may continue in the New Co.

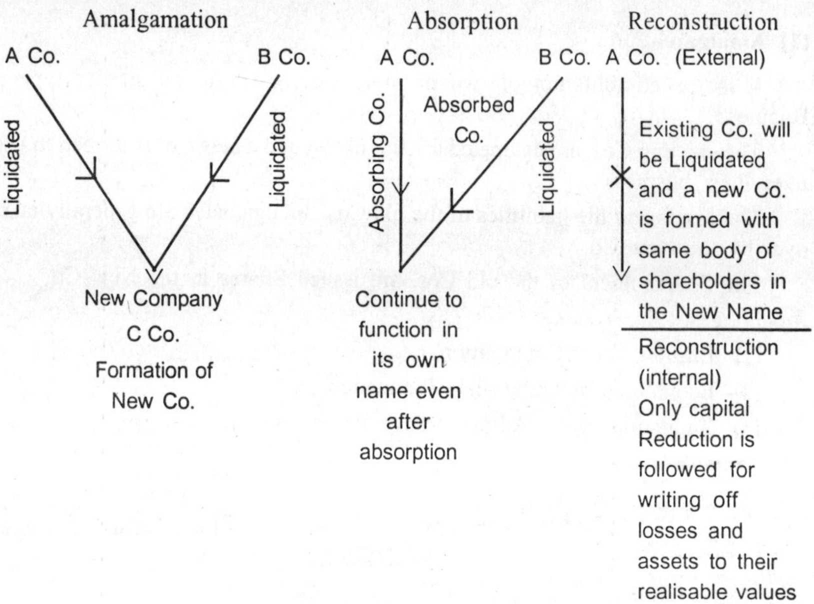

ACCOUNTING PROCEDURE

Amalgamation, Absorption and Reconstruction

A. (1) Liquidation of Companies amalgamated :

(a) Closing of the Books of the Companies in Liquidation :

(1) Open Realisation A/c (2) Shareholders A/c

(3) Debenture holders A/c (4) Purchasing Co. A/c

(5) Shares or Debentures in Purchasing Co. A/c

(6) Cash or Bank A/c if necessary.

(b) Opening Entries in the books of Purchasing Co.

B. Terms :

Purchase consideration is the price payable by the purchasing Co. to the Liquidator of the Co. in liquidation.

Purchase price is paid :

(a) in shares, (b) Cash, (c) Debentures etc. as agreed.

Methods of calculation of purchase consideration :

(a) Net Assets Method (b) Net Payment Method.

Net Assets Method :

Purchasing Co. agrees to pay purchase price — an amount equal to the Net Assets.

Net Assets = Assets taken over – Liabilities taken over.

Assets include all Assets taken over – (except accumulated losses i.e., Profit and Loss Debit Balance and Preliminary Expenses etc. Fictitious Assets). Liabilities include all liabilities and provisions taken over except – accumulated Profit Reserve and Reserve Fund.

Net Payment Method :

Purchasing Company agrees to pay a lumpsum fixed as purchase price.

Goodwill :

It is the result of excess payment of purchase price, over the Net Assets acquired.

Goodwill	=	Total Assets taken over	—
		Less Liabilities taken over	—
		Net Assets	—

Purchase Price $>$ Net Assets – Result in Excess payment, i.e. payment towards Goodwill.

Purchase Price $<$ Net Assets – results in under-payment — Capital gain treated as Capital Reserve.

(1) Journal entries to close the books of the companies in liquidation.

(2) Opening entries in the books of New Co. in case of Amalgamation (Or in case of Absorption entries in the books of Absorbing Co.).

Treatment of Accumulated Profits

(a) Undistributed Profit such as,
Reserves, Reserve funds, Dividend equilisation fund, Contingency Reserve.
Transfer directly to shareholders A/c — Credit side.

(b) Workmen's Profit sharing fund, Pension fund, Provident fund, Workmen's compensation fund are the accumulated liabilities transferred to Purchasing company.
Workmen's compensation fund or Accident compensation fund in this case after making payment of compensation to workers in case accident – the net balance on this account treated as accumulated Profit and transferred to Sharehoders Account.

(c) Depreciation fund : It should transferred to purchasing company alongwith assets taken over.

(d) Reserve for doubtful debts — It is treated as liability and transferred along with Debtors to purchasing company.

Problem No. 1

The following is the Balance Sheet of Shiva Ltd. as on 31-12-1997.

Balance Sheet as at 31-12-1997

Liabilities	Rs.	Assets	Rs.
Share Capital		Goodwill	97,000
30000 Preference shares of Rs. 5 each	1,50,000	Building	1,56,500
40000 Equity Shares of Rs. 5 each	2,00,000	Machinery	78,000
Reserves & Surplus		Debtors	32,000
Reserve Fund	11,000	Stock	52,500
Secured Loan		Bank	3,300
9% Debentures	75,000	Profit & Loss A/c	97,000
Unsecured Loan	—		
Current Liabilities			
Creditors	80,300		
	5,16,300		5,16,300

The company suffered heavy losses and found that Goodwill was worthless and that the Assets were overvalued to the following extent :

Building Rs. 26,500; Machinery Rs. 23,000; Stock Rs. 65,000; A Provision for doubtful debts @ 5% was necessary.

The following scheme of Reconstruction was adopted :

(a) The creditors to accept 9% Debenture to the extent of half of their dues and their balance to be paid six months after date.

(b) The preference shares to be reduced to Rs. 2.50 each.

(c) The Assets be reduced to the revalued figures and the Profit & Loss A/c debit balance be wiped out.

(d) Equity shares be reduced to Re. 0.50 paise each.

Draft the Journal entries to give effect to the above scheme and prepare Reconstructed Balance Sheet.

[K.U.D., April 1998(N)]

Solution :

Journal Entries		Dr. Rs.	Cr. Rs.
(1) Preference Share Capital A/c	Dr	75,000	
Equity Share Capital A/c	Dr	1,80,000	
To Capital Reduction A/c			2,55,000
(Preference shares of Rs. 5 each reduced to Rs. 2.50 each and equity shares of Rs. 5 each reduced to Re. 0.50 30000 × 2.50 = Rs. 75,000 + 40,000 × 4.50 = 1,80,000)			
(2) Capital Reduction A/c	Dr	2,55,000	
To Goodwill A/c			97,000
To Profit & Loss A/c			97,000
To Building A/c			26,500
To Machinery A/c			23,000
To Stock A/c			6,500
To Provision for Doubtful Debts			1,600
To Capital Reserve A/c			3,400
(Capital Reduction A/c utilised to write off Goodwill, Profit & Loss A/c Debit Balance and the Assets at reduced value and the Balance left credited to Capital Reserve A/c)			

Reconstructed Balance Sheet as at ....

Liabilities		Rs.	Assets	Rs.	Rs.
Share Capital			Goodwill	97,000	
30000 Pref. Shares of		75,000	*Less* Written off	97,000	—
Rs. 2.50 each			Building	1,56,500	
40000 Equity Shares of		20,000	*Less* Written off	26,500	1,30,000
Re. 0.50 each			Machinery	78,000	
Reserves & Surplus			*Less* Written off	23,000	55,000
Reserve Fund		11,000	Debtors	32,000	
Capital Reserve		3,400	*Less* 5% RDD	1,600	30,400
Secured Loan			Stocks	52,500	
9% Debentures	75,000		*Less* Written down	6,500	46,000
9% Issued to Credit	40,150	1,15,150	Bank A/c		3,300
Creditors A/c		40,150	Profit & Loss A/c	97,000	
			Less Written off	97,000	—
		2,64,700			2,64,700

Problem No. 2

K Ltd. is absorbed by 'A' Ltd.

The consideration being —

(i) Assumption of liabilities

(ii) Discharge of Debentures at a premium of 5% by the issue of 5% Debentures in 'A' Ltd.

(iii) A payment of cash of Rs. 30 per share.

(iv) The exchange of (3) three shares of Rs. 10 each in 'A' Ltd. at on agreed value of Rs. 15 per share for every share in K Ltd.

Balance Sheet of K Ltd. as at 31-12-1996

Liabilities	Rs.	Assets	Rs.
Share Capital		Goodwill	1,25,000
30000 shares of	15,00,000	Land & Building	3,82,500
Rs. 50 each fully paid		Plant of Machinery	11,00,000
Reserves & Surplus :		Patents	25,000
General Reserve	1,60,000	Patterns & Drawings	12,500
Profit & Loss A/c	15,000	Investments on	
Workman's Profit sharing		Compensation Fund	25,000
Fund	50,000	Works-in-progress	5,30,000
Accident Fund	25,000	Debtors	2,25,000
Secured Loan :		Banks	1,75,000
5% Debentures	7,50,000		
Current Liabilities creditors	1,00,000		
	26,00,000		26,00,000

Prepare Ledger Accounts to close the Books of B Ltd. and open the Books of 'A' Ltd.

[K.U.D., October 1997(N)]

Solution :

Calculation of Purchase Consideration

Assets taken			Purchase Consideration	
Sundry Assets		26,00,000	(1) 5% Debentures	7,50,000
Less Liabilities			*Add* Premium 5%	37,500
Workmen's profit			in Debenture	7,87,500
sharing fund	50,000		(2) Issue of shares @ Rs. 15	
Accident Fund	25,000		30,000 × 3 = 90,000 × 15 =	1,35,000
Creditors	1,00,000	–1,75,000		
Net Assets		24,25,000	(3) Cash Rs. 30	
Purchase Price		30,37,500	30000 × 30	9,00,000
Excess paid			Total	30,37,500
treated Goodwill		6,12,500	Purchase Proceeds Rs.	30,37,500

In the Books of K Ltd.
Realisation A/c

To Sundry Assets	26,00,000	By Workmen's Profit sharing Fund	50,000
To Premium on Debentures	37,500	By Accident Fund	25,000
To Profit on Realisation transferred to Shareholders	5,75,000	By Creditors	1,00,000
		By 'A' Ltd. (Purchase consideration)	30,37,500
	32,12,500		32,12,500

Purchasing Co. 'A' Ltd. A/c

To Realisation	30,37,500	By Debentures in 'A' Ltd.	7,87,500
		By Shares in 'A' Ltd.	13,50,000
		By Bank A/c	9,00,000
	30,37,500		30,37,500

Equity Shareholder A/c

To Shares in 'A' Ltd.	13,50,000	By Share Capital	15,00,000
To Bank A/c	9,00,000	By General Reserve	1,60,000
		By Profit & Loss A/c	15,000
		By Profit on Realisation	5,75,000
	22,50,000		22,55,000

Debenture holder A/c

To Debentures in 'A' Ltd.	7,87,500	By Debentures A/c	7,50,000
		By Premium on Debentures @ 5%	37,500
	7,87,500		7,87,500

In the Books of 'A' Ltd. (Absorbing Co.)

Opening Entries		Dr. Rs.	Cr. Rs.
(1) Business Purchase A/c	Dr	30,37,500	
To K Ltd. Co. (Vendor) A/c			30,37,500
(Purchase consideration payable)			
(2) Goodwill A/c (1,25,600 + 6,12,500)	Dr	7,37,500	
Land & Building A/c	Dr	3,82,500	
Plant & Machinery A/c	Dr	11,00,000	
Patents A/c	Dr	25,000	

Opening Entries		Dr. Rs.	Cr. Rs.
Patterns and Drawings A/c	Dr	12,500	
Investments on Accident Fund A/c	Dr	25,000	
Work-in-progress A/c	Dr	5,30,000	
Debtors A/c	Dr	2,25,000	
Bank A/c	Dr	1,75,000	
To Workers Profit sharing Fund A/c			50,000
To Accident Fund A/c			25,000
To Creditors A/c			1,00,000
To Business Purchase A/c			30,37,500
(Incorporation of Assets and Liabilities taken over)			
(3) K Ltd. Co. A/c (Vendor)	Dr	30,37,500	
To Equity Share Capital A/c			9,00,000
To Share Premium A/c			4,50,000
To 5% Debentures A/c			7,87,500
To Bank A/c			9,00,000
(Purchase consideration paid in by issue of 5% Debentures in discharge of Debentures at 5% premium, Issue of 3 equity shares of Rs. 10 each at Rs. 15 purchase in exchange of one share in old Co. and a payment of cash Rs. 30 per share.)			

Problem No. 3

The Balance Sheet of Mismage Ltd. stood as below :

Balance Sheet as at 31-12-1996

Liabilities	Rs.	Assets	Rs.
Share Capital		Patents	28,000
Equity shares of Rs. 10 each	1,20,000	Plant & Machinery	80,000
Preference shares of		Land & Building	31,200
Rs. 100 each	80,000	Stock	36,000
Reserves & Surplus	—	Cash	800
Secured Loan	—	Books Debts	24,000
Current Liabilities		Preliminary Expenses	8,000
Sundry Creditors	30,000	Profit & Loss Account	40,000
Bills Payable	18,000		
	2,48,000		2,48,000

The following scheme of Reconstruction is agreed to :

(a) The Existing equity shares be reduced to Rs. 5 each

(b) The existing preference shares be reduced to Rs. 75 each

(c) Preliminary expenses and Profit and Loss Account balance should be entirely written off.

(d) Assets are to be revalued as below :

(i) Plant & Machinery to be written down by 10%

(ii) Stocks to be revalued at Rs. 32,000

(iii) Patents to be written down by the amount available from Capital Reduction.

Pass the necessary journal entries to give effect to the above scheme of reconstruction and prepare the Balance sheet after Reconstruction.

(K.U.D., October 1997(O))

In the Books of Mismage Ltd.

Internal Reconstruction

Entries for Reconstruction Scheme (Reduction of Capital)		Dr Rs.	Cr Rs.
(1) Equity Shares Capital A/c	Dr	60,000	
Preference Share Capital A/c	Dr	20,000	
To Capital Reduction A/c			80,000
(Equity shares of Rs. 10 each reduced to Rs. 5 each 12000 × 5 = 60,000)			
(Preference shares of Rs. 100 each reduced to Rs. 75 each 800 × 25 = 20,000)			
(2) Capital Reduction A/c	Dr	80,000	
To Preliminary Expenses A/c			8,000
To Profit & Loss A/c			40,000
To Plant & Machinery A/c			8,000
To Stock A/c			4,000
To Patents A/c			20,000
(Capital Reduction A/c utilised to write off preliminary expenses and Profit & Loss A/c fully and, Plant & Machinery by 10%, stock revalued and reduced by Rs. 4,000 and Balance available used to write off patents)			

Balance Sheet as at 31-12-96 (After Reconstruction)

Liabilities	Rs.	Assets	Rs.	Rs.
Share Capital		Patents	28,000	
Equity shares of Rs. 5 each	60,000	*Less* Written off	20,000	8,000
12000 × 5		Plant of Machinery	80,000	
Preference shares of Rs. 75	60,000	*Less* Written off	8,000	72,000
800 × 75		Land & Building		31,200
Reserves & Surplus	—	Stock	36,000	
Secured Loan	—	*Less* Written off	4,000	32,000
Current Liabilities		Book Debts		24,000
Creditors	30,000	Cash		800
Bills payable	18,000	Preliminary Exp.	8,000	
		Less Written off	8,000	—
		Profit & Loss A/c	40,000	
		Less Written off	40,000	
	1,68,000			1,68,000

Problem No. 4

The following are the Balance sheets of S Ltd. & P Ltd. as on 31-3-1996

Balance Sheets as at 31-3-1996

Liabilities	S Ltd.	P Ltd.	Assets	S Ltd.	P Ltd.
Share Capital	Rs.	Rs.	Premises	2,00,000	5,00,000
Shares of Rs. 10 each	4,20,000	6,00,000	Plant	2,60,000	1,90,000
Reserves	1,00,000	1,50,000	Investments	40,000	—
Insurance Fund	20,000	10,000	Debtors	1,20,000	1,00,000
Secured Loan	40,000	—	Stocks	60,000	70,000
8% Bonds	—	1,00,000	Bank A/c	—	90,000
Creditors	1,00,000	1,00,000	Goodwill	—	10,000
	6,80,000	9,60,000		6,80,000	9,60,000

P Ltd. absorbed S Ltd. on the following terms :

(a) P Ltd. shall give 4 shares of Rs. 10 each at Rs. 15 per share for every 3 shares in S Ltd.

(b) P Ltd. shall pay sufficient cash to enable S Ltd. to discharge its secured Loan at a premium of 25%.

(c) The creditors of S Ltd. include Rs. 10,000 due to P Ltd.

(d) P Ltd. had valued investments of S Ltd. at Rs. 50,000

Prepare : (a) Realisation A/c and
(b) Shareholders A/c
in the Books of S Ltd.
(c) Journal entries in the Books of P Ltd.
(d) Balance sheet of P Ltd. after acquisition

[K.U.D., April 1997(N)]

Solution :

Calcualtion of Purchase Consideration

Assets taken over :		Purchase consideration paid in :	
Premises	2,00,000	By issue of equity shares	
Plant	2,60,000	$\frac{42,000 \times 4}{3}$ = 56000 shares	
Investments	50,000		
Debtors	1,20,000	of Rs. 10 each @ Rs. 15	
Stocks	60,000	share 56000 × 10 =	5,60,000
Less Liabilities taken	6,90,000	premium 56000 × 5	2,80,000
Creditors	1,00,000		8,40,000
Net Assets	5,90,000	Sufficient cash to	
Net Assets taken	5,90,000	discharge secure loan 40,000	
Purchase price paid Rs.	8,90,000	@ 25% premium 10,000	50,000
Net assets taken over	5,90,000		8,90,000
Excess payment		Purchase consideration	
Treated as Goodwill	3,00,000	paid Total Rs.	8,90,000

In the Books of S Ltd. (Vender Co.)

Realisation A/c

To Assets transferred		By Creditors	1,00,000
Premises	2,00,000	By P Ltd.	
Plant	2,60,000	(Purchasing Co.)	
Investments	40,000	Purchase consideration	8,90,000
Debtors	1,20,000		
Stocks	60,000		
To Secured Creditor			
Balance transferred	10,000		
To Profit transferred to			
Shareholders A/c	3,00,000		
	9,90,000		9,90,000

P. Ltd. Purchasing Co.

To Realisation A/c (Purchase consideration)	8,90,000	By Equity shares in P. Co.	8,40,000
		By Bank A/c	50,000
	8,90,000		8,90,000

Secured Loan A/c

To Bank A/c Secured Loan discharged @ 25% premium	50,000	By Balance b/d	40,000
		By Realisation A/c	10,000
	50,000		50,000

Bank A/c

To P. Ltd. A/c	50,000	By Secured Loan paid	50,000

Equity Shareholders A/c

To Equity shares in P. Ltd.	8,40,000	By Share Capital	4,20,000
		By Reserve A/c	1,00,000
		By Insurance Fund	20,000
		By Realisation P. Ltd.	3,00,000
	8,40,000		8,40,000

Journal Entries

			Dr. Rs.	Cr. Rs.
(1)	Business Purchase A/c	Dr	8,90,000	
	To S Ltd. A/c (Vendor Co.)			8,90,000
	(Purchase consideration payable)			
(2)	Premises A/c	Dr	2,00,000	
	Plant A/c	Dr	2,60,000	
	Investments A/c	Dr	50,000	
	Debtors A/c	Dr	1,20,000	
	Stock A/c	Dr	60,000	
	Goodwill A/c	Dr	3,00,000	
	To Sundry Creditors A/c			1,00,000
	To Business Purchase A/c			8,90,000
	(Incorporation of Assets and Liabilities of S Ltd. taken over)			

Journal Entries		Dr. Rs.	Cr. Rs.
(3) S Ltd. A/c	Dr	8,90,000	
To Equity Shares Capital A/c			5,60,000
To Share Premium A/c			2,80,000
To Bank A/c			50,000
(Purchase consideration paid to S Ltd. by issue of equity shares - 56000 of Rs. 10 each @ Market price Rs. 15 per share and sufficient cash to discharge secured loan @ 25% premium)			
(4) Creditors of S Ltd. A/c	Dr	10,000	
To Debtors of P Ltd.			10,000
(Inter company indebtedness cancelled)			

(After acquisition) Balance Sheet as at 31-3-96

Liabilities	Rs.	Rs.	Assets	Rs.	Rs.
Share Capital			Goodwill : P Ltd.	10,000	
Equity shares of			S Ltd.	3,00,000	3,10,000
Rs. 10 each P Ltd.	6,00,000		Premises : P Ltd.	5,00,000	
Issued to Vendor			S Ltd.	2,00,000	7,00,000
(56000 × 10)	5,60,000	11,60,000	Plant : P Ltd.	1,90,000	
Reserve P Ltd.		1,50,000	S Ltd.	2,60,000	4,50,000
Share Preimum		2,80,000	Investments S Ltd.	—	50,000
Insurance Fund		10,000	Debtors : P Ltd.	1,00,000	
5% Bonds P Ltd.		1,00,000	S Ltd.	1,20,000	
Creditors P Ltd.	1,00,000			2,20,000	
S Ltd.	1,00,000		*Less* Due form S Ltd.	10,000	2,10,000
	2,00,000		Stock : P Ltd	70,000	
Less due to P Ltd.	10,000	1,90,000	S Ltd.	60,000	1,30,000
			Bank : P Ltd.	90,000	
			Less Paid to S Ltd.	50,000	40,000
		18,90,000			18,90,000

Problem No. 5

On reconstruction of the company the following terms were agreed upon :

(a) The shareholders holding 100000 equity shares of Rs. 10 each were to receive—

(i) 2/5th of their holding in fully paid equity shares of Rs. 10 each and

(ii) 1/5 of their holding in 5% preference shares of Rs. 10 each fully paid in cancellation of old shares.

(b) Apply the credit Balance of General Reserve of Rs. 30,000 for reconstruction purpose.

(c) The Goodwill which stood at Rs. 3,00,000 was to be written of fully.

(d) The plant and premises which stood at Rs. 2,00,000 and Rs. 3,00,000 respectively were to be reduced by 25% each.

Pass Journal entries in the Books of the Company.

[K.U.D., April 1997(N)]

Solution :

Journal Entries (In the Books of the Co.)

		Dr Rs.	Cr Rs.
(1) Equity Share Capital A/c (Old)	Dr	10,00,000	
To Equity Share Capital A/c (New)			4,00,000
To 5% Preference Share Capital A/c			2,00,000
To Capital Reduction A/c			4,00,000
(Issue of 2/5 of 1,00,000 = 40,000 shares of Rs. 10 fully paid (New) and 1/5 5% pref. shares 1/5 × 1,00,000 (20000 × 10) of Rs. 10 each fully paid in cancellation of old shares and Balance to Capital Reduction A/c)			
(2) General Reserve A/c	Dr	30,000	
To Capital Reduction A/c			30,000
(General Reserve Cr. Balance utilised for Capital Reduction)			
(3) Capital Reduction A/c	Dr	4,30,000	
To Goodwill A/c			3,00,000
To Plant A/c			50,000
To Premises A/c			75,000
To Capital Reserve A/c			5,000
(Goodwill A/c written off—plant and premises reduced by 25% and Balance transferred to Capital Reserve A/c)			

Problem No. 6

On 31-3-1994 the Balance Sheet of Vivek Ltd. was as follows :

Balance Sheet as at 31-3-1994

Liabilities	Rs.	Assets	Rs.
Share Capital		Goodwill	40,000
6000 6% Preference		Patents	25,000
Shares of Rs. 10 each	60,000	Sundry Assets	1,64,500
15,000 Equity shares of		Cash	500
Rs. 10 each fully paid	1,50,000	Preliminary expenses	2,000
6% Debentures	30,000	Profit & Loss A/c	28,000
Creditors	20,000		
	2,60,000		2,60,000

The preference dividend is in arrears for four years. The following scheme of Reconstruction was agreed upon :

(a) A new company called "Naveen Ltd." to be formed with an authorised capital of Rs. 3,50,000 all in equity shares of Rs. 10 each.

(b) Two equity shares of Rs. 5 per share paid up in the new company to be issued for every three equity shares in the old company.

(c) Five equity shares as to Rs. 5 per shares paid up in the new company to be issued for every three preference shares in the old company.

(d) An issue of 500 equity shares of Rs. 10 each fully paid to be issued to satisfy the arrear of preference dividend.

(e) To pay cost of liquidation of Rs. 1,500 by the new company.

(f) The discharge of 6% Debentures of old company at a discount of 5% by issue of 8% Debentures in new company.

(g) Naveen company made a call of Rs. 5 on all partly paid equity shares and the call amount was fully received.

Show the necessary accounts to close the books of Vivek Co. Ltd. Pass opening entries and prepare the Balance Sheet of Naveen Ltd. Company.

[K.U.D., October 1996(O)]

Solution :

Note : Calculation of purchase consideration

Assets taken	Rs.	Purchase consideration paid in	Rs.
Goodwill	40,000	(1) To Equity shareholder	
Patents	25,000	$\frac{15000}{3} \times 2 = 10000 \times 5 =$	50,000
Sundry Assets	1,64,500		

	Rs.		Rs.
Cash	500	(2) To Pref. shareholders	
Total Assets	2,30,000	$\frac{6000}{3} \times 5 = 10000 \times 5 =$	50,000
Less Liabilities		(3) Preference Dividend	
Creditors	20,000	500 × 10 =	5,000
Net Assets	2,10,000	To Debenture holders	
Purchase price	1,33,500	8% debentures	
Capital Gain — Capital		6% Debentures 30,000	
Reserve	76,500	*Less* Discount @ 5% 1,500	28,500
		Purchase price	1,33,500

In the Book Vivek Ltd. (Old Company)

Realisation A/c

To Assets transferred		By Creditors	20,000
Goodwill	40,000	By 'Naveen Ltd'	1,33,500
Patents	25,000	Purchasing Co. A/c	
Sundry Assets	1,64,500	By Pref. Shareholders A/c	10,000
Cash	500	By Dividend in Arrears	9,400
To Preliminary expenses	2,000	By Debenture holders A/c	1,500
Profit & Loss A/c	28,000	By Loss on Realisation A/c	1,00,000
To Dividend in Arrears A/c	14,400	Transferred to Equity	
		Shareholders	
	2,74,400		2,74,400

Note : Cost of Liquidation paid by Naveen Ltd. New company not considered in the books of vendor company.

Naveen Ltd. (Purchasing Co.)

To Realisation A/c	1,33,500	By Equity shares in P. Co.		
		20000 × 5	1,00,000	
		500 × 10	5,000	1,05,000
		8% Debentures in P. Co.		28,500
	1,33,500			1,33,500

Equity Shareholders A/c

To Loss on Realisation	1,00,000	By Equity Share Capital	1,50,000
To Equity shares in P. Co.	50,000		
(10000 × 5)			
	1,50,000		1,50,000

Preference Shareholders A/c

To Equity shares in (P Co.) (10000 × 5)	50,000	By Pref. Share Capital	60,000
To Realisation A/c Balance Transfer	10,000		
	60,000		60,000

Dividend in Arrears A/c

To Equity shares in P. Co. (500 × 10)	5,000	By Realisation A/c dividend @ 6% on 60,000 3600 × 4 years	14,400
To Realisation A/c Balance Transfer	9,400		
	14,400		14,400

6% Debentures holders A/c

To 8% Debentures in (Naveen Ltd.)	28,500	By Debentures	30,000
To Realisation A/c Balance Transfer	1,500		
	30,000		30,000

Equity Shares in Naveen Ltd.

To Naveen Ltd (P. Co.)	1,05,000	By Preference Share holder A/c (10000 × 5)	50,000
		By Equity Shareholders A/c (10000 × 5)	50,000
		By Dividend in Arrears A/c (500 × 10)	5,000
	1,05,000		1,05,000

Books of Purchasing Co.
In the Books of Naveen Ltd.

Opening entries		Dr. Rs.	Cr. Rs.
(1) Business Purchase A/c	Dr.	1,33,500	
To Vivek Co. Ltd. (Vendor Co.)			1,33,500
(Purchase consideration payable)			
(2) Goodwill A/c	Dr.	40,000	
Patents A/c	Dr.	25,000	
Sundry Assets A/c	Dr.	1,64,500	
Cash A/c	Dr.	500	
To Creditors A/c			20,000
To Business Purchase A/c			1,33,500
To Capital Reserve A/c			76,500
(Incorporation of Assets of Liabilities taken over and the Balance by Capital Reserve)			

Opening entries		Dr. Rs.	Cr. Rs.
(3) Naveen Co. Ltd. A/c	Dr	1,33,500	
To Equity Share Capital A/c (20000 × 5)			1,05,000
To 8% Debentures			28,500
(Purchase consideration paid in by issue of 20000 equity shares of Rs. 5 paid up, 500 equity shares of Rs. 10 each fully paid, 8% Debentures)			
(4) Bank A/c	Dr	1,00,000	
To Equity Share Capital A/c			1,00,000
(Call money of Rs. 5 purchase on partly paid shares 20000 × 5 received)			
(5) Cost of Liquidaion A/c	Dr	1,500	
To Bank A/c			1,500
(Cost of Liquidation paid)			
(6) Capital Reserve A/c	Dr	41,500	
To Goodwill A/c			40,000
To Cost of Liquidation A/c			1,500
(Goodwill A/c and cost of Liquidation written off against Capital Reserve A/c)			

Books of Naveen Ltd. (New Company)

Balance Sheet as at 31-3-1994

Liabilities			Rs.	Assets		Rs.
Share Capital				Goodwill	40,000	
Authorised				*Less* Written off		
350000 Equity shares of				Capital Reserve	40,000	—
Rs. 10 each			3,50,000	Patents		25,000
Issued to vendor				Sundry Assets		1,64,500
20000 shares of				Cash		
Rs. 5		1,00,000		Balance	500	
20000 × 5 calls				Received	1,00,000	
Issued		1,00,000			1,00,500	
		2,00,000		*Less* Cost of		
500 × 10 shares as				Liquidation paid	1,500	99,000
fully paid		5,000	2,05,000			
Capital Reserve -		76,500				
Less Written off						
Goodwill	40,000					
Cost of						
Liquidation	1,500	41,500	35,000			
8% Debentures			28,500			
Creditors			20,000			
			2,88,500			2,88,500

Problem No. 7

The Balance Sheet of L. Ltd. on 31-3-1996

Liabilities	Rs.	Assets	Rs.
Share Capital		Goodwill	80,000
50000 equity shares		Building	1,80,000
of Rs. 10 each	5,00,000	Plant	2,00,000
Reserves & Surplus		Stock	1,20,000
Contingency Reserve	10,000	Debtors	90,000
Secured Loan		Bank	10,000
5% Debentures	2,00,000	Profit	1,60,000
Staff Provident Fund	30,000		
Creditors	1,00,000		
	8,40,000		8,40,000

The shareholders and creditors have as follows :

(1) A new company named 'A' Ltd. be formed with a Capital of Rs. 10,00,000 divided into equity shares of Rs. 10.

(2) The New Co. is to take over all Assets (except cash at Bank) 25% less than the Books value. The value of Goodwill is nil.

(3) The Debenture holders of Z Ltd. are to be satisfied by issuing 8% Debenture in 'A' Ltd. of Rs. 1,50,000 at par.

(4) Creditors have agreed to accept 75% of their claims in full settlement.

(5) The shareholders are to be issued 30000 equity shares in 'A' Ltd. fully paid.

(6) The liquidation expenses paid by Z Ltd. Rs. 10,000.

(7) A Ltd. issued 20000 shares to public at par and received the amount. Underwriting commission and brokerage amounted to Rs. 10,000.

You are required :

(1) (a) Realisation Account

(b) Shareholders Account in the Books of Z Ltd.

(2) Balance Sheet of 'A' Ltd. after implementing above decision.

[K.U.D., April 1996(N)]

Solution :

In the Books of Z Ltd.

Working Note

Calculation of Purchase Consideration

Assets taken		Rs.	Purchase consideration paid in	
(1) Building -	1,80,000		(1) 8% Debentures	1,50,000
Less 25%	45,000	1,35,000	(2) Creditors paid	
			@ 75% 1,00,000	75,000
(2) Plant	2,00,000		cash	
Less 25%	50,000	1,50,000	(3) Shareholders	
(3) Stocks	1,20,000		30000 shares of Rs. 10	
Less 25%	30,000	90,000	30000 × 10 =	3,00,000
(4) Debtors	90,000		Purchase price	5,25,000
Less 25%	22,500	67,500	Assets taken	4,12,500
Total Assets		4,42,500	Excess paid Good will	1,12,500
Less Staff provident fund		30,000		
Net Assets		4,12,500		

Realisation A/c

To Assets transferred		By Creditors	1,00,000
Goodwill	80,000	By Staff Provident Fund	30,000
Building	1,80,000	By 'A' Ltd. New Co.	5,25,000
Plant	2,00,000	(Purchase price)	
Stock	1,20,000	By Debentures holders	50,000
Debtors	90,000	By Loss on Realisation to	50,000
To Bank A/c	75,000	Shareholders A/c	
To Creditors paid		transferred	
Bank A/c Expenses	10,000		
	7,55,000		7,55,000

'A' Ltd. New Co.

To Realisation A/c	5,25,000	By Debentures in New Co.	1,50,000
		By Equity shares in New Co.	3,00,000
		By Cash/Bank A/c	75,000
	5,25,000		5,25,000

Equity Shareholders A/c

To Profit & Loss A/c	1,60,000	By Share Capital	5,00,000
To Loss an Realisation A/c	50,000	By Contingency Reserve	10,000
To Equity shares in New Co.	3,00,000		
	5,10,000		5,10,000

In the Books 'A' Ltd. New Company
(Reconstructed) Balance Sheet as at 31-3-1996

Liabilities	Rs.	Assets		Rs.
Share Capital		Goodwill	1,12,500	
Authorised			+ 10,000	1,22,500
100000 Equity shares of		Building		1,35,000
Rs. 10 each	10,00,000	Plant		1,50,000
Subscribed & paid		Stocks		90,000
Issued to Vendor Co.		Debtors		67,500
30000 equity shares of		Bank A/c		
Rs. 10 fully paid	3,00,000	Cash received	2,00,000	
Issued to Public		*Less* paid to		
20000 Equity Shares of		Vendor Co.	75,000	
Rs. 10 each	2,00,000		1,25,000	
Staff Provident Fund	30,000	*Less* Underwritting		
8% Debentures	1,50,000	Commission	10,000	1,15,000
	6,80,000			6,80,000

Note :	Goodwill	Rs. 1,12,500
	Excess price paid to Vendor Co.	
	Add Underwriting commission	
	Transferred to Goodwill	10,000
	Total Goodwill	Rs. 1,22,500

Extra Answer :

Opening Entries in the Books of 'A' Ltd.

			Dr Rs.	Cr Rs.
(1)	Business Purchase A/c	Dr	5,25,000	
	To 'Z' Ltd. A/c (Liquidator of)			5,25,000
	(Purchase price payable)			
(2)	Building A/c	Dr	1,35,000	
	Plant A/c	Dr	1,50,000	
	Stock A/c	Dr	90,000	
	Debtors A/c	Dr	67,500	
	Goodwill A/c	Dr	1,12,500	
	To Staff Provident Fund A/c			30,000
	To Business Purchase A/c			5,25,000
	(Incorporation of Assets and Liabilities taken and Goodwill paid)			
(3)	Bank A/c	Dr	2,00,000	
	To Equity Share Capital A/c			2,00,000
	(Issue of 20000 equity shares of Rs. 10 each fully paid to public and cash received)			
(4)	'Z' Ltd. A/c (Liquidator of)	Dr	5,25,000	
	To Equity Share Capital			3,00,000
	To 8% Debentures A/c			1,50,000
	To Bank A/c			75,000
	[Purchase consideration paid in by : (1) Issue of 30000 equity shares (2) Issue of 8% Debentures and (3) Payment of cash to pay off creditors]			
(5)	Underwriting Commission A/c	Dr	10,000	
	To Bank A/c			10,000
	(Underwriting commission paid)			
(6)	Goodwill A/c	Dr	10,000	
	To Underwriting Commission A/c			10,000
	(Underwriting commission paid to share capital and therefore transferred to Goodwill A/c)			

Problem No. 8

The assets of Krishna Ltd. on 31-3-1995 were composed of :

Fixed Assets	6,00,000
Current Assets	2,00,000
The liabilities were :	
7% Debentures	1,00,000
Loan from Jai Ltd.	30,000
Current Liabilities	70,000
The share capital of the company included :	
6% Preference shares of Rs. 100 each	1,00,000
Equity shares of Rs. 10 each	5,00,000

Jai Ltd. agreed to take over Krishna Ltd. on the following terms :

(a) Jai Ltd. shall issue 4 equity shares of Rs. 10 each at Rs. 15 per share in exchange of 5 equity shares of Krishna Ltd.

(b) 6% preference shares of Krishna Ltd. are to be exchanged by 8% preference shares of Rs. 100 each on Jai Ltd. at 25% premium.

(c) 7% Debenture holders are to be paid out in cash together with interest arrears of Rs. 7,000.

(d) Absorption expenses of Rs. 15,000 are to be paid by Jai Ltd.

(e) Jai Ltd. valued fixed assets of Krishna Ltd. Rs. 5,80,000.

Prepare a statement showing computation of purchase consideration and pass entries in the books of Jai Ltd.

(October 1996)

Solution :

Assets taken over :			
Fixed Assets		5,80,000	
Current Assets		2,00,000	
Total Assets		7,80,000	
Less : Liabilities :			
Current Liabilities	70,000		
Loan from Jai Ltd.	30,000	1,00,000	
Net Assets			6,80,000
(I) Issue of Equity shares			
50000 × 4 = 40,000 × 10 =		4,00,000	
Premium 40,000 × 5 =		2,00,000	
		6,00,000	
(II) Preference shares	1,00,000		
Premium 25%	25,000	1,25,000	
(III) Debentures	1,00,000		
Interest	7,000	1,07,000	
Total Purchase Price			8,32,000
	Goodwill		1,52,000

In the Books of Krishna Ltd.

Particulars	Amount	Particulars	Amount
To Fixed Assets	6,00,000	By Loan from Jai Ltd.	30,000
To Current Assets	2,00,000	By Current Liabilities	70,000
To Debentures Interest Arrears	7,000	By Jai Ltd. (Purchase Price)	8,32,000
To Pref. Share Premium	25,000		
To Profit transferred to Equity shareholders	1,00,000		
	9,32,000		9,32,000

Debentureholders Account

To Bank	1,07,000	By Debentures	1,00,000
		By Interest	7,000
	1,07,000		1,07,000

Preference Shareholder Account

Particulars	Amount	Particulars	Amount
To Pref. Shares in Jai Ltd.	1,25,000	By Pref. Share capital	1,00,000
		By Share Premium	25,000
	1,25,000		1,25,000

Equity Shareholder Account

To Equity shares in Jai Ltd.	6,00,000	By Share Capital	5,00,000
		By 6% Pref. Shares	1,00,000
	6,00,000		6,00,000

Jai Ltd. Account (Purchases Co.)

To Realisation Account	8,32,000	By Equity Shares	6,00,000
		By Pref. Shares	1,25,000
		By Cash	1,07,000
	8,32,000		8,32,000

Computation of Purchases consideration (As per Answer Provided) :

(I)	Equity shares $4/5 \times 5000 = 4,000 \times 15 =$	6,00,000
(II)	Preference shares Krishna Ltd. $1,00,000 \times \frac{100}{25}$	80,000
(III)	7% Debentures + Arrears of Interest 1,00,000 + 7,000 =	1,07,000
		7,87,000

Entries in the Books of Jai Ltd. :

Particulars		Dr. (Rs.)	Cr. (Rs.)
(1) Business Purchase A/c	Dr	8,32,000	
To Krishna (Vendor) A/c			8,32,000
(Purchase consideration payable)			
(2) Fixed Assets A/c	Dr	5,80,000	
Current Assets A/c	Dr	2,00,000	
Goodwill A/c	Dr	1,52,000	
To Loan from Jai Ltd.			30,000
To Current Liabilities			70,000
To Business Purchase A/c			8,32,000
(Assets & Liabilities taken over bought into Account)			
(3) Krishna Ltd. A/c	Dr	8,32,000	
To 8% Pref. Share capital			1,00,000
To Equity Share capital			4,00,000
To Premium A/c (2,00,000 + 25,000)			2,25,000
To Bank			1,07,000
(Purchase consideration paid in Equity shares of Rs. 10 each @ 15% shares, 8% Pref. shares of Rs. 100 each @ 25 premium and Balance in cash)			
(4) Loan from Jai Ltd. A/c	Dr	30,000	
To Krishna Ltd. A/c			30,000
(Inter company transaction cancelled)			
(5) Goodwill A/c	Dr	15,000	
To Bank A/c			15,000
(Liquidation Expenses paid transferred to Goodwill A/c)			

Entries in the Books of Jai Ltd. :

Particulars		Dr. (Rs.)	Cr. (Rs.)
(1) Business Purchases A/c	Dr	7,87,000	
To Krishna Ltd.			7,87,000
(Purchase consideration payable)			
(2) Fixed Assets A/c	Dr	5,80,000	
Current A/c	Dr	2,00,000	
Goodwill A/c	Dr	1,07,000	
To Loan from Jai Ltd.			30,000
To Current Liabilities			70,000
To Business purchases			7,87,000
(Assets & Liabilities taken over bought into Account)			
(3) Krishna Ltd. A/c	Dr	7,87,000	
To Equity Shares capital A/c			4,00,000
To 8% Pref. Share capital A/c			80,000
To Shares Premium A/c			2,00,000
To Bank A/c			1,07,000
(Purchase consideration paid in equity shares of Rs. 10 @ 15 per share, 8% Pref. shares and Balance in cash)			

Problem No. 9

Shiva Ltd. and Krishna Ltd. decided to amalgamate their business and form a new Shiva Krishna Ltd. with an authorised capital of Rs. 10,00,000 divided into equity share of Rs. 10 each.

Balance Sheet as on 31-3-1995

Liabilities	Shiva Ltd. Rs.	Krishna Ltd. Rs.	Assets	Shiva Ltd. Rs.	Krishna Ltd. Rs.
Equity share of Rs. 10	6,00,000	3,00,000	Goodwill	—	80,000
8% debentures	1,60,000	—	Premises	5,00,000	3,60,000
Reserve fund	—	1,10,000	Stock	90,000	60,000
Profit & Loss A/c	—	90,000	Debtors	1,10,000	30,000
Creditors	70,000	48,000	Bank	10,000	18,000
			B.R.	30,000	—
			Losses	90,000	—
Total	8,30,000	5,48,000	Total	8,30,000	5,48,000

The following were the terms :

(a) The assets of Shiva Ltd. were taken over subject to following adjustment : Premises and stock were depreciated by 10%, Provision at 5% was made against debtors and B.R. The liabilities were taken over at book values.

(b) The Assets of Krishna Ltd. were valued as follows :

Goodwill	50,000
Premises	3,75,000
Debtors	25,000

The stock of Krishna Ltd. included goods worth of Rs. 12,000 bought from Shiva Ltd. on which the latter company made a profit at 20% on cost. The creditors and bank balance were transferred at book values.

Purchase consideration is paid in fully paid shares.

Required :

(i) Computation of purchases consideration.

(ii) Balance Sheet of Shiva Krishna Ltd.

(October 1996)

Solution :

Computation of Purchase Consideration

Particulars	Shiva Ltd.	Krishna Ltd.
Assets taken over at agreed values :		
Premises	4,50,000	3,75,000
Goodwill	—	50,000
Stock (90,000 – 10%)	81,000	58,000
Krishna Ltd. 60,000 – 2,000 Loading)		
Debtors	1,10,000	25,000
B.R.	30,000	—
Bank	10,000	18,000
Total Assets	6,81,000	5,26,000
Less : Liabilities and Provisions :		
Creditors	70,000	48,000
8% Debentures	1,60,000	—
Provision for RDD (1,10,000 × 5%)	5,500	—
Provision against B.R. (30,000 × 5%)	1,500	—
Purchase Price (paid equity shares Rs. 10 each)	4,44,000	4,78,000

Balance Sheet of Shiva Krishna Ltd.

Liabilities	Rs.	Rs.	Assets	Rs.	Rs.
Share Capital :			Goodwill (Krishna)		50,000
Authorised Capital			Premises : Shiva	4,50,000	
Shares of Rs. 10.		10,00,000	Krishna	3,75,000	8,25,000
Issued to Vendor :			*Stock* : Shiva	81,000	
Shiva Ltd.	4,44,000		Krishna	58,000	1,39,000
Krishna Ltd.	4,78,000	9,22,000	Debtors :		
Reserve & Surplus		—	Shiva Ltd.1,10,000		
Secured Loan :			*Less* : RDD		
8% Debentures			5% 5,500	1,04,500	
Shiva Ltd.		1,60,000	Krishna Ltd.	25,000	1,29,500
Current Liabilities			B.R. : Shiva Ltd.	30,000	
Creditors Shiva	70,000		*Less* : Provision 5%	1,500	28,500
Creditors Krishna	48,000	1,18,000	*Bank* : Shiva Ltd.	10,000	
			Krishna Ltd.	18,000	28,000
		12,00,000			12,00,000

Note 1 : Inter Company transactions — Stock purchase and sales transactions result in a profit made by the selling and the stocks of purchasing company included are at a price cost + profit such profit is unrealised profit included in stock be eliminated i.e., deduct unrealised profit from stocks of purchasing company. For this purpose the entry is to be passed :

Entry : Goodwill/Capital Reserve A/c Dr.
To Stock A/c

Or : The assets of vendor company are debited at an agreed value while the stocks are taken at cost price only. This increases the amount of goodwill or Capital Reserve.

Note 2 : Elimination of Inter Co. indebtedness debts due to and due from one another company be deducted from debtors and creditors amount in the respective Debtors and Creditors.

Similarly Bills Receivable and Bills payable from one Company to another Co. i.e., Purchasing company to Vendor company. The amount due to and due from be deducted from respective Bills Payable & Bills Receivable. The Bills Receivable accepted by another company included in Bills receivable and part amount of the Bills are discounted only such amount of the Bills are in hand treated as common indebtedness and be deducted from Bills receivable and Bills payable respectively.

For Ex. : X Co. took over business of Y Co. X Co. draws Bills worth Rs. 35,000 on Y Co. and of the Bills X Co. discounted Bills worth of Rs. 20,000. Now Bills in hand are only 15,000 (35,000 – 20,000) be deducted from Bills receivable of X Co. Ltd. and Bills payable of Y Co. as common indebted.

Problem No. 10 (Extra)

Amar Co. Ltd. agrees to take over the business of Bangalore Co. Ltd. as on 31-12-1994 on which date their Balance Sheet are as follows :

Balance Sheet as at 31-12-1994

Liabilities	A Co. Ltd.	B Co. Ltd.	Assets	A Co. Ltd.	B Co. Ltd.
Share Capital :			*Fixed Assets* :	7,50,000	3,00,000
Equity shares of			*Current Assets* :		
Rs. 10 each	9,00,000	4,50,000	Stock	4,50,000	2,40,000
Reserve & Surplus :			Debtors	2,40,000	1,80,000
General Reserve	3,00,000	1,50,000	Bills Receivable	2,10,000	1,20,000
Profit & Loss A/c	3,00,000	1,50,000	Bank	1,50,000	90,000
Secured Loan	—	—			
Current Liabilities :					
Creditors	1,80,000	1,20,000			
Bills payable	1,20,000	60,000			
	18,00,000	9,30,000		18,00,000	9,30,000

The purchase consideration is agreed payable Rs. 8,40,000 in equity shares of Rs. 10 each in Amar Co. Ltd.

Additional Information :

(a) Sundry debtors of Amar Co. Ltd. include Rs. 90,000 due from Bangalore Co.

(b) Bills payable Amar Co. Ltd. include Rs. 36,000 due to Bangalore Co. Ltd.

(c) The stocks of Amar Co. Ltd. include Rs. 60,000 worth of goods purchased from Bangalore Co. Ltd. on which Bangalore Co. Ltd. made a profit 25% on cost. Whereas the stocks of Bangalore Co. Ltd. include Rs. 48,000 worth of goods purchased from Amar Co. Ltd. on which Amar Co. Ltd. made a profit 20% on sales. Show the entries in the books of both the Co.

Solution :

In the Books of Vendor Co. (Bangalore Co. Ltd.)

Entries :

(1) Realisation A/c	Dr	9,30,000	
To Fixed Assets A/c			3,00,000
To Stock A/c			2,40,000
To Debtors A/c			1,80,000
To Bills Receivable A/c			1,20,000
To Bank A/c			90,000
(Assets taken over transferred)			
(2) Creditors A/c	Dr	1,20,000	
Bills payable A/c	Dr	60,000	
To Realisation A/c			1,80,000
(Liabilities taken overn transferred)			
(3) Equity Shareholders A/c	Dr	7,50,000	
To Equity Shares Capital A/c			4,50,000
To General Reserve A/c			1,50,000
To Profit and Loss A/c			1,50,000
(Share capital and undistributed profits general Reserve & Profit & Loss transferred)			
(4) Amar Co. Ltd. A/c	Dr	8,40,000	
To Realisation			8,40,000
(Purchase consideration receivable)			
(5) Equity Share in Amar Co. Ltd. A/c	Dr	8,40,000	
To Amar Co. Ltd.			8,40,000
(Purchase consideration received in shares of Rs. 10 each)			
(6) Realisation A/c	Dr	90,000	
To Equity Shareholder A/c			90,000
(Profit on realisation transferred)			

In the Books of Amar Co. Ltd. (Purchasing Co.)

(1)	Business Purchase A/c	Dr	8,40,000	
	To Bangalore Co. Ltd.			8,40,000
	(Purchase consideration payable)			
(2)	Fixed Assets A/c	Dr	3,00,000	
	Stock A/c	Dr	2,40,000	
	Debtors A/c	Dr	1,80,000	
	Bills Receivable A/c	Dr	1,20,000	
	Bank A/c	Dr	90,000	
	Goodwill A/c (Balancing figure)	Dr	90,000	
	To Creditors A/c			1,20,000
	To Bills Payable A/c			60,000
	To Business Purchase A/c (8,40,000)			8,40,000
	(Assets and Liabilities takenover brought into account)			
(3)	Bangalore Co. Ltd. A/c	Dr	8,40,000	
	To Equity Share Capital A/c			8,40,000
	(Purchase consideration paid in equity shares of Rs. 10 each)			
(4)	Sundry Creditors A/c (of Bangalore Co. Ltd.)	Dr	90,000	
	To Sundry Debtors A/c (of Amar Co. Ltd.)			90,000
	(Entry for elimination of Inter Co. indebted)			
(5)	Bills Payable (of Amar Co.) A/c	Dr	36,000	
	To Bills Receivable (of Bangalore Co.)			36,000
	(Entry for elimination of Inter Co. Bills receivable and Bills payable)			
(6)	Goodwill A/c	Dr	12,000	
	To Stock A/c			12,000
	(Unrealised profit included in stock of Amar Co. Ltd. deducted from stock 60,000 × 25/125 = 12,000 unrealised profit)			
(7)	Goodwill A/c	Dr	9,600	
	To Stock A/c			9,600
	(Unrealised profit included in stock of Bangalore Co. Ltd. deducted from stock 48,000 × 20/100 = 9,600 unrealised profit)			

Amar Co. Ltd. Balance Sheet as at 31-12-1994 (After absorption)

Liabilities	Rs.	Rs.	Assets	Rs.	Rs.
Share Capital :			*Goodwill* :		
Equity shares of				90,000	
Rs.10 each				12,000	
Amar Co. Ltd.	9,00,000			9,600	1,11,600
Issued to Vendor	8,40,000	17,40,000	*Fixed Assets* :		
Reserve & Surplus :			Amar Co. Ltd.	7,50,000	
Amar Co. Ltd. :			B'lore Co. Ltd.	3,00,000	10,50,000
General Reserve		3,00,000	Stock : Amar Co. Ltd.	4,50,000	
Profit & Loss A/c		3,00,000	*Less* : Unrealised		
Secured Loan		—	profit	12,000	
Current Liabilities		—		4,38,000	
Creditors :			B'lore Co. Ltd.		
Amar Co. Ltd.	1,80,000		2,40,000		
B'lore Co. Ltd.	1,20,000		*Less* :		
	3,00,000		Unrealised		
Less : Due to			profit 9,600	2,30,400	6,68,400
Amar Co. Ltd.	90,000	2,10,000	Debtors : Amar Co.	2,40,000	
Bills Payable :			*Less* : Due from		
Amar Co. Ltd.	1,20,000		B'lore Co. Ltd.	90,000	
B'lore Co. Ltd.	60,000			1,50,000	
	1,80,000		B'lore Co. Ltd.	1,80,000	3,30,000
Less : Due to			*Bills Receivable* :		
B'lore Co. Ltd.	36,000	1,44,000	Amar Co. Ltd.		2,10,000
			B'lore Co. Ltd.	1,20,000	
			Less : Due from		
			Amar Co. Ltd.	36,000	84,000
			Bank : Amar Co.	1,50,000	
			B'lore Co. Ltd.	90,000	2,40,000
		26,94,000			26,94,000

Problem No. 11

(a) AMALGAMATION

Following are the Balance Sheet of A Ltd. and B Ltd. as on 31st March 1991.

Balance Sheet as at 31st March 1991

Liabilities	A Ltd.	B Ltd.	Assets	A Ltd.	B Ltd.
Share Capital			Sundry Assets	2,70,000	1,40,000
Equity shares of			Debtors	80,000	60,000
Rs. 10 each	3,00,000	1,50,000	Stock	50,000	40,000
Reserves & Surplus :			Bank	10,000	6,000
Reserve Fund	60,000	40,000	Bills receivable	15,000	4,000
Workmen's Compensation Fund	—	10,000			
Secured Loans	—	—			
Unsecured Loans	—	—			
Current Liabilities :					
Sundry Creditors	60,000	40,000			
Bills Payable	5,000	10,000			
	4,25,000	2,50,000		4,25,000	2,50,000

Both the companies have agreed to amalgamate and form C Ltd. which will takeover Assets and Liabilities of both companies.

(a) The shareholders of A Ltd. are issued 4 (four) shares of Rs. 10 each in C Ltd. at Rs. 12 per share in exchange of 3 (three) shares in A Ltd.

(b) The Assets and the Liabilities of B Ltd. are to be taken over at book values subject to 5% provision on Debtors and Bills receivable and 10% depreciation on Sundry assets. Goodwill of B Ltd. was valued @ Rs. 25,000.

You are required to :

(i) Compute purchase consideration due and

(ii) Prepare Balance Sheet of C Ltd.

(KUD, April 1994)

Solution :

Calculation :

A Ltd.			*Purchase Consideration paid in :*	
Total Assets		4,25,000	Equity shares of Rs. 10	
Less Liabilities :			@ Rs. 12 per share	
S. Creditors	60,000		30000×1/3 × 4 = 40,000 × 10	4,00,000
Bills payable	5,000	65,000	Premium 40,000 × 2 =	80,000
Net Assets		3,60,000	Purchase price	4,80,000
			Net Assets	– 3,60,000
			Excess paid — Goodwill	– 1,20,000

B. Ltd.			*Purchase Consideration paid in :*	
Assets taken :			Equity shares of Rs. 10 each	
Sundry Assets	1,40,000		20780 × 10	2,07,800
Less Depreciation	14,000	1,26,000	Net Assets Method.	
Debtors		60,000		
Stock		40,000		
Bank		6,000		
Bills Receivable		4,000		
		2,36,000		
Add Goodwill		25,000		
		2,61,000		
Less Liabilities :				
S. Creditors	40,000			
Bills payable	10,000			
R.D.D. 5% on 60,000	3,000			
5% on 4,000	200	53,200		
Net Assets		2,07,800		

Balance Sheet as at 31-3-1991 of C Ltd.

Liabilities	Rs.	Rs.	Assets	Rs.	Rs.
Share Capital :			Goodwill : A Ltd.	1,20,000	
Equity shares of Rs. 10			B Ltd.	25,000	1,45,000
A Ltd.	4,00,000		Sundry Assets : A	2,70,000	
B Ltd.	2,07,000	6,07,800	B	1,26,000	3,96,000
Share Premium		80,000	(1,40,000 – 14,000)		
Secured Loan		—	Debtors A Ltd.	80,000	
Unsecured Loan		—	B (60,000-3,000)	57,000	1,37,000
Current Liabilities :			Stock : A Ltd.	50,000	
Sundry Creditors			B Ltd.	40,000	90,000
A Ltd.	60,000		Bank : A Ltd.	10,000	
B Ltd.	40,000	1,00,000	B Ltd.	6,000	16,000
Bills payable			Bills receivable		
A Ltd.	5,000		A Ltd.	15,000	
B Ltd.	10,000	15,000	B Ltd. 4,000		
			Less RDD 200	3,800	18,800
		8,02,800			8,02,800

Extra Answer :

Books of A Ltd.

Realisation A/c

Particulars	Rs.	Particulars	Rs.
To Sundry Assets	2,70,000	By Sundry Creditors	60,000
To Debtors	80,000	By Bills Payable	5,000
To Stock	50,000	By C Ltd.	4,80,000
To Bank	10,000	(Purchase consideration)	
To Bills receivable	15,000		
To Equity Shareholders A/c (Profit transferred)	1,20,000		
	5,45,000		5,45,000

Equity Shareholders A/c

To Equity Shares in C Ltd.	4,80,000	By Share Capital	3,00,000
		By Reserve fund	60,000
		By Realisation (Profit)	1,20,000
	4,80,0000		4,80,000

C Ltd. A/c (Purchasing Co.)

To Realisation A/c	4,80,000	By Equity Shares in C Ltd.	4,80,000
	4,80,000		4,80,000

In the Books of B Ltd.

Realisation A/c

Particulars	Rs.	Particulars	Rs.
To Sundry Assets	1,40,000	By Sundry Creditors	40,000
To Debtors	60,000	By Bills Payable	10,000
To Stock	40,000	By C Ltd.	2,07,800
To Bank	6,000	(Purchasing Co.)	
To Bills receivable	4,000		
To Equity Shareholders A/c	7,800		
	2,57,800		2,57,800

Equity Shareholders A/c

Particulars	Rs.	Particulars	Rs.
To Equity Shares in C Ltd.	2,07,800	By Share Capital	1,50,000
		By Reserve Fund	40,000
		By Workmen's Compensation Fund	10,000
		By Realisation (Profit)	7,800
	2,07,800		2,07,800

C Ltd. A/c (Purchasing Co.)

To Realisation A/c	2,07,800	By Equity Shares in C Ltd.	2,07,800
	2,07,800		2,07,800

Opening Extries in C Ltd. :

(1) Business Purchase A/c	Dr	6,87,800	
To Liquidation of : A Ltd.			4,80,000
B Ltd.			2,07,800
(Purchase consideration payable)			
(2) S Assets A/c	Dr	2,70,000	
Debtors A/c	Dr	80,000	
Stock A/c	Dr	50,000	
Bank A/c	Dr	10,000	
Bills receivable A/c	Dr	15,000	
Goodwill A/c	Dr	1,20,000	
To S Creditors A/c			60,000
To Bills Payable			5,000
To Business Purchase			4,80,000
(Incorporation of Asscts & Liabilities of A Ltd. taken over)			
(3) Liquidation of A Ltd. A/c	Dr	4,80,000	
To Equity Share Capital			4,00,000
To Share Premium			80,000
(Purchase price paid in by issue of 40000 shares of Rs. 10 each at Rs. 10 per share)			

(4) S Assets A/c			
Debtors A/c	Dr	1,26,000	
Stock A/c	Dr	60,000	
Bank A/c	Dr	40,000	
Bills Receivable A/c	Dr	6,000	
	Dr	4,000	
To S Creditors A/c			40,000
To Bills Payable			10,000
To RDD – 5% on 60,000 – 3,000			
5% on 4,000 – 200			3,200
(Incorporation of Assets of Liabilities of of B Ltd. taken over)			
(5) Liquidation of B Ltd. A/c	Dr	2,07,800	
To Equity Share Capital A/c			2,07,800
(Purchase price paid in by issued of 20780 Equity shares of Rs. 10 each.)			

Problem No. 12

Following are the Balance Sheets of A Ltd. & B Ltd. as on 31-12-1991. On that date they decided to Amalgamate their business and form a New Co. AB Co. Ltd. The Authorised capital of AB Co. will be Rs. 14,00,000, divided into :

(a) Rs. 10,00,000 Equity shares of Rs. 10 each.

(b) Rs. 4,00,000 12% Preference shares of Rs. 100 each.

Balance Sheet as at 31-12-1991

Liabilities	A Co.	B Co.	Assets	A Co.	B Co.
Share Capital :			Goodwill	60,000	55,000
Equity shares of Rs. 10 each.	3,00,000	4,00,000	Land & Building	1,50,000	1,90,000
Reserves & Surplus :			Plant & Machinery	1,00,000	1,50,000
General Reserve	60,000	80,000	*Investments* :	—	—
Profit & Loss A/c	40,000	65,000	Stock	50,000	90,000
Secured Loan	—	—	Debtors	70,000	80,000
Current Liabilities :			Bank	30,000	65,000
Creditors	40,000	60,000			
Bills payable	20,000	25,000			
	4,60,000	6,30,000		4,60,000	6,30,000

The purchase consideration was agreed as under :

(1) A Co. : The Assets & Liabilities were taken over at Book values except :

(a) Land & Building at Rs. 1,75,000.

(b) Plant & Machinery at 10% less than Book value.

The consideration being :

(a) Equity shareholders of A Co. will be paid cash of Rs. 5 per share and

(b) Four (4) Equity shares of Rs. 10 each in AB Co. in exchange for every three (3) shares in A Co.

(2) B Co. : All Assets except goodwill and bank. Balance be taken over at Book values and the Liabilities in respect of Creditors only taken over. Whereas Bills payable were to be paid off before amalgamation by B Co.

The consideration being :

Equity shareholders will receive :

(a) Rs. 1,00,000 12% Preference shares of Rs. 100 each fully paid.

(b) Three (3) Equity shares of Rs. 10 each in AB Co. in exchange for every four (4) equity shares in B Co. and

(c) The balance in cash.

Of the remaining Equity shares of AB Co. 20,000 Equity shares were issued to public and cash was duly received.

(a) Calculate purchase consideration of both the Cos. and

(b) Write up the following Ledger A/cs in the Books of A Co. and B Co. in liquidation :

(1) Realisation A/c,

(2) Shareholders A/c and

(3) Bank A/c (only in B Co.)

(K.U.D., October 1993)

Solution

Calculations :

A Co.			*Purchase consideration*		
Assets taken over :			*paid in* :		
Land & Building		1,75,000	(a) Cash :		
Plant & Machinery	1,00,000		Rs. 5 per share for	30000	1,50,000
Less 10%	10,000	90,000	(5 × 30000)		
Stock		50,000	(b) In Equity shares :		
Debtors		70,000			
Bank		30,000	$\frac{30000}{3} \times 4 = 40000 \times 10$		4,00,000
Goodwill		60,000			
Total Assets		4,75,000			

Total Assets		4,75,000	Total purchase price	5,50,000
Less Liabilities :			Net Assets	4,15,000
Creditors	40,000		Excess payment	
Bills payable	20,000	60,000	treated as Goodwill	1,35,000
			Add Goowill in	
			Balance sheet	60,000
Net Assets taken		4,15,000	Total Goodwill	1,95,000

B Co.		Purchase consideration paid in :	
Assets takenover :		(a) Equity shareholders	1,00,000
Land & Building	1,90,000	12% Preference shares of Rs. 100 each	
Plant & Machinery	1,50,000	(b) Issue of Equity shares	
Stock	90,000	$\frac{40000}{4} \times 3 = 30000 \times 10$	3,00,000
Debtors	80,000		
Total Assets	5,10,000	(c) Balance in cash	
Less Liabilities :		4,50,000 – (1,00,000 + 3,00,000)	50,000
Creditors	60,000	Purchase price Equal	
Net Assets taken	4,50,000	to Net assets	4,50,000

In the Books of A Co.

Realisation A/c

To Sundry Assets :		By Sundry Creditors	40,000
Goodwill	60,000	By Bills Payable	20,000
Land & Building	1,50,000	By AB Co.	5,50,000
Plant & Machinery	1,00,000	(Purchase consideration)	
Stock	50,000		
Debtors	70,000		
Bank	30,000		
To Profit transferred			
to Equity shareholders	1,50,000		
	6,10,000		6,10,000

Equity Shareholders A/c

To Equity shares in AB Co.	4,00,000	By Share Capital	3,00,000
To Bank	1,50,000	By General Reserve	60,000
		By Profit & Loss A/c	40,000
		By Realisation A/c (Profit)	1,50,000
	5,50,000		5,50,000

In the Books of B Co.

Realisation A/c

To Sundry Assets :		By Sundry Creditors	60,000
Goodwill	55,000	By AB Co.	4,50,000
Land & Building	1,90,000	(Purchase consideration)	
Plant & Machinery	1,50,000	By Loss transferred to	
Stock	90,000	Equity shareholders	55,000
Debtors	80,000		
	5,65,000		5,65,000

Equity Shareholders A/c

To Realisation A/c (Loss)	55,000	By Share Capital	4,00,000
To Equity shares in AB Co.	3,00,000	By General Reserve	80,000
To Preference shares in		By Profit & Loss A/c	65,000
AB Co.	1,00,000		
To Bank balance transferred	90,000		
	5,45,000		5,45,000

Bank A/c

To Balance b/d	65,000	By Bills Payable paid	25,000
To AB Co.	50,000	By Balance transferred to	
		Equity shareholders	90,000
	1,15,000		1,15,000

In the Books of AB Co. (Purchasing Co.)

Journal Entries :

1.	Business Purchase A/c	Dr	10,00,000	
	To Liquidator of A Co.			5,50,000
	To Liquidator of B Co.			4,50,000
	(Purchase consideration payable)			
2.	Land & Building A/c	Dr	1,75,000	
	Plant & Machinery A/c	Dr	90,000	
	Stock A/c	Dr	50,000	
	Debtors A/c	Dr	70,000	
	Bank A/c	Dr	30,000	
	Goodwill A/c	Dr	1,95,000	
	(60,000 + 1,35,000)			
	To Creditors A/c			40,000
	To Bills Payable A/c			20,000
	To Business Purchase A/c			5,50,000
	(Incorporation of Assets & Liabilities of A Co. taken over)			
3.	Land & Building A/c		1,90,000	
	Plant & Machinery A/c		1,50,000	
	Stock A/c		90,000	
	Debtors A/c		80,000	
	To Creditors			60,000
	To Business Purchase A/c			4,50,000
	(Incorporation of Assets & Liabilities of B Co. taken over)			
4.	Liquidator of A Co. A/c	Dr	5,50,000	
	To Equity Share Capital			4,00,000
	To Bank			1,50,000
	(Purchase price paid in by issue of 40000 Equity shares of Rs. 10 each and 5 per share on 30000 shares.)			

5.	Liquidator of B Co. A/c	Dr	4,50,000	
	To 12% Preference Shares Capital			1,00,000
	To Equity Share Capital			3,00,000
	To Bank			50,000
	[Purchase price paid in by – (1) Issue of 1000 Preference shares of Rs. 100 (2) 30000 Equity shares of Rs. 10 each and Balance in cash.]			
6.	Bank A/c	Dr.	2,00,000	
	To Equity Share Capital A/c			2,00,000
	(20,000 Equity shares issued to public and cash received.)			

In the Books of AB Co.

Balance Sheet as at 31-12-1991 (Amalgamated)

Liabilities	Rs.	Rs.	Assets	Rs.	Rs.
Share Capital :			Goodwill – A Co.		1,95,000
Authorised :			Land & Building :		
100000 Equity shares			A Co.	1,75,000	
of Rs. 10	10,00,000		B Co.	1,90,000	3,65,000
12% Preference shares,			Plant & Machinery :		
4000 shares of			A Co.	90,000	
Rs. 100	4,00,000	14,00,000	B Co.	1,50,000	2,40,000
Issued Capital :			Investments :		
Vendor Cos.			Stock : A Co.	50,000	
A Co. 40000 × 10	4,00,000		B Co.	90,000	1,40,000
B Co. 30000 × 10	3,00,000		Debtors : A Co.	70,000	
Public 20000 × 10	2,00,000	9,00,000	B Co.	80,000	1,50,000
12% Preference			Bank A/c :		
shares 1000 × 100					
to B Co.	1,00,000	1,00,000	Balance A Co.	30,000	
Reserves & Surplus	—	—	Cash received	2,00,000	
Secured Loan	—	—		2,30,000	
Current Liabilities :			*Less* Paid :		
			A Co. 1,50,000		
Creditors : A Co.	40,000		B Co. 50,000	2,00,000	30,000
B Co.	60,000	1,00,000			
Bills payable : A Co.		20,000			
		11,20,000			11,20,000

Problem No. 13

Following are the Balance sheets of X Ltd. and Y Ltd. on 31st March, 1991, when they decided to Amalgamate and form a new Co. viz. Z Ltd.

Balance Sheets as at 31-12-1991

Liabilities	X Ltd. Rs.	Y Ltd. Rs.	Assets	X Ltd. Rs.	Y Ltd. Rs.
Share Capital :			*Fixed Assets* :		
Equity shares of Rs.10 each	7,00,000	2,50,000	Plant	3,80,000	1,10,000
9% Preference shares of Rs.10 each	—	2,50,000	Land & Building	4,20,000	1,50,000
Reserves & Surplus :			Investment	—	—
General Reserve	1,10,000	—	*Current Assets* :		
Profit & Loss A/c	70,000	—	Stock	1,00,000	1,20,000
Secured Loan	—	1,00,000	Debtors	70,000	1,50,000
Current Liabilities :			Bills Receivable	25,000	30,000
Creditors	1,40,000	50,000	Bank	65,000	40,000
Bills payable	40,000	30,000	Profit & Loss A/c	—	80,000
	10,60,000	6,80,000		10,60,000	6,80,000

Purchase consideration was agreed upon as under :

(I) *For X Ltd.* :

5 Equity shares of Rs.10 each in Z Ltd. in exchange for 4 Equity shares in X Ltd. at 20% premium for taking over Assets and Liabilities except Bills payable which are paid off before amalgamation.

(II) *For Y Ltd.* :

(a) The secured loan of Y Ltd. would be discharged by issuing equal amount of 8% debentures in Z Ltd. at 10% discount.

(b) The holders of Preference shares in Y Ltd. would be allotted 3 (three) 12% Preference shares of Rs. 100 each in Z Ltd. in exchange for every 4 (four) Preference shares held in Y Ltd.

(c) The Equity shareholders would be allotted sufficient Equity shares of Rs. 10 each in Z Ltd. to cover the balance on their account after writing off plant — by 10% and providing 5% on debtors and Rs. 5,000 for workers compensation.

Prepare : (1) Statement of purchase consideration.

(2) Balance Sheet of Z Ltd.

(K.U.D., October 1991)

Solution :

Calculations :

X Ltd.		*Rs.*
Assets taken :		
Plant		3,80,000
Land & Building		4,20,000
Stock		1,00,000
Debtors		70,000
Bills receivable		25,000
Bank	65,000	
Less Paid B.P.	40,000	25,000
Total Assets		10,20,000
Less Liabilities :		
Creditors		1,40,000
Net Assets		8,80,000

Purchase consideration paid in :	
(1) Equity shareholders	
$\frac{70000}{4} \times 5 = 87500 \times 10$	8,75,000
Add Premium 20%	1,75,000
Purchase price	10,50,000
Net Assets taken	8,80,000
Excess payment treated as Goodwill	1,70,000

Y Ltd.		Rs.
Assets taken :		
Plant	1,10,000	
Less 10%	11,000	99,000
Land & Building		1,50,000
Stock		1,20,000
Debtors		1,50,000
Bills Receivable		30,000
Bank		40,000
Total Assets		5,89,000
Less Liabilities :		
Creditors	50,000	
Bills payable	30,000	
RDD 5% on 15,000	7,500	
Provision for Workmen's Compensation	5,000	92,500
Net Assets taken	—	4,96,500

Purchase consideration paid in by :		
(1) Issue of Debentures		
8%	1,00,000	
Less Discount 10%	10,000	90,000
(2) Preference shareholders :		
$\frac{2500}{4} \times 3 = 1875 \times 100 =$		1,87,500
(3) Equity shareholders :		
Balance amount		
4,96,500 – 2,77,500		
Equity shares		
21900 × 10 =		2,19,000
		4,96,500

Amalgamated Balance Sheet as at 31-12-1991

Liabilities	Rs.	Rs.	Assets	Rs.	Rs.
Share Capital :			*Fixed Assets* :		
Equity shares of Rs.10 each :			Goodwill		1,70,000
X — 87500 × 10	8,75,000		Plant : X Ltd.	3,80,000	
Y — 21900 × 10	2,19,000	10,94,000	Y Ltd.	99,000	4,79,000
12% Preference shares			Land & Building :		
of Rs. 100 Y — 1875 × 10		1,87,500	X Ltd.	4,20,000	
Debenture :			Y Ltd.	1,50,000	5,70,000
Y Ltd.		90,000	Stock : X Ltd.	1,00,000	
Share premium		1,75,000	Y Ltd.	1,20,000	2,20,000
Current Liabilities :			Debtors : X Ltd.	70,000	
Creditors : X Ltd.	1,40,000		Y Ltd. 1,50,000		
Y Ltd.	50,000	1,90,000	*Less* RDD 7,500	1,42,500	2,12,500
Bills payable : Y Ltd.		30,000	Bills Receivable :		
Provision for Workers'			X Ltd.	25,000	
Compensation		5,000	Y Ltd.	30,000	55,000
			Bank : X Ltd.	25,000	
			Y Ltd.	40,000	65,000
		17,71,500			17,71,500

Additional Answer

In the Books of X Ltd.

Realisation A/c

To S Assets :		By S Creditors	1,40,000
Plant	3,80,000	By Z Ltd.	10,50,000
Land & Building	4,20,000	(Purchase consideration)	
Stock	1,00,000		
Debtors	70,000		
Bills receivable	25,000		
Cash	25,000		
To Shareholders A/c (Transferred)	1,70,000		
	11,90,000		11,90,000

Equity Shareholders A/c

	Rs.		Rs.
To Equity shares in Z Ltd.	10,50,000	By Share Capital	7,00,000
		By General Reserve	1,10,000
		By Profit & Loss	70,000
		By Realisation (Profit)	1,70,000
	10,50,000		10,50,000

Bank A/c

To Balance b/d	65,000	By Bills payable	40,000
		By Realisation	25,000
	65,000		65,000

In the Books of Y Ltd.

Realisation A/c

To Plant	1,10,000	By S Creditors	50,000
To Land & Building	1,50,000	By Bills payable	30,000
To Stock	1,20,000	By Z Ltd. (Purchase consideration)	4,96,500
To Debtors	1,50,000	By Debentures	10,000
To Bills Receivable	30,000	By Preference Shareholders	62,500
To Bank	40,000		
To Profit Transferred to Shareholders	49,000		
	6,49,000		6,49,000

Equity Shareholders A/c

To Profit & Loss A/c (Loss)	80,000	By Share Capital	2,50,000
		By Realisation (Profit)	49,000
To Equity shares in Z Ltd.	2,19,000		
	2,99,000		2,99,000

Preference Shareholders A/c

To Preference shares in Z Ltd.	1,87,500	By Preference Share Capital	2,50,000
To Realisation	62,500		
	2,50,000		2,50,000

Debenture-holders A/c

To Debentures in Z Ltd.	90,000	By Debentures	1,00,000
To Realisation (Transferred)	10,000		
	1,00,000		1,00,000

In the Books of Z Ltd.

Journal Entries :

(1) Business Purchase A/c	Dr	15,46,500	
To Liquidator of X Ltd.			10,50,000
To Liquidator of Y Ltd.			4,96,500
(Purchase consideration payable)			
(2) Plant A/c	Dr	3,80,000	
Land & Building A/c	Dr	4,20,000	
Stock A/c	Dr	1,00,000	
Debtors A/c	Dr	70,000	
Bills Receivable A/c	Dr	25,000	
Bank A/c	Dr	25,000	
Goodwill A/c	Dr	1,70,000	
To S Creditors A/c			1,40,000
To Business Purchase A/c			10,50,000
(Incorporation of Assets & Liabilities of X Ltd. taken over)			
(3) Plant A/c	Dr	99,000	
Land & Building A/c	Dr	1,50,000	
Stock A/c	Dr	1,20,000	
Debtors A/c	Dr	1,50,000	
Bills Receivable A/c	Dr	30,000	
Bank A/c	Dr	40,000	
To S Creditors A/c			50,000
To Bills payable			30,000
To Provision of Debtors			7,500
To Provision for workers' compensation			5,000
To Business Purchase A/c			4,96,500
(Incorporation of Assets & Liabilities of Y Ltd. taken over)			

(4) Liquidator of X Ltd. A/c	Dr	10,50,000	
To Equity Share Capital A/c			8,75,000
To Premium on Shares A/c			1,75,000
(Purchase consideration paid in by issue of 87500 Equity shares of Rs. 10 @ 20% premium)			
(5) Liquidator of Y Ltd. A/c	Dr	4,96,500	
To Equity Share Capital A/c			2,19,000
To Preference Share Capital A/c			1,87,500
To Debentures A/c			90,000
[Purchase consideration paid in by : (a) Issue of 21900 equity shares of Rs.10 each. (b) 1875 Preference shares of Rs. 100 each (c) Debentures]			

Problem No. 14

Shiva Ltd. and Krishna Ltd. decided to amalgamate. Their business and form a New Shiva-Krishna Ltd. with an authorised capital of Rs. 10,00,000 divided into shares of Rs. 10 each.

Balance Sheet as at 31-12-1987

Liabilities	Shiva Ltd.	Krishna Ltd.	Assets	Shiva Ltd.	Krishna Ltd.
Share Capital :			Goodwill	40,000	—
Equity shares of			Land & Building	1,80,000	2,50,000
Rs. 10 each	1,50,000	3,00,000	Stock	30,000	45,000
8% Debentures	—	80,000	Debtors	15,000	55,000
Reserve Fund	55,000		Cash at Bank	9,000	25,000
Profit & Loss A/c	45,000		Profit & Loss A/c	—	40,000
Creditors	24,000	35,000			
	2,74,000	4,15,000		2,74,000	4,15,000

The following are the terms of agreement :

(1) Shiva Ltd. — Assets and Liabilities are to be taken over at book values except Goodwill, Land & Building and stock which are to be valued at Rs. 56,000, 1,60,000 and Rs. 24,000 respectively.

(2) Krishna Ltd. — Assets except cash at Bank are valued at 10% less than the book values and the Liabilities are taken at book figures.

Required :

(1) Computation of purchase consideration.

(2) Amalgamated Balance Sheet of Shiva-Krishna Ltd.

(K.U.D., October 1988)

Solution :

Computation of Purchase Consideration

Shiva Ltd.

		Rs.
Assets taken over :		
Goodwill at revalued figure		56,000
Land & Building		1,60,000
Stock		24,000
Debtors		15,000
Cash at Bank		9,000
Total Assets		2,64,000
Less Liabilities :		
S Creditors		24,000
Net Assets		2,40,000
Purchase price paid in :		
Equity shares of Rs. 10		
24000 shares of Rs. 10 each		2,40,000

Ratio :

Old shares / New shares $= \frac{15000}{24000} = \frac{15}{24} = \frac{5}{8}$

For every five shares in Shiva Ltd. 8 shares of Rs. 10 are issued

$\frac{15000}{5} = 3000 \times 8 = 24000$ shares of Rs. 10 each Rs. 2,40,000

Krishna Ltd.

		Rs.
Assets taken over :		
Land & Building	2,50,000	
Less 10%	25,000	2,25,000
Stock	45,000	
Less 10%	4,500	40,500
Debtors		55,000
Cash at Bank		25,000
Total Assets		3,45,500
Less Liabilities :		
RDD @ 10% on 55,000	5,500	
Debentures	80,000	
S. Creditors	35,000	1,20,500
Net Assets		2,25,000
Purchase consideration paid in		
Equity Shares of Rs. 10		2,25,000

Ratio :

$\frac{30000 \text{ shares in Old Co.}}{22500 \text{ shares in New Co.}} = \frac{4}{3}$

For every four shares in Krishna Ltd. 3 shares of Rs. 10 are issued.

$= \frac{30000}{4} = 7500 \times 3 = 22500$ shares of Rs. 10 Rs. 2,25,000

Amalgamated Balance Sheet as at

Liabilities		Rs.	Assets		Rs.
Share Capital :			Goodwill — S		56,000
Authorised :			Land & Building :		
100000 shares			S	1,60,000	
of 10 each		10,00,000	K	2,25,000	3,85,000
Issued Capital :			Stock : S	24,000	
Shiva Ltd.			K	40,500	64,500
24000 shares of			Debtors : S	15,000	
Rs. 10 each	2,40,000		K	55,000	
Krishna Ltd.				70,000	
22500 shares of					
Rs. 10 each	2,25,000	4,65,000	*Less* RDD of K	5,500	64,500
Debentures		80,000	Cash at Bank : S	9,000	
Creditors : S	24,000		K	25,000	34,000
K	35,000	59,000			
		6,04,000			6,04,000

Entries :

Books of Shiva Ltd.

	Dr	Cr
(1) Realisation	2,74,000	
To Goodwill		40,000
To Land & Building		1,80,000
To Stock		30,000
To Debtors		15,000
To Cash		9,000
(Assets transferred)		
(2) S Creditors	24,000	
To Realisation		24,000
(Liabilities transferred)		
(3) Share Capital	1,50,000	
Reserve Fund A/c	55,000	
Profit & Loss A/c	45,000	
To Shareholders		2,50,000
(Share capital & Reserve Fund & Profit transferred)		

Books of Krishna Ltd.

	Dr	Cr
(1) Realisation	3,75,000	
To Land & Building		2,50,000
To Stock		45,000
To Debtors		55,000
To Cash		25,000
(Assets transferred)		
(2) Debentures A/c	80,000	
S. Creditors A/c	35,000	
To Realisation		1,15,000
(3) Share Capital A/c	3,00,000	
To Shareholders		3,00,000
(Share Capital transferred)		

	Dr	Cr
(4) Shiva-Krishna A/c	2,40,000	
To Realisation A/c		24,000
(Purchase Consideration Receivable)		
(5) Share in Shiva–Krishna Ltd.	2,40,000	
To Shiva-Krishna		2,40,000
(Purchase Consideration Received in 24000 shares of Rs. 10 each)		
(2) Debentures A/c	80,000	

	Dr	Cr
(4) Shiva-Krishna Ltd. A/c	2,25,000	
To Realisation A/c		2,25,000
(Purchase consideration receivable)		
(5) Share in purchasing Co. A/c	2,25,000	
To Shiva-Krishna		2,25,000
(Purchase consideration received in 22500 shares of Rs. 10 each)		
(6) Shareholders A/c	40,000	
To Profit & Loss A/c		40,000
(Loss transferred)		
(7) Shareholders A/c	35,000	
To Realisation A/c		35,000
(Loss transferred)		
Shareholders A/c	2,25,000	
To Share in P. Co.		2,25,000
(Shares in P Co. transferred)		

In the Books of Shiva Ltd.

Realisation A/c

	Rs.		Rs.
To Goodwill	40,000	By Creditors	24,000
To Land & Building	1,80,000	By Shiva-Krishna Ltd. (Purchasing Co.)	2,40,000
To Stock	30,000		
To Debtors	15,000	By Loss transferred to	
To Cash	9,000	Shareholders	10,000
	2,74,000		2,74,000

Shiva-Krishna Ltd. A/c

To Realisation A/c	2,40,000	By Share in Purchasing Co.	2,40,000

Shares in Purchasing Co.

	Rs.		Rs.
To Shiva-Krishna Ltd.	2,40,000	By Shareholders A/c	2,40,000

Shareholders A/c

To Realisation Loss	10,000	By Share Capital	1,50,000
To Share in Purchasing Co.	2,40,000	By Reserve Fund	55,000
		By Profit	45,000
	2,50,000		2,50,000

Books of Krishna Ltd.

Realisation A/c

To Land & Building	2,50,000	By Debentures	80,000
To Stock	45,000	By Creditors	35,000
To Debtors	55,000	By Shiva-Krishna Ltd. (Purchasing Co.)	2,25,000
To Cash	25,000	By Shareholders A/c (Loss transferred)	35,000
	3,75,000		3,75,000

Shiva-Krishna Ltd. A/c

To Realisation A/c	2,25,000	By Shares in Purchasing Co.	2,25,000

Shares in Purchasing Co.

To Shiva-Krishna Ltd.	2,25,000	By Shareholders	2,25,000

Shareholders A/c

To Profit & Loss	40,000	By Share Capital	3,00,000
To Realisation Loss	35,000		
To Shares in Purchasing Co.	2,25,000		
	3,00,000		3,00,000

Books of Shiva-Krishna Ltd.

Opening Entries :

(1)	Business Purchasing Co. A/c	Dr	4,65,000	
	To Liquidation of Shiva Ltd.			2,40,000
	To Liquidation of Krishna Ltd.			2,25,000
	(Purchase consideration payable to Shiva Ltd. & Krishna Ltd.)			
(2)	Goodwill A/c	Dr	56,000	
	Land & Building A/c	Dr	1,60,000	
	Stock A/c	Dr	24,000	
	Debtors A/c	Dr	15,000	
	Cash A/c	Dr	9,000	
	To S. Creditors			24,000
	To Business Purchase A/c			2,40,000
	(Assets & Liabilities of Shiva Ltd. brought in to A/c)			
(3)	Liquidator of Shiva Ltd. A/c	Dr	2,40,000	
	To Share Capital A/c			2,40,000
	(Issue of 24000 shares of Rs. 10 for payment of purchase consideration)			
(4)	Land & Building A/c	Dr	2,25,000	
	Stock A/c	Dr	40,500	
	Debtors A/c	Dr	55,000	
	Cash A/c	Dr	25,000	
	To R.D.D.			5,500
	To Debentures			80,000
	To S. Creditors			35,000
	To Business Purchase A/c			2,25,000
	(Incorporation of Assets & Liabilities taken over)			
5.	Liquidator of Krishna Ltd.	Dr	2,25,000	
	To Share Capital			2,25,000
	(Issue of 22500 shares of Rs. 10)			

Problem No. 15

A Ltd. and B Ltd. decided to Amalgamate their Business on 1st January 1984, and form a New Co. called AB Ltd. with an Authorised capital of 20000 shares of Rs. 100 each. Following are the Balance sheets of both Cos. on 1-1-1984 :

Balance Sheets as at 1-1-1984

Liabilities	A Ltd.	B Ltd.	Assets	A Ltd.	B Ltd.
Share Capital :			Goodwill	50,000	50,000
50000 Equity shares of Rs. 10 each	5,00,000		Land & Building	3,00,000	4,00,000
			Plant & Machinery	2,00,000	3,00,000
100000 Equity shares of Rs. 10 each		10,00,000	Patents	—	10,000
			Stock	20,000	1,00,000
Reserves & Surplus :			S. Debtors	20,000	1,20,000
Profit & Loss	50,000	—	Cash at Bank	60,000	50,000
Secured Loan	50,000	—	Profit & Loss A/c	—	50,000
Current Liabilities :					
S. Creditors	50,000	80,000			
	6,50,000	10,80,000		6,50,000	10,80,000

AB Ltd. took over all assets of A Ltd. & B Ltd. except cash at Bank but considered Goodwill of the B Ltd. as valueless. It also agreed to take over trade creditors for the purpose, it agreed to issue fully paid shares to the liquidators of the two companies. Give Journal entries in the books of both the Cos. to close their books.

Solution :

Calculation of purchase consideration :

Particulars	A Ltd.	B Ltd.
Assets taken over :		
Goodwill	50,000	—
Land & Building	3,00,000	4,00,000
Plant & Machinery	2,00,000	3,00,000
Patents	—	10,000
Stock	20,000	1,00,000
Sundry Debtors	20,000	1,20,000
Total Asscts	5,90,000	9,30,000
Less Liabilities Takenover :		
Sundry Creditors	50,000	8,50,000
	5,40,000	8,50,000
Purchase price :		
5400 × 100		
8500 × 100	5,40,000	8,50,000

Ratio :

A Ltd.			B Ltd.		
50,000	:	5400	1,00,000	:	8500
500	:	54	1000	:	85
250	:	27	200	:	17
10		100	10		100

Journal Entries :

Particulars	Books of A Ltd.		Books of B Ltd.	
(1) Realisation A/c Dr	5,90,000		9,80,000	
To Goodwill		50,000		50,000
To Land & Building		3,00,000		4,00,000
To Plant & Machinery		2,00,000		3,00,000
To Stock		20,000		1,00,000
To Sundry Debtors		20,000		1,20,000
To Patents		—		10,000
(Assets taken over transferred)				
(2) Sundry Creditors A/c Dr	50,000		80,000	
To Realisation		50,000		80,000
(Liabilities taken over transferred)				
(3) Share Capital A/c Dr	5,00,000		10,00,000	
Profit & Loss A/c Dr	50,000		—	
To Shareholders A/c		5,50,000		10,00,000
(Share capital & surplus transferred)				
(4) 6% Debentures A/c Dr	50,000			
To Debenture-holders A/c		50,000		
(Debentures transferred)				
(5) Shareholders A/c Dr	—		50,000	
To Profit & Loss A/c		—		50,000
(Loss transferred to shareholders)				
(6) AB Ltd. A/c Dr	5,40,000		8,50,000	
To Realisation A/c		5,40,000		8,50,000
(Purchase consideration receivable)				

Particulars		Books of A Ltd.		Books of B Ltd.	
(7) Shares in AB Ltd. A/c	Dr	5,40,000		8,50,000	
To AB Ltd. A/c			5,40,000		8,50,000
(Purchase consideration received in shares)					
(8) 6% Debenture-holders A/c	Dr	50,000		—	
To Bank A/c			50,000		—
(Debenture-holders paid cash)					
(9) Shareholders A/c	Dr	—		50,000	
To Realisation A/c			—		50,000
(Realisation loss transferred)					
(10) Shareholders A/c	Dr	5,50,000		9,00,000	
To Shares in AB Ltd.			5,40,000		8,50,000
To Bank			10,000		50,000
(Shares and Cash balance distributed to shareholders)					

Ledger A/cs in Books of A Ltd.

Realisation A/c

Debtors	Rs.	Creditors	Rs.
To Goodwill	50,000	By Sundry Creditors	50,000
To Land & Building	3,00,000	By AB Ltd.	5,40,000
To Plant & Machinery	2,00,000	(Purchase price)	
To Stock	20,000		
To Sundry Debtors	20,000		
	5,90,000		5,90,000

Shareholders A/c

To Shares in AB Ltd.	5,40,000	By Share Capital	5,00,000
To Bank	10,000	By Profit & Loss	50,000
	5,50,000		5,50,000

Debenture-holders A/c

	Rs.		Rs.
To Bank A/c	50,000	By 6% Debentures	50,000
	50,000		50,000.

Bank A/c

To Balance b/d	60,000	By Debenture-holders A/c	50,000
		By Shareholders A/c	10,000
	60,000		60,000

AB Ltd. A/c

To Realisation A/c	5,40,000	By Shares in AB Ltd.	5,40,000
	5,40,000		5,40,000

In the Books of B Ltd.

Realisation A/c

To Goodwill	50,000	By S Creditors	80,000
To Land & Building	4,00,000	By AB Ltd.	8,50,000
To Plant & Machinery	3,00,000	(Purchase Price)	
To Patent	10,000	By Loss Transferred to	
To Stock	1,00,000	Shareholders	50,000
To S Debtors	1,20,000		
	9,80,000		9,80,000

Shareholders A/c

To Profit & Loss A/c	50,000	By Share Capital A/c	10,00,000
(Loss transferred)			
To Realisation (Loss)	50,000		
To Shares in AB Ltd.	8,50,000		
To Bank	50,000		
	10,00,000		10,00,000

Bank A/c

To Balance b/d	50,000	By Shareholders A/c	50,000
	50,000		50,000

AB Ltd. A/c

	Rs.		Rs.
To Realisation A/c	8,50,000	By Shares in AB Ltd.	8,50,000
	8,50,000		8,50,000

Shares in AB Ltd. A/c

To AB Ltd.	8,50,000	By Shareholders A/c	8,50,000
	8,50,000		8,50,000

Amalgamated Balance Sheet of AB Ltd.

Liabilities	Rs.	Assets	Rs.
Share Capital :		Goodwill	50,000
Authorised :		Land & Building (3,00,000 + 4,00,000)	7,00,000
20000 shares of Rs. 10 each	20,00,000	Plant & Machinery (2,00,000 + 3,00,000)	5,00,000
Issued Capital :		Patent	10,000
5000 + 8500 13900 × 100	13,90,000	Stock (20,000 + 1,00,000)	1,20,000
S Creditors (50,000 + 80,000)	1,30,000	S Debtors (20,000 + 1,20,000)	1,40,000
	15,20,000		15,20,000

Problem No. 16

A Ltd. and B Ltd. agreed to amalgamate and form a New Co. C Ltd. which will take over all the assets and liabilities of the two companies.

In case of A Ltd. :

Assets and the Liabilities are to be taken at Book values in exchange for shares in C Ltd. The shares in C Ltd. were valued at a Premium of 10% and exchange was for every four (4) shares in A Ltd., five (5) shares of C Ltd.

In case of B Ltd. :

(1) Debentures of B Ltd. would be paid off by the issue of an equal number of Debentures in C. Ltd. @ 10% discount.

(2) The holders of 6% Preference shares of B Ltd. would be allotted four (4) 7% Preference shares in C Ltd. for every five (5) Preference shares held in B Ltd.

(3) The Equity shareholders would be allotted sufficient shares to cover the balance on their accounts after adjusting the Assets-values by reducing Plant & Machinery by 10% and providing 5% Reserve on Sundry debtors.

Balance Sheets of A Ltd. & B Ltd. as at

Liabilities	A Ltd.	B Ltd.	Assets	A Ltd.	B Ltd.
Shares Capital :					
Equity shares of Rs. 10 each	4,00,000	5,00,000	Plant & Machinery	8,00,000	8,00,000
6% Preference shares of Rs. 10	—	3,00,000	Stock	65,000	60,000
			Debtors	95,000	50,000
Reserves & Surplus	5,50,000	—	Cash at Bank	65,000	40,000
			Profit & Loss A/c	—	1,40,000
Secured Loan :					
4% Debentures	—	2,00,000			
Sundry Creditors	75,000	90,000			
	10,25,000	10,90,000		10,25,000	10,90,000

Ascertain purchase consideration payable to A Ltd. and B Ltd. and prepare the Balance sheet of C Ltd. assuming that the face value of shares in C Ltd. is Rs. 10 and of Debentures and Preference shares of Rs.100 each.

(K.U.D., October 1973)

Solution :

Amalgamation – Net Payment Method

A Ltd.		B Ltd.		
Assets taken over :	10,25,000	*Assets taken over :*		
Less Liabilities	75,000	Plant &		
	9,50,000	Machinery	8,00,000	
		Less 10%	80,000	7,20,000
Purchase consideration		Stock		60,000
paid in —		Debtors	50,000	
(a) Shares :		*Less* RDD 5%	2,500	47,500
$40000 \times \frac{1}{4} = 10000 \times 5 =$	50,000	Cash at Bank		40,000
		Total Assets		8,67,500
50,000 shares of Rs. 10	5,00,000	*Less Liabilities :*		
@ 10% Premium	50,000	Creditors	90,000	
	5,50,000	RDD	2,500	92,500
Net Assets	9,50,000	Net Assets		7,75,000
Purchase consideration	5,50,000	Purchase consideration		
Capital Gain		paid in :		
Capital Reserve	4,00,000	(a) Issue of		
Net Payment Method		Debentures	2,00,000	
		Less 10%		
		Discount	20,000	1,80,000

A Ltd.		B Ltd.	
Purchase Consideration		(b) Issue of Preference shares :	
Paid in -		$\frac{300000}{100} = \frac{3000}{5}$	
by issue of Equity Shares			
50000 shares of Rs. 10	5,00,000	$= 600 \times 4 = 2400 \times 100$	2,40,000
at a Premium of 10%	50,000	(c) Issue of Equity Shares	
Rs.	5,50,000	35750 shares of Rs.10 each	3,57,500
			7,77,500
		Net Assets Method.	

Balance Sheet as at

Liabilities	Rs.	Rs.	Assets	Rs.	Rs.
Share Capital :			Plant & Machinery :		
A Ltd. 50000 Equity shares of Rs.10 each	5,00,000		A Ltd.	8,00,000	
			B Ltd.	7,20,000	15,20,000
B Ltd. 35750 Equity shares of Rs.10 each	3,57,500	8,57,500	*Investments*		
2400 7% Preference shares of Rs. 100 each		2,40,000	*Loans & Advances*		
			Stock : A Ltd.	65,000	
			B Ltd.	60,000	1,25,000
Reserves & Surplus :					
Capital Reserve		4,00,000	Debtors : A Ltd.	95,000	
Share Premium		50,000	B Ltd.	50,000	
Secured Loan :		1,80,000		1,45,000	
Current Liabilities :			*Less* RDD	2,500	1,42,500
Debentures	75,000		Cash at Bank :		
Creditors	90,000	1,65,000	A Ltd.	65,000	
			B Ltd.	40,000	1,05,000
		18,92,500			18,92,500

Problem No. 17

X Co. Ltd. and Y Co. Ltd. decided to Amalgamate their business on 31-12-1978 and form a new company called XY Co. Ltd. with an Authorised capital of Rs. 60,00,000 divided into shares of Rs. 40 each.

The following are the Balance sheets of the two companies on the above date :

Balance Sheet as at 31-12-1978

Liabilities	X Co. Ltd.	Y Co. Ltd.	Assets	X Co. Ltd.	Y Co. Ltd.
Share Capital :			Goodwill	2,40,000	—
Equity shares			Machinery	12,80,000	14,40,000
of Rs. 40 each	8,00,000	15,00,000	Stock	1,18,000	1,38,000
Reserves & Surplus :			Debtors	1,71,000	98,000
Reserve Fund	2,90,000	—	Cash at Bank	1,17,000	84,000
Profit & Loss	7,00,000	—	Profit & Loss	—	3,20,000
Secured Loan :					
Debenture	—	4,00,000			
Current Liabilities :					
Creditors	1,36,000	1,80,000			
	19,26,000	20,80,000		19,26,000	20,80,000

The following are the terms of Amalgamation :

1. Assets and Liabilities of X Co. Ltd. are to be taken are Book value except :

   Goodwill valued at Rs. 3,60,000

   Machinery valued at Rs. 12,00,000

   Stock Rs. 1,28,000

2. The Assets of Y Co. Ltd. except cash at Bank and Debtors, are to be taken at 10% more than the book value and the liabilities, cash at Bank and debtors are taken over at Book values.

Prepare Amalgamated Balance Sheet of the new company.

(K.U.D., October 1979)

Solution :

Amalgamated Balance Sheet of XY Co. Ltd. as at 31-12-1979

Liabilities	Rs.	Rs.	Assets		Rs.	Rs.
Share Capital :			Goodwill X Co.			3,60,000
Authorised			Machinery :	X Co.	12,00,000	
Equity shares of				Y Co.	15,84,000	27,84,000
150000 Rs. 40 each		60,00,000	Stock :	X Co.	1,28,000	
Issued & Paid				Y Co.	1,51,800	2,79,800
Issued to			Debtors :	X Co.	1,71,000	
X Co. = 46000×40	18,40,000			Y Co.	98,000	2,69,000
Y Co. = 33445×40	13,37,800	31,77,800	Cash at Bank :			
Reserves & Surplus	—	—		X Co.	1,17,000	
Secured Loan				Y Co.	84,000	2,01,000
Debenture : X Co.	—	—				
Y Co.	4,00,000	4,00,000				
Current Liabilities						
Creditors : X Co.	1,36,000					
Y Co.	1,80,000	3,16,000				
		38,93,800				38,93,800

Calculation of X Co. Ltd.

Assets taken	Rs.
Goodwill	3,60,000
Machinery	12,00,000
Stock	1,28,000
Debtors	1,71,000
Cash at Bank	1,17,000
Total Assets	19,76,000
Less Liabilities :	
Creditors	1,36,000
Net Assets	18,40,000
Purchase consideration paid in Equity shares of Rs. 40 each 46000 × 40 =	18,40,000

Calculation of Y Co. Ltd.

Assets taken		Rs.
Machinery	14,40,000	
Add : 10%	1,44,000	15,84,000
Stock	1,38,000	
Add : 10%	13,800	1,51,800
Debtors		98,000
Cash at Bank		84,000
Total Assets		19,17,800
Less Liabilities :		
Debentures	4,00,000	
Creditors	1,80,000	5,80,000
Net Assets		13,37,800
Purchase consideration paid in equity shares of Rs. 40 each 33445 × 40 =		13,37,800

In the Books of X Co. Ltd.

Realisation A/c

Particulars	Rs.	Assets	Rs.
To Sundry Assets	19,26,000	By Creditors	1,36,000
To Equity Sharehoders A/c	50,000	By XY Co. Ltd.	18,40,000
	19,76,000		19,76,000

Equity Shareholders A/c

Particulars	Rs.	Assets	Rs.
To Equity shares in XY Co.	18,40,000	By Share Capital	8,00,000
		By Reserve Fund	2,90,000
		By Profit & Loss A/c	7,00,000
		By Realisation	50,000
	18,40,000		18,40,000

In the Books of Y Co. Ltd.

Realisation A/c

Particulars	Rs.	Assets	Rs.
To Sundry Assets	17,60,000	By Debtors	4,00,000
To Equity Shareholders	1,57,800	By Creditors	1,80,000
		By XY Co Ltd.	13,37,800
	19,17,800		19,17,800

Equity Shareholders A/c

Particulars	Rs.	Assets	Rs.
To Profit & Loss A/c	3,20,000	By Share Capital	15,00,000
To Equity shares in XY Co. Ltd.	13,37,800	By Realisation	1,57,800
	16,57,800		16,57,800

Books of XY Co. Ltd.

Entries :

Particulars		Amount	Amount
1. Business Purchase A/c	Dr	18,40,000	
To Liquidator of X Co. A/c			18,40,000
(Purchase consideration payable)			
2. Goodwill A/c	Dr	3,60,000	
Machinery A/c	Dr	12,00,000	
Stock A/c	Dr	1,28,000	
Debtors A/c	Dr	1,71,000	
Cash at Bank A/c	Dr	1,17,000	
To Creditors A/c			1,36,000
To Business Purchase A/c			18,40,000
(Incorporation of Assets & Liabilities taken over)			
3. Liquidation of X Co. Ltd. A/c		18,40,000	
To Equity Share Co. Ltd. A/c			18,40,000
(Purchase price paid in 46000 shares of Rs. 40 each)			
4. Business Purchase A/c	Dr	13,37,800	
To Liquidation of Y Co. A/c			13,37,800
(Purchase price payable)			
5. Machinery A/c	Dr	15,84,000	
Stock A/c	Dr	1,51,800	
Debtors A/c	Dr	98,000	
Cash at Bank A/c	Dr	84,000	
To Debentures A/c			4,00,000
To Creditors A/c			1,80,000
To Business Purchases A/c			13,37,800
(Incorporation of Assets & Liabilities taken over)			
6. Liquidation of Y Co. Ltd. A/c	Dr	13,37,800	
To Equity Share Capital A/c			13,37,800
(Purchase price paid in equity shares 33445 × 40)			

Problem No. 18

Following are the Balance sheets of X Ltd. and Y Ltd. which agree to amalgamate their business and form a new company XY Co. Ltd. with a Registered Capital of 50,00,000 divided into 50000 Equity shares of Rs. 100 each.

Balance Sheet as at 31-12-1980

Liabilities	X Co. Rs.	Y Co. Rs.	Assets	X Co. Rs.	Y Co. Rs.
Share Capital			*Fixed Assets*		
Equity share of	10,00,000	8,00,000	Goodwill	1,00,000	75,000
Rs. 100 each			Land & Building	3,00,000	2,50,000
Reserves & Surplus			Plant & Machinery	5,00,000	4,00,000
General Reserve	1,80,000	—	Investments in		
Profit & Loss A/c	2,00,000	—	Govt. Securities	5,00,000	3,00,000
Secured Loan			*Current Assets*		
8% Debentures	1,50,000	—	Stock	1,50,000	1,00,000
Unsecured Loan			Debtors	80,000	60,000
Public Deposits	—	4,00,000	Bills Receivable	30,000	20,000
Current Liabilities			Cash at Bank	1,20,000	50,000
Creditors	2,00,000	1,00,000	Profit & Loss A/c	—	75,000
Bills payable	50,000	30,000			
	17,80,000	13,30,000		17,80,000	13,30,000

Terms of Amalgamation are as follows :

The Assets and the Liabilities of both companies are taken over except Goodwill of Y Co. Ltd. at the following figures :

	X Co.	Y Co.
Land and Building	3,50,000	2,00,000
Plant & Machinery	4,00,000	3,50,000
Govt. Securities	5,00,000	3,00,000
Stocks	1,75,000	75,000
Debtors	80,000	60,000
Bills Receivable	30,000	20,000
Cash at Bank	1,20,000	50,000

The consideration being :

(a) *For X Co.*

1. Discharge of debentures at 20% premium by issue of 10% debentures of sufficient amount at 96%.
2. A cash payment of Rs. 20 per share of X Co. Ltd.

3. Issue of Three (3) equity shares of Rs. 100 each in XY Co. for every two equity shares in X Co. Ltd.

(b) *For Y Co.*

1. Sufficient amount of cash to pay off public deposits.
2. A cash payment of Rs. 10 per share of X Co. Ltd.
3. Issue Three (3) equity share in XY Co. for every five (5) equity shares in Y Co.

The cost of liquidators of X Co. Rs. 10,000 paid by itself and the cost of Liquidation of Y Co. Rs. 8,000 paid by XY Co.

(c) The equity shares of XY Co. 7000 shares of Rs. 100 issued to public and cash received duly.

You are required to :

(a) Calculate purchase consideration of both Cos.

(b) Close the books of both the companies by preparing Ledger A/cs.

(c) Prepare Amalgamated Balance sheet of XY Co. after passing opening entries in the books.

Solution :

Calculations of Purchase Considerations

Particulars	X Co.		Y Co.	
Assets taken				
Land & Building	3,50,000		2,00,000	
Plant & Machinery	4,00,000		3,50,000	
Govt. Securities	5,00,000		3,00,000	
Stocks	1,75,000		75,000	
Debtors	80,000		60,000	
Bills Receivable	30,000		20,000	
Cash at Bank	1,20,000		50,000	
Goodwill	1,00,000		—	
Total Assets		17,55,000		10,55,000
Less Liabilities				
Creditors	2,00,000		1,00,000	
Bills payable	50,000	2,50,000	30,000	1,30,000
Net Assets		15,05,000		9,25,000

Purchase consideration paid in :

Particulars		X Co.	Y Co.
1. Discharge of debentures	1,50,000		
@ 20% premium	30,000	1,80,000	—
2. Cash payment of X Co. Ltd.			
10000 × 20		2,00,000	—
Y Co. 8000 × 5		—	40,000
3. Issue of Equity shares is		15,00,000	
X Co. $\frac{10000}{2} \times 3 = 15000 \times 100$		15,00,000	—
Y Co. $\frac{8000}{5} \times 3 = 4800 \times 100$		—	4,80,000
4. Cash paid to payoff public deposit Y Co.		—	4,00,000
Purchase consideration paid		18,80,000	9,20,000
Net Assets		15,05,000	9,25,000
X Co. Excess paid treated Goodwill		3,75,000	
Y Co. Capital Gain Capital Reserve			5,000

Note : Discharge of debentures @ 20% premium by issue of sufficient amount of debenture @ 96%.

Debentures	1,50,000
@ 20% premium	30,000
Debentures	1,80,000

Face value of Debentures issued @ 96%.

$$1{,}80{,}000 \times \frac{100}{96} = 1{,}87{,}500$$

Entry : X Co. A/c Dr.	1,80,000	
Discount of Issue of Debentures	7,500	
To Debentures A/c		1,87,500
(Debentures issued @ 96%)		

In the Books of X Co. — Ledgers A/cs

Realisation A/c

Particular	Amount	Particular	Amount
To Sundry assets (All assets in book value)	17,80,000	By Sundry Creditors	2,00,000
		By Bills payable	50,000
To Debenture holders	30,000	By X Co. Purchase Co. (Purchase consideration)	18,80,000
To Bank A/c (Cost of liquidator)	10,000		
To Equity shareholders profit transfer	3,10,000		
	21,30,000		21,30,000

Debenture Holders A/c

To Debentures in Purchasing Co.	1,80,000	By Debentures	1,50,000
		By Realisation A/c (Balance transferred)	30,000
	1,80,000		1,80,000

Equity Share Holders A/c

To Equity shares in purchasing Co.	15,00,000	By Share Capital	10,00,000
To Bank A/c	1,90,000	By General Reserve	1,80,000
		By Profit& Loss A/c	2,00,000
		By Realisation A/c Profit transfer	3,10,000
	16,90,000		16,90,000

Bank A/c

To XY Co.	2,00,000	By Realisation (Cost of liquidation)	10,000
		By Equity Shareholders	1,90,000
	2,00,000		2,00,000

XY Co. A/c (Purchasing Co.)

To Realisation A/c	18,80,000	By Debentures in purchasing Co.	1,80,000
		By Equity shares in purchasing Co.	15,00,000
		By Bank	2,00,000
	18,80,000		18,80,000

In the Books of 'Y' Co. — Ledger A/c

Realisation A/c

Particular		Amount	Particular	Amount
To Sundry Assets	13,30,000		By Sundry Creditors	1,00,000
Less Loss	75,000	12,55,000	By Bills Payable	30,000
			By XY Co. Purchasing Co.	9,20,000
			By Equity Shareholders A/c (Loss transferred)	2,05,000
		12,55,000		12,55,000

Equity Shareholders A/c

To Profit & Loss A/c	75,000	By Share Capital A/c	8,00,000
To Realisation A/c (Loss)	2,05,000		
To Equity shares in purchasing Co.	4,80,000		
To Bank	40,000		
	8,00,000		8,00,000

XY Co. (Purchasing Co.)

To Realisation A/c	9,20,000	By Equity shares in purchasing Co.	4,80,000
		By Bank A/c (40,000 + 4,00,000)	4,40,000
	9,20,000		9,20,000

Bank A/c

To XY Co.	4,40,000	By Public Deposits	4,00,000
		By Equity Shareholders	40,000
	4,40,000		4,40,000

In the Books of 'XY' Co.

Note-1 : Goodwill :	
X Co.	4,75,000
Add : Cost of Liquidation of Y Co.	8,000
	4,83,000
Less : Capital Reserve of Y Co.	5,000
	4,78,000
Note-2 : *Bank A/c* :	
X Co.	1,20,000
Y Co.	50,000
	1,70,000
Add : Cash received 7000 × 100	7,00,000
	8,70,000
Less : Cash paid :	
X Co. 2,00,000	
Y Co. 4,40,000	
Cost of Liquidation 8,000	6,48,000
Cash at Bank balance	2,22,000

Amalgmated Balance Sheet of 'XY' Co. as at 31-12-1980

Liabilities	Amount	Amount	Assets	Amount	Amount
	Rs.	Rs.		Rs.	Rs.
Share Capital			Goodwill X Co.	4,75,000	
Authorised			*Add* : Cost of liquidation Y Co.	8,000	
50000 Equity shares of Rs. 100		50,00,000		4,83,000	
Issued Capital			*Less* : Capital Reserve Y Co.	5,000	4,78,000
X Co. 15000 × 100	15,00,000		Land & Building :		
Y Co. 4800 × 100	4,80,000		X Co.	3,50,000	
Public 7000 × 100	7,00,000	26,80,000	Y Co.	2,00,000	5,50,000
Reserves and Surplus		—	Plant & Machinery :		
Secured Loan :			X Co.	4,00,000	
10% debentures		1,87,500	Y Co.	3,50,000	7,50,000
Unsecured Loan		—			

Liabilities	Amount	Amount	Assets	Amount	Amount
	Rs.	Rs.		Rs.	Rs.
Current Liabilities			*Govt. Securities :*		
Creditors : X Co.	2,00,000		X Co.	5,00,000	
Y Co.	1,00,000	3,00,000	Y Co.	3,00,000	8,00,000
Bills Payable : X Co.	50,000		Stocks : X Co.	1,75,000	
Y Co.	30,000	80,000	Y Co.	75,000	2,50,000
			Debtors : X Co.	80,000	
			Y Co.	60,000	1,40,000
			Bills Receivable :		
			X Co.	30,000	
			Y Co.	20,000	50,000
			Cash at Bank Balance :		
			X Co.	1,20,000	
			Y Co.	50,000	
				1,70,000	
			Cash Received 7000 × 100	7,00,000	
				8,70,000	
			Less Paid		
			X Co. 2,00,000		
			Y Co. 4,40,000		
			Cost of liquidations 8,000		
				6,48,000	2,22,000
			Discount on issue of debenture		7,500
		32,47,500			32,47,500

Opening Entries in the Books of XY Co.

Particulars		Amount	Amount
1. Business Purchase A/c	Dr	28,00,000	
To Liquidators of X Co.			18,80,000
To Liquidators of Y Co.			9,20,000
(Purchase consideration payable)			
2. Land & Building A/c	Dr	3,50,000	
Plant & Machinery A/c	Dr	4,00,000	
Govt. Securities A/c	Dr	5,00,000	
Stocks A/c	Dr	1,75,000	
Debtors A/c	Dr	80,000	
Bills Receivable A/c	Dr	30,000	

Particulars		Amount	Amount
Cash at Bank A/c	Dr	1,20,000	
Goodwill (1,00,000+3,75,000) A/c	Dr	4,75,000	
To Creditors A/c			2,00,000
To Bills Payable A/c			50,000
To Business Purchase A/c			18,80,000
(Incorporation of Assets & Liabilities of X Co. ledger over)			
3. Land & Building A/c	Dr	2,00,000	
Plant & Machinery A/c	Dr	3,50,000	
Govt. Securities A/c	Dr	3,00,000	
Stocks A/c	Dr	75,000	
Debtors A/c	Dr	60,000	
Bills Receivable A/c	Dr	20,000	
Cash at Bank A/c	Dr	50,000	
To Creditors A/c			1,00,000
To Bills Payable A/c			30,000
To Business Purchase A/c			9,20,000
To Capital Reserve A/c			5,000
(In corporation of Assets & Liabilities of Y Co. taken over)			
4. Bank A/c	Dr	7,00,000	
To Equity Share Capital A/c			7,00,000
(7000 equity shares of Rs.100 issued to public and cash received)			
5. Liquidators of X Co. A/c	Dr	18,80,000	
Discount on Issue of debenture A/c	Dr	7,500	
To 10% Debentures			1,87,500
To Equity Share Capital A/c			15,00,000
To Bank A/c			2,00,000
(Purchase consideration paid in by issue of Debentures @ 96%, 15000 equity shares of Rs.100 and Balance in cash.)			
6. Liquidators of Y Co. A/c	Dr	9,20,000	
To Equity Share Capital A/c			4,80,000
To Bank (4,00,000+40,000) A/c			4,40,000
(Purchase consideration paid in by issue of 4800 equity shares of Rs.100 and balance in cash)			

Particulars		Amount	Amount
7. Cost of Liquidation A/c	Dr	8,000	
To Bank A/c			8,000
(Cost of Liquidation paid)			
8. Goodwill A/c	Dr	8,000	
To Cost of Liquidation A/c			8,000
(Cost of Liquidation transferred)			
9. Capital Reserve A/c	Dr	5,000	
To Goodwill A/c			5,000
(Capital reserve adjusted in Goodwill)			

(b) ABSORPTION

Problem No. 19

The Hubli Co Ltd. decided to sell its business to Belgaum Co. Ltd. as on 31-12-1994. On that date its Balance sheet was as follows :

Balance Sheet as at 31-12-1994

Liabilities	Rs.	Assets	Rs.
Share Capital :		Goodwill	4,000
Shares of Rs.10 each	20,000	Building	15,000
Reserves & Surplus :		Machinery	1,500
Reserve	5,000	Stock	3,500
Profit & Loss A/c	2,000	Sundry Debtors	4,000
Secured Loan		Bills Receivable	2,000
5% Debentures	10,000	Cash	10,000
Current Liabilities & Provisions			
Creditors	3,000		
	40,000		40,000

The Belguam Co. Ltd. agreed to take over the assets (Exclusive of goodwill and cash) at book value and to discharge the liabilities to trade creditors and to pay for goodwill Rs. 10,000.

The purchases price was paid by the absorbing Co.

Allotment of 1200 shares of Rs.10 each at market value of Rs. 12.50 each by the Belgaum Co. Ltd. and the balance in cash.

You are required to :

(a) Prepare Ledger Account in Hubli Co. Ltd. and

(b) Pass opening entries in Belguam Co. Ltd.

[K.U.D., April 1996 (a)]

Solution :

Working Note

(a) *Calculation of purchase consideration* :

Assets taken

Building	15,000	
Machinery	1,500	
Stock	3,500	
Sundry Debtors	4,000	
Bills Receivable	2,000	
Goodwill	10,000	
Total Assets	36,000	
Less : Liabilities : Creditors	3,000	
Net Assets	33,000	
Purchases price paid in by issue of 1200 shares of Rs. 10 each at market price of Rs. 12.50 each (1200 × 12.50)		15,000
Balance in cash		18,000
		33,000

In the Books Hubli Co. Ltd.

Realisation A/c

Particular	Amount	Particular	Amount
To Goodwill	4,000	By Creditors	3,000
To Building	15,000	By Belgaum Co. Ltd.	33,000
To Machinery	1,500		
To Stock	3,500		
To Sundry Debtors	4,000		
To Bills Receivable	2,000		
To Profit on Realisation A/c	6,000		
	36,000		36,000

Sharcholder A/c

To Shares in Belgaum Co. Ltd.	15,000	By Share Capital	20,000
To Cash Account	18,000	By Reserve	5,000
		By Profit & Loss A/c	2,000
		By Realisation A/c (Profit)	6,000
	33,000		33,000

Bank A/c

Particular	Amount	Particular	Amount
To Balance b/d	10,000	By Debenture A/c	10,000
To Belgaum cash	18,000	By Shareholder A/c	18,000
	28,000		28,000

Debenture A/c

To Cash	10,000	By Bank A/c	10,000
	10,000		10,000

In the Books of Belgaum Co. Ltd.

Opening Entries :

Particulars		Amount	Amount
(1) Business Purchases A/c	Dr	33,000	
To Liquidators of Hubli Co. Ltd.			33,000
(Purchase consideration payable)			
(2) Building A/c	Dr	15,000	
Machinery A/c	Dr	1,500	
Stock A/c	Dr	3,500	
Sundry Debtors A/c	Dr	4,000	
Bills Receivable A/c	Dr	2,000	
Goodwill A/c	Dr	10,000	
To Creditors A/c			3,000
To Business Purchases A/c			33,000
(Incorporation of Assets & Liabilities taken over)			
(3) Liquidators of Hubli Co. Ltd. A/c	Dr	33,000	
To Shares Capital A/c			12,000
To Share Premium A/c			3,000
To Bank A/c			18,000
(Purchase consideration paid by issue of 1200 shares of Rs. 10 each at Rs. 12.50 and balance in cash.)			

Problem No. 20

The Karnataka Co. Ltd. was incorporated with an authorised capital of Rs. 10,00,000 divided into equity shares of Rs. 100 each to take over the business of Hubli Co. Ltd. on 1-1-1994. The following is the Balance Sheet of Hubli Co. Ltd. :

Balance Sheet as at 1-1-1994

Liabilities	Rs.	Assets	Rs.
Share Capital (in shares of Rs. 100 each)	2,00,000	Buildings	1,00,000
General Reserve	50,000	Machinery	80,000
Profit and Loss A/c	40,000	Goodwill	20,000
5% Debentures	1,00,000	Investments	60,000
Employees Security Deposit	10,000	Stock	1,00,000
		Debtors	1,14,000
Sundry Creditors	85,000	Cash at Bank	26,000
Bills Payable	15,000		
Total	5,00,000		5,00,000

The terms agreed were as follows :

(1) The Karnataka Co. Ltd. is to issue 3 shares of Rs. 100 each for every 2 shares in Hubli Co. Ltd.

(2) The Karnataka Co. Ltd. is to issue 6% debentures and cash of Rs. 10,000 to discharge the 5% debentures of Hubli Co. Ltd. at 10% premium.

(3) The Karnataka Co. Ltd. to pay cash of Rs. 5 per share for every share in Hubli Co. Ltd.

(4) The realisation expenses are of Rs. 4,000 and is paid Karnataka Co. Ltd. The Karnataka Co. Ltd. issued 1,000 shares of Rs.100 each at par to the public for subscription which was fully subscribed and paid.

You are required to :

(i) Prcparc ncccssary Ledger accounts to close the books of Hubli Co. Ltd.

(ii) Give the opening Balance Sheet of Karnataka Co. Ltd.

(KUD, October 1995)

Solution :

Working Note

Assets taken :			Purchase consideration paid in :	
Sundry Assets		5,00,000	(a) To Equity sharesholders, in shares :	
Less : Liabilities			$\frac{2000}{2} \times 3 \times 100 =$	3,00,000
Employee Security Deposit	10,000			
Sundry Creditors	85,000			
Bills Payable	15,000	1,10,000	In cash : 2000 × 5	10,000
Net assets		3,90,000		

Purchase price	4,34,000	(b) Debenture holders		
Net Assets	3,90,000	Cash		10,000
Excess paid		6% Debenture	1,00,000	
treated as payment	44,000	@ 10% premium	10,000	1,10,000
Toward Goodwill :				4,30,000
Goodwill	44,000	*Add* : Realisation Exp.		4,000
Existing Goodwill	20,000	Purchase price		4,34,000
Total Goodwill	64,000	Total Cash	10,000	
			10,000	
			4,000	24,000
		Shares		3,00,000
		Debentures		1,10,000
				4,34,000

In the Books of Hubli Co. Ltd.

Realisation A/c

Particular	Amount	Particular	Amount
To Sundry Assets	5,00,000	By Sundry Liabilities	
To Debenture holders A/c	20,000	Employee securities	
To Bank A/c expenses	4,000	deposits	10,000
To Profit on Realisation	20,000	By Sundry Creditors	85,000
Transferred to equity		By Karnataka Co. Ltd.	4,34,000
Shareholder A/c		(Purchasing Co.)	
		purchase consideration	
	5,44,000		5,44,000

Equity Shareholders A/c

To Equity Shares		By Equity Shares	
Karnataka Co Ltd.	3,00,000	Capital	2,00,000
To Bank	10,000	By General Reserve	50,000
		By Profit and Loss A/c	40,000
		By Realisation A/c	20,000
		(Profit)	
	3,10,000		3,10,000

Debenture Holders A/c

Particular	Amount	Particular	Amount
To 6% Debenture in Karnataka Co. Ltd.	1,10,000	By Debentures A/c	1,00,000
To Bank	10,000	By Realisation A/c	20,000
	1,20,000		1,20,000

Bank A/c

To Karnataka Co. Ltd.	24,000	By Realisation exp.	4,000
		By Debenture holders A/c	10,000
		By Equity Sharesholder A/c	10,000
	24,000		24,000

Karnataka Co. Ltd. (Purchasing Co.)

To Realisation A/c	4,34,000	By Bank A/c	24,000
		By Equity shares in purchasing Co.	3,00,000
		By Debentures in purchasing Co.	1,10,000
	4,34,000		4,34,000

In the Books of Karnataka Co. Ltd.
Balance Sheet as at 1-1-1994

Liabilities	Rs.	Assets		Rs.
Share Capital		*Fixed Assets*		
Authorised Capital		Goodwill		64,000
10000 Equity shares of		Building		1,00,000
Rs. 100 each	10,00,000	Machinery		80,000
Issued & Paidup Capital		Investments		60,000
Vendor		*Current Assets*		
3000 Equity shares of		Stock		1,00,000
Rs. 100 each	3,00,000	Debtors		1,14,000
To public		Cash at Bank		1,02,000
1000 Equity shares of		Balance	26,000	
Rs. 100 each	1,00,000	*Add* : Cash recd.	1,00,000	
	4,00,000	Cash	1,26,000	

Liabilities	Rs.	Assets		Rs.
Reserves & Surplus	—	*Less* : Paid		
Secured Loan			10,000	
6% Debentures	1,10,000		10,000	
Unsecured Loan	—		4,000	24,000
Current Liabilities and Provisions				
Employees security deposit	10,000			
Sundry Creditors	85,000			
Bills Payable	15,000			
	6,20,000			6,20,000

In the Books of Karnataka Co. Ltd.

Extra Answer : Opening entries

Particulars		Amount	Amount
(1) Business Purchasing A/c	Dr	4,34,000	
To Liquidators of Hubli Co. A/c			4,34,000
(Purchase consideration payable)			
(2) Goodwill A/c	Dr	64,000	
Building A/c	Dr	1,00,000	
Machinery A/c	Dr	80,000	
Investment A/c	Dr	60,000	
Stock A/c	Dr	1,00,000	
Sundry Debtors A/c	Dr	1,14,000	
Cash at Bank A/c	Dr	26,000	
To Employee Security Deposit A/c			10,000
To Sundry Creditors A/c			85,000
To Bills Payable A/c			15,000
To Business Purchase A/c			4,34,000
(Incorporation of Assets and Liabilities taken over)			
(3) Bank A/c	Dr	1,00,000	
To Equity Shares Capital A/c			1,00,000
(Cash received on 1000 Equity shares issued to public)			
(4) Liquidators of Hubli Co. Ltd. A/c	Dr	4,34,000	
To Equity Share Capital A/c			3,00,000
To 6% Debentures A/c			1,10,000
To Bank A/c			24,000
[Purchase consideration paid in : (a) 3000 Equity shares of Rs. 100 (b) Debentures (c) Balance in cash.]			

Problem No. 21

(1) The following is the Balance Sheet of Chetana Ltd. as on 31-12-1990 :

Balance Sheet as at 31-12-1990

Liabilities	Rs.	Assets	Rs.
Share Capital : 20000 shares		Land and Building	3,00,000
of Rs. 25 each	5,00,000	Plant and Machinery	3,50,000
Reserve fund	75,000	Investment	97,500
Dividend equalisation fund	67,000	Furniture and Fittings	13,700
Workmen's compensation		Stocks	1,02,500
fund	73,100	Sundry debtors	1,06,300
Debentures	2,00,000	Cash at Bank	30,100
Sundry creditors	85,000		
	10,00,100		10,00,100

The company is absorbed by Parag Ltd. on the above date. The purchase consideration was the discharge of debentures at a permium of 10% taking over of the liabilities in respect of sundry creditors and payment of Rs. 15 in cash and issue of two shares of Rs. 10 each in Parag Ltd. at the market value of Rs. 15 per share in exchange for one share in Chetana Ltd. The cost of liquidation of Rs. 3,500 is met by purchasing company. Parag Ltd. valued land and building at 10% more and investment at Rs. 67,970. Show :

(a) Calculation of purchase consideration.

(b) Realisation account and shareholders account in the Books of Chetana Ltd.

(c) Opening entries in the books of Parag Ltd.

(K.U.D., October 1994)

Solution :

Calculation of Purchase Consideration

Assets taken over		Payment of purchase consideration	
Land & Building	3,00,000	(1) Debentures	2,00,000
Add : 10%	30,000	Premium 10%	20,000
	3,30,000		2,20,000
Plant & Machinery	3,50,000	(2) Shareholders cash payment 20000 × 15	3,00,000
Investments	67,970	Shares 20000 × 2 =	
Furniture	13,700	40000 × 15	6,00,000
Stock	1,02,500	Purchase price	11,20,000

Assets taken over		Payment of purchase consideration	
Sundry Debtors	1,06,300		11,20,000
Cash at Banks	30,100	Net Assets	9,15,570
	10,00,570	Excess payment	
Less : Liabilities :		treated as goodwill	2,04,430
Sundry Creditors	85,000		
Net Assets	9,15,570		

In the Books of Chetana Ltd.

Realisation A/c

Particular	Amount	Particular	Amount
To Land & Building	3,00,000	By Sundry Creditors	85,000
To Plant & Machinery	3,50,000	By Parag Ltd.	
To Investments	97,500	(Purchasing company)	11,20,000
To Furniture	13,700		
To Stock	1,02,500		
To Sundry Debtors	1,06,300		
To Cash at Bank	30,100		
To Premium on Debt	20,000		
To Profit transfer to shareholders	1,84,900		
	12,05,000		12,05,000

Shareholders A/c

To Shares in Parag Ltd.	6,00,000	By Share Capital	5,00,000
To Bank	3,00,000	By Reserve Fund	75,000
		By Dividend Equity Fund	67,000
		By Workmen's Compensation Fund	73,100
		By Profit on Realisation	1,84,900
	9,00,000		9,00,000

Parag Ltd. A/c (Purchasing Company)

Particular	Amount	Particular	Amount
To Realisation A/c	11,20,000	By Debentures in purchasing Co. A/c	2,20,000
		By Shares in purchasing Company	6,00,000
		By Bank A/c	3,00,000
	11,20,000		11,20,000

Debenture-holders A/c

To Debentures in purchasing Co.	2,20,000	By Debentures	2,00,000
		By Realisation A/c (Transfer)	20,000
	2,20,000		2,20,000

In the Books of Parag Ltd. (Purchasing company)

Opening Entries :

Particulars		Amount	Amount
(1) Business Purchase A/c	Dr	11,20,000	
To Equidator of Chetana Ltd.			11,20,000
(Purchase consideration payable)			
(2) Land & Building A/c	Dr	3,30,000	
Plant & Machinery A/c	Dr	3,50,000	
Investment A/c	Dr	67,970	
Furniture A/c	Dr	13,700	
Stock A/c	Dr	1,02,500	
Sundry Debtors A/c	Dr	1,06,300	
Cash at Bank A/c	Dr	30,100	
Goodwill A/c (Balancing figure)	Dr	2,04,430	
To Sundry Creditors			85,000
To Business Purchase A/c			11,20,000
(Incorporation of assets and liabilities taken over)			

Particulars		Amount	Amount
(3) Liquidator of Chetana Ltd. A/c	Dr	11,20,000	
To Debentures A/c			2,20,000
To Share Capital A/c			4,00,000
To Share Premium A/c			2,00,000
To Bank A/c			3,00,000
(Purchase consideration paid in debenture at 20% premium issue of 40000 shares of Rs.10 at market value of Rs.15 per share)			

Problem No. 22

Following is the Balance Sheet of Karnataka Ltd. Bangalore as on 31-12-1990 :

Balance Sheet as at 31-12-1990

Liabilities	Rs.	Assets	Rs.
Share Capital :		Land & Building	2,00,000
25000 Equity shares		Machinery	1,20,000
of Rs.10 each	2,50,000	Investments in Govt.	
1000 9% Preference shares		Securities	50,000
of Rs.100 each	1,00,000	Stock	40,000
Reserves & Surplus :	—	Debtors	20,000
Secured Loan :		Cash at Bank	20,000
11% Debentures	50,000	Profit & Loss A/c	41,000
Unsecured Loan	—		
Current Liabilities :			
Sundry Creditors	70,000		
Bills Payable	21,000		
	4,91,000		4,91,000

Prakash Ltd., Bangalore took over the Business of Karnataka Ltd. on the above date.

Terms agreed were as follows :

(1) The Assets were to be taken at Book values except – Land & Building, Machinery and Investments at Rs. 2,25,000, Rs. 1,02,000 and Rs. 4,500 respectively.

(2) Debentures were discharged by the issue of 10% debentures at 10% discount.

(3) Preference shares were paid by issue of four (4) 10% Preference shares of Rs.100 each in exchange for every five (5) Preference shares held in Karnataka Ltd., Bangalore.

(4) Equity shareholders are paid by issue of three (3) Equity shares of Rs.10 each in exchange for every five (5) Equity shares held in Karnataka Ltd. and Rs. 3 per share in cash.

(5) Cost of liquidation Rs. 6,000 paid by Prakash Ltd., Bangalore.

You are required to :

(a) Prepare Ledger Accounts to close the Books of Karnataka Ltd., Bangalore.

(b) Pass Journal Entries in the Books of Prakash Ltd., Bangalore.

(K.U.D., April 1993)

Solution :

Calculation :

Assets taken over :			*Purchase consideration paid in* :	
Land & Building		2,25,000	(1) 11% Debentures — discharged	
Machinery		1,02,000	@ 10% Discount	50,000
Investments		45,000	Discount	5,000
Stock		40,000		45,000
Debtors		20,000		
Bank A/c		20,000	(2) Preference shares :	
Total Assets		4,52,000	$\frac{1000}{5} \times 4 = 800 \times 100$	80,000
Less Liabilities :				
Sundry creditors	70,000		(3) Equity shareholders :	
Bills payable	21,000	91,000		
Net Assets		3,61,000	$\frac{25000}{5} \times 3 = 15000 \times 10$	1,50,000
Purchase price		3,50,000		
			25000 × 3 = Paid cash	75,000
Capital gain treated as Capital Reserve		11,000	Purchase price	3,50,000

In the Books of Karnataka Ltd. — Ledger A/cs

Realisation A/c

Particular	Amount	Particular	Amount
To Sundry Assets (4,91,000 – 41,000) (Loss)	4,50,000	By Sundry Creditors	70,000
		By Bills Payable	21,000
To Profit transferred to Equity Shareholders A/c	16,000	By Prakash Ltd. (Purchase price)	3,50,000
		By Debentures	5,000
		By Preference shares	20,000
	4,66,000		4,66,000

Prakash Ltd. A/c (Purchasing Co.)

Particular	Amount	Particular	Amount
To Realisation A/c	3,50,000	By Debentures in Prakash Ltd.	45,000
		By Preference shares in Prakash Ltd.	80,000
		By Equity shares in Prakash Ltd.	1,50,000
		By Bank	75,000
	3,50,000		3,50,000

Debenture-holders A/c

To Debentures in Prakash Ltd.	45,000	By Debentures	50,000
To Realisation A/c	5,000		
	50,000		50,000

Preference Shareholders A/c

To Preference shares in Prakash Ltd.	80,000	By Preference Share Capital	1,00,000
To Realisation	20,000		
	1,00,000		1,00,000

Equity Shareholders A/c

To Profit & Loss A/c	41,000	By Equity Share Capital	2,50,000
To Equity shares in Prakash Ltd.	1,50,000	By Realisation (Profit transferred)	16,000
To Bank A/c	75,000		
	2,66,000		2,66,000

In the Books of Prakash Ltd.

Journal Entries :

Particulars		Amount	Amount
(1) Business Purchase A/c	Dr	3,50,000	
To Liquidator of Prakash Ltd.			3,50,000
(Purchase consideration payable)			
(2) Land & Building A/c	Dr	2,25,000	
Machinery A/c	Dr	1,02,000	
Stock A/c	Dr	45,000	
Investments A/c	Dr	40,000	
Debtors A/c	Dr	20,000	
Bank A/c	Dr	20,000	
To Sundry Creditors A/c			70,000
To Bills Payable A/c			21,000
To Business Purchase A/c			3,50,000
To Capital Reserve A/c			11,000
(Incorporation of assets & liabilities taken over and Balance capital reserve)			
(3) Liquidator of Prakash Ltd. A/c	Dr	3,50,000	
Discount on Debenture A/c	Dr	5,000	
To 10% Debentures			50,000
To Preference Share Capital			80,000
To Equity Share Capital			1,50,000
To Bank A/c			75,000
[Purchase consideration paid in : (1) By issue of debentures @ Rs. 10% discount. (2) 800 Preference shares of Rs. 100 each. (3) 15000 Equity shares of Rs. 10 each and cash]			
(4) Cost of Liquidation A/c	Dr	6,000	
To Bank A/c			6,000
(Liquidation expenses paid)			
(5) Capital Reserve A/c	Dr	6,000	
To Cost of Liquidation			6,000
(Cost of liquidation written off)			

Problem No. 23

The following are the balance sheets of S Ltd. and P Ltd. as on 31st March 1991 :

Balance Sheets as at 31-3-1991

Liabilities	S Ltd. Rs.	P Ltd. Rs.	Assets	S Ltd. Rs.	P Ltd. Rs.
Share Capital :			*Fixed Assets* :		
Share of Rs. 10 each	2,00,000	3,00,000	Land & Building	1,00,000	2,50,000
Reserves & Surplus :			Plant & Machinery	1,30,000	95,000
Reserve fund	60,000	80,000	*Investments* :		
Worker's compensation fund	20,000	—	6% Debentures in P Ltd. (at par)	20,000	—
			Current Assets, Loans & Advances :		
Secured Loan :			Debtors	60,000	50,000
6% Debentures	—	50,000	Stock	30,000	70,000
Current Liabilities & Provisions :			Bank	—	15,000
Creditors	60,000	50,000			
	3,40,000	4,80,000		3,40,000	4,80,000

P Ltd. absorbed S Ltd. on the following terms :

(a) P Ltd. shall give one share of Rs. 15 each at Rs. 20 per share for every two shares in S Ltd.

(b) The creditors of S Ltd. included Rs. 10,000 due to P Ltd.

(c) The stock of S Ltd. consisted of goods worth Rs. 20,000 bought from P Ltd. on which the latter had made a profit of 20% on sales.

(d) The Land and Building and Plant and Machinery of S Ltd. were taken over at Rs. 1,20,000 and Rs. 1,00,000 respectively required :

(i) Realisation A/c, Shareholders A/c in S Ltd.

(ii) Journal entries relating to the acquisition in the books of P Ltd.

(iii) Balance-sheet of P Ltd. after absorption.

(K.U.D, October 1992)

Solution :

Calculations :

S Ltd.		Purchase consideration paid in :	
Assets taken :			
Land & Building	1,20,000	(1) Issue of one share Rs. 15 each @ Rs. 20 per share for every 2 shares in S Ltd.	
Plant & Machinery	1,00,000		
Investments :		20000 × 1/2 = 10000 shares	
Debentures	20,000	10000 shares of Rs. 15	
Debtors	60,000	each @ Rs. 20 per	
Stock	30,000	share (10000 × 20) =	2,00,000
Total Assets	3,30,000	Purchase Price	2,00,000
Less Liabilities :		Net assets	2,70,000
Creditors	60,000	Capital profit treated as Capital Reserve	70,000
Net Assets	2,70,000		

In the Books of S Ltd.

Realisation A/c

Particular	Amount	Particular	Amount
To S Assets	3,40,000	By Creditors	60,000
		By P Ltd. (Purchase consideration)	2,00,000
		By Loss transferred to Shareholders A/c	80,000
	3,40,000		3,40,000

Shareholders A/c

To Realisation A/c (Loss)	80,000	By Share Capital	2,00,000
		By Reserve Fund	60,000
To Shares in P Ltd.	2,00,000	By Workmen's compensation fund	80,000
	2,80,000		2,80,000

In the Books of P Ltd. (Absorbing Co.)

Journal Entries :

Particulars		Amount	Amount
(1) Business Purchase A/c	Dr	2,00,000	
To Liquidator of S Ltd.			2,00,000
(Purchase consideration payable)			
(2) Liquidator of S Ltd. A/c	Dr	2,00,000	
To Share Capital A/c			1,50,000
To Share Premium A/c			50,000
(Purchase consideration paid in by issue of 10000 shares of Rs. 15 @ Rs. 20 per share)			
(3) Land & Building A/c	Dr	1,20,000	
Plant & Machinery A/c	Dr	1,00,000	
Debentures in P Ltd. A/c	Dr	20,000	
Debtors A/c	Dr	60,000	
Stock A/c	Dr	30,000	
To Creditors A/c			60,000
To Capital Reserve A/c			70,000
To Business Purchase A/c			2,00,000
(Incorporation of Assets & Liabilities taken over)			

In the Books of P Ltd.

Balance Sheet as at 31-12-1991

Liabilities	Rs.	Rs.	Assets	Rs.	Rs.
Share Capital :			*Fixed Assets* :		
Share of Rs. 10			Land & Building :		
			P	2,50,000	
P Ltd. 30000×10 =	3,00,000		S	1,20,000	3,70,000
S Ltd. 10000×15 =	1,50,000	4,50,000	Plant & Machinery :		
Reserves & Surplus :			P	95,000	
Reserve Fund : P	80,000		S	1,00,000	1,95,000
S	—	80,000	*Investments* :		
			6% Debentures in		
Share Premium		50,000	P Ltd.	20,000	
Capital Reserve	70,000		Deduct Inter Co. incentives	20,000	—
Less Unrealised			Debtors : P	50,000	
profit	4,000	66,000	S	60,000	
6% Debentures – P	50,000			110,000	
Less held by S Ltd.	20,000	30,000	Less due from S Ltd.	10,000	1,00,000

Liabilities	Rs.	Rs.	Assets	Rs.	Rs.
Creditors : P Ltd.	50,000		Stock : P Ltd.	70,000	
S Ltd.	60,000		S Ltd.	30,000	
	1,10,000			1,00,000	
Less Due to P Ltd.	10,000	1,00,000	*Less* Unrealised profit	4,000	96,000
			Bank : P Ltd.	15,000	
			S Ltd.	—	15,000
		7,76,000			7,76,000

Problem No. 24

Zigma Limited was formed to take over the business of Stigma Limited. The following is the balance sheet of Stigma Limited on the date of purchase :

Balance Sheet of Stigma Limited

Liabilities	Rs.	Assets	Rs.
Capital		Plant	2,40,000
10000 Equity Shares		Building	3,20,000
of Rs. 50 each	5,00,000	Stock	1,00,000
3% Debentures	2,00,000	Debtors	48,000
Sundry Creditors	1,50,000	Cash	2,000
Bank Overdraft	20,000	Profit & Loss A/c (Dr)	1,00,000
Total	8,70,000		8,70,000

(a) The capital of Zigma Limited is to be 10,00,000 consisting of 100000 shares of Rs. 10 each.

(b) Zigma Limited agreed to issue five shares of Rs. 10 each and credited with Rs. 7 per share for every share held in Stigma Limited. The share-holders are to pay the balance of Rs. 3 per share in cash and the same has been duly collected by the company.

(c) The debenture-holders are to be issued 4% debentures in Zigma Ltd. Sufficient to discharge the debentures of Stigma Limited at a premium of 10%.

(d) Sundry creditors and Bank overdraft were taken over by Zigma Limited at the following values :
Plant Rs. 2,00,000, Building Rs. 3,00,000, Stock Rs. 1,25,000, Debtors Rs. 40,000, Cash Rs. 2,000.

(e) The expenses of liquidation of Rs. 2,000 were paid by Zigma Ltd.

Give Realisation A/c and Shareholders A/c in the books of Stigma Ltd. and the Balance Sheet of Zigma Ltd.

(K.U.D., October 1990)

Solution :

Working Notes

Assets taken over			*Purchase consideration*		
Plant		2,00,000	(1) Issue of shares		
Building		3,00,000	10000 × 5 = 50000 × 7 =		3,50,000
Stock		1,25,000	(2) *Debenture holders*		
Debtors		48,000	4% Debenture 2,00,000		
Cash		2,000	*Add* : 10%		
Total Assets		6,75,000	Premium	20,000	2,20,000
Less : Liabilities taken over			Total payment		5,70,000
Sundry Creditors	1,50,000		Assets taken		4,97,000
Bank Overdraft	20,000		Excess payment		
R.D.D.	8,000	1,78,000	(Payment towards		
Net Assets		4,97,000	goodwill)		73,000

In the Book of Stigma Ltd.

Realisation A/c

Particular	Amount	Particular	Amount
To Sundry Assets	7,70,000	By Sundry Creditors	1,50,000
To Debenture holders	20,000	By Bank Overdraft	20,000
(Premium on debenture)		By Purchasing Co. A/c	5,70,000
		By Loss on Realisation	50,000
		Transfer at shareholders	
	7,90,000		7,90,000

Shareholders A/c

To Profit & Loss (Loss)	1,00,000	By Share Capital	5,00,000
To Realisation Loss	50,000		
To Shares in purchasing company	3,50,000		
	5,00,000		5,00,000

3% Debenture-holders A/c

To Debentures in purchasing Co.	2,20,000	By Debentures A/c	2,00,000
		By Realisation A/c (Balance transferred)	20,000
	2,20,000		2,20,000

Zigma Limited
Balance Sheet as at

Liabilities	Rs.	Assets		Rs.
Share Capital		*Goodwill*	73,000	
50000 Share of Rs. 10	5,00,000	*Add* : Liquidator exp.	2,000	75,000
4% Debentures	2,20,000	Plant		2,00,000
Sundry Creditors	1,50,000	Building		3,00,000
Banks Overdraft	20,000	Stock		1,25,000
		Debtors	48,000	
		Less : RDD	8,000	40,000
		Cash balance	2,000	
		Add : Cash		
		50000 × 3	1,50,000	
			1,52,000	
		Less : Paid		
		Liquidator exp.	2,000	1,50,000
	8,90,000			8,90,000

Problem No. 25

The following was the Balance Sheet of General Co. Ltd. on 31st June 1989 on which date it was absorbed by Premier Co. Ltd. :

Balance Sheet as at 30-6-1989

Liabilities		Rs.	Assets	Rs.
Share Capital :				
5000, 5% Preference			Goodwill	40,000
shares of Rs. 50 each		2,50,000	Land & Building	3,00,000
150000 Equity shares			Machinery	3,00,000
of Rs. 5 each		7,50,000	Patents	1,30,000
Reserves & Surplus :			Stock	4,20,000
General Reserve		90,000	Sundry Debtors	3,00,000
Profit & Loss A/c			Bank	60,000
as per last B/s	1,500			
Profit for the year	18,500	20,000		
Secured Loan :				
Debentures of Rs. 100 each redeemable at the option of the Co. @ Rs. 105		1,20,000		
Current Liabilities :				
Sundry Creditors		3,20,000		
		15,50,000		15,50,000

(a) Premier Co. Ltd. took over the Assets only and the consideration for the absorption was :

(1) Payment of cash sufficient to discharge the debentures debt and liability to creditors.

(2) Payment of cash to the amount Rs. 1.50 for each equity share in General Co. Ltd.

(3) Allotment of one fully paid equity share of Re. 1 each (market value Rs. 1.75) in its capital to the shareholders of two equity shares in General Co. Ltd.

(4) Five (5) fully paid 6% preference shares of Rs. 10 each (value at par) in its capital duly allotted to the holders against one preference share of General Co. Ltd.

(b) Dividend due for the year on preference shares to be paid to them.

(c) General Co. Ltd. met its own liquidation expenses Rs. 5,250.

(d) Premier Co. Ltd. took over the Assets in its books, at the revalued figures : Appreciating Building by Rs. 16,500, Depreciating Machinery by Rs. 21,000, Depreciating Stock by Rs. 36,000 and Patents by Rs. 30,000.

You are required to show :

(1) The Ledger A/cs as they finally stood in the Books of General Co. Ltd.

(2) The Journal Entries in the Books of Premier Co. Ltd.

(3) The treatment of Goodwill in the absorbing Co.

(K.U.D., April 1990)

Solution :

Calculations :

Assets taken :			*Purchase consideration paid in :*	
Building	3,00,000			
Add Appreciation	16,500	3,16,500	(1) Cash to pay debentures	1,20,000
Machinery	3,00,000		Of @ Premium of 5%	6,000
Less Depreciation	21,000	2,79,000	Creditors	1,26,000
Stock	4,20,000		To Shareholders	3,20,000
Less Depreciation	36,000	3,84,000	150000 equity shares	
Patents	1,30,000		@ Rs. 1.50	2,25,000
Less Depreciation	30,000	1,00,000	Total cash	6,71,000
Debtors		3,00,000	(2) Issue of 5 Preference	
Bank		60,000	shares of Rs. 10 for 1	
Goowill		40,000	share in General Co.	
Total Assets		14,79,000	$\frac{5000 \times 5}{1} = 25000 \times 10$	2,50,000

Less Liabilities :		
Reserve for RDD		7,500
2-1/2% on 300000 =	6,000	
	1,500	
Net assets		14,72,000
Purchase price		10,52,250
Less payment capital gain		4,19,750
Capital Reserve		
Less Goodwill in B/s		40,000
Net capital reserve		3,79,750

(3) Equity Shareholders :		
Issue of one equity share of Re. 1 each @ Rs. 1.75		
Market value for 2 equity share in General Co.		1,31,250
Purchase Price		10,52,250
Equity share capital :		
75000 × 1.00 =	75,000	capital
75000 × 0.75 =	56,250	premium
	Rs. 1,31,250	

In the Books of General Co. Ltd.

Realisation A/c

Particular	Amount	Particular	Amount
To S Assets	15,50,000	By General Co. Ltd. (Purchase consideration)	10,52,250
To Debenture-holders A/c	6,000		
To Bank A/c (Liquidation exp.)	5,250	By Equity shareholders (Loss transferred)	5,09,000
	15,61,250		15,61,250

Equity Shareholders A/c

To Realisation Loss	5,09,000	By Equity share capital		7,50,000
To Equity shares in General Co. Ltd.	1,31,250	By General Reserve		90,000
To Bank	2,07,250	By Profit & Loss	20,000	
		Less Discount on preference shares	12,500	7,500
	8,47,500			8,47,500

Preference Shareholders A/c

To Preference in General Co. Ltd.	2,50,000	By Preference share capital	2,50,000
	2,50,000		2,50,000

Premier Co. Ltd. A/c (Purchasing Co.)

Particular	Amount	Particular	Amount
To Realisation A/c	10,52,250	By Bank A/c	6,71,000
		By Preference shares in General Co. Ltd.	2,50,000
		By Equity shares in General Co. Ltd.	1,31,250
	10,52,250		10,52,250

Bank A/c

To Premier Co.	6,71,000	By Debentures	1,26,000
		By Creditors	3,20,000
		By Dividend on preference shares	12,500
		By Realisation (Liquidation exp.)	5,250
		By Equity shareholders	2,07,250
	6,71,000		6,71,000

In the Books of Premier Co.

Journal Entries :

Particulars		Amount	Amount
(1) Business Purchase A/c	Dr	10,52,250	
To Liquidator of General Co. Ltd.			10,52,250
(Purchase consideration payable)			
(2) Goodwill A/c	Dr	40,000	
Land & Building A/c	Dr	3,16,500	
Machinery A/c	Dr	2,79,000	
Stock A/c	Dr	3,84,000	
Patents A/c	Dr	1,00,000	
Debtors A/c	Dr	3,00,000	
Bank A/c	Dr	60,000	
To Reserve for doubtful debts			7,500
To Business purchase A/c			10,52,250
To Capital Reserve A/c			4,19,750
(Incorporation of Assets taken and provision on debtors)			

Particulars		Amount	Amount
(3) Liquidator of General Co. Ltd.	Dr	10,52,250	
To Preference share capital A/c			2,50,000
To Equity share capital A/c			75,000
To Share premium A/c			56,250
To Bank A/c			6,71,000
[Purchase consideration paid in : (a) Issue of preference shares 25000 shares of Rs. 10. (b) Issue of 75000 equity shares of Re. 1 @ Rs. 1.75 Market value and in cash]			
(4) Capital Reserve A/c	Dr	40,000	
To Goodwill A/c			40,000
(Goodwill written against capital reserve)			

Problem No. 26

A Ltd. agreed to acquire the business of B Ltd. as on 31-12-1988. The Balance Sheet of B Ltd. as on that date was as follows :

Balance Sheet as at 31-12-1988

Liabilities	Rs.	Assets	Rs.
Share Capital :		Goodwill	2,00,000
Authorised		Land & Building	6,00,000
120000 Equity shares		Plant & Machinery	6,80,000
of Rs. 10 each	12,00,000	Stock	3,36,000
Subscribed & Paid-up :		Debtors	72,000
120000 Equity shares of		Cash in hand	12,000
Rs. 10 each	12,00,000	Cash at Bank	1,00,000
Reserves & Surplus :			
General Reserves	3,40,000		
Profit & Loss A/c	2,20,000		
Secured Loan :			
6% Debentures	2,00,000		
Current Liabilities :			
Creditors	40,000		
	20,00,000		20,00,000

The consideration payable by A Ltd. was agreed at as follows :

(a) Cash payment of Rs. 2.50 per share, in B Ltd.

(b) The issue of 180000 equity shares of Rs. 10 each in A Ltd. having an agreed value of Rs. 15 per share.

(c) The issue of such an amount of fully paid 8% debentures of A Ltd. at 96% as are sufficient to discharge the 6% debentures of B Ltd. at a premium of 20%.

While computing the agreed consideration, the Directors of A Ltd. valued Assets :

		Rs.
(1)	Land & Building	12,00,000
(2)	Plant & Machinery	12,00,000
(3)	Stock	2,84,000

(4) Debtors at their face value subject to an allowance of 5% to cover the doubtful debts.

The cost of liquidation come to be Rs. 10,000.

Show the necessary Ledger A/cs in the Books of B Ltd. and pass journal entries in the Books of A Ltd.

(K.U.D., October 1989)

Note : Cost of liquidation to be paid by the Vendor Co. (i.e. B Ltd.)

Solution :

(a) Assets taken over :

Land & Building		12,00,000
Plant & Machinery		12,00,000
Stock		2,84,000
Debtors		72,000
Goodwill		2,00,000
Cash at Bank		1,12,000
Total Assets taken over		30,68,000
Less Liabilities :		
Creditors	40,000	
RDD 5% on 72,000	3,600	43,600
Net Assets		30,24,400
Net Assets		30,24,400
Purchase price		32,40,000
Excess payment		2,15,600
Payment towards Goodwill		
Add Goodwill in B Ltd.		2,00,000
		4,15,600

(b) *Purchase consideration paid in :*

(1) To Shareholders :

Cash payment @ Rs. 2,50 per share 120000 × 2.50	3,00,000
Issue of shares in A Ltd. : 180000 shares of Rs. 10 each @ Rs. 15 per share 180000 × 15	27,00,000

(2) *Debenture-holders* :

Debentures discharged @ 20% premium	2,40,000

Issued @ 96% face value of debentures

issued : $\frac{2,40,000 \times 100}{96}$

= 2,50,000 face value

Purchase price	32,40,000

Discount on Issue of debentures 10,000

(2,50,000 – 10,000 = 2,40,000)

In the Books of B Ltd. (Vendor Co.)

Realisation A/c

Particular	Amount	Particular	Amount
To S Assets	20,00,000	By S Creditors	40,000
To Debentures premium	40,000	By A Ltd.	32,40,000
To Bank expenses	10,000	(Purchasing Co.)	
To Shareholders A/c	12,30,000		
(Profit transferred)			
	32,80,000		32,80,000

A Ltd. (Purchasing Co.)

To Realisation	32,40,000	By Bank A/c	3,00,000
		By Shares in A Ltd.	27,00,000
		By Debentures in A Ltd.	2,40,000
	32,40,000		32,40,000

Equity Shareholders A/c

To Shares in A Ltd.	27,00,000	By Share capital	12,00,000
To Bank A/c	2,90,000	By General reserve	3,40,000
		By Profit & Loss A/c	2,20,000
		By Realisation A/c	12,30,000
		(Profit)	
	29,90,000		29,90,000

Debenture-holders A/c

To Debentures in A Ltd.	2,40,000	By Debentures	2,00,000
		By Premium (realisation)	40,000
	2,40,000		2,40,000

Bank A/c

To A Ltd.	3,00,000	By Realisation expenses	10,000
		By Shareholders	2,90,000
		(transferred)	
	3,00,000		3,00,000

In the Books of A Ltd.

Journal Entries :

Particulars		Amount	Amount
		Rs.	Rs.
(1) Business Purchase A/c	Dr	32,40,000	
To Liquidator of B Ltd. (Vendor Co.)			32,40,000
(Purchase price payable)			
(2) Land & Building A/c	Dr	12,00,000	
Plant & Machinery	Dr	12,00,000	
Stock	Dr	2,84,000	
Debtors	Dr	72,000	
Cash at Bank	Dr	1,12,000	
Goowill	Dr	4,15,000	
(2,00,000 + 2,15,000)			
(Balancing figure)			
To Creditors A/c			40,000
To RDD			3,600
To Business Purchase A/c			32,40,000
(Assets & Liabilities taken over brought into A/c)			
(3) Liquidator of B Ltd. (Vendor Co.)	Dr	32,40,000	
Discount on issue of debentures	Dr	10,000	
To Debentures A/c			2,50,000
To Share capital A/c			18,00,000
To Share premium A/c			9,00,000
To Bank A/c			3,00,000
[Purchase consideration paid in :			
(a) Issue of debentures of 2,50,000 @ 96%			
(b) Issue of 180000 shares of Rs. 10 @ Rs. 15 per share.			
(c) Payment of cash @ Rs. 2.50 per share (120000 × 2.50)]			

Problem No. 27

White Ltd. of Bombay agreed to acquire the business of Green Ltd. of Bangalore as on 31st December 1974. The Balance Sheet of Green Ltd. as on that date was as follows :

Balance Sheet as at 31-12-1974

Liabilities	Rs.	Assets		Rs.
Share Capital :		Goodwill		1,00,000
60000 Share capital		Land & Building		4,00,000
of Rs. 10 each	6,00,000	Plant & Machinery		2,40,000
Reserves & Surplus :		Stock		1,68,000
Reserve fund	1,70,000	Debtors	40,000	
Profit & Loss A/c	1,10,000	*Less* Reserve	4,000	36,000
Secured Loan :		Cash at Bank		30,000
Debentures	1,00,000	Cash in hand		26,000
Current Liabilities :				
Creditors	20,000			
	10,00,000			10,00,000

The consideration payable by White Ltd. was agreed as follows :

(1) Cash payment equivalent to Rs. 2.50 per share for every share in Green Ltd.

(2) The issue of 90000 equity shares of Rs. 10 each fully paid, in White Ltd. at an agreed value of Rs. 15 per share.

(3) The issue of such an amount of fully paid debentures of White Ltd. @ 96% as is sufficient to discharge debentures of Green Ltd. at a Premium of 20%.

Pass Journal Entries in the Books of White Ltd. and prepare :

(a) Realisation A/c

(b) Shareholders A/c

in the Books of Green Ltd.

(KUD, April 1975)

Solution :

Green Ltd.		*Purchase consideration paid in* :	
Assets taken over	10,00,000	(a) Cash — Rs. 2.50 for every share in Green Ltd.	
Less Liabilities :		60000 × 2.50	1,50,000
Creditors	20,000	(b) Equity-shareholders;	
Net Assets	9,80,000	Issue of 90000 equity shares of Rs. 10 each @ Rs. 15 per share 90000 × 15	13,50,000

Net assets	9,80,000	(c) Debentures	1,00,000	
Purchase price	16,20,000	Discharged @		
Excess payment treated as Goodwill	6,40,000	premium 20%	20,000	1,20,000
Add Goodwill in B/s	1,00,000	Issued at 96%		
	7,40,000	(Debenture's face value $= 120000 \times \frac{100}{96} = 1,25,000$)		
		Purchase price		16,20,000

Solution :

In the Books of Green Ltd.

Realisation A/c

Particular	Amount	Particular	Amount
To Sundry assets	10,04,000	By Sundry creditors	20,000
To Debenture premium	20,000	By RDD	4,000
To Profit transferred to shareholders	6,20,000	By White Ltd. (Purchase consideration)	16,20,000
	16,44,000		16,44,000

White Ltd. A/c

To Realisation A/c	16,20,000	By Bank A/c	1,50,000
		By Equity shares in White Ltd.	13,50,000
		By Debentures in White Ltd.	1,20,000
	16,20,000		16,20,000

Equity Shareholders A/c

To Equity shares in White Ltd.	13,50,000	By Equity share capital	6,00,000
		By Reserve Fund	1,70,000
To Bank	1,50,000	By Profit & Loss A/c	1,10,000
		By Realisation profit	6,20,000
	15,00,000		15,00,000

Debenture-holders A/c

To Debentures in White Ltd.	1,20,000	By Debentures A/c	1,00,000
		By Realisation A/c (Transferred)	20,000
	1,20,000		1,20,000

In the Books of White Ltd.

Journal Entries :

Particulars		Amount	Amount
(1) Business Purchase A/c	Dr	16,20,000	
To Liquidation of Green Ltd. A/c			16,20,000
(Purchase consideration payable)			
(2) Land & Building A/c	Dr	4,00,000	
Plant & Machinery	Dr	2,40,000	
Stock A/c	Dr	1,68,000	
Debtors A/c	Dr	40,000	
Cash at Bank	Dr	30,000	
Cash in hand	Dr	26,000	
Goodwill A/c	Dr	7,40,000	
(1,00,000 + 6,40,000)			
To Creditors A/c			20,000
To RDD A/c			4,000
To Business purchase A/c			16,20,000
(Incorporation of Assets & Liabilities taken over)			
(3) Liquidation of Green Ltd. A/c	Dr	16,20,000	
Discount on debentures A/c	Dr	5,000	
To Debentures A/c			1,25,000
To Equity share capital A/c			9,00,000
(90000 × 10)			
To Share premium A/c			4,50,000
To Bank A/c (Purchase consideration paid)			1,50,000

Problem No. 28

Inter Company Indebtedness :

Ajanta Ltd. agreed to acquire the business of Elora Ltd. as on 31-12-1982. The Balance Sheet of Elora Ltd. as on that date was as follows :

Balance Sheet as at 31-12-1982

Liabilities	Rs.	Assets	Rs.
Share Capital :		Land & Building	3,00,000
1000 10% of Preference		Machinery	1,50,000
shares of Rs. 100 each	1,00,000	Furniture	45,000
40000 Equity shares of		Stock	2,00,000
Rs. 10 each	4,00,000	Debtors	1,00,000

Liabilities	Rs.	Assets	Rs.
Reserves & Surplus :		Bank	45,000
Reserve fund	60,000	Preliminary expenses	60,000
Profit & Loss A/c	40,000		
Secured Loan :			
8% Debentures	2,00,000		
Current Liabilities :			
Employees Savings Bank Deposit	20,000		
Trade Creditors	80,000		
	9,00,000		9,00,000

The consideration payable by Ajanta Ltd. was agreed as follows :

(a) To take over the Assets and Trade Liabilities.

(b) To allot 1100, 12% preference shares of Rs. 100 each fully paid in Ajanta Ltd. to be issued to preference shareholders in Elora Ltd.

(c) To pay cash at Rs. 3 per share for every equity share in Elora Ltd.

(d) To issue 15% debentures of Rs. 100 each at par in Ajanta Ltd. to discharge 8% debentures of Elora Ltd. at a discount of 5%.

(e) To issue 5 equity shares of Rs. 10 each in Ajanta Ltd. (Quoted in the Market @ Rs. 12.50 per share as fully paid for every 4 equity shares held in Elora Ltd.)

(f) Debtors of Elora Ltd. included to Rs. 20,000 due from Ajanta Ltd.

(g) Cost of liquidation amounted to Rs. 10,000.

Prepare Ledger A/cs in the books of Elora Ltd. and Pass Journal Entries in the Books of Absorbing Company.

Solution :

Calculation :

Assets taken over :			Purchase consideration :		
Total Assets	9,00,000		(1) Cash — Rs. 3 per share		
Less Preliminary	60,000	8,40,000	40000 × 3		1,20,000
Less Liabilities :			(2) *Preference Shareholders :*		
Creditors		80,000	Issue of 1100 shares of		
Net Assets		7,60,000	Rs. 100 each 1100 × 100		1,10,000
Purchase price		10,45,000	(3) *Debenture-holders :*		
Excess payment treated			Issue of 15%		
as Goodwill		2,85,000	Debentures	2,00,000	
			Discharged @		
			Discount 5%	10,000	1,90,000

(4) *Equity Shareholders :*

$$\frac{40000 \times 5}{4} = 50000 \times 12.50 \quad 6,25,000$$

Purchase price 10,45,000

In the Books of Elora Ltd.

Realisation A/c

Particular	Amount	Particular	Amount
To Sundry Assets	9,00,000	By Creditors	80,000
To Preference Shares Premium	10,000	By Ajanta Ltd.	10,45,000
		By Debentures	10,000
To Equity Shareholders (Profit transferred)	2,15,000		
	11,35,000		11,35,000

Ajanta Ltd. A/c

To Realisation A/c	10,45,000	By Cash	1,20,000
		By Preference shares in Ajanta Ltd.	1,10,000
		By Debentures	1,90,000
		By Equity shares	6,25,000
	10,45,000		10,45,000

Equity Shareholders A/c

To Equity shares A/c	6,25,000	By Equity share capital	4,00,000
To Bank	90,000	By Reserve Fund	60,000
		By Profit & Loss	40,000
		By Realisation profit	2,15,000
	7,15,000		7,15,000

Preference Shareholders A/c

To Preference shares in Ajanta Ltd.	1,10,000	By Preference share capital	1,00,000
		By Realisation A/c	10,000
	1,10,000		1,10,000

Debenture-holders A/c

Particular	Amount	Particular	Amount
To Debentures A/c	1,90,000	By Debentures A/c	2,00,000
To Realisation A/c	10,000		
	2,00,000		2,00,000

Bank A/c

To Ajanta Ltd. A/c	1,20,000	By Employees Savings Bank Deposit	20,000
		By Liquidation cost	10,000
		By Equity shareholders A/c (transferred)	90,000
	1,20,000		1,20,000

In the Books of Ajanta Ltd.

Journal Entries

Particulars		Amount	Amount
(1) Business purchase A/c	Dr	10,45,000	
To Liquidation of Elora Ltd. A/c			10,45,000
(Purchase consideration payable)			
(2) Land & Building A/c	Dr	3,00,000	
Machinery A/c	Dr	1,50,000	
Furniture A/c	Dr	45,000	
Stock A/c	Dr	2,00,000	
Debtors A/c	Dr	1,00,000	
Bank A/c	Dr	45,000	
Goodwill A/c	Dr	2,85,000	
To Creditors A/c			80,000
To Business purchase A/c			10,45,000
(Incorporation of Assets & Liabilities)			
(3) Liquidator of Elora Ltd.	Dr	10,45,000	
Discount on Debentures A/c	Dr	10,000	
To Preference share capital A/c 1100 × 100			1,10,000
To Equity share capital A/c 50000 × 10			5,00,000
To Share premium 50000 × 2.50			1,25,000
To Debentures A/c Rs. 100 @ 5% discount			2,00,000
To Bank A/c			1,20,000
(Purchase consideration paid)			
(4) Creditors of Ajanta Ltd. A/c	Dr	20,000	
To Debtors of Elora Ltd. A/c			20,000
(Debtors of Elora Ltd. included Rs. 20,000 due from Ajanta Ltd.)			

Problem No. 29

Inter Company Investments, Loans etc.

Following are the Balance Sheets of 'X' Ltd. & 'Y' Ltd. :

Balance Sheets as at 31-12-1989

Liabilities	X Ltd.	Y Ltd.	Assets	X Ltd.	Y Ltd.
Share Capital :			*Fixed Assets* :		
Equity shares of 100 each	5,00,000	4,00,000	Goodwill	2,00,000	1,00,000
2% Preference shares of Rs. 100 each	4,00,000	1,00,000	Buildings	3,00,000	2,00,000
Reserves & Surplus :			Machinery	4,00,000	3,00,000
General Reserve	1,00,000	50,000	*Investments* :		
Profit & Loss A/c	1,40,000	50,000	In Y Ltd. in 5000 equity shares @ cost	60,000	—
Secured Loan :			Stock	1,80,000	1,00,000
9% Debentures	2,00,000	1,00,000	Debtors	1,75,000	60,000
Unsecured Loan :			Bills Receivable	25,000	15,000
Loan from X Ltd.	—	50,000	Loan to Y Ltd.	50,000	—
Current Liabilities :			Bank	2,00,000	75,000
Creditors	2,50,000	70,000			
	15,90,000	8,20,000		15,90,000	8,20,000

'X' Ltd. decided to take over 'Y' Ltd. on the following terms :

(a) X Ltd. agreed to take over assets and the liabilities at book values except Building and Machinery @ revalued figures — Rs. 2,50,000 and Rs. 3,50,000 respectively and Stock at Rs. 70,000.

(b) X Ltd. will issue 7 equity shares of Rs. 10 each at a premium of 20% and Rs. 5 in cash in exchange for every five (5) equity shares of Y Ltd.

(c) Preference shareholders of Y Ltd. are redeemed at a premium of 5% and one 12% Preference share of Rs. 100 each at a premium of 5%.

(d) 9% Debentures of Y Ltd. are redeemed @ 8% premium by the issue 9% debentures in X Ltd. @ 10% discount.

(e) Cost of liquidation Rs. 10,000 be paid by X Ltd.

Close the Books of Y Ltd. and pass the Journal Entries in the Books of X Ltd. and prepare Balance sheet of X Ltd.

Solution :

Calculations :

(a) *Assets taken over :*

Goodwill		1,00,000
Building (2,00,000)		2,50,000
Machinery (3,00,000)		3,50,000
Stock		70,000
Debtors		60,000
Bills Receivable		1,50,000
Bank		75,000
Total Assets		9,20,000
Less Liabilities taken over :		
Loan from X Ltd.	50,000	
Creditors	70,000	1,20,000
Net Assets taken over		8,00,000

Purchase Consideration :

(1) Payment of Equity shareholders :

(a) No. of shares $\frac{4,00,000}{10}$

= 40000

Less held by X Ltd. 5000

35000

$\frac{35000}{5} \times 7 = 49000 \times 12$ 5,88,000

(b) Payment in cash

$\frac{35000}{5} = 7000 \times 5$ 35,000

(c) Discharge of shares held by X Ltd.

Proportionate :

$\frac{5000}{5} \times 7$

$= 7000 \times 12 = 84,000$

$\frac{5000}{5} \times 5 =$ 5,000 89,000

(2) Preference shareholders :

Face value	1,00,000	
Premium 5%	5,000	1,05,000

(3) Debentures

Debentures	1,00,000	
Premium 5%	8,000	1,08,000

Issue Rate :

$1,08,000 \times \frac{100}{90} = 1,20,000$

(4) Cost of liquidation 10,000

Purchase consideration 9,35,000

Ledger A/cs to close the Books
In the Books of 'Y' Ltd.
Realisation A/c

Particular	Amount	Particular	Amount
To Fixed Assets :			
Goodwill	1,00,000	By Loan from X Ltd.	50,000
Building	2,00,000	By Creditors	70,000
Machinery	3,00,000	By X Ltd.	9,35,000
Stock	70,000	(Purchase consideration)	
Debtors	60,000		
Bills receivable	15,000		
Bank	75,000		
To Debenture-holders A/c (Premium)	8,000		
To Preference Shareholders (Premium)	5,000		
To Bank expenses	10,000		
To Equity Shareholders A/c (Profit transferred)	12,000		
	10,55,000		10,55,000

X Ltd. A/c

To Realisation	9,35,000	By Equity shares in X Ltd.	5,88,000
		By Bank A/c (35,000+10,000)	45,000
		By Equity shares held by X Ltd. set off	89,000
		By Preference shares in X Ltd.	1,05,000
		By Debentures in X Ltd.	1,08,000
	9,35,000		9,35,000

Debenture-holders A/c

To Debentures in X Ltd.	1,08,000	By Debentures	1,00,000
		By Realisation (Premium on redemption)	8,000
	1,08,000		1,08,000

Preference Shareholders A/c

To Preference shares in X Ltd.	1,05,000	By Preference share capital	1,00,000
		By Realisation A/c (Premium on redemption)	5,000
	1,05,000		1,05,000

Equity Shareholders A/c

To Equity shares in X Ltd.	5,88,000	By Equity shares capital	4,00,000
To Bank A/c (45,000 – 10,000)	35,000	By General Reserve	50,000
To X Ltd. (Set-off)	89,000	By Profit & Loss A/c	50,000
		By Realisation (Profit)	2,12,000
	7,12,000		7,12,000

Bank A/c

To X Ltd.	45,000	By Realisation A/c (Expenses)	10,000
		By Equity shareholders	35,000
	45,000		45,000

In the Books of X Ltd.

Journal Entries :

Particulars		Amount	Amount
(1) Business purchase A/c	Dr	9,35,000	
To Liquidator of Y Ltd. (Vendor)			9,35,000
(Purchase consideration payable)			
(2) Building A/c	Dr	2,50,000	
Machinery A/c	Dr	3,50,000	
Stock A/c	Dr	70,000	
Debtors A/c	Dr	60,000	
Bills Receivable A/c	Dr	15,000	
Bank A/c	Dr	75,000	
Goodwill A/c (Balancing figure)	Dr	2,35,000	
To Business purchase A/c			9,35,000
To Loan from X Ltd.			50,000
To Creditors			70,000
(Assets & Liabilities taken brought into A/c)			

Particulars		Amount	Amount
(3) Liquidator of Y Ltd. A/c	Dr	9,35,000	
Discount on Issue of Debentures A/c	Dr	12,000	
To Equity share capital A/c			4,90,000
To 12% Preference share capital A/c			1,00,000
To Share premium A/c (98,000 + 5,000)			1,03,000
To 9% Debentures			1,20,000
To Shares in Y Ltd. (Investment)			89,000
To Bank A/c (35,000 + 10,000)			45,000
(Purchase consideration paid as above)			
(4) Shares in Y Ltd. A/c	Dr	29,000	
To Goodwill A/c (89,000 – 60,000)			29,000
(Profit on investment adjust on correlation)			
Note : See Purchase consideration [Page 190 — (c)] Dischare of shares held by X Ltd.			
(5) Loan from X Ltd.	Dr	50,000	
To Loan to Y Ltd.			50,000
(Mutual indebteness eliminated)			
(6) Share premium A/c	Dr	12,000	
To Discount on issue of debentures			12,000
(Discount on Issue of debentures adjusted)			

Balance Sheet as at 31-12-1989

Liabilities	Rs.	Rs.	Assets	Rs.	Rs.
Share Capital :			*Fixed Assets* :		
Equity Share Capital :			Goodwill X Ltd.	2,00,000	
Shares of Rs. 10			*Add* Goodwill	2,06,000	4,06,000
X Ltd. 50000	5,00,000		Buildings		
Issued to			(3,00,000+2,50,000)		5,50,000
Vendor 49000	4,90,000	9,90,000	Machinery A/c	4,00,000	
Preference Share Capital :				3,50,000	7,50,000
Shares of Rs. 100			Stock	1,80,000	
X Ltd.	4,00,000			70,000	2,50,000
Issued to Vendor	1,00,000	5,00,000	Bills Receivable	25,000	
Reserve & Surplus :				15,000	40,000
X Ltd. General Reserve		1,00,000			

Liabilities	Rs.	Rs.	Assets	Rs.	Rs.
Profit & Loss		1,40,000	*Bank A/c* :		
Share-premium		91,000	Balance : X	2,00,000	
(1,03,000 – 12,000)			Y	75,000	
Secured Loan :				2,75,000	
9% Debentures			*Less* Paid	45,000	2,30,000
X Ltd.	2,00,000		Debtors	1,75,000	
Issued to Vendor	1,20,000	3,20,000		60,000	2,35,000
Creditors :					
X Ltd.	2,50,000				
Vendor	70,000	3,20,000			
		24,61,000			24,61,000

Problem No. 30

The assets of Hubli Co. Ltd. are purchased of by Belgaum Co. Ltd. The purchase consideration was as follows :

(a) A payment in Cash Rs. 45 for every share in Hubli Co. Ltd.

(b) A further payment in cash Rs. 275 for every debenture in Hubli Co. Ltd. which the debenture-holders have agreed to accept in full discharge of their debentures.

(c) An exchange of 4 shares of Belgaum Co. Ltd. of Rs. 40 each of the Market value of Rs. 100 for every share in Hubli Co. Ltd.

The following was the Balance Sheet of Hubli Co. Ltd. on the date of absorption :

Balance Sheet as at

Liabilities	Rs.	Assets	Rs.
Share Capital :			
6000 Equity shares of		Buildings	5,00,000
Rs. 250 each	15,00,000	Machinery	8,00,000
Reserves & Surplus :		Furniture	1,00,000
Reserve fund	1,70,000	Stock	5,25,000
Profit & Loss A/c	30,000	Debtors	3,00,000
Secured Loan :		Cash	25,000
1300 Debentures of			
Rs. 250 each	3,25,000		
Current Liabilities :			
Worker's Savings Deposits	1,00,000		
Creditors	1,25,000		
	22,50,000		22,50,000

(KUD, October 1987)

Solution :

Calculations :

(1) Assets taken	22,50,000	*Purchase consideration paid in* :
Liabilities net taken	—	(a) Cash Rs. 45 per share
Total assets taken	22,50,000	Shares 6000 × 45 — 2,70,000
Total Assets	22,50,000	(b) Cash to debenture-holders
Purchase price	30,27,500	1300 × 275 — 3,57,500
Goodwill	7,77,500	6,27,500
		(c) Equity shares of Rs. 40 @ Rs. 100
		6000 × 4 = 24000×100 = 24,00,000
		Purchase price — 30,27,500

In the Books of Hubli Co. Ltd.

Realisation A/c

Particular	Amount	Particular	Amount
To S. Assets	22,50,000	By Belgaum Co. (Purchase consideration)	30,27,500
To Debenture-holders	32,500		
To Equity Shareholders A/c	7,45,000		
	30,27,500		30,27,500

Equity Shareholders A/c

To Equity shares in Belgaum Co.	24,00,000	By Share Capital	15,00,000
To Bank	45,000	By Reserve Fund	1,70,000
		By Profit & Loss	30,000
		By Realisation (Profit)	7,45,000
	24,45,000		24,45,000

Debenture-holders A/c

To Bank	3,57,500	By Debentures	3,25,000
		By Realisation (Balance transferred)	32,500
	3,57,500		3,57,500

Belgaum Co. Ltd. A/c

Particular	Amount	Particular	Amount
To Realisation	30,27,500	By Bank A/c	6,27,500
		By Equity shares in Belgaum Co.	24,00,000
	30,27,500		30,27,500

Bank A/c

To Belgaum Co. Ltd.	6,27,500	By Debenture-holders	3,57,500
		By Workers' Saving Deposit	1,00,000
		By Creditors	1,25,000
		By Equity Shareholders	45,000
	6,27,500		6,27,500

In the Books of Belgaum Co. Ltd.

Journal Entries :

Particulars		Amount	Amount
(1) Business Purchase A/c	Dr	30,27,500	
To Liquidation of Hubli A/c			30,27,500
(Purchase consideration)			
(2) Building A/c	Dr	5,00,000	
Machinery A/c	Dr	8,00,000	
Furniture A/c	Dr	1,00,000	
Stock A/c	Dr	5,25,000	
Debtors A/c	Dr	3,00,000	
Cash A/c	Dr	25,000	
Goodwill A/c (Balancing figure)	Dr	7,77,500	
To Business Purchase A/c			30,27,500
(Assets taken over brought into A/c)			
(3) Liquidator of Hubli Co. Ltd. A/c	Dr	30,27,500	
To Equity Share Capital A/c			9,60,000
To Share Premium A/c			14,40,000
To Bank A/c			6,27,500
(Purchase consideration paid in by : Issue of 24000 shares of Rs. 40 each at market value of Rs. 100 and in cash)			

Problem No. 31

B Ltd. agreed to take over the business of A Ltd. on the following terms :

(a) Taking over the assets and the liabilities at Book value.

(b) Discharge of debentures of A Ltd. are to be satisfied @ 9% debentures in B Ltd. @ Rs. 105.

(c) The equity shareholders of A Ltd. are to be satisfied by the issue of five (5) equity shares of Rs. 100 each in exchange for four (4) equity shares of A Ltd. @ an agreed value of Rs. 110 each.

The cost of liquidation of Rs. 4,000 be paid by B Ltd.

Following is the Balance sheet of A Ltd. on the date of acquisition :

Balance Sheet as at 31-12-1986

Liabilities	Rs.	Assets	Rs.
Share Capital :		Building	2,50,000
Equity shares of		Machinery	1,00,000
Rs. 100 each	4,00,000	Furniture	25,000
Reserves & Surplus :		Investments	5,000
Surplus	20,000	Stock	80,000
Accident compensation fund	5,000	Debtors	65,000
Secured Loan :		Cash at Bank	40,000
9% Debentures	1,00,000		
Current Liabilities :			
Creditors	40,000		
	5,65,000		5,65,000

You are required to prepare :

(1) Realisation A/c

(2) Shareholders A/c

(3) Debenture-holders A/c

(4) Purchasing Co. A/c in the Books of A Ltd. and also show opening entries in the Books of B Ltd.

(KUD, April 1986)

Solution :

Calculation :

Assets taken over :		Purchase consideration paid in :		
@ Book value	5,65,000	(1) 9% Debentures		
Less Liabilities taken over		of Rs. 100		1,00,000
S Creditors	40,000	@ Rs. 105		5,000
Net Assets	5,25,000			1,05,000
Purchase price	6,55,000	(2) Equity shareholders :		
Excess payment		$\frac{40000}{4} \times 5 = 5000 \times 100$		
Payment towards Goodwill	1,30,000		5,00,000	
		Premium 5000×10 =	50,000	5,50,000
		Total		6,55,000

In the Books of A Ltd.

Realisation A/c

Particular	Amount	Particular	Amount
To S. Assets	5,65,000	By Creditors	40,000
To Premium on Debentures	5,000	By B Ltd. (Purchasing Co.)	6,55,000
To Profit transferred to shareholders	1,25,000		
	6,95,000		6,95,000

Purchasing Co. A/c (B Ltd.)

To Realisation	6,55,000	By 9% Debentures in Purchasing Co.	1,05,000
		By Equity shares in purchasing Co.	5,50,000
	6,55,000		6,55,000

9% Debenture-holders A/c

To Debentures in purchasing Co.	1,05,000	By Debentures	1,00,000
		By Premium on debentures	5,000
	1,05,000		1,05,000

Equity Shareholders A/c

Particular	Amount	Particular	Amount
To Equity shares in purchasing Co.	5,50,000	By Share capital	4,00,000
		By Surplus	20,000
		By Accident compensation paid	5,000
		By Realisation (Profit)	1,25,000
	5,50,000		5,50,000

In the Books of B Ltd. (Absorbing Co.)

Opening Entries :

Particulars		Amount	Amount
(1) Business Purchase A/c	Dr	6,55,000	
To Liquidator of A Ltd.			6,55,000
(Purchase price payable)			
(2) Building A/c	Dr	2,50,000	
Machinery A/c	Dr	1,00,000	
Furniture A/c	Dr	25,000	
Investment A/c	Dr	5,000	
Stock A/c	Dr	80,000	
Debtors A/c	Dr	65,000	
Cash at Bank A/c	Dr	40,000	
Goodwill A/c	Dr	1,30,000	
To Creditors			40,000
To Business Purchase A/c			6,55,000
(Assets & Liabilities taken over brought into A/c)			
(3) Liquidator of A Ltd. A/c	Dr	6,55,000	
To Equity Share Capital A/c			5,00,000
To 9% Debentures A/c			1,05,000
To Share Premium			50,000
(Purchase price paid)			
(4) Cost of Liquidation A/c	Dr	4,000	
To Bank A/c			4,000
(Liquidation cost paid)			
(5) Goodwill A/c	Dr	4,000	
To Cost of Liquidation A/c			4,000
(Cost of Liquidation A/c transferred)			

Problem No. 32

A Co. Ltd. agreed to absorb the business of B Ltd. as on 31-12-1982. The following was the Balance sheet on the above date of B Co. Ltd. :

Balance Sheet as at 31-12-1982

Liabilities	Rs.	Assets	Rs.
Share Capital :		Goodwill	2,00,000
Equity shares of Rs. 10	8,50,000	Building	4,00,000
Reserve and Surplus		Machinery	3,00,000
General Reserves	2,25,000	Stocks	3,50,000
Profit and Loss A/c	1,25,000	Sundry debtors	1,00,000
Secured Loan		Cash at Bank	1,50,000
Debentures	2,50,000		
Current Liabilities			
Sundry Creditors	50,000		
Total	15,00,000		15,00,000

A Co. Ltd. agreed to take over the debenture and the assets except cash and Goodwill at book value and to pay Rs. 4,25,000 for goodwill.

The purchase consideration was settled by the allotment to B Co. Ltd. 10000 Equity shares of Rs. 100 each at a premium of 20% per share and the Balance in cash.

The liquidation expenses amounted Rs. 25,000 show the necessary ledger accounts in the books of B Co. Ltd. and the opening entries in the books of 'A' Co. Ltd.

[K.U.D., April 1983 (Modified)]

Solution :

Calculation of Net Assets and Purchase consideration :

Assets taken over :		
Sundry Assets		15,00,000
Less : Goodwill	2,00,000	
Cash	1,50,000	3,50,000
Net asset taken over		11,50,000
Less : Debenture		2,50,000
Net Asset		9,00,000
Goodwill		4,25,000
		13,25,000

Purchase consideration paid :	
Equity shares :	
10000 shares of Rs. 100 each	10,00,000
Add : 20% premium	2,00,000
	12,00,000
Balance in cash	1,25,000
Total	13,25,000

In the books of 'B' Co. Ltd.

Realisation A/c

Particular	Amount	Particular	Amount
To Sundry assets (15,00,000 – 1,50,000)	13,50,000	By Debentures	2,50,000
		By Sundry Creditors	50,000
To Sundry Creditors (Cash paid)	50,000	By 'A' Co Ltd. (Purchasing Co.)	13,25,000
To Bank (expenses)	25,000		
To Shareholders A/c (transferred)	2,00,000		
	16,25,000		16,25,000

Equity Shareholders A/c

To Equity Shares in 'A' Co Ltd.	12,00,000	By Share Capital	8,50,000
		By General Reserve	2,25,000
To Bank A/c	2,00,000	By Profit & Loss A/c	1,25,000
		By Realisation Profit	2,00,000
	14,00,000		14,00,000

Bank A/c

To Balance	1,50,000	By Realisation A/c (Sundry creditors)	50,000
To 'A' Co. Ltd.	1,25,000		
		By Liquidation expenses	25,000
		By Equity shareholders	2,00,000
	2,75,000		2,75,000

In the Books of 'A' Co Ltd.

(Opening Journal Entries)

Particulars		Amount	Amount
(1) Business Purchase A/c	Dr	13,25,000	
To Liquidators 'A'Co Ltd A/c			13,25,000
(Purchase consideration payable)			
(2) Goodwill A/c	Dr	4,25,000	
Building A/c	Dr	4,00,000	
Machinery A/c	Dr	3,00,000	
Stock A/c	Dr	3,50,000	
Sundry Debtors A/c	Dr	1,00,000	
To Debentures A/c			2,50,000
To Business Purchase A/c		13,25,000	
(Incorporation of assets and liabilities taken over)			
(3) Liqudators of B Co. Ltd. A/c	Dr	13,25,000	
To Equity Share Capital A/c			10,00,000
To Share Premium A/c			2,00,000
To Bank A/c			1,25,000
(Purchase consideration paid in 10000 shares of Rs. 100 at 20% premium and balance in cash.)			

Problem No. 33

Gulberga Trading Co. Ltd. has been absorbed by Dharwad Manufacturing and Trading Co. Ltd. with effect from 1st January 1981. The consideration was as follows :

(a) To taken over the assets and liabilities except debentures of Gulberga Trading Co. Ltd. at this Balance sheet values.

(b) To pay cash at Rs. 110 for every debenture in the Gulberga Trading Co. Ltd.

(c) To pay cash at Rs. 80 for every share in the Gulberga Trading Co. Ltd.

(d) To issue five (5) shares of Dharwad Manufacturing Co. Ltd. of Rs. 100 each at market price (quoted in the market at Rs. 180) for every share in the Gulberga Trading Co. Ltd.

Gulberga Trading Co. Ltd.

Balance Sheet as at 31-12-1980

Liabilities	Rs.	Assets	Rs.
Share Capital		*Fixed Assets*	
2000 Equity shares of		Goodwill	1,00,000
Rs. 600 each	12,00,000	Land & Building	5,00,000
Reserves & Surplus		Plant & Machinery	3,00,000
General Reserve	2,00,000	Furniture	50,000
Insurance fund	50,000	Patents	50,000
Profit & Loss A/c	50,000	*Investments*	
Secured Loan		Govt. securities	3,00,000
5000 6% Debentures of		*Loans & Advances*	
Rs. 100 each	5,00,000	Loans	2,00,000
Unsecured Loan	—	Stocks	5,00,000
Current Liabilities		Sundry debtors	2,00,000
Sundry creditors	2,00,000	Cash at Bank	1,00,000
Staff provident fund	50,000		
Bills payable	50,000		
	23,00,000		23,00,000

Give the necessary closing entries in the books of Gulberga Trading Co. Ltd. and opening entries in the books of Dharwad Manufacturing and Trading Co. Ltd.

(K.U.D., April 1981)

Solution :

In the Books of Gulberga Trading Co. Ltd.

Journal Entries :

Particulars		Dr Rs.	Cr Rs.
1. Realisation A/c	Dr	23,00,000	
To Goodwill A/c			1,00,000
To Land & Building A/c			5,00,000
To Plant & Machinery A/c			3,00,000
To Furnitures A/c			50,000
To Patents A/c			50,000
To Govt. securities A/c			3,00,000
To Loans A/c			2,00,000
To Stocks A/c			5,00,000
To Sundry debtors A/c			2,00,000
To Cash at bank A/c			1,00,000
(Assets taken over transferred)			

Particulars		Dr Rs.	Cr Rs.
2. Sundry creditors A/c	Dr	2,00,000	
Staff provident fund A/c	Dr	50,000	
Bills payable A/c	Dr	50,000	
To Realisation A/c			3,00,000
(Liabilities taken over transferred)			
3. 6% Debentures A/c	Dr	5,00,000	
To Debenture-holders A/c			5,00,000
(Debentures transferred to debenture-holders)			
4. Equity share capital A/c	Dr	12,00,000	
General Reserve A/c	Dr	2,00,000	
Insurance fund A/c	Dr	50,000	
Profit & Loss A/c	Dr	50,000	
To Equity shareholders A/c			15,00,000
(Equity share capital and undistributed profit transferred to shareholders A/c)			
5. Dharwad Trading & Manufacturing Co. Ltd. A/c	Dr	25,10,000	
To Realisation A/c			25,10,000
(Purchase consideration receivable)			
6. Equity share in purchasing Co. A/c	Dr	18,00,000	
Bank A/c	Dr	7,10,000	
To Dharwad Trading & Manufacturing Co. Ltd. A/c			25,10,000
(Purchase consideration received in equity shares and cash.)			
7. Debenture-holders A/c	Dr	5,50,000	
To Bank A/c			5,50,000
(Cash paid to debenture-holders)			
8. Realisation A/c	Dr	50,000	
To Debenture-holders A/c			50,000
(Balance on debenture-holders A/c transferred)			
9. Realisation A/c	Dr	4,60,000	
To Equity shareholders A/c			4,60,000
(Profit on realisation transferred)			
10. Equity shareholders A/c	Dr	19,60,000	
To Equity shares in purchasing Co. A/c			18,00,000
To Bank A/c			1,60,000
(Equity shares in purchasing Co. distributed cash paid to shareholders.)			

In the Books Dharwad Trading & Manufacturing Co. Ltd.

Opening Entries :

Particulars		Dr Rs.	Cr Rs.
1. Business purchase A/c	Dr	25,10,000	
To Liquidators Gulberga Trading Co. Ltd. A/c			25,10,000
(Purchase consideration payable to vendor)			
2. Land & Building A/c	Dr	5,00,000	
Plant & Machinery A/c	Dr	3,00,000	
Furniture A/c	Dr	50,000	
Patents A/c	Dr	50,000	
Govt. Securities A/c	Dr	3,00,000	
Loans A/c	Dr	2,00,000	
Stocks A/c	Dr	5,00,000	
Sundry debtors A/c	Dr	2,00,000	
Cash at Bank A/c	Dr	1,00,000	
Goodwill A/c	Dr	6,10,000	
Goodwill 1,00,000 Paid 5,10,000			
To Sundry creditors A/c			2,00,000
To Staff provident fund A/c			50,000
To Bills payable A/c			50,000
To Business purchase A/c			25,10,000
(Incorporation of Assets & Liabilities taken over)			
3. Liquidators of Gulberga Trading Co. Ltd. A/c	Dr	25,10,000	
To Equity share capital A/c			10,00,000
To Share premium A/c			8,00,000
To Bank A/c			7,10,000
(Purchase consideration paid in by issue of 10000 equity shares of Rs. 100 at Rs. 180 and balance in cash)			

In the Books of Gulberga Trading Co. Ltd.

Additional Work :

Realisation A/c

Particulars	Amount	Particulars	Amount
To Goodwill A/c	1,00,000	By Sundry creditors A/c	2,00,000
To Land & Building A/c	5,00,000	By Staff P.F. A/c	50,000
To Plant & Machinery A/c	3,00,000	By Bills payable A/c	50,000
To Patent A/c	5,00,000	By Dharwad Trading & Manufacturing Co. Ltd. (Purchase consideration)	25,10,000
To Furnitures A/c	50,000		
To Govt. securities A/c	3,00,000		
To Loans A/c	2,00,000		
To Stock A/c	5,00,000		
To Sundry debtors A/c	2,00,000		
To Cash at bank A/c	1,00,000		
To Debenture-holders A/c	50,000		
To Profit transferred to equity shareholders A/c	4,60,000		
	28,10,000		28,10,000

Debenture-holder A/c

To Bank A/c	5,50,000	By Debentures	5,00,000
		By Realisation (Balance transferred)	50,000
	5,50,000		5,50,000

Equity Shareholders A/c

To Equity shares in purchasing Co.	18,00,000	By Share Capital	12,00,000
To Bank A/c	1,60,000	By General Reserve	2,00,000
		By Insurance Fund	50,000
		By Profit & Loss A/c	50,000
		By Realisation A/c (Profit)	4,60,000
	19,60,000		19,60,000

Dharwad Trading & Manufacturing Co. Ltd.

To Realisation A/c	25,10,000	By Equity shares in purchasing Co.	18,00,000
		By Bank	7,10,000
	25,10,000		25,10,000

Bank A/c

Particulars	Amount	Particulars	Amount
To Dharwad Trading & Manufacturing Co. Ltd.	7,10,000	By Debenture-holders	5,50,000
		By Equity shareholders	1,60,000
	7,10,000		7,10,000

Problem No. 34

Following was the Balance-Sheet of General Co. Ltd. on 31-12-1989, on which date was absorbed by Premier Co. Ltd. :

General Co. Ltd. — Balance Sheet as at 31-12-1989

Liabilities	Rs.	Assets	Rs.
Share Capital		Goodwill	40,000
5000 9% Preference shares of Rs. 50 each	2,50,000	Land & Building	3,00,000
75000 Equity shares of Rs. 10 each	7,50,000	Machinery	3,00,000
Reserves & Surplus :		Patents	1,30,000
General Reserve	85,000	Stock	4,20,000
Profit & Loss A/c	25,000	Sundry Debtors	3,00,000
Debentures of Rs. 100 each redeemable at the option of the Co. @ Rs. 105	1,20,000	Bank balance	60,000
Sundry creditors	3,20,000		
	15,50,000		15,50,000

The dividend due on preference shares to be paid to them.

The terms of absorption :

(1) The Premier Co. took over the Assets only and the consideration after absorption was :

(a) Payment of cash sufficient to discharge debentures debt and liability to sundry creditors.

(b) Payment of cash to the equity shareholders of General Co. Ltd. @ Rs. 3 per share.

(c) Allotment of fully paid shares of Rs. 10 each at market value of Rs. 12 per share in exchange for every three shares in General Co. Ltd. and two shares in Premier Co. Ltd.

(d) Five fully paid 11% preference shares of Rs. 10 each at par be allotted to preference shareholders of General Co. Ltd. for every preference shares held.

(2) The General Co. Ltd. met its own Liquidation expenses of Rs. 5,250.

(3) Premier Co. Ltd. took over the Assets in its books at the revalued figures by appreciating – Land & Building by Rs. 16,500 and depreciating — machinery, stock and patents by Rs. 24,000, 36,000, and Rs. 30,000 respectively and by creating a bad debt reserve of 2-1/2% on debtors.

You are required to show :

The Ledger A/cs as they finally stood in the books of General Co. Ltd. and pass the Journal Entries required to incorporate the absorption of Assets in the Books of Premier Co. Ltd.

[C.A. Final (Modified)]

Solution :

Calculation of Purchase Consideration

Total Assets takenover :			*Purchase Consideration* :		
Land & Building	3,00,000		(1) Debentures discharged		
Add Appreciate	16,500	3,16,500	@ Rs. 105	1,20,000	Cash
Machinery	3,00,000		*Add* : 5%	6,000	
Less Depreciation	24,000	2,76,000		1,26,000	Cash
Stock	4,20,000		Creditors paid	3,20,000	Cash
Less Reduced	36,000	3,84,000	(2) To Equity sharehoders :		
Patents	1,30,000		75000 × 3	2,25,000	Cash
Less Depreciation	30,000	1,00,000	75000 × 1/3 × 2		
Debtors		3,00,000	= 50000 × 12	6,00,000	Equity shares
Total Assets		13,76,500			
Less Liabilities :			(3) Preference Shareholders :		
Reserve for Doubtful			5000×5 = 25000×10		
Debts 2-1/2% on 3,00,000		7,500		2,50,000	11% Pref. shares
Net Assets		13,69,000			
			Purchase price	15,21,000	
			Purchase Price		15,21,000
			Net assets acquired		13,69,000
			Excess payment treated as goodwill		1,52,000

In the Books of General Co. Ltd.

Realisation A/c

Particulars	Amount	Particulars	Amount
To Goodwill	40,000	By Premier Co. Ltd.	15,21,000
To Land & Building	3,00,000	(Purchase consideration)	
To Machinery	3,00,000		
To Patents	1,30,000		
To Stock	4,20,000		
To Debtors	3,00,000		
To Debenture-holders	60,000		
To Bank — expenses	5,250		
To Profit (Transferred to shareholders)	19,750		
	15,21,000		15,21,000

Premier Co. Ltd. A/c

Particulars	Amount	Particulars	Amount
To Realisation A/c (Purchase consideration)	15,21,000	By Equity shares in purchasing Co.	6,00,000
		By 11% Preference shares in purchasing Co.	2,50,000
		By Bank A/c	6,71,000
	15,21,000		15,21,000

Debenture-holders A/c

To Bank	1,26,000	By Debentures	1,20,000
		By Realisation (Transferred)	6,000
	1,26,000		1,26,000

Creditors A/c

To Bank	3,20,000	By Balance b/d	3,20,000
	3,20,000		3,20,000

9% Preference Shareholders A/c

Particulars	Amount	Particulars	Amount
To 11% Preference shares in purchasing Co.	2,50,000	By Preference share capital A/c	2,50,000
	2,50,000		2,50,000

Equity Shareholders A/c

To Equity shares in Premier Co.	6,00,000	By Equity share capital	7,50,000
To Bank	2,57,250	By General Reserve	85,000
(Balance transferred)		By Profit & Loss	
		Balance – 25,000	
		Less Paid 22,500	2,500
		By Realisation (Profit)	19,750
	8,57,250		8,57,250

Bank A/c

To Balance b/d	60,000	By Debenture A/c	1,26,000
To Purchasing Co. A/c	6,71,000	By Creditors	3,20,000
		By Preference dividend	22,500
		By Realisation — exp.	5,250
		By Equity sharesholders (transferred)	2,57,250
	7,31,000		7,31,000

In the Books of Premier Co. Ltd.

Journal Entries :

Particulars		Dr Rs.	Cr Rs.
(1) Business purchase A/c	Dr	15,21,000	
To Liquidator of Vendor Co.			15,21,000
(Purchase consideration payable)			
(2) Land & Building A/c		3,16,500	
Machinery A/c		2,76,000	
Stock A/c		3,84,000	
Patent A/c		1,00,000	
Debtors A/c		3,00,000	

Particulars		Dr Rs.	Cr Rs.
Goodwill A/c (Balancing figure)		1,52,000	
To RDD A/c			7,500
To Business Purchase A/c			15,21,000
(Assets taken over brought into A/c)			
(3) Liquidator of Purchasing Co. (General Co. Ltd.)	Dr	15,21,000	
To Equity share capital A/c			5,00,000
To Share premium A/c			1,00,000
To 11% Preference share capital A/c			2,50,000
To Bank A/c			6,71,000
(Purchase consideration paid in 50000 equity shares of Rs. 10 @ Rs. 12% issue of 11% preference shares of Rs. 10 and balance in cash.)			

Problem No. 35

The following is the Balance sheet of AB Ltd. as on 31-12-1976 :

Balance Sheet as at 31-12-1976

Liabilities	Rs.	Assets		Rs.
Share Capital :	5,00,000	Goodwill		95,000
5000 Shares of Rs.10 each fully paid		Land & Building		1,00,000
		Plant & Machinery		2,20,000
Reserves & Surplus :		Patents & Trade Mark		15,000
General Reserve	40,000	*Investments*		—
Contingency Reserve	15,000	*Current Assets* :		
Profit & Loss A/c	35,000	Stock		1,05,000
Workmen's compensation fund	25,000	Sundry debtors	90,000	
		Less RDD	6,000	
Secured Loan	—			84,000
Unsecured Loan	—	Cash at Bank		66,000
Current Liabilities & Provisions :		Preliminary expenses		10,000
Sundry creditors	80,000			
	6,95,000			6,95,000

The company is acquired by X. Ltd. which pays Rs. 7,00,000 in all. Rs. 6,00,000 in fully paid shares of Rs. 100 each and the balance in cash. There was a contingent liability in respect of a claim for compensation under Workmen's

Compensation Act. The claim was not taken over by the XY Ltd. and AB Ltd. had to pay ultimately a sum of Rs.10,000 against the claim.

The Balance sheet of XY Ltd. as on 31-12-1976 was as under :

Balance Sheet as at 31-12-1976

Liabilities	Rs.	Assets	Rs.
Share Capital :		Goodwill	1,10,000
10000 Shares of Rs.100	10,00,000	Land & Building	3,00,000
Reserves & Surplus :		Plant & Machinery	4,00,000
General Reserve	1,00,000	*Investments*	—
Profit & Loss A/c	50,000	*Current Assets* :	
Secured Loan :		Stock	2,50,000
8% Debentures	2,00,000	Sundry Debtors	1,50,000
Unsecured Loan	—	Cash at Bank	2,20,000
Current Liabilities :			
Sundry Creditors	80,000		
	14,30,000		14,30,000

The expenses of liquidation of AB Ltd. come to Rs. 5,000. These were met by XY Ltd.

(a) Draft Journal Entries to close the books of the AB Ltd. and show important Accounts.

(b) Give Journal Entries in the Books of XY Ltd. and redraft Balance sheet of XY Ltd. after absorption is completed assuming Land & Building of AB Ltd. are valued at Rs.1,40,000.

Solution :

Purchase consideration :

Total Assets takenover :			*Purchase consideration paid in* :	
Goodwill		95,000	Equity shares 6000 × 100	6,00,000
Land & Building		1,00,000	Balance in cash	1,00,000
Plant & Machinery		2,20,000	Total purchase price	7,00,000
Patents & Trade marks		15,000	Net Assets	6,45,000
Stock		1,05,000	Excess payment, payment	
Sundry debtors		90,000	towards Goodwill	55,000
Cash at Bank		66,000		
Total Assets		7,31,000	Goodwill	55,000
Less Liabilities :			*Add* : Existing Goodwill	
S. Creditors	80,000		in B/s	95,000
Provision R.D.D.	6,000	86,000	Total Goodwill	1,50,000
Net Assets		6,45,000		

In the Books AB Ltd.

Realisation A/c

Particulars	Amount	Particulars	Amount
To Goodwill	95,000	By Sundry Creditors	80,000
To Land & Building	1,00,000	By Provision on	
To Plant & Machinery	2,20,000	S. Creditors	6,000
To Patents & Trade mark	15,000	By XY Ltd.	7,00,000
To Stock	1,05,000		
To Sundry debtors	90,000		
To Cash at bank	66,000		
To Preliminary exp.	10,000		
	7,01,000		
To Shareholders A/c	85,000		
	7,86,000		7,86,000

XY Ltd. A/c

To Realisation A/c	7,00,000	By Shares in XY Ltd.	6,00,000
		By Bank	1,00,000
	7,00,000		7,00,000
To Bank A/c (Liquidation exps.)	5,000	By Bank A/c	5,000
	5,000		5,000

Shareholders A/c

To Shares in XY Ltd.	6,00,000	By Share Capital	5,00,000
To Bank	90,000	By General Reserve	40,000
		By Contingency Reserve	15,000
		By Profit & Loss A/c	35,000
		By Workmen's Compensation Fund	15,000
		By Realisation	85,000
	6,90,000		6,90,000

Workmen's Accident Compensation Fund A/c

To Bank	10,000	By Balance b/d	25,000
To Shareholders (Balance transferred)	15,000		
	25,000		25,000

Shares in XY Ltd. A/c

Particulars	Amount	Particulars	Amount
To XY Ltd.	6,00,000	By Shareholders A/c	6,00,000
	6,00,000		6,00,000

Bank A/c

To XY Ltd.	1,00,000	By XY Ltd.	5,000
To XY Ltd. (liquidation exps.)	5,000	(Liquidation exps.)	
		By Workmen's accident Compensation fund	10,000
		By Shareholders A/c	90,000
	1,05,000		1,05,000

In the Books of XY Ltd.

Particulars		Dr Rs.	Cr Rs.
(1) Business purchase A/c	Dr	7,00,000	
To Liquidator of AB Ltd.			7,00,000
(Purchase consideration payable)			
(2) Goodwill A/c	Dr	1,50,000	
Land & Building A/c	Dr	1,40,000	
Patents & Trade Mark A/c	Dr	15,000	
Plant & Machinery A/c	Dr	2,20,000	
Stock A/c	Dr	1,05,000	
Sundry Debtors A/c	Dr	90,000	
Cash A/c	Dr	66,000	
To Sundry creditors			80,000
To Provision for DD			6,000
To Business purchase A/c			7,00,000
(Assets and Liabilities taken over brought into A/c)			
(3) Liquidator of AB Ltd.	Dr	7,00,000	
To Equity share capital			6,00,000
To Bank			1,00,000
(Purchase price paid in 6000 shares of Rs. 100 each and balance in cash)			
(4) Goodwill A/c	Dr	5,000	
To Bank A/c			5,000
(Cost of Liquidation paid in AB Ltd. transferred to Goodwill)			

Balance Sheet as at 31-12-1976

Liabilities	Rs.	Assets		Rs.
Share Capital :		Goodwill : XY	1,10,000	
XY—10000 Equity shares		AB	1,50,000	
of Rs.100 each	10,00,000	Cost of Liquidation	5,000	2,65,000
AB—6000 Equity shares		Land & Building :		
of Rs.100 each	6,00,000	XY	3,00,000	
Reserves & Surplus :		AB	1,40,000	4,40,000
General Reserve XY	1,00,000	Plant & Machinery :		
Profit & Loss A/c	50,000	XY	4,00,000	
Secured Loan		AB	2,20,000	6,20,000
8% Debentures	2,00,000	Patents & Trade		
Unsecured Loan	—	Mark : XY	—	
Current Liabilities :		AB	15,000	15,000
S. Creditors	1,60,000	*Current Liabilities* :		
(80,000 + 80,000)		Stock : XY	2,50,000	
		AB	1,05,000	3,55,000
		Sundry Debtors :		
		XY	1,50,000	
		AB	90,000	
			2,40,000	
		Less Provision R.D.D.	6,000	2,34,000
		Bank Balance	2,20,000	
		Add AB	66,000	
			2,86,000	
		Less Paid	1,05,000	1,81,000
	21,10,000			21,10,000

Problem No. 36

A Co. Ltd. agreed to acquire the business of B Co. Ltd. as on 31-12-1980. Following is the Balance Sheet of B. Co. Ltd. :

B. Co. Ltd. — Balance Sheet as at 31-12-1980

Liabilities	Rs.	Assets	Rs.
Share Capital :		*Fixed Assets :*	
60000 shares of Rs.10 each	6,00,000	Goodwill	1,00,000
Reserves & Surplus :		Land & Building	4,00,000
General Reserve	1,70,000	Plant & Machinery	2,40,000
Profit & Loss A/c	1,10,000	*Investments*	—
Secured Loan :		*Loans & Advances*	36,000
Debentures	1,00,000	Debtors	1,68,000
Unsecured Loan	—	Stock in Trade	56,000
Current Liabilities :		Bank	
Sundry Creditors	20,000		
	10,00,000		10,00,000

The consideration is payable as follows :

(1) A cash payment equivalent to Rs. 2.50 for every share in B Co. Ltd.

(2) The issue of 90,000 shares of Rs.10 each fully paid @ Rs.15 per share.

(3) The issue of such an amount of fully paid Debentures of A Co. Ltd. @ Rs. 96 per share as is suffcient to discharge the debentures of B Co. Ltd. at a Premium of 20%.

Prepare Realisation A/c, Shareholders A/c in the books of B Co. Ltd. and also pass Journal Entries in the books of A Co. Ltd.

Solution :

Calculations :

(a) Total Assets	10,00,000	*Purchase price payable in :*		
Less Liabilities taken over	20,000	(1) *Shareholders* :		*Form*
Net Assets	9,80,000	60000 shares @ Rs. 2.50		
Purchase Price	16,20,000	each 60000×2.50 =	1,50,000	Cash
Net Assets	9,80,000	(2) Issue of 90000 shares		
Excess payment	6,40,000	of 10 each @ Rs. 15		
Treated as Goodwill		90000 × 15 =	13,50,000	Shares
Add Existing	1,00,000	(3) Debenture-holders		
	7,40,000	discharged @ 20%		
		premium		
		1,00,000 + 20,000 =	1,20,000	
			16,20,000	

Note :

Debentures discharged	1,00,000	In the books of A Co.Ltd.	
@ 20% Premium	20,000	*Journal Entry* :	
	1,20,000	Liquidator of B Co. Ltd. A/c Dr 1,20,000	
Payable to debenture-holders in B Co. Ltd.		(Debenture-holders of B Co. Ltd.)	
A Co. Ltd. (Purchasing Co.)		Discount on issue of Debentures A/c Dr 5,000	
Issued debentures @ 96%	1,20,000	To Debentures A/c	1,25,000
Therefore face value of Debentures issued by A Co. Ltd. is :		(Debentures issued @ 96% per debenture)	
$120000 \times \frac{100}{96}$ = Rs. 1,25,000			
Face value of debentures issued	1,25,000		

In the Books of B Co. Ltd. A/c

Realisation A/c

Particulars	Amount	Particulars	Amount
To S. Assets	10,00,000	By S. Creditors	20,000
To Debenture-holders	20,000	By A Co. Ltd.	16,20,000
To Shareholders	6,20,000	(Purchase consideration)	
	16,40,000		16,40,000

A Co. Ltd. A/c (Purchasing Co.)

To Realisation	16,20,000	By Debentures in A Co.	1,20,000
		By Shares in A Co.	13,50,000
		By Bank A/c	1,50,000
	16,20,000		16,20,000

Debentures in A Co. Ltd. A/c

To A Co. Ltd.	1,20,000	By Debenture-holders A/c	1,20,000
	1,20,000		1,20,000

Shareholders A/c

To Shares in A Co. Ltd.	13,50,000	By Share Capital	6,00,000
To Bank A/c	1,50,000	By General Reserve	1,70,000
		By Profit & Loss A/c	1,10,000
		By Realisation A/c	6,20,000
	15,00,000		15,00,000

Debenture-holders A/c

To Debentures in A Co. Ltd.	1,20,000	By Debentures	1,00,000
		By Realisation A/c	20,000
	1,20,000		1,20,000

Bank A/c

To A Co. Ltd.	1,50,000	By Shareholders A/c	1,50,000
	1,50,000		1,50,000

In the Books of B Co. Ltd.

Journal Entries :

Particulars		Dr Rs.	Cr Rs.
(1) Realisation A/c	Dr	10,00,000	
To Sundry Assets			10,00,000
(Assets transferred)			
(2) Sundry Creditors A/c	Dr	20,000	
To Realisation A/c	Dr		20,000
(Liabilities Transferred)			
(3) Share Capital A/c	Dr	6,00,000	
General Reserve	Dr	1,70,000	
Profit & Loss A/c	Dr	1,10,000	
To Shareholders A/c			8,80,000
(Share capital & undistributed profit transferred to shareholders)			
(4) Debentures A/c	Dr	1,00,000	
To Debenture-holders A/c			1,00,000
(Debentures transferred to debenture-holders)			
(5) A Co. Ltd. A/c	Dr	16,20,000	
To Realisation A/c			16,20,000
(Purchase price receivable)			
(6) Debentures in A Co. Ltd. A/c	Dr	1,20,000	
Shares in A Co. Ltd. A/c		13,50,000	
Bank A/c		1,50,000	
To A Co. Ltd. A/c			16,20,000
(Purchase price received in debentures in shares & cash)			
(7) Debenture-holders A/c	Dr	1,20,000	
To Debentures in A Co. Ltd.			1,20,000
(Debentures distributed)			
(8) Realisation A/c	Dr	20,000	
To Debenture-holders A/c			20,000
(Balance transferred to realisation)			
(9) Realisation A/c	Dr	6,20,000	
To Shareholders A/c			6,20,000
(Profit on realisation transferred to shareholders)			

(10) Shareholders A/c	Dr	15,00,000	
To Shares in A Co. Ltd.			13,50,000
To Bank A/c			1,50,000
(Shares in A Co. Ltd. & cash distributed to shareholders)			

In the Books of A Co. Ltd.

Journal Entries :

Particulars		Dr Rs.	Cr Rs.
(1) Business Purchase A/c	Dr	16,20,000	
To Liquidation of B Co. Ltd.			16,20,000
(Purchase consideration payable)			
(2) Goodwill A/c	Dr	7,40,000	
Land & Building A/c	Dr	4,00,000	
Plant & Machinery A/c	Dr	2,40,000	
Debtors A/c	Dr	36,000	
Stock A/c	Dr	1,68,000	
Bank A/c	Dr	56,000	
To S. Creditors A/c			20,000
To Business Purchase A/c			16,20,000
(Assets & Liabilities taken over brought into books and the balancing being Goodwill)			
(3) Liquidator of A Co. Ltd. A/c	Dr	16,20,000	
Discount on issue of debentures A/c	Dr	5,000	
To Debentures A/c			1,25,000
To Share capital A/c			9,00,000
To Share premium A/c			4,50,000
To Bank A/c			1,50,000
(Purchase price paid in : (a) By the issue of debentures @ 96%. (b) Issue of 90000 shares of Rs. 10 each at a Premium of Rs. 5 per share and a cash payment of Rs. 2.50 for 60000 shares.)			

Problem No. 37

The Amar Co. Ltd. is absorbed by Bharat Co. Ltd., the consideration being :

(a) Taking over the liabilities.

(b) The payment of cost of absorption (as part of purchase consideration) not exceeding Rs. 8,000.

(c) The repayment of B debentures at a Premium of 5%.

(d) The discharge of A debentures at a Premium of 10% by the issue of 6% debentures in Bharat Co. Ltd.

(e) A payment of Rs. 15 per share in cash and allotment of one 7%

Preference share of Rs. 100 each and 5 Equity shares of Rs. 100 each fully paid for every 4 shares in Amar Co. Ltd. The market value of Equity shares of Bharat Co. Ltd. is Rs. 140 but it is desired that entries should be made on the basis of par value only.

(f) The actual cost of Absorption came to Rs. 10,000.

Following is the Balance Sheet of Amar Co. Ltd. :

Balance Sheet as at

Liabilities	Rs.	Assets		Rs.
Share Capital :		Goodwill		4,00,000
20000 shares of 100 each	20,00,000	Land & Building		16,00,000
Reserves & Suplus :		Plant & Machinery		14,00,000
Reserve fund	5,00,000	Patents		3,50,000
Sinking fund	1,00,000	*Investment against Sinking Fund*		1,00,000
Workmen's Accident Compensation fund (Estimated liability 9000)	50,000	*Current Assets* :		
Employees' profit sharing fund	1,00,000	Stock		2,00,000
Staff provident fund	1,50,000	Debtors	4,00,000	
Secured Loan :		*Less* Provisions	40,000	3,60,000
A Debentures	4,00,000	Bank		30,000
B Debentures	10,00,000			
Unsecured Loan	—			
Current Liabilities :				
Sundry creditors	1,40,000			
	44,40,000			44,40,000

Pass Journal Entries to close the Books of Amar Co. Ltd. and the opening entries in the Books of Bharat Co. Ltd.

Solution :

In the Books of Amar Co. Ltd.

Calculations :

Purchase consideration taken :		*Purchase consideration paid in* :			*Form*
Total Assets :					
Goodwill	4,00,000	(1) Cost of Absorption		8,000	Cash
Land & Building	16,00,000	(2) B Debentures	10,00,000		
Plant & Machinery	14,00,000	*Add* 5% premium	50,000	10,50,000	Cash
Patent Rights	3,50,000				
Investments	1,00,000	(3) A Debentures	4,00,000		
Stock	2,00,000	*Add* 10% Pre.	40,000	4,40,000	Debentures

Debtors	4,00,000	
Bank	30,000	
	44,80,000	44,80,000
Less Liabilities :		
Sundry creditors	1,40,000	
Provision for DD	40,000	
Employees profit sharing fund	1,00,000	
Staff provident fund	1,50,000	4,30,000
Net Assets		40,50,000
Total Goodwill	7,48,000	
Goodwill in B/s	4,00,000	11,48,000

(4) Shareholders :

20000×15	3,00,000	Cash
$\frac{20000}{4} \times 1 \times 100$	5,00,000	Pref. shares
$\frac{20000}{4} \times 5 \times 100$	25,00,000	Shares
Purchase price	47,98,000	

Total cash 8,000	Purchase price 47,98,000
10,50,000	N. Assets 40,50,000
3,00,000	
13,58,000	Excess 7,48,000 Goodwill.

Bharat Co. Ltd. A/c

Particulars	Amount	Particulars	Amount
To Realisation A/c	47,98,000	By Debentures in Bharat Co. Ltd.	4,40,000
		By Pref. shares in Bharat Co.	5,00,000
		By Equity shares in Bharat Co. Ltd.	25,00,000
		By Bank A/c	13,58,000
	47,98,000		47,98,000

In the Books of Amar Co.

Realisation A/c

To Goodwill	4,00,000	By S. Creditors	1,40,000
To Land & Building	16,00,000	By Provision for RDD	40,000
To Plant & Machinery	14,00,000	By Employees profit sharing fund	1,00,000
To Patent Rights	3,50,000	By Staff PF	1,50,000
To Investment	1,00,000	By Bharat Co. Ltd.	47,98,000
To Stock	2,00,000		
To Debtors	4,00,000		
To Bank	30,000		
Bank A/c (Cost of liquidation)	10,000		
To A Debentures	40,000		
To B Debentures	50,000		
	45,80,000		
To Shareholders A/c (Profit transferred)	6,48,000		
	52,28,000		52,28,000

Shareholders A/c

Particulars	Amount	Particulars	Amount
To Preference shares in Bharat Co. Ltd.	5,00,000	By Share capital	20,00,000
To Equity shares in Bharat Co. Ltd.	25,00,000	By Reserve fund	5,00,000
To Bank	2,89,000	By Sinking fund	1,00,000
		By Workmen's Accident Compensation fund	41,000
		By Realisation	6,48,000
	32,89,000		32,89,000

Workmens' Accident Compensation Fund A/c

To Bank	9,000	By Balance	50,000
To Shareholders A/c	41,000		
	50,000		50,000

'A' Debenture-holders A/c

To Debentures in Bharat Co. Ltd.	4,40,000	By Balance of debentures	4,00,000
		By Realisation	40,000
	4,40,000		4,40,000

'B' Debenture-holders A/c

To Bank	10,50,000	By Debentures	10,00,000
		By Realisation	50,000
	10,50,000		10,50,000

Bank A/c

To Bharat Co. Ltd.	13,58,000	By Workmen's Accident Compensation fund	9,000
		By Realisation (Cost of liquidation)	10,000
		By Debenture-holders (B)	10,50,000
		By Shareholders A/c	2,89,000
	13,58,000		13,58,000

In the Books of Bharat Co. Ltd.

Opening Entries :

Particulars		Dr Rs.	Cr Rs.
(1) Business Purchase A/c	Dr	47,98,000	
To Liquidator of Amar Co. Ltd.			47,98,000
(Purchase consideration payable)			
(2) Land & Building A/c	Dr	16,00,000	
Plant & Machinery A/c	Dr	14,00,000	
Patent Rights A/c	Dr	3,50,000	
Investment A/c	Dr	1,00,000	
Stocks A/c	Dr	2,00,000	
Debtors A/c	Dr	4,00,000	
Bank A/c	Dr	30,000	
Goodwill A/c	Dr	11,48,000	
[Existing in B/s 4,00,000+7,48,000 (Excess paid)]			
To Sundry creditors A/c			1,40,000
To Provision for doubtful debts			40,000
To Employees profit sharing fund			1,00,000
To Staff provident fund			1,50,000
To Business purchase A/c			47,98,000
(Incorporation of Assets & Liabilities taken over)			
(3) Liquidators of Amar Co. Ltd. A/c	Dr	47,98,000	
To Debentures A/c			4,40,000
To Preference share capital A/c			5,00,000
To Equity share capital A/c			25,00,000
To Bank A/c			13,58,000
(Purchase consideration paid in by issue of debentures, preference shares, equity shares and the balance in cash.)			

Problem No. 38

The following is the Balance-Sheet of XYZ Co. Ltd. :

Balance Sheet as at 31-12-1976

Liabilities	Rs.	Assets	Rs.
Share Capital :		Land & Building	1,00,000
20000 shares of Rs. 10 each	2,00,000	Plant & Machinery	1,50,000
Reserves & Surplus :		Work-in-progress	30,000
Reserve fund	25,000	Stock	60,000
Dividend equalisation fund	20,000	Furniture & Fittings	2,500
Profit & Loss appro-priation account	5,100	Sundry debtors	25,000
		Cash at Bank	12,600
Secured Loan :			
Debentures	1,00,000		
Unsecured Loan	—		
Current Liabilities :			
Sundry Creditors	30,000		
	3,80,100		3,80,100

The company is absorbed by ABC Ltd. on the above date. The consideration for the absorption is :

(a) The discharge of the Debentures at a Premium of 5%.

(b) Taking over the liabilities in respect of sundry creditors and

(c) A payment of Rs. 7 in cash and one share of Rs. 5 in the ABC Ltd. at the market value of Rs. 8 per share in exchange for one share in XYZ Co. Ltd.

(d) The cost of liquidation is to be met by the purchasing Co.

Pass Journal Entries in the books of both the Cos. Show how the purchase price is arrived.

Solution :

Calculation :

Purchase consideration :		Purchase price paid in :			Form
Total Assets	3,80,100	(a) Discharge of debentures @ 5% premium			
Less Liabilities :		Debentures	1,00,000		
S. Creditors	30,000	*Add* Premium 5%	5,000	1,05,000	Cash
Net Assets	3,50,100				
Purchase price	4,05,000	(b) *Payment to Share-holders* :			
Goodwill	54,900	20000 shares Rs. 7 per share		1,40,000	Cash
		20000 shares one share of Rs. 5 cost @ Rs. 8 per share 20000 × 8		1,60,000	Shares
		Total Price		4,05,000	

In the Books of XYZ Ltd.

Realisation A/c

Particulars	Amount	Particulars	Amount
To Land & Building	1,00,000	By S. Creditors	30,000
To Plant & Machinery	1,50,000	By ABC Ltd. A/c (Purchasing Co.)	4,05,000
To Work-in-progress	30,000		
To Stock	60,000		
To Furniture & Fittings	2,500		
To Sundry debtors	25,000		
To Cash at bank	12,600		
To Debentures	5,000		
	3,85,000		
To Shareholders A/c (Transferred)	49,900		
	4,35,000		4,35,000

Shareholders A/c

Particulars	Amount	Particulars	Amount
To Shares in ABC Co. Ltd.	1,60,000	By Share capital	2,00,000
To Bank A/c	1,40,000	By Reserve fund	25,000
		By Dividend equilisation fund	20,000
		By Profit & Loss A/c	5,100
		By Realisation A/c	49,900
	3,00,000		3,00,000

Debenture-holders A/c

To Bank	1,05,000	By Debentures	1,00,000
		By Realisation	5,000
	1,05,000		1,05,000

ABC Co. Ltd. A/c

To Realisation	4,05,000	By Shares in ABC Co. Ltd.	1,60,000
		By Bank	2,45,000
	4,05,000		4,05,000

Shares in ABC Co. Ltd. A/c

To ABC Co. Ltd.	1,60,000	By Sharesholders A/c	1,60,000
	1,60,000		1,60,000

Bank A/c

To ABC Co. Ltd.	2,45,000	By ABC Co. Ltd. (Cost of liquidation)	5,000
To ABC Co. Ltd. (Cost of liquidation recovered)	5,000	By Debenture-holders	1,05,000
		By Shareholders	1,40,000
	2,50,000		2,50,000

Journal Entries :

Particulars		Dr Rs.	Cr Rs.
(1) Realisation A/c	Dr	3,80,000	
To Land & Building A/c			1,00,000
To Plant & Machinery A/c			1,50,000
To Work-in-progress A/c			30,000
To Stock A/c			60,000
To Furniture & Fittings A/c			2,500
To Sundry debtors A/c			25,000
To Cash at bank A/c			12,600
(Assets taken over transferred)			
(2) Sundry Creditors A/c	Dr	30,000	
To Realisation A/c			30,000
(Liabilities taken over transferred)			
(3) Share capital A/c	Dr	2,00,000	
Reserve fund A/c	Dr	25,000	
Dividend equalisation fund A/c	Dr	20,000	
Profit & Loss appropriation A/c	Dr	5,100	
To Shareholders A/c			2,50,100
(Share capital and undistributed profit transferred)			
(4) ABC Co. Ltd. A/c	Dr	4,05,000	
To Realisation A/c			4,05,000
(Purchase consideration recurable)			
(5) Shares in ABC Co. Ltd.	Dr	1,60,000	
Bank A/c	Dr	2,45,000	
To ABC Co. Ltd. A/c			4,05,000
(Purchase price received in shares & cash)			
(6) Debenture-holders A/c	Dr	1,05,000	
To Bank			1,05,000
(Debenture-holders paid cash at 5% premium)			
(7) Realisation A/c	Dr	5,000	
To Debenture-holders A/c			5,000
(Balance transferred)			
(8) Realisation A/c	Dr	49,000	
To Shareholders A/c			49,000
(Balance transferred to shareholders)			

Particulars		Dr Rs.	Cr Rs.
(9) ABC Co. Ltd. A/c	Dr	5,000	
To Bank A/c			5,000
(Cost of liquidation)			
(10) Bank A/c	Dr	5,000	
To ABC Co. Ltd. A/c			5,000
(Cost of liquidation recovered)			
(11) Shareholders A/c	Dr	3,00,000	
To Shares in ABC Ltd.			1,60,000
To Bank A/c			1,40,000
(Shares and cash distributed to shareholders)			

In the Books of Purchasing Company
XYZ Co. Ltd.

(1) Business Purchase A/c	Dr	4,05,000	
To Liquidator of ABC Co. Ltd. A/c			4,05,000
(Purchase price payable)			
(2) Land & Building A/c	Dr	1,00,000	
Plant & Machinery A/c	Dr	1,50,000	
Work-in-progress A/c	Dr	30,000	
Stock A/c	Dr	60,000	
Furniture & Fittings A/c	Dr	2,500	
Sundry debtors A/c	Dr	25,000	
Cash at Bank A/c	Dr	12,600	
Goodwill A/c	Dr	54,900	
To S. Creditors A/c			30,000
To Business purchase A/c			4,05,000
(Assets & Liabilities taken over brought into A/c and the balance being Goodwill)			

Particulars		Dr Rs.	Cr Rs.
(3) Liquidator of ABC Co. Ltd. A/c	Dr	40,50,000	
To Share capital A/c			1,00,000
To Share premium A/c			60,000
To Bank A/c			2,45,000
[Purchase price paid in : (a) Shares 20000 of Rs. 5 each at premium of Rs. 3 per share. (b) Rs. 7 per share in cash. (c) Debentures paid in cash @ 5% Premium.]			
(4) Goodwill A/c	Dr	5,000	
To Bank A/c			5,000
(Cost of liquidation paid transferred to Goodwill A/c)			

Problem No. 39

The Balance Sheet of Z Ltd. on 31-3-1996 was as follows :

Liabilities	Rs.	Assets	Rs.
Share Capital :		Goodwill	80,000
50000 shares of Rs. 10	5,00,000	Building	1,80,000
Reserve & Surplus :		Plant	2,00,000
Contingency Reserve	10,000	Stock	1,20,000
Secured Loan :		Debtors	90,000
5% Debentures	2,00,000	Bank	10,000
Current Liabilities & Provision :		Profit & Loss A/c	1,60,000
Staff provident fund	3,000		
Creditors	1,00,000		
	8,40,000		8,40,000

The shareholders and creditors have decided as follows :

(1) A new company named A Ltd. be formed with a capital of Rs. 10,00,000 divided into shares of Rs. 10 each.

(2) The new company is to take over all the Assets (Except cash at Bank) 25% less than the book value. The value of goodwill is nil.

(3) The debenture-holders of Z Ltd. are to be satisfied by issuing 8% debenture in A Ltd. of Rs. 1,50,000 at par.

(4) The creditors have agreed to accept 75% of their claims in full settlement.

(5) The shareholders are to be issued 30000 equity shares in A Ltd. fully paid.

(6) The liquidation expenses paid by Z Ltd. Rs. 10,000 at par.

(7) A Ltd. issued 20000 shares to public at par and received the amount underwriting commission and brokerage amounted to Rs. 10,000.

You are required to prepare :

(a) Realisation Account (b) Shareholders Account in the books of 'Z' Ltd. and (c) Balance Sheet of A Ltd. after employing above decision.

[K.U.D., April 1996(N)]

Solution :

Calculation of purchase consideration :

Assets taken over :		
Building	1,80,000	
Less : 25%	45,000	1,35,000
Plant	2,00,000	
Less : 25%	50,000	1,50,000
Stock	1,20,000	
Less : 25%	30,000	90,000
Debtors	90,000	
Less : Written off 25%	22,500	67,500
Total Assets		4,42,500
Less : Liabilities :		
Staff P.F.	30,000	
Creditors	1,00,000	1,30,000
Net Assets		3,12,500

Purchase consideration paid in :	
(1) Issue of 8% debenture in A Ltd.	1,50,000
(2) Issue of 30000 equity shares of Rs. 10 in fully paid shares	3,00,000
Purchase price	4,50,000
Net Assets	3,12,500
Excess paid (Goodwill)	1,37,500

Note : It is assumed that the creditors are paid by the New Co. and therefore creditors transferred to New Co.

In the Books of Z Ltd.

Particulars	Amount	Particulars	Amount
To Goodwill A/c	80,000	By Staff provident fund	30,000
To Building	1,80,000	By Creditors	1,00,000
To Plant	2,00,000	By A Ltd. (Purchase consideration)	4,50,000
To Stock	1,20,000	By Debenture-holders A/c	50,000
To Debtors	90,000	By Loss transferred to	
To Bank liqudation exp.	10,000	shareholders A/c	50,000
	6,80,000		6,80,000

Shareholders A/c

To Profit & Loss A/c	1,60,000	By Share Capital	5,00,000
To Share in 'A' Ltd.	3,00,000	By Contingency Reserves	10,000
To Realisation Loss	50,000		
	5,10,000		5,10,000

Debenture-holders A/c

To 6% Debentures	1,50,000	By Debentures	2,00,000
To Realisation A/c	50,000		
	2,00,000		2,00,000

In the Books of New Co. A Ltd.

Opening Entries :

Particulars		Dr Rs.	Cr Rs.
(1) Business Purchase A/c	Dr	4,50,000	
To Liquidator of Z Ltd.			4,50,000
(Purchase Price payable)			
(2) Building A/c	Dr	1,35,000	
Plant A/c	Dr	1,50,000	
Stock A/c	Dr	90,000	
Debtors A/c	Dr	67,500	
Goodwill A/c	Dr	1,37,500	
(Balancing figure)			
To Creditors A/c			1,00,000
To Staff Provident Fund A/c			30,000
To Business Purchase A/c			4,50,000
(Being incorporation of Assets & Liabilities taken over)			

Particulars		Dr Rs.	Cr Rs.
(3) Bank A/c	Dr	2,00,000	
To Equity Share Capital A/c			2,00,000
[20000 Shares issued to public and recurred (20000 × 10)]			
(4) Liquidator of Z Ltd. A/c	Dr	4,50,000	
To Equity Share Capital			3,00,000
To 8% Debentures A/c			1,50,000
(Purchase Price paid in by issue of 30000 Equity Shares of Rs. 10 fully paid and issue 8% debentures to debenture holdes in Z Ltd.)			
(5) Creditors A/c	Dr	1,00,000	
To Bank A/c			75,000
To Goodwill A/c			25,000
(Creditors were paid at 75% of their claims and the balance unpaid being capital profit and transferred to Goodwill A/c against excess paid)			
(6) Goodwill A/c	Dr	10,000	
To Bank A/c			10,000
(Underwriting commission paid being expenses transferred to Goodwill A/c)			

Balance Sheet of A Ltd. as at 31-03-1996

Liabilities	Rs.	Assets		Rs.
Share Capital :		Goodwill	1,37,500	
Authorised 100000 equity		*Less* : Adj. in Crs	25,000	
share of Rs. 10 each	10,00,000		1,12,500	
Issued & Paid up :		*Add* Cost of under-		
Issued to Vendor Co.		writing comm.	10,000	1,22,500
30000 share of Rs. 10 each	3,00,000	Building		1,35,000
Issued to public 20000	2,00,000	Plant		1,50,000
Reserves & Surplus	—	Stock		90,000
Secured Loan :		Debtors	90,000	
8% debentures	1,50,000	*Less* : RDD	22,500	67,500
Current Liabilities :		Bank A/c		
Staff providend fund	30,000	Cash realised	2,00,000	
		Less : Paid to Crs		
		75% of 100000	75,000	
			1,25,000	
		Less : Underwriting		
		cost	10,000	1,15,000
	6,80,000			6,80,000

(c) RECONSTRUCTION

Problem No. 40

The following is the Balance sheet of Pickwick Ltd. as on 31st December 1993.

Balance Sheet as at 31-12-1993

Liabilities	Rs.	Assets	Rs.
Share Capital :			
30000 Preference shares		Goodwill	1,94,000
of Rs. 10 each	3,00,000	Building	3,13,000
40000 Equity shares		Machinery	1,56,000
of Rs. 10 each	4,00,000	Debtors	64,000
Reserve fund	22,000	Stock	1,05,000
9% Debentures	1,50,000	Bank	6,600
Creditors	1,60,600	Profit & Loss A/c	1,94,000
	10,32,600		10,32,600

The company suffered heavy losses and found that Goodwill was worthless and that assets were overvalued to the following extent : Building Rs. 53,000, Machinery Rs. 46,000, Stock Rs. 13,000. A provision for doubtful debt at 5% was necessary. The following scheme of reconstruction was adopted :

(a) The creditors to accept 9% debentures to the extent of half their dues and the balance to be paid six months after date.

(b) The preference shares to be reduced to Rs. 5 each.

(c) The assets to be reduced to the revalued figures and Profit and Loss Account debit balance be wiped out.

(d) Ordinary share be reduced to share of Re. 1 each.

Draft Journal entries for giving effect to the above scheme and prepare the reconstructed Balance Sheet.

(K.U.D., April 1995)

Solution :

Journal Entries :

Particulars		Dr Rs.	Cr Rs.
(1) Preference share capital A/c	Dr	1,50,000	
Equity share capital A/c	Dr	3,60,000	
To Capital reduction A/c			5,10,000
(Pref. shares of Rs. 10 each reduced to Rs. 5 each and equity share of Rs. 10 each reduced to Re. 1 per share.)			

Particulars		Dr Rs.	Cr Rs.
(2) Capital Reduction A/c	Dr	5,10,000	
To Goodwill A/c			1,94,000
To Building A/c			53,000
To Profit & loss A/c			1,94,000
To Machinery A/c			46,000
To Stock A/c			13,000
To Provision for doubtful debts			3,200
To Capital reserve A/c			6,800
(Capital reduction amount utilised to write off Goodwill and Profit and Loss A/c and other assets as per written down, as per the scheme of reconstruction and the Balance on A/c transferred to capital reserve account.)			
(3) Creditors A/c	Dr	80,300	
To 9% Debentures A/c			80,300
(Creditors accept 9% Debentures half of their dues and the balance payable after six months till then shown as creditors half of the amount)			

Balance Sheet as at (Reconstructed)

Liabilities	Rs.	Rs.	Assets	Rs.	Rs.
Share Capital :			Goodwill	1,94,000	
30000 Preference share			Written off	1,94,000	—
of Rs. 5		1,50,000	Building	3,13,000	
40000 Equity share of Re. 1			*Less* : Reduced	53,000	2,60,000
each (reduced)		40,000	Machinery	1,56,000	
Reserve & Surplus :			*Less* : Reduced	46,000	1,10,000
Reserve fund		22,000	Stock	1,05,000	
Capital Reserve		6,800	*Less* : Reduced	13,000	92,000
Secured Loan :			Debtors	64,000	
9% Debentures	1,50,000		*Less* : RDD	3,200	60,800
Add : Issued to Crs.	80,300	2,30,300	Bank		6,600
Current Liabilities :			Profit & Loss A/c	1,94,000	
Creditors	1,60,600		Written off	1,94,000	—
Less : 9% Debenture	80,300	80,300			
		5,29,400			5,29,400

Problem No. 41 (Internal-Reduction of Share Capital)

Following is the Balance-sheet of X Co. Ltd. as on 31-12-1992 :

Balance Sheet as at 31-12-1992

Liabilities	Rs.	Assets	Rs.
Share Capital :		Goodwill	50,000
2000 9% Preference shares		Building	1,50,000
of Rs.100 each	2,00,000	Machinery	1,50,000
30000 Equity shares		Patents	40,000
of Rs. 10 each	3,00,000	Stock	65,000
Reserves & Surplus	—	Debtors	45,000
Secured Loan	—	Cash at Bank	15,000
Current Liabilities :		Profit & Loss A/c	1,35,000
Creditors	1,05,000		
Bank Overdraft	45,000		
	6,50,000		6,50,000

Note : Dividend on preference shares was in arrears for 3 years.

The company facing financial difficulties due to heavy losses, decided to adopt the scheme of reconstruction :

(1) Preference shares be reduced to Rs. 50 per share fully paid.

(2) Equity shares be reduced to Rs. 5 each, Rs. 2.50 per share paid up and the final call of Rs. 2.50 per share was duly received from the shareholders.

(3) The amount available on Capital reduction A/c be utilised to write off : Losses, Goodwill and Patents.

The other Assets be written off as :

Building less 10%, Machinery less 20%, Stock revalued @ Rs. 40,000 and a provision on debtors @ 5% be made.

(4) Bank Overdraft be paid off.

Give the Journal Entries to give effect to the above and prepare Balance sheet thereafter.

(K.U.D., April 1992)

Solution :

Journal Entries :

Particulars		Dr Rs.	Cr Rs.
(1) Preference share capital A/c (2000 shares — Rs. 50 each)	Dr	1,00,000	
Equity share capital A/c (30000 shares — Rs. 7.50 each)	Dr	2,25,000	
To Capital reduction A/c			3,25,000
(Capital reduced 2000 preference shares of Rs. 100 each, @ Rs. 50 per share and 30000 equity shares of Rs. 10, Rs. 7.50 per share)			
(2) Capital Reduction A/c	Dr	3,25,000	
To Profit & Loss A/c			1,35,000
To Goodwill A/c			50,000
To Patents A/c			40,000
To Building A/c			15,000
To Machinery A/c			30,000
To Stock A/c			25,000
To Reserve for doubtful debts A/c			2,250
To Capital Reserve A/c (Balancing figure)			27,750
(Capital Reduction A/c utilised to write off fictitious Assets, losses and other assets as per resolution and the Balance transferred to Capital Reduction.)			
(3) Bank A/c	Dr	75,000	
To Equity share capital A/c			75,000
(Cash received on final call on 30000 shares @ Rs. 2.50 each)			
(4) Bank Overdraft A/c	Dr	45,000	
To Bank A/c			45,000
(Bank Overdraft A/c paid)			

(Revised) Balance Sheet as at 31-3-1992

Liabilities	Rs.	Assets		Rs.
Share Capital :		Building	1,50,000	
2000, 9% Pref. shares		*Less* 10%	15,000	1,35,000
of Rs. 50 each fully paid	1,00,000	Machinery	1,50,000	
30000 equity shares of		*Less* 20%	30,000	1,20,000
Rs. 5 each fully paid	1,50,000			
Reserves & Surplus :		Stock	65,000	
Capital Reserve	27,750	*Less*	25,000	40,000
Secured Loan :	—	Debtors	45,000	
Current Liabilities		*Less* RDD 5%	2,250	42,750
Creditors	1,05,000	Bank balance	15,000	
		Add Received	75,000	
			90,000	
		Less Paid	45,000	45,000
	3,82,750			3,82,750

Problem No. 42

Following is the Balance Sheet of Ajit Co. Ltd. :

Balance Sheet as at 31-12-1989

Liabilities	Rs.	Assets	Rs.
Share Capital :		Goodwill	40,000
Authorised :		Building	90,000
100000 equity shares		Machinery	3,75,000
of Rs. 10 each	10,00,000	Patents	45,000
2000, 12% Preference		Furniture	30,000
shares of Rs. 100 each	2,00,000	Stock	1,45,000
	12,00,000	Debtors	90,000
Subscribed and paid up :		Cash at bank	10,000
50000 Equity shares of		Preliminary expenses	30,000
Rs. 10 each	5,00,000	Profit & Loss A/c	1,55,000
1000, 12% Preference			
shares of Rs. 100 each	1,00,000		
9% Debentures	2,50,000		
Secured loan (Mortgage on			
Building)	75,000		
Creditors (unsecured)	85,000		
	10,10,000		10,10,000

The company suffered heavy losses and was not getting on well.

The Board of Directors in the meeting of creditors and shareholders decided to adopt the scheme of reconstruction.

The following resolutions were passed in the meeting :

(a) Equity shares of Rs. 10 each be reduced to Rs. 3 per share, paid up, and further agreed to pay a call money of Rs. 2 per share. The amount was received from all the shareholders.

(b) 12% Preference shares of Rs. 100 each, were reduced by Rs. 25 per share.

(c) 9% Debenture-holders, has agreed to accept new 11% Debentures of the amount of Rs. 2,25,000 by cancelling the old debentures.

(d) Secured loan amount was paid at 80% of their claims. For this purpose security building was sold for Rs. 95,000.

(e) The amount available as a result of capital reduction, is utilised to write off :

(i) All fictitious assets including goodwill and patents.

(ii) The remaining assets were revalued as follows :
Machinery less 20%
Furniture less 25%
Stock valued at Rs. 1,10,000
Provision on debtors at 5%.

Pass the Journal entries to give effect to the above and also prepare revised Balance sheet in the books of Ajit Co. Ltd.

(K.U.D., April 1991)

Solution :

Journal Entries :

Particulars		Dr Rs.	Cr Rs.
(1) Equity share capital A/c (50000 × 7)	Dr	3,50,000	
12% Preference share capital A/c (1000 × 25)	Dr	25,000	
To Capital reduction A/c			3,75,000
(Equity shares of Rs. 10 each reduced to Rs. 3 per share, reduction (10 – 3) = Rs. 7 per share and 12% preference shares of Rs. 100 reduced by Rs. 25 per share, reduction Rs. 25 per share)			
(2) 9% Debenture A/c	Dr	2,50,000	
To 11% Debentures			2,25,000
To Capital reduction A/c			25,000
(Cancellation of old debentures and issue of new 11% debentures of Rs. 2,25,000 and the balance transferred to capital reduction.)			

Particulars		Dr Rs.	Cr Rs.
(3) Bank A/c	Dr	95,000	
To Building A/c			90,000
To Capital reserve A/c			5,000
(Secured building sold for payment of secured Cos. and profit on sale of building transferred to capital reserve.)			
(4) Secured Loan A/c	Dr	75,000	
To Bank A/c			60,000
To Capital Reserve A/c			15,000
(Cash paid to secured loan @ 80% of Rs. 75,000 = Rs. 60,000 and the balance on A/c transferred to capital reserve).			
(5) Bank A/c	Dr	1,00,000	
To Equity share capital A/c			1,00,000
(Call money of Rs. 2 per share on 50000 shares received).			
(6) Capital Reduction A/c	Dr	4,20,000	
To Goodwill A/c			40,000
To Patents A/c			45,000
To Preliminary exp. A/c			30,000
To Profit & Loss A/c			1,55,000
To Machinery A/c (20% on Rs. 3,75,000)			75,000
To Furniture A/c (25% on Rs. 30,000)			7,500
To Stock A/c (Rs. 1,45,000 – 1,10,000)			35,000
To Reserve for doubtful debts A/c (5% on Rs. 90,000)			4,500
To Capital Reserve A/c (Balancing figure)			28,000
(All fictitious assets including Goodwill and patents written off and Assets — Machinery, Furniture, Stock and R.D.D. written off as per Resolution and the Balance on A/c transferred to capital reserve)			

(Revised) Balance Sheet as at 31-12-1989

Liabilities	Rs.	Assets		Rs.
Share Capital :		Machinery	3,75,000	
Authorised :		*Less* Written off	75,000	3,00,000
100000 equity shares of		Furniture	30,000	
Rs. 10 each	10,00,000	*Less* Written off	7,500	22,500
2000, 12% Preference shares		Stock	1,45,000	
of Rs. 100 each	2,00,000	*Less* Written off	35,000	1,10,000
	12,00,000	Debtors	90,000	
Subscribed and paid up :		*Less* R.D.D.	4,500	85,500
50000 equity shares of		Cash at Bank :		
Rs. 10 each, Rs. 5 paid up	2,50,000	Balance	10,000	
1000, 12% preference shares		*Add* Received from		
of Rs. 100 each, Rs. 75		sale of building	95,000	
paid up	75,000		1,05,000	
Capital Reserve	28,000	*Less* Paid to		
11% Debentures	2,25,000	secured creditors	60,000	
Creditors (Unsecured)	85,000		45,000	
		Add Received call		
		money	1,00,000	1,45,000
	6,63,000			6,63,000

Problem No. 43

RECONSTRUCTION — INTERNAL

The following is the Balance sheet of M/s Nirama Ltd. as on 31-12-1988

Balance Sheet as at 31-12-1988

Liabilities	Rs.	Assets	Rs.
Share Capital :		*Fixed Assets* :	50,000
Authorised :		Goodwill	3,50,000
6000, 9% Preference shares		Land & Building	6,00,000
of Rs. 100 each	6,00,000	Plant & Machinery	
10000 equity shares of		*Current Assets* :	
Rs. 100 each	10,00,000	Stock	1,70,000
Issued and paid up :		Debtors	2,10,000
4000, 9% Preference shares		Profit & Loss A/c	3,80,000
of Rs. 100 each	4,00,000		

Liabilities	Rs.	Assets	Rs.
8000 Equity shares of Rs. 100 each	8,00,000		
Reserves & Surplus	—		
Secured Loan :			
6% Debentures	2,40,000		
Unsecured Loan :			
Bank Overdraft	1,10,000		
Current Liabilities :			
Creditors	2,10,000		
	17,60,000		17,60,000

The following scheme of Reconstruction was approved by the court and was given effect to :

(1) The preference shares and the equity shares were reduced to Rs. 80 and Rs. 50 per share fully paid up respectively.

(2) Debenture-holders agreed to receive 2000 preference in full satisfaction of their claim.

(3) The Goodwill A/c and the debit balance of Profit & Loss A/c were written off and

(4) Land & Building and Plant & Machinery were depreciated by 20% and 10% respectively.

Pass Journal Entries to give effect to the above and draw revised Balance Sheet after reconstruction.

(K.U.D., April 1989)

Solution :

Journal Entries :

Particulars		Dr Rs.	Cr Rs.
(1) 9% Preference share capital A/c	Dr	80,000	
Equity share capital A/c	Dr	4,00,000	
To Capital reduction A/c			4,80,000
[4000 preference share of Rs. 100 each reduced by Rs. 20 each (and Rs. 80 fully paid), 8000 equity share of Rs. 100 each reduced by Rs. 50 each (Rs. 50 as fully paid).]			
(2) 6% Debenture A/c	Dr	2,40,000	
To 9% Preference share capital A/c			1,60,000
To Capital reduction A/c			80,000
(2000, 9% preference shares of Rs. 80 fully paid issued in full satisfaction of their due.)			

Particulars		Dr Rs.	Cr Rs.
(3) Capital Reduction A/c	Dr	5,60,000	
(4,80,000 + 80,000)			
To Goodwill A/c			50,000
To Profit and Loss A/c			3,80,000
To Freehold Property			70,000
To Plant and Machinery			60,000
(Goodwill & Profit & Loss A/c written off also freehold property and Plant & Machinery depreciated by 20% and 10% respectively.)			

Balance Sheet as at 31-12-1988

Liabilities	Rs.	Assets		Rs.
Share Capital :		*Fixed Assets :*		
Authorised Capital :		Goodwill written off		—
6000, 9% preference shares of Rs. 80 each	4,80,000	Freehold property (Buildings)	3,50,000	
10000 Equity shares of Rs. 50 each	5,00,000	*Less* 10% Depreciation	70,000	2,80,000
Issued & paid-up :		Plant & Machinery	6,00,000	
6000, 9% preference shares of Rs. 80 each fully paid	4,80,000	*Less* 10% Depreciation	60,000	5,40,000
8000 equity shares of Rs. 50 fully paid	4,00,000	Stock		1,70,000
		Debtors		2,10,000
Bank overdraft	1,10,000	Profit & Loss A/c	3,80,000	
S. Creditors	2,10,000	Written off	3,80,000	—
	12,00,000			12,00,000

Problem No. 44

RECONSTRUCTION — EXTERNAL

The Creditors and the Shareholders having agreed upon a scheme of Reconstruction. The United Trading Co. went into voluntary liquidation.

The Balance Sheet on the date of reconstruction stood as follows :

Balance Sheet as at 31-12-1989

Liabilities	Rs.	Assets	Rs.
Capital :		Goodwill	40,000
25000 shares of Rs. 10 each	2,50,000	Building	95,000
Reserve Fund :		Plant	1,05,000
5% Debentures	1,00,000	Stock	50,000
Creditors	40,000	Debtors	60,000
		Bank	2,000
		Profit & Loss A/c	65,000
	4,17,000		4,17,000

The following are the terms of Reconstruction :

(1) The New Co., called "National Trading Co. Ltd." be formed with a capital of Rs. 5,00,000 in 50000 shares of Rs. 10 each.

(2) The New Co. is to take over from the above company the stock and debtors @ 20% less than the Book value and Buildings and Plant @ Rs. 77,000 and Rs. 1,00,000 respectively.

(3) The debenture-holders were to be satisfied by the issue of 6% debentures of Rs. 1,50,000 in the New Co. in exchange for old debentures.

(4) Creditors agreed to receive Rs. 35,000 from the New Co. in full settlement of their (claims) Accounts.

(5) The shareholders agreed to receive 25,000 shares of Rs. 10 each. Creditors with Rs. 5 per share paid up from the New Co., they further agreed to pay call of Rs. 2.50 per share immediately to the New Co.

(6) The Balance @ Bank was utilised in payment of Reconstruction expenses.

Prepare : (1) Realisation A/c and

(2) Shareholders A/c in the books of old Co.

Also prepare the Balance sheet of the New Co. assuming that call money is duly received.

(K.U.D., October 1990)

Solution :

Calculations :

Assets taken over :			Purchase consideration :	
Stock	50,000		(1) 6% Debentures	1,50,000
Less 20%	10,000	40,000	(2) *Shareholders* :	
Debtors (20% RDD)		60,000	Issue of 25000 shares of Rs. 10, Rs. 5 paid-up	1,25,000
Building		77,000	Total Purchase consideration	2,75,000
Plant		1,00,000	Net Assets	2,65,000
Goodwill (Book value)		40,000	Excess payment treated as Goodwill	10,000
Total Assets		3,17,000		
Less Liabilities :			*Add* Goodwill shown in Balance sheet or existing Goodwill	40,000
S. Creditors	40,000			
RDD 20% on book value	12,000	52,000	Total Goodwill	50,000
Net Assets		2,65,000		

In the Books of United Trading Co. (Old Co.)

Realisation A/c

Particulars	Rs.	Particulars	Rs.
To Goowill	40,000	By S. Creditors	40,000
To Building	95,000	By Purchasing Co. A/c	2,75,000
To Plant	1,05,000	By Shareholders A/c (Loss) transferred.	87,000
To Stock	50,000		
To Debtors	60,000		
To Debenture-holders	50,000		
To Bank (expenses)	2,000		
	4,02,000		4,02,000

Shareholders A/c

To Profit & Loss A/c (Loss)	65,000	By Share capital	2,50,000
		By Reserve fund	27,000
To Realisation (Loss)	87,000		
To Shares in purchasing Co.	1,25,000		
	2,77,000		2,77,000

Debenture-holders A/c

Particulars	Rs.	Particulars	Rs.
To 6% Debentures in purchasing Co.	1,50,000	By Debentures	1,00,000
		By Realisation (Transferred)	50,000
	1,50,000		1,50,000

Bank A/c

To Balance b/d	2,000	By Realisation A/c (expenses)	2,000
	2,000		2,000

In the Books of National Trading Co.

Entries :

Particulars		Dr Rs.	Cr Rs.
(1) Business purchase A/c	Dr	2,75,000	
To Liquidator of Vendor Co.			2,75,000
(Purchase price payable)			
(2) Goodwill A/c (40,000 + 10,000)	Dr	50,000	
Stock A/c	Dr	40,000	
Debtors A/c	Dr	60,000	
Building A/c	Dr	77,000	
Plant A/c	Dr	1,00,000	
To S. Creditors A/c			40,000
To RDD A/c			12,000
To Business purchase A/c			2,75,000
(Assets & Liabilities taken over brought into A/c.)			
(3) Liquidator of Vendor Co. A/c	Dr	2,75,000	
To Share capital A/c			1,25,000
To 6% Debentures A/c			1,50,000
(Purchase price paid in issue of 25000 shares of Rs. 10, Rs. 5 paid up and 6% debentures.)			

Particulars		Dr Rs.	Cr Rs.
(4) Bank A/c	Dr	6,25,000	
To Share capital A/c			6,25,000
(Cash received on calls @ Rs. 2.50 2.50 × 25,000)			
(5) S. Creditors A/c	Dr	40,000	
To Bank A/c			35,000
To Goodwill A/c			5,000
(Paid in full settlement)			

Balance Sheet as at 31-12-1989 (Reconstructed)

Liabilities	Rs.	Assets		Rs.
Share Capital:		Goodwill	50,000	
Authorised :		(40,000 + 10,000)		
25000 shares of Rs. 10 each	5,00,000	*Less* Provision on creditors	5,000	45,000
Paid up Capital :		Building		77,000
25000 shares of Rs. 10,		Plant		1,00,000
Rs. 7.50 paid up	1,87,000	Stock		40,000
6% Debentures	1,50,000	Debtors	60,000	
		Less R.D.D.	12,000	48,000
		Cash	62,500	
		Less Paid	35,000	27,500
	3,37,000			3,37,000

RECONSTRUCTION – INTERNAL

Problem No. 45

Capital Reduction

Rao & Co. Ltd. had the following Balance Sheet as at 30-6-1987 :

Balance Sheet as at 30-6-1987

Liabilities	Rs.	Assets	Rs.
Share Capital :		Goodwill	40,000
1500, 8% preference		Land & Building	2,00,000
shares of Rs. 100 each	1,50,000	Patents	70,000
30000 Equity shares of		Stock	1,00,000
Rs. 10 each	3,00,000	Debtors	80,000
Reserves & Surplus :		Profit & Loss A/c	95,000
Profit prior to Incorporation	15,000		

Liabilities	Rs.	Assets	Rs.
Secured Loan :			
9% Debentures	1,00,000		
Unsecured Loan	—		
Current Liabilities :			
Creditors	20,000		
	5,85,000		5,85,000

The following Scheme of Reconstruction was adopted :

(1) 8% preference shares were to be reduced to a share of Rs. 50 each.

(2) Equity shares were to be reduced to a share of Rs. 40 each.

(3) Debenture-holders have agreed to accept 800, 10% debentures of Rs. 100 each in full satisfaction of their claim.

(4) All the fictitious assets including Goodwill, Patents were to be eliminated.

(5) Land & Building reduced by 20% and Stock 25%.

(6) A Provision of 10% on Debtors for doubtful debts was to be created.

Pass the entries and prepare Balance Sheet after reconstruction has been carried out.

(K.U.D., April 1988)

Solution :

Journal Entries :

Particulars		Dr Rs.	Cr Rs.
(1) 8% Preference share capital A/c	Dr	75,000	
Equity share capital A/c	Dr	1,80,000	
(100 – 40 = 60) 60 × 3000			
To Capital reduction A/c			2,55,000
(Preference Share capital of Rs. 100 each reduced Rs. 50 per share and Equity share capital of Rs. 100 each reduced Rs. 60 per share.)			
(2) Profit Prior to incorporation A/c	Dr	15,000	
To Capital reduction A/c			15,000
(Profit prior to incorporation transferred)			

Particulars		Dr Rs.	Cr Rs.
(3) 9% Debentures A/c	Dr	1,00,000	
To 10% Debentures A/c			80,000
To Capital reduction A/c			20,000
(Balance transferred)			
(4) Capital Reduction A/c	Dr		
(2,55,000 + 15,000 + 20,000)		2,90,000	
To Profit & Loss A/c			95,000
To Goodwill A/c			40,000
To Patents A/c			70,000
To Land & Building A/c			40,000
To Stock A/c			25,000
To Provision for DD A/c			8,000
To Capital Reserve A/c			12,000
(Capital Reduction A/c is utilised to write off Profit & Loss, Goodwill and Assets as above and the balance transferred to Capital Reserve A/c.)			

Balance Sheet as at 30-6-1988

Liabilities	Rs.	Assets		Rs.
Preference shares	75,000	Land & Building	2,00,000	
Equity shares	1,20,000	*Less* 20%	40,000	1,60,000
Debentures	80,000	Stock	1,00,000	
Capital Reserve	12,000	*Less* Reduction	25,000	75,000
Creditors	20,000	Debtors	80,000	
		Less R.D.D.	8,000	72,000
	3,07,000			3,07,000

RECONSTRUCTION — EXTERNAL

Problem No. 46

X Ltd. having proved unsuccessful decided to wind up its affairs and reconstruct itself by forming a new company called Y Ltd. The following was the Balance sheet on the date of reconstruction.

Balance Sheet as at 31-12-1989

Liabilities	Rs.	Assets	Rs.
Share Capital :		Building	1,50,000
40000 Shares of Rs. 10 each	4,00,000	Machinery	1,00,000
Loan from Bank	4,000	Stock	80,000
Creditors	20,000	Debtors	60,000
Bills payable	16,000	Cash	10,000
		Profit & Loss A/c	40,000
	4,40,000		4,40,000

The following are the terms of reconstruction :

(1) The New Co. is to take over all the Assets of the Old Co. but not the liabilities.

(2) The capital of the New Co. is to be Rs. 10,00,000 in shares of Rs. 5 each.

(3) The New Co. is to issued 100000 shares of Rs. 5 each credited with Rs. 3 per share as paid up and also to pay Rs. 50,000 in cash on account of purchase consideration to the Old Co.

(4) The balance of Rs. 2 per share due by members of the New Co. is to be paid on application and allotment and the same has been duly collected in full.

(5) The expenses of reconstruction amounted to Rs. 10,000.

Show the necessary accounts to close the books of the old company and the Balance sheet of the New company.

(K.U.D., April 1987)

Solution :

Calculation :

Total Assets	4,00,000	*Purchase consideration :*	
Purchase price	3,50,000	(1) To Shareholders :	
Less Payment capital gain treated as capital reserve	50,000	Issue 100000 shares of Rs. 5, Rs. 3 paid up	3,00,000
		(2) Cash payment	50,000
		Total Purchase price	3,50,000

In the Books of X Co. Ltd.

Realisation A/c

Particulars	Rs.	Particulars	Rs.
To Building	1,50,000	By Y Ltd. (P. consideration)	3,50,000
To Machinery	1,00,000	By Shareholders A/c	60,000
To Stock	80,000	(Loss transferred)	
To Debtors	60,000		
To Cash	10,000		
To Bank — expenses	10,000		
	4,10,000		4,10,000

Shareholders A/c

To Profit & Loss A/c	40,000	By Share Capital	4,00,000
To Realisation	60,000		
To Shares in Y Ltd.	3,00,000		
	4,00,000		4,00,000

Y Ltd. A/c (Purchasing Co.)

To Realisation A/c	3,50,000	By Shares in Y Ltd.	3,00,000
		By Bank A/c	50,000
	3,50,000		3,50,000

Bank A/c

To Y Ltd.	50,000	By Realisation A/c – exps.	10,000
		By Bank loan	4,000
		By Creditors	20,000
		By Bills payable	16,000
	50,000		50,000

Balance Sheet as at 31-12-1989 (Y Ltd.)

Liabilities	Rs.	Assets		Rs.
Share Capital :		Building		1,50,000
Authorised Capital :		Machinery		1,00,000
200000 shares of Rs. 5 each	10,00,000	Stock		80,000
Issued & paid up :		Debtors		60,000
100000 shares of Rs. 5		Cash balance	10,000	
fully paid	5,00,000	*Add* Received	2,00,000	
Reserves & Surplus :			2,10,000	
Capital Reserve	50,000	*Less* Paid	50,000	1,60,000
	5,50,000			5,50,000

Problem No. 47

The Balance Sheet of A Ltd. showed the following position as on 31-3-1984.

Balance Sheet as at 31-3-1984

Liabilities	Rs.	Assets	Rs.
Share Capital :		Building	90,000
20000 equity shares of		Machinery	80,000
Rs. 10 each	2,00,000	Stock	70,000
Reserves & Surplus	—	Debtors	50,000
Secured Loan	—	Profit & Loss A/c	60,000
Unsecured Loan	—		
Current Liabilities :			
Creditors	1,50,000		
	3,50,000		3,50,000

The shareholders and creditors resolved as follows :

(1) That the company be taken into voluntary liquidation a new company namely B Ltd. be formed with a Registered capital of 50,000. Equity shares of Rs. 10 each to take over the Assets and Liabilities of B Ltd.

(2) That the assets be valued as follows :
Building – Rs. 1,10,000, Machinery – Rs. 70,000, Stock – Rs. 55,000, Debtors – Rs. 35,000.

(3) That 20000 equity shares of Rs. 10 each be issued to the shareholders of A Ltd. as Rs. 6 per share paid up.

(4) That the balance of Rs. 4 per share are to be paid by the shareholders.

(5) That the creditors are to be paid 1/3 of their amount in cash and the issue of 12% debentures as to the balance.

Prepare : Realisation A/c and Shareholders A/c in the Books of A Ltd. and the Balance Sheet of B Ltd.

(K.U.D., October 1985)

Solution :

Calculation :

Assets taken over :		*Purchase price paid up :*	
Building	10,000	(1) To Shareholders :	
Machinery	70,000	Issue of shares of Rs. 10	
Stock	55,000	each as Rs. 6 paid up.	
Debtors	35,000	20000 × 6 =	1,20,000
Total Assets	2,70,000		
Less Liabilities :			
Creditors	1,50,000		
Net Assets	1,20,000		

In the Books of A Ltd. (Vendor Co.)

Realisation A/c

Particulars	Rs.	Particulars	Rs.
To Building	90,000	By Creditors	1,50,000
To Machinery	80,000	By B Ltd.	1,20,000
To Stock	70,000	(Purchasing Co.)	
To Debtors	50,000	By Shareholders A/c	20,000
		(Loss transferred)	
	2,90,000		2,90,000

B Ltd. A/c (Purchasing Co.)

Realisation A/c	1,20,000	By Shares in B Ltd. A/c	1,20,000
	1,20,000		1,20,000

Shareholders A/c

To Profit & Loss A/c	60,000	By Share Capital	2,00,000
To Realisation A/c	20,000		
To Shares in B Ltd.	1,20,000		
	2,00,000		2,00,000

In the Books of B Ltd. (Purchasing Co.)

Entries :

Particulars		Dr Rs.	Cr Rs.
(1) Business Purchase A/c	Dr	1,20,000	
To Liquidator of A Ltd. A/c			1,20,000
(Purchase consideration payable)			
(2) Building A/c	Dr	1,10,000	
Machinery A/c	Dr	70,000	
Stock A/c	Dr	55,000	
Debtors A/c	Dr	50,000	
To Provision on debtors A/c			15,000
To Creditors A/c			1,50,000
To Business purchase A/c			1,20,000
(Assets and Liabilities taken over brought into A/c.)			

Particulars		Dr Rs.	Cr Rs.
(3) Liquidator of A Ltd. A/c	Dr	1,20,000	
To Share capital A/c			1,20,000
(Purchase price paid in 20000 shares of Rs. 10 each, Rs. 6 per share paid up)			
(4) Bank A/c	Dr	80,000	
To Share capital A/c			80,000
(Cash received on 20000 shares 20000 × 4)			
(5) Creditors A/c	Dr	1,50,000	
To Bank A/c			50,000
To 12% Debentures A/c			1,00,000
(Creditors claim settled by payment of 1/3 in cash & 2/3 in debentures)			

Balance Sheet as at 31-3-1984 (B Ltd.)

Liabilities	Rs.	Assets		Rs.
Share Capital :		Building		1,10,000
Authorised :		Machinery		70,000
50000 shares of Rs. 10 each	5,00,000	Stock		55,000
Issued Capital :		Debtors	50,000	
20000 shares of Rs. 10 each	2,00,000	*Less* RDD	15,000	35,000
12% Debentures	1,00,000	Bank		30,000
	3,00,000			3,00,000

Problem No. 48

The Unlucky Ltd. having proved unsuccessful, decided to wind up its affairs and to reconstruct itself by forming a new Co. called Lucky Ltd.

The following was the Balance Sheet on the date of reconstruction :

Balance Sheet as at 30-6-1983

Liabilities	Rs.	Assets	Rs.
Share Capital :		Building	75,000
20000 shares of Rs. 10 each fully paid	2,00,000	Machinery	50,000
Reserve & Surplus	—	Stock	40,000
Loan from Bank	2,000	Debtors	30,000
Creditors	10,000	Cash	5,000
Bills payable	8,000	Profit & Loss A/c	20,000
	2,20,000		2,20,000

The following are the terms of reconstruction :

(1) The New Co. is to take over all the Assets of the Old Co., but not the liabilities.

(2) The capital of the New Co. is to be Rs. 5,00,000 in shares of Rs. 5 each.

(3) The New Co. is to issue 50000 shares of Rs. 5 each credited with Rs. 3 per share as paid up, and also to pay Rs. 25,000 in cash on account of purchase consideration to the Old Co.

(4) The balance of Rs. 2 per share due by the members of the New Co. is to be paid on application and allotment and the same has been duly collected in full.

(5) The expenses of reconstruction amounted Rs. 5,000.

Show the necessary A/cs to close the books of the Old Co. and the balance sheet of the New Co.

(K.U.D., October 1984)

Solution :

Calculation :

Total Assets taken over	2,00,000	*Purchase consideration :*	
Purchase price	1,75,000	(1) To Shareholders :	
Capital gain treated as capital reserve	25,000	50000 shares of Rs. 5 each, Rs. 3 per share paid up	1,50,000
		(2) Cash	25,000
		Total Purchase consideration	1,75,000

In the Books of Unlucky Ltd.

Realisation A/c

Particulars	Rs.	Particulars	Rs.
To Building	75,000	By Lucky Ltd. (Purchase consideration)	1,75,000
To Machinery	50,000	By Shareholders A/c (Loss transferred)	30,000
To Stock	40,000		
To Debtors	30,000		
To Cash	5,000		
To Bank—expenses	5,000		
	2,05,000		2,05,000

Lucky Ltd. A/c (New Co.)

To Realisation A/c	1,75,000	By Shares in New Co.	1,50,000
		By Bank	25,000
	1,75,000		1,75,000

Shareholders A/c

Particulars	Rs.	Particulars	Rs.
To Profit & Loss A/c	20,000	By Share Capital	2,00,000
To Realisation (Loss)	30,000		
To Shares in New Co.	1,50,000		
	2,00,000		2,00,000

Bank A/c

To Lucky Co.	25,000	By Realisation (Expenses)	5,000
		By Bank loan	2,000
		By Creditors	10,000
		By Bills payable	8,000
	25,000		25,000

In the Books of Lucky Ltd.

Balance Sheet as at 30-6-1993

Liabilities	Rs.	Assets		Rs.
Share Capital :		Building		75,000
Authorised :		Machinery		50,000
100000 shares of		Stock		40,000
Rs. 5 each	5,00,000	Debtors		30,000
Issued & paid up :		Cash : Balance	5,000	
50000 shares of Rs. 5		*Add* Received	1,00,000	
fully paid	2,50,000		1,05,000	
Capital Reserve	25,000	*Less* paid	25,000	80,000
	2,75,000			2,75,000

Problem No. 49

X Co's Balance Sheet showed the following position :

Balance Sheet as at 31-12-1970

Liabilities	Rs.	Assets	Rs.
Share Capital :		*Fixed Assets* :	
20000 equity shares		Building	90,000
of Rs. 10 each	2,00,000	Plant	80,000
Reserves & Surplus	—	Investment	—
Secured Loan	—	*Current Assets* :	
Current Liabilities :		Stock	70,000
Creditors	1,80,000	Debtors	50,000
		Cash at Bank	30,000
		Profit & Loss A/c	60,000
	3,80,000		3,80,000

The Committee of shareholders and the creditors as follows :

1. That the company be taken into voluntary liquidation and the new company namely Y Co. Ltd. be formed with a registered capital of 50000 equity shares of Rs. 10 each to take over the Assets and Liabilities of the existing company.
2. That the assets be valued as follows :

   Building – Rs. 1,10,000 Debtors – Rs. 35,000

   Stocks – Rs. 55,000 Plant – Rs. 70,000
3. That 20000 equity shares of Rs. 10 each be issued to the shareholders of X Co. Ltd. at Rs. 6 per share paid up.
4. That the shareholders are to pay Rs. 4 per share (the balance) in cash.
5. That the Creditors of the Co. be satisfied by payment to them 1/3 amount in cash and by issue of 9% debentures as to the balance (2/3).
6. Of the Equity shares 10000 shares be issued to public for cash. Amount was duly received.

Prepare : (a) Realisation A/c

(b) Shareholders A/c in the Books of X Co. Ltd. and

(c) Balance Sheet of Y Co. Ltd.

(K.U.D., October 1970)

Solution :

Calculation :

Assets taken :			Purchase consideration paid in :	
Building	1,10,000		(1) By issue of 20000 equity	
Plant	70,000		shares of Rs.10 @	
Stocks	55,000		Rs. 6 per share.	
Debtors	50,000		20000 × 6 = 1,20,000	
Bank	30,000		Purchase consideration	1,20,000
Total Assets		3,15,000	Equal to net assets	1,20,000
Less :			No Profit/No Loss	-Nil-
Liabilities taken :				
Creditors	1,80,000			
Provision for doubtful debt	15,000	1,95,000		
		1,20,000		

In the Books of X Co.
Ledger A/c
Realisation A/c

Particulars	Rs.	Particulars	Rs.
To Sundry Assets :		By Sundry creditors	1,80,000
Building	90,000	By Y Co. Ltd. (Purchasing Co.)	1,20,000
Plant	80,000		
Stock	70,000	By Equity shareholders (Loss transferred)	20,000
Debtors	50,000		
Cash at Bank	30,000		
	3,20,000		3,20,000

Equity Shareholders A/c

To Profit & Loss A/c	60,000	By Share capital	2,00,000
To Realisation (Loss)	20,000		
To Equity shares in Y Co. Ltd.	1,20,000		
	2,00,000		2,00,000

'Y' Co. Ltd.
Balance Sheet as at 31-12-1970 (Reconstructed)

Liabilities		Rs.	Assets		Rs.
Share Capital :			Building		1,10,000
Authorised Capital :			Plant		70,000
50000 equity shares			Stock		55,000
of Rs. 10 each		5,00,000	Debtors	50,000	
Issued Capital :			*Less* RDD	15,000	35,000
To X Co.=20000×10	2,00,000		Cash at Bank :		
To public			Balance	30,000	
= 10000 × 10	1,00,000	3,00,000	*Add* Reserved		
Reserves & Surplus		—	20000 × 4	80,000	
Secured Loan :			Eq. shares issued to		
10% Debentures		1,20,000	public 10,000×10	1,00,000	
				2,10,000	
Current Assets		—	*Less* Paid to creditors		
			1/3 × 1,80,000	60,000	1,50,000
		4,20,000			4,20,000

Opening Entries in the Books of 'Y' Co. Ltd. :

Particulars		Dr Rs.	Cr Rs.
1. Business purchase A/c	Dr	1,20,000	
To Liquidators of X Co. Ltd.			1,20,000
(Purchase consideration payable)			
2. Building A/c	Dr	1,10,000	
Plant A/c	Dr	70,000	
Stock A/c	Dr	55,000	
Debtors A/c	Dr	50,000	
Cash at bank A/c	Dr	30,000	
To Credit A/c			1,80,000
To Reserve for doutful debts A/c			15,000
To Business purchase A/c			1,20,000
(Incorporation of Assets & Liabilities taken over.)			
3. Liquidators of X Co. Ltd. A/c	Dr	1,20,000	
To Equity share capital A/c			1,20,000
(Purchase consideration paid in by issue of 20000 equity shares of Rs. 10 each, Rs. 6 paid up.)			
4. Bank A/c	Dr	80,000	
To Equity share capital A/c			80,000
(Cash received on 20,000 × 4.2			
5. Bank A/c	Dr	1,00,000	
To Equity share capital A/c			1,00,000
(Cash received on public issue 10000 equity share @ Rs. 10 per share.)			
6. Creditors A/c	Dr	1,80,000	
To 10% Debentures A/c			1,20,000
To Bank A/c			60,000
(Creditors paid 1/3 in cash and 2/3 by issue of 10% debentures.)			

3

Liquidation (Voluntary)

LIQUIDATION OF COMPANIES

Joint Stock Company, being an artificial person comes into existence under the Joint Stock Companies Act, with a view to undertake Commercial Activities. Normally the Company continues to function so long as business earns profits. If the Company due to competition or otherwise could not withstand and was incurring losses the members of the Company may propose to close down. In other situations where the purpose of the Company for which came into existence was over and the members may decide to close down the business.

Liquidation of the Company means the termination of the legal existence of the Company and stop thereby all the business activities when the joint stock company is in liquidation the assets are realised and the outside liabilities are paid; if still cash balance remains it will be distributed to shareholders at pro-rata.

Modes of Winding-up (or Liquidation)

(a) Compulsory winding-up by the Court

(b) Voluntary winding-up by members & creditors

(c) Voluntary winding-up under the supervision of the Court.

Procedure of the Liquidation

When the Company is in Liquidation, the process of Liquidation is carried by a person appointed by the appropriate authority. The Liquidator appointed for the purpose is vested with powers, to realise assets and pay off all the liabilities. He prepares a list of assets and the liabilities of the company. For the services rendered by the Liquidator, he is paid remuneration in the form-fixed amount and/or commission on amount realised and amount paid to creditors and amount distributed to preference shareholders as capital and dividend.

Liquidator prepares a final statements of accounts showing receipts and payments.

Order of payment of liabilities (Voluntary Liquidation) :

(1) Secured Creditors

(2) Cost of Liquidation :

(i) Legal Expenses

(ii) Liquidator's remuneration – Fixed amount

(iii) Commission on assets realised and amount collected from shareholder on calls.

(iv) Commission on amount paid to unsecured creditors (including preferential creditors).

(v) Commission on amount paid to preference shareholders as capital and dividend.

(3) Debentures having floating charge on general assets including interest on debentures up to the date of payment.

(4) Preferential creditors.

(5) Unsecured creditors.

(6) Refund of capital :

(a) Preference share capital and arrears of dividend (if any).

(b) Equity share capital – at pro-rata.

Preferential Creditors

(1) All taxes or amounts due to Government : Central/State/Local Bodies etc.

(2) Wages to workers.

(3) Salaries to clerks etc.

Preferential creditors are paid first before unsecured creditors.

For the purpose of calculations of commission on preferential creditors are treated as unsecured creditors.

Liquidator's Commission

(a) As a percentage on assets realised amount includes the amount of assets — securities realised by secured creditors.

Cash in hand and cash at banks some times it is included in the amount of total assets realised for the purpose of calculation of commission. In some other cases it is not included (not taken). Suitable note be given where cash included or not in calculations of commissions.

(b) As a percentage on amount paid to unsecured creditors and preference shares capital and dividend. If the amount available is sufficient to pay liquidator's commissions and unsecured creditors' in full. Commission is directly calculated on unsecured creditors amount and preference share capital and dividend.

(1) If the amount available is insufficient to pay unsecured creditors in full; the amount available also includes liquidator's commission on the amount payable to unsecured creditors. Therefore first the liquidator's commission be paid from the amount available and thereafter balance amount left (reduced by the amount of commission) be paid to unsecured creditors at pro-rata.

The calculation of liquidator's commission in such cases; the following formula be applied :

$$\text{Commission} = \frac{\text{Percentage of commission (\%)}}{100 + \text{percentage of commission}} \times \text{Amount available}$$

$$\text{OR} \quad \frac{\%}{100 + \%} \times \text{Amount available}$$

i.e. 100 + %

Now we get commission.... This amount commission is deducted from the amount available and the net balance of amount be distributed to unsecured creditors at pro-rata. To verify the correctness of the calculations; now directly calculate commission at % given on amount distributed to unsecured creditors. This amount should be the same as calculated in the first instance.

(2) Calculation of commission on the amount paid to preference share capital and dividend. The amount available being insufficient to pay them and results in deficiency. The deficiency amount is to be shared by equity shareholders of having different paid up capital. The calls will be made on such shares where paid up amount is less than the amount of deficiency. Similarly where paid up amount is more than the deficiency excess amount contributed be refunded.

Here once again calculation of commission becomes unusual i.e. the amount required to pay preference share capital & dividend is the net amount and the commission is not included. Net + Commission = 100% is the gross amount required to be collected from uncalled shares.

Problem No. 1

The Dharwad Co. Ltd. went into voluntary Liquidation on 31st December, 1997.

Balance Sheet as at 31-12-1997

Liabilities		Rs.	Assets	Rs.
Share Capital			Goodwill	20,000
Paid up Capital			Building	45,000
10000 Shares of Rs. 10 each			Plant	50,000
Rs. 8 Called up	80,000		Stock	4,300
Less Calls in arrear	2,000	78,000	Debtors	13,850
Debentures		25,000	Cash	1,500
Sundary Creditors :			Profit & Loss A/c	56,850
Preferential Creditors		9,250		
Secured Creditors		31,500		
(Secured on Plant)				
Unsecured Creditors		43,250		
Bank Overdraft		4,500		
		1,91,500		1,91,500

The liquidator realised the Assets as under :

	Rs.
Building	21,250
Plant	24,000
Stock	5,200
Debtors	13,550

Liquidation expenses amounted to Rs. 215

Liquidators Remuneration was fixed @ 3% on amount of Assets realised and @ 2% on the amount paid to unsecured creditors.

Prepare Liquidators Final Statement of A/c.

[K.U.D., April 1998(N)]

Solution :

Liquidators Final Statement of A/c

		Rs.			Rs.
To Assets Realised			By Liquidation Expenses		215
Building	21,250		By Liquidation Remuneration		
Plant	24,000		@ 3% on assets Realised		
Secured Creditors	31,500		3% on 64,000 =	1,920	
Unpaid Balance transferred to Unsecured			2% on amount paid to Unsecured Creditors		
			2% on Pref. Creditors		
Creditors	7,500		2% on 9,250	185	
Stock		5,200	2% on 24,049	481	2,586
Debtors		13,550	By Debenture holders		25,000
Cash		1,500	By Preferential Creditors		9,250
Calls on shares		19,600	By Unsecured Creditors		24,049
Shares	10,000				
Less 200 Calls Unpaid	200				
	9,800				
Shares 9,800 × 2 =					
		61,100			61,100

Working Note

(1) Assets Realised

Building		21,250
Plant		24,000
Stock		5,200
Debtors		13,550
Total amount realised		64,000
Less Paid to		
Secured Creditors		24,000
On Plant Sec.		40,000
Add Cash in hand		1,500
Total Cash in hand		41,500
Less paid		
Liquidation Exp.	215	
Commission		
1,920 + 185 =	2,105	
Deben. holders	25,000	
Preferential		
Creditors	9,250	36,570
		4,930

(2) Liquidator's Commission

3% on Assets realised	
3% on 64,000 =	1,920
2% Preferential Creditors	
2% on 9,250	185
2% Commission	481
Amount includes commission	2,586

2/102 × 24530 = 481

$\frac{481}{24049}$ = 481 Commission Cash paid

(3) Total Unsecured Creditors

Unsecured Creditors	43,250
Unpaid by Secured Crs.	7,500
Bank Overdraft	4,500
Total Unsecured Crs.	55,250

(4) Cash left to pay Unsecured Creditors

Creditors		4,930
Call on shares	10,000	
Less Calls unpaid	200	
	9,800	
9800 × 2		19,600
Total Cash		24,530

Problem No. 2

The Ashok Company Ltd. went into Voluntary Liquidation on 31-12-1996 when the state of affairs was as follows : unsecured creditors Rs. 40,000 including preferential creditors of Rs. 5,000.

Secured creditors : secured on Plant and Machinery stood at Rs. 20,000

Cash in hand Rs. 1,000

The Liquidator realised :

Plant & Machinery for Rs. 15,000

and other Assets realised for Rs. 10,000

The liquidation expenses amouned to Rs. 1,000

Liquidator's remuneration was fixed at 4% of the amount realised including cash Balance and 2% of the amount distributed to unsecured creditors including preferential creditors.

Prepare Liquidator's Final Statement of Account showing dividend paid to unsecured creditors.

[K.U.D., October 1997(N)]

Solution :

Liquidator's Final Statement of A/c

To Assets realised :			By Liquidation Expenses		1,000
Cash in hand		1,000	By Liquidation remuneration		
Plant & Machinery	15,000		@ 4% on amount realised		
Paid to secured creditors			excluding cash		
on Plant & Machinery	20,000		(1,000 + 15,000 + 10,000)		
Unpaid balance transferred			4% on 26,000	1,040	
to unsecured creditors	5,000		2% on 5,000	100	
Other Assets		10,000	+ 2% on 3,784	76	1,216
			Unsecured creditors :		
			By Preferential creditors		5,000
			By Unsecured creditors		3,784
			(40,000 – 5,000 + 5,000) 40,000		
		11,000	Dividend Paid to Unsecured creditors. $\frac{3,784}{40,000}$ = 0.095		11,000

Note : Cash in hand		11,000	Cash available includes
Less cash paid :			Liquidators commission
Liquidation expenses	1,000		Therefore 100 + 2% = 102 gross
4% commission	1,040		Calculation of comm.
Pref. creditors	5,000		Comm. = 2/102 × 3,860 = 75.68 = 76
2% comm. on 5000	100	7,140	Amount in Bond 3,860
Cash debt to pay		3,860	*Less* Commission 76 = 3,784
Unsecured creditors + 2% comm.			Comm. 2% on 3,784 = 75.68 = 76

Problem No. 3

Park Avenue Ltd. went into voluntary Liquidation on 31-12-1995, on which date its Balance sheet stood as below :

Balance Sheet as at 31-12-1995

Liabilities		Rs.	Assets	Rs.
Share Capital			Plant & Machinery	12,000
8000 equity shares of			Vehicles	10,000
Rs. 5 each		40,000	Goodwill	6000
Reserves & Surplus		—	Books Debts	13,600
Current Liabilities :			Stocks	18,000
Preferential	1,600		Bank Balance	400
Unsecured	22,400		Profit & Loss A/c	20,000
Partly Secured	8,000	32,000		
Banks Overdraft		8,000		
		80,000		80,000

The Liquidator realised the following sums of money — Vehicles Rs. 4,800, Plant and Machinery Rs. 10,000, Stocks Rs. 12,000, Book Debts Rs. 5,200

The Liquidation Expenses amounted Rs. 1,840

The Liquidators remuneration was fixed as under :

4% of the amount realised by him.

2% of the amount distributed to unsecured creditors.

Prepare Liquidators Final Statement of Account.

[K.U.D., October 1997(O)]

Solution :

Liquidators Final Statement of A/c

Assets realised			By Liquidation Expenses		1,840
Vehicles —	4,800		Liquidators remuneration		
Less paid to partly			4% on amount realised		
secured creditors	8,000		4% on 32,000	1,280	
(Uncovered Balance	3,200		2% on 1,600 pref. crs.	32	
transferred to unsecured			2% on 22,400	448	1,760
Creditors)			By Preferential creditors		1,600
To Plant & Machinery		10,000	By Unsecured creditors paid		22,400
To Stocks		12,000	(33,600) (66.67% prorata)		
To Books Debts		5,200			
To Bank Balance		400			
		27,600			27,600

			Rs.	
Cash in hand			27,600	Whose cash available to pay unsecured creditors includes the Liquidators commission also therefore cash available 100 + 2 = 102
Less cash paid				
Liquidation Expenses		1,840		
Liquidators remuneration : 4% on amount realised				
Vehicles	4,800			
Plant & Machinery	10,000			Calculation of Liquidators commission
Stock	12,000			
Books Debts	5,200			= 2%/102 × 22,848 = 448
	32,000			
(Excluding cash)				
4% on 32,000		1,280		
		3,120		
Preferential creditors		1,600		
2% comm. on 1,600		32	4,752	
Cash left to pay Unsecured creditors			22,848	

Unsecured creditors	22,400	*Less* Comm.	448		
Unpaid Balance of partly secured	3,200	Net amount paid	22,400	Amount available	22,848
Bank overdraft	8,000			*Less* 2% Com.	448
Total Unsecured creditors	33,600	Comm. 2%	448	Amount Paid to creditors	22,400
Cash available to pay is insufficient	Rs. 22,848		22,848	Com. 2% on 22,400 =	Rs. 448

Problem No. 4

The share capital of A Ltd. at the time of Liquidation consisted of :

(1) 1000 5% preference shares of Rs. 100 each fully paid

(2) 2500 equity shares of Rs. 10 each fully paid

(3) 1500 equity shares of Rs. 10 each Rs. 7 paid up

(4) Rs. 37,500 6% Debentures holding floating charge

(5) Rs. 4,500 preference claims

(6) Rs. 12,500 Unsecured Creditors

(7) Rs. 6,000 Liquidators remuneration

(8) The liquidators realised assets Rs. 1,60,000

Prepare Liquidators Final Statement of Account

[K.U.D., October 1997(N)]

Liquidator's Final Statement of A/c

	Rs.		Rs.
To Assets Realised	1,60,000	By Liquidator's Remuneration	6,000
To Calls on shares on 1500 shares at Rs. 2 per share 1500 × 2 =	3,000	By Debentures holding floating charges	37,500
		By Preferential creditors	4,500
		By Unsecured creditors	12,500
		By Refund of capital Preference share capital	1,00,000
		Equity share capital 2500 shares Re. 1 per share 2500 × 1 =	2,500
	1,63,000		1,63,000

Cash in hand		1,60,000
Less Cash paid		
Liquidator's Remuneration	6,000	
Debentures	37,500	
Preferential Creditors	4,500	
Unsecured Creditors	12,500	60,500
Cash debt to pay		99,500
Pref. share capital	1,00,000	
Paid	99,500	
	500	

2500 eq. shares of Rs. 10 fully paid	25,000
1500 eq. shares Rs.10 each Rs. 7 paid	10,500
	35,500
Cash required to pay	+ 500
Total Deficiency	36,000

Total Deficiency amount Rs. 36,000 be shared by Equity shareholders

$$\frac{\text{Deficiency}}{\text{No. of Equity Shares}} = \frac{36,000}{(2500+1500)} = \frac{36,000}{4000} = \text{Rs. 9 per share}$$

Still cash required :	
To pay equity share capital	– 35,500
Cash required to pay pref. capital	500
Deficiency	36,000

(1) Equity shares 2500 Rs. 10 paid –

Loss – Refund

Rs. 9 – Re. 1

Loss 9

(2) Equity shares 1500 Rs. 7 paid

loss 9 = Rs. 2 call.

Calls on share 1500 × 2 = Rs. 3,000

Refund on 2500 × 1 = Rs. 2,500

Problem No. 5

Dharwad Co. Ltd. went into voluntary liquidation on 1-4-1994 on which date dividend on preference shares were in for 3 years. The following was the position of the company :

I. *Share Capital* :

6000 equity shares of Rs. 100 each Rs. 50 paid up

3000 6% preference shares of Rs. 100 each fully paid

II. *Liabilities* :

	Rs.
Secured Loan against Machinery	30,000
Unsecured Creditors	70,000
Bills payable	40,000
Preferential Creditors	8,100

III. *Assets Realised* :

Machinery	50,000
Other Assets	3,64,000

The Liquidator is enlisted to a remuneration of Rs. 12,000 and 5% commission on amount paid to preference shareholder as capital & dividend and 5% on amount collected by him the legal expenses and the cost of winding up amounted to Rs. 1,000 and Rs. 3,000 respectively.

Show : (a) Computation of calls on shares

(b) Prepare Liquidators Final Statement of Account.

[K.U.D., April 1997(N)]

Solution :

Liquidator's Final Statement of A/c

Particulars		Rs.	Particulars		Rs.
To Assets realised			By Liquidation Expenses :		
Machinery	50,000		Legal Expenses	1,000	
Less Secured Loan			Cost of winding up	3,000	4,000
Surplus	30,000	20,000	Liquidator's Remuneration		12,000
To Other Assets		3,64,000	Commission on amount		
To Calls on Equity shares			paid to Pref. share		
Rs. 21.37 per share		1,28,220	capital & Dividend		
on 6000 shares			5% on 3,54,000	17,700	
6000 × 21.37			5% on collected	,411	24,120
Actual amount required			By 5% on 1,28,220		
Rs. 1,28,211 only			Preferential creditors		8,100
Calls on shares			Unsecured creditors		70,000
Rs. 21.3685 = 37			By Bills payable		40,000
.0015 Rs. per share excess called			By Preferential shareholders		
the amount paid to Liquidator			pref. share capital	3,00,000	
			Dividend 6% on 3,00,000		
			= 18,000 × 3 years	54,000	3,54,000
		5,12,220			5,12,220

Working Note

Total cash in hand		3,84,000	Amount payable to	
Less Cash paid			Pref. Shareholders	
Cost of Liquidator	4,000		Capital	3,00,000
Remuneration	12,000		Dividend @ 6% for 3 years	
Commission	17,700		6% on 3,00,000 = 18,000 × 3=	54,000
Pref. Crs.	8,100		Amount Required	3,54,000
Unsecured crs.	70,000		Amount available	2,32,200
Bills payable	40,000	1,51,800	Amount required	
Cash left to pay			to pay pref. shareholders	1,21,800
Pref. share cap. & Dividend		2,32,200	+ 5% commission on amount collected	

Amount payable to pref. shareholders

Rs. 1,21,800 being 95% + 5% com. = 100% amount to be collected from shareholders. i.e. for 95 for 1,21,800 / 100

$= 1,21,800 \times \frac{100}{95}$ = Rs. 1,28,211 amount to be collected from Shareholders

$= 6411$ Less $\frac{6411}{1,21,800}$ 5% Commission

$\frac{\text{Total amount required}}{\text{No. of shares}} = \frac{1,28,211}{6,000}$ = Rs. 21.37 per share to be collected.

Problem No. 6

X Co. Ltd. went into voluntary liquidation on 31-12-1994. The following was the position of the company on that date :

Balance Sheet as at 31-12-1994

Liabilities	Rs.	Assets	Rs.
Share Capital		Goodwill	30,000
1455 Equity shares		Leasehold property	25,000
of Rs. 100 each	1,45,500	Sundry Assets	1,42,120
Reserves of Surplus	—	Cash at Bank	500
Current Liabilities		Profit & Loss	61,380
Preferential creditors	4,000		
Partly secured creditors	29,180		
Unsecured creditors	79,160		
Bank overdraft	1,160		
	2,59,000		2,59,000

The Liquidator realised the Assets as follows :

	Rs.
(1) Leasehold property which was first used to pay partly secured creditors	18,000
(2) Sundry Assets	99,500
(3) Cash at Bank	500
Total	1,18,000

The Liquidation expenses amounted Rs. 1,170

The Liquidators commission was at

2½% on amount realised by him and 2% on the amount distributed to unsecured creditors

Prepare Liquidator's Final Statement of Account

[K.U.D., October 1996(O)]

Solution :

Liquidator's Final Statement of A/c

Particulars		Rs.	Particulars		Rs.
To Assets Realised			By Liquidation Expenses		1,170
Leasehold property	18,000		By Liquidator's Remuneration		
Partly secured crs.	29,180		2½% on 1,18,000	2,950	
Uncovered Balance	11,180		2% on 4,000	80	
transferred to			2% on 90,000	1,800	4,830
Unsecured creditor			By Preferential creditors		4,000
To Sundry Assets		99,500	By Unsecured creditors		90,000
To Cash at Bank		500			
		1,00,000			1,00,000

		Rs.
Cash in hand		1,00,000
Less Payment :		
Liquidation exp.	1,170	
Commissions	2,450	
	50	
Pref. creditors	4,000	8,200
Cash available to pay unsecured creditors + 2% com.		91,800

	Rs.
Unsecured creditors	79,160
Uncovered balance	
Of partly seemed creditors	11,180
Bank overdraft	1,160
Total unsecured creditors	91,500

The amount available Rs. 91,800
To pay unsecured creditors Rs. 91,500
after deducting liquidators commission
@ 2% on amount distributed to
unsecured creditors
Therefore liquidator's commission
is to be ascertained and paid first

$$\text{Commission} = \frac{2\% \times 91,800}{100 + 2}$$

= 2/102 × 41,800 = 1,800 Commission

	Rs.
Total amount	Rs. 91,800
Less Commission	1,800
	90,000

	Rs.
Amount available	Rs. 90,000
Com. @ 2% on 90,000	1,800

Amount available to pay unsecured creditors Rs. 90,000.

Problem No. 7

The share capital of X Ltd. (in liquidation) consisted of :

(a) 2000, 10% preference shares of Rs. 100 each fully paid.

(b) 5000 equity shares of Rs. 10 each fully paid.

(c) 3000 equity shares of Rs. 10 each, Rs. 7 paid up.

Rs. 75,000 — 12% Debentures holding floating charge.
Rs. 9,000 — Preferential claims.
Rs. 25,000 — Unsecured creditors.
Rs. 12,000 — Liquidators remuneration.

The liquidator realised Rs. 3,20,000.

Determine the amount of call to be made on partly paid shares and prepare the liquidators statement of account.

(October 1996)

Solution :

Liquidator's Final Statement Account

Liabilities	Rs.	Assets	Rs.
To Assets realised	3,20,000	By Liquidator's Remuneration	12,000
To Calls on shares 3000 × @ Rs. 2 per share	6,000	By Debenture-holder	75,000
		By Preferential claims	9,000
		By Unsecured creditors	25,000
		By Preference shareholders	2,00,000
		By Refund of capital 5000 equity share of Re. 1	5,000
Total	3,26,000		3,26,000

Working Note : Total deficiency Rs. 72,000 is to be shared by equity shareholders i.e., 5,000 + 3,000 = 8,000.

$$\frac{\text{Total deficiency}}{\text{Total No. of shares}} = \frac{72{,}000}{8{,}000} = \text{Rs. } 9$$

5000 share of Rs. 10—9 = Re. 1 refund.
3000 share of Rs. 7—9 = Rs. 2 call to be made.

Determination of Call to be made on partly paid equity shares

		Rs.
Assets realised		3,20,000
Less : Payment made :		
Liquidators remuneration	12,000	
Debenture-holders	75,000	
Preferential claims	9,000	
Unsecured creditors	25,000	1,21,000
Cash in hand		1,99,000

			Rs.
Share capital to be refund :			
Preference shares capital – 2000 × 100		2,00,000	
Equity share capital — 5000 × 10		50,000	
Equity share capital — 3000 × 7		21,000	2,71,000
Total deficiency			72,000

Problem No. 8

The following is the Balance Sheet of Rashiko Ltd. on 31-12-1995

Balance Sheet as at 31-12-1995

Liabilities	Rs.	Assets	Rs.
Share Capital :		Building	1,00,000
2000, 6% preference		Machinery	2,50,000
shares of Rs. 100 each	2,00,000	Plants	40,000
1000 equity shares of		Stock	65,000
Rs. 100 each, Rs. 75 paid up	75,000	Debtors	1,00,000
3000 equity shares of		Bank	30,000
Rs. 100 each, Rs. 60 paid up	1,80,000	Profit & Loss A/c	1,20,000
Reserve & Surplus	—		
Secured Loan :			
10% debenture (having floating charges on assets)	1,00,000		
Interest on debentures due	5,000		
Sundry creditors	1,05,000		
Bills payable	30,000		
Preferential creditors for taxes	10,000		
	7,05,000		7,05,000

On the above date the company went into voluntary liquidation.

(a) The dividend on preference shares was in arrears for two years.

(b) The sundry creditors included a Loan of Rs. 50,000 on mortgage on building.

(c) The liquidators realised the assets as follows :
Building – 1,20,000, Machinery – 2,00,000, Plants – 30,000, Stock – 60,000 and Debtors – 80,000.

(d) The legal expenses and cost of winding up amounted to Rs. 2,000 and Rs. 8,000 respectively.

(e) The liquidator is entitled to a commission of 3% on assets realised by him and 2% on amount paid to unsecured creditors. All payments were made on 31-3-1996.

Prepare the liquidators final statement of account, also give working note.

[K.U.D., April 1996 (N)]

Solution :

Liquidator's Final Statement of A/c

Liabilities	Rs.	Rs.	Assets	Rs.
To Assets realised :			By Legal expenses	2,000
Building	1,20,000		By Cost of winding up	8,000
Less Mortgage loan			By Liquidator's commission :	
on Building	– 50,000	70,000	(a) 3% on assets realised (3% on 5,20,000)	15,600
To Machinery		2,00,000	(b) 2% on account paid to unsecured creditors (2% on 95,000)	1,900
To Plants		30,000	By Debenture-holders [*see* note (a)]	1,07,500
To Stocks		60,000	By Preferential creditors	10,000
To Debtors		80,000	By Unsecured creditors [*see* note (b)]	85,000
To Bank-cash		30,000	Total	2,30,000
			By Refund of capital : Pref. share capital 2,00,000 Arrears of dividend 2 years 2×12,000 24,000	2,24,000
			By Equity share capital : 1000 shares of Rs. 75 paid @ Rs. 15.25×1000	15,250
			3000 shares of Rs. 60 paid @ Re. 0.25×3000	750
		4,70,000		4,70,000

Working Note-I

Note (a) Debenture-holders

10% Debentures	1,00,000
Interest due upto 31-12-1995	5,000
Interest due upto date of payment 31-3-96 i.e. 3 months 1,00,000 × 10% = 10,000	
10,000 × 3/12 =	2,500
Total amount	1,07,500

Note (b) Unsecured creditors

Sundry creditors	1,05,000
Less Mortgage loan on Building	50,000
	55,000
Bills payable	30,000
Total Unsecured creditors	85,000
Add Preferential credit	10,000
Total Unsecured creditors for calculation of 2% commission.	95,000

Note (c) : Calculation of Liquidator's Commission

(1) On Assets realised	5,20,000
1,20,000 + 2,00,000 + 30,000 + 60,000 + 80,000 + 30,000	
Commission on 5,20,000 × 3%	15,600
(2) On amount paid to unsecured	
creditors on 85,000 + 10,000 = 95,000 × 2%	1,900
Total Commission	17,500

Working Note-II

	Rs.	Rs.
Cash in hand		4,70,000
Less Payments :		
Cost of liquidation (2,000 + 8,000)	10,000	
Commission	17,500	
Debenture-holders	1,07,500	
Preferential creditors	10,000	
Unsecured creditors	85,000	2,30,000
Cash left to pay		2,40,000
Preferential shareholders		
Pref. share capital	2,00,000	
Dividend arrears for 2 years	24,000	2,24,000
Cash balance available to pay equity shareholders		16,000
Equity shareholders :		
1000 shares of Rs. 75 paid		75,000
3000 shares Rs. 60 paid		1,80,000
Amount payable		2,55,000
Cash in hand		16,000
Amount of deficiency		2,39,000
Deficiency shared by equity shareholders.		

		Rs.
Total deficiency		2,39,000
Total No. of shares		4,000
Deficiency per shares		59.75

Loss per share

	Loss	Refunded
1000 shares Rs. 75 paid	59.75	15.25
3000 shares Rs. 60 paid	59.75	0.25

Refund of share capital :

Equity shares 1000 × 15.25 =	15,250
Equity shares 3000 × 0.25 =	750
	Rs. 16,000

Problem No. 9

The following is the Trial Balance of Bombay Co. Ltd. on 1-4-1994 on which date the dividend on preference shares were arrears for three years :

Particulars	Dr	Cr
Shares capital	—	1,50,000
3000 equity shares of Rs. 100 each,		
Rs. 50 per share paid up.		
1500, 6% preference shares of Rs. 100	—	1,50,000
each fully paid up.		
Secured loans against machinery	—	15,000
Preferential creditors	—	4,050
Machinery	1,50,000	—
Other assets	1,95,000	—
Profit & Loss account	29,050	
Unsecured creditors	—	35,000
Bills payable	—	20,000
Total	3,74,050	3,74,050

The company went into voluntary liquidation. Liquidators realised assets as follows :

(a) Machinery Rs. 35,000

(b) Other assets Rs. 1,72,000

The liquidation expenses amounted to Rs. 2,300. The liquidator is entitled to a remuneration of Rs. 6,000 and a commission @ 5% on the amount paid to preference shareholders as capital and dividend and 5% on the amount collected by him.

Prepare liquidators final statement of account.

[K.U.D., April 1996 (a)]

Solution :

Liquidator's Final Statement of Account

Particulars	Rs.	Rs.	Particulars	Rs.
To Assets realised			By Liquidation expenses	2,300
Machinery	35,000		By Liquidation remuneration	6,000
Less : secured			By Commission amount collected :	
loan	15,000	20,000	5% on 2,07,000 = 10,350	
To Other assets		1,72,000	5% on 66,000 = 3,300	13,650
To Calls on equity		66,000	By Preferential creditors	4,050
shareholders (3000 × 22)			By Unsecured creditors	35,000

Particulars	Rs.	Particulars		Rs.
		By Bills payable		20,000
		By Refund of capital :		
		Preference shareholders capital	1,50,000	
		Dividend @ 6% for 3 years @ 6% on 1,50,000 (9,000 × 3)	27,000	1,77,000
	2,58,000			2,58,000

Working Note

(1) *Liquidation Commission :*

(a) 5% on amount collected :

35,000 + 1,72,000 =	2,07,000	
5% on 2,07,000 =		10,350
(b) 5% commission on amount collected from equity shareholders (66,000 × 5%)		3,300
		13,650

(2) *Cash in hand* : (20,000 + 1,72,000)		1,92,000
Less : Paid : Expenses	2,300	
Remuneration	6,000	
Commission	10.350	
Pref. Creditors	4,050	
Unsecured Crs.	35,000	
Bills Payable	20,000	77,700
Cash left to pay : Pref. share capital		1,14,300
Dividend	1,50,000	
3 × 9000	27,000	1,77,000
Deficit		62,700

If the amount required is Rs. 100, 5% commission is to be paid, net amount is 100 – 5 = 95 Net = 62,700 × 100/95 = 66,000 (Gross)

Problem No. 10

The Bangalore Co. Ltd. went into voluntary liquidation on 31-12-1994 at which date its capital consisted of :

(a) 10,000, 8% preference shares of Rs. 10 each fully paid.

(b) 20000 equity shares of Rs. 10 each fully paid.

The assets realised Rs. 1,60,000. The liquidation expenses amounted to Rs. 4,000. The unsecured creditors were Rs. 68,000 including Rs. 10,000 for preferential creditors. The liquidators remuneration was fixed at :

(i) 4% commission on the assets realised.

(ii) 2% commission on the amount distributed to the shareholders.

Preference shares carry preferential right as to payment of capital and assume no arrears of dividend.

Prepare the liquidator's final statement of account.

(K.U.D., October 1995)

Solution :

Liquidator's Final Statement of A/c

Particulars	Rs.	Particulars		Rs.
To Assets realised	1,60,000	By Liquidation expenses		4,000
		By Liquidators remuneration commission		
		4% on 1,60,000	6,400	
		Commission 2% on 80,000	1,600	8,000
		By Preferential creditors		10,000
		By Unsecured creditors (68,000 – 10,000)		58,000
		By Refund of capital to Preference shareholders		80,000
	1,60,000			1,60,000

Note : Cash in hand		1,60,000	Cash Balance include 2% commission		81,600
Less : Paid expenses	4,000		commission 2/102 × 81,600		1,600
Commission 4%	6,400		Cash balance	81,600	
Pref. Crs	10,000		*Less* : 2% commission	1,600	
Unsecured Crs	58,000	78,400	Cash payable to Pref. shares	80,000	
Cash available to pay pref. shareholder & 2% commission		81,600	Commission 2% on 80,000 = 1,600		

Problem No. 11

Goodwill Ltd. went into voluntary liquidation on 31st December 1990, on which date its balance sheet as follows :

Balance Sheet as at 31-12-1990

Liabilities	Rs.	Assets	Rs.
Share Capital			
6% Preference shares		Plant & Machinery	4,50,000
of Rs. 10 each	2,40,000	Stock	2,25,000
Equity shares of Rs. 10 each	4,00,000	Debtors	3,68,000
Reserves & Surplus	—	Cash	3,000
Secured Loan :		Profit & Loss A/c	1,28,000
10% Debentures	1,20,000		
Current Liabilities			
Creditors	4,14,000		
	11,74,000		11,74,00

(a) There was arrears of preference dividend Rs. 28,800.

(b) The liquidator realised Plant & Machinery Rs. 4,40,000 and Stock Rs. 2,07,000.

(c) He collected debts from debtors with exception of Rs. 15,000 which was found to be irrecoverable.

(d) Creditors of which Rs. 12,000 was preferential and were paid in full.

(e) The debentures were paid with interest of Rs. 3,000 on 31st March 1991.

(f) Liquidation expenses amounted to Rs. 12,400 and liquidator's remuneration was agreed at 2% on amount realised and 3% on the amount distributed to the equity shareholders.

Show liquidator's final statement of account.

(K.U.D., April 1995)

Solution :

Liquidator's Final Statement of Account

Particulars	Rs.	Particulars		Rs.
To Assets realised		By Liquidators expenses		12,400
Plant & Machinery	4,40,000	By Remuneration :		
Stock	2,07,000	2% on 10,00,000		20,000
Debtors	3,53,000	3% on 1,60,000		4,800
Cash	3,000	Preferential creditors		12,000
		Debenture	1,20,000	
		Plus Interest	3,000	1,23,000

Particulars	Rs.	Particulars	Rs.
		By Creditors	4,02,000
		By Refund of Capital :	
		Preference share capital 2,40,000 + 28,800 dividend	2,68,800
		By Equity shareholders	1,60,000
	10,03,000		10,03,000

Note : (1) 2% commission on amount realised :

		Rs.
Assets realised :	Plant & Machinery	4,40,000
	Stock	2,07,000
	Debtors	3,53,000
	Total amount	10,00,000

		Rs.
Total cash in hand		10,03,000
Less Payments :		
1. Liquidators Exp.	12,400	
2. Remuneration (2% on 10,00,000)	20,000	
3. Pref. Creditors	12,000	
4. Debentures	1,23,000	
5. Creditors (4,14,000 – 12,000)	4,02,000	
6. Refund of Capital Pref. Shareholders	2,68,800	– 8,38,200
Amount left to pay		1,64,800

Equity shareholder — is less than the amount payable Rs. 4,00,000.

In such case commission is calculated as follows :

$$\text{Commission} = \frac{\%}{100 + \%} \times \text{Amount} = \frac{3}{103} \times 1,64,800 = 4,800$$

Amount in hand	Rs. 1,64,800	*Verification*
Less Commission	4,800	3% Comm. on 1,60,000 = Rs. 4,800
Net Amount paid to Equity Shareholders	1,60,000	

Problem No. 12

Dhanalaxmi Ltd. went into voluntary liquidation on 31st December 1992. The following was the position on that date :

Balance Sheet as at 31-12-1992

Liabilities	Rs.	Assets	Rs.
Share capital		Land & Building	50,000
1000, 6% Preference		Machinery	1,25,000
shares of Rs. 100 each	1,00,000	Furniture	20,000
500 equity shares of		Stock	27,500
Rs. 100 each, Rs. 75 paid	37,500	Sundry debtors	55,000
1500 equity shares of		Cash at bank	15,000
Rs. 100 each, Rs. 60 paid	90,000	Profit and Loss A/c	60,000
5% debentures having a			
floating charge on all assets	50,000		
Interest outstanding	2,500		
Creditors	72,500		
	3,52,500		3,52,500

The preference dividend were in arrears for two years. Creditors include a loan of Rs. 25,000 on the mortgage of land and building.

The assets were realised as follows :

Land and Building	60,000
Machinery	1,00,000
Furniture	15,000
Stock	30,000
Sundry debtors	40,000

The expenses of liquidation amounted to Rs. 5,450. The liquidator entitled to a commission of 3% on all assets realised except cash at Bank and a commission of 2% on amounts distributed among unsecured creditors. Preferential creditors amounted to Rs. 7,500. The payment was made on June 30th, 1993.

Prepare the liquidator's final statement of accounts.

(K.U.D., October 1994)

Liquidator's Final Statement of Account

Particulars		Rs.	Particulars		Rs.
To Assets realised :			By Liquidation expenses		5,450
Land & Building	60,000		By Liquidator's commission :		
Less : Loan paid	25,000		3% on 2,45,000	7,350	
Surplus		35,000	2% on 7,500	150	
Machinery		1,00,000	2% on 40,000	800	8,300
Furnitures		15,000	By Debentures	50,000	
Stock		30,000	*Add* Int. for 6 months		
Sundry debtors		40,000	@ 5% $\frac{2500}{1250}$ =	1,250	51,250

Particulars	Rs.	Particulars		Rs.
Cash at Bank	15,000	Preferential creditors		7,500
		Interest outstanding		2,500
		Unsecured creditors		40,000
		Refund of Capital		
		Preference Shareholders		
		Capital	1,00,000	
		Arrears of Dividend		
		2 years = 6,000 × 2	12,000	1,12,000
		Refund of Capital		
		Equity Shareholders :		
		500 × 15.25 =	7,625	
		1,500 × 00.25 =	375	8,000
	2,35,000			2,35,000

Working Notes

	Rs.
(1) *Assets realised*	2,20,000
Add : Cash at bank	15,000
Total Cash	2,35,000
Less Payments :	
(1) 5,450	
(2) 8,300	
(3) 51,250	
(4) 7,500	
(5) 2,500	
(6) 40,000	
(7) 1,12,000	– 2,27,000
Cash Balance available to pay Equity shareholders	8,000

(2) Amount payable to Equity Shareholders

	Rs.
500 Equity Shares Rs. 75 paid	37,500
1500 Equity Shares Rs. 60 paid	90,000
Total Payment to be made to Equity Shareholders	1,27,500
Cash Available	8,000
Deficiency	Rs. 1,19,500

Deficiency shared by Equity Shareholders

$$\frac{\text{Deficiency}}{\text{No. of Shares}} = \frac{1,19,500}{(500 + 1500)} = \text{Rs. } 59.75$$

Loss per share.

(3) Creditors	Rs. 72,500
Less Loan Creditors	25,000
	47,500
Less Preferential Creditors	7,500
Unsecured Creditors	40,000

Equity Shares	– Paid up	– Loss	= Refund
500	– 75	– 59.75	= 15.25
1500	– 60	– 59.75	= 00.25
500 × 15.25 =			7,625
1500 × 00.25 =			375
Total Refund			Rs. 8,000

Problem No. 13

X Ltd. went into voluntary liquidation on 31st March 1991 and their position is given below :

2000, 6% preferential shares of Rs. 100 each fully paid

1000 equity shares of Rs. 100 each fully paid.

1000 equity shares of Rs. 100 each, Rs. 60 per share paid up.

	Rs.
Calls in arrears	6,000
Calls in advance	4,000
Total assets realised	3,00,000
Sundry creditors (secured)	40,000
Sundry creditors (unsecured)	20,000
Preferential creditors	8,000

There is arrears of preference dividend for one year which has preferential claim over equity-holders.

The liquidator made necessary call on partly paid shares and received in full.

You are required to prepare :

(a) Statement showing determination of call amount.

(b) Liquidator's final statement of account.

(K.U.D., April 1994)

Solution :

Liquidator's Final Statement of Account

Particulars	Rs.	Particulars	Rs.
To Assets realised	3,00,000	By Call in advance	4,000
To Less secured credit	40,000	By Pref. creditors	8,000
	2,60,000	By Unsecured creditors	20,000
To Calls in arrears	6,000	By Preferential shares	2,00,000
To Calls on 1000 × 9	9,000	By Dividend	12,000
		By *Refund* :	
		Equity shares 1000 × 31	31,000
	2,75,000		2,75,000

Total cash	2,66,000
Less Paid	32,000
Cash in hand	2,34,000

Amount required to pay : 6% preferential shareholders

	2000 × 100	2,00,000
	Dividend 6% of 2,00,000	12,000
		2,12,000
Equity shareholders		
1000 × 100		1,00,000
1000 × 60		60,000
		3,72,000
Less : Cash in hand		2,34,000
	Total Deficiency	1,38,000

Shared by 2000 equity shares $\frac{1,38,000}{2000}$ = 69 deficiency per share

Equity shareholder's deficiency 1000 : 100 – 69 = 31 refund.

1000 : 60 – 69 = 9 calls on shares.

Problem No. 14

Ambica Limited went into voluntary liquidation on 31-12-1990. The following informations are available to the liquidator :

Sundry creditors Rs. 75,660 including Rs. 8,160 are preferential creditors, 6% debentures – Rs. 80,000. Debentureholders were paid interest upto 30-6-1989.

The assets realised as follows :

		Rs.
Stock		84,000
Machinery	–	60,000
Cash in hand	–	500

Debentures were paid off on 30th July 1991 with interest. The secured creditors realised the securities. Building and handed over & surplus of Rs. 3,000 to the liquidator. The cost of liquidation expenses come to Rs. 1,902.

The liquidator is entitled to a remuneration at 2% on the amount realised and 2% on the amount distributed to unsecured creditors.

Prepare liquidator's final statement of account.

(K.U.D., April 1993)

Solution :

Liquidator's Final Statement of Account

Particulars	Rs.	Particulars	Rs.
To Assets realised :		By Liquidation expenses	1,902
Stock	84,000	By Liquidator remuneration on	
Machinery	60,600	Assets realised :	
Cash in hand	500	2% on 1,47,600	2,952
Surplus from		2% on pref. crs. (Unsecured)	
secured creditors	3,000	8,160 × 2%	163
		2% on 44,043 =	880
		By Preferential creditor	8,160
		6% debentures 80,000	
		Interest (for 6 + 12 + 7 months) 10,000	90,000
		2% Unsecured creditors	44,043
	1,48,100		1,48,100

Working Notes

(1) Assets realised :

	Rs.
Stock	84,000
Machinery	60,600
Surplus from secured crs.	3,000
including cash in hand Rs.	1,47,600

Commission 2% on 1,47,600 = 2,952.

(2) Sundry creditors		75,660
Preferential creditors		8,160
Unsecured creditors		67,500

(3) 6% Debentures	80,000
Interest upto 31-12-89 for 6 months of 4,800	2,400
For 1990 one year upto	4,800
30-7-91 4,800 × 7/12 =	2,800
Total	90,000

(4) Total amount		1,48,100
Less cash paid		
Cost of Liquidation	1,902	
Commission	3,115	
Pref. creditors	8,160	
Debenture	90,000	
Total payable		1,03,177
Cash available to pay unsecured creditors		44,923

(5) Unsecured creditors 67,500

Amount available to pay 44,923 cash is sufficient to pay in full amount available includes liquidator remuneration @ 2% on amount distributed to unsecured creditors.

Commission $= 2/102 \times 44{,}923$

$$= \frac{44{,}923}{51}$$

Commission = 880.8

44,923 – 880.8 = 44,043.20.

Problem No. 15

X Company went into voluntary liquidation on 31-12-1991. The capital of the company consisted of :

(1) 2000, 12% preference shares of Rs. 100 each fully paid.

(2) 25000 equity shares of Rs. 10 each fully paid.

(3) 30000 equity shares of Rs. 10 each, Rs. 8 paid up.

(4) 40000 equity shares of Rs. 10 each, Rs. 7 paid up.

The dividend on preference shares was in arrears for one year.

The unsecured creditors Rs. 1,00,000 included Rs. 25,000 towards preferential creditors.

The assets realised Rs. 4,49,000.

The liquidation expenses Rs. 7,520.

Liquidators remuneration fixed Rs. 8,000.

Commission of 2% on amount paid to preference shareholders as capital and dividend preference shareholders have priority in regard to the repayment of capital and dividend over equity shareholders.

Prepare liquidator's final statement of accounts.

(K.U.D., October 1993)

Liquidator's Final Statement of A/c

Particulars	Rs.	Particulars		Rs.
To Assets realised	4,49,000	By Liquidation exp.		7,520
		By Liquidators remuneration		
		Fixed		8,000
		2% commission of 2,24,000		4,480
		By Preferential creditors		25,000
		By Unsecured creditors		75,000
		By Refund of capital preferential shares		
		Capital	2,00,000	
		Dividend	24,000	2,24,000
		Refund of excess money		
		Equity shareholders		
		25,000 × 3		75,000
		30,000 × 1		30,000
	4,49,000			4,49,000

Working Notes

(1) Cash in hand		4,49,000
Less Paid :		
Liquidation expenses	7,520	
Remuneration	8,000	
Commission	4,480	
Creditors	25,000	
	75,000	1,20,000
		3,29,000
Less Paid to preference :		
Share capital	2,00,000	
Dividend	24,000	2,24,000
Amount available to pay Equity shareholders		1,05,000
Amount payable to equity shareholders :		
(1) 25,000 × 10 =	2,50,000	
(2) 30,000 × 8 =	2,40,000	
(3) 40,000 × 7 =	2,80,000	
95,000	7,70,000	7,70,000
Deficiency		6,65,000
Total deficiency to be shared by total No. of equity shareholders		6,65,000
		95,000

Deficiency per share $= \dfrac{6,65,000}{95,000}$

= Rs. 7 deficiency per share

Now,

Equity shareholders

(1) 25000 shareholders paid Rs. 10 – 7 loss = 3 refund

(2) 30000 shareholders paid Rs. 8 – 7 loss = 1 refund

(3) 4000 Shareholders 7 – 7 loss = 0

Refund to shareholders :

(1) 25000 × 3 =	75,000
(2) 30000 × 1 =	30,000
Total payment	1,05,000

Problem No. 16

The position of X Company Ltd. (in liquidation) was as follows :

2000, 6% preference shares of Rs. 100 each fully paid.

(Dividend for one year in arrears)

1000 equity shares of Rs. 100 each fully paid.

1000 equity shares of Rs. 75 each, Rs. 60 paid.

Calls in arrears Rs. 8,000

Calls in advance Rs. 12,000

Cash in hand Rs. 2,18,500

Articles provide priority to preference shareholder as to capital and dividend.

(a) Ascertain the call to be on shares.

(b) Prepare liquidator's final statement of account.

(K.U.D., October 1992)

Liquidator's Final Statement of Account

Particulars	Rs.	Particulars	Rs.
To Cash in hand	2,18,500	By Calls in advance	12,000
To Calls in arrears	8,000	By Refund of capital & dividend pref. share capital	2,00,000
To Calls on shares 1000 of Rs. 75	7,500	Dividend 6% of 2,00,000	12,000
		By Refund of capital on Equity shares	10,000
	2,34,000		2,34,000

Working Notes

Cash in hand (2,18,500 + 8,000)		2,26,500
Less Cash paid		12,000
		2,14,500
Less Paid to pref. share + dividend		2,12,000
Cash balance left to pay		2,500
Equity shareholders		
1000 share of Rs. 100 =	1,00,000	
1000 share of Rs. 75, Rs. 60 paid	60,000	1,60,000
Deficiency is to be shared proportionally		1,57,500

1000 equity share of Rs. 100 = 4/7

1000 equity share of Rs. 75 = 3/7

Ratio 4 : 3 = 7.

Deficiency of Rs. 1,57,500. Equity shares of Rs. 1·00 = 1,57,500 × 4/7 = 90,000 for 1000 shares of Rs. 90,000 = 90 Rs. per share.

Equity share of Rs. 75 : 1,57,500 × 3/7 = 67,500 for 100 shares of Rs. 67.50.

% of Deficiency : 90/100 × 100 = 90% refund Rs. 10

67.50/75 × 100 = 90% call on shares 67.50 – 60 = 7.50 Rs.

Calls on share of Rs. 7.50 per share.

Problem No. 17

X Company Ltd., went into voluntary liquidation on 1-1-1990. The following was the position on that date :

Balance Sheet as at 1-1-1990

Liabilities	Rs.	Assets	Rs.
Share Capital :		Goodwill	50,000
Equity shares of Rs. 10	3,00,000	Building	50,000
Reserves & Surplus		Machinery	90,000
Sundry creditors :		Furnitures	60,000
(a) Secured against		Stock	68,500
machinery	65,000	Debtors	82,000
(b) Creditors having lien		Cash at Bank	4,500
on stock	75,000	Profit & Loss A/c	1,51,000
(c) Preferential credit	25,000		
(d) Unsecured	91,000		
	5,56,000		5,56,000

The liquidator was appointed to carry over the process of liquidation.
The secured creditors exercised their claims against the securities offered.
Machinery was sold @ Rs. 70,000
Stock realised at 30% only
The liquidator realised the remaining assets :

Building	30,000
Furnitures	27,000
Debtors	60,250
Cash at Bank	4,500

The liquidator's expenses — Rs. 1,439
The liquidator's remuneration was agreed as follows :

(a) 2% commission on assets realised and

(b) 3% commission on the amount paid to unsecured creditors.

Prepare liquidators final statement of A/c.

(K.U.D., April 1992)

Liquidator's Final Statement of Account

Particulars		Rs.	Particulars	Rs.
To Assets realised :			By Liquidation expenses	1,439
Machinery	70,000		By Liquidator's remuneration	
Less Paid to			On assets realised	
secured creditors	65,000	5,000	2% commission on 1,26,750	2,535
To Stock	20,550		On amount paid to unsecured creditors	
Less on stock secured creditors	75,000		3% commission on 25,000	750
Unsatisfied credit			3% commission on 94,200	2,826
transferred to			By Preferential creditors	25,000
unsecured creditors	54,450		By Unsecured creditors	94,200
Other Assets :				
Building		30,000		
Furnitures		27,000		
Debtors		60,250		
Cash at Bank		4,500		
		1,26,750		1,26,750

Note : Liquidators Remuneration

(a) Assets realised : 2% on 1,26,750 = 2,535

(b) On amount paid to unsecured creditors	91,000	
Add Transfer from partly share (Unsatisfied)	54,450	
Preferential creditors	25,000	1,70,450

Amount Available : Assets Realised =		1,26,750	
Less : Paid liquidator expenses	1,439		
Commission	2,535	3,974	1,22,776 cash available to pay.

Unsecured creditors is in sufficient to pay in full.

Calculation of commission included in amount available :

Formula $\dfrac{\text{\% of com.}}{100 + \text{\% com.}} \times$ Amount available

$$= \frac{3}{100 + 3} \times 1,22,776 =$$

$$= \frac{3}{103} \times 1,22,776 = 3,575.99$$

$$= \underline{3,576}$$

Amount Available =		1,22,776
Less Preferential creditors	25,000	
Add Commission 3%	750	25,750
		97,026
Less Commission	3,576	
	– 750	2,826
		94,200

Total commission :		Amount paid to	
On pref. crs.		unsecured creditors	94,200
25,000 × 3%	750	Verification of Com. — Rs. 94,200	
Unsecured crs		Commission @ 3%	= Rs. 2,826
94,200 × 3%	2,826		
	3,576		

Problem No. 18

Shri Laxmi Narayan Company Ltd. went into voluntary liquidation on 1-1-1989. The following was the position on that date :

Share Capital :

(a) 3000, 12% preference shares of Rs. 100 each fully paid.

(b) 50000 equity share of Rs. 10 each fully paid.

(c) 40000 equity shares of Rs. 10 each Rs. 8 paid up.

(d) 30000 equity shares of Rs. 10 each Rs. 6 paid up.

(i) Dividend on preference shares was in arrears for one year

(ii) Preference shareholders have priority over equity shareholders as regards capital and dividend.

Liability :	Rs.
Mortgage on Building	65,000
Preferential creditors	15,000
Unsecured creditors	7,20,000
Assets realised :	
Building	75,000
Other assets	10,11,000
Liquidation expenses amounted	4,440

Liquidator's remuneration :

(1) 1% commission on Assets realised

(2) 2% commission on amount paid to unsecured creditors.

Prepare liquidator's final statement of account.

(K.U.D., April 1991)

Solution :

Liquidator's Final Statement of Account

Particulars	Rs.	Rs.	Particulars	Rs.	Rs.
To Assets realised :			By Liquidation expenses		4,440
Building	75,000		Liquidator's remuneration :		
Less : Secured creditors	65,000	10,000	1% com. on 10,86,000		10,860
Surplus		—	2% on 15,000		300
Other assets		10,11,000	2% on 7,20,000		14,400
Calls on shares			Preferential creditors		15,000
40,000 × 1 =	40,000		Unsecured creditors		7,20,000
30,000 × 3 =	90,000	1,30,000	Refund of capital :		
			Preference capital	3,00,000	
			Dividend	36,000	3,36,000
			Refund of capital on Equity shareholder		50,000
		11,51,000			11,51,000

Working Notes

Cash in hand		10,21,000	(10,000 + 10,11,000)
Less Cash paid liquidation exp.	4,440		
Liquidators remuneration			
Commission 10,860 + 300 + 14,400	25,560		
	30,000		
Unsecured creditors	7,35,000	7,65,000	
Cash left to pay for pref. share capital + dividend + equity share capital		2,56,000	

Amount payable to :

(1) Preferential share capital 3000 × 100 =	3,00,000
Dividend on 3,00,000 of 12%	36,000
(2) Equity share capital 5,00,000+3,20,000+1,80,000	10,00,000
Total amount payable	13,36,000
Less : Cash balance left	2,56,000
Deficiency	10,80,000

Deficiency Rs. 10,80,000 be shared by equity shareholders 50,000+40,000+30,000 = 1,20,000

Deficiency per share = 10,80,000/1,20,000 = Rs. 9 per share Loss

50000 Equity shares of Rs. 10 each : Rs. 10 paid – Rs. 9 deficiency = excess Re. 1 refund

40000 " " " Rs. 8 paid – 9 = short Re. 1 call money

30000 " " " Rs. 6 paid – 9 = short Rs. 3 call money

Calls on shares : 40000 × 1 = 40,000

30000 × 3 = 90,000 = 1,30,000.

Problem No. 19

Fair Deal Ltd. went into voluntary liquidation on 31st March 1991 on which date its position was as under :

		Rs.
(I)	Liabilities :	
	Mortgage on Machinery	15,000
	Trade creditors	35,000
	Bills payable	20,000
	Preferential claims for salary & wages	3,000
	Government taxes	1,050
(II)	Share capital :	
	3000, 6% preference shares of Rs. 50 (pref. dividend due for 3 years)	1,50,000
	6000 equity shares of Rs. 50 each, Rs. 25 paid	1,50,000
(III)	Assets realised :	
	Machinery	35,000
	Other assets	1,72,000

The liquidation cost and legal expenses amounted to Rs. 1,500 and 500 respectively. The liquidator is entitled to a remuneration of Rs. 6,000 plus 5% commission on amount paid to preference shareholders as capital & dividend and 5% commission on total amount collected (including calls on shares).

Give : (a) Working notes on determination of call per share

(b) Liquidator's final statement of account.

(K.U.D., October 1991)

Solution :

Liquidator's Final Statement of Account

Particulars		Rs.	Particulars	Rs.
To Assets realised :			By Cost of liquidation	1,500
Machinery	35,000		By Legal expenses	500
Less : Paid	15,000	20,000	By Liquidators remuneration	6,000
Other assets		1,72,000	By 5% commission	10,350
Cash received from			By 5% commission on 75,000	3,750
6000 equity shareholders @ Rs. 12.50% per shares		75,000	By 5% on amount paid to pref. shares amount	8,850
			By Preferential credit	3,000
			By Govt. taxes	1,650
			By Trade creditors	35,000
			By Bills payable	20,000
			By Refund to pref. 6% share capital	1,50,000
			By Dividend	27,000
		2,67,000		2,67,000

Working Note

(1) Cash in hand		1,92,000	
Less : Amount paid		86,250	1,05,750 cash available
(2) Calculation of commission :			
(a) 5% on assets realised		35,000	
		1,72,000	
5% on 2,07,000		2,07,000	10,350
(b) Amount collected from shareholders 5%			3,750
(c) Amount paid to pref. share capital + dividend 1,77,000 on 5%			8,850
Amount payable to pref. capital	1,50,000		
Add : Dividend for 3 years @ 6%	27,000	1,77,000	
Less amount available		1,05,750	71,250

Total amount required 71,250+5% commission on amount to be collected = Rs. 75,000

Total amount required including 5% commission Rs. 75,000 (i.e. $71{,}250 \times \frac{100}{95} = 75{,}000$)

This amount is to be collected from shareholders equity 75,000/6,000 = Rs. 12.50 per share to be collected.

Problem No. 20

Belgaum Co. Ltd. went into voluntary liquidation on 1-4-1989 on which date dividend on preference shares were in arrears for three years. The following is the position of the company :

Share capital

3000 equity shares of Rs. 100 each, Rs. 50 paid up

1500, 6% preference shares of Rs. 100 each fully paid up

	Rs.
Liabilities :	
Secured loans against machinery	15,000
Unsecured creditors	35,000
Preferential creditors	4,050
Bills payable	20,000
Assets realised :	
Machinery	35,000
Other assets	1,72,000

The liquidation expenses and legal expenses amounted to Rs. 1,500 and Rs. 1,250 respectively liquidators is entitled to a remuneration of Rs. 6,000 and a commission of 5% on the amount paid to preference shareholders as capital and dividend and 5% commission on the amount collected by him.

(K.U.D., April 1990)

Solution :

Liquidator's Final Statement of Account

Particulars		Rs.	Particulars	Rs.
To Assets realised :			By Liquidation exp.	1,500
Machinery	35,000		By Legal expenses	1,250
Less Secured loan	15,000	20,000	By Remuneration	6,000
Other assets		1,72,000	By Commission 5% on assets	10,350
Calls on shares 3000×24		72,000	By 5% on pref. capital + dividend	8,850
			By Preferential creditors	4,050
			By Unsecured creditors	55,000
			By Preferential share capital + dividend	1,77,000
		2,64,000		2,64,000

Total amount in hand		1,92,000
Less Amount paid		87,000
Cash balance in hand		1,05,000
Amount payable to pref. share capital	1,50,000	
Dividend @ 6%	27,000	1,77,000
Amount required to pay		72,000

Calls on shares 3000 × 24 = 72,000

Problem No. 21

A company went into voluntary liquidation on which date the following balance sheet was prepared. The dividend on pref. shares was in arrears for one year.

Balance Sheet as on 30-6-1990

Liabilities	Rs.	Assets	Rs.
1000 Equity shares of Rs. 25 each, Rs. 15 paid up.	15,000	Buildings	15,000
1000, 6% Pref. shares of Rs. 10 each	10,000	Furnitures	6,000
Sundry creditors	30,000	Stock	9,000
		Debtors	8,000
		Cash	3,000
		Profit & Loss A/c	14,000
	55,000		55,000

(a) Of Sundry creditors Rs. 6,000 were preferential and creditors of Rs. 8,000 were secured by a charge over building.

(b) The assets were realised by the liquidator as follows :
Building Rs. 12,000, Furniture Rs. 4,500
Stock Rs. 7,900, S. Debtors Rs. 6,000, Cash Rs. 3,000.

(c) The liquidator is entitled to a commission of 2½% on the amount paid to the unsecured creditors and 2% on the amount realised.

(d) Liquidation expenses amounted to Rs. 600.

(e) Preference shareholders have priorities over equity shareholders to return of capital and dividend.

Prepare liquidators final statement of account.

(K.U.D., October 1990)

Solution :

Liquidator's Final Statement A/c

Particulars		Rs.	Particulars		Rs.
To Assets Realised :			By Liquidation expenses		600
Building	12,000		By Liquidators commission :		
Less : Paid to secured crs.	8,000	4,000	(a) 2½% on amount paid to unsecured credit (6,000 + 16,000) 22,000		550
To Furnitures		4,500	(b) 2% on amount realised		
To Stock		7,900	2% on 33,400	668	
To Debtors		6,000		172	840
To Cash		3,000	By Preferential creditors		6,000
To Calls on equity shares :			By Unsecured creditors		16,000
1000 shares @ 8.59		8,590	By Refund of share capital preference shareholders		10,000
		33,990			33,990

Working Notes

Assets Realised :		
Building		12,000
Furnitures		4,500
Stock		7,900
Debtors		6,000
Cash		3,000
		33,400
Cash in hand :		25,400
Less Cash paid :		
Liquidate exp.	600	
2½% commission	550	
2% on 33,400	668	
Pref. crs.	6,000	
Unsecured crs.	16,000	23,818
Cash balance left to pay pref. share capital		1,582
Pref. share capital		10,000
Less : Cash available		1,582
Deficit Amount		8,418

to be collected from equity shareholders + 2% commission payable to liquidators on amount collected.

Sundry creditors	30,000
Less : Preferential crs.	6,000
Less : Secured creditors	24,000
Charge on building	8,000
Unsecured creditors	16,000

(1) Commission on amount paid to Unsecured creditors :

(6,000 + 16,000) 22,000

2½% on 22,000 = Rs. 550

For amount required to pay pref. share capital 98% of 8,418

100 Gross amount to be collected

$$= 8{,}418 \times \frac{100}{98} = \text{Rs. } 8{,}590$$

Amount to be collected from equity shareholders	8,590
Less : 2% commission of liquidator	172
Amount required to pay pref. share capital	8,418
Add : Cash balance	1,582
	10,000

If the Gross Amount collected is 100 on this 2% liquidators commission payable.... Net amount is 100 – 2 = Rs. 98.

Amount required of Rs. 10,000.

Problem No. 22

The following was the Balance Sheet of Miniature Ltd. as on 31-12-1983 which went into voluntary liquidation :

Balance Sheet as at 31-12-1983

Liabilities	Rs.	Assets	Rs.
Share Capital :		Goodwill	50,000
1000, 10% pref. shares		Freehold property	48,000
of Rs. 100 each	1,00,000	Plant & Machinery	65,500
15000, equity shares of		Stock	56,800
Rs. 10 each, Rs. 8 paid up	1,20,000	Debtors	64,820
Sundry Creditors :		Cash	2,500
Preferential	24,000	Profit & Loss A/c	98,380
Partly secured	55,310		
Unsecured	86,690		
	3,86,000		3,86,000

The assets were realised by the liquidator as follows :

(a)	Freehold property which was used in the first instance to pay partly secured creditors (at pro-rata)	35,000
(b)	Plant & Machinery	51,000
(c)	Stock	39,000
(d)	Debtors	58,500
	Total	1,83,500

The expenses of liquidation amounted to Rs. 800.

The liquidator's remuneration was agreed 3% on the total assets realised (including cash on hand) and 2% on the amount paid to unsecured creditors. The preference shares Dividend was in arrears for one year. Prepare liquidators final statement of account.

(Gulbarga, 1984 & K.U.D., 1990)

Solution :

Liquidator's Final Statement of A/c

Particulars		Rs.	Particulars	Rs.
To *Assets Realised* :			By Liquidation exp.	800
Freehold property	35,000		By Liquidator's remuneration	
Less : Paid to partly secured creditors	35,000	—	3% Commission on assets realised (3% on 1,86,000)	5,580
To Plant & Machinery		51,000	By 2% Com. on amount paid to unsecured creditors including Pref. creditors (2% on 1,31,000)	2,620
To Stock		39,000	By Pref. creditors	24,000
To Debtors		58,500	By Unsecured creditors (see note-2)	1,07,000
To Cash		2,500	By Refund of capital	
To Calls on partly paid Equity shares (15000 × 2)		30,000	Pref. shares capital (1000 × 41)	41,000
Total		1,81,000	Total	1,81,000

Working Note-1

Cash in hand Assets Realised (1,51,000 + 35,000)		1,86,000
Less : *Cash paid*		
(1) Liquidation exp.	800	
(2) 3% com. on 1,86,000	5,580	
(3) Pref. creditors	24,000	
(4) Partly secured creditors	35,000	65,380
Cash available		1,20,620
Less : Paid commission 2% on 1,31,000		2,620
		1,18,000
Less : Paid to unsecured creditors		1,07,000
Amount available		11,000
Add : Calls equity shares (15000 × 2)		30,000
Amount available to pay Pref. Shares capital at pro-rata		41,000

$$\text{Pref. share} = \frac{41,000}{1000} = \text{Rs. } 41.$$

Working Note-2

Unsecured creditors		86,690
Partly secured	55,310	
Less : Paid	35,000	
Unsecured creditors		20,310
Total		1,07,000

Working Note-3

Calculation of commission on amount paid to unsecured creditors	1,07,000
Add : Pref. creditors	24,000
Total	1,31,000
Commission 2% on 1,31,000	2,620

Problem No. 23

The Hubli Co. Ltd. went into voluntary liquidation on 31st December 1988. Its Balance Sheet on that date was as under :

Balance Sheet as at 31-12-1988

Liabilities	Rs.	Assets	Rs.
Share capital :		Goodwill	20,000
10000 Equity share		Building	45,000
of Rs. 10 each, Rs. 8 paidup	80,000	Plant	50,000
Less Calls in arrears	2,000	Stock	4,300
	78,000	Debtors	13,850
Debentures	25,000	Cash	1,500
Preferential creditors	9,250	Profit & Loss A/c	56,850
Secured creditors (Secured on plant)	31,500		
Unsecured creditors	43,250		
Bank overdraft	4,500		
	1,91,500		1,91,500

The liquidator realised assets as under :

Building Rs. 21,150, Plant Rs. 24,000, Stock Rs. 5,200, Debtors Rs. 31,550, Liquidation expenses amounted to Rs. 215, liquidator's remuneration was agreed at 3% on the assets realised and 2% on the amount paid to unsecured creditors.

Prepare liquidators final statement of A/c.

(K.U.D., April 1989)

Solution :

Liquidator's Final Statement of Account

Particulars		Rs.	Particulars	Rs.
To Assets realised :			By Liquidation expenses	215
Building		21,250	By Liquidator's remuneration :	
Plant	24,000		3% commission on 64,000	1,920
Secured creditors	31,500		2% on 9,250	185
	7,500		2% on 26,402	528
To Balance uncovered treated as unsecured Creditors transferred			By Debentures	25,000
			By Preferential creditors	9,250
			By Unsecured creditors	26,402
Stock		5,200		
Debtors		13,550		
Cash		1,500		
Calls in arrears		2,000		
Calls on shares 10000 × 2		20,000		
		63,500		63,500

Working Note

Liquidators Commission :

Note : (1) 3% on assets realised

Building	21,250
Plant	24,000
Stock	5,200
Debtors	13,550
Excluding cash	64,000

Commission :

1. 3% on 64,000	1,920
2. 2% commission amount paid to unsecured pref. creditors (2% on 9,250)	185

Total Unsecured Creditors :

Bank overdraft	43,250
Add : Uncovered balance transferred	4,500
	7,500
Total unsecured creditors	55,250

Calculation of commission

Formula : $\text{Com.} = \frac{\%}{100+\%} \times \text{Amount}$

$= \frac{2}{102} \times 26{,}930 = \text{Rs. } 528$

Note (2) Amount paid :

Liquidation Exp.	215
3% commission	1,920
2% on 9,250	185
	2,320
Debentures	25,000
Pref. creditors	9,250
Total amount paid	36,570

(3) Cash in hand 43,500

(1) *Assets Realised*

Building	21,250
Stock	5,200
Debtors	13,550
Cash	1,500
Calls in Arrears	2,000
Add : Calls on shares 10000 × 2	20,000
Total Cash	63,500
Less : Cash paid	36,570
	26,930
Amount available to pay unsecured creditors	26,930
Plus 2% commission	26,930
$= \frac{2}{102} \times 26{,}930$	– 528
= 528	
Amount paid to unsecured creditors	26,402

Verification

Com. 2% on 26,402 = Rs. 528

Problem No. 24

The Luckless Ltd. went into voluntary liquidation on 31-12-1988, on which date dividend on the preference shares was in arrears for one year. The capital of the company consisted of :

(a) 1000, 8% preference shares of Rs. 10 each fully paid.

(b) 1000 equity shares of Rs. 10 each, Rs. 8 paid up.

(c) 2000 equity shares of Rs. 10 each, Rs. 7 paid up.

The assets realised Rs. 13,000.

The expenses of liquidation came to Rs. 400.

The liquidator is entitled to a fixed remuneration of Rs. 1,200 in all.

The unsecured creditors were Rs. 5,600 including Rs. 600 preferential creditors.

The preference shareholders have priority over equity shareholders with regard to payment of capital and dividend as provided in the article.

Prepare liquidator's final statement of account assuming that he made the necessary calls, which are duly received for payment to preference shareholders.

(K.U.D., October 1989)

Solution :

Liquidator's Final Statement of Account

Particulars	Rs.	Particulars	Rs.
To Assets realised	13,000	By Liquidation expenses	400
To Call on equity shares :		By Liquidator's remuneration	1,200
On 2000 share of Rs. 7 paid		By Preferential creditors	600
at Rs. 2 each	4,000	By Unsecured creditors	5,000
On 1000 share of Rs. 8		By Refund of capital to	
paid at Re. 1 each	1,000	preference shareholder	10,000
		By Arrears of dividend on	
		10000 at 8%	800
	18,000		18,000

Note :

Cash in hand	13,000
Less Paid	7,200
Cash left	5,800
Amount payable	10,800
Cash required	5,000

Amount payable to preference shareholders 10,000

Add Dividend 8% for one year 800 = 10,800.

Equity shareholders 1000 shares of Rs. 10 – 9 = 1000 × 1 – 1,000

2000 shares of Rs. 10 – 8 = 2000 × 2 = 4,000.

Problem No. 25

The Moon Ltd. went into voluntary liquidation on 31-3-1987, on which date its capital consisted of (1) 12000, 10% preference shares of Rs. 10 fully paid (2) 15000 equity shares of Rs. 10 each fully paid.

The assets realised Rs. 1,80,000.

Expenses of liquidation amounted to Rs. 11,200.

The liquidator's remuneration was fixed @ 4% commission on assets realised and 2% commission on the amount distributed to shareholders.

Unsecured creditors were Rs. 75,000.

Preferential creditors were Rs. 5,000.

Preferential shares carry preferential rights as to payments of capital.

Prepare liquidator's final statement of A/c.

(K.U.D., April 1988)

Solution :

Liquidator's Final Statement of Account

Particulars	Rs.	Particulars	Rs.
To Assets realised	1,80,000	By Liquidation expenses	11,200
		Liquidator's remuneration :	
		4% on 1,80,000 assets	7,200
		2% on 80000 preference share	1,600
		Preferential creditors	5,000
		Unsecured creditors	75,000
		Refund of capital pref. shareholders	80,000
	1,80,000		1,80,000

Problem No. 26

Following is the position of the company in liquidation on 1-1-1987 :

Share Capital :

3000, 5% preference shares of Rs. 100 each fully paid.

1000 equity share of Rs. 80 each fully paid.

2000 equity share of Rs. 80 each Rs. 50 paid.

6% debentures	1,50,000
Mortgage on building	40,000
Preferential creditors	10,000
Unsecured creditors	90,000
Assets realised :	
Building	1,25,000
Bank	30,000
Other assets	5,15,000

Preference dividend was in arrears for one year. The preference share have priority over equity share as regards capital and dividend.

The cost of winding up come to Rs. 3,000.

The liquidator is entitled to a commission of Rs. 6,000 plus 5% on the amount paid to unsecured creditors.

All payments were made on 1-9-1987.

Prepare liquidator's final statement of account.

(K.U.D., October 1988)

Solution :

Liquidator's Final Statement of Account on 1-9-1987

Particulars		Rs.	Particulars	Rs.
To Assets realised :			By Cost of winding up	3,000
Building	1,25,000		By Liquidator's commission	6,000
Less Mortgage on building (secured crs.)	40,000	85,000	5% on (10,000+90,000) 1,00,000 unsecured credit	5,000
Bank		30,000	6% Debentures	1,50,000
Other assets		5,15,000	Interest on debit upto 1-9-87 on 1,50,000 × 6% for 12 months for 8 months	6,000
			Preferential creditors	10,000
			Unsecured creditors	90,000
			Refund of capital : Preference capital	3,00,000
			Dividend 5% on 3,00,000	15,000
			Refund of capital Equity shareholders	
			1000 × 35	35,000
			2000 × 5	10,000
		6,30,000		6,30,000

Working Note

Cash in hand		6,30,000
Less : Cash paid		5,85,000
Cash left to pay		45,000
Equity shareholders 1000 × 80 =	80,000	
2000 × 50 =	1,00,000	1,80,000
Deficiency		1,35,000

Deficiency is shared by equity shareholders 1000 + 2000 = 3000

Deficiency per share = 1,35,000/3000 = Rs. 45 per share (loss)

Equity shares 1000 shares Rs. 80 paid – 45 deficiency = Rs. 35 refund.

2000 shares paid Rs. 50 – 45 = Rs. 5 refund.

Problem No. 27

Unlucky Ltd. went into voluntary liquidation on 31-12-1986 on which date dividend on preference shares were in arrears for one year.

The subscribed capital of the Co. consisted of :

(a) 15000, 10% preference shares of Rs. 10 each fully paid.

(b) 24000 equity shares of Rs. 10 each, Rs. 5 per share paid up.

The assets realised Rs. 1,40,000.

The expenses of liquidation amounted to Rs. 4,250.

The liquidator is entitled to a commission of 2% on the assets realised and 3% on the amount distributed to preference shareholders as capital and dividend.

The liquidator has paid the liabilities of Rs. 23,000.

Prepare liquidator's final statement of account.

(K.U.D., April 1987)

Solution :

Liquidator's Final Statement of Account

Particulars	Rs.	Particulars	Rs.
To Assets realised	1,40,000	By Liquidation exp.	4,250
To Calls made on 24000 Equity shares @ Rs. 2.50	60,000	By Liquidators commission :	
		2% on 1,40,000 assets	2,800
		3% on 1,65,000	4,950
		By Liabilities	23,000
		By Preferences share capital	1,50,000
		By Dividend @ Rs. 10 on 1,50,000	15,000
	2,00,000		2,00,000

Note :

	Rs.
Cash in hand	1,40,000
Less : Paid	30,050
Cash Balance	1,09,950

	Rs.
Cash required to pay Pref. Share Capital	1,50,000
Add Dividend for one year @ 10%	15,000
	1,65,000
Add 3% Commission on 1,65,000	4,950
Total Amount required	1,69,950
Less Cash Balance	1,09,950
Amount required be collected from Equity Shareholders	60,000

$$\frac{\text{Rs. } 60,000}{24,000} = \text{Per Share Rs. 2.50 Call is to be made}$$

Problem No. 28

Binny Ltd. went into voluntary liquidation on 31-12-1985. The Balance of the company on that date was as follows :

Balance Sheet as on 31-12-1985

Liabilities	Rs.	Assets	Rs.
Share Capital :		*Fixed Assets*	2,00,000
3000 Equity shares of		Investment	1,00,000
Rs. 10 each, Rs. 8 paid up	2,40,000	Stock	78,000
Calls in advance	4,000	Debtors	22,000
Sundry Creditors :		Cash	11,380
(a) Secured against building	80,000	Profit & Loss A/c	88,620
(b) Preferential	12,600		
(c) Unsecured	1,63,400		
	5,00,000		5,00,000

The assets were realised as follows :

(1) Fixed assets realised Rs. 1,85,000 (including building Rs. 85,000)

(2) Stock Rs. 60,000

(3) Investment Rs. 1,20,000

(4) Debtors Rs. 20,000

(5) Remuneration to liquidator :

(a) 2% on the amount realised (except cash in hand).

(b) 1% on the amount paid to unsecured creditor.

(c) 2% on the amount paid to shareholders

Prepare liquidator's final statement of account.

(K.U.D., April 1986)

Solution :

Liquidator's Final Statement of Account

Particulars		Rs.	Particulars		Rs.
To Assets realised :			By Calls in advance		4,000
Fixed assets	1,85,000		By *Liquidator's Remuneration :*		
Less : Building	85,000	1,00,000	(a) 2% on 3,05,000	6,100	
Building	85,000		(b) 1% on 1,76,000	1,760	
Less : Secured crs.	80,000		(c) 2% on 1,26,000	2,520	10,380
Surplus		5,000	By Pref. creditors		12,600
Stock		60,000	By Unsecured creditors		1,63,400
Investments		1,20,000	By Refund to share-		
Debtors		20,000	holders capital		1,26,000
Cash		11,380			
Total		3,16,380			3,16,380

Note : Calculation of liquidator's remuneration :

(a) 2% on amount realised (except cash in hand)

Amount realised :	
Fixed assets	1,00,000
Surplus from :	
Secured creditors	5,000
Stock	60,000
Investments	1,20,000
Debtors	20,000
	3,05,000
Amount realised	3,05,000
Commission @ 2%	6,100

(b) Commission @ 1% on amount paid to unsecured creditors :

Preferential creditors	12,600
Unsecured creditors	1,63,400
	1,76,000
Commission @ 1% 1,76,000 =	1,760

(c) Commission @ 2% on amount paid to shareholder :

Cash in hand	Rs.	3,16,380
Less : Paid :		
(1) Calls in advance	4,000	
(2) Commission @ 2%	6,100	
Commission @ 1%	1,760	
(3) Preferential creditors	12,600	
(4) Unsecured creditors	1,63,400	1,87,860
Amount available to pay shareholders		1,28,520

This amount included liquidator's commission @ 2% on amount paid to shareholders.

Commission = 2/102 × 1,28,520 =		2,520
Gross amount available	Rs. 1,28,520	
Less : Commission @ 2%	2,520	
Amount paid to shareholders	1,26,000	
Commission @ 2% on 1,26,000 =	2,520.	

Problem No. 29

X Co. Ltd. went into voluntary liquidation on 31-12-1985. The following are the particulars provided by the company :

	Rs.
1500 equity shares of Rs. 100 each, Rs. 75 paid	1,12,500
750 equity shares of Rs. 100 each, Rs. 60 paid	45,000
Unsecured creditors	3,60,000
Secured creditors (Security on plant)	1,50,000
Preferential creditors	30,000
The liquidator's realised assets as under :	
Cash	15,000
Stock	90,000
Land & Building	3,00,000
Plant	2,10,000

The liquidator expenses amounted to Rs. 4,200. The liquidator is entitled to a commission @ 3% on the assets realised (excluding cash) and 2% on the amount paid to unsecured creditors.

Prepare liquidator's final statement of account.

(K.U.D., October 1986)

Solution :

Liquidator's Final Statement of Account

Particulars		Rs.	Particulars	Rs.
To Assets Realised :			By Liquidator's exp.	4,200
Cash		15,000	By Liquidator's commission :	
Stock		90,000	(a) @ 3% on 6,00,000	18,000
Land & Building		3,00,000	(b) @ 2% on 3,90,000	7,800
Plant	2,10,000		By Preferential creditors	30,000
Less : Secured crs.	1,50,000	60,000	By Unsecured creditors	3,60,000
			Refund of Capital :	
			1500 equity @ Rs. 25	37,500
			750 equity @ Rs. 10	7,500
Total		4,65,000		4,65,000

Note : Calculations :

Cash in hand		4,65,000
Less : Cash paid :		
(1) Liquidation Exp.	4,200	
(2) Commission	25,800	
(3) Unsecured crs. (30,000+3,60,000)	3,90,000	4,20,000
Cash left to pay shareholder		45,000

There are two types of equity shareholders having same face value but, different paid up value :

(a) 1500 equity shares of Rs. 100 each, Rs. 75 paid up	1,12,500
(b) 750 equity shares of Rs. 100 each, Rs. 60 paid up	45,000
Total amount payable	1,57,500
Less : Cash available	45,000
Deficiency	1,12,500

Method : (A) *Equalisation of rights of shareholders*

In such cases it is advised to equalise the right of shareholders of two types.

1500 equity shares of Rs. 100 each paid Rs. 75 more than the other shareholder who paid only Rs. 60. The excess amount paid by first type shareholders i.e., (75–60) = Rs. 15 per share be refunded *i.e.*, 1500 × 15 = 22,500.

Now both the type of shareholders paid up value is Rs. 60 per share. The balance amount of Rs. 22,500 (45,000 – 22,500) be distributed among both type of shareholders i.e., 1500 + 750 = 2250 shareholder

$$\text{Balance amount Rs. } \frac{22{,}500}{2{,}250} = \text{Rs. 10 per shareholder}$$

Now total amount paid to :

1500 equity shareholders Rs. 25 (15+10)	37,500
750 equity shareholders Rs. 10	7,500
Total	45,000

Method : (B) *Total Deficiency Method*

Total amount required to pay shareholders :

(1) 1500 equity shares of Rs. 100 each at Rs. 75	1,12,500
(2) 750 equity shares of Rs. 100 each at Rs. 60	45,000
Total amount required	1,57,500
Cash in hand	45,000
Total deficiency	1,12,500

The amount of deficiency Rs. 1,12,500 is shared by equity shareholders = 1,500 + 750 = 2,250

$$\text{Deficiency per share} = \frac{\text{Total deficiency}}{\text{No. of shares}}$$

$$= \frac{1{,}12{,}500}{2{,}250}$$

$$= \text{Rs. 50 per share loss.}$$

(1) 1500 equity shares of Rs. 75 each paid up loss Rs. 50.
Rs. 25 per share refund.
Refund = 1500 × 25 = Rs. 37,500

(2) 750 equity shares of Rs. 60 each paid up loss = Rs. 50.
Rs. 10 per share refund.
Refund 750 × 10 = Rs. 7,500

Total capital refund :

1500 × 25 = Rs.	37,500
750 × 10 = Rs.	7,500
Total Rs.	45,000

Problem No. 30

The Mody Co. Ltd. went into voluntary liquidation on 1-1-1984. The subscribed capital of the company on that was as follows :

(a) 100000, 6% preference share of Rs. 10 each fully paid which were preferential both as regards capital and dividend.

(b) 200000 equity shares of Rs. 10 each, Rs. 6.25 per share paid up.

(c) 150000 equity shares of Rs. 10 each, Rs. 7.50 per share paid up.

(1) Assets were realised for Rs. 26,27,500.

(2) Cost and liquidation amounted to Rs. 1,15,000.

(3) Liabilities amounted to Rs. 22,00,000.

Prepare liquidator's final statement of account.

(Gulbarga, 1990; April 1991)

Solution :

Liquidator's Final Statement of Account

Particulars	Rs.	Particulars	Rs.
To Assets realised	26,27,500	By Cost of liquidation	1,15,000
To Calls on equity shares :		By Liabilities	22,00,000
200000 × 2.50	5,00,000	By Refund of capital	
150000 × 1.25	1,87,500	preference shareholders	10,00,000
Total	33,15,000		33,15,000

Note : Cash in hand		26,27,500
Less : Cash paid :		
Cost of liquidation	1,15,000	
Liabilities	22,00,000	23,15,000
Cash in hand		3,12,500
Amount payable to pref. shareholders		10,00,000
Amount required to pay pref. shareholders		6,87,500

Amount required to pay :

(1) Pref. shareholders	6,87,500
(2) Equity shareholders	
200000 × 6.25	12,50,000
150000 × 7.50	11,25,000
Total deficiency	30,62,500

$$\text{Deficiency per share} = \frac{30,62,500}{3,50,000}$$

$$= 8.75$$

Deficiency per share Rs. 8.75 i.e. loss per share is to be shared by equity shareholders.

200000 equity shares of Rs. 10 each paid	Rs. 6.25
Less : Loss	Rs. 8.75
is to be called	Rs. 2.50

Calls on 200000 × 2.50 = Rs. 5,00,000

150000 equity shares of Rs. 10 each	Rs. 7.50 paid
Less : Loss	Rs. 8.75
is to be called	Rs. 1.25

Calls on 150000 × 1.25 = Rs. 1,87,500

Total calls on

200000 × 2.50 =	Rs. 5,00,000
150000 × 1.25 =	Rs. 1,87,500
Total	Rs. 6,87,500

Problem No. 31

X Co. Ltd. went into voluntary liquidation on 31-12-1983. The following was the position of the company.

Balance Sheet as at 31-12-1983

Liabilities	Rs.	Assets	Rs.
Share Capital :		Goodwill	30,000
14550 shares of Rs. 10 each	1,45,500	Land & Building	25,000
Preferential creditors	4,000	Sundry assets	1,42,120
Partly secured creditors	29,180	Cash at Bank	500
Unsecured creditors	79,160	Profit & Loss A/c	61,380
Bank overdraft (Unsecured)	1,160	(Debit balance)	
	2,59,000		2,59,000

The liquidators realised the assets as follows :

(1) Land and Building which was used to pay first partly secured creditors at pro-rata	18,000
(2) Sundry assets	99,500
(3) Cash at Bank	500
Total	Rs. 1,18,000

The expenses of liquidation 1,170

The liquidator's remuneration :

2½% on amount realised and 2% on amount paid unsecured creditors.

Prepare liquidator's final statement of account.

(K.U.D., April 1985)

Liquidator's Final Statement of Account

Particulars		Rs.	Particulars	Rs.
To Assets realised :			By Liquidators expenses	1,170
Land & Building	18,000		By Liquidator's commission :	
Partly secured			(a) 2½% on 1,18,000	2,950
Creditors	29,180		(b) 2% on 4,000	80
Unsecured balance	11,180		(c) 2% on 90,000	1,800
transferred to			By Preferntial creditors	4,000
unsecured crs.			By Unsecured creditors	90,000
To Sundry assets		99,500		
To Cash at Bank		500		
Total		1,00,000	Total	1,00,000

Cash in hand		1,00,000	Unsecured creditors	79,160
Less : Paid	1,170		Bank overdraft	1,160
	2,950		Partly secured creditors	
	80		(Uncovered Balance)	11,180
	4,000	8,200		
Cash left to pay unsecured creditors		91,800		91,500

This amount of Rs. 91,800 includes the amount of commission @ 2%.

$$\therefore \text{Commission} = \frac{\%}{100 + \%} \times \text{Amount.}$$

$$= \frac{2}{102} \times 91,800 = 1,800 \text{ commission.}$$

	Rs.
Cash available =	91,800
Less : 2% commission	1,800
	90,000

Cash left to pay unsecured creditors is less than the actual amount payable to unsecured creditors 91,500.

Problem No. 32

Shaky Co. Ltd. went into voluntary liquidation on 31-12-1983 on which date dividend on preference shares was in arrears for one year. The subscribed capital of the company consisted of :

(a) 30000, 10% preference shares of Rs. 10 each fully paid.

(b) 48000 equity shares of Rs. 10 each Rs. 5 per share paid up.

The assets realised Rs. 2,80,000.

The expenses of liquidation Rs. 8,500.

The liquidator's commission :

@ 2% on assets realised and

@ 3% on amount distributed to preference shareholders as capital and dividend.

The liquidator's paid liabilities Rs. 46,000.

Prepare liquidator's final statement of accounts.

(K.U.D., April 1984)

Solution :

Liquidator's Final Statement of Account

Particulars	Rs.	Particulars		Rs.
To Assets realised	2,80,000	By Liquidation exp.		8,500
To Calls on shares	1,20,000	By Liquidation commission :		
(48000 × 2.50)		(a) 2% on 2,80,000		5,600
		(b) 3% on 3,30,000		9,900
		By Liabilities		46,000
		By refund pref. shareholders :		
		Capital	3,00,000	
		Dividend	30,000	3,30,000
	4,00,000			4,00,000

Cash in hand		2,80,000
Less : paid	8,500	
	5,600	
	9,900	
	46,000	70,000
		2,10,000
Cash left to pay pref. shareholders		3,60,000
Amount required		1,20,000

Amount required to pay pref. shareholders is collected from partly paid equity shareholders 1,20,000

$$\frac{1,20,000}{48000} = 2.50 \text{ per share}$$

$48000 \times 2.50 =$ Rs. 1,20,000

Problem No. 33

The following particulars related to the Bad Luck Co. Ltd. which went into voluntary liquidation on 31-12-1982 :

Particulars	Rs.
4000, 8% preference shares of Rs. 100 each	4,00,000
2000 equity shares of Rs. 100 each, Rs. 75 paid	1,50,000
6000 equity shares of Rs. 100 each, Rs. 60 paid	3,60,000
5% debentures (having floating charge) on all assets	2,00,000
Creditors	2,90,000
The liquidator realised to the assets as follows :	
Land and Building	2,40,000
Plant and Machinery	4,00,000
Patents	60,000
Stock	1,20,000
Debtors	1,60,000

The dividend on preference shares was in arrears for two years which was to be paid on liquidation as per the Articles of the company. The interest on debentures was due for the year 1982.

The creditors include Rs. 1,00,000 loan on mortgage of Land and Building and Rs. 30,000 preferential creditors.

The expenses of liquidation amounted to Rs. 19,800.

The liquidator is entitled to a commission @ 5% on the assets realised and 2% on the amount distributed among the creditors.

All the payments were made on 30-6-1983.

Prepare liquidator's final statement of accounts.

(Gulbarga, April 1984)

Solution :

Liquidator's Final Statement of Account on 30-6-1983

Particulars		Rs.	Particulars		Rs.
To Assets realised :			By Liquidator's expenses		19,800
Land & Building	2,40,000		By Liquidator remuneration		
Less : Paid to			Commission :		
Secured Crs.	1,00,000	1,40,000	(a) 5% on 9,80,000		49,000
To Plant & Machinery		4,00,000	(b) 2% on 2,90,000		5,800
To Patents		60,000	By Preferential creditors		30,000
To Stock		1,20,000	By Debentures	2,00,000	
To Debtors		1,60,000	*Add* : Interest for		
To Calls on equity shares			6 months		
6000 × 11.70		70,200	5% on 2,00,000		
			(10,000 + 5,000)	15,000	2,15,000
			By Unsecured		
			creditors	2,90,000	
			Less : Secured crs.	1,00,000	
				1,90,000	
			Less : Pref. crs.	30,000	1,60,000
			By Refund of capital :		
			Pref. shareholders		
			capital	4,00,000	
			Dividend (32,000×2)	64,000	4,64,000
			By Refund to equity share-		
			holders (2,000×3.30)		6,600
Total		9,50,200			9,50,200

Note : Calculations :

	Commission on assets realised		
(a)	Commission @ 5% on 9,80,000		49,000
(b)	Commission @ 2% on 2,90,000		5,800
	Cash in hand		8,80,000
	Less : Paid 1	19,800	
	2	49,000	
	3	5,800	
	4	30,000	
	5	2,05,000	
	6	1,60,000	
		4,79,600	4,79,600
	Cash Balance left to pay Pref. Share Capital & Dividend		4,00,400

Cash left to pay Pref. Shareholders	4,00,400
Less Preference share capital & dividend	4,64,000
Deficiency	63,600
Cash payable to equity shareholders :	
2000 × 75	1,50,000
6000 × 60	3,60,000
Amount payable	5,10,000
Total Deficiency :	
Payable to preference shares	63,600
Payable to equity shares	+5,10,000
Total deficiency	5,73,000

Shared by Total No. of equity shares =

$$\frac{5,73,600}{8,000} = \text{Rs. } 71.70 \text{ Loss per share.}$$

2000 – 100 – 75 (loss) 71.70 = Refund = Rs. 3.30

6000 – 100 – 60 – (loss) 71.70 = calls to be made Rs. 11.70

Calls on shares :

6000 × 11.70	Rs. 70,200
Less : Paid to preference shares	63,600
Balance refund to 2000 equity shares	
2000 × 3.30 = Rs. 6,600 refund.	6,600

Problem No. 34

Unlucky Co. Ltd. went into voluntary liquidation when its liabilities were as under :

Secured creditors	2,00,000
Preferential creditors	40,000
Unsecured creditors	50,000

The liquidator realised Rs. 2,50,000 from the securities hold by secured creditors and Rs. 60,000 from other assets, cash in hand amounted to Rs. 11,000.

The cost of liquidation amounted to Rs. 19,900 and the liquidator's remuneration was fixed @ 3% on the assets realised and 2% on the amount distributed to unsecured creditors (including preferential creditors).

Prepare liquidator's final statement of account.

(K.U.D., April 1983)

Solution :

Liquidator's Final Statement of Account

Particulars		Rs.	Particulars	Rs.
To Assets realised :			By Cost of liquidation	19,900
Securities	2,50,000		By Liquidator's remuneration :	
Less : Secured			(a) 3% com. on 3,10,000	9,300
creditors	2,00,000		(b) 2% on pref.	
			creditors 40,000	800
Surplus		50,000	(c) 2% on unsecured	
			creditors 50,000	1,000
Other assets		60,000	By Pref. creditors	40,000
Cash		11,000	By Unsecured creditors	50,000
		1,21,000		1,21,000

Calculation of Commission :

3% on assets realised :	
Securities	2,50,000
Other assets	60,000
Total assets	3,10,000

3% on 3,10,000 = 9,300

2% on pref. crs. = 800

Cash in hand		1,21,000
Less : Paid	19,900	
	9,300	
	800	
	30,000	
Pref. crs.	40,000	70,000
Cash left to pay		51,000

Unsecured creditors of 50,000 includes 2% commission = 1,000 (2/100 × 50,000)

Cash	51,000
Less : Commission	1,000
	50,000

Problem No. 35

The following particulars related to Goodluck Co. Ltd. which went into voluntary liquidation on 31-12-1982 :

4000, 8% preference shares of Rs. 100 each	4,00,000
2000 equity shares of Rs. 100 each, Rs. 75 paid up	1,50,000
6000 equity shares of Rs. 100 each, Rs. 60 paid up	3,60,000
5% debentures (having folding on all assets)	2,00,000
Creditors	2,90,000

The liquidator realised assets as follows :

Land and Building	2,40,000

Plant and Machinery	4,00,000
Patents	60,000
Stock	1,20,000
Debtors	1,60,000

The dividend on preference shares was in arrears for two years which was to be paid on liquidation as per Articles of the company. The interest on debentures was due for the year 1982. The creditors includes Rs. 1,00,000 loan on mortgage of Land & Building.

Preferential creditors Rs. 30,000.

The liquidator's expenses amounted to Rs. 19,800.

The liquidator is entitled to a commission @ 5% on the assets realised and 2% on the amount distributed to creditors.

All payments were made on 30-6-1983.

Prepare liquidator's final statement of accounts.

(Gulbarga, April 1982)

Solution :

Liquidator's Final Statement of Account

Particulars		Rs.	Particulars		Rs.
To Assets realised :			By Liquidation expenses		19,800
Land & Building	2,40,000		By Liqudation Commission :		
Less : Secured crs.	1,00,000		@ 5% on 9,80,000		49,000
Surplus		1,40,000	@ 2% on 2,90,000		5,800
Plant & Machinery		4,00,000	By Preferential creditors		30,000
Patents		60,000	By Debenture-holders :		
Stock		1,20,000	@ 5% Debentures	2,00,000	
Debtors		1,60,000	*Add* : Interest		
Calls on equity shares			for ½ year	15,000	2,15,000
6,000 × 11.70		70,200	By Creditors	2,90,000	
			Less : Secured	1,00,000	
				1,90,000	
			Less : Pref. Crs.	30,000	1,60,000
			By Refund of capital		
			Pref. shares	4,00,000	
			Dividend for 1982	64,000	4,64,000
			By Refund of capital :		
			Equity shareholder		
			2000 × 3.30		6,600
Total		9,50,200			9,50,200

Note : Calculation of liquidator's commission :

	Rs.
(1) @ 5% on Assets realised :	
Land and Building	2,40,000
Plant & Machinery	4,00,000
Patents	60,000
Stock	1,20,000
Debtors	1,60,000
Total Assets	9,80,000
Commission 5% on 9,80,000 = Rs. 49,000	
(2) 2% on amount paid to creditors :	
Creditors	2,90,000
Commission @ 2% on 2,90,000	5,800
(3) Creditors	2,90,000
Less : Secured creditors	1,00,000
	1,90,000
Less : Preferential creditors	30,000
Unsecured creditors	1,60,000
(4) Cash in hand	+ 8,80,000
Less : Payments	4,79,600
Cash Balance Left	4,00,400
Pref. Share Capital & Dividend Deficit	4,64,000
	63,600

Amount payable to shareholders :

2000 equity share @ Rs. 75 each (2000 × 75)	1,50,000
6000 equity shares @ Rs. 60 each (6000 × 60)	3,60,000
Total	5,10,000
Add : Amount required	63,600
Total deficit	5,73,600

Deficit per share – $\frac{5,73,600}{8000}$ = 71.70 Loss per share.

Equity shares of Rs. 100 each paid up.

2000 × 75 = Loss Rs. 71.70 = 3.30 Refund.

6000 × 60 = Loss Rs. 71.70 = 11.70 is to be called (calls be made).

Note :

Calls on shares : 6000 × 11.70 =	70,200
Less : Refund 2000 × 3.30 =	6,600
Amount required [see note No. (4)]	Rs. 63,600

Problem No. 36

Poona Co. Ltd. went into voluntary liquidation on 1-1-1978 on which date dividend on preference shares were in arrears for three years. The following is the position of the company :

Liabilities	Rs.
Share Capital	
6000 equity shares of Rs. 100 each Rs. 50 per share paid	3,00,000
3000 6% preference shares of Rs. 100 each fully paid	3,00,000
Liabilities :	
Secured Loan against machinery	30,000
Unsecured creditors	70,000
Preferential creditors	8,100
Bills payable	40,000
Assets Realised :	
Machinery	70,000
Other Assets	3,44,000

The liquidation expenses and legal expenses amounted to Rs. 30,000 and Rs. 1,000 respectively. The liquidator is entitled to a remuneration of Rs. 1,20,000 and a commission of 5% on the amount paid to the preference shareholder as capital and dividend and 5% commission on the amount collected by him from equity shareholders.

Prepare liquidator's final statement of account.

(K.U.D., October 1978)

Solution :

Liquidator's Final Statement Account

Particulars	Rs.	Particulars		Rs.
To Assets realised :		By Liquidation :		
Machinery 70,000		Expenses		3,000
Less : Secured Crs. 30,000		Legal expenses		1,000
Surplus	40,000	By Liquidator's remuneration		12,000
Other assets	3,44,000	(a) 5% commission 3,54,000		17,700
Calls on equity shares		(b) 5% comm.4,19,000 20,700		
amount collected		5% comm. 1,50,000 7,500		28,200
6000 × 25	1,50,000	By Preferential creditors		8,100
		Unsecured creditors		70,000
		Bills payable		40,000
		By Refund of capital pref.		
		shareholders Capital	3,00,000	
		Dividend for 3 years		
		6% on 3,00,000		
		(18,000 × 3)	54,000	3,54,000
Total	5,34,000			5,34,000

Cash in hand		3,84,000
Less : Paid	3,000	
	1,000	
	12,000	
	17,700	
	8,100	
	70,000	
	40,000	
Add 5% Comm. on Assets Realised 4,14,000	20,700	1,72,500
Cash left to pay		2,11,500
Pref. share capital & dividend		3,54,000
Deficiency	(95%)	1,42,500
Add : 5% commission	(5%)	—
	(100%)	?

If Rs. 100 is collected, 5% commission be paid and 95 paid preferential shares capital and dividend.

Amount required to collect from shareholders.

$$1{,}42{,}500 \times \frac{100}{95} = 1{,}50{,}000$$

Amount collected	1,50,000
Commission 5%	7,500
Amount of Deficiency	1,42,500

Amount to be collected Rs. from shareholders $\dfrac{1{,}50{,}000}{6000}$ = Rs. 25 per share

Total Commission —

On amount Realised (Assets)

5% on 4,14,000 = 20,700

On amount collected from

Shareholders 5% on 1,50,000 = 7,500

Total Commission 28,200

4

Holding Company Accounts

Meaning

Holding Company is one which directly or indirectly acquires either all or more than half the number of shares in one or more companies which are known as subsidiary companies.

There cannot be Holding company without a subsidiary company according to section 4 of Companies Act 1956.

A company is a subsidiary of another company if the other company :

(a) Controls the composition of its Board of Directors, or

(b) Holds more than half in nominal value of its cquity shares capital.

Or

Eg.

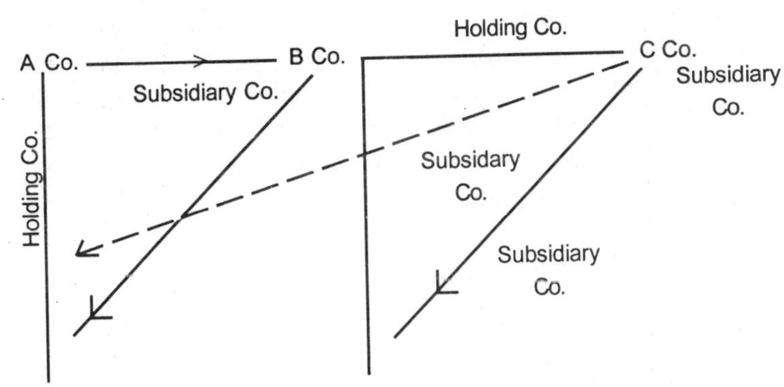

Note :

A Co. is a holding company of B Company – B Company is a subsidiary to A Company.

B Company is a holding company of C Company – C Company is a subsidiary to B Co. & A Co.

A Company is a holding company of B Co. & C Co.

Preparation of consolidated Balance sheet of Holding Co. and its subsidiary company :

(1) Date of Balance sheets – The date of Balance sheet of Holding company and Subsidiary company should be the same.

(2) Aggregation of assets and liabilities – All the assets and liabilities of the subsidiary company shall be added up to the figures of holding company.

In doing so the following points be remembered :

(a) Revaluation of Assets of subsidiary company (increase or decrease in the value of assets be treated as capital profit or capital loss).

(b) Inter company transactions resulting in profit, the purchase and sale of goods between holding company and subsidiary company and the profit earned by the selling company on goods sold.

In the closing stocks of purchasing company includes goods purchased from another company (selling company) the profit on unsold stocks, be treated as *unrealised profit* of the selling company and the closing stocks of purchasing company, be deducted.

(c) Eliminate mutual indebtedness such as amounts due to holding company and due from subsidiary company and *vice versa*.

Debtors (Asset side)	*Creditors (Liability side)*
Included due from holding Co./ subsidiary company deduct such amount from debtors.	Included due to subsidiary company/holding company deduct such amount from creditors.
Similarly bills receivable the amount of bills in hand be deducted from bills receivable	Bills payable the amount of bills in hand be deducted from bills payable.

(d) Share capital of the holding company be shown as it is.

(e) Share capital and undistributed profits such as General Reserve Profit & Loss A/c (Cr. Bal.) of the subsidiary company :

(a) Share of holding company is to be calculated.

(b) and also share of out side shareholder i.e. minority shareholders. Known as minority interest.

Ascertainment of share of holding company in the share capital and undistributed profit of subsidiary company. In doing so we can divide the figures – as (a) prior to acquisition & (b) after acquisition, of such amount, the share of holding company will be treated as capital gain and transferred to capital reserve.

Revaluation of Assets of subsidiary company : If the assets of subsidiary company is revalued – i.e. under valuation of assets shown in Balance sheet, it means the value of such assets is increased by the amount of undervalued, i.e. increase in the value of asset is a capital profit and transferred capital reserve similarly. Over valuation of assets mean decrease in the value of assets i.e. capital loss and the share of holding company is to be deducted from capital reserve.

Goodwill or Cost of Control

It is the excess of cost price of shares in subsidiary company over its nominal value. Excess paid is treated payment towards goodwill. If this goodwill amount is more than the capital reserve (share of holding company in the undistributed profit prior to acquisition), the capital reserve shown on liability side be deducted from goodwill and *vice versa*.

Undistributed profits — General Reserve Profit & Loss A/c (Credit Balance), Share of holding company be treated as capital profit & capital reserve and after acquisition – Current – General Reserve Current – Profit.

The following working table will show the above figures.

Working Table

Particulars	Total	Holding Company	Minority Interest
Ratio		80% 4/5 or 75% 3/4	20% 1/5 25% 1/4
(1) Share Capital (Subsidiary Co.)	—	—	—
(2) General Reserve as per B/s :			
(a) Prior to acquisition			
Bal. + Up to date of acquisition	—	CR	—
(b) After acquisition	—	—	—
(3) Profit & Loss A/c (as per B/s) :			
(a) Prior to acquisition			
Bal. + Up to date of acquisition	—	CR	—
(b) After acquisition			
Total miniority interest			

Capital Reserve : Minority interest as above

Share of holding company in subsidiary company

In general reserve Marked as CR above

and profit and loss

Assets overvalued deducted from Capital Reserve (–)

(Capital loss)

Undervalued Add to CR +

Capital Gain Net CR

Capital Reserve

General Reserve and Profit and Loss accounts (Cr. Balance) of subsidiary company the share of Holding Co.

If the Balance sheet of subsidiary company shows General Reserve and Profit & Loss Accounts (Credit balance) before the date of acquisition.

Proforma

Consolidated Balance Sheet of Holding Company and its Subsidiary Company as at....

Liabilities	Rs.	Assets	Rs.
(1) *Share Capital*		*Goodwill*	
H. Co.		Or *Cost of control*	
Preference shares of Rs.		Cost price of shares in S. Co.	
Equity shares of Rs.		Nominal value	
(2) *Reserves & Surplus*		Excess paid treated as Goodwill	
(a) General Reserve H. Co.		Deduct capital reserve	
S. Co.		(per contra)	
(b) *Capital Reserve*		*Add* Goodwill in B/s : H. Co.	
Share of H. Co. in the		S. Co.	
undistributed profits of		Total *Goodwill*	
S. Co. prior to acquisition		*Building* : H. Co.	
deducted from goodwill		S. Co.	
(per contra)		Undervalued Add to Assets	
(c) Profit & Loss A/c H. Co.		*Machinery* : H. Co.	
Share in S. Co.		S. Co.	
Total		Overvalued less	
Less Unrealised profit		*Investments*	
(3) *Secured Loan*		In shares in S. Co.	
Debentures : H. Co.		(as above)	
S. Co.		Debentures S. Co.	
Less Held by H. Co./S. Co.		*Less* Held by H. Co.	
(4) *Unsecured Loan*		Stock : H. Co.	
H. Co.		S. Co.	
S. Co.		*Less* Unrealised profit	
(5) *Current Liabilities*		*Debtors* : H. Co.	
H. Co.		S. Co.	
S. Co.		Deduct due from	
Deduct due to		Bills receivable : H. Co.	
(6) *Bills payable*		S. Co.	
H. Co.		Deduct due from	
S. Co.		Cash at Banks	
Less Bills due to		H. Co.	
(only amount of bills in hand)		S. Co.	
(7) *Minority Interest*			
Share of minority			
Share capital			
General Reserve,			
Profit & Loss			
Total		Total	

Problem No. 1

From the Balance Sheets as on 31-12-1997, and the information given below, prepare the Consolidated Balance Sheet of H. Ltd. with its Subsidiary S Ltd. as on 31-12-1997.

Balance Sheets as at 31-12-1997

Liabilities	H Ltd. Rs.	S Ltd. Rs.	Assets	H Ltd. Rs.	S Ltd. Rs.
Share Capital			Goodwill	50,000	1,00,000
Shares of Rs. 100 each	30,000	2,00,000	Building	1,00,000	75,000
Reserves & Surplus			Machinery	50,000	50,000
Profit & Loss A/c			Investment		
Balance 1-1-97	35,000	30,000	1500 Shares in S Ltd.	1,80,000	—
Profit for the year	50,000	45,000	Govt. Securtities	25,000	30,000
General Reserve	30,000	20,000	Stock	75,000	37,500
Secured Loan			Debtors	1,00,000	60,000
12 Debentures	1,00,000	87,500	Bills Receivable	—	10,000
Current Liabilities			Cash at Bank	10,000	20,000
Creditors	60,000	—			
Bills payable	15,000	—			
	5,90,000	3,82,500		5,90,000	3,82,500

Information :

(a) H Ltd. acquired the shares in S Ltd. on 1-5-1997

(b) The General Reserve of S Ltd. on 1-1-1997 was Rs. 17,000

(c) Bills Receivable of S Ltd. were all accepted by H Ltd.

(d) The Debtors of S Ltd. induded the amount of Rs. 10,000 for the supply of goods to H Ltd.

(e) The stock of H Ltd. included goods purchased from S Ltd. worth Rs. 5,000. The goods were supplied by S Ltd. at cost + 25%.

[K.U.D., April 1998(N)]

Solution :

Working Table

		Total	Holding Co.	Minority Interest
No. of shares		2000	1500	500
Ratio			3/4	1/4
Share Capital		2,00,000	1,50,000	50,000
General Reserve		20,000CR		
Balance 1-1-97		17,000		
Additions during year 3,000				
1-1-97 to 1-5-97				
1/3 × 3,000	1,000	1,000		
(a) Prior to acquisition		18,000	13,500 CR	4,500
(b) After acquisition		2,000	1,500	500
Profit & Loss A/c				
on 1-1-1997		30,000		
Profit for the year 45,000				
Profit 1-1-97 to 1-5-97				
4/12 × 45,000	15,000	+15,000 30,000		
(a) Prior to acquisition		45,000	33,750CR	11,250
(b) Profit after acquisition		30,000	22,500	7,500
				73,750

Summary

(a) Minority Interest		73,750
(b) *Capital Profit*		
General Reserve	13,500	
Profit & Loss A/c	33,750	47,250
Revenue		
(a) General Reserve		1,500
(b) Profit & Loss		22,500

Calculation of unrealised profit

Sales price — 5,000

Cost + 25%

Profit 1/5 × 5,000 = Rs. 1,000

Unrealised Profit Rs. 1,000

Share of Holding Co. 3/4 × 1,000 = 750

Unrealised Profit Rs. 750

Consolidated Balance Sheet of H Ltd. of its Subsidiary S Ltd. as at 31-12-1997

Liabilities	Rs.	Rs.	Assets	Rs.	Rs.
Share Capital			Cost of Control		
Shares of Rs. 100 each H Ltd.		3,00,000	Cost Price	1,80,000	
Reserve & Surplus			*Less* Nominal value	1,50,000	
General Reserve H Ltd.	30,000		Excess paid Goodwill	30,000	
Share in S Ltd. 3/4	1,500	31,500	*Add* Goodwill in		
Profit & Loss A/c			B/s of S Ltd.	1,00,000	
Balance 1-1-97 H Ltd.		35,000		1,30,000	

Liabilities	Rs.	Rs.	Assets		Rs.	Rs.
Profit for the year					1,30,000	
H Ltd.	50,000		Dedct Capital Reserve per contra		47,250	
Less Unrealised Profit	750				82,750	
	49,250		*Add* Goodwill of H Ltd.		50,000	1,32,750
Add Share in S Ltd.	22,500	71,750	Building : H Ltd.		1,00,000	
Cap. Reserve deducted	47,250		S Ltd.		75,000	1,75,000
from Goodwill			Machinery : H Ltd.		50,000	
(Per contra)			S Ltd.		50,000	1,00,000
Secured Loan			Investments			
12% Debentures H Ltd.	1,00,000		(in S Ltd. as above)			
S Ltd.	87,500	1,87,500	in Govt. Securities			
Current Liabilities			H Ltd.		25,000	
Creditors H Ltd.	60,000		S Ltd.		30,000	55,000
Less due to S Ltd.	10,000	50,000	Stock H Ltd.		75,000	
Bills payable H Ltd.	15,000		*Less* Unrealised Profit		750	
Less due to S Ltd.	10,000	5,000			74,250	
Minority Interest		73,750	*Add* S Ltd.		37,500	1,11,750
			Debtors : H Ltd.		1,00,000	
			S Ltd.	60,000		
			Less due from			
			H Ltd.	10,000	50,000	1,50,000
			Bills Receivable S Ltd.		10,000	
			Less due from H Ltd.		10,000	—
			Cash at Bank H Ltd.		10,000	
			S Ltd.		20,000	~~30,000~~
		7,54,500				7,54,500

Problem No. 2

A Co. Ltd. acquired 75% of Equity shares in B Co. Ltd. on 1-7-1996. The following are the Balance sheets of two companies on 31-12-1996 :

Balance Sheets as at 31-12-1996

Liabilities	A Co. Rs.	B Co. Rs.	Assets	A Co. Rs.	B Co. Rs.
Share capital	3,00,0000	1,80,000	Land & Building	75,000	60,000
Shares of Rs. 10			Machinery	85,000	87,500
each			Furniture	4,000	3,000
Reserves & Surplus			Investments in		
General Reserve	30,000	20,000	13500 shares in	1,60,000	—
Profit & Loss A/c	20,000	15,000	B.Co.		
(on 1-1-1996)			in Govt. Securities	—	42,500
Profit for the year	45,000	30,000	Stocks	46,000	32,000
Current Liabilities			Debtors	30,000	20,000
Creditors	87,500	50,000	Bills Receivable	12,500	10,000
Bills payable	10,000	10,000	Bank A/c	80,000	50,000
	4,92,500	3,05,000		4,92,500	3,05,000

Additional Information

(a) On 1-1-1996 the Books of B Co. Ltd. showed a Balance of General Reserve Rs. 10,000.

(b) Sundry Debtors of B Co. Ltd. include Rs. 7,500 due from A Co. Ltd.

(c) All the Bills payable of B Co. Ltd. were drawn by A Co. Ltd. of which bills worth Rs. 7,500 were discounted by A Co. Ltd.

(d) Land & Buildings of B Co. Ltd. were overvalued by Rs. 5000

Prepare the Consolidated Balance Sheet of A Co. Ltd. and its subsidiary B Co. Ltd.

[K.U.D., October 1997(N)]

Solution :

Working Note

	Total	Holding Co.	Minority Interest
Shares	100	75%	25%
ratio		3/4	1/4
	Rs.	Rs.	Rs.
Share Capital	1,80,000	1,35,000	45,000
General Reserve	20,000		

		Total	Holding Co.	Minority Interest
On 1-1-96 Balance		10,000		
1-1-96 to 31-12-96	10,000			
Upto 1-7-96	5,000	5000		
Prior to acquisition		15,000	11,250 CR	3,750
After acquisition		5,000	3,750	1,250
Profit & Loss A/c				
on 1-1-96		15,000		
Profit for the year	30,000			
Upto 1-7-96	15,000			
Prior to acquisition		15,000		
Total		30,000	22,500 CR	7,500
After acquisition		15,000	11,250	3,750
				61,250 (MI)

Capital Profit		Minority Interest
General Reserve	11,250	61,250
Profit & Loss A/c	22,500	
	33,750	61,250
Land & Building of B Co. overvalued		
be reduced by – 5,000	– 3,750	– 1,250
	30,000	60,000

Now : Capital Reserve	30,000	(1)
Revenue		
(a) General Reserve	3,750	(2)
(b) Profit & Loss A/c	11,250	(3)
Minority Interest	60,000	(4)

Consolidated Balance Sheet of Holding Co. A Co. and its Subsidiary B Co. as at 31-12-96

Liabilities	Rs.	Rs.	Assets	Rs.	Rs.
Share capital			Cost of control		
Shares of Rs. 10			Cost Price	1,60,000	
each A Co.		3,00,000	Norminal value	1,35,000	
Reserve & Surplus			Excess paid—		
General Reserve			Goodwill	25,000	
A Co.	30,000		Deducted from		
B Co.	3,750	33,750	Capital Reserve		
Capital Reserve	30,000		(Per contra)	25,000	—
Less Goodwill			Land & Building		
(Per contra)	25,000	5,000	A Co.	75,000	
Profit & Loss A/c 1-1-96			B. Co. 60,000		
A.Co.		20,000	*Less* Overvalued 5,000	55,000	1,30,000
Profit for the year			Machinery : A Co.	85,000	
A Co.	45,000		B Co.	87,500	1,72,500
B Co.	11,250	56,250	Furniture : A Co.	4,000	
Current Liabilities			B Co.	3,000	7,000
Creditors A Co.	87,500		Investments		
Less Due to B Co.	7,500		(in B Co. as above)		
	80,000		in Govt. Securities B Co.		42,500
Add B Co.	50,000	1,30,000	Stock : A Co.	46,000	
Bills payable A Co.	10,000		B Co.	32,000	78,000
B Co. 10,000			Debtors : A Co.	30,000	
Less Bills			B Co. 20,000		
due to			*Less* due from		
A Co. 2,500	7,500	17,500	A Co. 7,500	12,500	42,500
			Bills Receivable A Co.	12,500	
Minority Interest		60,000	*Less* Due from B Co.	2,500	
				10,000	
			Add B. Co.	10,000	20,000
			Bank A/c : A Co.	80,000	
			B Co.	50,000	1,30,000
		6,22,500			6,22,500

Note : All the Bills payable of B Co.	Rs. 10,000
are drawn by A Co. of which Bills worth	
are discounted by A Co.	7,500
Therefore Bills in hand of A Co.	2,500
are due from B Co.	

Common indebtedness Rs. 2,500 Bills in hand are deduced from

B.P. of B Co. — 10,000 – 2,500 = 7,500

B.R. of A Co. — 12,500 – 2,500 = 10,000

Problem No. 3

On 1st August 1995 Stern Ltd. purchased 6000 shares of Rs. 10 each fully paid for Rs. 20 each in Strict Ltd. At the time of acquisition of shares the Real Estate of Strict Ltd. was undervalued by Rs. 15,000.

Balance Sheets of two Cos. as at 31-12-1995

Liabilities	Stern Ltd. Rs.	Strict Ltd. Rs.	Assets	Stern Ltd. Rs.	Strict Ltd. Rs.
Shares Capital			Real Estate	30,000	37,500
Shares of			Machinery	15,000	18,000
Rs. 10 each	1,50,000	75,000	Investments		
Reserves & Surplus			Shares in Strict Ltd.	1,20,000	
General Reserve	30,000	22,500	Stock	60,000	48,000
Profit & Loss A/c			Debtors	27,000	37,500
Balance on 1-1-95	15,000	7,500	Cash	10,500	9,000
Profit for the year	45,000	15,000			
Secured Loan	—	—			
Current Liabilities					
Creditors	22,500	30,000			
	2,62,500	1,50,000		2,62,500	1,50,000

Debtors of Strict Ltd. included Rs. 7,500 due from Stern Ltd.

Prepare Consolidated Balance sheet as on 31-12-1995

[K.U.D., October 1997(O)]

Solution :

Working Note

Calculation of Minority Interest

		Total	Holding Co.	Minority Interest	Summery	
No. of shares		7500	6000	1500		
Ratio			4/5	1/5	(1) Capital Profit	
(1) Share Capital		75,000	60,000	15,000	Gen. Reserve	10,500
(2) General Reserve		22,500			P & L. A/c	13,000
(a) Prior to acquisition					Assets revalued	23,500
1-1-95 to 1-7-95		13,125	10,500CR	2,625	Increase	12,000
7:5					Total Capital	
(b) after acquisition		9,375	7,500	1,875	Reserve	35,500
(3) Profit & Loss A/c					(2) Revenue :	
Balance on 1-1-95		7,500			General Reserve	7,500
Profit for the year	15,000	8,750			Profit & Loss	5,000
Upto 1-1-95 1-8-95					(3) Minority Interest	27,000
7:5	8,750					
(a) Prior to acquisition		16,250	13,000CR	3,250		
(b) after acquisition		6,250	5,000	1,250		
General Reserve			10,500	24,000		
Profit & Loss			13,000			
Real Estate undervalued increase			23,500			
		15,000	12,000	3,000		
			35,500	27,000		

Consolidated Balance Sheet of Stern Ltd. and its Subsidiary Strict Ltd. as at 31-12-95

Liabilities	Rs.	Rs.	Assets	Rs.	Rs.
Share Capital			Cost of Control		
Shares of Rs. 10			Cost Price	1,20,000	
each Stern Ltd.		1,50,000	Norminal value	60,000	
Reserved & Surplus			Excess paid Goodwill	60,000	
Capital Reserve	35,500		Capital Reserve		
Deducted from			deducted per contra	35,500	
Goodwill	35,500		Goddwill		24,500
Gen. Reserve Stern Ltd.	30,000		Real Estate Stern Ltd.	30,000	
Add Share in Strict Ltd.	7,500	37,500	Strict Ltd. 37,500		
			Add Increase 15,000	52,500	82,500

Liabilities	Rs.	Rs.	Assets	Rs.	Rs.
Profit & Loss A/c			Machinery : Stern Ltd.	15,000	—
Stern Ltd.			Strict Ltd.	18,000	33,000
Balance 1-1-95		15,000	Investments		—
Profit for the year Stern	45,000		(as above)		
Add Share in Strict	5,000	50,000	Stock : Stern Ltd.	60,000	
Secured Loan		—	Strict Ltd.	48,000	1,08,000
Current Liabilities			Debtors Stern Ltd.	27,000	
Creditors : Stern Ltd.	22,500		*Less* Due from		
Strict Ltd. 30,000			Strict Ltd.	7,500	
Less Due to				19,500	
Stern Ltd. 7,500	22,500	45,000	*Add* Strict Ltd.	37,500	57,000
Minority Interest		27,000	Cash : Stern Ltd.	10,500	
			Strict Ltd.	9,000	19,500
		3,24,500			3,24,500

Problem No. 4

Balance Sheets of H Ltd. and S Ltd. as on 31-3-1996

Liabilities	H Ltd.	S Ltd.	Assets	H Ltd.	S Ltd.
Share Capital			Goodwill	20,000	30,000
Equity shares of			Fixed Assets	2,00,000	1,50,000
Rs. 10 each	3,00,000	2,00,000	Investments :		
Secured Loan :			(i) 16000 shares in		
10% Debentures	1,00,000	—	S Ltd.	1,20,000	—
Creditors	63,000	20,000	(ii) Govt. Securities	10,000	5,000
Bills payable	10,000	10,000	Debtors	60,000	25,000
			Stock	40,000	10,000
			Bills Receivable	3,000	—
			Profit & Loss A/c	20,000	10,000
	4,73,000	2,30,000		4,73,000	2,30,000

Notes :

(a) The shares of S Ltd. were acquired on 31-12-1995

(b) The Profit & Loss A/c of S Ltd. on 1-4-1995 had a Debt Balance of Rs. 80,000.

(c) Bill payable of S Ltd. were all in favour of H Ltd. of which bills of Rs. 8,000 were endorsed by H Ltd.

(d) Fixed Assets of S Ltd. were undervalued by Rs. 25000
(e) Stock H Ltd. includes goods valued Rs. 10,000 sold by S Ltd. at a profit of 20% on selling price.

Prepare a Consolidated Balance Sheet of H Ltd. as on 31-3-1996. Give Working Note.

[K.U.D., April 1997(N)]

Solution :

Working Note

(1) Calculation of unrealised Profit

S Ltd. sales price Rs. 10,000
Profit on sales 20% 2,000
Share of Holding Co. 4/5 × 2,000 = 1,600
Minority Interest 200

Unrealised profit share of Holding Co. included in stock of Holding Co. be deducted and similarly in the Profit of Loss A/c in H Ltd. be deduced i.e. Debited to P & L A/c

(2) Calculation of Minority Interest

	Total	Holding Co.	Minority Interest	
No. of shares	20000	16000	4000	
Ratio		4/5	1/5	
	Rs.	Rs.	Rs.	
(1) Share Capital	2,00,00	1,60,000	40,000	
(2) Profit & Loss A/c				
On 1-4-95 Balance (Dr)	80,000			
On 31-3-96 Balance (Dr)	10,000			
Profit during the year	70,000			
(a) Prior to acquisition				
1-4-95 to 31-12-95				
9 months 9/12 × 70,000	52,500			
(b) Profit after acquisition	17,500	+ 14,000	+ 3,500	Current profit or Reserve Profit
Profit prior to acquisition	52,500			
Loss on 1-4-95	80,000			
Loss prior to acquisition	27,500	– 22,000	– 5,500	Capital loss
Fixed Assets of S Ltd. undervlaued by Rs. 25,000 i.e. to be increased it is capital profit	25,000	+ 20,000	+ 5,000	
		– 2,000	– 500	Net Capital Loss
		Capital Loss	43,000 Minority Interest	

(3) Cost of Control

Face value of shares	1,60,000
Cost price	1,20,000
Gain Capital profit	40,000
Less Capital loss	– 2,000
Capital Profit or Capital Reserve	38,000
Goodwill : H Ltd. 20,000	
S Ltd. 30,000	50,000
Goodwill	12,000

(4) Profit Loss A/c of H Ltd.

Balance on 31-3-96	– 20,000
Profit share in S Ltd.	+ 14,000
Loss Balance	– 6,000
Add (Debit) Unrealised Profit	– 1,600
Net Loss	– 7,600
Balance on Profit & Loss Debit (Loss after above adjustment)	– 7,600

(5) Bills payable of S Ltd. all are in favour of H Ltd. Bills Rs. 8,000 endorsed. Bill in hand Rs. 2,000 be deducted.

Consolidated Balance Sheet of H Ltd. and its Subsidiary S Ltd. as at 31-3-96

Liabilities	Rs.	Rs.	Assets	Rs.	Rs.
Share Capital			Goodwill		12,000
Equity share of Rs. 10			(Cost of control		
each H Ltd.		3,00,000	see note-3)		
Reserves & Surplus			Fixed Assets : H Ltd.	2,00,000	
Secure Loan			S Ltd. 1,50,000		
10% Debentures H Ltd.		1,00,000	*Add* Increased 25,000	1,75,000	3,75,000
Creditors : H Ltd.	63,000		Investments		
S Ltd.	20,000	83,000	Shares in S Ltd.		
Bills payables H Ltd.	10,000		(see Note No. 3 cost		
S Ltd. 10,000			of control)		
Less Bills in hand			(ii) Govt. Security :		
due to H Ltd. 2,000	8,000	18,000	H Ltd.	10,000	
Minority Interest		43,000	S Ltd.	5,000	15,000
(see Note-2)			Debtors : H Ltd.	60,000	
			S Ltd.	25,000	85,000
			Stock . H Ltd.	40,000	
			S Ltd.	10,000	
				50,000	
			Less Share of unrealised		
			Profit	1,600	48,400
			(See Note-1)		
			Bills Receivable H. Ltd.	3,000	
			Less Due from S. Ltd	2,000	1,000
			Profit & Loss A/c		7,600
			(Debit Balance) Loss		
			(See Note No. 4)		
		5,44,000			5,44,000

Note : Clarification :

Bills payable of S Ltd. Rs. 10,000 all are in favour of H Ltd. of which H. Ltd. endorsed Bills worth Rs. 8,000. Therefore now on 31-3-96 Bills in hand with H S Ltd. (10,000–8,000) Rs. 2,000 are treated as B R due from S Ltd. such Bills in hand are deducted from B R of H Ltd. as due from and B R of S Ltd. due to H Ltd.

Problem No. 5

On 1st April 1994, H Ltd. acquired 80% of Equity shares and 30% of Preference shares in S Ltd. for Rs. 1,95,000 and Rs. 30,500 respectively. On that date, the General Reserve and Profit & Loss Account showed a credit Balance of Rs. 30,000 and Rs. 4,000 respectively.

On 31st March 1995, the Balance Sheets of the two companies were as follows :

Balance Sheets as at 31-3-1995

Liabilities	H Ltd. Rs.	S Ltd. Rs.	Assets	H Ltd. Rs.	S Ltd. Rs.
Share Capital			Sundry Assets	13,54,500	4,76,000
Equity shares of			Investments in		
Rs. 10 each	10,00,000	2,00,000	S Ltd.		
10% Preference shares			80% Equity shares	1,95,000	—
of Rs. 100 each	—	1,00,000	30% Pref. shares	30,500	—
Reserves & Surplus					
General Reserve	3,00,000	40,000			
Profit & Loss A/c	1,00,000	39,000			
Current Liabilities					
Creditors	1,80,000	97,000			
	15,80,000	4,76,000		15,80,000	4,76,000

You are required to draw Consolidated Balance Sheet & H Ltd. with its subsidiary S. Ltd. assuming that there were no arrears of Dividend on preference shares on 1-4-1994.

[K.U.D., October 1996(O)]

Solution :

Working Note
Calculation of Minority Interest

		Total	Holding Co.	Minority Interest	Summary		
% of Holding & ratio		100	80% 4/5	20% 1/5	(1) Minority Interest		1,25,800
Equity share capital		2,00,000	1,60,000	40,000	(2) Capital Reserve :		
Preference share capital		1,00,000	30,000	70,000	(a) Gen. Reserve	24,000	
General Reserve	40,000	40,000			(b) P & L	3,200	27,200
Balance on 1-4-94	30,000	30,000	24,000 CR	6,000	Revenue :		
(a) Prior to acquisition		10,000	8,000	2,000	G R		800
(b) After acquisition					P & L		28,000
Profit & Loss A/c		39,000					
(a) Prior to acquisition		4,000	3,200 CR	800			
(b) After acquisition		35,000	28,000	7,000			
				1,25,800			

In the Books of H Ltd. Holding Co.
Consolidated Balance Sheet of H Ltd. and its Subsidiary S Ltd. as at 31-3-1995

Liabilities	Rs.	Rs.	Assets		Rs.	Rs.
Share Capital			Cost of Control			
Equity shares of			Equity shares cost		1,95,000	
Rs. 10 each H Ltd.		10,00,000	Pref. Share Capital		30,500	
Reserves & Surplus					2,25,500	
Capital Reserve	27,200		Nominal value			
Deducted from G W	27,200	—	80% of 2,00,000	1,60,000		
(per contra)			30% of 1,00,000	30,000		
General Reserve					1,90,000	
H Ltd.	3,00,000		Excess paid Goodwill		35,500	
Add Share in S. Ltd.	8,000	3,08,000	Deduct Capital Reserve		27,200	
Profit & Loss A/c			(per contra)			8,300
H Ltd.	1,00,000		Net Goodwill			
Add Share in S Ltd.	28,000	1,28,000	Sundry Assets : H Ltd.		13,54,500	
Current Liabilities			S Ltd.		4,76,000	18,30,500
Creditor H Ltd.	1,80,000		Investments as above		—	—
Add S Ltd.	97,000	2,77,000				
Minority Interest		1,25,800				
		18,38,800				18,38,800

Problem No. 6

The following were the Balance sheets of H Ltd. and S Ltd. as on 31-3-1996 :

Balance Sheets as at 31-3-1996

Liabilities	H Ltd. Rs.	S Ltd. Rs.	Assets	H Ltd. Rs.	S Ltd. Rs.
Share Capital					
Equity shares of			Fixed Assets	1,00,000	75,000
Rs. 10 each	2,50,000	1,25,000	*Investments*		
Reserves & Surplus			1000 shares in		
General Reserve	30,000	25,000	S. Ltd. at cost	1,20,000	—
Profit & Loss A/c	15,000	20,000	Govt. securities	5,000	40,000
Secured Loan	—	—	Stocks	35,000	37,500
Current Liabilities			Debtors	20,000	17,500
Creditors	10,000	7,500	Bills Receivable	7,500	7,500
Bills payable	5,000	12,500	Banks	22,500	12,500
	3,10,000	1,90,000		3,10,000	1,90,000

Additional Information :

(1) When H Ltd acquired the shares in S Ltd. the latter Co. had Rs. 10,000 and Rs. 7,500 to the credit of General Reserve and Profit & Loss account respectively.

(2) Bills payable of S Ltd. include Rs. 2,500 accepted in favour of H. Ltd.

(3) The Debtors of H. Ltd. include Rs. 2,500 due from S. Ltd.

(4) The stock of S. Ltd included Rs. 6,000 supplied by H. Ltd. at cost + 20%.

Prepare a Consolidated Balance Sheet. Give Working Notes.

[K.U.D., April 1996(N)]

Solution :

Working Note : Calculation of Minority Interest

Particulars	Total	Holding Co.	Minority Interest	Summary		
No. of Shares	12500	1000	2500			
Ratio		4/5	1/5			
	Rs.	Rs.	Rs.			
I. Share Capital	1,25,000	1,00,000	25,000	(1) Minority Interest		34,000
II. General Reserve	25,000			(2) Capital Profit		
(a) Prior to acquisition	10,000	8,000 CR	2,000	G.R.	8,000	
(b) After acquisition	15,000	12,000	3,000	P & L	6,000	14,000
III. Profit & Loss A/c	20,000			Capital Reserve		
(a) Prior to acquisition	7,500	6,000 CR	1,500	Reserve Profit		
(b) After acquisition	12,500	10,000	2,500	G.R.	12,000	
Minority Interest			34,000	P & L	10,000	

Calculation of unrealised profit

Sales price cost + 20 = 120   20/120 = 1/6

Sales price Rs. 6,000 × 1/6 = Rs. 1000 unrealised profit

Share of Holding Co. 4/5 × 1,000 = Rs. 800 unrealised profit

Consolidated Balance Sheet as at 31-3-1996

Liabilities	Rs.	Rs.	Assets	Rs.	Rs.
Share Capital			*Cost of Control*		
Equity shares of			Cost Price	1,20,000	
Rs. 10 each H Ltd.		2,50,000	Nominal value	1,00,000	
Reserves & Surplus			Excess paid	20,000	
Capital Reserve	14,000		Deduct Capital Reserve	14,000	
Deducted for G.W.			(per contra)		
(per contra)	14,000	—	Goodwill		6,000
General Reserve H Ltd.	30,000		Fixed Assets : H Ltd.	1,00,000	
Share in S Ltd.	12,000	42,000	S Ltd.	75,000	1,75,000
Profit & Loss A/c :			Investment in		
H Ltd.	15,000		S Ltd. as above		
Add Share in S Ltd.	10,000		In Government		
	25,000		Securities : H Ltd.	5,000	
Less Unrealised profit	800	24,200	S Ltd.	40,000	45,000
Secured Loan	—	—	Stock H Ltd.	35,000	
Current Liabilities			*Less* Unrealised Profit	800	
Creditors : H Ltd.	10,000			34,200	
S Ltd. 7,500			*Add* S Ltd.	37,500	71,700
Less Duc to H Ltd. 2,500	5,000	15,000	Debtors H Ltd.	20,000	
Bills payable : H Ltd.	5,000		*Less* due from S Ltd.	2,500	
S Ltd. 12,500				17,500	
Less Due to H Ltd. 2,500	10,000	15,000	*Add* S Ltd.	17,500	35,000
Minority Interest		34,000	Bills Receivable H Ltd.	7,500	
			Less due from S Ltd.	2,500	
				5,000	
			Add S Ltd.	7,500	12,500
			Bank A/c : H Ltd.	22,500	
			S Ltd.	12,500	35,000
		3,80,200			3,80,200

Problem No. 7

From the following Balance Sheets of Rashmi Ltd. and Rakhi Ltd. prepare a consolidated Balance Sheet on 31-3-1996 :

Liabilities	Rashmi Ltd. Rs.	Rakhi Ltd. Rs.	Assets	Rashmi Ltd. Rs.	Rakhi Ltd. Rs.
Share Capital :			Goodwill	20,000	10,000
Equity share of Rs. 10	3,00,000	1,50,000	Land & Building	1,50,000	50,000
General Reserve	60,000	—	Plant & Machinery	1,30,000	80,000
Profit & Loss A/c	60,000	30,000	Share in Rakhi Ltd. (12000 shares)	1,30,000	—
Creditors	40,000	20,000			
Bills payable	15,000	5,000	Stock	20,000	35,000
			Debtors	25,000	25,000
			B.R.	—	5,000
Total	4,75,000	2,05,000		4,75,000	2,05,000

Additional information :

(a) Rashmi Ltd. acquired shares in Rakhi Ltd. on 1-7-1995.

(b) The Balance Sheet of Rakhi Ltd. showed a debit balance of Rs. 30,000 on its Profit and Loss account on 1-4-1995.

(c) All Bills payable of Rakhi Ltd. were drawn by Rashmi Ltd.

(d) Plant and Machinery of Rakhi Ltd. was overvalued by Rs. 10,000 and Land and Building were undervalued by Rs. 20,000.

(e) Stock of Rakhi Ltd. included goods worth Rs. 6,000 by Rashmi Ltd. at a profit of 20% on cost Rakhi Ltd. had not made any payment towards this transaction.

(K.U.D., October 1996)

Solution :

Working Table

Share of Holding Co. and Minority Interest

		Total Rs.	Holding Co. Rs.	Minority Interest Rs.
No. of shares in subsidiary Co.		15000	12000	3000
Ratio			4 :	1
		Rs.	Rs.	Rs.
(I) Share Capital		1,50,000	1,20,000	30,000
(II) General Reserve		—	—	—
(III) Profit & Loss Account				
Debit balance as on 1-4-95		–30,000		
Profit as on 31-3-96	30,000			
Add : Loss as on 1-4-95	30,000			
Total profit during year	60,000			
Profit upto 1-7-95 60,000 × 3/12 =		15,000	Capital loss	
		– 15,000	– 12,000	– 3,000
(IV) Revenue profit :				
Profit after acquisition				
60,000 × 9/12		45,000	36,000	9,000
				36,000
Capital Loss			– 12,000	36,000
Revaluation of Assets :				
Plant and Machinery overvalued decrease	– 10,000			
Land and Building undervalued – increase	+ 20,000			
Net Capital profit	10,000	+ 10,000	+ 8,000	+ 2,000
Net Capital loss			– 4,000	38,000
Capital loss	4,000			
Minority interest	38,000			
Unrealised profit				
6,000 × 20/120=	800			
Revenue profit	36,000			

Consolidated Balance Sheet of Holding Co. Rashmi Ltd. and Its Subsidiary Rakhi Ltd. as at 31-3-1996

Liabilities	Rs.	Rs.	Assets	Rs.	Rs.
Share Capital :			*Cost of Control* :		
Equity shares of			Cost price	1,30,000	
Rs. 10 each Rashmi Ltd.		3,00,000	Nominal value	1,20,000	
Reserve & Surplus :			Excess paid Goodwill	10,000	
General Reserve			*Add* : Capital loss	4,000	
Rashmi Ltd.		60,000		14,000	
Profit & Loss A/c			*Add* : *Goodwill* :		
Rashmi Ltd.	60,000		Rashmi Ltd.	20,000	
Add : Share in Rakhi	36,000		Rakhi Ltd.	10,000	44,000
	96,000		*Land & Building* :		
Less : Unrealised profit	800	95,200	Rashmi Ltd.	1,50,000	
Current Liabilities :			Rakhi Ltd. 50,000		
Creditors :			*Add* : Incr. 20,000	70,000	2,20,000
Rashmi Ltd.	40,000		*Plant & Machinery* :		
Rakhi Ltd.	20,000		Rashmi Ltd.	1,30,000	
	60,000		Rakhi Ltd. 80,000		
Less : Due to Rashmi	6,000	54,000	*Less* : Decr. 10,000	70,000	2,00,000
Bills payable :			*Stock* :		
Rashmi Ltd.	15,000		Rashmi Ltd.	20,000	
Rakhi	5,000	20,000	Rakhi Ltd.	35,000	
Minority Interest		38,000		55,000	
			Less : Unrealised profit	800	54,200
			Debtors :		
			Rashmi Ltd.	25,000	
			Rakhi Ltd.	25,000	
				50,000	
			Less : Due from		
			Rakhi Ltd.	6,000	44,000
			Bills receivable		
			Rakhi Ltd.		5,000
		5,67,200			5,67,000

Note :

(1) Rakhi Ltd. purchased goods on credit included in creditors.

(2) All Bills payable in favour of Rashmi were discounted and therefore no Bills are in hands no deduction from Bills receivable.

Problem No. 8

The following were the Balance Sheets of H Ltd. and S Ltd. as on 31-3-1996 :

Balance Sheets as at 31-3-1996

Liabilities	H Ltd.	S Ltd.	Assets	H Ltd.	S Ltd.
Share Capital			Fixed Assets	1,00,000	75,000
Share of Rs. 10	2,50,000	1,25,000	*Investments :*		
Reserve & Surplus			Shares in S Ltd.		
General Reserve	30,000	25,000	10000 shares at	1,20,000	—
Profit & Loss A/c	15,000	20,000	Govt. Securities	5,000	40,000
Secured Loan	—	—	Stock	35,000	37,500
Current Liabilities			Debtors	20,000	17,500
Creditors	10,000	7,500	Bills receivable	7,500	7,500
Bills payable	5,000	12,500	Bank balance	22,500	12,500
	3,10,000	1,90,000		3,10,000	1,90,000

Notes :

(1) When H Ltd. acquired the sharp in S Ltd. the latter Co. had Rs. 10,000 and Rs. 7,500 to the credit of General Reserve and Profit & Loss account respectively.

(2) Bills payable of S Ltd. include Rs. 2,500 accepted in favour of H Ltd.

(3) The debtors of H Ltd. included Rs. 2,500 due from S Ltd.

(4) Stock of S Ltd. included Rs. 6,000 supplied by H Ltd. at cost plus 20%.

Prepare a Consolidated Balance Sheet and give working notes.

[K.U.D., April 1996(N)]

Solution :

It is assured that the date of purchase of shares of S Ltd. as 1-4-1995.

Working Note

	Total	Holding	Minority Interest
No. of shares	125000	100000	25000
Ratio		4/5	1/5
	Rs.	Rs.	Rs.
Share Capital	1,25,000	1,00,000	25,000
General Reserve			
on 1-4-1995	25,000		
(a) Prior to acquisition	10,000	8,000 CR	2,000
(b) After acquisition	15,000	12,000	3,000
Profit & Loss Account			
on 1-4-1995	20,000		
(a) Prior to acquisition	7,500	6,000 CR	1,500
(b) After acquisition	12,500	10,000	2,500
			34,000

Capitals Profit :

(a) G.R. (General Reserve) 8,000

(b) Profit & Loss Account 6,000

Capital Reserve 14,000

Minority Interest 34,000

Unrealised profit :

Sales price 6,000

Profit cost + 20% $\frac{20}{120} \times 6{,}000 = 1{,}000$

Profit 4/5 share of H Ltd. 800 Unrealised profit.

Consolidated Balance Sheet of H Ltd. as at 31-3-96

Liabilities	Rs.	Rs.	Assets	Rs.	Rs.
Share Capital			*Goodwill*		
Shares of Rs. 10			Cost price	1,20,000	
each H Ltd.		2,50,000	Normal value (–)	1,00,000	
Reserve & Surplus				20,000	
Capital Reserve	14,000		*Deduct* Capital		
Deducted from			Reserve	14,000	6,000
Goodwill (per contra)			Fixed Assets : H Ltd.	1,00,000	
General Reserve			S Ltd.	75,000	1,75,000
H Ltd.	30,000		*Investment*		
S Ltd.	12,000	42,000	In Govt. Securities		
Profit & Loss A/c			H Ltd.	5,000	
H Ltd.	15,000		S Ltd.	40,000	45,000
S Ltd.	10,000		Stock : H Ltd.	35,000	
	25,000		S Ltd.	37,500	
Less : Unrealised	800	24,200		72,500	
Creditors			*Less* : Unsecured	800	71,700
H Ltd.	10,000		Debtors : H Ltd.	20,000	
S Ltd.	7,500		S Ltd.	17,500	
	17,500			37,500	
Less : Due to	2,500	15,000	*Less* : Due from S Ltd.	2,500	35,000
Bills receivable	5,000		Bills receivable :		
S Ltd.	12,500		H Ltd.	7,500	
	17,500		S Ltd.	7,500	
Less : Due to H Ltd.	2,500	15,000		15,000	
Minority Interest		34,000	*Less* : Due from	2,500	12,500
			Bank : H Ltd.	22,500	
			S Ltd.	12,500	35,000
		3,80,200			3,80,200

Problem No. 9

The following are the Balance Sheets of Sun Ltd. and Moon Ltd. as on 31-12-1993 :

Liabilities	Sun Ltd.	Moon Ltd.	Assets	Sun Ltd.	Moon Ltd.
Share Capital			Building	1,00,000	28,000
Share of Rs. 5 each	2,00,000	50,000	Machinery	80,000	12,000
Reserve & Surplus			*Investments*		
General Reserve	50,000	—	Share in Moon Ltd.		
Profit & Loss A/c	30,000	—	7500 at cost	30,000	—
Secured Loan	—	—	Stock	32,500	22,500
Current Liabilities			Debtors	17,500	10,000
Creditors	20,000	15,000	Bills receivable	25,000	—
Bills payable	—	35,000	Cash at Bank	15,000	7,500
			Profit & Loss A/c	—	20,000
Total	3,00,000	1,00,000		3,00,000	1,00,000

(a) The Sun Ltd. acquired shares in Moon Ltd. on 1-5-1993.

(b) The Profit & Loss A/c of Moon Ltd. showed a debit balance of Rs. 32,000 on 1-1-1993.

(c) Creditors of Moon Ltd. included Rs. 5,000 for purchase from Sun Ltd.

Prepare a consolidated balance sheet on 31-12-1993.

[K.U.D., April 1996(a)]

Solution :

Working Table

Particulars	Total	Holding Co.	Minority Interest
No. of shares	10000	7500	2500
Ratio		3/4	1/4
	Rs.	Rs.	Rs.
Share Capital	50,000	37,500	12,500
General Reserve	—	—	—
Profit & Loss A/c			
Loss on 1-1-93	32,000		
Loss as on 31-12-93	20,000		
Profit during the period	12,000		

Particulars		Total	Holding Co.	Minority Interest
Pre-acquisition profit :				
12,000 × 1/3 =	4,000			
Post acquisition =	8,000			
Loss as on 1-1-1993		32,000		
Profit from 1-1-93 to 1-4-93		4,000		
Loss prior to acquisition		28,000	– 21,000 Loss	– 7,000 Loss
Profit after acquisition Revenue		8,000	+ 6,000 Profit	+ 2,000 Profit
Capital Loss			– 21,000	M.I. 7,500

Consolidated Balance Sheet of Sun Ltd. Holding Co. Assets and Subsidiary Moon Co. Ltd. as at 31-12-1993

Liabilities	Rs.	Rs.	Assets	Rs.	Rs.
Share Capital			Cost price	30,000	
Share of Rs. 5			Nominal value	37,500	
each Sun Ltd.		2,00,000	Capital Gain	7,500	
Reserve & Surplus			Capital Loss	21,000	
General Reserve S. Ltd.		50,000	Net total Goodwill		13,500
Profit & Loss A/c	30,000		Building : S Ltd.	1,00,000	
Share in M Ltd.	6,000	36,000	M Ltd.	28,000	1,28,000
Current Liabilities			Machinery : S Ltd.	80,000	
Creditors : S Ltd.	20,000		M Ltd.	12,000	92,000
M Ltd.	15,000		Investment (as above)		—
	35,000		Stock : S Ltd.	32,500	
Less : Due to S Ltd.	5,000	30,000	M Ltd.	22,500	55,000
Bills payable M Ltd.		35,000	Debtors : S Ltd.	17,500	
Minority Interest		7,500	M Ltd.	10,000	
					22,500
			Less Due to from M Ltd.		25,000
			Bills receivable S Ltd.	15,000	
			M Ltd.	7,500	
			Cash at Bank		22,500
Total		3,58,500			3,58,500

Problem No. 10

A Co. Ltd. acquired 75% of equity shares in B Co. Ltd. on 1-1-1994. The following are the Balance Sheets of two companies on 31-12-1994 :

Balance Sheets as at 31-12-1994

Liabilities	A Co. Rs.	B Co. Rs.	Assets	A Co. Rs.	B Co. Rs.
Share Capital (in shares of Rs. 10 each)	6,00,000	3,60,000	Land & Building	1,50,000	1,20,000
			Machinery	1,70,000	1,75,000
General Reserve	60,000	40,000	Furniture	8,000	6,000
Profit & Loss A/c on 1-1-94	40,000	30,000	Investments : 27000 shares in B Co.	3,20,000	—
Profit for the year	90,000	60,000	At Cost in Govt. Securities	—	85,000
Creditors	75,000	50,000			
Bills payable	20,000	20,000	Stock	92,000	64,000
			Sundry debtors	60,000	40,000
			Bills receivable	25,000	20,000
			Cash at Bank	60,000	50,000
	8,85,000	5,60,000		8,85,000	5,60,000

Additional Information :

(1) On the date of acquisition of shares in B Co. Ltd. the books of B Co. Ltd. showed a balance of General Reserve of Rs. 20,000.

(2) Sundry debtors of B Co. Ltd. include Rs. 15,000 due from A Co. Ltd.

(3) All the Bills payable of B Co. Ltd. were drawn by A Co. Ltd., of which bills worth Rs. 15,000 were discounted by A Co. Ltd.

(4) Land and Buildings of B Co. Ltd. were overvalued by Rs. 20,000 and Machinery was undervalued by Rs. 10,000.

Prepare a Consolidated Balance Sheet of A Co. Ltd. with its subsidiary of B Co. Ltd. as on 31-12-1994.

(K.U.D., October 1995)

Solution :

Working Note

Particulars	Total	Holding Co.	Minority Interest
Total No. of shares	36000	27000	9000
Ratio		75% 3/4	25% 1/4
	Rs.	Rs.	Rs.
(1) Share Capital	3,60,000	2,70,000	90,000
(2) General Reserve	40,000	—	—
(a) Prior to acquisition	20,000	16,000 CR	4,000
(b) After acquisition	20,000	16,000	4,000
(3) Profit & Loss A/c			
(a) Prior to acquisition	30,000	22,500 CR	7,500
(b) After acquisition	60,000	45,000	15,000
			1,20,500

Total Capital profit & Minority interest :		Capital profit	Minority interest
		16,000	
		22,500	
		+ 38,500	+ 1,20,500
Capital Profit or Loss :			
(a) Building overvalued by reduced/loss	– 20,000		
(b) Machinery undervalued by (increased/profit)	+ 10,000		
Net Capital loss	– 10,000	– 7,500	– 2,500
Net Capital profit and Minority Interest		31,000	1,18,000

Summary :

(1) Capital Profit	31,000
(2) Revenue Profit	
General Reserve	16,000
(3) Profit & Loss A/c	45,000
(4) Minority Interest	1,18,000

CR = Capital Profit

Consolidated Balance Sheet of Holding Co., A Co. Ltd. and its Subsidiary B Co. Ltd. as at 31-12-1994.

Liabilities	Rs.	Rs.	Assets	Rs.	Rs.
Share Capital A Co.			*Fixed Assets*		
Equity shares			Goodwill		
of Rs. 10		6,00,000	*Cost of Control*		
Reserve & Surplus			Face value	3,20,000	
General Reserve A Co.	60,000		*Less* : Nominal value	2,70,000	
3/4 shares in B Co.	16,000	76,000	Excess paid		
Capital (Profit)			Goodwill	50,000	
Reserve	31,000		Deducted Capital		
Deducted from			Reserve (per contra)	31,000	
Goodwill (per contra)	31,000	—	Net Goodwill		19,000
Profit & Loss A/c			*Land & Building*		
A Co. on 1-1-1994	40,000		A Co. Ltd.	1,50,000	
Profit for the year	90,000		B Co. Ltd.		
	1,30,000		(1,20,000 – 20,000)	1,00,000	2,50,000
3/4 shares in B Co.	45,000	1,75,000	Machinery : A Co.	1,70,000	
Secured Loan		—	B Co. 1,75,000		
Unsecured Loan		—	*Add* : 10,000	1,85,000	3,55,000
Current Liabilities			Furnitures : A Co.	8,000	
Sundry Creditors :			B Co.	6,000	14,000
A Co.	75,000		Investment A Co.		
B Co.	50,000		Shares in B Co.		
	1,25,000		(as above in Goodwill)		
Less : Due to A Co.	15,000	1,10,000	B Co. in Govt. Securities		85,000
Bills payable :			*Current Assets*		
A Co.	20,000		Stock : A Co. Ltd.	92,000	
B Co.	20,000		B Co. Ltd.	64,000	1,56,000
	40,000		Sundry debtors : A Co.	60,000	
Less : Due to A Co.	5,000	35,000	B Co.	40,000	
Minority Interest		1,18,000		1,00,000	
			Less : Due from	15,000	85,000
			Bills receivable :		
			A Co. Ltd.	25,000	
			B Co. Ltd.	20,000	
				45,000	
			Less : Due from B Co.	5,000	40,000
			Cash at Bank : A Co.	60,000	
			B Co.	50,000	1,10,000
		11,14,000			11,14,000

Note : Bills payable accepted by : B Co. in favour

of A Co. Ltd.	20,000
A Co. discounted bills	15,000
Bills in hand	5,000

Only bills in hand Rs. 5,000 be deducted from bills payable of B Co. Ltd. and bills receivable of A Co. Ltd. as inter Co. indebted.

Problem No. 11

The following are the Balance Sheets of Maya and Chaya Ltd. :

Balance Sheets as on 31-12-1992

Liabilities	Maya Ltd. Rs.	Chaya Ltd. Rs.	Assets	Maya Ltd. Rs.	Chaya Ltd. Rs.
Share Capital			Building	3,65,000	1,50,000
Equity shares of			Machinery	2,00,000	1,30,000
Rs. 10 each	8,00,000	1,80,000	14400 shares in		
General Reserve	80,000	60,000	Chaya Ltd. at cost	1,60,000	—
Profit & Loss a/c	80,000	—	Stock	1,35,000	30,000
Creditors	60,000	1,10,000	Debtors	80,000	30,000
Bills payable	25,000	15,000	Bank	1,05,000	15,000
			Profit & Loss A/c	—	20,000
	10,45,000	3,65,000		10,45,000	3,65,000

Maya Ltd. acquired shares in Chaya Ltd. on 1-7-1992. Chaya Ltd. has Rs. 60,000 credit to its General Reserve and Rs. 15,000 to its Profit and Loss Account. Machinery of Chaya Ltd. were found overvalued to the extent of Rs. 20,000. Creditors of Chaya Ltd. include Rs. 25,000 for goods supplied by Maya Ltd.

Prepare the Consolidated Balance Sheet as on 31st December 1992.

(K.U.D., April 1995)

Solution :

Working Table

Particulars		Total	Holding Co.	Minority Interest
No. of Shares/Ratio		18000	14400/ 80%	3600/ 20%
		Rs.	Rs.	Rs.
Share Capital		1,80,000	1,40,000	36,000
General Reserve 60,000				
(a) Prior to acquisition		60,000	48,000 CR	12,000
(b) After acquisition				
Profit & Loss A/c				
Profit on 1-1-92	15,000			
Loss during year	20,000			
Total Loss	35,000			
Loss 1-1-92 to 1-7-92	17,500			
½ Less	+ 15000			
(a) Prior to acquisition (+15,000 – 17,500) Loss		– 2,500	– 2,000 CL	– 500
(b) After acquisition		– 17,500	– 14,000	– 3,500
Machinery decrease		– 20,000	– 16,000 CL	– 4,000
				40,000

Capital Reserve – General Reserve		48,000
Profit & Loss A/c (loss)	– 2,000	
Machinery overvalued by 20,000	– 16,000	– 18,000
Capital Reserve		30,000
Minority Interest	+ 48,000	
Less : Loss	– 8,000	
	40,000	

CR – Capital Profit

CL – Capital Loss

Consolidated Balance Sheet as at 31-12-1992

Liabilities	Rs.	Rs.	Assets	Rs.	Rs.
Share Capital			*Goodwill*		
Equity shares of			Cost price	1,60,000	
Rs. 10 each		8,00,000	Nominal value	1,44,000	
Reserve & Surplus			Excess paid	16,000	
General Reserve	80,000		Deducted from		
Chaya Ltd.	—	80,000	Capital Reserve	16,000	—
Capital Reserve	30,000		Building : Maya Ltd.	3,65,000	
Deducted Goodwill	16,000	14,000	Chaya Ltd.	1,50,000	5,15,000
Profit & Loss a/c			Machinery: Maya Ltd.	2,00,000	
Maya Ltd.	80,000		Chaya Ltd.	1,10,000	3,10,000
Less : Loss Chaya Ltd.	–14,000	66,000	Stock : Maya Ltd.	1,35,000	
Creditors : Maya Ltd.	60,000		Chaya Ltd.	30,000	1,65,000
Chaya Ltd.	1,10,000		Debtors : Maya Ltd.	80,000	
	1,70,000		Chaya Ltd.	20,000	
Less Due to Maya Ltd.	25,000	1,45,000		1,00,000	
Bills payable :			*Less* Due from Chaya	25,000	75,000
Maya Ltd.	25,000		Bank : Maya Ltd.	1,05,000	
Chaya Ltd.	15,000	40,000	Chaya Ltd.	15,000	1,20,000
Minority Interest		40,000			
		11,85,000			11,85,000

Problem No. 12 (Holding Company)

The following are the Balance Sheets of Rin Ltd. and Nirma Ltd. as at 31-12-1993. Nirma Ltd. is a subsidiary company of Rin Ltd.

Balance Sheets as at 31-12-1993

Liabilities	Rin Ltd. Rs.	Nirma Ltd. Rs.	Assets	Rin Ltd. Rs.	Nirma Ltd. Rs.
Share Capital			Plant & Machinery	5,00,000	2,50,000
Ordinary shares of					
Rs. 10 each	7,20,000	4,00,000	Investments :		
Reserve fund	50,000	30,000	32000 shares		
(on 1-1-93)			in Nirma Ltd.	3,30,000	—
Profit & Loss A/c	1,40,000	25,000	Debtors	2,35,000	1,43,000
Creditors	1,80,000	60,000	Stock	90,000	1,67,000
Bills payable	90,000	45,000	Bills Receivable	25,000	—
	11,80,000	5,60,000		11,80,000	5,60,000

Rin Ltd. acquired shares in Nirma Ltd. on 1st May 1993. Nirma Ltd. has a credit balance on Profit and Loss account of Rs. 10,000 on 1-1-1993. All bills receivable of Rin Ltd. were accepted by Nirma Ltd. The plant and machinery of Nirma Ltd. were undervalued to the extent of Rs. 10,000. Creditors of Rin Ltd. include Rs. 30,000 payable to Nirma Ltd.

Prepare the Consolidated Balance Sheet on 31-12-1993.

(K.U.D., October 1994)

Solution :

Working Table

Particulars	Total	Holding Co.	Minority Interest
No. of shares	40000	32000	8000
Ratio		4/5	1/5
	Rs.	Rs.	Rs.
(1) Shares Capital	4,00,000	3,20,000	80,000
(2) Reserve Fund on 1-1-1993	30,000		
(a) Prior to acquisition	—	24,000 CR	6,000
(b) After acquisition	—	—	—
(3) Profit & Loss A/c	25,000		
On 1-1-1993	10,000		
Add : upto 1-5-1993 15,000 × 4/12	5,000		
(a) Prior to acquisition	15,000	12,000 CR	3,000
(b) After acquisition	10,000	8,000	2,000
			91,000
Capital profit	CR	36,000	
Plant & Machinery under-valued increase	10,000	8,000 CR	2,000
		44,000	93,000

(1) *Capital Profit*	
(a) Reserve fund	24,000
(b) Profit & Loss a/c	12,000
(c) Plant & Machinery increase	8,000
Capital Reserve	44,000
(2) Minority Interest	93,000

Consolidated Balance Sheet of Holding Company Rin Ltd. and its Subsidiary Nirma Ltd. as at 31-12-1993

Liabilities	Rs.	Rs.	Assets	Rs.	Rs.
Share Capital			*Cost of Control*		
Equity shares of Rs. 10 each			Cost price	3,30,000	
only Holding Co.		7,20,000	Nominal value	3,20,000	
Reserve & Surplus			Excess paid Goodwill	10,000	
Capital Reserve	44,000		Deducted from Capital Reserve	10,000	—
Deducted Goodwill	10,000	34,000			
Reserve fund :			Plant & Machinery : Rin Ltd.	5,00,000	—
Rin Ltd.	50,000				
Nirma Ltd.	—	50,000	Nirma Ltd. 2,50,000		
Profit & Loss A/c			*Add* : Increase 10,000	2,60,000	7,60,000
Rin Ltd.	1,40,000		Investments as above	—	—
Nirma Ltd.	8,000	1,48,000	Debtors : Rin Ltd.	2,35,000	
Secured Loan		—	Nirma Ltd.	1,43,000	
Current Liabilities :				3,78,000	
Creditors : Rin Ltd.	1,80,000		*Less* : Due from Rin Ltd.	30,000	3,48,000
Nirma Ltd.	60,000				
	2,40,000		Stocks : Rin Ltd.	90,000	
Less : Due to Nirma Ltd.	30,000	2,10,000	Nirma Ltd.	1,67,000	2,57,000
Bills payable : Rin Ltd.	90,000		Bills receivable Rin Ltd.	25,000	
Nirma Ltd.	45,000		*Less* : Nirma Ltd.	25,000	—
	1,35,000				
Less : Due to Rin Ltd.	25,000	1,10,000			
Minority Interest		93,000			
		13,65,000			13,65,000

Problem No. 13

Following are the Balance Sheets of H Ltd. and S Ltd. as on 31st December 1990 :

Balance Sheets as at 31-12-1990

Liabilities	H Ltd. Rs.	S Ltd. Rs.	Assets	H Ltd. Rs.	S Ltd. Rs.
Share Capital :			Building	1,50,000	1,50,000
Equity shares			Machinery	2,05,000	1,95,000
of Rs. 10 each	6,00,000	3,00,000	*Investments*		
Reserve & Surplus			24000 shares in		
General Reserve	80,000	60,000	S Ltd. at cost	3,00,000	—
Profit & Loss A/c	90,000	75,000	Govt. Securities	—	50,000
Secured Loans			Stocks	80,000	65,000
Debentures	—	80,000	Cash at Bank	35,000	35,000
Unsecured Loans	—	—	Debtors	40,000	55,000
Current Liabilities					
Sundry creditors	40,000	25,000			
Bills payable	—	10,000			
	8,10,000	5,50,000		8,10,000	5,50,000

Other Informations :

(a) H Ltd. acquired 80% of equity shares of S Ltd. on 1-5-1990.

(b) In the Balance Sheets of S Ltd. on 1-1-1990, the General Reserve showed a balance of Rs. 15,000 and to the credit of Profit & Loss account was Rs. 30,000.

(c) The Bills payable of S Ltd. are all in favour of H Ltd.

(d) Plant & Machinery of S Ltd. are overvalued by Rs. 2,000.

(e) The Stock of H Ltd. includes Rs. 5,000 brought from S Ltd. which made company profit of 20% on sales.

You are required to prepare :

(i) Consolidated Balance Sheet.

(ii) Give Working Notes.

(K.U.D., April 1994)

Solution :

Date of acquisition 1-5-1990.

Working Notes

Particulars		Total	Holding Co. Share	Minority Interest
Ratio		100%	80% (4/5)	20% (1/5)
		Rs.	Rs.	Rs.
(1) Share Capital – S Ltd.		3,00,000	2,40,000	60,000
(2) General Reserve 31-12-90		60,000		
On 1-1-1990	15,000			
from 1-1-90 to 1-5-90				
4/5 × 45,000 =	15,000			
			CR	
(a) Prior to acquisition		30,000	24,000	6,000
(b) After acquisition 8/12 × 45,000		30,000	24,000	6,000
(3) Profit & Loss A/c 31-12-90		75,000		
On 1-1-1990	30,000			
from 1-1-90 to 1-5-90				
4/12 × 45,000	15,000			
(a) Prior to acquisition		45,000	36,000 CR	9,000
(b) After acquisition 8/12 × 45,000		30,000	24,000	6,000
Capital Reserve (24,000+36,000)	60,000			87,000
(4) Assets revalued				
Plant & Machinery overvalue decrease in value loss		2,000	– 1,600	– 400
			58,400	86,600

(5) *Unrealised Profit*

Goods in stock sales price	5,000
Profit 20% on sales 1/5 × 5,000 =	1,000
Share of Holding company 4/5 × 1,000 =	800
Unrealised profit	
Now Capital Reserve	58,400
(a) Minority Interest	86,600
(b) Unrealised profit	800

Cosolidated Balance Sheet of H Ltd. as at 31-12-1990

Liabilities	Rs.	Rs.	Assets	Rs.	Rs.
Share Capital			*Cost of Control*		
Equity shares of			Cost price	3,00,000	
Rs. 10 each — H Ltd.		6,00,000	*Less* : Nominal value	24,000	
Reserve & Surplus				60,000	
General Reserve			Deduct Capital		
H Ltd.	80,000		Reserve per contra	58,400	
Add : Share in S Ltd.	24,000	1,04,000	Goodwill		1,600
Profit & Loss A/c			Building : H Ltd.	1,50,000	
H Ltd.	90,000		S Ltd.	1,50,000	3,00,000
Share in S Ltd.	24,000		Plant & Machinery :		
	1,14,000		H Ltd.	2,05,000	
Less : Unrealised			S Ltd. 1,95,000		
profit	– 800	1,13,200	*Less* : Over 2,000	1,93,000	3,98,000
Capital Reserve	58,400		*Investments*		
Deducted from			In shares of S		
Goodwill	—		as above in		
Secured Loan			Goods security S Ltd.		5C,000
Debentures S Ltd.		80,000	Stock : H Ltd.	80,000	
Unsecured Loan		—	S Ltd.	65,000	
Current Liabilities				1,45,000	
Sundry Creditors :			*Less* : Unsecured profit	800	1,44,200
H Ltd.	40,000		Debtors : H Ltd.	40,000	
S Ltd.	25,000	65,000	S Ltd.	55,000	95,000
Bills payable — S Ltd.		10,000	Cash at Bank :		
Minority Interest		86,600	H Ltd.	35,000	
			S Ltd.	35,000	70,000
		10,58,800			10,58,800

Note : Bills payable of S Ltd. in favour of H Ltd. were all discounted by H Ltd. Therefore there is no need to deduct bills payable and bills receivable.

Problem No. 14

X Company acquired 75% of equity shares in Y Company on 1-4-1991. Following are the Balance Sheets of two companies on 31-12-91 :

Balance Sheets as at 31-12-1991

Liabilities	X Co. Rs.	Y Co. Rs.	Assets	X Co. Rs.	Y Co. Rs.
Share Capital			Goodwill	60,000	90,000
Equity shares of			Land & Building	1,50,000	2,00,000
Rs. 10 each	5,00,000	4,00,000	Machinery	2,10,000	2,50,000
Reserves & Surplus			*Investments*		
General Reserve	3,00,000	2,00,000	30000 shares in Y Co.	4,00,000	
Profit & Loss	1,20,000	90,000	Stocks	80,000	1,10,000
Current Liabilities			Debtors	60,000	50,000
Creditors	60,000	75,000	Bills receivable	20,000	30,000
Bills payable	40,000	25,000	Banks	40,000	60,000
	10,20,000	7,90,000		10,20,000	7,90,000

Additional Information :

(1) On 1-1-1991 Y company showed :

(a) General Reserve and

(b) Profit & Loss account a credit balance of Rs. 1,20,000 and Rs. 60,000 respectively.

(2) Creditors of Y company included Rs. 30,000 for goods supplied by X company sales price being cost + 25% profit. All goods were in stocks of Y company on 31-12-1991.

(3) Bills payable of Y company included Bills drawn by X company Rs. 15,000.

(K.U.D., October 1993)

Solution :

Working Table

Particulars		Total	Holding Co. Share	Minority Interest
No. of shares		40000	30000	10000
Ratio			3/4	1/4
		Rs.	Rs.	Rs.
(1) Share Capital		4,00,000	3,00,000	1,00,000
(2) General Reserve		2,00,000		
On 1-1-1991	1,20,000			
Upto 1-4-1991				
80,000 × 3/12 =	20,000			
(a) Pre-acquisition		1,40,000	1,05,000 CR	35,000
(b) After acquisition		60,000	45,000	15,000
(3) Profit & Loss account		90,000		
1-1-1991	60,000			
Upto 1-4-1991				
30,000 × 3/12 =	7,500			
(a) Pre-acquisition		67,500	50,625 CR	16,875
(b) After acquisition		22,500	16,875	5,625
				1,72,500

(1) Capital Profits :

(a) General Reserve	1,05,000
(b) Profit & Loss A/c	50,625
Capital Reserve	1,55,625

(2) Minority Interest 1,72,500

(3) Unrealised profit :

Sale price 30,000

Cost + 25%

25/125 × 30,000 = 6,000

Share of Holding company 4/5 × 6,000 = 4,500

Consolidated Balance Sheet of X Company as at 31-12-1991

Liabilities	Rs.	Rs.	Assets	Rs.	Rs.
Share Capital			*Cost of Control*		
Equity share			Cost price	4,00,000	
of Rs. 10 each			Nominal value	3,00,000	
X Co.		5,00,000	Goodwill	1,00,000	
Reserve & Surplus			*Add* : Goodwill in		
General Reserve			X Co.	60,000	
X Co.	3,00,000		Y Co.	90,000	
Y Co.	45,000	3,45,000		2,50,000	
Capital Reserve	1,55,625		Deduct Capital		
Deducted from			Reserve per contra	1,55,625	94,375
Goodwill	—		Land & Building :		
Per contra			X Co.	1,50,000	
Profit & Loss A/c			Y Co.	2,00,000	3,50,000
X Co.	1,20,000		Machinery : X Co.	2,10,000	
Y Co.	16,875		Y Co.	2,50,000	4,60,000
	1,36,875		Investments as above		
Less : Unrealised			Stock : X Co.	80,000	
Profit	4,500	1,32,375	Y Co.	1,10,000	
Current Liabilities				1,90,000	
Creditors :			*Less* : Unrealised profit	4,500	1,85,500
X Co.	60,000		Debtors : X Co.	60,000	
Y Co.	75,000		Y Co.	50,000	
	1,35,000			1,10,000	
Less : Due to X Co.	30,000	1,05,000	*Less* : Due from Y Co.	30,000	80,000
Bills payable : X Co.	40,000		Bills receivable X Co.	20,000	
Y Co.	25,000		Y Co.	30,000	
	65,000			50,000	
Less : Due to X Co.	15,000	50,000	*Less* : Due from Y Co.	15,000	35,000
Minority Interest		1,72,500	Banks : X Co.	40,000	
			Y Co.	60,000	1,00,000
		13,04,875			13,04,875

Problem No. 15

The Balance Sheets of R Ltd. and S Ltd. companies are given below :

Balance Sheets as at 31-12-1990

Liabilities	R Ltd. Rs.	S Ltd. Rs.	Assets	R Ltd. Rs.	S Ltd. Rs.
Share Capital			Building	80,000	30,000
Equity shares of Rs. 10 each	2,00,000	1,00,000	Machinery	70,000	75,000
			Investments		
Reserves & Surplus			8000 shares in		
General Reserve	25,000	20,000	S Ltd. at cost	1,20,000	
Profit & Loss A/c	40,000	30,000	Govt. Securities	—	10,000
Secured Loan			Stocks	60,000	30,000
6% Debentures	7,500		Debtors	40,000	15,000
Unsecured Loan	—	—	Bills receivable	20,000	10,000
Current Liabilities			Cash at Banks	20,000	10,000
Sundry Creditors	50,000	20,000			
Bills payable	20,000	10,000			
	4,10,000	1,80,000		4,10,000	1,80,000

Other Informations :

(1) R Ltd. acquired 8000 shares of Rs. 10 each at Rs. 15 per share in S Ltd. on 1-4-1990.

(2) Rs. 10,000 and Rs. 15,000 were to the credit of General Reserve and Profit and Loss account on 1-1-1990 of S Ltd.

(3) The creditors of S Ltd. include Rs. 15,000 for purchase of goods from R Ltd.

(4) The Stocks of S Ltd. include goods of Rs. 10,000 supplied by R Ltd. at cost plus 25% profit.

(5) The Bills payable of S Ltd. were all in favour of R Ltd. and they were discounted.

(6) The Building of S Ltd. was overvalued to the entent of Rs. 5,000.

Prepare Consolidated Balance Sheet of on 31-12-1990.

(K.U.D., April 1993)

Solution :

Working Table

Particulars		Total	Holding Company	Minority Interest
No. of shares		10000	8000	2000
Ratio			4/5	1/5
		Rs.	Rs.	Rs.
(1) Share Capital		1,00,000	80,000	20,000
(2) General Reserve		20,000		
On 1-1-90	10,000			
Upto 1-4-90				
20,000 – 10,000 = 10,000 × 3/12 =	2,500	12,500	10,000 CR	2,500
(a) Prior to acquisition		—	—	—
(b) After acquisition		7,500	6,000	1,500
(3) Profit & Loss A/c		30,000		
On 1-1-90	15,000			
Upto 1-4-1990				
30,000-15,000 = 15,000 × 3/12 =	3,750			
(a) Prior to acquisition		18,750	15,000 CR	3,750
(b) After acquisition		11,250	9,000	2,250
Minority Interest				30,000
Capital Reserve			25,000	
Less : Capital Loss				
Building overvalue		5,000	– 4,000	– 1,000
			21,000	29,000

(1) Capital Reserve 21,000

(2) Minority Interest 29,000

(3) Unrealised profit

Stock 10,000

Profit 25/125 2,000

Holding Co. share 4/5 × 2000 = 1,600 unrealised profit.

Consolidated Balance Sheet of Holding Company as at 31-12-90

Liabilities	Rs.	Rs.	Assets	Rs.	Rs.
Share Capital			Goodwill		
Equity shares of			Cost of Control		
Rs. 10 each		2,00,000	Cost price	1,20,000	
General Reserve			Face value	80,000	
R Ltd.	25,000			40,000	
4/5 share in S Ltd.	6,000	31,000	Deducted Capital		
Capital Reserve			Reserve per contra	21,000	
4/5 share in S Ltd.	21,000		Goodwill		19,000
Deducted from			Building : R Ltd.	80,000	
G.W. per contra	21,000	—	S Ltd. 30,000		
Profit & Loss			*Less* : 5,000	25,000	1,05,000
Account : R Ltd.	40,000		Machinery : R Ltd.	70,000	
4/5 shares in S Ltd.	9,000		S Ltd.	75,000	1,45,000
	49,000		Investments S Ltd.		
Less : Unrealised profit	1,600	47,400	in Govt. securities		10,000
Secured Loan			Stocks : R Ltd.	60,000	
Debentures R Ltd.		75,000	S Ltd.	30,000	
Current Liabilities				90,000	
Sundry Creditors :			*Less* : Unrealised Profit	1,600	88,400
R Ltd.	50,000		Debtors : R Ltd.	40,000	
S Ltd.	20,000		S Ltd.	15,000	
	70,000			55,000	
Less : Due from R Ltd.	15,000	55,000	*Less* : Due from S Ltd.	15,000	40,000
Bills payable :			Bills receivable :		
R Ltd.	20,000		R Ltd.	20,000	
S Ltd.	10,000	30,000	S Ltd.	10,000	30,000
Minority Interest		29,000	Banks : R Ltd.	20,000	
			S Ltd.	10,000	30,000
		4,67,400			4,67,400

Problem No. 16

The following are the Balance Sheets on 31 March 1991 :

Balance Sheets as at 31-3-1991

Liabilities	H Ltd. Rs.	S Ltd. Rs.	Assets	H Ltd. Rs.	S Ltd. Rs.
Share Capital			*Fixed Assets*		
Equity shares of Rs. 10 each	3,60,000	2,00,000	Goodwill	20,000	10,000
Reserves & Surplus			Sundry Assets	2,40,000	1,70,000
General Reserve		—	Investments		
Profit & Loss A/c	—	5,000	(1) 12,000 shares in		
Secured loan			S Ltd. at cost	1,00,000	
Debentures	40,000	—	(2) Debenture in		
Current Liabilities			H Ltd. at par		25,000
Creditors	80,000	50,000	*Current Assets*		
Bills payable	10,000	5,000	Stock	60,000	20,000
			Debtors	50,000	30,000
			Bills receivable	—	5,000
			Profit & Loss A/c	20,000	
	4,90,000	2,60,000		4,90,000	2,60,000

Notes :

(1) Shares in S Ltd. were acquired by X Ltd. 31st October, 1990.

(2) The Profit and Loss account of S Ltd. on 1st April 1990 showed credit Balance of Rs. 50,000.

(3) Sundry Assets of S Ltd. was undervalued by Rs. 10,000.

(4) Bills payable of S Ltd. were all in favour of H Ltd.

(5) The Stock of H Ltd. included goods worth Rs. 12,000 sold by S Ltd. at cost plus 20%.

Required :

Prepare Consolidated Balance Sheet with necessary working notes.

(K.U.D., October 1992)

Working Table

Date of Balance Sheet 1-4-1990 to 31-3-1991.

Date of acquisition 1-10-1990

Particulars		Total	Holding Company	Minority Interest
No. of shares		20000	12000	8000
Ratio			3/5	2/5
		Rs.	Rs.	Rs.
(1) Share Capital of S Ltd.		2,00,000	1,20,000	80,000
(2) General Reserve		Nil		
(3) Profit & Loss A/c 31-3-91		5,000		
Profit on 1-4-1991	50,000			
Profit on 31-3-1991	5,000			
Loss during the year	45,000			
(a) Loss prior to acquisition from 1-4-90 to 1-10-90 6 months 6/12 × 45,000 =		– 22,500	– 13,500 CL	– 9,000
(b) After acquisition (loss)		– 22,500	– 13,500	– 9,000
Profit on 1-4-90 Capital profit		50,000	+ 30,000 CR	+ 20,000
(4) Sundry assets undervalued (capital profit) *add* increase		10,000	+ 6,000 CR	+ 4,000
				– 86,000

(A) Capital profit	Rs.
(a) Profit & Loss on 1-4-90	30,000
Add : Sundry assets profit	6,000
	36,000
Less : Capital loss 1-4-90 to 1-10-90	-13,500
Capital Profit or Capital Reserve	22,500
(B) Minority Interest	86,000
(C) Unrealised profit :	
Goods in stock sales price	1,20,000
Cost + 20% profit 20/120 × 1,20,000 =	2,000
Shares of Holding company 3/5 × 2,000 =	1,200
Unrealised profit	1,200

CR = Capital Profit CL = Capital Loss

Consolidated Balance Sheet of H Ltd. Company Holding company and Subsidiary S Ltd. as at 31-3-1991

Liabilities	Rs.	Rs.	Assets	Rs.	Rs.
Share Capital			*Goodwill*		
Equity share			Cost of Control		
of Rs. 10 each		3,60,000	Cost price	1,00,000	
Reserve & Surplus			Nominal value	1,20,000	
(a) General Reserve	Nil		Capital gain	20,000	
(b) Capital Reserve			Goodwill in B/s :		
(see working notes)	22,500		H Ltd. 20,000		
Deduct Goodwill			S Ltd. 10,000	30,000	
per contra	10,000	12,500	Net result Goodwill	10,000	
Secured loan			Deducted from		
Debentures H Ltd.	40,000		Capital reserve		
Less : Held by S Ltd.	25,000	15,000	per contra	—	—
Current Liability			Sundry Assets H Ltd.	2,40,000	
Bills payable : H Ltd.	10,000		S Ltd. 1,70,000		
S Ltd.	5,000	15,000	*Add* : Interest 10,000	1,80,000	4,20,000
			Investment in		
Creditors : H Ltd.	80,000		Shares (as above)		
S Ltd.	50,000	1,30,000	Debenture H Ltd.	25,000	
Minority Interest		86,000	*Less* : Held by S Ltd.	25,000	—
(see working notes)			Current Assets :		
			Stock : H Ltd.	60,000	
			S Ltd.	20,000	
				80,000	
			Less : Unrealised profit	1,200	78,800
			Debtors : H Ltd.	50,000	
			S Ltd.	30,000	80,000
			Bills Receivable: H Ltd.	Nil	
			S Ltd.	5,000	5,000
			Profit & Loss A/c		
			H Ltd. Debit balance		
			31-3-90	20,000	
			Add : Loss during year	13,500	
			Share in S Ltd.	33,500	
			Add : Unrealised profit	1,200	34,700
		6,18,500			6,18,500

Problem No. 17

A Company Ltd. acquired both the types of shares 80% in B Company Ltd. on 1-7-1991.

Following are the Balance Sheets of two companies :

Balance Sheets as at 31-12-1991

Liabilities	A Co. Ltd. Rs.	B Co. Ltd. Rs.	Assets	A Co. Ltd. Rs.	B Co. Ltd. Rs.
Capital Share			Goodwill	75,000	50,000
Equity shares of Rs. 10 each	4,50,000	2,00,000	Building	1,50,000	1,00,000
9% preference share of Rs. 10 each	2,00,000	1,00,000	Machinery	2,00,000	2,00,000
Reserve & Surplus			Investments :		
General Reserve	80,000	60,000	In B Co. Ltd. in		
Profit & Loss A/c	1,10,000	80,000	Equity shares	2,20,000	
Current Liabilities			Preference shares	90,000	—
Creditors	65,000	45,000	Stocks	80,000	70,000
Bills payable	25,000	15,000	Debtors	40,000	30,000
			Bills receivable	15,000	—
			Cash at Bank	60,000	50,000
	9,30,000	5,00,000		9,30,000	5,00,000

Additional Information :

(1) B Company Ltd. had to its credit of General Reserve and Profit and Loss accounts Rs. 40,000 and Rs. 30,000 respectively on 1-1-91.

(2) Creditors of B Company Ltd. included Rs. 25,000 for goods supplied by A Company Ltd. at a profit of 20% on sales price. Goods worth Rs. 10,000.

(3) Machinery of B Company Ltd. were found overvalued Rs. 20,000.

Prepare Consolidated Balance Sheet of A Company Ltd.

(K.U.D., April 1992)

Solution :

Working Notes

Particulars		Total	Holding Company	Minority Interest
Ratio			80%	20%
		Rs.	Rs.	Rs.
(1) Share Capital				
Preference shares		1,00,000	80,000	20,000
Equity shares capital		2,00,000	1,60,000	40,000
(2) General Reserve		60,000		
(a) Prior to acquisition on 1-1-1991	40,000			
from 1-1-91 to 1-7-92	10,000	50,000	40,000	10,000
(b) After acquisition		10,000	8,000	2,000
(3) *Profit & Loss Account*				
(a) Pre-acquisition on 1-1-91	30,000			
Upto 1-7-92	25,000	55,000	44,000	11,000
(b) After acquisition		25,000	20,000	5,000
				88,000
(4) Machinery				
Less : Overvaluation		– 20,000	– 16,000	– 4,000
				84,000

(1) Capital Profit : (a) General Reserve	40,000	
(b) Profit and Loss A/c	44,000	
	84,000	
Less : Capital loss	16,000	
Capital Reserve	68,000	
(2) Goodwill Cost price : Preference share	90,000	
Equity share	2,20,000	3,10,000
Less : Face value		2,40,000
Excess paid		70,000
Less : Capital Reserve		68,000
Goodwill		2,000
Add : Goodwill in B/s A Co.	75,000	
B Co.	50,000	1,25,000
Net Goodwill		1,27,000

Consolidated Balance Sheet of Holding Company A Co. Ltd. and its Subsidiary B Company Ltd. as at 31-12-1991

Liabilities	Rs.	Rs.	Assets	Rs.	Rs.
Share Capital			*Goodwill*		
(A Company only)			Cost price	2,20,000	
Equity shares of				90,000	
Rs. 10 each		4,50,000		3,10,000	
9% pref. shares of			Face value 1,60,000		
Rs. 10 each		2,00,000	80,000	2,40,000	
Reserve & Surplus			Earn paid	70,000	
Gen. Reserve : A Co.	80,000		Capital Reserve	68,000	
B Co.	8,000	88,000		2,000	
Profit & Loss A/c			*Add* : Goodwill in B/s :		
A Co.	1,10,000		A Co.	75,000	
B Co.	20,000		B Co.	50,000	
	1,30,000		Goodwill Net		1,27,000
Less : Unrealised			Building : A Co.	1,50,000	
profit	1,600	1,28,400	B Co.	1,00,000	2,50,000
Current Liability			Machinery : A Co.	2,00,000	
Creditors : A Co.	65,000		B Co.		
B Co.	45,000		(2,00,000 – 2,000)	1,80,000	3,80,000
	1,10,000		Investment (as above)		
Less : Due to B Co.	25,000	85,000	Stock : A Co.	80,000	
Bills payable : A Co.	25,000		B Co.	70,000	
B Co.	15,000	40,000		1,50,000	
Minority Interest		84,000	*Less* : Unrealised profit	1,600	1,48,400
			Debtors : A Co.	40,000	
			B Co.	30,000	
				70,000	
			Less : Due from B Co.	25,000	45,000
			Bills receivable : A Co.		15,000
			Cash at Bank : A Co.	60,000	
			B Co.	50,000	1,10,000
		10,75,400			10,75,400

Problem No. 18

The Balance Sheets of H Ltd. and S Ltd. as on 31-3-1991 :

Balance Sheets as at 31-12-1991

Liabilities	H Ltd. Rs.	S Ltd. Rs.	Assets	H Ltd. Rs.	S Ltd. Rs.
Share Capital			Fixed Assets :		
Share of Rs. 100 each	4,00,000	2,00,000	Premises	1,50,000	1,28,000
Reserve & Surplus :			Equipments	1,07,000	1,00,000
General Reserve			Furniture	20,000	10,000
on 1-4-1990	80,000	50,000	Investment :		
Profit & Loss A/c	70,000	50,000	1500 shares of S. Ltd.	1,80,000	
Current Liabilities :			Current assets Loans & Advances		
Bills payable	—	10,000	Bills receivable	5,000	
Creditors	30,000	20,000	Stocks	80,000	60,000
			Debtors	30,000	25,000
			Banks	8,000	7,000
	5,80,000	3,30,000		5,80,000	3,30,000

Notes :

(1) H Ltd. purchased shares in S Ltd. on 1-4-1990 when Profit and Loss A/c of Ltd. showed a credit balance of Rs. 30,000.

(2) S Ltd. paid a Dividend at 10% in October 1990 for the year 89-90 and the dividend received by H Ltd. was credited to its Profit & Loss account.

(3) H Ltd. had received from S Ltd. bills amounted to Rs. 5,000 of which it holds on 31-3-1991 bills worth Rs. 3,000 only.

(4) Creditors of S Ltd. includes Rs. 20,000 due to H Ltd. for supply of goods on which latter Company made a profit at 25% on sales price.

(5) Stocks of S Ltd. include half of the goods bought from H Ltd.

Prepare :

(1) Consolidated Balance Sheet.

(2) Working Notes.

(K.U.D., October 1991)

Solution :

Working Table

Particulars	Total	Holding Company	Minority Interest
No. of share	2000	1500	500
Ratio		(3/4)	(1/4)
	Rs.	Rs.	Rs.
Share Capital	2,00,000	1,50,000	50,000
General Reserve :			
(a) Prior acquisition	50,000	37,500 CR	12,500
(b) After acquisition	—	—	—
Profit & Loss A/c :			
(a) Prior to acquisition	30,000	22,500 CR	7,500
(b) After acquisition	20,000	15,000	5,000
			75,000

(1) Capital Profit	
(a) General Reserve	37,500
(b) Profit & Loss A/c	22,500
Capital Reserve	60,000
Add : Dividend 10% on 1,50,000 for 1989-90	15,000
	75,000

Unrealised profit	
Sales	20,000
Profit 25% on sales price	5,000
1/2 of goods on stock	2,500
Unrealised profit	2,500

Share of Holding Company 3/4 × 2,500 = 1,875.

Consolidated Balance Sheet of H Ltd. and its Subsidiary S Ltd.
as at 31-12-91

Liabilities	Rs.	Rs.	Assets	Rs.	Rs.
Share Capital			*Goodwill*		
Share of Rs. 100 each		4,00,000	Cost of Control		
Reserve & Surplus			Cost price	1,80,000	
Gen. Reserve H Ltd.	80,000	80,000	*Less* Nominal value	1,50,000	
Capital Reserve	75,000			30,000	
Deduct Goodwill	30,000	45,000	Deducted per contra Capital Reserve	—	—
Profit & Loss A/c	70,000		*Fixed Assets*		
Less Dividend for 89	15,000		Premises : H Ltd.	1,50,000	
	55,000		S Ltd.	1,28,000	2,78,000
Transfer to C.R.	15,000		Equipments : H Ltd.	1,07,000	
Share in S Ltd. shares	70,000		S Ltd.	1,00,000	2,07,000
Less Unrealised profit	1,875	68,125	Furniture : H Ltd.	20,000	
Current Liabilities			S Ltd.	10,000	30,000
Bills payable : H Ltd.	—		*Investment* as above		
S Ltd.	10,000		*Current Assets* :		
Less Due to H Ltd.	3,000	7,000	Stock : H Ltd.	80,000	
Creditors : H Ltd.	30,000		S Ltd.	60,000	
S Ltd.	20,000			1,40,000	
	50,000		*Less* Unrealised profit	1,875	1,38,125
Less Due to H Ltd.	20,000	30,000	Bills receivable : H Ltd.	5,000	
Minority Interest		75,000	*Less* Bills due from S	3,000	2,000
			Debtors : H Ltd.	30,000	
			S Ltd.	25,000	
				55,000	
			Less Due from S Ltd.	20,000	35,000
			Banks : H Ltd.	8,000	
			S Ltd.	7,000	15,000
		7,05,125			7,05,125

Problem No. 19

Following are the Balance Sheets of A Ltd. & B Ltd. :

Balance Sheets as at 31-12-1989

Liabilities	A Ltd. Rs.	B Ltd. Rs.	Assets	A Ltd. Rs.	B Ltd. Rs.
Share Capital			Goodwill	75,000	40,000
Equity shares			Land & Building	4,50,000	1,20,000
of Rs. 10 each	9,00,000	1,50,000	Plant & Machinery	3,00,000	90,000
10% pref. share			Investments in		
of Rs. 100 each	1,00,000		B Ltd. 12000		
Reserve & Surplus			Shares	1,90,000	—
Gen. Reserve	90,000	60,000	Current Assets :		
Profit & Loss			Stock	2,40,000	75,000
on 1-1-89	60,000	15,000	Debtors	1,50,000	80,000
For the year	1,50,000	60,000	Bills Receivable	25,000	10,000
Secured loan	—	—	Cash at Bank	95,000	10,000
Current Liabilities :					
Creditors	1,85,000	1,05,000			
Bills payable	40,000	35,000			
	15,25,000	4,25,000		15,25,000	4,25,000

Additional Information :

(a) A Ltd. acquired shares in B Ltd. on 1-4-1989.

(b) General Reserve of B Ltd. on 1-1-1989 was Rs. 10,000.

(c) Bills payable of B Ltd. included Rs. 20,000 accepted in favour of A Ltd. out of which A Ltd. discounted the Bills worths Rs. 12,000.

(d) Creditors of B Ltd. included Rs. 60,000 for goods supplied by A Ltd. at cost plus 25%. Half of the goods purchase included in stock of B Ltd.

(e) Plant & Machinery of B Ltd. were undervalued by Rs. 20,000.

Prepare a Consolidated Balance Sheet of A Ltd. and its subsidiary B Ltd. on 31-12-1989.

(K.U.D., April 1991)

Solution :

Working Notes (Date of acquisition)

Particulars		Total	Holding Company	Minority Interest
No. of shares		15000	12000	3000
Ratio			4/5	1/5
		Rs.	Rs.	Rs.
(1) Share Capital B Ltd.		1,50,000	1,20,000	30,000
(2) General Reserve		60,000		
On 1-1-1989	10,000			
For the year	50,000			
(a) Prior to acquisition				
On 1-1-1989	10,000			
Upto 1-4-89				
3/12 × 50,000	12,500	22,500	18,500	4,500
(b) After acquisition 9/12 × 30,000		37,500	30,000	7,500
(3) Profit and Loss Account				
on 1-1-1989	15,000			
For the year	60,000			
(a) Prior to acquisition				
On 1-1-1989	15,000			
Upto 1-4-89				
3/12 × 60,000	5,000	30,000	24,000	6,000
(b) After acquisition 9/12 × 60,000		45,000	36,000	9,000
				57,000
Assets Revalued				
Plant & Machinery				
Undervalued increase		20,000	16,000	4,000
				61,000
Capital Profit				
General Reserve		18,000		

Consolidated Balance Sheet of Holding Company A Ltd. and its Subsidiary B Ltd. as at 31-12-89

Liabilities	Rs.	Rs.	Assets	Rs.	Rs.
Share Capital			*Goodwill*		
of A Ltd.			Cost of Control		
Equity shares of			Cost price	1,90,000	
Rs. 10 each		9,00,000	Nominal value	1,20,000	
10% pref. share			Excess paid Goodwill	70,000	
of Rs. 100 each		1,00,000	*Add* : Goodwill in B/s :		
Reserve & Surplus			A Ltd.	75,000	
General Reserve :			B Ltd.	40,000	
A Ltd.	90,000			1,85,000	
B Ltd.	30,000	1,20,000	Deduct Capital		
Capital Reserve	58,000		Reserve (per contra)	58,000	
(see working note)			Total Goodwill		1,27,000
Deducted from			Land & Building :		
Goodwill (per contra)	—		A Ltd.	4,50,000	
Profit & Loss A/c			B Ltd.	1,20,000	5,70,000
A Ltd. on 1-1-89	60,000		Plant & Machinery :		
For the year	1,50,000		A Ltd.	3,00,000	
	2,10,000		B Ltd. 90,000		
			Add : incr. 20,000	1,10,000	4,10,000
Add : B Ltd.	36,000		*Investments*		
	2,46,000		(as above)		
Less : Unrealised profit	4,800	2,41,200	*Current Assets*		
Secured Loan	—	—	Stock : A Ltd.	2,40,000	
Current Liabilities :			B Ltd.	75,000	
Creditors : A Ltd.	1,85,000			3,15,000	
B Ltd.	1,05,000		*Less* : Unrealised Profit	4,800	3,10,000
			Debtors : A Ltd.	1,50,000	
	2,90,000		B Ltd.	80,000	
Less : Due to A Ltd.	60,000	2,30,000		2,30,000	
Bills payable : A Ltd.	40,000		*Less* : Due to B Ltd.	60,000	1,70,000
B Ltd.	35,000		Bills receivable :		
	75,000		A Ltd.	25,000	
Less : Due to A Ltd.	8,000	67,000	B Ltd.	10,000	
Minority Interest		61,000		35,000	
			Less Due to B Ltd.	8,000	27,000
			Cash at Bank : A Ltd.	95,000	
			B Ltd.	10,000	1,05,000
		17,19,200			17,19,200

Problem No. 20

The following are the Balance Sheets of Ameer Company Ltd. and Sameer Company Ltd. as on 31-12-1990 :

Liabilities	Ameer Ltd. Rs.	Sameer Ltd. Rs.	Assets	Ameer Ltd. Rs.	Sameer Ltd. Rs.
Share Capital			Building	28,000	—
Equity shares of			Machinery	24,000	26,000
Rs. 10 each	1,00,000	60,000	Furnitures	15,000	9,000
6% pref. shares	20,000	—	Investments in Sameer		
Reserve & Surplus :			Ltd. share	50,000	
General Reserve	15,000	7,000	Current Assets :		
Profit & Loss A/c	18,000	6,000	Stock	22,000	18,000
Secured loan	—	—	Debtors	18,000	15,000
Current Liabilities :			Bills receivable	—	4,000
Creditors	15,000	3,000	Cash at Bank	13,000	8,000
Bills payable	2,000	4,000			
	1,70,000	80,000		1,70,000	80,000

Additional Information :

(1) Ameer Company acquired 75% of shares of Sameer Company on 30-9-1989 on which date the General Reserve of Sameer company stock at Rs. 4,000 and the Profit and Loss account had a credit balance of Rs. 2,000 on that date.

(2) Bills payable of Ameer Company were all payable to Sameer Company debtors of Ameer Company included Rs. 2,000 due from Sameer.

(3) Stocks of Sameer Company included stock worth Rs. 5,000 purchased from Ameer Company and there goods were sold by Ameer Company to Sameer Company at cost plus 25%.

Prepare Consolidate Balance sheet as at 31-3-1990.

(K.U.D., October 1990)

Solution :

Working Table

Particulars		Total	Holding Company	Minority Interest
Ratio		100%	75%	25%
		Rs.	Rs.	Rs.
(1) Share Capital		60,000	45,000	15,000
(2) General Reserve 31-3-90	7,000			
(a) Prior to acquisition		4,000	3,000	1,000
(b) After acquisition		3,000	2,250	750
(3) Profit & Loss account 31-3-90				
(a) Prior to acquisition		2,000	1,500	500
(b) After acquisition		4,000	3,000	1,000
				18,250

Minority Interest Rs. 18,250

(1) Capital Profit

(a) General Reserve	3,000
(b) Profit & Loss A/c	1,500
Capital Reserve	4,500

(2) Unrealised Profit

Stock include 5,000

Sales price = Cost + 25% profit 1/5 × 5,000 = 1,000

Share of holding company 3/4 × 1,000 = 750.

Consolidated Balance Sheet of Ameer Company Holding company and its Subsidiary Sameer company as at 31-3-1990

Liabilities	Rs.	Rs.	Assets	Rs.	Rs.
Share Capital			*Goodwill*		
Equity shares			Cost of Control		
of Rs. 10 each			Cost price	50,000	
A Company		1,00,000	*Less* Nominal value	45,000	
6% preference share		20,000	Excess paid	5,000	
Reserve & Surplus			Deducted Capital		
General Reserve :			Reserve per contra	4,500	500
A Co.	15,000		Building : A Co.	28,000	
S Co.	2,250	17,250	S Co.	—	28,000
Capital Reserve	4,500		Machinery : A Co.	24,000	
Deducted from Goodwill			S Co.	26,000	50,000
per contra	—	—	Furniture : A Co.	15,000	
Profit & Loss A/c :			S Co.	9,000	24,000
A Co.	18,000		Investments		—
S Co.	3,000		*Current Assets*		
	21,000		Stocks : A Co.	22,000	
Less Unrealised profit	750	20,250	S Co.	18,000	
Current Liabilities				40,000	
Creditors : A Co.	15,000		*Less* Unrealised profit	750	39,250
S Co.	3,000		Debtors : A Co.	18,000	
	18,000		S Co.	15,000	
Less Due to A Co.	2,000	16,000		33,000	
Bills payable : A Co.	2,000		*Less* Due from S Co.	2,000	31,000
S Co.	4,000		Bills receivable : A Co.	Nil	
	6,000		S Co.	4,000	
Less Due to S Co.	2,000	4,000		4,000	
Minority Interest		18,250	*Less* Due from : A Co.	2,000	2,000
			Cash at Bank :		
			A Co.	13,000	
			S Co.	8,000	21,000
		1,95,750			1,95,750

Problem No. 21

Major Ltd. acquired 80% of shares in Minor Ltd. on 1st January 1989 at a total cost of Rs. 4,25,000. The Balance Sheets of the two companies are follows :

Balance Sheets

Liabilities	Major Rs.	Minor Rs.	Assets	Major Rs.	Minor Rs.
Share Capital :			Land & Building	4,65,000	1,85,000
Equity shares of			Plant & Machinery	15,000	1,09,000
Rs. 10 each	5,00,000	2,50,000	Investments :		
10% pref. shares of			Shares in minor	4,25,000	
Rs. 100 each	2,00,000	—	Stock	1,55,000	70,800
Reserve & Surplus :			Debtors	1,20,000	62,700
General Reserve	3,50,000	15,000	Cash at Bank	1,05,000	52,500
Profit & Loss A/c	3,00,000	1,50,000			
Current Liabilities :					
Creditors	70,000	65,000			
	14,20,000	4,80,000		14,20,000	4,80,000

The following further information is relevant :

(a) Sundry creditors of Major Ltd. include Rs. 20,000 for goods purchased from Minor Ltd. on which the subsidiary company made a profit of Rs. 5,000.

(b) Half of the goods sold as above were still in stocks of Major Company Ltd.

(c) Profit & Loss A/c balance on 1-1-89 was Rs. 50,000 out of which dividend @ 10% was paid for the year 1988.

The General Reserve of Minor Ltd. respresents the balance on as 1st January 1989.

(d) The Plant & Machinery of Minor Ltd. are undervalued by Rs. 25,000.

You are required to prepare Consolidated Balance Sheet of Major Ltd. and its Subsidiary Minor Ltd.

(K.U.D., October 1990)

Solution :

Working Table

Particulars		Total	Holding Company	Minority Interest
No. of share / (Ratio)			80%	20%
		Rs.	Rs.	Rs.
(1) Share Capital		2,50,000	2,00,000	50,000
(2) General Reserve	15,000			
On 1-1-1989 :				
(a) Pre-acquisition		15,000	12,000	3,000
(b) After acquisition		—	—	—
(3) Profit & Loss A/c	1,50,000			
1-1-1989	50,000			
Less Dividend paid 10% on 2,50,000	25,000			
(a) Pre-acquisition		25,000	20,000 CR	5,000
(b) After acquisition		1,25,000	1,00,000	25,000
Add : Capital profit machinery undervalue		25,000	20,000 CR	5,000
				88,000

(1) Capital Profit :

(a) General Reserve	12,000
(b) Profit & Loss A/c	20,000
(c) Machinery Capital profit	20,000
(d) Dividend for 1988 25,000 × 4/5 =	20,000
Capital Reserve	72,000

(2) Minority interest 88,000

(3) Unrealise profit

Sale price	20,000
Profit on above	5,000
1/2 Goods in stock	10,000
Profit 1/2	2,500

Share of holding company unrealised 4/5 × 2,500 = Rs. 2,000.

Consolidated Balance Sheet of Holding Company as at 31-12-1989

Liabilities	Rs.	Rs.	Assets	Rs.	Rs.
Share Capital			*Goodwill*		
Equity share of Rs. 10			*Cost of Control*		
Major Ltd.		5,00,000	Cost price	4,25,000	
10% pref. share of 100			Nominal value	2,00,000	
Major Ltd.		2,00,000	Excess paid Goodwill	2,25,000	
Reserve & Surplus			Deduct Capital		
Gen. Reserve :			per contra	72,000	1,53,000
Major Ltd.		3,50,000	Land & Building :		
Capital Reserve	72,000		Major Ltd.	4,65,000	
Deducted from Goodwill (per contra)	—	—	Minor Ltd.	1,85,000	6,50,000
Profit & Loss A/c	3,00,000		Plant & Machinery :		
Less Dividend recd.			Major Ltd.	1,50,000	
transfer to C.R.	20,000		Minor Ltd.	1,34,000	2,84,000
	2,80,000		*Investment* :		
Less Unrealised profit	2,000		as above		
	2,78,000		Stock : Major Ltd.	1,55,000	
Add Profit of Minor	1,00,000	3,78,000	Minor Ltd.	70,800	
Current Liabilities				2,25,800	
Creditors : Major	70,000		*Less* Unrealised profit	2,000	2,23,800
Minor	65,000		Debtors : Major Ltd.	1,20,000	
			Minor Ltd.	62,700	
	1,35,000			1,82,700	
Less Due to Minor	20,000	1,15,000	*Less* Due from		
Minority Interest		88,000	Major Ltd.	20,000	1,62,700
			Cash at Bank :		
			Major	1,05,000	
			Minor Ltd.	52,500	1,57,500
		16,31,000			16,31,000

Problem No. 22

From the following Balance Sheet as on 31-12-1988 and the adjustments given below, prepare a Consolidated Balance Sheet.

Balance Sheets as at 31-12-1988

Liabilities	H Ltd. Rs.	S Ltd. Rs.	Assets	H Ltd. Rs.	S Ltd. Rs.
Share Capital			Fixed Assets	8,00,000	1,20,000
Equity shares of			Investments :		
Rs. 10 each	10,00,000	2,00,000	14000 shares		
Reserves & Surplus			in S Ltd. at cost	1,50,000	
Reserve Fund	1,20,000	60,000	Current Assets :		
Profit & Loss A/c	4,00,000	1,20,000	Stock	6,00,000	2,40,000
Current Liabilities :			Debtors	1,50,000	1,70,000
Creditors	2,20,000	1,20,000	Bills receivable	40,000	
Bills payable	—	30,000	Cash at Bank		
	17,40,000	5,30,000		17,40,000	5,30,000

Adjustments :

(1) The bills accepted by S Ltd. are all in favour of H Ltd.

(2) The Stock of H Ltd. includes Rs. 50,000 bought from S Ltd. at a profit to the latter company of 20% on sales price.

(3) All the profits of S Ltd. has been earned since the shares were acquired by H Ltd. but there was already Reserve fund of Rs. 60,000 at that date.

(K.U.D., October 1989)

Solution :

Working Table

Particulars	Total	Holding Company	Minority Interest
No. of share	20000	14000	6000
Ratio		7/10	3/10
	Rs.	Rs.	Rs.
(1) Share Capital	2,00,000	1,40,000	60,000
(2) Reserve Fund			
(a) Pre-acquisition	60,000	42,000	18,000
(b) After acquisition			
(3) Profit & Loss A/c			
(a) Pre-acquisition			
(b) After acquisition	1,20,000	84,000	36,000
			1,14,000

(1) Capital profit

(a) Reserve fund	42,000
(b) Profit & Loss A/c	—
Capital Reserve	42,000

(2) Minority Interest 1,14,000

(3) Unrealised Profit

Stock in due 50,000

Profit 20% on sales price

profit 1/5 × 50,000 = 10,000

Share of holding company 7/10 × 10,000 = Rs. 7,000

Consolidated Balance Sheet of H Ltd. and its Subsidiary S Ltd. as at 31-12-1988

Liabilities	Rs.	Rs.	Assets	Rs.	Rs.
Share Capital			*Goodwill*		
Equity shares of			Cost of Control		
Rs. 10 each — H Ltd.		10,00,000	Cost price	1,50,000	
Reserves & Surplus			Nominal value	1,40,000	
Reserve fund : H Ltd.	1,20,000		Excess paid Goodwill	10,000	
S Ltd.	Nil	1,20,000	Deduct from Capital		
Capital Reserve	42,000		Reserve per contra	10,000	—
Deduct Goodwill					
per contra	10,000	32,000	Fixed assets : H Ltd.	8,00,000	
Profit & Loss A/c :			S Ltd.	1,20,000	9,20,000
H Ltd.	4,00,000		Investments (as above)		—
S Ltd.	84,000		*Current Assets*		
	4,84,000		Stocks : H Ltd.	6,00,000	
Less : Unrealised profit	7,000	4,77,000	S Ltd.	2,40,000	
Secured Loan		—		8,40,000	
Current Liabilities			*Less* Unrealise profit	7,000	8,33,000
Creditors : H Ltd.	2,20,000		Debtors : H Ltd.	1,50,000	
S Ltd.	1,20,000	3,40,000	S Ltd.	1,70,000	3,20,000
Bills payable : H Ltd.	—		Bills receivable : H Ltd.	40,000	
S Ltd.	30,000		S Ltd.	—	
	30,000			40,000	
Less Due to H Ltd.	30,000	—	*Less* : Due from S Ltd.	30,000	10,000
Minority Interest		1,14,000			
		20,83,000			20,83,000

Problem No. 23

From the following Balance Sheet and particulars given below prepare a Consolidated Balance Sheets of Holding Company Asha Ltd. and Nisha Ltd. as at 31-12-1988.

Liabilities	Asha Ltd. Rs.	Nisha Ltd. Rs.	Assets	Asha Ltd. Rs.	Nisha Ltd. Rs.
Share Capital			Goodwill	16,000	12,000
Equity shares of Rs. 100 each	2,00,000	80,000	Land & Building	50,000	40,000
Reserves & Surplus			Machinery	80,000	44,000
General Reserve			Furniture	14,000	4,000
as on 1-1-1988	40,000	24,000	Investments		
Profit & Loss A/c	56,000	36,000	600 equity shares		
Secured loan	—	—	in Nisha Ltd.	96,000	
Current Liabilities :			Current Assets :		
Creditors	32,000	20,000	Stock	40,000	36,000
Bills payable	—	16,000	Debtors	8,000	30,000
			Cash at Bank	24,000	10,000
	3,28,000	1,76,000		3,28,000	1,76,000

(1) Asha Ltd. acquire the shares in Nisha Ltd. on 1-7-1988.

(2) All the Bills payable of Nisha Ltd. were in favour of Asha Ltd. All the Bills have been discounted by the latter company.

(3) Creditors of Nisha Ltd. included Rs. 8,000 by payable to Asha Ltd. for goods supplied.

(4) The stock of Nisha Ltd. included the goods Rs. 3,200 supplied by Asha Ltd. at cost plus 33-1/3%.

(5) The Profit and Loss account of Nisha Ltd. showed a credit Balance of Rs. 8,000 on 1-1-1988.

(K.U.D., April 1989)

Solution :

Working Table

Particulars		Total	Holding Company	Minority Interest
No. of shares		800	600	200
Ratio			3/4	1/4
		Rs.	Rs.	Rs.
(1) Share Capital		80,000	60,000	20,000
(2) General Reserve				
on 1-1-88	24,000			
(a) Pre-acquisition		24,000	18,000 CR	6,000
(b) After acquisition		—	—	—
(3) Profit & Loss A/c	36,000			
(a) Pre-acqusition				
1-1-1988	8,000			
+ 1-7-1988	14,000	22,000	16,500 CR	5,500
(b) After acquisition		14,000	10,500	3,500
				35,000

CR — Capital Profit

(1) *Capital Profit*

General Reserve	18,000
Profit & Loss A/c	16,500
Capital Reserve	34,500

(2) Minority Interest 35,000

Unrealised Profit

Goods in Stocks 3,200

Profit cost + 33-1/3 i.e. 1/4 × 3,200 = 800

Share of Holding company 3/4 × 800 = 600.

Consolidated Balance Sheet of Holding Company Asha Ltd. and its Subsidiary Nisha Ltd. as at 31-12-1988

Liabilities	Rs.	Rs.	Assets	Rs.	Rs.
Share Capital			*Goodwill*		
Equity share of Rs. 100		2,00,000	*Cost of Control*		
Reserves & Surplus			Cost price	96,000	
General Reserve :			Nominal value	60,000	
Asha Ltd.	40,000		Excess paid Goodwill	36,000	
Nisha Ltd.	—	40,000	*Add* Goodwill in B/s :		
Capital Reserve	34,500		Asha Ltd.	16,000	
Deducted from			Nisha Ltd.	12,000	
Goodwill (per contra)	—	—	Total Goodwill	64,000	
Profit & Loss A/c :			*Deduct* Capital		
Asha Ltd.	56,000		Reserve (per contra)	34,500	29,500
Nisha Ltd.	10,500		Land & Building :		
	66,500		Asha Ltd.	50,000	
Less Unrealised profit	600	65,900	Nisha Ltd.	40,000	90,000
Secured Loan		—	Machinery : Asha Ltd.	80,000	
Current Liabilities			Nisha Ltd.	44,000	1,24,000
Asha Ltd.	32,000		*Investments*		
Nisha Ltd.	20,000		(As above)		
	52,000		*Current Assets*		
Less Due to Asha Ltd.	8,000	44,000	Stock : Asha Ltd.	40,000	
Bills payable :			Nisha Ltd.	36,000	
Asha Ltd.	—			76,000	
Nisha Ltd.	16,000	16,000	*Less* Unrealised profit	600	75,400
Minority Interest		35,000	Debtors : Asha Ltd.	8,000	
			Nisha Ltd.	30,000	
				38,000	
			Less Due from Asha	8,000	30,000
			Cash at Bank :		
			Asha Ltd.	24,000	
			Nisha Ltd.	10,000	34,000
		4,00,900			4,00,900

Problem No. 24

From the following Balance Sheets and the adjustments given below prepare the Consolidated Balance Sheet as at 31-12-1987.

Balance Sheets as at 31-12-1987

Liabilities	H Ltd. Rs.	S Ltd. Rs.	Assets	H Ltd. Rs.	S Ltd. Rs.
Share Capital			Plant & Machinery	4,00,000	60,000
Share of Rs. 10	5,00,000	1,00,000	Investments :		
Reserves & Surplus :			7500 shares in S Ltd.	1,50,000	
Reserve fund			Stocks	2,30,000	1,20,000
on 1-1-87	50,000	30,000	Debtors	65,000	85,000
Profit for year 87	1,50,000	40,000	Bills receivable	5,000	—
Profit & Loss A/c	1,50,000	40,000			
Current Liabilities :					
Creditors	1,00,000	60,000			
Bills payable	—	15,000			
	8,50,000	2,65,000		8,50,000	2,65,000

Adjustments :

(a) The shares were acquired by H Ltd. in S Ltd. on 1-4-1987.

(b) The bills receivable of H Ltd. were all accepted by S Ltd.

(c) Creditors of H Ltd. included Rs. 20,000 payable to S Ltd.

(d) The stock of H Ltd. included goods purchased from S Ltd. worth Rs. 10,000. The goods were supplied by S Ltd. at cost plus 25%.

(e) The Plant and Machinery of S Ltd. was overvalued to the extent of the Rs. 5,000.

(K.U.D., October 1988)

Solution :

Working Table

Particulars		Total	Holding Company	Minority Interest
No. of shares		10000	7500	2500
Ratio			3/4	1/4
		Rs.	Rs.	Rs.
(1) Share Capital of S Ltd.		1,00,000	75,000	25,000
(2) General Reserve on 1-1-1987		30,000		
(a) Prior to acquisition			22,500 CR	7,500
(b) After acquisition		Nil	—	—
(3) Profit & Loss A/c on 1-1-1987	40,000			
from 1-1-87 to 1-4-87 3/12 × 20,000	5,000			
(a) Prior to acquisition		45,000	33,750 CR	11,250
(b) After acquisition 9/12 × 20,000		15,000	11,250	3,750
Capital Reserve (22,500 + 33,750)			56,250	47,500
(4) Assets Revalued Plant & Machinery over-valued — decrease in value		5,000	– 3,750	– 1,250
			52,500	46,250

Unrealise Profit :

Goods included in stocks at sales price 10,000

Sales prices cost + 25% profit 25/125 × 10,000 = 2,000

Share of Holding Company 3/4 × 2,000 = 1,500

Note : (1) Capital Reserve – Rs. 52,500

(2) Minority interest – Rs. 46,250

(3) Unrealised Profit – Rs. 1,500

Consolidated Balance Sheet of H Ltd. Holding company and its Subsidiary S Ltd. as at 31-12-1987

Liabilities	Rs.	Rs.	Assets	Rs.	Rs.
Share Capital			*Goodwill*		
Equity shares			Cost of Control		
of Rs. 10 each					
H Ltd.	5,00,000		Cost price	1,50,000	
Reserves & Surplus			Nominal value	75,000	
General Reserve :			Earn paid Goodwill	75,000	
H Ltd.	50,000		*Deduct* Capital Res.		
S Ltd.	Nil	50,000	Goodwill	52,500	2,25,000
Capital Reserve	52,500		Plant & Machinery :		
(see working notes)			H Ltd.	4,00,000	
Profit & Loss A/c			S Ltd. 60,000		
H Ltd.			*Less* : Decrease 5,000	55,000	4,55,000
1-1-1987	1,50,000				
For the year	50,000		Investments (as above)		
	2,00,000		*Current Assets*		
S Ltd.	11,250		Stocks : H Ltd.	2,30,000	
	2,11,250		S Ltd.	1,20,000	
Less : Unrealised				3,50,000	
Profit	1,500	2,09,750	*Less* Unrealised profit	1,500	3,48,500
Secured Loan		—	Debtors : H Ltd.	65,000	
Current Liabilities			S Ltd.	85,000	
Creditors : H Ltd.	1,00,000			1,50,000	
S Ltd.	60,000		*Less* Due from H Ltd.	20,000	1,30,000
	1,60,000		Bills receivable : H Ltd.	5,000	
Less Due to S Ltd.	20,000	1,40,000	S Ltd.	Nil	
Bills payable : H Ltd.	Nil			5,000	
S Ltd.	15,000		*Less* Due from S Ltd.	5,000	—
	15,000				
Less Due to H Ltd.	5,000	10,000			
Minority Interest		46,250			
		9,56,000			9,56,000

Problem No. 25

The following Balance Sheets were presented to you :

Balance Sheets as at 31-12-1987

Liabilities	A Co. Rs.	B Co. Rs.	Assets	A Co. Rs.	B Co. Rs.
Share Capital			Fixed Assets	1,75,000	80,000
Equity share of Rs. 10	2,50,000	1,00,000	Investments :		
Reserve & Surplus			8000 shares in B	65,000	
General Reserve	50,000	—	8% debentures	30,000	—
Profit & Loss A/c	40,000	—	Current Assets :		
Secured Loan			Stock	45,000	20,000
8% Debentures	—	50,000	Debtors	30,000	15,000
Current Liabilities :			Cash at Bank	30,000	10,000
Creditors	35,000	25,000	Profit & Loss A/c	–	50,000
	3,70,000	1,75,000		3,70,000	1,75,000

A Company acquired shares in B Company on 1st May 1987.

(a) The Profit & Loss Account of B Company showed a debit balance (loss) Rs. 80,000 on 1-1-1987.

(b) Creditors of B Company included Rs. 10,000 for goods supplied by A Company on which A Company made a profit of Rs. 1,000. Half of the goods have been sold.

Prepare the Consolidated Balance Sheet.

(K.U.D., April 1988)

Solution :

Working Table

Particulars		Total	Holding Company	Minority Interest
No. of shares		10000	8000	2000
Ratio			4/5	1/5
		Rs.	Rs.	Rs.
(1) Share Capital		1,00,000	80,000	20,000
(2) General Reserve				
(3) Profit & Loss A/c				
Balance 1-1-87	80,000			
Loss on 31-12-87	50,000			
Profit during year	30,000			
(a) Prior acquisition 1-1-87 to 1-5-87				
4/12 × 30,000 =	10,000			
Loss on 1-1-87	80,000	– 70,000	– 56,000	– 14,000
(b) After acquisition profit		+ 20,000	+ 16,000	+ 4,000
			Minority Interest	10,000

Consolidated Balance Sheet of A Company and its Subsidiary B Company as at 31-12-1987

Liabilities	Rs.	Rs.	Assets	Rs.	Rs.
Share Capital			*Goodwill*		
Equity shares			*Cost of Control*		
of Rs. 10 each			Cost price	65,000	
A Co.		2,50,000	*Less* Nominal value	80,000	
Reserves & Surplus			Capital gain	15,000	
General Reserve : A Co.	50,000		*Deduct* Capital loss	56,000	
B Co.	—	50,000	Capital loss	41,000	
Capital Reserve		—	Treated Goodwill		41,000
Profit & Loss A/c :			Fixed Assets :		
A Co.	40,000		A Co.	1,75,000	
B Co.	16,000		B Co.	80,000	2,55,000
	56,000		Investments as above		
Less Unrealised profit	400	55,600	*Current Assets*		
Secured Loan			Stock : A Co.	45,000	
8% Debentures B Co.	50,000		B Co.	20,000	
Less Held by A Co.	30,000	20,000		65,000	
Current Liabilities			*Less* Unrealised profit	400	64,600
Creditors : A Co.	35,000		Debtors : A Co.	30,000	
B Co.	25,000		B Co.	15,000	
	60,000			45,000	
Less Due to A Co.	10,000	50,000	*Less* Due from A Co.	10,000	35,000
Minority Interest		10,000	Cash at Bank A Co.	30,000	
			B Co.	10,000	40,000
		4,35,600			4,35,600

Problem No. 26

From the following Balance Sheets of H Ltd. and its Subsidiary S Ltd. prepare a Consolidated Balance Sheet as on 31-12-1986.

Balance Sheets as at 31-12-1986

Liabilities	H Ltd. Rs.	S Ltd. Rs.	Assets	H Ltd. Rs.	S Ltd. Rs.
Share Capital			Goodwill	—	70,000
Equity shares			Building	60,000	27,500
of Rs. 10 each	2,50,000	1,00,000	Machinery	1,50,000	35,000
General Reserve	80,000	20,000	Share in S Ltd.		
Profit & Loss A/c	50,000	16,000	7500 shares	90,000	
Current Liabilities			Stock	50,000	25,000
Creditors	27,500	9,000	Debtors	40,000	10,000
Bills payable	15,000		Bills receivable	10,000	15,000
			Cash at Bank	22,500	22,500
	4,22,500	1,45,000		4,22,500	1,45,000

Additional Information :

(1) H Ltd. acquired 7500 shares in S Ltd. on 1-7-1986.

(2) The balance to the credit of General Reserve and Profit & Loss A/c of S Ltd. stock at Rs. 10,000 and Rs. 8,000 respectively on 1-1-1986.

(3) Out of Rs. 15,000 bills payable of H Ltd. bills amounting Rs. 10,000 were payable to S Ltd. and the S Ltd. had discount bills worth Rs. 8,000.

[K.U.D., October 1987 (Mod.)]

Solution :

Working Table

Particulars		Total	Holding Company	Minority Interest
No. of shares / ratio		10000	7500 / 3/4	2500 / 1/4
		Rs.	Rs.	Rs.
(1) Share Capital		1,00,000	75,000	25,000
(2) General Reserve	– 20,000			
Balance on 1-1-86	10,000			
Upto 1-7-86 – 6/12 × 10,000 = 5,000				
(a) Pre-acquisition		15,000	11,250 CR	3,750
(b) After acquisition		5,000	3,750	1,250
(3) Profit & Loss A/c	– 16,000			
(a) Pre-acquisition		12,000	9,000 CR	3,000
Balance 1-1-1986	8,000			
Upto 1-7-86 – 6/12 × 8,000 = 4,000				
	12,000			
(b) After acquisition		4,000	3,000	1,000
				34,000

Capital Profit	Rs.
(1) General Reserve	11,250
(2) Profit & Loss A/c	9,000
Capital Reserve	20,250

Minority Interest – Rs. 34,000.

Consolidated Balance Sheet of H Ltd. and its Subsidiary S Ltd. as at 31-12-1986

Liabilities	Rs.	Rs.	Assets	Rs.	Rs.
Share Capital			*Goodwill*		
Equity share of			Cost of Control		
Rs. 10 — H Ltd.		2,50,000	Cost price	90,000	
Reserve & Surplus			*Less* : Nominal value	75,000	
General Reserve :			Excess paid	15,000	
H Ltd.	80,000		B/s Goodwill	10,000	
S Ltd.	3,750	83,750		25,000	
Capital Reserve	20,250		*Deducted* Capital		
Deducted to Goodwill	20,250	–	Reserve per contra	20,250	4,750
Profit & Loss A/c :			Building : H Ltd.	60,000	
H Ltd.	50,000		S Ltd.	27,500	87,500
S Ltd.	3,000	53,000	Machinery : H Ltd.	1,50,000	
Current Liabilities			S Ltd.	35,000	1,85,000
Creditors : H Ltd.	27,500		*Investments* as above		
S Ltd.	9,000	36,500	*Current Assets* :		
Bills payable : H Ltd.	15,000		Stocks : H Ltd.	50,000	
S Ltd.	–		S Ltd.	25,000	75,000
	15,000		Debtors : H Ltd.	40,000	
Less Bills due to S Ltd.	2,000	13,000	S Ltd.	10,000	50,000
Minority Interest		34,000	Bills Receivable : H Ltd.	10,000	
			S Ltd.	15,000	
				25,000	
			Less Due for H Ltd.	2,000	23,000
			Cash at Bank : H Ltd.	22,500	
			S Ltd.	22,500	45,000
		4,70,250			4,70,250

Note : Bills payable of H Ltd. included Bills worth Rs. 10,000 payable to S Ltd. out of which Bills worth Rs. 8,000 estimated by S Ltd. Therefore, Bills in hand (Rs. 10,000 – 8,000) 2,000 be treated as mutual indebtedness and are eliminated from Bills payable of H Ltd. and Bills receivable of S Ltd.

Problem No. 27

The following were the Balance Sheets of H Ltd. and S Ltd. as on 31-12-1986 :

Balance Sheets as at 31-12-1986

Liabilities	H Ltd. Rs.	S Ltd. Rs.	Assets	H Ltd. Rs.	S Ltd. Rs.
Share Capital			Fixed Assets	3,60,000	80,000
Equity shares of			Investments :		
Rs. 10 each	4,00,000	1,00,000			
Reserve & Surplus			7500 shares in S Ltd.		
General Reserve	1,00,000		at cost	60,000	
Profit & Loss A/c	60,000		12% debentures in		
Secured Loan :			S Ltd. at par	50,000	
12% Debentures		70,000	Current Assets :		
Current Liabilities :			Stocks	65,000	45,000
Creditors	40,000	30,000	Debtors	35,000	20,000
			Cash at Bank	30,000	15,000
			Profit & Loss A/c		40,000
	6,00,000	2,00,000		6,00,000	2,00,000

Additional information :

(1) H Ltd. acquired shares on 1-5-1986 in S Ltd.

(2) Profit & Loss A/c of S Ltd. showed a debit balance of Rs. 64,000 on 1-1-86.

(3) Creditors of S Ltd. include Rs. 10,000 for goods. Purchased from H Ltd. on which the latter company made a profit of Rs. 2,400 and half of goods were still in stock on 31-12-1986.

Prepare Consolidated Balance sheet as on 31-12-1986.

(K.U.D., April 1987)

Solution :

Working Table

Particulars		Total	Holding Company	Minority Interest
No. of shares | Ratio		100000	7500 | 3/4	3500 | 1/4
		Rs.	Rs.	Rs.
(1) Share Capital		1,00,000	75,000	25,000
(2) General Reserve		Nil		
(3) Profit & Loss A/c				
Loss on 1-1-86	64,000			
Loss on 31-12-86	40,000			
Profit during the year	24,000			
(a) Pre-acquisition loss on 1-1-86	64,000			
Profit up to 1-5-86 4/12 × 24,000	8,000	56,000 (loss)	– 42,000 (loss)	14,000 (loss)
(b) After acquisition profit 8/12 × 24,000		16,000	+ 12,000	4,000
		Minority Interest		15,000

Capital Loss = 42,000 treated as Goodwill.

Consolidated Balance Sheet of H Ltd. and its Subsidiary S Ltd. as at 31-12-1986

Liabilities	Rs.	Rs.	Assets	Rs.	Rs.
Share Capital			*Goodwill*		
Equity shares			*Cost of Control*		
of Rs. 10 each — H Ltd.		4,00,000	Cost price	60,000	
			Nominal value	75,000	
Reserve & Surplus			Capital gain	15,000	
General Reserve H Ltd.		1,00,000	Capital profit		
Profit & Loss A/c			Capital Loss	– 42,000	
			Capital loss treated		
H Ltd.	60,000		as Goodwill		27,000
S Ltd.	12,000		Fixed Assets : H Ltd.	3,60,000	
	72,000		S Ltd.	80,000	4,40,000
			Investments in		
Less Unrealised profit	900	71,100	shares as above		
Secured Loan			12% Debentures in		
12% Debentures S Ltd.	70,000		H Ltd.	50,000	
Less Held by H Ltd.	50,000	20,000	*Less* Held by H Ltd. (Deducted per control)	– 50,000	—

Liabilities	Rs.	Rs.	Assets	Rs.	Rs.
Current Liabilities			*Current Assets*		
Creditors : H Ltd.	40,000		Stocks : H Ltd.	65,000	
S Ltd.	30,000		S Ltd.	45,000	
	70,000			1,10,000	
Less Due to H Ltd.	10,000	60,000	*Less* Unrealised		
Minority Interest		15,000	profit	900	1,09,100
			Debtors : H Ltd.	35,000	
			S Ltd.	20,000	
				55,000	
			Less Due from S Ltd.	10,000	45,000
			Cash at Bank : H Ltd.	30,000	
			S Ltd.	15,000	45,000
		6,66,100			6,66,100

Problem No. 28

The following were the Balance Sheets of H Ltd. and S Ltd. as on 31-12-1986 :

Balance Sheets as at 31-12-1986

Liabilities	H Ltd. Rs.	S Ltd. Rs.	Assets	H Ltd. Rs.	S Ltd. Rs.
Share Capital			Fixed Assets	3,60,000	80,000
Equity share of Rs. 10	4,00,000	1,00,000	Investments in S Ltd. 7500 shares		
Reserve & Surplus			at cost	60,000	
General Reserve	1,00,000	—	12% debentures in S Ltd.		
Profit & Loss A/c	60,000	—	acquired at par	50,000	—
Secured Loan :			Stock	65,000	45,000
12% Debentures		70,000	Debtors	40,000	25,000
Current liabilities :			Bills receivable	20,000	15,000
Creditors	40,000	30,000	Cash at Bank	30,000	15,000
Bills payable	25,000	20,000	Profit & Loss A/c	—	40,000
	6,25,000	2,20,000		6,25,000	2,20,000

Additional Information :

(1) H Ltd. acquired shares on 1-5-1986 in S Ltd.

(2) Profit & Loss A/c of S Ltd. showed a debit Balance of Rs. 64,000 on 1-1-1986.

(3) Creditors of S Ltd. include Rs. 10,000 for goods supplied by H Ltd. on which the latter company has made a profit of Rs. 2,400 and half of the goods were still in stock as on 31-12-1986.

(4) Bills payable of S Ltd. included Rs. 15,000 bills accepted in favour of H Ltd. out of which bills worth Rs. 10,000 were discounted by H Ltd.

Prepare Consolidated Balance Sheet as on 31-12-1986.

(K.U.D., April 1987)

Solution :

Working Table

Particulars		Total	Holding Company	Minority Interest
No. of shares | Ratio		100000	7500 | 3/4	3500 | 1/4
		Rs.	Rs.	Rs.
(1) Share Capital		1,00,000	75,000	25,000
(2) General Reserve		–	–	–
(3) Profit & Loss A/c				
Loss on 1-1-86	64,000			
Profit upto 1-5-86				
24,000 × 4/12 =	8,000			
(a) Prior to acquisition				
Capital loss		– 56,000	– 42,000	– 14,000
(b) After acquisition				
profit 24,000 × 8/12		16,000	+ 12,000	+ 4,000
				15,000

(1) Minority Interest Rs. 15,000

(2) Capital loss – Rs. 42,000

(3) Unrealised profit

Profit on sales for sales of	10,000
Profit	2,400
For 1/2 good in stock	5,000
Profit	1,200
Share of H Ltd. 3/4 × 1,200 =	900

Unrealised profit Rs. 900.

Consolidated Balance Sheet of H Ltd. & its Subsidiary company S Ltd. as at 31-12-1986

Liabilities	Rs.	Rs.	Assets	Rs.	Rs.
Share Capital			*Goodwill*		
Equity shares			Cost of Control		
of Rs. 10 each		4,00,000	Cost price	60,000	
Reserve & Surplus			Nominal value	75,000	
General Reserve H Ltd.		1,00,000	Capital Gain	+15,000	
Capital Reserve			Capital Loss	–42,000	
(resulted in loss			Capital Loss		
shown in goodwill)			treated goodwill		27,000
Profit & Loss A/c			Fixed Assets : H Ltd.	3,60,000	
H Ltd.	60,000		S Ltd.	80,000	4,40,000
S Ltd.	12,000		Investments :		
	72,000		In shares of S Ltd. as above		—
Less Unrealised profit	900	71,100	12% Debentures S Ltd.	50,000	
Secured loan :			*Less* : Held by H Ltd.	50,000	—
12% Debentures S Ltd.	70,000		Stocks : H Ltd.	65,000	
Less : Held by H Ltd.	50,000	20,000	S Ltd.	45,000	
Current Liabilities :				1,10,000	
Creditors : H Ltd.	40,000		*Less* : Unrealised profit	900	1,09,100
S Ltd.	30,000		Debtors : H Ltd.	40,000	
	70,000		S Ltd.	25,000	
Less : Due to H Ltd.	10,000	60,000		65,000	
Bills payable : H Ltd.	25,000		*Less* : Due from S Ltd.	10,000	55,000
S Ltd.	20,000		Bills receivable		
	45,000		H Ltd.	20,000	
Less : Due to H Ltd.	5,000	40,000	S Ltd.	15,000	
Minority Interest		15,000		35,000	
			Less : Due from S Ltd.	5,000	30,000
			Cash at Bank :		
			H Ltd.	30,000	
			S Ltd.	15,000	45,000
		7,06,100			7,06,100

Problem No. 29

The following were the Balance Sheets of Harihar Ltd. and its Subsidiary Sagar Ltd. as on 31-12-1985 :

Balance Sheets as at 31-12-1985

Liabilities	H Ltd. Rs.	S Ltd. Rs.	Assets	H Ltd. Rs.	S Ltd. Rs.
Share Capital			Building	90,000	–
Equity shares			Machinery	2,00,000	41,000
of Rs. 10 each	2,00,000	75,000			
Reserve & Surplus			Investments :		
General Reserve	45,000	15,000	450 shares in S Ltd.		
Profit & Loss A/c :			at cost	97,500	
Balance on 1-1-85	60,000	30,000	*Current Assets*		
Profit for year	75,000	37,500	Stocks	60,000	1,27,500
Secured Loan			Debtors	15,000	4,000
Debentures	50,000	30,000	Bills receivable		15,000
Current Liabilities			Cash at Bank	15,000	15,000
Creditors	25,000	15,000			
Bills payable	22,500	–			
	4,77,500	2,02,500		4,77,500	2,02,500

From the following information prepare : Consolidated Balance Sheet as on 31-12-1985 :

(a) Shares in Sagar Ltd. were purchased by Harihar Ltd. on 1-7-1985.

(b) As on 1-1-1985 balance on General Reserve of Sagar Ltd. was Rs. 10,000.

(c) Bills receivable held by Sagar Ltd. were all accepted by Harihar Ltd.

(d) Debtors of Sagar Ltd. included the amount of Rs. 9,000 for goods supplied to Harihar Ltd.

(e) Stock of Harihar Ltd. included goods from the above purchased worth Rs. 6,000. The goods supplied by Sagar Ltd. to Harihar Ltd. were at cost + 33-1/3%.

(K.U.D., October 1986)

Solution :

Working Table

Particulars		Total	Holding Company	Minority Interest
No. of shares | Ratio		750	450 | 3/5	300 | 2/5
		Rs.	Rs.	Rs.
(1) Share Capital		75,000	45,000	30,000
(2) General Reserve	15,000			
(a) Prior to acquisition				
On 1-1-1985	10,000			
Upto 1-7-1985				
5,000 × 1/2 =	2,500	12,500	7,500	5,000
(b) After acquisition		2,500	1,500	1,000
(3) Profit & Loss A/c				
(a) Prior to acquisition				
On 1-1-1985	30,000			
Upto 1-7-1985				
1/2 × 37,500 =	18,750	48,750	29,250	19,500
(b) After acquisition				
1/2 × 37,500		18,750	11,250	7,500
				63,000

	Rs.
(1) Minority Interest Rs. 63,000	
(2) Capital Reserve : General Reserve	7,500
Profit & Loss A/c	29,250
	36,750

(3) Unrealised profit : Sales price 60,000

Profit 1/4 of sales price = 1,500

Share of Holding company 3/5 × 1,500 = Rs. 900 unrealised profit.

Consolidated Balance Sheet of Holding Company H Ltd. and its Subsidiary S Ltd. as at 31-12-1985

Liabilities	Rs.	Rs.	Assets	Rs.	Rs.
Share Capital			*Goodwill*		
Equity share			Cost of Control		
of Rs. 100 H Ltd.		2,00,000	Cost price	97,500	
Reserves & Surplus			Nominal value	45,000	
General Reserve :				52,500	
H Ltd.	45,000		*Deduct* Capital		
S Ltd.	1,500	46,500	Res. per contra	36,750	15,750
Capital Reserve	36,750		Building : H Ltd.		90,000
Deducted from			Machinery : H Ltd.	2,00,000	
Goodwill per contra	—		S Ltd.	41,000	2,41,000
Profit & Loss A/c :			Investments (as above)		
H Ltd. on 1-1-85	60,000		*Current Assets :*		
Profit for year	75,000		Stock : H Ltd.	60,000	
S Ltd.	11,250		S Ltd.	1,27,500	
	1,46,250			1,87,500	
Less : Unrealised profit	900	1,45,350	*Less* Unrealised profit	900	1,86,600
Secured Loan			Debtors : H Ltd.	15,000	
Debentures : H Ltd.	50,000		S Ltd.	4,000	
S Ltd.	30,000	80,000		19,000	
Current Liabilities			*Less* : Due from H Ltd.	9,000	10,000
Creditors : H Ltd.	25,000		Bills recoverable :		
S Ltd.	15,000		H Ltd.	—	
	40,000		S Ltd.	15,000	
Less : Due to S Ltd.	9,000	31,000		15,000	
Bills payable H Ltd.	22,500		*Less* Due from H Ltd.	15,000	—
Less Due S Ltd.	15,000	7,500	Cash at Bank : H Ltd.	15,000	
Minority Interest		63,000	S Ltd.	15,000	30,000
		5,73,350			5,73,350

Problem No. 30

A Company Ltd. acquired 75% of equity shares in B Company Ltd. on 1-1-1984. On the date of acquisition their Balance sheets were as follows :

Balannce Sheets as at 31-12-1984

Liabilities	A Ltd. Rs.	B Ltd. Rs.	Assets	A Ltd. Rs.	B Ltd. Rs.
Share Capital			*Fixed Assets*		
Equity share of Rs. 10	6,00,000	3,60,000	Building	1,50,000	1,20,000
Reserve & Surplus			Machinery	1,70,000	1,75,000
General Reserve	60,000	40,000	Furniture	8,000	6,000
Surplus balance 1-1-84	40,000	30,000	*Investments*		
Profit for the year	90,000	60,000	27000 shares B Ltd.	3,20,000	
Current Liabilities			In Govt. security		85,000
Creditors	75,000	50,000	*Loan & Advances*		
Bills payable	20,000	20,000	Stock	92,000	64,000
			Bills receivable	25,000	20,000
			Cash at Bank	60,000	50,000
	8,85,000	5,60,000		8,85,000	5,60,000

Additional Information :

(1) On the date of acquisition of shares in B Ltd. the books of B Ltd. showed the General Reserve of Rs. 20,000.

(2) Debtors of B Ltd. include Rs. 15,000 due from A Ltd.

(3) All the Bills payable of B Ltd. were drawn by A Ltd. of which bills worth Rs. 15,000 were discounted by A Ltd.

(4) Building of B Ltd. were overvalued by Rs. 20,000 and Machinery was undervalued by Rs. 10,000.

Prepare Consolidated Balance Sheet as on 31-12-1984.

(K.U.D., April 1986)

Solution :

Working Table

Particulars		Total	Holding Company	Minority Interest
No. of shares | Ratio			75% | 3/4	25% | 1/4
		Rs.	Rs.	Rs.
(1) Share Capital		3,60,000	2,70,000	90,000
(2) General Reserve	40,000			
(a) Prior acquisition		20,000	15,000	5,000
(b) After acquisition		20,000	15,000	5,000
(3) Profit & Loss Account				
(a) Prior acquisition		30,000	22,500	7,500
(b) After acquisition		60,000	45,000	15,000
			CR 37,500	1,22,500
Less : Building overvalued		– 20,000	– 15,000	– 5,000
Add : Machinery undervalued		+ 10,000	+ 7,500	+ 2,500
			30,000	1,20,000

(1) Minority Interest – Rs. 1,20,000

(2) Capital Reserve – Rs. 30,000.

Consolidated Balance Sheet of Holding Co. A Ltd. and its subsidiary B Ltd. as at 31-12-1984

Liabilities	Rs.	Rs.	Assets	Rs.	Rs.
Share Capital			Goodwill		
Equity share of			Cost of Control		
Rs. 10 — A Ltd.		6,00,000	Cost price	3,20,000	
Reserve & Surplus			Nominal value	2,70,000	
General Reserve :			Excess paid Goodwill	50,000	
A Ltd.	60,000		*Deduct* Capital Res.	30,000	20,000
B Ltd.	15,000	75,000	Building : A Ltd.	1,50,000	
Capital Reserve	30,000		B Ltd.		
Deducted from			(1,20,000–20,000)	1,00,000	2,50,000
Goodwill (per contra)	—	—	Machinery : A Ltd.	1,70,000	
Profit & Loss A/c			B Ltd.		
Balance on 1-1-84	40,000		(1,75,000+10,000)	1,85,000	3,55,000
Profit for year	90,000		Investments as above		
	1,30,000		in Govt. security		85,000
			Stocks : A Ltd.	92,000	
Add : B Ltd.	45,000	1,75,000	B Ltd.	64,000	1,56,000

Liabilities	Rs.	Rs.	Assets	Rs.	Rs.
Current Liabilities			Debtors : A Ltd.	60,000	
Creditors : A Ltd.	75,000		B Ltd.	40,000	
B Ltd.	50,000			1,00,000	
	1,25,000		*Less* : Due from A Ltd.	15,000	85,000
Less : Due to B Ltd.	15,000	1,10,000	Bills receivable: A Ltd.	25,000	
Bills payable : A Ltd.	20,000		B Ltd.	20,000	
B Ltd.	20,000			45,000	
	40,000		*Less* : Due from B Ltd.	5,000	40,000
Less : Due to A Ltd.	5,000	35,000	Cash at Bank : A Ltd.	60,000	
Minority Interest		1,20,000	B Ltd.	50,000	1,10,000
			Furniture : A Ltd.	8,000	
			B Ltd.	6,000	14,000
		11,15,000			11,15,000

Problem No. 31

The following were the Balance Sheets of Senior Ltd. and its Subsidiary Junior Ltd. as on 31-12-1984.

Balance Sheets as at 31-12-1984

Liabilities	Sr. Ltd. Rs.	Jr. Ltd. Rs.	Assets	Sr. Ltd. Rs.	Jr. Ltd. Rs.
Share Capital			Building	60,000	85,000
Equity shares			Machinery	40,000	30,000
of Rs. 10 each	2,40,000	1,25,000	Investments in		
Reserve and Surplus			Jr. Ltd. 10,000		
General Reserve	30,000	25,000	at cost share	1,25,000	
Current Liabilities			*Current Assets*		
Creditors	10,000	7,500	Stock	35,000	37,500
Bills payable	5,000	12,500	Debtors	23,000	20,000
			Bills receivable	5,000	5,000
			Cash at Bank	12,000	12,500
	3,00,000	1,90,000		3,00,000	1,90,000

(1) When the Senior Ltd. acquired 80% of shares in the Junior Ltd. had Rs. 7,500 and Rs. 10,000 to the credit of Profit and Loss A/c and General Reserve respectively.

(2) Debtors of Senior Ltd. included Rs. 2,000 due from Junior Ltd.

(3) The Bills payable of Junior Ltd. included Rs. 2,000 Bills accepted in favour of Senior Ltd.

Prepare Consolidated Balance Sheet as on 31-12-1984.

(K.U.D., October 1985)

Solution :

Working Table

Particulars	Total	Holding Company	Minority Interest
No. of shares | Ratio	1,25,000	1,00,000 | 4/5	25,000 | 1/5
	Rs.	Rs.	Rs.
(1) Share Capital	1,25,000	1,00,000	25,000
(2) General Reserve 25,000			
(a) Prior to acquisition	10,000	8,000	2,000
(b) After acquisition	15,000	12,000	3,000
(3) Profit & Loss A/c 20,000			
(a) Prior to acquisition	7,500	6,000	1,500
(b) After acquisition	12,500	10,000	2,500
			34,000

Capital Reserve – Rs. 14,000.

Consolidated Balance Sheet of Holding Company Senior Ltd. and its Subsidiary Junior Ltd. as at 31-12-1984

Liabilities	Rs.	Rs.	Assets	Rs.	Rs.
Share Capital			*Goodwill*		
Equity shares of Rs. 10			Cost of Control		
S Ltd.		2,40,000	Cost price	1,25,000	
Reserve & Surplus			Nominal value	1,00,000	
General Reserve S Ltd.	30,000		Excess paid goodwill	25,000	
J Ltd.	12,000	42,000	Deduct Capital Res.		
Capital Reserve	14,000		per contra	14,000	11,000
Deducted per contra	—		Building : S Ltd.	60,000	
Profit & Loss A/c :			J Ltd.	85,000	1,45,000
S Ltd.	15,000		Machinery : S Ltd.	40,000	
J Ltd.	10,000	25,000	J Ltd.	30,000	70,000
Current Liabilities			Investments as above		
Creditors : S Ltd.	10,000		*Current Assets*		
J Ltd.	7,500		Stock : S Ltd.	35,000	
	17,500		J Ltd.	37,500	72,500
Less Due to S Ltd.	3,000	14,500	Debtors : S Ltd.	23,000	
Bills payable : S Ltd.	5,000		J Ltd.	20,000	
J Ltd.	12,500			43,000	
	17,500		*Less* Due from J Ltd.	3,000	40,000
Less : Due to S Ltd.	2,000	15,500	Bills Receivable : S Ltd.	5,000	
Minority Interest		34,000	J Ltd.	5,000	
				10,000	
			Less : Due from J Ltd.	2,000	8,000
			Cash at Bank : S Ltd.	12,000	
			J Ltd.	12,500	24,500
		3,71,000			3,71,000

Problem No. 32

From the Balance Sheets as on 31-12-1983 and the information given below, prepare a Consolidated Balance Sheet of H Ltd. with its Subsidiary S Ltd. as on 31-12-1983.

Balance Sheets as at 31-12-1983

Liabilities	H Ltd. Rs.	S Ltd. Rs.	Assets	H Ltd. Rs.	S Ltd. Rs.
Share Capital			Goodwill	50,000	1,00,000
Equity share of			Building	1,00,000	75,000
Rs. 100	3,00,000	2,00,000			
Reserve & Surplus			Machinery	50,000	50,000
General Reserve	30,000	20,000	Investments		
Profit & Loss A/c			1500 equity shares		
Balance on 1-1-83	35,000	30,000	in S Ltd.	1,80,000	
Profit for the year	50,000	45,000	In Govt. Security	25,000	30,000
Secured Loan			*Current Assets*		
Debentures	1,00,000		Stock	75,000	37,500
Current Liabilities			Debtors	1,00,000	60,000
Creditors	60,000	87,500	Bills Receivable		10,000
Bills payable	15,000	–	Cash at Bank	10,000	20,000
	5,90,000	3,82,500		5,90,000	3,82,500

Additional Information :

(1) H Ltd. acquired shares in S Ltd. on 1-5-1983.

(2) General Reserve of S Ltd. on 1-1-1983 was Rs. 17,000.

(3) Bills Receivable of S Ltd. were all accepted by H Ltd.

(4) Debtors of S Ltd. included the amounts of Rs. 10,000 for goods supplied to H Ltd.

(5) The stock of H Ltd. included goods purchased from S Ltd. worth Rs. 5,000. The goods supplied by S Ltd. at cost + 25%.

(K.U.D., April 1984)

Solution :

Working Table

Particulars		Total	Holding Company	Minority Interest
No. of shares | Ratio		2000	1500 | 3/5	500 | 1/4
		Rs.	Rs.	Rs.
(1) Share Capital		2,00,000	1,50,000	50,000
(2) General Reserve 20,000				
(a) Prior to acqusition				
Balance on 1-1-1983	17,000			
Upto 1-5-83 =				
4/12 × 3,000 =	1,000	18,000	13,500	4,500
(b) After acquisition				
From 1-5-83 to 31-12-83				
8/12 × 3,000		2,000	1,500	500
(3) Profit & Loss A/c				
(a) Prior to acquisition				
Balance on 1-1-83	30,000			
Upto 1-5-83				
4/12 × 4,500 =	15,000	45,000	33,750	11,250
(b) After acquisition				
1-5-83 to 31-12-83		15,000	22,500	7,500
				73,750

(1) Minority Interest – Rs. 73,750

(2) Capital Reserve :

(a) General Reserve	Rs. 13,500
(b) Profit & Loss Account	Rs. 33,750
	47,250

Unrealised Profit in stock sales price Rs. 5,000

Cost + 25% i.e. profit on sales 20% of 5,000 = Rs. 1,000

Unrealised profit share of H Ltd. 3/4 × 1,000 = Rs. 750.

Consolidated Balance Sheet of H Ltd. and its Subsidiary S Ltd. as at 31-12-1983

Liabilities	Rs.	Rs.	Assets	Rs.	Rs.
Share Capital			*Goodwill*		
Equity share of Rs. 100			Cost of Control		
each — H Ltd.		3,00,000	Cost of price	1,80,000	
Reserve & Surplus			Nominal value	1,50,000	
General Reserve :			Excess paid goodwill	30,000	
H Ltd.	30,000		*Add* : Goodwill in B/s :		
S Ltd.	1,500	31,500	H Ltd.	50,000	
Capital Reserve	47,250		S Ltd.	1,00,000	
Deducted (per contra)	–	–		1,80,000	
Profit & Loss A/c			*Deduct* Capital Res.	47,250	1,32,750
on 1-1-1983	35,000		Building : H Ltd.	1,00,000	
Profit for year	50,000		S Ltd.	75,000	1,75,000
	85,000		Machinery : H Ltd.	50,000	
3/4 shares in S Ltd.	22,500		S Ltd.	50,000	1,00,000
	1,07,500		*Investment* in shares		
Less Unrealised profit	750	1,06,750	S Ltd. as above		–
Secured Loan			In Govt. Security :		
Debenture : H Ltd.		1,00,000	H Ltd.	25,000	
Current Liability			S Ltd.	30,000	55,000
Creditors : H Ltd.	60,000		Stock : H Ltd.	75,000	
S Ltd.	87,500		S Ltd.	37,500	
	1,47,500			1,12,500	
Less Due to S Ltd.	10,000	1,37,500	*Less* Unrealised profit	750	1,11,750
Bills payable H Ltd.	15,000		Debtors : H Ltd.	1,00,000	
Less Due to S Ltd.	10,000	5,000	S Ltd.	60,000	
Minority Interest		73,750		1,60,000	
			Less Due from H Ltd.	10,000	1,50,000
			Bills receivable S Ltd.	10,000	
			Less Due to H Ltd.	10,000	–
			Cash at Bank : H Ltd.	10,000	
			S Ltd.	20,000	30,000
		7,54,500			7,54,500

Problem No. 33

The following Balance Sheet of H Ltd. and its Subsidiary S Ltd. as on 31-12-1976 are presented to you.

Balance Sheets as at 31-12-1976

Liabilities	H Ltd. Rs.	S Ltd. Rs.	Assets	H Ltd. Rs.	S Ltd. Rs.
Share Capital			Fixed Assets	3,50,000	1,50,000
Equity shares of			*Investments*		
Rs. 10 each	5,00,000	2,00,000	15000 shares in		
Reserve & Surplus			S Ltd. at cost	1,20,000	
General Reserve	1,00,000	–	8% Debentures in		
Profit & Loss A/c	80,000	–	S Ltd. at par	60,000	
Secured Loan			*Current Assets*		
8% Debentures	–	1,00,000	Stocks	90,000	40,000
Current Liabilities			Debtors	60,000	30,000
Creditors	75,000	45,000	Cash at Bank	75,000	25,000
			Profit & Loss	—	1,00,000
	7,55,000	3,45,000		7,55,000	3,45,000

Additional Information :

(1) H Ltd. acquired the shares in S Ltd. on 1-5-1976.

(2) The Profit & Loss A/c of S Ltd. showed debit balance of Rs. 1,60,000 on 1-1-1976.

(3) Creditors of S Ltd. include Rs. 20,000 for goods supplied by H Ltd. on which H Ltd. made a profit of Rs. 2,000. Half of the goods were in stock on 31-12-1976.

Prepare Consolidated Balance Sheet as on 31-12-1976.

(K.U.D., April 1980)

Solution :

Working Table

Particulars		Total	Holding Company	Minority Interest
No. of shares | Ratio		20000	15000 | 3/4	5000 | 1/4
		Rs.	Rs.	Rs.
(1) Share Capital		2,00,000	1,50,000	50,000
(2) General Reserve		–	–	–
(3) Profit & Loss A/c				
on 1-1-75 – loss	– 1,60,000			
Profit up to 1-5-76				
60,000 × 4/12 =	+ 20,000			
	1,40,000			
(a) Prior to acquisition		– 1,40,000	1,05,000	35,000
(b) After acquisition				
60,000 × 8/12 =		+ 40,000	30,000	10,000
				25,000

(1) Minority Interest Rs. 25,000

(2) Profit & Loss A/c

On 1-1-1976 loss	1,60,000
On 31-12-76 loss	1,00,000
Profit during years	60,000

Profit from 1-1-1976 to 1-5-1976

4 months 4/12 × 60,000 = 20,000 prior to acquisition

Profit after acquisition 8/12 × 60,000 = Rs. 40,000

Now loss 1-1-1976	1,60,000
Less Profit upto 1-5-76	20,000
Loss prior to acquisition	1,40,000

Unrealised profit – sales 20,000

Profit on it 2,000

1/2 of goods in stocks = 10,000

Profit on 10,000 = Rs. 1,000
(1/2% 2,000)

Unrealised profit share of H Ltd. 3/4 × 1,000 = Rs. 750.

Consolidated Balance Sheet of Holding Company H Ltd. and its Subsidiary S Ltd. as at 31-12-1976

Liabilities	Rs.	Rs.	Assets	Rs.	Rs.
Share Capital			*Goodwill*		
Equity shares of Rs. 10 each — H Ltd.		5,00,000	Cost of Control	1,20,000	
Reserves & Surplus			Nominal value	1,50,000	
General Reserve — H Ltd.		1,00,000	Capital gain	+ 30,000	
Capital Reserve (resulted in loss shown in goodwill)		—	Capital loss	– 1,05,000	
Profit & Loss A/c :				75,000	
H Ltd.	80,000		Capital loss is Goodwill		75,000
S Ltd.	30,000		Fixed Assets : H Ltd.	3,50,000	
	1,10,000	—	S Ltd.	1,50,000	5,00,000
Less Unrealised profit	750	1,09,250	*Investment*		
Secured Loan			In shares of S Ltd.		
8% Debenture in S Ltd.	1,00,000		8% Debentures in S Ltd.	60,000	
Less Held by H Ltd.	60,000	40,000	*Less* Held by H Ltd.	60,000	—
Current Liabilities			*Current Assets*		
Creditors : H Ltd.	75,000		Stocks : H Ltd.	90,000	
S Ltd.	45,000		S Ltd.	40,000	
	1,20,000			1,30,000	
Less Due to H Ltd.	20,000	1,00,000	*Less* Unrealised profit	750	1,29,250
Minority Interest		25,000	Debtors : H Ltd.	60,000	
			S Ltd.	30,000	
				90,000	
			Less Due from S Ltd.	20,000	70,000
			Cash at Bank : H Ltd.	75,000	
			S Ltd.	25,000	1,00,000
		8,74,250			8,74,250

Problem No. 34

A Company Ltd. acquired 80% of equity shares in B Company Ltd. on 31-12-1977. On that date B Company Ltd. had to its credit of Profit and Loss account Rs. 15,000 and General Reserve Rs. 20,000. The stock of B Company Ltd. includes goods worth Rs. 5,000, purchased from A Company Ltd. The profit bearing 20% on sales price.

Prepare Consolidated Balance Sheet of Holding Co.

Balance Sheets as at 31-12-1977

Liabilities	A Ltd. Rs.	B Ltd. Rs.	Assets	A Ltd. Rs.	B Ltd. Rs.
Share Capital			Land & Building	2,30,000	20,000
Equity share			Machinery	2,00,000	1,00,000
of Rs. 10	5,00,000	1,00,000			
Reserve & Surplus			Furnitures	15,500	3,000
Reserve Fund	2,20,000	30,000	*Investments*		
Profit & Loss A/c	40,000	10,000	B Co. shares	1,20,000	
Current Liabilities			Stock	2,14,000	23,000
Creditors	1,49,700	36,000	Debtors	87,000	27,400
Bills payable	21,300	7,400	Cash	64,500	10,000
	9,31,000	1,83,400		9,31,000	1,83,400

(K.U.D., October 1979)

Solution :

Working Notes

Particulars		Total	Holding Company	Minority Interest
No. of shares | Ratio			80% | 3/4	20% | 1/4
		Rs.	Rs.	Rs.
(1) Share Capital		1,00,000	80,000	20,000
(2) General Reserve	30,000			
(a) Prior to acquisition		20,000	16,000	4,000
(b) After acquisition		10,000	8,000	2,000
(3) Profit & Loss A/c	10,000			
(a) Prior to acquisition		15,000	12,000	3,000
(b) After acquisition		– 5,000	– 4,000	– 1,000
				28,000

Capital Reserve –	General Reserve	16,000
	Profit & Loss A/c	12,000
		28,000

Unrealised profit – Sales price – 5,000

Profit 20% of 5,000 profit = 1,000

Unrealised share of Holding company 80% of 1,000 = Rs. 800

Unrealised profit = Rs. 800

Minority Interest = Rs. 28,000.

Consolidated Balance Sheet of Holding Company A and its Subsidiary B Company as at 31-12-1977

Liabilities	Rs.	Rs.	Assets	Rs.	Rs.
Share Capital			Cost of Control		
Equity shares of Rs. 10 each		5,00,000	Cost price	1,20,000	
			Nominal value	80,000	
Reserve & Surplus			Excess paid	40,000	
General Reserve			*Deduct* Capital Res.		
A Co.	2,20,000		per contra goodwill	28,000	12,000
B Co.	8,000	2,28,000	Land & Building :		
Capital Reserve	28,000		A Co.	2,30,000	
Deducted from Goodwill	—	—	B Co.	20,000	2,50,000
			Machinery : A Co.	2,00,000	
Profit & Loss A/c			B Co.	1,00,000	3,00,000
A Co.	40,000		Furniture : A Co.	15,500	
Less Share in B Co.	4,000		B Co.	3,000	18,500
	36,000		*Investments* as above		
Less Unrealised profit	800	35,200	*Current Assets*		
Current Liabilities			Stocks : A Co.	2,14,000	
Creditors : A Co.	1,49,700		B Co.	23,000	
B Co.	36,000	1,85,700		2,37,000	
Bills payable : A Co.	21,300		*Less* Unrealised profit	800	2,36,200
B Co.	7,400	28,700	Debtors : A Co.	87,000	
Minority Interest		28,000	B Co.	27,400	1,14,400
			Cash : A Co.	64,500	
			B Co.	10,000	74,500
		10,05,600			10,05,600

Problem No. 35

Following are the Balance Sheets of A Ltd. and B Ltd. as at 31-12-1989 :

Balance Sheets as at 31-12-1989

Liabilities	A Ltd. Rs.	B Ltd. Rs.	Assets	A Ltd. Rs.	B Ltd. Rs.
Share Capital			*Fixed Assets*		
Equity shares of			Building	3,00,000	1,50,000
Rs. 10 each	8,00,000	4,00,000	Machinery	4,75,000	2,00,000
Reserve & Surplus			*Investments*		
General Reserve	1,25,000	20,000	B Ltd. shares 32000 at		
Profit & Loss A/c	90,000		cost & debentures	2,90,000	
Secured Loan			400 @ Rs. 90 each	36,000	
12% Debentures	2,00,000	1,00,000	*Current Assets*		
(of Rs. 100 each)			Stock	1,20,000	60,000
Current Liabilities			Debtors	80,000	25,000
Creditors	95,000	45,000	Bills receivable	40,000	
Bills payable	60,000	25,000	Cash at Bank	29,000	25,000
			Profit & Loss A/c		1,30,000
	13,70,000	5,90,000		13,70,000	5,90,000

Additional Information :

(1) A Ltd. acquired shares in B Ltd. on 1-4-1989.

(2) The Balance Sheet of B Ltd. showed on 1-1-1989 General Reserve of Rs. 40,000 and Profit & Loss A/c debit balance (loss) of Rs. 70,000.

(3) It was found that Buildings of B Ltd. was undervalued by Rs. 20,000 and Machinery was overvalued by Rs. 30,000.

(4) Creditors of B Ltd. included Rs. 25,000 for goods supplied by A Ltd. on which A Ltd. made a profit 20% on sales.

(5) The stock of B Ltd. included goods worth Rs. 15,000 purchased from A Ltd.

(6) Bills payable of B Ltd. all are in favour of A Ltd. out of which A Ltd. discounted Bills worth Rs. 20,000 with the Banker.

(K.U.D. — A)

Solution :

Working Notes

(1) General Reserve		
On 1-1-1989 credit Balance		40,000
On 31-12-1989 credit Balance		20,000
Loss during the year		20,000
Loss from 1-1-89 to 1-4-89 = 3/12 × 20,000 =	5,000	
On 1-1-1989 credit Balance	40,000	
Net credit Balance		35,000
Capital profit		+35,000
(a) Prior to acquisition		33,000
(b) After acquisition loss 9/12 × 20,000 = –15,000		– 15,000
(2) Profit & Loss A/c		
Loss on 1-1-1989		70,000
Loss on 31-12-1989		1,30,000
Loss during the year		60,000
Now loss from 1-1-989 to 1-4-1989 3/12 × 60,000 =		– 15,000
Loss on 1-1-1989		70,000
Now Capital : (a) Prior to acquisition		85,000
(b) After acquisition 9/12 × 60,000 =		– 45,000
Reserve Loss Rs. – 45,000		
(3) Assets Revalued		
(1) Building undervalued increase in value Capital profit		+ 20,000
(2) Machinery overvalued decrease in value Capital loss		– 30,000
Net result Capital loss		– 10,000

(4) Capital Profit/Loss

(a) General Reserve prior to acquisition

Capital profit 35,000

(1) Share of Holding Company 4/5 × 35,000 = 28,000 A Ltd.

1/5 × 35,000 = 7,000 M.I.

(b) Profit & Loss Account

Prior to acquisition Loss – Rs. 85,000

Share of Holding Company 4/5 × 85,000 = 68,000 A Ltd.

1/5 × 85,000 = 17,000 M I

(c) Assets revalued Capital loss 10,000

Share of Holding Company 4/5 × 10,000 = 8,000 A Ltd.

1/5 × 10,000 = 2,000 M I

Total Capital Profit/Loss

Share of Holding Company

(1) General Reserve	Profit	28,000
(2) Profit & Loss A/c	Loss	– 68,000
(3) Assets revalued	Loss	– 8,000
Net Capital loss		– 48,000

(5) Minority Interest

(1) Share Capital 4,00,000 × 1/5 =		80,000
(2) Capital Loss		
(a) General Reserve	+ 7000	
(b) Profit & Loss	– 17000	
(c) Assets Revalue	– 2000	– 12,000
(3) Revenue loss after acquisition		
(i) General Reserve 1/5 × 15,000 =		– 3,000
(ii) Profit & Loss A/c 1/5 × 45,000 =		– 9,000
Total Minority Interest		56,000

Alternatives

Working Notes

Particulars	Total	Holding Company	Minority Interest
No. of shares | Ratio	40000	32000 | 4/5	8000 | 1/5
	Rs.	Rs.	Rs.
(1) Share Capital	4,00,000	3,20,000	80,000
(2) General Reserve 20,000			
(a) Prior to acquisition	35,000	28,000	7,000
(b) After acquisition	15,000	– 12,000	– 3,000
(3) Profit & Loss A/c 1,30,000			
(a) Prior to acquisition	85,000	– 68,000	– 17,000
(b) After acquisition	45,000	– 36,000	– 9,000
			58,000
Assets Revalued			
(a) Building undervalued increase in value	+ 20,000	+ 16,000	+ 4,000
(b) Machinery overvalued decrease in value	– 30,000	– 24,000	– 6,000
			56,000

Capital Profit/Loss		
(1) General Reserve	28,000	
(2) Profit & Loss A/c	– 68,000	
		– 40,000
Assets Revalued		
Building	+ 16,000	
Machinery	– 24,000	– 8,000
Capital Loss treated as Goodwill.		– 48,000

Minority Interest – 56,000
Unrealised profit : Goods in stocks sales price 15,000
Profit 20% of 15,000 = 3,000
Share of Holding Company 4/5 × 3,000 = Rs. 2,400.

Consolidated Balance Sheet of A Ltd. Holding Company and its Subsidiary B Ltd. as at 31-12-1989

Liabilities	Rs.	Rs.	Assets	Rs.	Rs.
Share Capital			Cost of Control		
Equity shares of Rs. 10 each — A Ltd.		8,00,000	(a) Cost price of shares	2,90,000	
Reserves & Surplus			Nominal value	3,20,000	
General Reserve			Capital gain	30,000	
A Ltd.	1,25,000		(b) Debentures cost price 36,000		
Share in B Ltd. loss 4/5 × 15,000	– 12,000	1,13,000	Nominal value 40,000	4,000	
Capital Reserve			Total Capital gain	34,000	
Profit & Loss A/c			Total Capital loss	48,000	
A Ltd.	90,000		Capital loss	14,000	
Share in B Ltd.			Treated as Goodwill		14,000
loss 4/5 × 45,000	– 36,000		*Fixed Assets*		
	54,000		Building : A Ltd.	3,00,000	
Less Unrealised profit	2,400	51,600	B Ltd. 1,50,000		
Secured Loan			*Add* : Increase 20,000	1,70,000	4,70,000
12% Debentures :			Machinery : A Ltd.	4,75,000	
A Ltd.	2,00,000		B Ltd.		
B Ltd. – 1,00,000			(2,00,000–30,000)	1,70,000	6,45,000
Less by A Ltd. 40,000	60,000	2,60,000	*Investments* as above		
Current Liabilities			*Current Assets*		
Creditors : A Ltd.	95,000		Stocks : A Ltd.	1,20,000	
B Ltd.	45,000		B Ltd.	60,000	
	1,40,000			1,80,000	

Liabilities	Rs.	Rs.	Assets	Rs.	Rs.
Less Due to A Ltd.	25,000	1,15,000	*Less* Unrealised profit	2,400	1,77,600
Bills payable : A Ltd.	60,000		Debtors : A Ltd.	80,000	
B Ltd.	25,000		B Ltd.	25,000	
	85,000			1,05,000	
Less Due to A Ltd.	5,000	80,000	*Less* Due from B Ltd.	25,000	80,000
Minority Interest		56,000	Bills Receivable A Ltd.	40,000	
			Less Due from B Ltd.	5,000	35,000
			Cash at Bank : A Ltd.	29,000	
			B Ltd.	25,000	54,000
		14,75,600			14,75,600

Problem No. 36

Following are the Balance Sheets of A Ltd. and B Ltd. as at 31-12-1989 :

Balance Sheets as at 31-12-1989

Liabilities	A Ltd. Rs.	B Ltd. Rs.	Assets	A Ltd. Rs.	B Ltd. Rs.
Share Capital			*Fixed Assets*		
Shares of Rs. 10 each	6,00,000	2,00,000	Building	2,00,000	90,000
General Reserve	75,000	10,000	Machinery	3,75,000	1,40,000
Profit & Loss A/c	60,000	–	Investments in B Ltd.		
12% Debentures	2,00,000	1,00,000	shares 16000 @ cost	1,45,000	
(of Rs. 100 each)			and 12% debentures		
Current Liabilities			(400 @ Rs. 90 each)	36,000	
Bills payable	30,000	25,000	Stock	1,20,000	45,000
Creditors	60,000	45,000	Debtors	80,000	25,000
			Bills receivable	40,000	—
			Cash at Bank	29,000	15,000
			Profit & Loss	—	65,000
	10,25,000	3,80,000		10,25,000	3,80,000

(1) A Ltd. acquired shares in B Ltd. on 1-1-1989 when the Balance Sheet of B Ltd. showed a General Reserve Rs. 20,000 and Profit and Loss Account (Debit Balance of) Rs. 35,000.

(2) It was found that the Building of B Ltd. was undervalued by Rs. 10,000 and that of Machinery was overvalued by Rs. 15,000.

(3) Creditors of B Ltd. included Rs. 25,000 for goods supplied by it A Ltd. on which the latter company made a profit of Rs. 5,000.

(4) The Stock of B Ltd. included goods worth Rs. 15,000 purchased from A Ltd.

(5) Bills payable of B Ltd. all are in favour of A Ltd. out of which A Ltd. discounted the Bills worth Rs. 20,000 with its Banker.

Prepare Consolidated Balance Sheet of A Ltd. and its Subsidiary B Ltd. as at 31-12-1989.

(K.U.D. – B)

Solution :

Working Notes

(I) *Capital Loss*

On 1-1-1989 Profit & Loss A/c (Debit Balance) loss		35,000
Less : General Reserve (Credit Balance) 1-1-1989		20,000
Net loss		15,000
Add : Machinery – overvalued by loss		15,000
		30,000
Less : Building – undervalued by		10,000
Loss reduced to		20,000

Net Capital loss – 20,000

4/5 share of holding company – 4/5 × 20,000 = 16,000

1/5 Minority Interest – 1/5 × 20,000 = 4,000.

Deducted from cost of control.

(II) *Current Loss*

Profit and Loss Account debit Balance on 31-12-1989	65,000	
Less : on 1-1-1989	35,000	
Loss during the year		30,000
Add : General Reserve on 1-1-1989	20,000	
Less : 31-12-1989	10,000	
Loss in General Reserve		10,000
Total Current loss – Rs. 40,000		40,000
4/5 Holding Company of 40,000 =	32,000	
1/5 Minority Interest of 40,000 =	8,000	

(III) *Cost of Control*

Cost of shares purchased	1,45,000
Less : Face (Nominal) value of shares	1,60,000
Capital gain	15,000

12% Debentures cost price (400 × 90)	36,000	
Face value (400 × 100)	40,000	
Profit on purchase		4,000
Total Capital gain or profit		19,000
Less : Capital loss		16,000
Net Capital gain		3,000

Realised as Capital Reserve (shown on Balance sheet liability side)

(IV) *Minority Interest :*

1/5 Share Capital 2,00,000 × 1/5		40,000
Less : Capital loss 1/5 × 20,000 =	4,000	
Current loss 1/5 of 40,000 =	8,000	12,000
Net Minority Interest		28,000

Shown in Balance sheet liability side.

(V) *Unrealised Profit*

Sales price	25,000	
Profit on above	5,000	

Profit on stocks – 15,000

$$\frac{15,000}{25,000} \times 5,000 = 3,000$$

25,000

Unrealised Profit = Rs. 3,000.

4/5 share of Holding Company of 3,000 = 2,400

deducted from holding company Profit and Loss Account and also from stocks of B company.

Working Table

Particulars	Total	Holding Company	Minority Interest
No. of shares | Ratio	20000	16000 | 4/5	4000 | 1/5
	Rs.	Rs.	Rs.
(1) Share Capital	2,00,000	1,60,000	40,000
(2) General Reserve			
(a) Prior to acquisition	20,000	16,000	4,000
(b) After acquisition (loss)	– 10,000	– 8,000	–2,000
(3) Profit & Loss A/c			
(a) Prior to acquisition loss	35,000	28,000	–7,000
(b) After acquisition	30,000	24,000	6,000
			29,000

		Capital Reserve		Minority Interest	
General Reserve	+ 16,000				
Profit & Loss	– 28,000	– 12,000		+ 29,000	
Add Building increase		+ 8,000		+ 2,000	
Less : Machinery decrease		– 12,000	– 16,000	– 3,000	Rs. 28,000

Consolidated Balance Sheet of Holding Company A Ltd. and its Subsidiary B Ltd. as at 31-12-1989

Liabilities	Rs.	Rs.	Assets	Rs.	Rs.
Share Capital (A Ltd.)			*Cost of Control*		
Share of Rs. 10 each		6,00,000	Cost price of share	1,45,000	
Reserve & Surplus			Nominal value of shares	1,60,000	
General Reserve — A Ltd.		75,000	Capital gain	15,000	
Capital Reserve		3,000	12% Debentures 400×90		
Profit & Loss A/c	60,000		Cost price 36,000		
Less : Unrealised profit	2,400		Nominal value 40,000	4,000	
	57,600		Total Capital profit	19,000	
Less 1/5 shown loss	32,000	25,600	Total Capital loss	16,000	
Secured Loan			Net Capital profit	3,000	
12% Debenture :			Deducted as CR	—	—
A Ltd.	2,00,000		*Fixed Assets*		
B Ltd. 1,00,000			Building : A Ltd.	2,00,000	
Less A Ltd. 40,000	60,000	2,60,000	B Ltd. (90,000+10,000)	1,00,000	3,00,000
Current Liability			Machinery : A Ltd.	3,75,000	
Bills payable : A Ltd.	30,000		B Ltd. (1,40,000–15,000)	1,25,000	5,00,000
B Ltd.	25,000		*Investments* as above		
	55,000		Stock : A Ltd.	1,20,000	
Less Due to A Ltd.	5,000	50,000	B Ltd.	45,000	
Creditors : A Ltd.	60,000			1,65,000	
B Ltd.	45,000		*Less* Unrealised profit	2,400	1,62,000
	1,05,000		Debtors : A Ltd.	80,000	
Less Due to A Ltd.	25,000	80,000	B Ltd.	25,000	
Minority Interest		28,000		1,05,000	
			Less Due from B Ltd.	25,000	80,000
			Bills receivable A Ltd.	40,000	
			Less Due B Ltd.	5,000	35,000
			Cash at Bank : A Ltd.	29,000	
			B Ltd.	15,000	44,000
		11,21,600			11,21,600

Problem No. 37

Following are the Balance Sheets of A Ltd. and B Ltd. as at 31-12-1988 :

Balance Sheets as at 31-12-1988

Liabilities	A Ltd. Rs.	B Ltd. Rs.	Assets	A Ltd. Rs.	B Ltd. Rs.
Share Capital			*Fixed Assets*		
Shares of Rs. 10 each	6,00,000	2,50,000	Goodwill	60,000	40,000
Reserve & Surplus			Building	2,40,000	1,50,000
General Reserve			Machinery	2,50,000	1,35,000
on 1-1-1988	90,000	50,000	*Investments*		
Profit & Loss A/c	1,20,000	60,000	20000 shares in		
Secured Loan			B Ltd. @ cost	2,65,000	
8% Debentures	2,00,000	1,00,000	8% Debentures in B Ltd.	60,000	
Current Liabilities			Stock	1,20,000	1,10,000
Bills payable	20,000	20,000	Debtors	40,000	55,000
Creditors	45,000	40,000	Bills receivable	20,000	
			Cash at Bank	20,000	30,000
	10,75,000	5,20,000		10,75,000	5,20,000

Other Information :

(1) A Ltd. acquired shares in B Ltd. on 1-4-1988. The Profit and Loss Account of B Ltd. showed a credit balance on Rs. 35,000 on 1-1-1988. Out of which a dividend @ 10% was paid in July 1988 for the year 1987.

(2) All the bills payable of B Ltd. were issued in favour of A Ltd. which discounted the same with Banker.

(3) Debtors of A Ltd. include Rs. 20,000 for goods supplied to B Ltd. @ cost + 25%.

(4) Building of B Ltd. were undervalued by Rs. 25,000 and Machinery were overvalued by Rs. 15,000.

(K.U.D. – C)

Solution :

Working Notes

		Rs.
(a) *Profit & Loss A/c*		
Profit on 1-1-1988		35,000
Less Dividend @ 10% on 2,50,000 paid for 1987, on 1-7-1988		25,000
Balance of profit on 1-1-1988		10,000
Profit & Loss A/c on 31-12-1988		60,000
Less : Profit on 1-1-1988		10,000
Profit for the year 1988		50,000
Less Profit from 1-1-1988 to 3-4-1988		
Prior to acquisition 3/12 × 50,000 = 12,500.		
After acquisition 9/12 × 50,000 = 37,500.		
(b) *Capital Profit*		
(1) General Reserve – Rs. 50,000 on 1-1-1988		
Share of Holding Company 4/5 × 50,000 = 40,000		
Share of Minority Interest 1/5 × 50,000 = 10,000		
(2) *Profit*		
On 1-1-1988	10,000	
Add : Profit prior to acquisition from 1-1-1988 to 1-4-1988	12,500	
Total	22,500	
Share of Holding Company A Ltd. 4/5 × 22,500 =		18,000
Share of Minority Interest 1/5 × 22,500 =		4,500
Total Capital Reserve		
Prior to acquisition : (a) General Reserve		40,000
(b) Profit & Loss A/c		18,000
Total		58,000
Add : Building	25,000 × 4/5 =	20,000
		78,000
Less : Machinery	15,000 × 4/5 =	12,000
	Capital Profit	66,000
Add : Dividend		20,000
Total Capital Profit or Capital Reserve		86,000
(c) *Revenue Profit*		
Profit for 1-4-1988 to 31-12-1988		37,500
Share of Holding Company 4/5 × 37,500 = 30,000		
Minority Interest 1/5 × 37,500 = 7,500		

Minority Interest

1/5 Share Capital	50,000
General Reserve	10,000
Capital Profit	4,500
Revenue Profit	7,500
	72,000
Add : Building increase 1/5 × 25,000	5,000
	77,000
Less Machinery decrease 1/5 × 15000 =	3,000
Minority Interest	74,000

Unrealised Profitn :

Sales price 20,000

Profit cost + 25% of

20% on sales price

$$\frac{20}{100} \times 20{,}000 = \quad 4{,}000$$

Unrealise profit Rs. 4,000

4/5 share of Holding Company A Ltd. 4/5 × 4,000 = 3,200

Unrealised profit 3,200 deducts from Profit & Loss A/c and Stocks of A Ltd.

Working Table

Particulars		Total	Holding Company	Minority Interest
No. of shares | Ratio		25000	20000 | 4/5	5000 | 1/5
		Rs.	Rs.	Rs.
(1) Share Capital		2,50,000	2,00,000	50,000
(2) General Reserve :				
(a) Prior to acquisition		50,000	40,000	10,000
(b) After acquisition		—	—	—
(3) *Profit & Loss A/c*				
Profit on 1-1-1988	35,000			
Less Dividend paid for 1987 on 1-7-1988	25,000			
Balance of profit 1-1-88	10,000			
Profit on 31-12-1988	60,000			
Less Balance of profit 1-1-1988	10,000			
Profit for 1988	50,000			

Particulars		Total	Holding Company	Minority Interest
Profit upto 1-4-1988				
3/12 × 50,000 =	12,500			
Profit after	37,500			
Now Profit & Loss A/c				
(a) Prior to acquisition 1-1-1988			CR	
(10,000+12,500)		22,500	18,000	4,500
(b) After acquisition		37,500	30,000	7,500
Capital Profit (a) General Reserve		40,000		72,000
(b) Profit & Loss A/c		18,000	58,000	
Add : Building increase by 25,000			20,000	5,000
			78,000	77,000
Less : Machinery decrease by 15,000			12,000	3,000
			66,000	74,000
Add : Dividend 4/5 of 25,000 =			20,000	
Capital Reserve			86,000	

Unrealised Profit on sales Rs. 20,000.

Profit cost + 25% on sales price 20/100 × 20,000 = 4,000

4/5 share of Holding Company of 4,000 = Rs. 3,200.

Consolidated Balance Sheet of Holding Company A Ltd. and its Subsidiary B Ltd. as at 31-12-1988

Liabilities	Rs.	Rs.	Assets	Rs.	Rs.
Share Capital			*Goodwill*		
Equity shares of			Cost price	2,65,000	
Rs. 10 each — A Ltd.		6,00,000	*Less* Nominal value	2,00,000	
Reserve & Surplus			Excess paid	65,000	
General Reserve of			*Add* Goodwill : A Ltd.	60,000	
A Ltd.		90,000	B Ltd.	40,000	
Capital Reserve	86,000			1,65,000	
Deducted from GW	—	—	*Less* Capital Reserve	86,000	79,000
Profit & Loss A/c	1,20,000		Building : A Ltd.	2,40,000	
Less Dividend for			B Ltd. 1,50,000		
1987 in July 88			*Add* Increase 25,000	1,75,000	4,15,000
transferred to CR	20,000		Machinery : A Ltd.	2,50,000	
	1,00,000		B Ltd. 1,35,000		
Less Unrealised profit	3,200		*Less* Decrease 15,000	1,20,000	3,70,000
	96,800				

Liabilities	Rs.	Rs.	Assets	Rs.	Rs.
Add Share in B Ltd.	30,000	1,26,800	*Investments* as above in share		
Secured Loan			In debentures	60,000	
8% Debenture : A Ltd.		2,00,000	*Less* B Ltd.	60,000	—
B Ltd. 1,00,000			Stocks : A Ltd.	1,20,000	
Less by A Ltd. 60,000	40,000	2,40,000	B Ltd.	1,10,000	
Current Liabilities				2,30,000	
Bills payable : A Ltd.	20,000		*Less* Unrealised profit	3,200	2,26,800
B Ltd.	20,000	40,000	Debtors : A Ltd.	40,000	
Creditors : A Ltd.	45,000		B Ltd.	55,000	
B Ltd.	40,000			95,000	
	85,000		*Less* Due from B Ltd.	20,000	75,000
Less Due to A Ltd.	20,000	65,000	Bills Receivable A Ltd.		20,000
Minority Interest		74,000	Cash at Bank : A Ltd.	20,000	
			B Ltd.	30,000	50,000
		12,35,800			12,35,800

Problem No. 38

X Ltd. acquired 80% of both the types of shares in Y Ltd. on 1-7-1988. The Balance Sheets of X Ltd. and Y Ltd. on 31-12-1988 are as follows :

Balance Sheets as at 31-12-1988

Liabilities	X Ltd. Rs.	Y Ltd. Rs.	Assets	X Ltd. Rs.	Y Ltd. Rs.
Share Capital			*Fixed Assets*		
Equity shares of			Land & Building	4,75,000	2,50,000
Rs. 10 each	6,00,000	3,00,000	Machinery	2,20,000	3,00,000
12% Preference			*Investments*		
share of Rs. 100	3,00,000	2,00,000	in Y Ltd. equity shares		
Reserve & Surplus			24,000 cost	3,00,000	
General Reserve	2,50,000	40,000	12% pref. shares		
Profit & Loss	3,50,000	2,00,000	1600 at cost	1,80,000	
Current Liabilities			Stocks	2,00,000	75,000
Bills payable	25,000	20,000	Debtors	80,000	60,000
Creditors	60,000	45,000	Bills Receivable	25,000	30,000
			Banks	1,05,000	90,000
	15,85,000	8,05,000		15,85,000	8,05,000

Other Information :

(1) On 1-1-1988 Y Ltd. Balance sheet showed to the credit of :

(a) General Reserve – Rs. 25,000 and

(b) Profit & Loss A/c – Rs. 1,20,000.

The dividend on equity shares was paid in October 1988 for the year 1987 @ 12%. The dividend on preference shares be provided for the year 1988.

(2) Creditors of Y Ltd. include Rs. 35,000 for goods supplied by X Ltd. at a profit of 20% on sales price.

(3) Stocks of Y Ltd. includes the goods purchased from X Ltd. Rs. 20,000.

(4) Bills payable of Y Ltd. are all in favour of X Ltd. out of which Bills worth Rs. 15,000 were discounted with Banker.

Prepare Consolidated Balance sheet.

(K.U.D. — D)

Solution :

Working Table

Particulars			Total	Holding Company	Minority Interest
No. of shares : Equity shares			30000	24000	6000
Pref. shares			2000	1600	400
Ratio				4/5	1/5
			Rs.	Rs.	Rs.
(1) Share Capital : Equity shares			3,00,000	2,40,000	60,000
Preference shares			2,00,000	1,60,000	40,000
(2) General Reserve		40,000			
(a) Prior to acquisition on 1-1-1988		25,000			
Balance 15000 × ½		7,500	32,500	26,000 CR	6,500
(b) After acquisition 15000 × ½			7,500	6,000	1,500
(3) Profit & Loss A/c		2,00,000			
(a) Prior to acquisition 1-1-1988	1,20,000				
Less Dividend paid for 1987 @ 12% on 3,00,000	36,000	84,000			
Profit & Loss A/c	2,00,000				
Less Balance	84,000				
	1,16,000				
Profit for the year 1988 of		58,000	1,42,000	1,13,600	28,400
(b) Profit after acquisition		58,000			
Less Provision for preference dividend @ 12% on 2,00,000		24,000	34,000	27,200	6,800
Dividend on preference shares			24,000	19,200	4,800
					1,48,000

(1) Capital Profit : General Reserve		26,000	
Profit & Loss A/c		1,13,600	
		1,39,600	
Add : Dividend on equity shares for 1987 paid 1988 : 36,000 × 4/5		28,800	1,68,400
Deduct goodwill excess paid			80,000
Capital Reserve			88,400
(2) Cost of control : Cost price of :	Equity shares		3,00,000
	Preference shares		1,80,000
			4,80,000
Less : Face value			4,00,000
Treated as Goodwill			Rs. 80,000

Consolidated Balance Sheet of X Ltd. Holding Company and its Subsidiary Company Y Ltd. as at 31-12-1988

Liabilities	Rs.	Rs.	Assets	Rs.	Rs.
Share Capital			*Cost of Control*		
Equity shares of			Cost price		
Rs. 10 each		6,00,000	Equity shares	3,00,000	
12% Preference			Preference shares	1,80,000	
share of Rs. 100		3,00,000		4,80,000	
Reserve & Surplus			*Less* : Nominal value	4,00,000	
General Reserve :				80,000	
X Ltd.	2,50,000		*Deducted* from CR		–
Y Ltd.	6,000	2,56,000	Land & Building :		
Capital Reserve	1,39,600		X Ltd.	4,75,000	
Add : Dividend	28,800		Y Ltd.	2,50,000	7,25,000
	1,68,400		Machinery : X Ltd.	2,20,000	
Deducted from GW	80,000	88,400	Y Ltd.	3,00,000	5,20,000
Profit & Loss			*Investment* as above		
X Ltd.	3,50,000		Stocks : X Ltd.	2,00,000	
Less : Dividend 1987	28,800		Y Ltd.	75,000	
	3,21,200			2,75,000	
Less : Unrealised profit	3,200		*Less* : Unrealised profit	3,200	2,71,800
	3,18,000		Debtors : X Ltd.	80,000	
Add : Profit of Y Ltd.	27,200		Y Ltd.	60,000	
Profit Dividend	19,200	3,64,400		1,40,000	

Liabilities	Rs.	Rs.	Assets	Rs.	Rs.
			Less : Due from Y Ltd.	35,000	1,05,000
Current Liabilities			Bills receivable : X Ltd.	25,000	
Bills payable : X Ltd.	25,000		Y Ltd.	30,000	
Y Ltd.	20,000			55,000	
	45,000		*Less* : Due from Y Ltd.	5,000	50,000
Less : Due X Ltd.	5,000	40,000		1,05,000	
Creditors : X Ltd.	60,000		Banks : X Ltd.		
Y Ltd.	45,000		Y Ltd.	90,000	1,95,000
	1,05,000				
Less : Due to X Ltd.	35,000	70,000			
Minority Interest		1,48,000			
		18,66,800			18,66,800

Problem No. 39

Following are the Balance Sheets of H Ltd. and S Ltd. as at 31-12-1988 :

Liabilities	H Ltd. Rs.	S Ltd. Rs.	Assets	H Ltd. Rs.	S Ltd. Rs.
Equity share Capital			Goodwill	80,000	45,000
of Rs. 10 each	6,00,000	2,50,000	Building	2,75,000	1,60,000
Reserve & Surplus			Machinery	2,80,000	1,55,000
General Reserve			*Investments*		
1-1-19881	1,20,000	75,000	20000 shares in S Ltd.	2,65,000	
Profit & Loss	1,30,000	80,000	12% Debentures		
Secured Loan			in B Ltd. at par	60,000	
12% Debentures	2,00,000	1,00,000	*Current Assets*		
Current Liabilities			Stock	1,20,000	90,000
Creditors	95,000	50,000	Debtors	30,000	75,000
Bills payable	30,000	30,000	Bills receivable	20,000	10,000
			Cash at Bank	45,000	50,000
	11,75,000	5,85,000		11,75,000	5,85,000

Additional Information :

(1) H Ltd. acquired shares in S Ltd. on 1-4-1988. The Profit & Loss Account of S Ltd. showed a credit Balance of Rs. 50,000 on 1-1-1988, out of which a dividend of 12% on equity share capital was paid in July 1988 for the year 1987.

(2) All the Bills payable of S Ltd. were issued in favour of H Ltd. which discounted Bills worth Rs. 20,000.

(3) Debtors of H Ltd. include Rs. 20,000 for goods supplied to S Ltd. at cost plus 25%.

(4) The stock of S Ltd. include goods worth Rs. 10,000. Still in stock purchased from H Ltd.

(5) Building of S Ltd. undervalued by Rs. 20,000.

(6) Machinery of S Ltd. overvalued by Rs. 15,000.

Prepare Consolidated Balance Sheet of H Ltd. and its Subsidiary S Ltd. as at 31-12-1988.

(K.U.D. — E)

Solution :

Date of acquisition 1-4-1988

Working Notes

(1) Profit and Loss Account of S Ltd.

	Rs.
Profit on 1-1-1988	50,000
Less : Dividend paid for 1987 in 1988 @ 12% on 2,50,000	30,000
Balance of profit on 1-1-1988	20,000
Profit & Loss A/c on 31-12-1988	80,000
Less : Profit for the year 1988	20,000
Profit for the year 1988	60,000

Profit from 1-1-1988 to 1-4-1988 i.e. 3/12 × 60,000 = 15,000

(i) Profit prior to acquisition	15,000
(ii) Profit after acquisition 9/12 × 60,000 =	45,000

Now Total Capital Profit

Profit on 1-1-1988	20,000	
Add : Profit upto date of acquisition	15,000	
Capital Profit (20,000 + 15,000)		35,000

Prior to acquisition : Share Holding Company 4/5 × 35,000 = 28,000 CR

1/5 × 35,000 = 7,000 MI

Total Capital Reserve : (i) General Reserve on 1-1-1988 – 75,000

(a) Prior to acquisition	75,000
(b) After acquisition	—

Share of Holding Company prior to acquisition 4/5 × 75,000 = 60,000

1/5 × 75,000 = 15,000

Dividend Received for 1987

4/5 × 30,000 = 24,000 H Ltd.

Assets Revalued :

(1) Building undervalued increase in value	+ 20,000
(2) Machinery overvalued decrease in value	– 15,000
Net Capital profit	5,000
Share of Holding Company	4/5 × 5,000 = 4,000 CR
	1/5 × 5,000 = 1,000 MI

Total Capital Reserve

	Rs.	
(1) General Reserve	60,000	
(2) Profit & Loss A/c	28,000	
(3) Dividend	24,000	
(4) Profit on Assets revalued	4,000	
	1,16,000	Total Capital Reserve

Minority Interest :

(1) Share Capital 1/5 × 2,50,000 =	50,000
(2) Profit & Loss A/c	
Prior to acquisition	7,000
After acquisition 1/5 × 45,000	9,000
(3) General Reserve	
Prior to acquisition	15,000
(4) Assets Revalued profit	1,000
Minority Interest	82,000

Unrealised Profit

Goods in Stock

Sales Price	10,000
Cost + 25%	
Profit 1/5 × 10,000 =	2,000
Profit unrealised =	2,000
Share of Holding Company	
4/5 × 2,000 =	Rs. 1,600

Working Chart

Particulars		Total	Holding Company	Minority Interest
No. of shares		25000	20000	5000
Ratio			4/5	1/5
		Rs.	Rs.	Rs.
(1) Share Capital of S Ltd.		2,50,000	2,00,000	50,000
(2) General Reserve 75,000				
(a) Prior to acquisition 1-1-88		75,000	60,000 CR	15,000
(b) After acquisition		Nil	–	–
(3) Profit & Loss A/c				
Profit on 1-1-1988	50,000			
Less : Dividend paid for 89 @ 12% on 2,50,000	30,000			
Balance of profit	20,000			
Add : Profit upto date acquisition 1-4-89	15,000			
(a) Prior to acquisition		35,000	28,000 CR	7,000
(b) After acquisition		45,000	36,000	9,000
				81,000
Assets Revalued				
(1) Building undervalued increase in value		20,000	+ 16,000	4,000
(2) Machinery overvalued decrease in value		–15,000	–12,000	–3,000
				82,000

Unrealised profit : Sales of goods 20,000

Sales price cost + 25% profit 1/5 × 20,000 = 4,000

Goods in Stock = 10,000

Profit 1/5 × 10,000 = 2,000

Share of Holding Company 4/5 × 2,000 = 1,600

Now Total Capital Profit	Rs.
(1) General Reserve	60,000
(2) Profit & Loss A/c	28,000
(3) Assets Revalued (16,000 – 12,000)	4,000
(4) Dividend for 1987	24,000
Capital Reserve	1,16,000

Consolidated Balance Sheet of H Ltd. Holding Co. and its Subsidiary S Ltd. as at 31-12-1988

Liabilities	Rs.	Rs.	Assets	Rs.	Rs.
Share Capital of H Ltd.			*Goodwill*		
Equity share of Rs. 10		6,00,000	Cost of Control		
Reserves & Surplus			Cost price	2,65,000	
General Reserve			Nominal value	2,00,000	
on 1-1-1988 H Ltd.		1,20,000	Excess paid	65,000	
Capital Reserve	1,16,000		*Add* Goodwill : H Ltd.	80,000	
			S Ltd.	45,000	
Deducted from goodwill	—	—	Total Goodwill	1,90,000	
Profit & Loss A/c			*Deduct* Capital		
H Ltd.	1,30,000		Reserve	1,16,000	74,000
Less Dividend for 87			Building : H Ltd.	2,75,000	
paid in July 88	24,000		S Ltd. 1,60,000		
	1,06,000		*Add* : Increase 20,000	1,80,000	4,55,000
Add : S Ltd.	36,000		Machinery : H Ltd.	2,80,000	
			S Ltd. 1,55,000		
	1,42,000		*Less* Decrease 15,000	1,40,000	4,20,000
Less Unrealised profit	1,600	1,40,400	*Investments* as above		
Secured Loan			Shares in S Ltd.		
12% Debenture :			12% Debentures		
H Ltd.	2,00,000		S Ltd.	60,000	
S Ltd. 1,00,000			*Less* : Held by H Ltd.	60,000	—
Less : H Ltd. 60,000	40,000	2,40,000	*Current Assets*		
Current Liabilities			Stock : H Ltd.	1,20,000	
			S Ltd.	90,000	
Creditors : H Ltd.	95,000			2,10,000	
S Ltd.	50,000		*Less* : Unrealised profit	1,600	2,08,400
	1,45,000		Debtors : H Ltd.	30,000	
			S Ltd.	75,000	
Less Due to H Ltd.	20,000	1,25,000		1,05,000	
Bills payable : H Ltd.	30,000		*Less* : Due from S Ltd.	20,000	85,000
S Ltd.	30,000		Bills receivable : H Ltd.	20,000	
	60,000		S Ltd.	10,000	
Less Due to H Ltd.	10,000	50,000		30,000	
Minority Interest		82,000	*Less* Due from S Ltd.	10,000	20,000
			Cash at Bank : H Ltd.	45,000	
			S Ltd.	50,000	95,000
		13,57,400			13,57,400

Notes : S Ltd. Bills payable Rs. 30,000 in favour of H Ltd.

H Ltd. discounted Bills Rs. 20,000. Now Bills in hand only Rs. 10,000 deducted.

Problem No. 40

X Ltd. acquired 80% of the types of shares in Y Ltd. on 1-7-1988. The Balance Sheets of X Ltd. and Y Ltd. as on 31-12-1988 were as follows :

Balance Sheets as at 31-12-1988

Liabilities	X Ltd. Rs.	Y Ltd. Rs.	Assets	X Ltd. Rs.	Y Ltd. Rs.
Share Capital			*Fixed Assets*		
12% Preference			Building	4,50,000	2,75,000
share of Rs. 100	2,50,000	1,50,000	Machinery	2,00,000	2,80,000
Equity share Rs. 10	5,50,000	3,00,000	*Investments*		
Reserve & Surplus			In Y Ltd.		
General Reserve	2,25,000	50,000	Equity shares		
Profit & Loss A/c	3,75,000	1,75,000	24000 at cost	3,00,000	
Current Liabilities			Preference shares		
Creditors	90,000	60,000	1200 at cost	3,00,000	
Bills payable	30,000	25,000	*Current Assets*		
			Stock	2,00,000	75,000
			Bills receivable	45,000	20,000
			Debtors	80,000	50,000
			Cash at Bank	1,05,000	60,000
	15,20,000	7,60,000		15,20,000	7,60,000

Additional Information :

(1) On 1-1-1988 Y Ltd. Balance Sheet showed to the credit of (a) General Reserve Rs. 25,000 and (b) Profit & Loss A/c 1,00,000. Dividend on equity shares @ 12% paid in October 1988 for the year 1987. The Dividend on preference shares be proceeded for the year 1988.

(2) Creditors of Y Ltd. include Rs. 35,000 for goods supplied by X Ltd. at a profit of 20% on sales price.

(3) Stock of Y Ltd. include Rs. 20,000. Goods purchased from X Ltd.

(4) Bills payable of Y Ltd. are all in favour of X Ltd., out of which X Ltd. discounted the Bills amount to Rs. 15,000 with its bank.

(5) Building of Y Ltd. undervalued Rs. 25,000 and Machinery overvalued by Rs. 5,000.

Prepare Consolidated Balance Sheet of X Ltd. and its Subsidiary Y Ltd.

(K.U.D. – F)

Solution :

Date of acquisition 1-7-1988

Working Table

Particulars		Total	Holding Company	Minority Interest
Ratio		100%	80% 4/5	20% 1/5
		Rs.	Rs.	Rs.
(1) Share Capital Equity		3,00,000	2,40,000	60,000
Preference share		1,50,000	1,20,000	30,000
(2) General Reserve on 1-1-88				
Balance on 1-1-88	25,000			
Upto date of acquisition i.e. from 1-1-88 to 1-7-1988 (6/12)	12,500			
(a) Prior to acquisition		37,500	30,000 CR	7,500
(b) After acquisition		12,500	10,000	2,500
(3) Profit & Loss A/c on 31-12-1988	1,75,000			
Balance on 1-1-1988	1,00,000			
Less Dividend on equity share @ 12% on 3,00,000 paid for 1987 in July 1988	36,000			
Balance 1-1-1988	64,000			
Now profit on 31-12-1988	1,75,000			
Profit on 1-1-1988	64,000			
Profit during the year 1988	1,11,000			
Profit upto date of acquisition i.e. 1-1-88 to 1-7-88 — 6 months 1/2 × 1,11,000 =	55,500			
Profit prior to acquisition				
Now Total Capital Profit				
Balance on 1-1-88	64,000			
Add : Profit upto 1-7-88	55,500			
(a) Prior to acquisition		1,19,500	95,600	23,900
(b) After acquisition	55,500	—	—	—
Revenue Profit :				
Less : Dividend on pref. shares provide for 88	18,000	37,500	30,000	7,500
Dividend on pref. shares for 88		18,000	14,400	3,600
Add : Revalued Building increase		25,000	20,000	5,000
Machinery decrease		5,000	–4,000	–1,000
		Minority Interest		1,39,000

Note 1 :

Total Capital Profit

(1) General Reserve	30,000
(2) Profit & Loss A/c	95,600
(3) Dividend for 1987	
4/5 × 36,000 =	28,800
(4) Assets Revalued	
(20,000 – 4,000)	16,000
Total Capital Reserve	1,70,400

Note 2 :

Minority Interest

(1) Share Capital	
(a) Equity shares	60,000
(b) Preference shares	30,000
(2) General Reserve	7,500
	2,500
(3) Profit & Loss CR	23,900
R	7,500
Dividend for profit R	3,600
Assets Revalued	4,000
Total Minority Interest	1,39,000

Unrealise Profit

Goods included in stock of Y Ltd. 20,000

Profit 20% on sales price — 20% of 20,000 = 4,000

Share of Holding Company 4/5 × 4,000 = 3,200.

Unrealised profit = Rs. 3,200.

Consolidated Balance Sheet of X Ltd. Holding Company and its Subsidiary Y Ltd. as at 31-12-1988

Liabilities	Rs.	Rs.	Assets	Rs.	Rs.
Share Capital of X Ltd.			*Goodwill*		
12% preference			Cost price equity	3,00,000	
share of Rs. 100		2,50,000	Nominal value	2,40,000	60,000
Equity share of Rs. 10		5,50,000	Preference shares	1,40,000	
Reserve & Surplus			Nominal value	1,20,000	20,000
General Reserve :			Total Goodwill		80,000
X Ltd.	2,25,000		*Deducted* from		
Y Ltd.	10,000	2,35,000	Capital Reserve		—
Capital Reserve	1,70,400		Building : X Ltd.	4,50,000	
Deduct Goodwill	80,000	90,400	Y Ltd. 2,75,000		
Profit & Loss A/c	3,75,000		*Add* Increase 25,000	3,00,000	7,50,000
Less Dividend for			Machinery : X Ltd.	2,00,000	
1987 transferred			Y Ltd. 2,80,000		
to Capital Reserve	28,800		*Less* Decrese 5,000	2,75,000	4,75,000
	3,46,200		*Current Assets*		
Add : S Ltd. profit	30,000		Stocks : X Ltd.	2,00,000	
	3,76,200		Y Ltd.	75,000	
Add : Dividend on pref.				2,75,000	
shares for year 1988	14,400		*Less* Unrealised profit	3,200	2,71,800
	3,90,600		Debtors : X Ltd.	80,000	
Less : Unrealised profit	3,200	3,87,400	Y Ltd.	50,000	
Current Liabilities				1,30,000	
Creditors : X Ltd.	90,000		*Less* : Due from Y Ltd.	35,000	95,000
Y Ltd.	60,000		Bills receivable : X Ltd.	45,000	
	1,50,000		Y Ltd.	20,000	
Less Due to X Ltd.	35,000	1,15,000		65,000	
Bills payable : X Ltd.	30,000		*Less* : Due from Y Ltd.	10,000	55,000
Y Ltd.	25,000		Cash at Bank : X Ltd.	1,05,000	
	55,000		Y Ltd.	60,000	1,65,000
Less Due to X Ltd.	10,000	45,000			
Minority Interest		1,39,000			
		18,11,800			18,11,800

5

Bank Accounts

The Banking Companies Act of 1949

Specifies the proforma for presenting Balance Sheet and the Profit and Loss Account for the year ended.... The Third Schedule Form-A is prescribed the Pro-Forma of Balance Sheet the manner in which it is to be prepared to show the financial position of the Banking companies i.e., Balance Sheet expose the Capital—Authorised, issued and subscribed and paid up capital, and also Reserves and Surplus Deposits — classified and other liabilities. Similarly Assets are shown in order of liquidity of funds and classified and fixed Assets etc.

The performance of the Banking companies is known by preparing Profit and Loss Account for the year i.e., the Profit or Loss.

The Profit and Loss Account is prepared in a proforma specified in Schedule III. Form-B as per the provisions of the Banking Companies Act, it is stated that the Incomes – *Less* Provisions made during the year for Bad and Doubtful debts, Rebate on bills discounted and Investment fluctuation Reserve i.e., Interest and Discount Received.

Less : Provisions for Bad and Doubtful debts.

Rebate on Bills Discounted

Taxation

Investment fluctuation Reserve etc.

Net amount of Interest and Discount is shown under Incomes of Profit and Loss Account.

All the Banking Companies were following the Provisions of the Act in preparing :

(a) Profit and Loss Account for the year ended in Form-B, Schedule-III.

(b) Balance Sheet as at ... in Form-A, Schedule-III.

Now recently, Reserve Bank of India issued circular letter directing all the Banking companies to prepare the Final Accounts as on 31st March every year in the prescribed form under Schedule Third — Form-A — Balance Sheet and Form-B — Profit and Loss Account.

The following are the new Pro-forma as per Schedule Third :

Form-A, Balance Sheet and

Form-B, Profit and Loss Account.

(*Note* : Till recently the Profit and Loss Account and the Balance Sheets of the Banks were prepared as per the provision earlier, the problems were answered accordingly. On receipt of advise of R.B.I. — the proforma provided in Schedule Third — Form-A, Balance Sheet and Form-B — Profit and Loss Account are prepared accordingly.)

Proforma—Schedule Third—Form-A, Balance Sheet.

Proforma—Schedule Third—Form-B, are as follows :

(Students are advised to follow the new Pro-Forma as given in answering the Problems/Questions in the Examinations.)

BANK ACCOUNTS

Third Schedule *(Section 20)*

Form-A — Name of the Bank

Balance Sheet as at 31-12-19....

Capital and Liabilities	Schedule	Current Year	Previous Year
(1) Capital	1		
(2) Reserves & Surplus	2		
(3) Deposits	3		
(4) Borrowings	4		
(5) Other Liabilities and Provision	5		
Total			
Property and Assets			
(1) Cash and Balance with Reserve Bank of India	6		
(2) Balance with Banks and money at call & short Notice	7		
(3) Investments	8		
(4) Advances	9		
(5) Fixed Assets	10		
(6) Other Assets	11		
Total			
(7) Contingent liabilities	12		
Bills for collections	—		

All the liabilities are classified and shown under Schedule 1 to 5 and all the Assets under schedule 6 to 11. The contingent liabilities shown under Schedule 12 — Bills for collection no provision in Schedule proposed and therefore shown outside Balance Sheet. The main schedules mentioned in Balance Sheets required to be proposed separately showing all the prescribed particulars and details and only the total amount of the schedule is to be shown. The total liabilities agree with the total Assets.

Schedule 1 — Capital

	Rs.
(1) Authorised Capital	
... Shares of Rs. ... each	
(2) Issued Capital	
Shares of Rs. ... each	
(3) Subscribed Capital	
Shares of Rs. ... each	
(4) Called up Capital	
Shares of Rs. ... each	
Less Calls unpaid	
Add Forfeited shares	
Total	

The total of this schedule be shown in Balance Sheet

Schedule 2 — Reserves & Surplus

(1) Statutory Reserve	
Opening Balance	
Add during the year	
(2) Capital Reserves	
Opening Balance	
Add during the year	
(3) Share Premium	
Opening Balance	
Add during the year	
Deductions during the year	
(4) Revenue and other Reserves	
Opening Balance	
Add during the year	
Deductions during the year	
(5) Balances in profit & Loss A/c	
Opening Balance	
Add during the year	
Deductions during the year	
Total	

Schedule 3 — Deposits Rs.

(1) Demand Deposits

From Banks

From Others

(2) Savings Banks Deposits

(3) Term Deposits

From Banks

From Others

(i) Deposits of branches in India

(ii) Deposits of branches outside India

Total

Schedule 4 — Borrowings

(1) Borrowing in India

From Reserve Bank of India

From Other Banks

From Other Institutions and Other Agencies

(2) Borrowing outside India

Total

Schedule 5 — Other Liabilities and Provisions

(1) Bills payable

(2) Inter Office Adjustments

(3) Interest accrued

(4) Others (including provisions)

Total

Schedule 6 — Cash and Balances with Reserve Bank of India

(1) Cash in hand (including foreign currency Notes)

(2) Balances with Reserve Bank of India

(a) In Current A/c

(b) In Other A/cs.

Total

Schedule 7 — Balances with Banks and Money at Call and Short Notice

Rs.

(I) In India
- (i) Balance with Banks
  - In Current A/c
  - In Other Deposit A/c
- (ii) Money at Call and Short Notice
  - with Banks
  - with other Institutions

(2) Outside India.
- (a) In Current A/c
- (b) In Other Deposit A/cs
- (c) Money at Call and Short Notice

Total

Schedule 8 — Investments

(1) Investments in India
- (a) Government securities
- (b) Other approved securities
- (c) Shares
- (d) Debentures and Bonds
- (e) Subsidiaries and for joint ventures
- (f) Others

(2) Investments outside India
- (a) Government securities (including local Authorities)
- (b) Subsidiaries and loss joint ventures
- (c) Others

Total

Schedule 9 — Advances

(1) Bills purchased and Discounted
- (b) Cash Credits, Overdrafts and loan (repayable on Demands)
- (c) Term Loans

(2) (a) Secured by Tangible Assets
- (b) Covered by Bank/Government Guarantee
- (c) Unsecured

Rs.

(i) Advance in India

(a) Priority sectors

(b) Private sectors

(c) Banks

(d) Others

(ii) Advances outside India

(a) Due from Banks

(b) Due from Others

(c) Bills purchased and discounted others

Total

Schedule 10 — Fixed Assets

(1) Premises

at cost as per last B/S

Additions during the year

Deductions during the year

Depreciation to date

(2) Other Assets (including Furnitures and Fixtures)

at cost as per last B/S

Additions during the year

Deductions during the year

Depreciation to date

Total

Schedule 11 — Other Assets

(a) Inter Office Adjustment

(b) Interest accrued

(c) Tax paid in Advance/Tax deducted at source

(d) Stationery and Stamps

(e) Non-Banking Assets acquired in satisfaction of claims

(f) Others

Total

Schedule 12 — Contingent Liabilities Rs.

(a) Claims against the Banks not acknowledged as debts
(b) Liabilities for partly paid Investments
(c) Liabilities outstanding forward incharge contracts
(d) Guarantee given on behalf of constituent
  (i) In India
  (ii) Outside India
(e) Acceptances, Endorsements and other obligations
(f) Other item, for which Bank is contingents liable

Total

BILLS OF COLLECTION

It should be shown outside Balance Sheet

No Schedule is provided for this

Form-B

Profit and Loss Account for the year ended 31-3-19...

Income	Schedule	Current Year	Previous Year
Interest earned	13		
Other incomes	14		
Total			
Expenditure			
Interest expended	15		
Operating expenses	16		
Provisions & contingencies			
Total			
Profit/Loss			
Net profit for the year			
Profit brought forward			
Total			
Appropriation			
Transfer to Statutory Reserve			
Transfer to other Reserve			
Balance carried over to B/S			
Total			

Schedule 13— Interest Earned Rs.

(1) Interest Discount on Advances / B/S
(2) Income on Investment
(3) Interest on Balances with RBI and other inter-Bank Funds
(4) Others

Total

Schedule 14 — Other Income

(1) Commission, Exchange and Brokerage
(2) Profit on sale of Investment
Less Loss on sale of Investment
(3) Profit on Revaluation of
Revaluation of Investments

Less :
(4) Profit on Sales of Land & Building and other Assets
Less Loss on sales of Land and Building and other Assets
(5) Profit on Exchange Transactions
Less Loss on exchange Transactions
(6) Incomes earned by way of Dividends abroad and in India
(7) Miscellaneous Income

Total

Schedule 15 — Interest Expended

(1) Interest on deposits
(2) Interest on Reserve Bank of India inter-Bank Borrowings
(3) Other

Total

Schedule 16 — Operating Expenses

(1) Payment to and provisions to employees
(2) Rent, Taxes and Lighting
(3) Printing and Stationery
(4) Advertisement and publicity
(5) Depreciation on Bank property
(6) Directors fees and allowances
(7) Auditors fees (including branch auditors)
(8) Law charges
(9) Postage, Telegrams, Telephone etc.
(10) Repairs and Maintenances
(11) Insurances
(12) Other Expenses

Total

Provisions & Contingencies

Problem No. 1

The following is the Trial Balance of Mahalaxmi Bank Ltd. as on 31-3-1997

Trial Balance as on 31-3-1997

		Dr Rs.	Cr Rs.
1.	Share Capital (in shares of Rs. 100 each)	—	1,25,000
2.	Reserves	—	87,500
3.	Fixed deposits	—	2,37,500
4.	Investment (at cost)	6,50,000	—
5.	Current Accounts	—	17,50,000
6.	Profit & Loss A/c (Cr) 1-4-1996	—	52,500
7.	Premises (original cost Rs. 10,75,000	10,50,000	—
8.	Cash in hand	40,000	—
9.	Cash with RBI	3,25,000	—
10.	Loans from other Banks	—	1,75,000
11.	Bills discounted and purchased	4,00,000	—
12.	Savings Bank Account	—	10,00,000
13.	Bills payable	—	2,00,000
14.	Unclaimed dividend	—	7,500
15.	Branch Adjustment A/c (Cr)	—	7,500
16.	Non Banking Assets	60,000	—
17.	Stamps on hand	2,500	—
18.	Stock of Printing and Stationery	7,500	—
19.	Advance to Building Contractor	5,000	—
20.	Loans Advances and Cash Credits	11,68,500	—
21.	Profit for the year 31-3-1997	—	66,000
		37,08,500	37,08,500

Adjustments :

(a) Make necessary provision for statutory reserve

(b) Directors proposed dividend at 20%

(c) Provide for rebate on Bills discounted Rs. 750

(d) Acceptances and Endorsement Rs. 7,500

(e) Bills for collection Rs. 5,000

Prepare Balance Sheet in prescribed Schedules and Forms.

[K.U.D., April 1998(N)]

Solution :

Form-A

Mahalaxi Bank Ltd.

Balance sheet as at 31-3-1997

	Schedule	Rs.
(I) *Capital & Liabilities*		
(1) Capital	1	1,25,000
(2) Reserves & Surplus	2	1,80,250
(3) Deposits	3	29,87,500
(4) Borrowings	4	1,75,000
(5) Other Liabilities	5	2,40,750
Total		37,08,500
(II) *Property and Assets*		
(6) Cash and Balances with RBI	6	3,65,000
(7) Balances with other Banks and Money at Call and Short Notice	7	Nil
(8) Investments	8	6,50,000
(9) Advances	9	15,68,500
(10) Fixed Assets	10	10,50,000
(11) Other Assets	11	75,000
Total		37,08,500
(12) Contingent Liabilities	12	
(a) Bills for Collection		5,000
(b) Acceptances and Endorsements etc.		7,500
		12,500

Form-B

Profit & Loss A/c for the year ended 31-3-1997

Incomes			
Interest Earned	13		
Other Incomes	14		
Total			
Expenditure			
Interest Expended	15		
Operating Expenses	16		
Provisions & Contingencies			
Total			
Profit for the year, 31-3-1997			66,000
Less Provision for Rebate on Bills discounted		750	750
			65,250
Appropriation			
(a) Statutory Reserve u/s 17 — 20% on 65,250		13,050	
(b) Proposed Dividend — 20% on 1,25,000		25,000	38,050
Net Profit			27,200

Schedule to Balance sheet as at 31-3-1997

		Rs.
Schedule 1 — Capital		
Authorised Capital		
Issued and Paid up — Shares of Rs. 100 each		1,25,000
Total		1,25,000
Schedule 2 — Reserves & Surplus		
Reserve		87,500
Statutory Reserves up 17		13,050
Surplus — Profit 1-4-1996	52,500	
Add Profit for the year	27,200	79,700
Total		1,80,250
Schedule 3 — Deposits		
(a) Fixed Deposits		2,37,500
(b) Current Account		17,50,000
(c) Saving Bank Account		10,00,000
Total		29,87,500
Schedule 4 — Borrowings		
Loans from other Banks		1,75,000
Total		1,75,000
Schedule 5 — Other Liabilities		
Bills payable		2,00,000
Unclaimed dividend		7,500
Branch adjustment		7,500
Proposed Dividend		25,000
Rebate on Bills discounted		750
Total		2,40,750
Schedule 6 — Cash in hand and with RBI		
Property & Assets		
(a) Cash in hand		40,000
(b) Cash with RBI		3,25,000
Total		3,65,000

		Rs.
Schedule 7 — Balances with other Banks and Money at Call and Short Notice		—
Total		Nil
Schedule 8 — Investments		
Investments (at Cost)		6,50,000
Total		6,50,000
Schedule 9 — Advances		
Loans advances and Cash Credits		11,68,500
Bills discounted and purchased		4,00,000
Total		15,68,500
Schedule 10 — Fixed Assets		
Promises		
Less Depreciation (Cost 10,75,000)	10,50,000	
Total		10,50,000
Schedule 11 — Other Assets		
Non Banking Assets		60,000
Stamps in hand		2,500
Stock of Printing & Stationery		7,500
Advance to Building Contractor		5,000
Total		75,000
Schedule 12 — Contingent Liabilities		
(a) Bills for Collection		5,000
(b) Acceptances, Endorsements etc.		7,500
Total		12,500

Problem No. 2

From the following information :

Prepare the Profit & Loss A/c of Modern Banks for the year ending 31-3-1996 with the necessary schedules.

	Rs.
Interest of Discount	4,60,000
Income on Investments	40,000
Interest on Balances with R.B.I.	20,000
Commission and Exchange	1,60,000
Profit on sale of Investments	20,000
Interest on Deposits	1,30,000
Interest on Borrowings from R.B.I.	30,000
Payments to and provision for employees	1,40,000
Rent, Taxes and Lighting	40,000
Printing and Stationery	30,000
Advertisement and Publicity	12,000
Depreciation on Bank's property	8,000
Auditors fees and allowances	16,000
Directors fees	24,000
Law charges	10,000
Postages, Telegrams & Phones	4,000
Repairs and Maintenance	14,000
Insurance	2,000

Other Informations :

(1) Make provision for Income Tax Rs. 20,000

(b) Provision for Bad and Doubtful Debts Rs. 12,000

(c) Provide for Rebate on Bills discounted Rs. 8,000

(d) 20% of the Profit to be transferred to Statutory Reserve

(e) The Directors have proposed a Dividend of Rs. 40,000.

[K.U.D., October 1997(N)]

Solution :

Form-B

Modern Bank Ltd.

Profit & Loss A/c for the year ended 31-3-1996

Particulars		Schedule	Amount Rs.
Income			
Interest Earned		13	4,80,000
Other Incomes		14	2,20,000
	Total		7,00,000
Expenditure			
Interest Expended		15	1,60,000
Operating Expenses			
Provisions & Contingencies		16	3,00,000
	Total		4,60,000
Provisions	Total		40,000

		Rs.
Incomes — Schedule 13 & 14	Total	7,00,000
Less Expenditure — Schedule 15 & 16		4,60,000
		2,40,000
Less Provisions		40,000
Net Profit for the year		2,00,000
Add Profit brought forward		—
	Total Profit	2,00,000
Appropriation		
(1) Terms for to Statutory Reserve 20%		– 40,000
(2) Proposed Dividend		– 40,000
Profit Transferred to B/s		1,20,000

Schedules for Profit & Loss A/c for the year ended 31-3-1996

Particulars		Schedule	Amount
Incomes — Interest Earned		13	
Interest & Discount			4,60,000
Interest on Balances with R.B.I.			20,000
	Total		4,80,000
Other Incomes		14	
Incomes on Investment			40,000
Commission and Exchange			1,60,000
Profit on sale of Investments			20,000
	Total		2,20,000

Particular	Schedule	Amount
Expenses		Rs.
Interest on Deposit	15	1,30,000
Interest on Borrowings from R.B.I.		30,000
Total		1,60,000
Operating Expenses	16	
Payments to and provisions to employees		1,40,000
Rent, Taxes and Lighting		40,000
Printing and Stationery		30,000
Advertisement & Publicity		12,000
Depreciation on Bank's property		8,000
Auditors fees and Allowances		16,000
Directors fees		24,000
Law charges		10,000
Postage, telegrams and phones		4,000
Repairs and maintenances		14,000
Insurance		2,000
Total		3,00,000
Provisions and Contingencies		
(1) Provision for Income Tax		20,000
(2) Provision for Bad Debts		12,000
(3) Provision for Rebate on Bills discounted		8,000
Total		40,000

Problem No. 3

Shri Durdundishwar Banks Ltd.'s Trial Balance as on 31-3-1995

	Dr. Rs.	Cr. Rs.
Share Capital :		
Authorised — 6000 Equity shares of Rs. 100 each		
2000 Preference shares of Rs. 100 each		
Issued — 4000 Equity shares of Rs. 100 each		
2000 Pref. shares of Rs. 100 each		
Called up — 4000 Equity shares of Rs. 80		3,20,000
2000 Preference shares fully paid		2,00,000
Statutory Reserve		1,60,000
Capital Reserve		40,000
Cash in hand	2,00,000	—

	Dr. Rs.	Cr. Rs.
C.D. with R.B.I.	3,00,000	—
F.D. with R.B.I.	2,40,000	—
Profits for the year 1994-95 (before Appropriation)	—	2,84,000
Profit & Loss A/c (1-4-94)	—	60,000
Unpaid expenses	—	8,000
Balance with other Banks (Current A/c)	6,00,000	—
Money at Call and Short Notice	1,20,000	—
Current Deposits	—	8,00,000
Savings Bank Deposits	—	5,00,000
Fixed Deposits	—	3,20,000
Recurring Deposits	—	60,000
Cumulative Deposits	—	40,000
Investments in Govt. Securities	2,00,000	—
Investments in Treasury Bills	1,00,000	—
Borrowing from other Banks	—	1,60,000
Unexpired Discount	—	20,000
Bills Purchased & Discounted	2,80,000	—
Cash Credits, Overdrafts etc.	6,40,000	—
Term Loans	2,40,000	—
Provision for Doubtful Debts	—	1,20,000
Provision for Income Tax	—	56,000
Advance Income Tax paid	20,000	—
Furnitures & Fixtures (cost Rs. 30,000)	20,000	—
Stationery and Stamps	10,000	—
Non Banking Assets	1,10,000	—
Unclaimed Dividend	—	12,000
Advance to Staff for expenses	16,000	—
Electricity & Telephone deposits	6,000	—
Advance to Builders	36,000	—
Prepaid expenses	2,000	—
Investment in shares	20,000	—
	31,60,000	31,60,000

Adjustments :

(a) Bills for collection Rs. 1,00,000

(b) Acceptances, Endorsements etc. Rs. 1,50,000

(c) Create Statutory Reserve for current year

Prepare Balance Sheet of Bank as on 31-3-95 with relevant schedules.

[K.U.D., April 1997(N)]

Solution :

Form-A

Shri Durdundishwar Bank Ltd.

Balance Sheet as at 31-3-1995

	Schedule	Rs.
(I) *Capital & Liabilities*		
(1) Capital	1	5,20,000
(2) Reserves & Surplus	2	5,44,000
(3) Deposits	3	17,20,000
(4) Borrowings	4	1,60,000
(5) Other Liabilities & Provisions	5	2,16,000
Total		31,60,000
(II) *Property and Assets*		
(6) Cash and Balances with Reserve Bank of India	6	7,40,000
(7) Balances with Banks and Money at Call & Short Notice	7	7,20,000
(8) Investments	8	3,20,000
(9) Advances	9	11,60,000
(10) Fixed Assets	10	20,000
(11) Other Assets	11	2,00,000
Total		31,60,000
(12) Contingent Liabilities		
(a) Bills for collection		1,00,000
(b) Acceptances, Endorsements etc.		1,50,000
Total		2,50,000

Profit & Loss A/c for the year ended 31-3-1995

	Schedule	Rs.
Incomes		
Interest Earned	13	
Other Incomes	14	
Total		
Expenditure		
Interest Expended	15	
Operating Expenses	16	
Provisions & Contingencies		
Total		

	Schedule	Rs.
Profit for the year — 1994-95		2,84,000
Appopriation		
Statutory Reserve 20% of 2,84,000		56,800
Profit & Loss A/c on 1-4-94		2,27,200
		60,000
Total		2,87,200
Schedule 13 — Interest Earned		
Interest and Discount		
Commission & Exchange		
Total		
Schedule 14 — Other Incomes		
Total		
Schedule 15 — Interest Expended		
Interest on FD & S B A/c		
Total		
Schedule 16 — Operating Expenses		
Salaries		
Rent, Taxes and Insurance		
Other Expenditure		
Depreciation on Banks Property		
Total		

Schedule to Balance Sheet as at 31-3-1995

	Schedule	Rs.
Schedule 1 — Capital		
Authorised :		
6000 Equity shares of Rs. 100 each		6,00,000
2000 Preference shares of Rs. 100 each		2,00,000
Issued — 4000 Equity shares of Rs. 100 each		4,00,000
2000 Preference shares of Rs. 100 each		2,00,000
Subscribed and paid up capital		
4000 Equity shares of Rs. 80 per share		3,20,000
2000 Preference shares of Rs. 100 each fully paid		2,00,000
Total		5,20,000

	Schedule	Rs.
Schedule 2 — Reserves & Surplus		
Statutory Reserve		1,60,000
Add Statutory Reserve for 1994-95		56,800
		2,16,800
Capital Reserve		40,000
Profit & Loss A/c		2,87,200
Total		5,44,000
Schedule 3 — Deposits		
Current Deposits		8,00,000
Saving Bank Deposits		5,00,000
Fixed Deposits		3,20,000
Recurring Deposits		60,000
Cumulative Deposits		40,000
		17,20,000
Schedule 4 — Borrowings		
Borrowing from other Banks		1,60,000
Total		1,60,000
Schedule 5 — Other Liabilities & Contingency		
Unpaid Expenses		8,000
Unexpired discount		20,000
Provision for Doubtful Debts		1,20,000
Provision for Income Tax		56,000
Unclaimed Dividend		12,000
Total		2,16,000

Property & Assets	Rs.
Schedule 6 — Cash in hand and Balances with R.B.I.	
Cash in hand	2,00,000
C.D. with R.B.I.	3,00,000
F.D. with R.B.I.	2,40,000
Total	7,40,000
Schedule 7 — Balances with other Banks and Money at Call & Short Notice	
Balances with other Banks (Current A/c)	6,00,000
Money at Call and Short Notice	1,20,000
Total	7,20,000

	Schedule	Rs.
Schedule 8 — Investments		
Investments : in Govt. Securities		2,00,000
in Treasury Bills		1,00,000
in Shares		20,000
Total		3,20,000
Schedule 9 — Advances		
Bills purchased and Discounted		2,80,000
Cash credits, overdrafts etc.		6,40,000
Term Loans		2,40,000
Total		11,60,000
Schedule 10 — Fixed Assets		
Furnitures & Fixtures (cost Rs. 30,000)		20,000
Total		20,000
Schedule 11 — Other Assets		
Non-Banking Assets		1,10,000
Advance Income Tax paid		20,000
Stationery and Stamps		10,000
Advance to Staff for expenses		16,000
Electricity and Telephone Deposit		6,000
Advance to Builders		36,000
Prepaid Expenses		2,000
Total		2,00,000
Schedule 12 — Contingent Liabilities		
Bills for collections		1,00,000
Acceptances, Endorsement etc.		1,50,000
Total		2,50,000

Problem No. 4

From the following balances taken from the books of Chartered Bank Ltd. prepare :

(1) Profit & Loss Account for the year ended 31-3-1996 and the

(2) Balance Sheet as on that date in a prescribed Schedule.

	Rs.
(1) Share Capital (Authorised and Issued) 10000 equity shares of Rs. 100 each, Rs. 30 paid up	3,00,000
(2) Reserved Fund	1,00,000
(3) Money at Call and Short Notice	1,25,000
(4) Investments @ Cost	10,00,000
(5) Interest Paid	75,000
(6) Salaries (including Remuneration to Managing Director Rs. 10,000 and Directors Rs. 6,000	45,000
(7) Rent and Taxes	4,000
(8) General Expenses (Stationery Rs. 3,000, Auditors fees Rs. 5,000 and other Rs. 2,000)	10,000
(9) Fixed Deposits	5,00,000
(10) Savings Bank and Current Account	25,00,000
(11) Premises (after depreciation upto 31-3-95 Rs. 25,000)	1,75,000
(12) Furniture (after depreciation upto 31-3-95 Rs. 5,000)	15,000
(13) Cash in hand	35,000
(14) Cash with Travancore State Bank Ltd.	2,00,000
(15) Cash with other Banks	3,00,000
(16) Borrowings from other Banks	2,50,000
(17) Interest and Discount	2,23,250
(18) Profit & Loss A/c (Credit)	50,000
(19) Dividend for the year 1995	30,000
(20) Loans, cash credits and overdrafts	16,14,250
(21) Bills payable	25,000
(22) Bills discounted and purchased	3,50,000
(23) Unclaimed dividend	5,000
(24) Gratuity Fund	12,500
(25) Commission and Exchange	22,500
(26) Library Books	6,000
(27) Repairs to Bank's property	4,000
(28) Bills for collection	50,000
(29) Acceptances on behalf of Customers	1,00,000

Adjustments :

(a) Provide Depreciation @ 5% on premises and @ 10% on Furniture.

(b) Provide Rs. 20,000 for Bad and Doubtful Debts.

(c) Provide for Taxation Rs. 25,000.

(d) Rebate on Bills discounted for unexpired period amounted to Rs. 2,500.

[K.U.D., October 1997(O)]

Solution :

Form-A

Chartered Bank Ltd.

Balance Sheet as at 31-3-1996

	Schedule	Rs.
(I) *Capital & Liabilities*		
(1) Capital	1	3,00,000
(2) Reserves & Surplus	2	1,80,750
(3) Deposits	3	30,00,000
(4) Borrowings	4	2,50,000
(5) Other Liabilities & Provisions	5	77,500
Total		38,08,250
(II) *Property & Assets*		
(1) Cash and Balance with R.B.I.	6	35,000
(2) Balances with other Banks and Money at call and short notice	7	6,25,000
(3) Investments	8	10,00,000
(4) Advances	9	19,64,250
(5) Fixed Assets	10	17,800
(6) Other Assets	11	6,000
Total		38,08,250
(7) Contingent Liabilities	12	
(a) Bills collections		50,000
(b) Acceptances on behalf of Customers		1,00,000
Total		1,50,000

Form-B

Profit & Loss A/c for the year ended 31-3-1996

	Schedule	Rs.
Incomes		
Interest Earned	13	2,23,250
Other Incomes	14	22,500
Total		2,45,750
Expenditures		
Interest Expended	15	75,000
Operating Expenses	16	7,500
Provisions and Contingencies Provisions		47,500
Total		1,97,500

	Schedule	Rs.
Profit for the year 1995-96		
Incomes — Schedules 13 & 14		2,45,750
Less Expenses — Schedules 15 & 16		1,97,500
Net profit for the year		48,250
Add Profit brought forward		50,000
Appropriation		98,250
Statutory Reserve u/s 17 20% of 48,250		9,650
		88,600
Less Dividend paid in 1995		30,000
		58,600
Schedule to Profit & Loss A/c		
Incomes : Interest Earned	13	
Interest of Discount		2,23,250
Total		2,23,250
Other Incomes	14	
Commission and Exchange		22,500
Total		22,500
Expenses		
Schedule Expenses	15	
Interest paid		75,000
Interest on Borrowings		
Total		75,000
Operating Expenses	16	
Salaries :		
Remuneration to Managing Director		10,000
Directors fees		6,000
Salaries		29,000
Rent and Taxes		4,000
General Expenses :		
Stationery		3,000
Auditors fees		5,000
Others		2,000
Repairs is Bank's property		4,000
Depreciation on Bank Property :		
Premises : cost = Rs. 2,00,000 @ 5% 10,000		
Furniture : cost = Rs. 20,000 @ 10% 2,000		12,000
Total		75,000

Provisions & Contingencies	Rs.
(1) Provision for Bad & Doubtful Debts	20,000
(2) Provision for Taxation	25,000
(3) Provision for Rebate on Bills discounted for unexpired period	2,500
Total	47,500

Schedules to Balance Sheet as at 31-3-1996

	Schedule	Rs.
Schedule 1 — Capital		
Authorised — 10000 equity shares of Rs. 100 each		10,00,000
Issued — 10000 equity shares of Rs. 100 each		10,00,000
Subscribed and paid up — 10000 equity shares of Rs. 100 each, Rs. 30 paid up		3,00,000
Total		3,00,000
Schedule 2 — Reserves & Surplus		
Reserve Fund		1,00,000
Statutory Reserve		9,650
Surplus — Profit & Loss A/c (Cr. Balance)		58,600
Gratuity Fund		12,500
Total		1,80,750
Schedule 3 — Deposits		
Fixed Deposit		5,00,000
Savings Bank and Current A/c		25,00,000
Total		30,00,000
Schedule 4 — Borrowings		
Borrowings from other Banks		2,50,000
Total		2,50,000
Schedule 5 — Other Liabilities		
Unclaimed Dividend		5,000
Provision for Bad & Doubtful Debts		20,000
Provision for Taxation		25,000
Provision for Rebate on Bills discounted		2,500
Bills payable		25,000
Total		77,500

	Schedule	Rs.
(II) *Property & Assets*		

Schedule 6

Cash in hand		35,000
Cash with R.B.I.		—
		35,000

Schedule 7 — Balances with other Banks

Cash with Travancore State Bank		2,00,000
Cash with other Banks		3,00,000
Money at Call and Short Notice		1,25,000
	Total	6,25,000

Schedule 8 — Investments

Investments @ Cost		10,00,000
	Total	10,00,000

Schedule 9 — Advances

Loans, cash creditors, overdrafts		16,14,250
Bills discounted and purchased		3,50,000
	Total	19,64,250

Schedule 10 — Fixed Assets

Premises — Cost		2,00,000	
Less Depreciation upto 31-3-95	25,000		
Add for the year	10,000	35,000	1,65,000
Furniture — Cost		20,000	
Less Depreciation upto 31-3-95	5,000		
Add for the year	2,000	7,000	13,000
	Total		1,75,000

Schedule 11 — Other Assets

Library Books		6,000
	Total	6,000

Problem No. 5

The following is the Trial Balance of Karnatak Bank Ltd. as on 31-3-1995 :

Trial Balance

		Dr. Rs.	Cr. Rs.
(1)	6000 Equity shares of Rs. 100 each	—	6,00,000
(2)	3000, 8% preference shares of Rs. 100 each	—	3,00,000
(3)	Fixed Deposit		3,50,000
(4)	Savings Bank A/c		2,50,000
(5)	Current A/c		6,00,000
(6)	Reserve Fund		3,00,000
(7)	Interest and Discount		3,00,000
(8)	Money at Call and Short Notice	3,00,000	—
(9)	Cash in hand	3,00,000	—
(10)	Cash at Bank of India	3,60,000	—
(11)	Investments in Govt. securities	1,80,000	—
(12)	Loans and Cash Credits	13,48,200	—
(13)	Furniture *Less* Depreciation	30,000	—
(14)	Premises *Less* Depreciation	2,52,000	—
(15)	Borrowing from Central Bank	—	1,20,000
(16)	Unclaimed Dividend	—	36,000
(17)	Pension Fund	—	90,000
(18)	Rent	—	12,000
(19)	Commission Received	—	48,000
(20)	Interest paid on Deposits & Borrowings	1,80,000	—
(21)	Salaries and allowances to staff	48,000	—
(22)	Audit fees	6,000	
(23)	Directors fees	3,000	—
(24)	Depreciation on Bank property	6,000	—
(25)	Printing & Stationery	3,000	—
(26)	Non-Banking Assets	30,000	—
(27)	Other Expenditures	1,800	—
(28)	Profit & Loss A/c (1-4-1994)	—	42,000
		30,48,000	30,48,000

Adjustments :

	Rs.
(1) Provide for Bad Debts	1,500
(2) Provide for Rebate on Bills Discounted	3,000
(3) Current Deposit include Rs. 5000 being Debit Balance representing overdraft	
(4) Acceptences on behalf of customers	4,50,000
(5) Bills for collection amounted to	4,20,000

You are required to prepare Final Statements as on 31-3-1995 in the prescribed forms and schedules.

[K.U.D., October 1996(O)]

Solution :

Form-A

Karnatak Bank Ltd.

Balance Sheet as at 31-3-1995

	Schedule	Rs.
Capital & Liabilities		
(1) Capital	1	9,00,000
(2) Reserves & Surplus	2	4,49,700
(3) Deposits	3	11,95,000
(4) Borrowing	4	1,20,000
(5) Other Liabilities & Provisions	5	1,30,500
Total		27,95,200
Property & Assets		
(6) Cash in hand and Balances with R.B.I.	6	3,00,000
(7) Balances with other Banks and Money at Call and Short Notice	7	6,60,000
(8) Investments	8	1,80,000
(9) Advances	9	13,43,200
(10) Fixed Assets	10	2,82,000
(11) Other Assets	11	30,000
Total		27,95,200
Contingent Liabilities	12	
Bills for collection		4,20,000
Acceptances & Endorsements		4,50,000
Total		8,70,000

Form-B

Profit & Loss A/c for the year ended 31-3-1995

	Schedule	Rs.
Incomes		
Interest Earned	13	3,00,000
Other Incomes	14	60,000
Total		3,60,000
Expenditures		
Interest Expended	15	1,80,000
Operating Expenses	16	67,800
Total		2,47,800
Provisions & Contingencies		4,500
Profit or Loss		
Incomes — Schedules 13 & 14		3,60,000
Less Expenditures — Schedules 15 & 16		−2,47,800
		1,12,200
Less Provisions & Contingencies		4,500
Net profit for the year		1,07,700
Profit brought forward		42,000
Total Profit		1,49,700
Appropriation		
Statutory Reserve u/s 17 — 20% of 1,07,700		21,540
Net Profit carried to Balance Sheet		1,28,160

Schedule to Balance Sheet as at 31-3-1995

	Rs.
Schedule 1 — Capital	
Authorised :	
Issued & Subscribed & paid up	
6000 Equity shares of Rs. 100 each	6,00,000
3000, 8% Preference shares of Rs. 100 each	3,00,000
Total	9,00,000
Schedule 2 — Reserves & Surplus	
Statutory Reserve	21,540
Opening Balance	—
Additions during the year	—
Reserve Fund Opening Balance	3,00,000
Balance in Profit & Loss A/c	1,28,160
Total	4,49,700

Schedule 3 — Deposits

		Rs.
Fixed Deposits		3,50,000
Savings Bank A/c		2,50,000
Current A/c	6,00,000	
	5,000	5,95,000
Total		11,95,000

Schedule 4 — Borrowings

Borrowing from Central Bank	1,20,000
Total	1,20,000

Schedule 5 — Other Liabilities

Unclaimed Dividend	36,000
Pension Fund	90,000
Provision for Bad Debts	1,500
Rebate on Profits discounted	3,000
Total	1,30,500

Property & Assets

Schedule 6 — Cash and Balance with R.B.I.

	Rs.
Cash in hand	3,00,000
Total	3,00,000

Schedule 7 — Balances with other Banks

Cash at Bank of India	3,60,000
Money at Call and Short Notice	3,00,000
Total	6,60,000

Schedule 8 — Investments

Investments in Govt. Securities	1,80,000
Total	1,80,000

Schedule 9 — Advances

Loans advances, cash credits etc.	13,48,200	
Less Deposits toward Overdrafts included in current Deposit (per contra)	5,000	13,43,200
Total		13,43,200

	Rs.
Schedule 10 — Fixed Assets	
Premises *Less* Depreciation	2,52,000
Furniture *Less* Depreciation	30,000
Total	2,82,000

Schedule — 11 Other Assets	
Non-Banking Assets	30,000
Total	30,000

Schedule 12 — Contingent Liabilities	
Bills for collection	4,20,000
Acceptances on behalf of customers	4,50,000
Total	8,70,000

Schedule to Profit & Loss A/c for the year ended 31-3-1995

	Rs.
Schedule 13 — Interest Earned	
Interest and Discount	3,00,000
Interest accrued	—
Total	3,00,000

Schedule 14 — Other Incomes	
Commission received	48,000
Rent	12,000
Total	60,000

Schedule 15 — Interest Expended	
Interest paid on Deposits & Borrowings	1,80,000
Total	1,80,000

Schedule 16 — Operating Expenses	
Salaries and allowances to staff	48,000
Audit fees	6,000
Directors fees	3,000
Depreciation on Bank's property	6,000
Printing & Stationery	3,000
Other expenditures	1,800
Total	67,800

	Rs.
Provisions & Contingencies	
(1) Provide for Bad Debts	1,500
(2) Provide for Rebate on Bills Discounted	3,000
Total	4,500

Problem No. 6

The following is the Trial Balance of Dhanalaxmi Bank Ltd. as on 31-3-1996 :

Trial Balance as on 31-3-96

	Particulars	Dr. Rs.	Cr. Rs.
(1)	Share Capital — Equity shares of Rs. 100 each	—	5,00,000
(2)	Reserves		3,50,000
(3)	Fixed Deposit		9,50,000
(4)	Investments at Cost	26,00,000	—
(5)	Current Accounts	—	70,00,000
(6)	Profit & Loss Account Cr. (1-4-1995)	—	2,10,000
(7)	Premises (Original cost Rs. 43,00,000)	42,00,000	
(8)	Cash in hand	1,60,000	
(9)	Cash with R.B.I.	13,00,000	
(10)	Loans from other Banks	—	7,00,000
(11)	Bills discounted and purchased	16,00,000	—
(12)	Savings Bank Account	—	40,00,000
(13)	Bills payable	—	8,00,000
(14)	Unclaimed dividend	—	30,000
(15)	Branch Adjustment Account (Cr.)	—	30,000
(16)	Non-Banking Assets	2,40,000	—
(17)	Stamps on hand	10,000	—
(18)	Stock of Printing and Stationery	30,000	—
(19)	Advance to Building Contractor	20,000	—
(20)	Loans, Advances and Cash Credits	46,74,000	—
(21)	Profit for the year on 31-3-96	—	2,64,000
		1,48,34,000	1,48,34,000

Adjustments :

(a) Make necessary provision for Statutory Reserve

(b) Directors proposed dividend @ 20%

(c) Provide for Rebate on Bills discounted Rs. 3,000

(d) Acceptances and Endorsements Rs. 30,000

(e) Bills for collections Rs. 20,000

Prepare Balance Sheet in prescribed schedule and form.

[K.U.D., April 1996(N)]

Solution :

Form-A

Dhanalaxmi Bank Ltd.

Balance Sheet as at 31-3-1996

	Schedule	Amount
Capital & Liabilities		Rs.
(1) Capital	1	5,00,000
(2) Reserves & Surplus	2	7,21,000
(3) Deposits	3	1,19,50,000
(4) Borrowings	4	7,00,000
(5) Other Liabilities	5	9,63,000
Total		1,48,34,000
Property and Assets		
(6) Cash in hand and Balances with R.B.I.	6	14,60,000
(7) Balances with other Banks and Money at call and short notice	7	Nil
(8) Investments	8	26,00,000
(9) Advances	9	62,74,000
(10) Fixed Assets	10	42,00,000
(11) Other Assets	11	3,00,000
Total		1,48,34,000
(12) Contingent Liabilities :	12	
(a) Bills for collections		20,000
(b) Acceptances and Endorsements		30,000
Total		50,000

Form-B

Profit & Loss A/c for the year ended ...

	Schedule	Amount Rs.
Incomes		
Interest Earned	13	
Other Incomes	14	
Total		
Expenditures		
Interest expended	15	
Operating expenses	16	
Provisions & Contingencies :		
Rebate on Bills discounted		3,000
Total		3,000

Profit for the year ended 31-3-1996	
Incomes — Schedules 13 & 14	
Less Expenditures	
Profit for the year	2,64,000
Less Provisions	3,000
Net Profit for the year	2,61,000
Add Profit brought forward (1-4-95)	2,10,000
Total Profit	4,71,000
Appropriation	
Statutory Reserve u/s 17 — 20% of 2,61,000	52,200
	4,18,800
Proposed Dividend 20% on 5,00,000	1,00,000
Profit, carried to Balance Sheet	3,18,800

Schedule to Balance sheet as at 31-3-1996

Schedule 1 — Capital	
Authorised	
Issued Capital	
Subscribed and paid up	
5000 Equity shares of Rs. 100 each	5,00,000
Total	5,00,000

	Rs.
Schedule 2 — Reserves & Surplus	
Reserves	3,50,000
Statutory Reserve	52,200
Surplus — Profit for the year	3,18,800
Total	7,21,000
Schedule 3 — Deposits	
(a) Fixed Deposits	9,50,000
(b) Current A/cs	70,00,000
(c) Savings Bank A/c	40,00,000
Total	1,19,50,000
Schedule 4 — Borrowings	
Loans from other Banks	7,00,000
Total	7,00,000
Schedule 5 — Other Liabilities	
Bills payable	8,00,000
Unclaimed Dividend	30,000
Branch Adjustment	30,000
Rebate on Bills Discounted	3,000
Proposed Dividend	1,00,000
Total	9,63,000
Property & Assets	
Schedule 6 — Cash in hand & with RBI	
Cash in hand	1,60,000
Cash Balance with RBI	13,00,000
Total	14,60,000

	Rs.
Schedule 7 — Balances with other Banks	
Balances with other Banks	—
Money at Call and Short Notice	—
Total	—
Schedule 8 — Investment	
Investments at cost	26,00,000
Total	26,00,000
Schedule 9 — Advances	
Loans, Advances, cash credits etc.	46,74,000
Bills discounted and purchased	16,00,000
Total	62,74,000
Schedule 10 — Fixed Assets	
Premises *Less* Depreciation (Cost Rs. 43,00,000)	42,00,000
Furnitures *Less* Depreciation	—
Total	42,00,000
Schedule 11 — Other Assets	
Non-Banking Assets	2,40,000
Stamps on hand	10,000
Stock of Printing & Stationery	30,000
Advance to Building Contractor	20,000
	3,00,000
Schedule 12 — Contingent Liabilities	
Bills for collection	20,000
Acceptances, and Endorsements	30,000
Total	50,000

Problem No. 7

Following are the Ledger balances of Indian Banking Corporation as on 31st March 1996. Prepare Profit and Loss Account in prescribed schedules and forms as required under law :

Interest and Discount	2,46,000
Payment and Provisions to Employees	85,000
Contribution to staff P.F.	15,000
Advertising	8,000
Directors fees	7,000
Auditors fees	5,000
Depreciation on Banks property	9,200
Printing and Stationery	3,700
Law charges	3,100
Interest on deposits and borrowings	1,05,000
Profit on sale of non-banking assets	25,000
Loss on sale of Investment	10,000
Commission and Exchange	54,000
Other Income	6,000
Profit and Loss Account on 1-4-1995 (Cr)	85,000

Additional Information :

(a) Make provision for income tax Rs. 5,000 and Rs. 10,000 for investment fluctuation reserve.

(b) Make provision for unexpired discount on bills Rs. 5,000 and accrued interest on investment Rs. 2,500.

(c) Directors declare a dividend at 15% on share capital of Rs. 2,50,000.

(d) Make Provision for statutory reserves.

(K.U.D., October 1996)

Solution :

Schedules for Profit and Loss Account of Indian Banking Corporation as on 31st March 1996

Particulars		Sch. No.	Amount Rs.
Income			
Interest and Discount		13	2,46,000
Add : Accrued interest on Investment			2,500
			2,48,500
Other Incomes		14	
Profit on sale of non-banking Assets	25,000		
Less : Loss on sale of Investment	– 10,000		15,000
Commission and Exchange			54,000
Other Income			6,000
			75,000
Expenses		15	
Interest on Deposit			1,05,000
Operating Expenses		16	
Payment and provisions to employees			85,000
Contribution to staff P.F.			15,000
Rent, Rates			—
Printing & Stationery			3,700
Advertisement			8,000
Depreciations on Bank's properties			9,200
Directors Fees			7,000
Auditors Fees			5,000
Law Charges			3,100
Postage and Telegrams			—
Insurances			—
Other Expenses			—
			1,36,000
Provisions for :			
Income tax			5,000
Investment Fluctuation Reserve			10,000
Rebate on bills discounted			5,000
			20,000

Form-B

Profit & Loss A/c for the year ended 31-3-1996

	Schedule	Amount Rs.
Incomes		
Interest Earned	13	2,48,500
Other Incomes	14	75,000
Total		3,23,500
Expenditures		
Interest Expended	15	1,05,000
Operating Expenses	16	1,36,000
Provisions		20,000
Total		2,61,000

Profit for the year ended 31-3-1996	
Incomes — Schedules 13 & 14	3,23,500
Less Expenditures — Schedules 15 & 16	2,61,000
Net Profit for the year	62,500
Add Profit & Loss A/c Cr. Bal. b/fd	85,000
Total Profits	1,47,500
Appropriation	
Less Statutory Reserve u/s 17	
20% of Current Profit of 62,500	12,500
	1,35,000
Less Proposed Dividend	
15% on share capital of Rs. 2,50,000	37,500
Balance of Profit carried forward to Balance Sheet	97,500

Problem No. 8

The following is the Trial Balance of Laxmi Bank Ltd. as on 31-3-1994 :

Trial Balance

		Dr. Rs.	Cr. Rs.
	Share Capital : Subscribed and Paid up Equity shares of Rs. 10 each		2,00,000
(2)	Statutory Reserve		50,000
(3)	Reserve fund		10,000
(4)	Deposits		10,00,000
(5)	Profit and Loss Account 1-4-93		25,000
(6)	Interest and Discount		1,00,000
(7)	Borrowings from other Banks		30,000
(8)	Commission and Brokerage		12,000
(9)	Rent		15,000
(10)	Profit on sale of Investment		30,000
(11)	Loss on sale of Investment	5,500	
(12)	Cash	30,000	
(13)	Payment and Provisions to Employers	55,000	
(14)	Taxes and Lighting	3,000	
(15)	Directors fees	12,000	
(16)	Audit fees	10,000	
(17)	Balances with Union Bank	18,000	
(18)	Money at call and short notice	13,000	
(19)	Investment in Govt. securities	1,80,000	
(20)	Premises *Less* : Depreciation	36,000	
(21)	Furnitures *Less* : Depreciation	7,000	
(22)	Interim Dividend paid	8,000	
(23)	Loans advances and cash credits	10,60,000	
(24)	Income tax paid	5,000	
(25)	Printing and Stationery	2,000	
(26)	Postage and Telegrams	3,500	
(27)	Depreciation	2,000	
(28)	Interest paid on Deposit	32,000	
		14,72,000	14,72,000

Adjustments

(a) Interest accrued on Investment Rs. 14,000.

(b) Provide for Bad and Doubtful Debts Rs. 6,000

(c) The interim dividend declared was at 5%.

(d) Acceptances and Endorsements were Rs. 2,00,000.

(f) The market value of Investment was Rs. 1,70,000 and Investment fluctuation reserve to be created for the fall in value.

Prepare : (a) Profit and Loss Account.
(b) The Balance Sheet.

[K.U.D., April 1996 (a)]

Solution :

Balance Sheet of Laxmi Bank Ltd. as at 31-3-94

		Schedule	Rs.
Capital and Liabilities			
Share Capital		1	2,00,000
Reserve and Surplus		2	1,10,000
Deposits		3	10,00,000
Borrowings		4	30,000
Other Liabilities and Provision		5	2,000
Total			13,42,000
Property and Assets			
Cash and Balances with Reserve Bank of India		6	20,000
Balances with other Bank and Money at call and short notice		7	31,000
Investments		8	1,80,000
Advances		9	10,54,000
Fixed Assets		10	43,000
Other Assets		11	14,000
Total			13,42,000
Contingent Liabilities :		12	
Bills for collection	50,000		
Acceptances and Endorsement	2,00,000		2,50,000
Total			2,50,000

Profit and Loss Account for the year ended 31-3-1994

	Schedule		Rs.
Incomes			
Interest Earned	13		1,14,000
Other Incomes	14		51,500
Total			1,65,500
Expenditure			
Interest Expended	15		32,000
Operating Expenses	16		87,500
Total			1,19,500
Provisions and Contingencies			16,000
Profit or Loss :			
Incomes — Schedule 13 and 14			1,65,500
Less : Expenditures (15 & 16)		1,19,500	
Less : Provision & Contingencies		16,000	1,35,500
Net - Profit for the year			30,000
Profit brought forward			25,000
Profit Total			55,000
Appropriation			
Transfer to Statutory Reserve 20% of current profit of 30,000		6,000	
Interim dividend declared @ 5% on 2,00,000		10,000	
Income tax paid		5,000	21,000
Profit transferred to B/S			34,000

Schedule the Balance Sheet as at 31-3-1994

Schedule 1 — Capital	
Equity share capital : Authorised capital equity shares of Rs. 10 each subscribed and paid up capital 20000 Equity shares of Rs. 10 each	2,00,000
Total	2,00,000

Schedule 2 — Reserve and Surplus		Rs.
Statutory Reserve : Opening Balance	50,000	
Additions during the year	6,000	56,000
Reserve Fund :		
Opening Balance	10,000	
Addition during the year	—	10,000
Investment Fluctuation Reserve		10,000
Balance in Profit and Loss A/c		34,000
Total		1,10,000

Schedule 3 — Deposits	
Demand Deposits	10,00,000
Savings Bank Deposits	—
Term Deposits (Fixed)	—
Total	10,00,000

Schedule 4 — Borrowings	
Borrowings from other Banks	30,000
Total	30,000

Schedule 5 — Other Liabilities	
Rebate on Bills discounted	—
Pension fund, provident fund etc.	—
Interim dividend payable	2,000
Total	2,000

Property and Assets :

Schedule 6 — Cash and Balance with R.B.I.	
Cash in Hand	20,000
Balances with Reserve Bank of India	—
Total	20,000

Schedule 7 — Balances with other Banks and Money at call and short notice	
Balance with Union Bank	18,000
Money at call and short notice	13,000
Total	31,000

Schedule 8 — Investments		Rs.
Investment in Govt. Securities		1,80,000
Total		1,80,000

Schedule 9 — Advances		
Loans, Advances, cash credits etc.		10,60,000
Less : Provision for Bad debts		6,000
Total		10,54,000

Schedule 10 — Fixed Assets		
Premises *Less* Depreciation		36,000
Furniture *Less* Depreciation		7,000
Total		43,000

Schedule 11 — Other Assets		
Interest accrued on Investment		14,000
Total		14,000

Schedule 12 — Contingent Liabilities		
Bills for collections		50,000
Acceptance and Endorsement		2,00,000
Total		2,50,000

Schedule to Profit & Loss A/c

Schedule 13 — Interest Earned		
Interest and Discount		1,00,000
Add : Interest accrued on Investment		14,000
Total		1,14,000

Schedule 14 — Other Incomes		
Commission and Brokerage		12,000
Rent		15,000
Profit on Sales of Investment	30,000	
Less : on Sale of Investment	5,500	24,500
Total		51,500

Schedule 15 — Interest Expended		
Interest on Deposits		32,000
Total		32,000

Schedule 16 — Opening Expenses		Rs.
Payments and provisions to Employees		55,000
Taxes and Lighting		3,000
Director fees		12,000
Auditors fees		10,000
Printing and Stationery		2,000
Postage and Telegram		3,500
Depreciation		2,000
	Total	87,500

Provision and Contingency :		
Provision for Bad doubtful debts		6,000
Investment Fluctuation Reserve	1,80,000	
	– 1,70,000	10,000
	Total	16,000

Alternatively

The same Problem may be answered as follows :

Laxmi Bank Ltd.

Profit and Loss A/c for the year ended 31-3-1994

Particulars	Rs.	Particulars		Rs.
To Interest on Deposit	32,000	By Interest & Discount		98,000
To Payments and Provision to employees	55,000	By Commission & Brokerage		12,000
To Taxcs and Lighting	3,000	By Rent		15,000
To Direct Fees	12,000	By Profit on sale of		
To Auditors fees	10,000	Investment	30,000	
To Printing & Stationery	2,000	*Less* : Loss on sale		
To Postage and Telegram	3,500	of Investment	5,500	24,500
To Depreciation	2,000			
To Net Profit	30,000			
Total	1,49,500	Total		1,49,500

Profit and Loss Appropriation Account

Particulars	Rs.	Particulars	Rs.
To Transfer to statutory reserve 20% of 30,000	6,000	By Profit for the year	30,000
To Interim Dividend @ 5% on 2,00,000	10,000	By Profit and Loss A/c brought forward	25,000
To Income tax paid	5,000		
To Net Profit transfer to Balance Sheet	34,000		
Total	55,000	Total	55,000

Working Note

Interest and Discount		1,00,000
Add : Interest accrued		14,000
		1,14,000
Less : Provisions :		
(a) For Doubtful debts	6,000	
(b) Investment fluctuation reserve for fall in value of investment	10,000	16,000
		98,000

Balance Sheet of Laxmi Bank Ltd. as at 31-3-1994

Capital & Liabilities	Rs.	Rs.	Property & Assets	Rs.	Rs.
Share Capital			Cash in Hand		20,000
20000 Equity shares			With R.B.I.		—
of Rs. 10 each		2,00,000	With other Bank		18,000
Reserve & Surplus					
Statutory Reserve			Money at call &		
balance b/d	50,000		short Notice		13,000
Additions during			*Investment in* :		
the year	6,000	56,000	Govt. Securities		1,80,000

Capital & Liabilities	Rs.	Rs.	Property & Assets	Rs.	Rs.
Reserve Fund		10,000	*Advances* :		
Investment Fluctuation			Loans and advances	10,60,000	
Reserve		10,000	*Less* : R.D.D.	6,000	
Deposits :					10,54,000
F.D., Savings Current A/c		10,00,000	Bills Receivable being bills for collection (per contra)		50,000
Borrowings from other Bank		30,000	Acceptance, Endorsement (per contra)		2,00,000
Bills payable		—	Premises *Less* : Depr.		36,000
Bills for collection			Furniture *Less* : Depr.		7,000
being B.R per contra		50,000	Non-Banking Assets		—
Other Liabilities :			*Other Assets* :		
Rebate on Bills discounted		—	Interest accrued on Investment		14,000
Interim dividend payable		2,000			
Acceptance, Endorsement : (per contra)		2,00,000			
Profit & Loss A/c					
Balance b/d	25,000				
Add : Profit for the year	30,000				
	55,000				
Less : Statutory Reserve	6,000				
	49,000				
Less : Interim dividend	10,000				
	39,000				
Less : Income Tax	5,000	34,000			
Total		15,92,000	Total		15,92,000

Problem No. 9

The following is the Trial Balance of Dhanalaxmi Bank Ltd. as on 31-3-1996:

Trial Balance

	Particulars	Dr. Rs.	Cr. Rs.
(1)	Share Capital (in shares of Rs. 100 each)	—	5,00,000
(2)	Reserve		3,50,000
(3)	Fixed Deposits		9,50,000
(4)	Investment @ cost	26,00,000	—
(5)	Current Account		70,00,000
(6)	Profit and Loss Account (Cr) (1-4-95)		2,10,000
(7)	Premises (Original Cost) Rs. 43,00,000	42,00,000	—
(8)	Cash in hand	1,60,000	—
(9)	Cash with R.B.I.	13,00,000	—
(10)	Loans from other Banks	—	7,00,000
(11)	Bills discounted and purchases	16,00,000	—
(12)	Savings Bank Account		40,00,000
(13)	Bills payable		8,00,000
(14)	Unclaimed Dividend		30,000
(15)	Branch Adjustment (Cr)		30,000
(16)	Non-Banking Assets	2,40,000	—
(17)	Stamps on hand	10,000	—
(18)	Stock : Printing and Stationery	30,000	—
(19)	Advance to Building contractors	20,000	—
(20)	Loans advance and cash credits	46,74,000	—
(21)	Profit for the year on 31-3-1996	—	2,64,000
		1,48,34,000	1,48,34,000

Adjustments :

(a) Make necessary provision for Statutory Reserve.

(b) Directors proposed dividend @ 20%.

(c) Provide for rebate on bills discounted Rs. 3,000.

(d) Acceptances and Endorsement Rs. 30,000.

(e) Bills for collection Rs. 20,000.

Prepare Balance Sheet in prescribed schedules and forms.

[K.U.D., April 1996 (N)]

Solution :

THIRD SCHEDULE

Form-A

Dhanalaxmi Bank Ltd.

Balance Sheet as at 31-3-1996

	Schedule	Amount Rs.
Capital and Liabilities		
Share Capital	1	5,00,000
Reserve and Surplus	2	7,21,000
Deposits	3	1,19,50,000
Borrowings	4	7,00,000
Other Liabilities and Provision	5	9,63,000
Total		1,48,34,000
Property and Assets		
Cash and balances with R.B.I.	6	14,60,000
Balances with other Banks and Money at call short notice	7	—
Investments	8	26,00,000
Advances	9	62,74,000
Fixed Assets	10	42,00,000
Other Assets	11	3,00,000
Total		1,48,34,000
Contingent Liabilities :	12	
Bills for Collection		20,000
Acceptances and Endorsement		30,000
Total		50,000

Profit and Loss Account for the year ended 31-3-1996

Incomes		
Interest Earned	13	—
Other Incomes	14	—
Total		—
Expenditures		
Interest Expended	15	—
Operating Expenses	16	—
Total		—

Profit or Loss	Rs.
Profit and Loss A/c for the year ended 31-3-1996	2,64,000
Less : Provision for rebate on bills discounted	3,000
Net Profit for the year	2,61,000
Profit brought forward 1-4-1995	2,10,000
Profit Total	4,71,000
Appropriation :	
Statutory Reserve 20% of Current Profit (20% of 2,61,000)	– 52,200
	4,18,800
Less : Proposed Dividend 20% of 5,00,000	1,00,000
Balance of profit transferred to Balance Sheet	3,18,800

Schedule the Balance Sheet as at 31-3-1996

Schedule 1 — Capital	
Equity Share Capital	
Authorised Capital	
Equity shares of Rs. 100 each subscribed and Paid up Capital 5000 Equity shares of Rs. 100 each	5,00,000
Total	5,00,000

Schedule 2 — Reserve and Surplus	
Statutory Reserve : Opening balance	
Additions during the year	52,200
Reserve Fund :	
Opening Balance	3,50,000
Additions during the year	—
Balance in Profit and Loss Account	3,18,800
Total	7,21,000

Schedule 3 — Deposits	
Demand Deposit Current Account	70,00,000
Savings Bank Deposits (SB A/c)	40,00,000
Term Deposits — Fixed Deposits	9,50,000
Total	1,19,50,000

Schedule 4 — Borrowings	
Borrowings from the Banks	7,00,000
Total	7,00,000

Schedule 5 — Other Liabilities

Bills payable	8,00,000
Unclaimed Dividend	30,000
Branch Adjustment A/c	30,000
Rebate on Bills discounted	3,000
Proposed Dividend	1,00,000
Total	9,63,000

Property and Assets

Schedule 6 — Cash and Balance with R.B.I.

Cash in Hand	1,60,000
Balance with R.B.I.	13,00,000
Total	14,60,000

Schedule 7 — Balance with other Banks and Money at call and short notice

Balance with other Banks	—
Money at call and short notice	—
Total	—

Schedule 8 — Investments

Investment (@ cost)	26,00,000
Total	26,00,000

Schedule 9 — Advances

Bills discounted and purchased	16,00,000
Loans, advances and cash credits	46,74,000
Total	62,74,000

Schedule 10 — Fixed Assets

Premises original cost	43,00,000	
Less : Depreciation up to this day	1,00,000	42,00,000
Furnitures cost	—	
Less : Depreciation	—	—
Total		42,00,000

Schedule 11 — Other Assets	Rs.
Non-Banking Assets	2,40,000
Stamps on hand	10,000
Stock — Printing and Stationery	30,000
Advances to Building contractor	20,000
Total	3,00,000

Schedule 12 — Contingent Liabilities	
Bills for collection	20,000
Acceptance and Endorsement	30,000
	50,000

Schedule to Profit and Loss Account for the year ended 31-3-96

Schedule 13 — Interest Earned	
Interest and Discount	—
Total	—

Schedule 14 — Other Incomes	
Commission and Brokerages	—
Rent	
Profit on sale of Investment	—
Total	—

Schedule 15 — Interest Expended	
Interest on Deposits	—
Total	—

Schedule 16 — Operating Expenses	—
Total	—

Provisions and Contingencies :	
Rebate on Bills Discounted	3,000
Total	3,000

Alternatively

The same problem may be answered as follows :

Balance Sheet of Dhanalaxmi Bank Ltd. as at 31-3-1996

Capital & Liabilities	Rs.	Rs.	Property & Assets	Rs.	Rs.
Share Capital			Cash in hand		1,60,000
5000 Equity shares of			Balance with R.B.I.		13,00,000
Rs. 100 each		5,00,000			14,60,000
Reserve and Reserve fund					
Statutory Reserve	52,200		Balance with other Banks		—
Reserve fund	3,50,000	4,02,200	Money at call and		
Deposits :			short notice		—
Demand Deposit	70,00,000		Investment		26,00,000
Savings Bank	40,00,000				
Term Deposit	9,50,000	1,19,50,000	*Loans & Advances :*		
Borrowings from			Bills Discounted and		
other Banks		7,00,000	Purchases	16,00,000	
Bills payable		8,00,000	Loans and advances		
Bills for collection			cash credit	46,74,000	
being bills receivable					62,74,000
(per contra)		20,000	Bills Receivable		
Other Liabilities :			Being bills for collection		
Unclaimed dividend	30,000		(per contra)		20,000
Rebate on Bills			Acceptances and endor-		
discounted	3,000		sement (per contra)		30,000
Branch Adjustment	30,000		Premises Original	43,00,000	
Proposed Dividend	1,00,000	1,63,000	*Less* : Depreciation		
Acceptances & endorsement			up to this day	1,00,000	
(per contra)		30,000			42,00,000
Profit and Loss A/c			Non-Banking Assets		2,40,000
Balance 1-4-95	2,10,000		*Other Assets :*		
Add : Profit 31-3-96	2,64,000		Stamps on Hand	10,000	
	4,74,000		Stock : Printing &		
Less : Rebate on			Stationery	30,000	
bills Disc.	3,000		Advances to Building		
	4,71,000		contractor	20,000	60,000
Less : Statutory Reserve 20% on 2,61,000	52,500				
	4,18,800				
Less : Proposed Dividend	1,00,000	3,18,800			
Total		1,48,84,000	Total		1,48,84,000

Problem No. 10

The following is the Trial Balance of Ideal Bank Ltd. as on 31-3-1994 :

Trial Balance

	Particulars	Dr. Rs.	Cr. Rs.
1.	Share Capital in shares of Rs. 10 each		4,00,000
2.	Reserve fund		1,20,000
3.	Cash in hand and with R.B.I.	40,000	
4.	Payments and Provisions to employees	1,10,000	
5.	Deposits		20,00,000
6.	Profit and Loss Account (1-4-1993)		50,000
7.	Rent and Taxes	6,000	
8.	Directors fees	24,000	
9.	Auditors fees	20,000	
10.	Interest and Discount		2,50,000
11.	Balance with Central Bank	36,000	
12.	Money at call and short notice	26,000	
13.	Investment of Government securities	3,60,000	
14.	Commission and brokerage		24,000
15.	Premises *Less* depreciation	72,000	
16.	Furniture *Less* depreciation	14,000	
17.	Cash credit, overdraft and loans	21,36,000	16,000
18.	Borrowing from Bank of India		44,000
19.	Income tax paid	10,000	
20.	Printing and Stationery	5,000	
21.	Rent		30,000
22.	Postage and Telegrams	6,500	
23.	Interest on Deposits etc.	64,000	
24.	Depreciation	4,500	
	Total	29,34,000	29,34,000

Adjustments :

(1) Interest accrued on investment was Rs. 28,000.

(2) Provide Rs. 6,000 for Bad debts.

(3) Provide for rebate on bills discounted Rs. 6,000.

(4) Bills for collection amounted to Rs. 80,000.

(5) Acceptance and endorsement on behalf of customers amounted to Rs. 1,00,000.

Prepare Profit and Loss Account and Balance Sheet in prescribed form.

(K.U.D., October 1995)

Solution :

Ideal Bank Ltd.
Balance Sheet as at 31-3-1994

Capital and Liabilities	Schedule	Amount Rs.
Capital	1	4,00,000
Reserves and Surplus	2	2,40,000
Deposits	3	20,00,000
Borrowings	4	44,000
Other Liabilities and Provisions	5	12,000
Total		26,96,000
Property and Assets		
Cash in hand and Balance with R.B.I.	6	40,000
Balances with other Bank and Money at call and short notice	7	62,000
Investments	8	3,60,000
Advances	9	21,20,000
Fixed Assets	10	86,000
Other Assets	11	28,000
Total		26,96,000
Contingent Liabilities	12	
Bills for collection		80,000
Acceptances, Endorsement etc.		1,00,000
		1,80,000

Profit and Loss A/c for the year ended 31-3-1994

Income		
Interest earned	13	2,78,000
Other Income	14	54,000
Total		3,32,000
Expenditure		
Interest expended	15	64,000
Operating Expenses	16	1,86,000
Provisions and Contingency (6,000 + 6,000)	—	12,000
Total		2,62,000

	Rs.
Profit or Loss	
Net Profit for the year	70,000
Profit brought forward	50,000
Total Profit	1,20,000
Appropriations	
Transfer to Statutory Reserve u/s 17 : 20% of 70,000	14,000
Balance carried over to Balance Sheet	1,06,000

Schedule to Balance Sheet as at 31-3-1994

Schedule 1 — Capital		
Authorised Capital shares of Rs. 10 each		
Issued Capital — shares of Rs. 10 each		
Subscribed Capital — shares of Rs. 10 each		
Called up Capital — shares of Rs. 10 each fully paid		4,00,000
Total		4,00,000
Schedule 2 — Reserves and Surplus		
Statutory Reserve	—	
Opening Balance	—	
Additions during the year	14,000	
Reserve Fund		
Opening Balance	1,20,000	
Additions during the year		
(Profit and Loss A/c Balance)	1,06,000	2,40,000
Total		2,40,000
Schedule 3 — Deposits		
Demand Deposits		20,00,000
Savings Bank Deposits		—
Term Deposits (Fixed Deposits)		—
Total		20,00,000
Schedule 4 — Borrowings		
Borrowings from Bank of India		44,000
Total		44,000
Schedule 5 — Other Liabilities and Provisions		
Rebate on Bills Discounted		6,000
Bad Debts		6,000
Total		12,000

Property & Assets

Schedule 6 — Cash in hand and with Balance with R.B.I.

Cash in hand and with R.B.I.	40,000
Total	40,000

Schedule 7 — Balances with Other Banks and Money at call and short notice

Balance with Central Bank	36,000
Money at call and short notice	26,000
Total	62,000

Schedule 8 — Investments

Investment in Govt. Securities	3,60,000
Total	3,60,000

Schedule 9 — Advances

Cash credit, Overdraft and Loans	21,36,000
Less : Creditors	16,000
Total	21,20,000

Schedule 10 — Fixed Assets

Premises *Less* Depreciation	72,000
Furniture *Less* Depreciation	14,000
Total	86,000

Schedule 11 — Other Assets

Interest accrued on Investments	28,000
Total	28,000

Schedule 12 — Contingent Liabilities

Bills for collection	80,000
Acceptance, Endorsement etc.	1,00,000
Total	1,80,000

Schedule to Profit and Loss A/c for the year ended 31-3-1994

Schedule 13 — Interest Earned

Interest and Discount	2,50,000	
Interest accrued	28,000	2,78,000
Total		2,78,000

Schedule —14 Other Income

Commission and Brokerage		24,000
Rent		30,000
Total		54,000
Total — Schedule 13	2,78,000	
Total — Schedule 14	54,000	3,32,000
Total		3,32,000

Schedule 15 — Interest Expended

Interest on Deposit etc.	64,000
Total	64,000

Schedule 16 — Operating Expenses

Payments and Provisions to employees	1,10,000
Rent and Taxes	6,000
Directors fee	24,000
Audit fees	20,000
Income Tax paid	10,000
Printing & Stationery	5,000
Postage & Telegrams	6,500
Depreciation	4,500
Total	1,86,000

Total Incomes :		
Schedule 13		2,78,000
Schedule 14		54,000
Total		3,32,000
Less : Expenses		
Schedule 15	64,000	
Schedule 16	1,86,000	2,50,000
		82,000
Less : Provision and Contingency		12,000
Net Profit		70,000
Less : Transfer to Statutory Reserve 20% on 70,000		14,000
Balance of Profit carried to Balance Sheet		56,000

Alternately : The same problem may be answered in Traditional way.

Profit and Loss Account for the year ended 31-3-1994

Expenditure	Rs.	Income (*Less* Provisions)	Rs.
Interest on Deposits	64,000	Interest and Discount	2,66,000
Payments and Provisions	1,10,000	Commission & Exchange	
Directors Fees	24,000	Brokerage	24,000
Rent and Taxes	6,000	Rent	30,000
Postage & Telegram	6,500		
Audit Fees	20,000		
Printing & Stationery	5,000		
Depreciation	4,500		
Income Tax Paid	10,000		
Net Profit	70,000		
Total	3,20,000	Total	3,20,000

Note :

Interest and Discount		2,50,000
Add : Interest Accrued		28,000
		2,78,000
Less : Provisions :		
(a) for Bad Debts	6,000	
(b) Rebate on Bills discounted	6,000	12,000
		2,66,000
(2) Loan and Advances		21,36,000
Less : Creditors		16,000
		21,20,000
Provision :		
Less : Bad Debts		6,000
		21,14,000

Ideal Bank Ltd.
Balance Sheet as at 31-3-1994

Capital & Liabilities	Rs.	Rs.	Property & Assets	Rs.	Rs.
Share Capital			Cash in Hand and with R.B.I.		40,000
Authorised Capital Shares of Rs. 10 each			With Other Banks		—
Subscribed and Paidup			Central Bank		36,000
Equity shares Rs. 10 each		4,00,000	Money at call and short notice		26,000
Reserves & Surplus			Investments		3,60,000
Reserve Fund	1,20,000		*Loans & Advances*		
Statutory Reserve	14,000	1,34,000	Cash Credit, Overdraft & Loan	21,36,000	
Deposits					
Fixed Deposits		20,00,000	*Less* : Creditors	16,000	
Savings Bank A/c		—		21,20,000	
Current A/c		—	*Less* : R.D.D.	6,000	21,14,000
Borrowings from other Banks			Bills Receivable being bills for collection (per contra)		80,000
Bank of India		44,000			
Bills payable		—	Contingent Liabilities for Acceptances & Endorsement (per contra)		1,00,000
Bills for collection being bills receivable (per contra)		80,000	Premises *Less* Depr.		72,000
Other Liabilities			Furniture *Less* : Depr.		14,000
			Other Assets		
Rebate on Bills Discounted		6,000	Interest Accrued on Investment		28,000
Acceptances, Endorsement etc. (per contra)		1,00,000	Loss (if any)		—
Profit and Loss A/c		1,06,000			
Balance 1-4-93	50,000				
Profit for the year	70,000				
	1,20,000				
Less : Statutory Reserve 20% on 70,000	14,000				
		28,70,000			28,70,000

Problem No. 11

The following Balances have been extracted from the books of Chetana Bank Ltd. as on 31-12-1991 :

		Rs.
(1)	Subscribed and Paid up Capital Shares of Rs. 10 each	10,00,000
(2)	Reserve Fund	8,70,000
(3)	Fixed Deposit Account	13,00,000
(4)	Money at call and short notice	1,00,000
(5)	Investment in shares	7,50,000
(6)	Investments in Government securities	4,00,000
(7)	Current Accounts	60,00,000
(8)	Gold bullion	1,50,000
(9)	Savings Bank Account	12,17,000
(10)	Borrowing from other banks	3,28,000
(11)	Contingency Accounts	3,10,000
(12)	Interest and Discounts (Cr)	7,26,000
(13)	Commission and Brokerage (Cr)	1,20,000
(14)	Premises	7,48,000
(15)	Depreciation fund on premises	1,54,000
(16)	Salaries	2,89,000
(17)	Interest on Fixed Deposits and Savings Bank Deposit	1,96,000
(18)	Rent, Rates and Insurance	27,000
(19)	Depreciation on Bank property	32,500
(20)	Other Expenditures	57,300
(21)	Bills payable	1,35,000
(22)	Cash on hand and with other Banks	6,12,000
(23)	Unexpired discount	24,500
(24)	Loans, cash credits and overdrafts	46,83,200
(25)	Bills discounted and purchased	40,58,500
(26)	Branch Adjustment Account (Dr)	77,300
(27)	Interest accrued on Investment	7,500
(28)	Silver	50,000
(29)	Profit and Loss Account (Cr)	89,200
(30)	Furniture	35,400

The following information is to be considered :

(a) Bills for collection amounted to Rs. 3,50,000.

(b) Rebate on Bills discounted has been overcalculated Rs. 2,500.

(c) Liability for acceptances, endorsement on behalf of customers amounted to Rs. 5,25,000.

(d) Provision for taxation is to be made for Rs. 100,000 for the year.

(c) Prepare Profit and Loss Account and Balance Sheet as on 31-12-1991.

(K.U.D., April 1995)

Solution :

Form-A

Chetan Bank Limited

Balance Sheet as at 31-12-1991

	Schedule	Amount Rs.
(I) *Capital and Liabilities*		
(1) Capital	1	10,00,000
(2) Reserves and Surplus	2	12,59,900
(3) Deposits	3	85,17,000
(4) Borrowings	4	3,28,000
(5) Other Liabilities and provisions	5	5,67,000
Total		1,16,71,900
(II) *Property and Assets*		
(6) Cash and Balance with Reserve Bank of India	6	6,12,000
(7) Balance with Banks and Money at call and short notice	7	1,00,000
(8) Investments	8	13,50,000
(9) Advances	9	87,41,700
(10) Fixed Assets	10	7,83,400
(11) Other Assets	11	84,800
Total		1,16,71,900
(12) Contingent Liabilities	12	5,25,000
Bills for collections	—	3,50,000

Profit and Loss Account for the year ended 31-12-1994

		Schedule	Amount Rs.
Incomes			
Interest earned		13	8,46,000
Other Incomes		14	2,500
Total			8,48,500
Expenditure			
Interest Expended		15	1,96,000
Operating Expenses		16	4,05,800
Provision & Contingencies			
Provision for taxation			1,00,000
Total			7,01,800
Profit & Loss	8,48,500		
	– 7,01,800		
Net Profit			1,46,700
Add Profit Brought forward			89,200
			2,35,900
Less Appreciation			
Statutory Reserve 20% on 1,46,900			29,340
Profit & Loss Account			2,06,560

Schedule to Balance Sheet as at 31-12-1994

Schedule 1 — Capital	
Authorised Capital	
Shares of Rs. 100 each	
Issued Capital	
Shares of Rs. 100 each	
Subscribed and Paid up Capital	
10000 shares of Rs. 100 each	10,00,000
Total	10,00,000

Schedule 2 — Reserves & Surplus	
Statutory Reserve	29,340
Reserve Fund	8,70,000
Depreciation Fund	1,54,000
Balance in Profit & Loss Account	2,06,560
Total	12,59,900

Schedule 3 — Deposits		Rs.
Demand Deposits : Current Account		60,00,000
Savings Bank Deposit		12,77,000
Term Deposits : Fixed Deposits		13,00,000
Total		85,17,000

Schedule 4 — Borrowings		
From other Banks		3,28,000
Total		3,28,000

Schedule 5 — Other Liabilities		
Contingency Account		3,10,000
Bills payable		1,35,000
Rebate on Bills discounts	24,500	
Less : Overcalculate	2,500	22,000
Provision for taxation		1,00,000
Total		5,67,000

Schedule 6 — Cash in hand and Balance with RBI	6,12,000
Schedule 7 — Balances with other Banks and Money at call and short notice	1,00,000

Schedule 8 — Investments	
In Shares	7,50,000
In Govt. securities	4,00,000
Gold Bullion	1,50,000
Silver	50,000
Total	13,50,000

Schedule 9 — Advances	
Bills purchased and discounted	40,58,500
Cash credits, overdraft etc.	46,83,200
Total	87,41,700

Schedule 10 — Fixed Assets	
Premises at cost *less* depreciation	7,48,000
Furniture at cost *less* depreciation	35,400
Total	7,83,400

Schedule 11 — Other Assets	Rs.
Branch Adjustment	77,300
Interest accrued on Investment	7,500
Total	84,800

Schedule 12 — Contingent Liabilities	
Acceptance, endorsement and other obligations	5,25,000
Total	5,25,000

Schedule to Profit & Loss Account

Schedule 13 — Interest Earned	
Interest & Discount	7,26,000
Commission and Exchange	1,20,000
Total	8,46,000

Schedule 14 — Other Incomes	
Rebate on Bills Discount Overcalculated A/c	2,500
Total	2,500

Schedule 15 Interest Expended	
Interest on F.D. & S.B. Account	1,96,000
Total	1,96,000

Schedule 16 — Operatory Expenses	
Salaries	2,89,000
Rent, Taxes and Insurance	27,000
Other Expenditures	57,300
Depreciation on Bank's property	32,500
Total	4,05,800

Problem No. 12

Following is the Trial Balance of Suvarna Bank Ltd. as on 31-12-1990 :

Trial Balance

	Particulars	Dr. Rs.	Cr. Rs.
1.	Share Capital equity shares of Rs. 100 each Rs. 50 paid up		10,00,000
2.	Profit and Loss Account		40,333
3.	Current Accounts		34,12,829
4.	Fixed Deposits Accounts		38,95,554
5.	Savings Bank Accounts		25,68,000
6.	Director fees	4,980	
7.	Audit fees	1,000	
8.	Furniture	37,280	
9.	Interest and Discounts		2,10,223
10.	Commission and exchange		1,02,000
11.	Investment Reserve Fund		35,000
12.	Branch Adjustment		46,894
13.	Postage	1,156	
14.	Printing and Stationery	3,390	
15.	Rent and Taxes	8,507	
16.	Provident Fund contributes	10,000	
17.	Salary	52,150	
18.	Building	2,05,000	
19.	Law charges	1,650	
20.	Cash in hand and with RBI	8,16,324	
21.	Cash with other Banks	12,05,125	
22.	Investments	8,87,125	
23.	Loans, cash credits, overdrafts etc.	70,00,000	
24.	Bills discounted	14,00,520	
25.	Unexpired Insurance	437	
26.	Stamps in Hand	189	
27.	Statutory Reserve Fund		65,000
28.	Reserve Fund		2,50,000
		1,16,25,833	1,16,25,833

Other Information :

(a) Rebate on Bills discounted Rs. 5,900.

(b) Provide depreciation on Building @ 5%; on Furniture @ 10%.

(c) Acceptances and Endorsement Rs. 2,00,000.

(d) Market value of Investment Rs. 850,000.

The Investments are to be written down to its figure.

(e) Bills for collection Rs. 3,75,000.

(f) Provide for doubtful debts on debtors Rs. 25,000.

Prepare :

(1) Profit and Loss Account and

(2) Balance Sheet as on 31-12-1990.

(K.U.D., October 1994)

Solution :

Form-A

Suvarna Bank Limited

Balance Sheet as at 31-12-1990

	Schedule	Amount
(I) *Capital and Liabilities*		
(1) Capitals	1	10,00,000
(2) Reserves & Surplus	2	5,46,720
(3) Deposits	3	98,76,383
(4) Borrowings	4	—
(5) Other Liabilities	5	52,794
Total		1,14,75,897
(II) *Property and Assets*		
(6) Cash in hand and Balance with RBI	6	8,16,324
(7) Balance with other Banks	7	12,05,125
(8) Investments	8	8,50,000
(9) Advances	9	83,75,520
(10) Fixed Assets	10	2,28,302
(11) Other Assets	11	626
Total		1,14,75,897
Contingent Liabilities :	12	
Bills for collection		3,75,000
Acceptances and Endorsement		2,00,000
Total		5,75,000

Profit & Loss Account for the year ended 31-12-1990

Incomes		
Interest earned	13	2,81,323
Other Incomes	14	—
Total		2,81,323
Expenditure		
Interest Expended	15	—
Operating Expenses	16	96,811
Total		96,811
Provision & Contingencies :		—
Profit and Loss		
Net Profit		1,84,512
Add Profit brought forward		40,333
		2,24,845
Less Appropriation		
Less Statutory Reserve 20% of 1,84,512		36,902
Balance c/fd to B/s		1,87,943

Schedule to Balance Sheet at 31-12-1990

Schedule — 1 Capital

Authorised Capital	
Shares of Rs. 100 each	
Issued Capital	
Shares of Rs. 100 each	
Subscribed and Paid up Capital	
20000 shares of Rs. 100 each, Rs. 50 paid up	10,00,000

Schedule 2 — Reserve and Surplus

(a)	Statutory Reserve		
	Opening Balance	65,000	
	Additions during the year	36,902	1,01,902
(b)	Reserve Fund		
	Opening Balance		—
	Additions during the year		2,50,000
(c)	Investment Reserve Fund	35,000	
	Loss on revaluation	– 28,125	6,875
(d)	Balance of Profit and Loss A/c		1,87,943
	Total		5,46,720

Schedule 3 — Deposits

Current Account		34,12,829
Fixed Deposit		38,95,554
Savings Bank A/c		25,68,000
Total		98,76,383

Schedule 4 — Borrowings

		—
Total		—

Schedule 5 — Other Liabilities

(a) Rebate on Bills Discounted		5,900
(b) Provision for taxation		—
(c) Contingency Account		—
(d) Branch Adjustment		46,894
(e) Bills payable		
Total		52,794

Schedule 6 — Property and Assets

Cash in hand and balance with RBI		8,16,324

Schedule 7

Balance with other Banks and Money at call and short notice		12,05,125

Schedule 8 — Investments

	8,78,125	
Loss on Revaluation	28,125	8,50,000
Total		8,50,000

Schedule 9 — Advances

(a) Bills discounted and purchased		14,00,520
(b) Loans, cash credits, overdraft etc.	70,00,000	
Less RDD	25,000	69,75,000
Total		83,75,520

Schedule 10 — Fixed Assets

Building	2,05,000	
Less : Depreciation	10,250	1,94,750
Furniture	37,280	
Less : Depreciation	3,728	33,552
Total		2,28,302

Schedule — 11 Other Assets	Rs.
Unexpired Insurance	437
Stamp in hand	189
Branch Adjustment	—
Total	626

Schedule 12 — Contingent Liabilities	
(1) Bills for collections	3,75,000
(2) Acceptance Endorsement	2,00,000
Total	5,75,000

Alternatively : The same problem is answered as follows :

Profit and Loss Account for the year ended as 31-12-1990

Expenditure		Rs.	Income (*Less* Provisions)	Rs.
(1) Interest paid on Deposits and Borrowers		—	(1) Interest and Discount	1,79,323
			(2) Commission & Exchange	1,02,000
(2) Salaries and Allowances		52,150	(3) Rent	
(3) Contribution to PF		10,000	(4) Net profit on sale or revaluation of assets of Investment	
(4) Director fees		4,980		
(5) Rent, Taxes and Insrurance		8,507		
(6) Law charges		1,650	(5) Other receipts	
(7) Postage & Telegrams		1,156	(6) Loss is any	
(8) Auditors Fees		1,000		
(9) Depreciation :				
Building	10,250			
Furniture	3,728	13,978		
(10) Stationery and Printing		3,390		
(11) Loss from sale of Non-Bank assets		—		
(12) Other expenses		—		
(13) Net Profit		1,84,512		
		2,81,323		2,81,323

Note : (a) Interest & Discounts		2,10,223
Less : (i) Rebate on Bills Discount	5,900	
(ii) RDD	25,000	30,900
		1,79,323

(b) Investment Reserve Fund		35,000
Investment	8,78,125	
Market value	8,50,000	
Loss	28,125	28,125
		6,875
(c) Loans Advance cash	70,00,000	
	– 25,000	
	69,75,000	

Balance Sheet as at 31-12-1990

Capital & Liabilities	Rs.	Rs.	Properties & Assets	Rs.	Rs.
Share Capital			Cash in hand & with RBI		8,16,324
Equity shares of Rs. 100 each Rs. 50 paid up		10,00,000	Other Banks		12,05,125
Reserve & Reserve fund			Money at Call & Short Notice		—
Reserve fund	2,50,000		Investments	8,78,125	
Statutory Reserve 65,000			Loss	28,125	8,50,000
Add for the year 36,902	1,01,902		Loans Advance		69,75,000
			Bills Discounted		14,00,520
Investment Reserve	6,875	3,58,777	Bills Receivable being bills for collection per contra		3,75,000
Deposit & Other A/c :					
Fixed Deposit	38,95,554				
Savings Bank	25,68,000				
Current A/c	34,12,829	98,76,383	Contingent Liability for acceptances endorsement		2,00,000
Borrowing from other Banks :		—	Building	2,05,000	
Bills payable			*Less* Depre.	10,250	1,94,750
Bills for collection being BR (per control)		3,75,000	Furniture	37,280	
Others Liabilities			*Less* : Depre.	3,728	33,552
Branch Adjustment	46,894		*Other Assets*		
Rebate on Bills	5,900	52,794	Stamps on hand	437	
Acceptances, endorsement & other obligations		2,00,000	Unexpired insurance	189	626
Net Profit	40,333		Non-Banking Assets		—
Add : Profit for the year	1,84,512		Loss (if any)		—
	2,24,845				
Less : Statutory Res. 20% of 1,84,512	36,902	1,87,943			
		1,20,50,897			1,20,50,897

Problem No. 13

Following is the Trial Balance of Mahalaxmi Bank Ltd., Bombay as on 31st March 1991 :

Trial Balance

	Particulars	Dr. Rs.	Cr. Rs.
(1)	Share Capital : Shares of Rs. 100 each		6,00,000
(2)	Reserve Fund		2,10,000
(3)	Borrowings from Commercial Bank		2,28,000
(4)	Interest and Discount		3,75,000
(5)	Deposits		10,32,000
(6)	Commission and Exchange		37,500
(7)	Bills payable		26,000
(8)	Unclaimed Dividend		5,000
(9)	Pension Fund		2,000
(10)	Cash in hand	1,44,000	
(11)	Cash with Reserve Bank	2,74,000	
(12)	Money at call and short notice	2,37,500	
(13)	Investments	5,49,000	
(14)	Loans and Advances	9,01,500	
(15)	Premises *less* Depreciation	1,47,000	
(16)	Furniture *less* Depreciation	28,500	
(17)	Interest paid	1,50,000	
(18)	Salaries and Allowances	48,000	
(19)	Directors fees	12,000	
(20)	Postage	3,000	
(21)	Auditors fees	4,500	
(22)	Depreciation on Banks property	6,000	
(23)	Printing and Stationery	3,000	
(24)	Stamps in hand	500	
(25)	Branch Adjustment	7,000	
		25,15,500	25,15,500

Adjustments :

(1) Provision for unexpired discount on bills Rs. 3,000.

(2) Provision for taxation Rs. 5,000.

(3) Bills for collection amounted to Rs. 4,00,000.

(4) Acceptances on behalf of customers Rs. 2,00,000.

(5) Provide for Bad Debts Rs. 1,500.

You are required to prepare :

(a) Profit and Loss Account for the year ended 31-3-1991.

(b) Balance Sheet as at 31-3-1991.

(K.U.D., April 1994)

Solution :

Form-B

Profit and Loss Account for the year ended 31-3-1991

	Schedule	Amount Rs.
Incomes		
Interest earned	13	4,03,000
Other Incomes	14	—
Total		4,03,000
Expenditure		
Interest expended	15	1,50,000
Operatory expenses	16	—
Provision and Contingents		76,500
Total		2,26,500
Profit and Loss		
Net profit		1,76,500
Add : Profit brought forward		
Less : Appreciation		—
Statutory Reserve 20% of 1,76,500		35,300
Balance of profit C/fd to B/S		1,41,200

Form-A

Mahalaxmi Bank Ltd., Bombay

Balance Sheet as at 31-3-1991

	Schedule	Amount
(I) *Capital and Liabilities*		
(1) Capital	1	6,00,000
(2) Reserves and Surplus	2	3,86,500
(3) Deposits	3	10,32,000
(4) Borrowings	4	2,28,000
(5) Other Liabilities	5	41,000
Total		22,87,500

		Schedule	Amount Rs.
(II) *Property and Assets*			
(6)	Cash in hand and balance with RBI	6	4,18,000
(7)	Balance with others Banks	7	2,37,500
(8)	Investments	8	5,49,000
(9)	Advances	9	9,00,000
(10)	Fixed Assets	10	1,75,500
(11)	Other Assets	11	7,500
	Total		22,87,500
Contingent Liabilities :		12	
	Bills for collection		4,00,000
	Acceptance on behalf of customer		2,00,000
	Total		6,00,000

Schedule to Balance Sheet as at 31-3-1991

Schedule 1 — Capital

		Amount
Authorised Capital		
	.... Shares of Rs. 100 each	
Issued Capital		
	.... Shares of Rs. 100 each	
Subscribed and Paid up Capital		
	6000 shares of Rs. 100 each	6,00,000
	Total	6,00,000

Schedule 2 — Reserves and Surplus

		Amount
(a)	Statutory Reserves	35,300
	Opening Balance	—
	Additions during the year	—
(b)	Reserve Fund	2,10,000
	Opening Balance	—
	Additions during the period	—
(c)	Other Reserves	—
(d)	Balance of Profit	1,41,200
	Total	3,86,500

Schedule 3 — Deposits

		Amount
		10,32,000
(a)	Current Accounts	
(b)	Fixed Deposits Accounts	
(c)	Savings Bank Accounts	
	Total	10,32,000

Schedule 4 — Borrowings

From other Banks	2,28,000
Total	2,28,000

Schedule 5 — Other Liabilities

(a)	Rebate on Bills Discounted	3,000
(b)	Provision for taxation	5,000
(c)	Contingent A/c / Unclaimed dividend	5,000
(d)	Pension Fund	2,000
(e)	Bills payable	26,000
	Total	41,000

Schedule 6 — Cash and Balances with RBI

(a)	Cash in hand	1,44,000
(b)	Balances with Reserve Bank	2,74,000
	Total	4,18,000

Schedule 7 — Balances with Banks

(c)	Balance with other Banks	—
(d)	Money at call and short notice	2,37,500
	Total	2,37,500

Schedule 8 — Investments

	5,49,000
Total	5,49,000

Schedule 9 — Advances

Loan Advances, cash credit, overdraft etc.	9,01,500	
Less : R.D.D.	1,500	9,00,000
Bills discounted and purchased		—
Total		9,00,000

Schedule 10 — Fixed Assets

Premises *less* Depreciation	1,47,000
Furniture *less* Depreciation	28,500
Total	1,75,500

Schedule 11 — Other Assets

Stamps in hand	500
Branch Adjustment	7,000
Total	7,500

Schedule 12 — Contingent Liabilities

Acceptances, endorsement etc.	2,00,000
Bills for collection	4,00,000
Total	6,00,000

Schedule to Profit and Loss Account for the year ended 31-3-1991

Schedule 13 — Interest Earned

(a)	Interest & Discount		3,75,000	
	Less : Provisions :			
	(1) Unexpired discount	3,000		
	(2) For Taxation	5,000		
	(3) For Bad debts	1,500	9,500	3,65,500
(b)	Commission and Exchange			37,500
	Total			4,03,000

Schedule 14 — Other Incomes —

Schedule 15 — Interest Expended

Interest paid on Deposits & Borrowing	1,50,000
Total	1,50,000

Schedule 16 — Operating Expenses

Salaries & Allowances	48,000
Directors fees	12,000
Audit fees	4,500
Postage	3,000
Printing & Stationery	3,000
Rent & Taxes	—
Law Charges	—
Depreciation	6,000
Total	76,500

Alternatively : The same Problem is answered as follows :

Profit and Loss Account for the year ended 31-3-1991

Expenditure	Rs.	Income (*Less* Provisions)	Rs.
To Interest paid on Deposits and Borrowing	1,50,000	By Interest & Discounts	3,65,500
		By Commission & Exchange	37,500
To Salaries & Allowances	48,000	By Rent	—
To Directors fees	12,000	By Net profit on sale or Revaluation of interest	—
To Rent, Rate, Taxes, Insurance	—	By Income from non-Banking Assets	—
To Law charges	—		
To Postage and Telegrams	3,000	By Other Incomes	—
To Audit fees	4,500	By Loss (if any)	—
To Depreciation	6,000		

Expenditure	Rs.	Income (*Less* Provisions)	Rs.
To Stationery and Printing	3,000		
Less on Sale of Non-bought Assets			
To Other expenses			
To Net Profit	1,76,500		
	4,03,000		4,03,000

Interest and Discount		3,75,000
Less : Provision for Rebate on Bills Discounted	3,000	
For Taxation	5,000	
For RDD	1,500	9,500
		3,65,500

Mahalaxmi Bank, Bombay

Balance Sheet as at 31-3-1991

Capital & Liabilities	Rs.	Rs.	Property & Assets	Rs.	Rs.
1. Share Capital : share of Rs. 100		6,00,000	1. Cash in hand	1,44,000	
			With Reserve Bank	2,74,000	4,18,000
2. Reserve Fund & Other Reserves			2. With other Banks		—
Reserve Fund	210,000		3. Month at call & Short notice		2,37,500
Statutory Reserve	35,300	2,45,300	4. Investments		5,49,000
3. Deposits & Other A/c			5. Loans & Advances	9,01,500	
(a) Current A/c	—		*Less* RDD	1,500	9,00,000
(b) Fixed Deposits	10,32,000		6. Bills Receivable being Bills for collection per contra		4,00,000
(c) Provision for taxation	5,000	10,37,000	7. Contingent liability for acceptance, endorsement per contra		—
4. Borrowings from other Banks Commercial Bank		2,28,000	8. Premises *Less* Depreciation		1,47,000
5. Bills payable		26,000	9. Furniture *Less* Depreciation		28,500
6. Bills for collection being BR per contra		4,00,000	10. Other Assets		
7. Other Liability :			(a) Stamp in hand	500	
(a) Unclaimed dividend	5,000		(b) Branch Adjustment	7,000	7,500
(b) Pension fund	2,000				
(c) Rebate on Bills discount	3,000	10,000	11. Non-banking Assets		—

Capital & Liabilities	Rs.	Rs.	Property & Assets	Rs.	Rs.
8. Acceptance endorsement and other obligation per contra		2,00,000	12. Profit & Loss A/c (if any)		—
9. Profit and Loss A/c Balance	—				
For the year	1,76,500				
Less 20% Statutory	35,300	1,41,200			
		28,87,500			28,87,500

Problem No. 14

The Dhan Varsha Bank Ltd. has an Authorised Capital of Rs. 10,00,000 in equity share of Rs. 10 each. The following is the Trial Balance of the Bank :

Trial Balance as on 31-12-1991

	Particulars	Dr. Rs.	Cr. Rs.
(1)	Subscribed Capital		6,00,000
(2)	Reserve fund		2,40,000
(3)	Deposits and other account		18,00,000
(4)	Investment in Government securities	3,60,000	
(5)	Money at call and short notice	72,000	
(6)	Borrowings from other Banks		1,80,000
(7)	Interest and Discounts		3,45,600
(8)	Commission and Exchange		36,000
(9)	Salaries	96,000	
(10)	Rent, Taxes etc.	6,000	
(11)	Profit and Loss Account on 1-1-1991		48,000
(12)	Cash in hand	1,44,000	
(13)	Cash with RBI	60,000	
(14)	Cash with other Banks	1,92,000	
(15)	Unclaimed Dividend		7,200
(16)	Pension Fund		9,600
(17)	Loans, cash credits, etc.	17,70,000	
(18)	Bills discounted and purchased	3,00,000	
(19)	Interest paid	84,000	
(20)	Bills payable		34,000
(21)	Premises *less* depreciation	1,14,000	
(22)	Furniture *less* depreciation	32,400	
(23)	Depreciation	9,600	
(24)	Non-Banking assets	18,000	
(25)	Other receipts		1,800
(26)	Stationery in hand	10,000	
(27)	Postage and Telegram	3,000	
(28)	Directors fees	16,800	
(29)	Auditors fees	14,400	
		33,02,200	33,02,200

Additional Information :

(1) Provide for doubtful debts Rs. 20,000
(2) Provide for taxation Rs. 25,000
(3) Rebate on bills discounted Rs. 25,000
(4) Bills for collection Rs. 3,00,000
(5) Acceptances and Endorsements Rs. 2,00,000

Prepare :

(1) Profit and Loss Account and
(2) Balance Sheet in prescribed Form.

(K.U.D., October 1993)

Solution :

Profit and Loss Account for the year ended 31-12-1991

Expenditure	Rs.	Income (*Less* Provisions)	Rs.
Interest paid on		By Interest & Discount	2,75,600
Borrowing deposits	84,000	By Commission, exchange etc.	36,000
Salaries & Allowance	96,000	By Rent	—
Directors fees	16,800	By Profit on sale of	
Rent, Insurance, Taxes	6,000	revaluation of Investment	—
Law charges		By Income from Non-banking	
Postage & Telegrams	3,000	assets	—
Audit fees	14,400	By Other receipts	1,800
Depreciation	9,600	By Loss (if any)	—
Stationery and Printing	—		
Loss on sale of non-Banking assets	—		
Other expenses	—		
Net profit	83,600		
	3,13,400		3,13,400

Note :

(1) Interest and Discounts		3,45,600
Less : (a) Provision for doubtful debts	20,000	
(b) Provision for taxation	25,000	
(c) Rebate on Bills discount	25,000	70,000
Net		2,75,600
(2) Loans, cash credits, etc.	17,70,000	
Less : RDD	20,000	
	17,50,000	

Dhan Varsha Bank Ltd.

Balance Sheet as at 31-12-1991

Capital & Liability	Rs.	Rs.	Property & Assets	Rs.	Rs.
1. Share Capital			1. Cash in hand	1,44,000	
Authorised 100000			With RBI	60,000	
Equity share of Rs. 10		10,00,000	2. With other Banks	1,92,000	3,96,000
Issued & paid up			3. Money at call &		
60000 equity			short notice		72,000
share of Rs. 10		6,00,000	4. Investments		3,60,000
2. Reserve Fund and			5. Loans, cash credits,		
Other Reserve	2,40,000		overdrafts etc.	17,50,000	
Statutory Reserve	16,720	2,56,720	Bills discounted	3,00,000	20,50,000
3. Deposit & other Assets					
(a) Fixed		—	6. Bills receivable		
(b) Current A/c		18,00,000	being bills for		
(c) Saving Banks		25,000	collection		3,00,000
4. Borrowing from			7. Constituent liabilities		
other Banks		1,80,000	for acceptance, endorse-		
5. Bills payable		34,000	ment etc. per contra		2,00,000
6. Bills for collection			8. Premises *less* depreciation		1,14,000
being bill be receivable		3,00,000	9. Furniture *less* depreciation		32,400
7. Other Liabilities :			10. Other Assets :		
(a) Unclaimed			Stationery		10,000
dividend	7,200		11. Non-banking Assets		18,000
(b) Premises fund	9,600		12. Profit & Loss A/c		—
(c) Rebate on bills	25,000	41,800			
8. Acceptance, Endorsement					
and other obligations		2,00,000			
9. Net Profit on					
1-1-91	48,000				
Add Profit					
in the year	83,600				
	1,31,600				
Less Statutory					
Reserve 20%	16,720	1,14,880			
		35,52,400			35,52,400

Problem No. 15

The following is the Trial Balance as on 31-3-1991 of Grindlays Bank :

Trial Balance

	Particulars	Dr. Rs.	Cr. Rs.
(1)	Equity share of Rs. 10 each		4,00,000
(2)	Salaries and Allowances	15,000	
(3)	Rent	15,000	40,000
(4)	Interest and Discount		1,40,000
(5)	Directors fees	15,000	
(6)	Printing and Stationery	10,000	
(7)	Postage and Telegram	6,000	
(8)	Subscription to school Magazines	5,000	
(9)	Audit fees	6,000	
(10)	Depreciation on Banks property	7,000	
(11)	Stock of Stationery	2,000	
(12)	General Expenses	10,000	
(13)	Cash in hand and with RBI	60,000	
(14)	Money at call and short notice	1,40,000	
(15)	Deposits in Canara Bank	60,000	
(16)	Loans and cash credits	3,50,000	
(17)	Overdrafts	1,80,000	
(18)	Bills discounted and purchased	90,000	
(19)	Furniture *less* depreciation	30,000	
(20)	Premises *less* depreciation	80,000	
(21)	Commission and exchange		80,000
(22)	Reservc Fund		90,000
(23)	Profit and Loss A/c on 1-4-90		50,000
(24)	Provident fund balance		10,000
(25)	Borrowings from State Bank		30,000
(26)	Money transfers payable		5,000
(27)	Indian Govt. Securities	1,00,000	
(28)	Shares	1,19,000	
(29)	Savings Bank Deposits		50,000
(30)	Recurring deposits		55,000
(31)	Current account		1,00,000
(32)	Fixed deposit		2,50,000
		13,00,000	13,00,000

Other Information :

(a) Provision for bad and doubtful debts required at Rs. 5,000.

(b) Rebate on Bills discounted amounted to Rs. 10,000.

(c) Endorsement made on behalf of customers Rs. 60,000.

(d) Bills for collection amounted to Rs. 50,000.

(e) Provide Rs. 15,000 for taxation.

(f) Indian Govt. securities market value was Rs. 90,000.

Prepare :

(1) Profit and Loss Account

(2) Balance Sheet as on 31-3-1991.

(K.U.D., April 1993)

Solution :

Grindlays Bank Ltd.

Profit and Loss Account for the year ended 31-3-1991

Expenditure	Rs.	Income (*Less* Provisions)	Rs.
Interest paid on Deposit and Borrowing	7,000	By Interest and Discounts	1,00,000
Salaries and allowances	15,000	By Commission and Exchange	80,000
Directors fees	15,000	By Rent	40,000
Rent, Rates, Taxes etc.	15,000	By Net profit on sale of Revaluation of Investment	—
Law charges		By Income from non-banking Assets	—
Postage and Telegrams	6,000	By Other Incomes	—
Audit fees	6,000	By Loss (if any)	—
Stationery and Printings	10,000		
Loss on sale of non-banking Assets			
Other expenses :			
General expenses	10,000		
Subscription to school Magazines	5,000		
Net Profit	1,31,000		
	2,20,000		2,20,000

Note : Interest & Discounts		1,40,000
Less : Provisions for		
(1) RDD	5,000	
(2) Rebate	10,000	
(3) Taxation	15,000	
(4) Investment	10,000	40,000
Net Interest and Discount		1,00,000

Balance Sheet as at 31-3-1991

Capital & Liability	Rs.	Rs.	Property & Assets	Rs.	Rs.
Share of Capital			Cash in Hand &		
Equity share of Rs. 10		4,00,000	with RBI		60,000
Reserve Fund & other			With other Banks		60,000
Reserve			Money at Call & Short		
Reserve fund	90,000		Notice		1,40,000
Statutory Reserve	26,200		Investment in		
Investment :			Govt. security	1,00,000	
Fluctuation Reserve	10,000	1,26,200	in shares	1,19,000	2,19,000
Deposits & other A/c :			Loans and cash		
Recurring deposit	55,000		credit	3,50,000	
Savings banks	50,000		Overdrafts	1,80,000	
Current A/c	1,00,000			5,30,000	
Fixed deposit	1,50,000		*Less* RDD	5,000	
Provision for Tax	15,000	4,70,000			5,25,000
Borrowing from other			Bills recoverable being		90,000
Bank : State Bank		30,000	Bills for collection		
Bills payable		—	per contra		50,000
Bills for collection			Constituent liability		
being bills receivable		50,000	for acceptances and		
Other Liabilities :			endorsement (per contra)		60,000
PF Balance	10,000		Premises *less* depreciation		80,000
Rebate	10,000		Furniture *less* depreciation		30,000
Money transport			Other Assets :		
payable	15,000	25,000	Stock of Stationery		2,000
Profit & Loss A/c :			Non-Banking assets		—
Balance 1-4-90	50,000		Profit and Loss A/c		—
Add Profit for year	1,31,000				
	1,81,000				
Less Statutory reserve					
20% of 1,31,000	26,200	1,54,800			
		13,16,000			13,16,000

Problem No. 16

Shri Mahalaxmi Bank Ltd., Hubli
Trial Balance as on 31 March 1991

Particulars	Dr. Rs.	Cr. Rs.
Share Capital 25,000 : Equity shares of Rs. 10 each		2,50,000
Reserve fund		1,00,000
Money at call and short notice	30,000	
Fixed deposits		3,50,000
Borrowings from banks		75,000
Investments in Government securities	1,50,000	
Savings banks deposits		2,50,000
Interest and discount		1,84,000
Commission, Exchange and brokerage		15,000
Rent and tax	2,500	
Salaries and allowances to staff	65,000	
Current Account		1,50,000
Salary to Manager	15,000	
Profit and Loss Account (1-4-1990)		20,000
Cash in hand	60,000	
Cash with other banks	80,000	
Provident fund		7,500
Cash with R.B.I.	25,000	
Loans, cash credit and overdraft	7,37,500	
Depreciation	4,000	
Directors fee	7,000	
Audit fees	6,000	
Postage and Telegrams	500	
Stationery on hand	1,500	
Non-Banking Assets	7,500	
Bills payable		14,000
Income from non-banking assets		1,000
Branch adjustment account		2,000
Bills discounted and purchased	1,25,000	
Profit on sale of investment		5,000
Premises	50,000	
Furniture	15,000	
Transfer fees		1,500
Interest on deposits	35,000	
Interim dividend paid	8,500	
	14,25,000	14,25,000

Notes :

(a) Provide for Taxation Rs. 10,000 and for doubtful debts Rs. 12,500.
(b) Unexpired discount Rs. 5,000.
(c) Interest accrued on investment Rs. 10,000.
(d) Bills for collection Rs. 60,000.
(e) Acceptances, endorsements on behalf of customers Rs. 75,000.
(f) Interim dividend declared @ 4%.
(g) Provide for employee contribution to provident fund Rs. 5,000.
(h) The market value of Government securities was Rs. 1,60,000.

Prepare Final Accounts.

(K.U.D., October 1992)

Solution :

Working Note

(1)	Interest and Discount		1,84,000
	Add : Interest on Investments		10,000
			1,94,000
	Less : (a) Taxation	10,000	
	(b) Doubtful Debts	12,500	
	(c) Unexpired discount	5,000	
	(d) Contribution to P.F.	5,000	32,500
			1,61,500
(2)	Interim Dividend :		8,500
	Interim Dividend @ 4% on 2,50,000		10,000
	Dividend payable		1,500
(3)	Loans, Cash Credits and Overdraft		7,37,500
	Less : R.D.D.		12,500
			7,25,000

Profit and Loss Account for the year ended 31-3-92

Expenditure	Rs.	Income (*Less* Provisions)	Rs.
Interest paid on Deposit and Borrowings	35,000	Interest and Discount	1,61,500
Salaries & Allowances	65,000	Commission, Exchange and Brokerage	15,000
Salaries to Manager	15,000	Rent	5,000
Directors fees	7,000	Net Profit on sale of Investment	—
Rent, Taxes Insurance etc.	2,500	Net Profit on Revaluation of Investment	—
Law charges			
Postage, telegrams	500	Income from non-Banking Assets	1,000
Audit fees	6,000	Other Receipts	—
Depreciation on Banks property	4,000	Transfer fees	1,500
Stationery Printing etc.	—	Loss if any	—
Loss from sale of Non-Banking Assets	—		
	—		
Other Expenses			
Net Profit	49,000		
	1,84,000		1,84,000

Mahalaxmi Bank Ltd.

Balance Sheet as on 31-3-1992

Capital & Liability	Rs.	Rs.	Property & Assets	Rs.	Rs.
Capital			Cash in Hand	60,000	
Share Capital			With Reserve Bank	25,000	85,000
25000 Equity shares of Rs. 10 each		2,50,000			
Reserves & Reserve fund :			With other Bank		80,000
Reserve fund	1,00,000		Money at call & short notice		30,000
Statutory Reserve	9,800	1,09,800	Investments in Govt. Securities	1,60,000 (market value)	1,50,000
Deposits & Other A/c					
(a) Fixed Deposits	3,50,000		Loans, Advances,		
(b) Savings Bank	2,50,000		& cash credit	7,25,000	
(c) Current A/c	1,50,000				
	10,000	7,60,000	Bills Disc. & purchased	1,25,000	8,50,000
Borrowing from other Bank			Bills Receivable		
Bills payable		14,000	being Bills for collection (per contra)		60,000
Bills for collections being Bills Receivable (per contra)		60,000	Constituent Liabilities for acceptance, endorsement and other obligation (per contra)		75,000
Other Liabilities					
(a) Provident fund	7,500		Premises *Less* : Depr.		50,000
(b) Branch Adj.	5,000		Furniture *Less* : Depr.		15,000
(c) Unexpired Disc.	2,000				
Contribution to PF	5,000				
Dividend pay	1,500	21,000	*Other Assets*		
Acceptances, Endorsement			(a) Stationery on hand	1,500	
and other obligation			(b) Interest on		
per contra		75,000	Investment	10,000	11,500
Profit and Loss A/c			Non-Banking Assets		7,500
Balance on 1-4-90	20,000		Profit and Loss A/c		—
Less : Dividend	10,000				
	10,000				
Add : Profit for year	49,000				
	59,000				
Less : Statutory Reserve 20% on 49,000	9,800	49,200			
		14,14,000			14,14,000

Problem No. 17

Following is the Trial Balance Sheet of Citizen Bank Ltd. as on 31-3-1991. The Authorised Capital of the Bank was Rs. 10,00,000 in Equity Shares of Rs. 10 each.

Trial Balance as on 31-3-1991

	Particulars	Dr. Rs.	Cr. Rs.
(1)	Subscribed and Paid up Capital 50000 Equity shares of Rs. 10 each		5,00,000
(2)	Reserve Fund		2,50,000
(3)	Bank Premises	1,05,000	
(4)	Loans & Advances	4,85,000	
(5)	Investments in Govt. security	4,50,000	
(6)	Bills Discounted and purchased	46,000	
(7)	Deposits and Contingency accounts		4,90,000
(8)	Salaries and Allowances	30,000	
(9)	Interest paid on Deposits	50,000	
(10)	General expenses	27,400	
(11)	Rent, Taxes etc.	2,300	
(12)	Directors fees	1,800	
(13)	Profit and Loss A/c on 1-4-1990		40,000
(14)	Interest and discount		2,48,000
(15)	Money at call and short notice	80,000	
(16)	Audit fees	3,000	
(17)	Income tax paid	8,500	
(18)	Provision for taxation		21,000
(19)	Rebate on Bills discounted		900
(20)	Interim dividend paid	40,000	
(21)	Cash in Hand	1,04,000	
(22)	Cash with Reserve Bank	1,10,000	
(23)	Interest accrued	8,000	
(24)	Commission and Exchange		10,100
(25)	Depreciation	9,000	
		15,60,000	15,60,000

Adjustments :

(1) Provide for doubtful debts Rs. 16,000
(2) Final dividend declared @ 10% on capital
(3) Bills for collection Rs. 1,00,000
(4) Acceptances, Endorsements etc. Rs. 1,25,000
(5) Market value of Investments Rs. 4,25,000.

Make provision for fall in value of Investment.

(K.U.D., April 1992)

Profit and Loss Account for the year ended 31-3-1991

Expenditure	Rs.	Income (Less Provisions)	Rs.
Interest paid on deposits	50,000	By Interest & Discount	2,07,000
Salaries & Allowance	30,000	By Commission & Exchange	10,100
Directors fees	1,800	By Rent	—
Rent, Tax & etc.	2,300	By Profit on sale or Revalue	
Law charges	—	of interest	—
Postage & Telegram	—	By Income from Non-banking	
Auditor fees	3,000	Assets	—
Depreciation	9,000	By Other receipts	—
Stationery and Printing	—	By Loss (if any)	—
Loss on sale of assets	—		
Other expenses			
General expenditure	27,400		
Net Profit	93,600		
	2,17,100		2,17,100

(1) Interest and Discount		2,48,000
Less Provision for RDD	16,000	
Provision for fall in value of interest	25,000	41,000
Interest & Discount		2,07,000
(2) Interim Dividend	40,000	
Final dividend 10% on 5,00,000 =	50,000	
Unclaimed dividend	10,000	

Rs. 50,000 be deducted from Profit and Loss Account in Balance sheet.

Balance Sheet as at 31-3-1991

Capital & Liability	Rs.	Rs.	Property & Assets	Rs.	Rs.
Share Capital			Cash in Hand		1,04,000
Authorised			With RBI		1,10,000
100000 Equity shares			With other Banks		—
of Rs. 10 each		10,00,000	Money at call & short		
Subscribed & Paid up			notice		80,000
50000 Equity share of Rs. 10		5,00,000	Investments	4,25,000	4,50,000
Reserve & Surplus			Loans & Advance	4,85,000	
Reserve fund		2,50,000	Bills discount	46,000	
Statutory Reserve		18,720		5,31,000	
Investment fluctuation fund		25,000	*Less* RDD	16,000	5,15,000
Deposits & Others			Bills receivable bearing		
F.D., S.B & Current		4,90,000	Bills for collection		1,00,000
Provision for taxation		21,000	Premises *less* depreciation		1,05,000
Borrowing from other Bank		—	Furniture *less* depreciation		—
Bills payable		—	Other Assets		—
Bills for collection		—	Interest accrued		8,000
Being Bills receivable			Constituent liability		
per contra		1,00,000	for acceptance,		
Other Liabilities			endorsements		1,25,000
Rebate on Bills	900		Non-banking assets		—
Unclaimed dividend	10,000	10,900	Profit & Loss A/c (if any)		—
Acceptance, Endorsements					
per contra		1,25,000			
Profit & Loss A/c		56,380			
Balance 1-4-1990	40,000				
Less Income Tax paid	8,500				
	31,500				
Add Profit for year	93,600				
	1,25,100				
Less Dividend	50,000				
	75,100				
Less : Statutory					
Reserve 20%	18,720				
		15,97,000			15,97,000

Problem No. 18

Prepare the Final Account of the Guilol Bank Ltd. for the year ended 31 March 1991.

Ledger Balance

	Particulars	Rs.
(1)	Share Capital	
	Authorised : 10000 equity shares of Rs. 50 each	5,00,000
	Issued 6000 equity shares of Rs. 50 each	3,00,000
(2)	Statutory Reserve	50,000
(3)	Interest paid on deposits	22,500
(4)	Contingency accounts	12,500
(5)	Unexpired Insurance	500
(6)	Unexpired discount	2,500
(7)	Law charges	2,500
(8)	Investment Reserve	15,000
(9)	Directors fees	6,000
(10)	Auditors fees	5,000
(11)	Premises	75,000
(12)	Furniture and Fixtures	20,000
(13)	Interest and discount	1,77,000
(14)	Stamps on hand	2,000
(15)	Cash with RBI	1,00,000
(16)	Bills discounted and purchased	1,50,000
(17)	Salaries and allowances	35,000
(18)	Depreciation	5,500
(19)	Profit and Loss A/c (1-4-1990)	7,500
(20)	Loans	9,00,000
(21)	Cash	1,25,000
(22)	Contribution to provident fund	6,500
(23)	Investment	4,25,000
(24)	Rent, Insurance and Tax	12,000
(25)	Savings Bank deposits	4,00,000
(26)	Cash credit	3,00,000
(27)	Branch Adjustment (Dr.)	10,000
(28)	Commission, exchange etc.	8,000
(29)	Overdraft	1,95,000
(30)	Current account	7,20,000

		Rs.
(31)	Cash with Banks	1,75,000
(32)	Fixed Deposits	8,80,000
(33)	Other expenses	10,000
(34)	Provident Fund	10,000

Adjustments :

(a) Municipal tax owing Rs. 10,000
(b) Provide for taxation Rs. 25,000
(c) For Doubtful debts Rs. 25,000
(d) The market value of Investment is Rs. 4,20,000 and they are to be written down.
(e) Bills for collection Rs. 50,000
(f) Acceptances and Endorsement on behalf of customers Rs. 30,000
(g) Contingent liabilities against Bills re-discounted.

(K.U.D., October 1991)

Profit and Loss A/c for the year ended 31-3-1991

Expenditure	Rs.	Income (*Less* Provisions)		Rs.
To Interest paid on Deposits on Borrowings	22,500	By Interest & Discount *Less* : Provisions :		1,77,000
To Salaries & Allowance	35,000	(a) Taxation 25,000		
Contribution to PF	6,500	(b) RDD 25,000	50,000	1,27,000
To Directors Fee	6,000	By Commission & Exchange		8,000
To Rent, Insurance, taxes	12,000	By Rent		—
Less : Municipal Taxes	10,000	By Profit on sale of		
To Law charges	2,500	revaluation of investment		—
To Postage & Telegram	—	By Income from Non-		
To Auditors fees	5,000	banking assets		—
To Depreciation	5,500	By Other receipt		—
To Stationery & Printing	—	By Net Loss, if any		—
To Loss on sale of Non-Banking assets	—			
To Other expenses	10,000			
To Net Profit	20,000			
	1,35,000			1,35,000

Balance Sheet as at 31-3-1991

Capital & Liability	Rs.	Rs.	Property & Assets	Rs.	Rs.
Share Capital			Cash in Hand	1,25,000	
Authorised Capital			With RBI	1,00,000	
10,000 Equity			With other Banks	1,75,000	4,00,000
shares of Rs. 50 each		5,00,000	Money at Call &		
Issued Capital			Short Notice		4,20,000
6000 Equity share of Rs. 50 each		3,00,000	Investments	4,25,000	4,20,000
Reserve Fund and Others			Loans cash credits		
Statutory Reserve	50,000		Draft loans 9,00,000		
Add :	4,000	54,000	*Less* RDD 25,000	8,75,000	
Investment Reserve	15,000		Overdrafts	1,95,000	
Less fall in value	5,000	10,000	Cash Credits	3,00,000	
Deposits & Other A/c			Bills Discount &		
Fixed	8,80,000		Purchased	1,50,000	15,20,000
Saving Banks	4,00,000		Bills receivable		
Current A/c	7,20,000		being bills for		
Contingency	12,500		collection		50,000
Provision for taxation	25,000	20,37,500	Contingent liability		
Borrowing from other banks			for acceptance, endorsement		30,000
Bills payable		—	Premises		75,000
Bills for collection			Furniture		20,000
being bills receivable		50,000	Other Assets		
Other liabilities :			Unexpired insurance	500	
Unexpired discount	2,500		Stamps in hand	2,000	
Provident fund	10,000		Branch adjustment	10,000	12,5000
Municipal taxes	10,000	22,500	Non-banking assets		—
Acceptance, Endorsement		30,000	Profit & Loss A/c		—
Net Profit :			(if any)		
Balance	7,500				
Add Profit for year	20,000				
	2,72,500				
Less Statutory reserve					
20% of 20,000	4,000	23,500			
		25,27,500			25,27,500

Problem No. 19

Following is the Trial Balance of Dhan-Vridhi Bank Ltd. as on 31-12-89 :

Trial Balance as on 31-12-1989

	Particulars	Dr. Rs.	Cr. Rs.
(1)	Share Capital : Equity shares of Rs. 100 each fully paid		24,00,000
(2)	Money at call and short notice	9,30,000	
(3)	Borrowings from other banks		9,90,000
(4)	Cash in hand	6,45,000	
(5)	Cash with Reserve Bank	8,25,000	
(6)	Cash with other banks	6,00,000	
(7)	Reserve fund		8,10,000
(8)	Deposits		33,00,000
(9)	Investments	9,75,000	
(10)	Investment fluctuation fund		36,000
(11)	Pension fund		30,000
(12)	Loans Cash credits etc.	39,75,000	
(13)	Premises *less* Depreciation	2,40,000	
(14)	Furniture *less* Depreciation	1,50,000	
(15)	Rent		99,000
(16)	Commission and Brokerage		90,000
(17)	Interest paid on Deposits and Borrowings	4,20,000	
(18)	Interest and Discounts		12,00,000
(19)	Salaries	2,10,000	
(20)	Non-banking Assets	60,000	
(21)	Contribution to pension fund	6,000	
(22)	Directors fee	15,000	
(23)	Law charges	6,000	
(24)	Audit fees	9,000	
(25)	Postage and Telegram	7,500	
(26)	Printing and Stationery	15,000	
(27)	Depreciation on banks property	10,500	
(28)	Profit and Loss Account as on 31-12-1989		1,44,000
		90,99,000	90,99,000

Additional information :

(a)	Provide rebate on bills discounted	45,000
(b)	Provide for doubtful debts on debtors	25,000
(c)	Provide for Income tax	75,000
(d)	Bills for collections	8,75,000
(e)	Acceptances and endorsements	6,25,000
(f)	Market value of intvestments	9,25,000

Prepare : (i) Profit and Loss Account; and
(ii) Balance Sheet of the bank.

(K.U.D., April 1991)

Solution :

Profit and Loss A/c for the year ended 31-12-89

Expenditure	Rs.	Income (*Less* Provisions)	Rs.
To Interest paid on Deposits on Borrowings	4,20,000	By Interest on	11,16,000
		By Commission and Brokerage	90,000
To Salaries & Allowances	2,10,000	By Rent	99,000
To Contribution to pension fund	6,000	By Net Profit on sales or Revaluation of investment	—
To Directors fees	15,000	By Income from other sources	
To Rent, Taxes etc.	—		
To Law charges	6,000	Non Banking Assets	—
To Postage & Telegram	7,500	Other Receipts	—
To Audit fees	9,000	Loans, if any	—
To Depreciation on banks property	10,500		
To Loss from sale of non-Banking Assets	—		
To Other Expenses	—		
To Net Profit	6,06,000		
	13,05,000		13,05,000

Investments	9,75,000	Interest of Discount		12,00,000
Market value	9,25,000	*Less* : Provisions :		
	50,000	Rebate on Bills		
Investment fluctuation fund	36,000	Discount	45,000	
Loss uncovered deducted		R.D.D.	25,000	
from interest and discount	14,000	Uncovered Balance	14,000	84,000
		Loss on Revaluation of Investment		11,16,000

Dhan Vridhi Bank Ltd.

Balance Sheet as on 31-12-1989

Capital & Liability	Rs.	Rs.	Property & Assets	Rs.	Rs.
Capital : Authorised,			Cash in Hand		6,45,000
Subscribed and			With Reserve Bank		8,25,000
Paid up			With other Banks		6,00,000
Equity shares of			Money at call and		
Rs. 100 each			short notice		9,30,000
fully paid		24,00,000	Investments		9,75,000
Reserve and			*Loans, Advances,*		
Reserve fund			*Cash credits*		
Reserve fund		8,10,000	Bills Discounted and		
Statutory Reserve		1,21,200	purchased		39,50,000
Investment fluctuation fund		50,000	Bills Receivable being Bills		
Deposits		33,75,000	for collection (per contra)		8,75,000
(a) Fixed	33,00,000		Constituent Liabilities for		
(b) Savings bank	—		Acceptance, Endorsement		
(c) Current A/c	—		and other obligations		
Income Tax	75,000		(per contra)		6,25,000
Borrowing from			Premises *less* depreciation		2,40,000
other Banks		9,90,000	Furniture *less* depreciation		1,50,000
Bills payable		—	Other Assets :		
Bills for collection			Non-Banking Assets		60,000
being Bills Receivable			Profit & Loss A/c (Loss if any)		—
(per contra)		8,75,000			
Other Liabilities		75,000			
(a) Rebate on Bills discounted	45,000				
(b) Pension fund	30,000				
(c) Provident fund	—				
(d) Unclaimed Dividend	—				
(e) Branch Adjustment	—				
Acceptances, Endorsement and other obligation					
(per contra)		6,25,000			
Profit and Loss A/c		5,53,800			
Balance in 1-1-89	1,44,000				
Less : Provision for Income Tax	75,000				
	69,000				
Add : Profit for the year	6,06,000				
	6,75,000				
Less : Statutory Reserve fund @ 20% on 6,06,000	1,21,200				
		98,75,000			98,75,000

Problem No. 20

From the following Trial Balance of Citizen Bank Ltd. as on 31-12-1989. Prepare : (1) Profit and Loss Account and (2) Balance Sheet.

Trial Balance

	Particulars	Dr. Rs.	Cr. Rs.
(1)	Share Capital : shares of Rs. 100 each fully paid		15,00,000
(2)	Reserve Fund		2,00,000
(3)	Cash in hand	1,51,500	
(4)	Fixed Deposits & Savings Bank A/c		15,00,000
(5)	Investment	6,00,000	
(6)	Current Account		10,00,000
(7)	Cash with Reserve Bank	2,00,000	
(8)	Bills payable		1,25,000
(9)	Provident fund		50,000
(10)	Branch Adjustment account	25,000	
(11)	Money at call and short notice	3,00,000	
(12)	Interest on deposit paid	1,50,000	
(13)	Rent		25,000
(14)	Loans and overdraft	30,00,000	
(15)	Interest on discount		6,00,000
(16)	Salaries and allowance	1,30,000	
(17)	Premises *less* depreciation	2,00,000	
(18)	Directors fees	20,000	
(19)	Non-Banking assets	25,000	
(20)	Furniture *less* depreciation	25,000	
(21)	Auditors fees	12,000	
(22)	Profit and Loss Account		1,25,000
(23)	Interest accrued on Investment	15,000	
(24)	Postage and Telegram	10,000	
(25)	Rent, Taxes, Insurance etc.	17,500	
(26)	Balance with other Banks	1,98,000	
(27)	Printing and Stationery	21,000	
(28)	Silver	10,000	
(29)	Depreciation	15,000	
		51,25,000	51,25,000

Adjustments :

(1) Provide Rs. 5,000 for Rebate on Bills discounted
(2) Make provision for Bad and doubtful debts Rs. 15,000
(3) Bills for collection concerted to Rs. 1,00,000
(4) Rent, taxes, insurance etc. include Insurance of Rs. 2,000 paid for the year ending 31-3-1990
(5) Current account includes Rs. 50,000 debit balance representing over-drafts.

(K.U.D., October 1990)

Solution :

Citizen Bank Ltd.

Profit and Loss Account for the year ended 31-12-1989

Expenditure	Rs.	Income (*Less* Provisions)	Rs.
To Interest paid on Deposits & Borrowings	1,50,000	By Interest & Discounts	5,80,000
To Salaries & Allowances	1,30,000	By Commission & exchange	—
To Directors fees	20,000	By Tent	25,000
To Rent	17,000	By Net profit on sale or revaluation of investment and other assets	—
To Postages & Telegram	10,000	By Income from non-banking assets	—
To Auditors fees	12,000	By Other receipts	—
To Depreciation on Bank	15,000	By Loss, if any	—
To Stationery & Printing	21,000		
To Loss on sale of non-banking assets	—		
To Other expenses	—		
To Net Profit	2,30,000		
	6,05,000		6,05,000

(1)	Interest and Discounts		6,00,000
	Less : Rebate on B D	5,000	
	RDD	15,000	20,000
			5,80,000
(2)	Rent, Rates, Insurances		17,500
	Less Insurances paid		500
			17,000

Citizen Bank Ltd.

Balance Sheet as at 31-12-989

Capital & Liability	Rs.	Rs.	Property & Assets	Rs.	Rs.
Share Capital			Cash in hand		1,51,500
Authorised			With Reserve Bank		2,00,000
Issued and paid up shares			Balance with other Banks		1,98,000
Rs. 100 each fully paid		15,00,000	Money at call & short		
Reserves & Fund			notice		3,00,000
Reserve fund	2,00,000		Investments		6,00,000
Statutory Reserve	46,000	2,46,000	Loans, advance, cash		
Deposits and Other A/c		25,00,000	credits etc.		
Fixed Deposit]			Bills Discounted and pur-		
Sayings Banks A/c]	15,00,000		chased (30,00,000 – 15,000)		29,85,000
Current A/c &			Bills receivable being		
Contingency	10,00,000		bills for collection		1,00,000
Borrowings from other Banks			Customers liabilities for		
Bills payable		2,25,000	acceptance, endorsement		
Bills for collection being			and other obligations		
bills receivable (per contra)		1,00,000	Premises *less* Depreciation		2,00,000
Other Liabilities			Furniture *less* Depreciation		25,000
Provident fund	50,000		*Other Assets*		
Rebate on Bills			Branch Adjustment	25,000	
Discounts	5,000	55,000	Silver	10,000	
Acceptance, endorsement &			Interest accounted		
other obligation per contra		—	on Investment	15,000	
Profit & Loss A/c			Insurance prepaid	500	50,500
Balance	1,25,000		Non-banking Assets		25,000
Profit for year	2,30,000		Profit and Loss A/c		—
	3,55,000				
Less : 20% Statutory					
Reserve of 2,30,000	46,000	3,09,000			
		48,35,000			48,35,000

Problem No. 21

From the following Trial Balance of Marchant Bank Ltd. as on 31-3-1990. Prepare : (1) Profit & Loss A/c and (2) Balance Sheet

Trial Balance as on 31-3-1990

Particulars	Dr. Rs.	Cr. Rs.
Share Capital :		
Shares of Rs. 100 each fully paid		10,00,000
Reserve fund		1,00,000
Fixed Deposit and Savings :		
Bank Accounts		12,00,000
Current Accounts		6,00,000
Provident fund		20,000
Pension fund		12,000
Bills payable		96,000
Cash in hand	1,00,000	
Money at call and short notice	2,40,000	
Cash with other banks	70,000	
Cash with Reserve Bank of India	1,85,000	
Borrowings from other Banks		1,14,000
Investments (In Govt. securities)	4,85,000	
Branch Adjustment Account	20,000	
Loans and advances	22,00,000	
Interest and discounts		4,80,000
Commission and exchange		2,12,000
Interest on deposits paid	1,40,000	
Directors fees	12,000	
Salaries and allowances	1,13,000	
Audit fees	7,000	
Premises *less* depreciation	96,000	
Rent received		15,000
Taxes and Insurance	12,000	
Postage and Telegram	4,000	
Printing and Stationery	6,000	
Furniture *less* depreciation	1,40,000	
Non-Parking Assets	45,000	
Depreciation	25,000	
Profit and Loss A/c Balance		1,11,000
	39,60,000	39,60,000

Adjustments :

(1) Bills for collection on behalf of customers amounted Rs. 85,000
(2) Acceptances, Endorsement etc. on behalf of customers Rs. 36,000
(3) Provide Rs. 6,000 for rebate on bills discounted.
(4) Make provision for bad and doubtful debts. Rs. 12,000
(5) Interest accrued on investment amounted to Rs. 6,000.

(K.U.D., October 1990)

Profit and Loss A/c for the year ended 31-3-90

Expenditure	Rs.	Income (*Less* Provisions)	Rs.
To Interest paid Borrowing & Deposit	1,40,000	By Interest & Discount	4,68,000
To Salaries & Allowances	1,13,000	By Commission & Exchange	2,12,000
To Directors fees	12,000	By Rent Received	15,000
To Rent, Taxes, Insurance	12,000	By Profit on sales or of Investment	—
To Postage & Telegram	4,000	By Profit on sale of non-Banking property	—
To Printing and Stationery	6,000	By Other Receipts	—
To Audit fees	7,000	By Loss if any	—
To Depreciation	25,000		
To Loss on sales of non-banking A/c	—		
To Other Expenses	—		
To Net Profit	3,76,000		
	6,95,000		6,95,000

Note : (1)

Interest & Discounts	4,80,000	
Add : Interest accrued	6,000	4,86,000
Provision for		
Rebate on Bills Discount	6,000	
R.D.D.	12,000	18,000
		4,68,000

Balance Sheet as at 31-3-1990

Liabilities	Rs.	Rs.	Assets	Rs.	Rs.
Share Capital			Cash in Hand		1,60,000
Authorised			With Reserve Bank		1,85,000
Paidup Capital			With other Banks		70,000
Shares of Rs. 100 each fully paidup		10,00,000	Money at call & short notice		2,40,000
Reserve & Reserve Fund			Investments in Govt. Securities		4,85,000
Reserve Fund	1,00,000		Loans & Advances		
Stationery Reserve	75,200	1,75,200	Cash credit	22,00,000	
Deposit & Other A/c			*Less* : R.D.D.	12,000	21,88,000
Fixed Deposit & Savings A/c	12,00,000		Bills Receivable		
Current A/c	6,00,000	18,00,000	being Bills for collection (per contra)		85,000
Borrowing from Other Banks		1,14,000	Constituents Liabilities for Acceptances, Endorsement etc. (per contra)		36,000
Bills payable		96,000	Premises *Less* depreciation		96,000
Bills for collection being Bills Receivable (per contra)		85,000	Furnitures *Less* depreciation		1,40,000
Other Liabilities			*Other Assets*		
(a) Provident Fund	20,000		(a) Branch Adj.	20,000	
(b) Pension Fund	12,000		(b) Interest on Investment accrued	6,000	26,000
(c) Rebate on Bills discounted	6,000	38,000			
Acceptances, Endorsement & Other obligation (per contra)		36,000	Non Banking Assets		45,000
Profit & Loss A/c		4,11,800			
Balance	1,11,000				
Add : Profit	3,76,000				
	4,87,000				
Less : 20% U/s 17 Transfer 3,76,000 × 20/100	75,200				
		37,56,000			37,56,000

Problem No. 22

The following is the Trial Balance of Kadamba Bank Ltd. as on 31-12-1989 :

	Particulars	Dr. Rs.	Cr. Rs.
1.	Subscribed and Paid up Capital		2,00,000
2.	Stationery Reserve		50,000
3.	Capital Reserve		10,000
4.	Deposits		10,00,000
5.	Profit and Loss Account on 1-1-1989		25,000
6.	Interest and Discount		1,25,000
7.	Borrowing from State Bank India		30,000
8.	Commission and Brokerage		12,000
9.	Rent		15,000
10.	Cash	20,000	
11.	Salaries	55,000	
12.	Tax and Insurance	3,000	
13.	Directors fee	12,000	
14.	Auditors fee	10,000	
15.	Balances with other Banks	18,000	
16.	Money at call and short notice	13,000	
17.	Investments to Government securities	1,80,000	
18.	Interim Devidend paid	8,000	
19.	Loans and Advances	10,60,000	
20.	Income Tax paid	5,000	
21.	Printing and Stationery	2,500	
22.	Postage and Telegram	3,500	
23.	Depreciation	2,000	
24.	Interest on Deposits	32,000	
		14,67,000	14,67,000

The following information is to be considered :

(1) The authorised capital was 40,000 Equity shares of Rs. 10 each.

(2) Interest accrued on investment was Rs. 14,000.

(3) Provision for Bad and Doubtful debts is to be made Rs. 6,000.

(4) The interest Dividend declared was @ 5% in the paid up capital.

(5) Bills for collections amounted to Rs. 40,000.

(6) Acceptances, Endorsement etc. on behalf of customers amounted Rs. 60,000.

(7) The market value of investments was Rs. 1,70,000 and the investment fluctuation reserve to be created for the fall in value.

(K.U.D., April 1990)

Profit and Loss Account for the year ended 31-12-1989

Expenditure	Rs.	Income (*Less* Provisions)	Rs.
To Interest paid on		By Interest & Discount	1,23,000
Deposit & Borrowing	32,000	By Commission and	12,000
To Salaries	55,000	Exchange	
To Directors fees	12,000	By Rent	15,000
To Rent paid, Taxes,	3,000	By Net Profit on sale	
Insurances		or revaluation of	
To Law charges	—	Investment	—
To Postage & Telegram	3,500	By Income from non-	
To Audit fees	10,000	Banking property	—
To Depreciation	2,000	By Other receipt	—
To Stationery and Printing	2,500	By Loss (if any)	—
To Loss on sale of non-Banking Assets	—		
To Other Expenses	—		
To Balance of Profit	—		
To Net Profit	30,000		
	1,50,000		1,50,000

Note : Interest and Discount		1,25,000
Add : Interest accrued		14,000
		1,39,000
Less : Provision for D.D.	6,000	
Investment Fluctuation Reserve	10,000	16,000
		1,23,000

Kadamba Bank Ltd.

Balance Sheet as at 31-12-1989

Capital & Liabilities	Rs.	Rs.	Property & Assets	Rs.	Rs.
Share Capital			Cash in hand and		
Authorised Capital			with R.B.I.		20,000
40000 equity shares			Balance with other Banks		18,000
of Rs. 10 each		4,00,000	Money at call and short		
Subscribed & Paidup			notice		13,000
20000 Equity shares			Investements in Govt.		
of Rs. 10 each		2,00,000	securities	1,70,000	1,80,000
Reserve Fund and			Loans & Advances	10,60,000	
Other Reserve			*Less* : R.D.D.	6,000	10,54,000
Capital Reserve		10,000	Bills Receivable being		
Statutory Reserve	50,000		bills for collection		
Add : 20% U/s 17	6,000	56,000	(per contra)		40,000
Investment		10,000	Acceptances, endorse-		
Fluctuation Reserve			ment etc.		60,000
Deposits & Other A/c		10,00,000	Premises *Less* Depreciation		36,000
(a) Fixed			Furnitures *Less* Depreciation		7,000
(b) Saving Bank			*Other Assets*		
(c) Current A/c			Interest accrued		14,000
Borrowing from S.B.I.		30,000			
Bills payable being					
bills for collection (per contra)		40,000			
Other Liabilities					
Dividend payable		2,000			
Acceptances, Endorsement					
etc. (per contra)		60,000			
Profit & Loss A/c					
balance 1-1-89	25,000				
Less : Income Tax	5,000				
	20,000				
Add : Profit for the					
year	30,000				
	50,000				
Less : 20% Statutory					
Reserves	6,000				
	44,000				
Less : Dividend	10,000	34,000			
Total		14,42,000	Total		14,42,000

Problem No. 23

From the following Trial Balance of Corporation Bank Ltd., prepare the (1) Profit and Loss Account for the year ended 31-12-1987 and the (2) Balance Sheet on that date.

Trial Balance

	Particulars	Dr. Rs.	Cr. Rs.
(1)	Share Capital : shares of Rs. 10 each fully paid		8,00,000
(2)	Cash in Hand	3,10,000	
(3)	Reserve fund		3,30,000
(4)	Money at call and short notice	2,15,000	
(5)	Borrowings from other Banks		2,70,000
(6)	Cash with other Banks	4,75,000	
(7)	Deposits		11,00,000
(8)	Investments in Govt. securities	3,25,000	
(9)	Loans, cash credits etc.	13,25,000	
(10)	Promises *less* depreciation	80,000	
(11)	Furniture *less* depreciation	50,000	
(12)	Rent		30,000
(13)	Commission, Brokerage etc.		33,000
(14)	Interest and Discount		4,00,000
(15)	Salaries and allowances to staff	70,000	
(16)	Interest paid	1,40,000	
(17)	Directors fees	5,000	
(18)	Postages	2,000	
(19)	Auditors fees	3,000	
(20)	Legal charges	2,500	
(21)	Depreciation on Banks property	5,000	
(22)	Printing and Stationery	3,500	
(23)	Profit and Loss A/c		48,000
		30,11,000	30,11,000

Adjustments :

(1) Make provision for Income tax Rs. 20,000.

(2) Provide Rs. 6,000 for rebate on Bills Discounted.

(3) Provision for Doubtful debts to be made is Rs. 4,000.

(4) Acceptances and endorsement on behalf of customers amounted to Rs. 2,00,000 and Bills for collected Rs. 3,00,000.

(5) Market value of Govt. securities is Rs. 3,50,000.

(K.U.D., October 1988)

Solution :

Corporation Bank Ltd.

Profit and Loss Account for the year ended 31-12-1987

Expenditure	Rs.	Income (*Less* Provisions)	Rs.
Interest paid on deposits		Interest and Discount	3,70,000
and borrowings	1,40,000	Commission exchange	
Salaries and allowances	70,000	and brokerage	33,000
Directors fees	5,000	Rent	30,000
Rent, taxes, insurance		Net profit on sale	
Law charges	2,500	of revaluation of	
Postage, Telegram, stamps	2,000	Investments	—
Auditors fees	3,000	Income from other non-	
Depreciation on banking property	5,000	banking assets	—
Stationery & Printing	3,500	Other receipts	
Loss from sales of non-banking assets	—	Net Loss (if any)	—
Other expenditures	—		
Balance of profit	2,02,000		
	4,53,000		4,53,000

(1) Interest & Discounts			4,00,000
Less :	Rebate on Bills discount	6,000	
	R.D.D.	4,000	
	Provision for income	20,000	30,000
			3,70,000

Note : Loans, cash credit	13,25,000
Less : R.D.D.	4,000
	13,21,000

Balance Sheet as at 31-12-1987

Capital & Liabilities	Rs.	Rs.	Property & Assets	Rs.	Rs.
Capital			*Cash*		
Authorised Issued			In hand	3,10,000	
Capital : Share of			With Reserve	4,75,000	7,85,000
Rs. 100 fully paid		8,00,000	With other Banks		—
Reserve Fund & Other			Money at call & short		
Reserve Fund	3,30,000		notice		2,15,000
Statutory	40,400	3,70,400	Investments	3,50,000	3,25,000
Deposits & Other			Loan, cash credit	13,25,000	
Fixed deposits &			*Less* : RDD	4,000	13,21,000
Savings Bank A/c	11,00,000		Bills Receivable		
Current A/c	—		being bills for collection		3,00,000
Contingency	20,000	11,20,000	Contingent liabilities		
Borrowings from other			for acceptance		2,00,000
Banks		2,70,000	Premises *less* depreciation		80,000
Bills payable		—	Furniture *less* depreciation		50,000
Bills for collection			Other assets :		
being bills receivable		3,00,000	Non-banking assets		—
Other Liabilities					
Rebate in Bills		6,000			
Acceptance, endorsement					
and other obligation		2,00,000			
Profit & Loss A/c					
Balance 1-1-87	48,000				
Profit for year	2,02,000				
	2,50,000				
Less 20% Statutory	40,400	2,09,600			
		32,76,000			32,76,000

Problem No. 24

The Krishna Bank Ltd. has an authorised capital of Rs. 10,00,000 divided into shares of Rs. 10 each. The following is the Trial Balance as on 31-12-1984 :

Trial Balance

Particulars	Dr. Rs.	Cr. Rs.
Subscribed & Paid up Capital		5,00,000
Statutory Reserve		1,25,000
Capital Reserve		25,000
Profit & Loss Account on 1-1-1984		62,500
Deposit		25,00,000
Interest & Discount		3,12,500
Commission & Exchange		30,000
Borrowings from State Bank		75,000
Rent		37,500
Salaries & Allowances	1,25,000	
Directors' Fees	30,000	
Taxes & Insurance	20,000	
Audit fees	25,000	
Money at Call & Short Notice	32,500	
Balance with other Banks	45,000	
Investments in Government Securities	4,50,000	
Premises *Less* Depreciation	90,000	
Furniture *Less* Depreciation	20,000	
Cash in Hand	50,000	
Interim Dividend paid	17,500	
Loans & Advances	26,50,000	
Income tax paid	12,500	
Printing & Stationery	8,000	
Postage & Telegrams	7,000	
Depreciation	5,000	
Interest on Deposits, etc.	80,000	

The following information is to be considered :

(1) Interest accrued on investments Rs. 35,000.

(2) Provision for doubtful debts to be made Rs. 15,000.

(3) Interim dividend declared was at 5% on the paid up capital.

(4) Bills for collection amounted to Rs. 1,00,000.

(5) Acceptances, endorsements, etc., on behalf of customers amounted to Rs. 1,50,000.

(6) The market value on investments was Rs. 4,25,000 and the investment fluctuation reserve is to be created for fall in the value of investments.

Prepare the Profit and Loss Account for the year ending 31-12-1984 and the Balance Sheet as on that date.

(Karnataka, April 1986)

Profit and Loss A/c for the year ended 31-12-84

Expenditure	Rs.	Income (Less Provisions)	Rs.
To Interest paid on Deposits and Borrowings	80,000	By Interest & Discount	3,06,500
To Salaries & allowances	1,25,000	By Commission, Exchange and brokerage	30,000
To Directors fees	30,000	By Rent	37,500
To Rent, Taxes & Insurance	20,000	By Net Profit on sale of Investment and other assets	—
To Law Charges	—	By Net Profit on revaluation of Investment and other assets	—
To Postage & Telegram	7,000		
To Audit fees	25,000	By Income from Non-Banking Assets	—
To Depreciation on Banking property	5,000	By Other Receipts	—
To Printing & Stationery	8,000	By Loss (if any)	—
To Loss from sale of non-Banking Assets	—		
To Other Expenditure	—		
To Balance of Profit	75,000		
	3,75,000		3,75,000

Interest & Discount		3,12,500	
Add : Interest accrued		35,000	
		3,47,500	
Less : Provision for doubtful debts	15,000		
Provision for Investment fluctuation reserve (fall value)	25,000	40,000	
Interest and Discount		3,07,500	

Interim Dividend declared @ 5% on paid up 5,00,000 @ 5%	25,000
Less : Paid	17,500
Unclaimed Dividend shown in Balance sheet	7,500

The Krishna Bank Ltd.
Balance Sheet as at 31-12-1984

Capital & Liabilities	Rs.	Rs.	Property & Assets	Rs.	Rs.
Authorised Capital			Cash in Hand		50,000
100000 shares of Rs. 10 each		10,00,000	With Reserve Bank		—
Subscribed & Paid up Capital 50000 shares of Rs. 10 each fully paid		5,00,000	Balance with Other Banks		45,000
Reserve Fund & Other Reserves			Money at call & short notice		32,500
Statutory Reserve U/s 17 20%	1,25,000		Investments in Govt. securities (Market value)	4,25,000	4,50,000
Add : For the Year 20%	15,000	1,40,000	Advances, Loans, Cash credit and Over-draft etc.	26,50,000	26,35,000
Capital Reserve		25,000	*Less*	15,000	
Deposits					
Fixed Deposit	25,00,000	25,25,000	Bills Receivable beings bills for collection (per contra)		1,00,000
S.B. & Current A/c					
Contingency					
Investment Reserve	25,000		Customers Liabilities for acceptances & Endorsements (per contra)		1,50,000
Borrowings from Other Banks			Premises *Less* Depr.		90,000
State Bank		75,000	Furniture *Less* Depr.		20,000
Bills payable			*Other Assets*		
Bills for collection being Bills Receivable (per contra)		1,00,000	Interest accrued		35,000
Other Liabilities			Non-Banking Assets		—
Pension Fund			Profit & Loss (Loss if any)		—
Insurance Fund		—			
Unclaimed Dividend		7,500			
Rebate on Bills discount —					
Acceptances, Endorsement Other Obligation etc.		1,50,000			
(per contra)		—			
Profit & Loss A/c		85,000			
Balance	62,500				
Less : Interim Dividend 5% paid	25,000				
	37,500				
Less : Income Tax paid					
Add : Profit Year	12,500				
	25,000				
Less : 20% Statutory Reserve	75,000				
	1,00,000				
	15,000				
		36,07,500			36,07,500

Problem No. 25

The Karnataka Bank Ltd. has an authorised capital of Rs. 5,00,000 in shares of Rs. 100 each. From the following balances extracted from the books of the bank prepare the Profit & Loss Account for the year ending 31-12-1984 and the Balance Sheet as on that date :

Issue Capital : 3000 shares of Rs. 100 each	3,00,000
Reserve Fund	1,00,000
Money at call & short notice	1,25,000
Investments	10,00,000
Interest paid	75,000
Salaries & Allowances	39,000
Directors Fees	6,000
Rent, Taxes	4,000
Other Expenses	10,000
Deposits	30,00,000
Premises (after depreciation upto 31-12-1983 Rs. 25,000)	1,75,000
Furniture (after depreciation upto 31-12-83 Rs. 5,000)	15,000
Cash in hand	35,000
Cash with other Banks	5,00,000
Borrowings from the Banks	2,50,000
Interest and Discount	2,23,250
Profit & Loss A/c (Cr balance 1-1-84)	50,000
Dividend for the year 1983	30,000
Loans, Cash Credit etc.	16,14,250
Bills payable	25,000
Bills discount & purchased	3,50,000
Unclaimed Dividend	5,000
Gratuity fund	12,500
Commission & Brokerage	22,500
Library Books	6,000
Auditors Fees	4,000
Bills for collection	50,000
Acceptances, Endorsements, etc.	1,00,000

Adjustments :

(1) Provide depreciation at 5% on premises and at 10% on furniture.

(2) Provide Rs. 20,000 for bad and doubtful debts and Rs. 25,000 for taxation.

(3) Rebate on bills discounted amounted to Rs. 2,500.

(K.U.D., October 1985)

Profit & Loss Account for the year ended 31-12-84

Expenditure		Income (*Less* provision during the year for Bad and doubtful debt and other usual or necessary provision)	
Interest paid on deposits, borrowing etc.	75,000	Interest and Discount	1,75,750
Salaries and Allowances and Provident Fund contribution	39,000	Commission, Exchange and Brokerage	22,500
Directors and Local Committee Members fees and allowances	6,000	Rent	—
Rent, Taxes, Insurance, Lighting etc.	4,000	Net Profit on sale of investment, gold, silver, Land, Premises and other assets (not credited to Reserve or any particular fund or account)	—
Law Charges	—	Net Profit on revaluation of investments, gold, silver, land, premises a and other assets (not credited to Reserve or any particular fund or account)	—
Postage, Telegram and Stamp	—		
Audit Fees	4,000		
Depreciation on and Repair to Bank's property (8,750 + 1,500)	10,250	Income from non-banking assets and profit on sale of or dealing with such assets	—
Stationery, Printing, Advertisement etc.	—	Other receipts	—
Loss from sale of or dealing with non-Banking assets	—	Loss (if any)	—
Other Expenditure	10,000		
Balance of Profit	50,000		
	1,98,250		1,98,250

Note : Interest and Discount 2,23,250

Less : Provision for doubtful debts	20,000	
Provision for taxation	25,000	
Rebate on Bills Discounted	2,500	47,500
Net Income taken to Profit and Loss Account		1,75,750

Balance Sheet as at 31-12-1984

Capital & Liabilities	Rs.	Rs.	Property & Assets	Rs.	Rs.
Capital Authorise of			Cash		35,000
5000 shares of Rs. 100 each		5,00,000	Balances with Other Banks		5,00,000
3000 shares of Rs. 10 each fully paid		3,00,000	Money at call and short notice		1,25,000
Reserve Fund and Other Reserves Fund	1,00,000		Investments		10,00,000
Add : 20% of Profit	10,000	1,10,000	*Advances :*		
Deposit and Other A/c			Loans, Cash credit and Overdrafts		15,94,250
Deposits (30,00,000)		30,00,000	Bills Discounted and purchases		3,50,000
Contingency A/c		25,000	Bills Receivable being bills for collection (as per contra)		50,000
Borrowings From other Banking Companies, Agents etc.		2,50,000	Constituent Liabilities for Acceptances, Endorsements and Other obligation (per contra)		1,00,000
Other Liabilities			*Premises Less Depr.*		
Unclaimed Dividend		5,000	Cost	2,00,000	
Gratuity Fund		12,500	*Less* : Depr.		
Rebate on Bills		2,500	Up to 31-12-83 25,000		
Bills for collection as being receivable (per contra)		50,000	For the year 8,750	33,750	1,66,250
Acceptances, Endorsements and Other obligations (per contra)		1,00,000	Furniture & Fixtures	20,000	
Profit & Loss Account			*Less* : Depreciation		
As per left B/s	50,000		Upto 31-12-83 5,000		
Less : Dividend paid	30,000		For year 1,500	6,500	13,500
	20,000		Other Assets (including silver)		
Add : Profit for the year	50,000		Library books		6,000
	70,000		Non-Banking Assets		—
Less : 20% of Profit transferred to Reserve fund	10,000	60,000	Acquired in satisfaction of claims		—
Contingent Liabilities		—	Profit & Loss		—
Total		39,40,000	Total		39,40,000

Note : Loans, cash credit etc.	16,14,250
Less : Provision for doubtful debts	20,000
Net Amount taken to be Balance sheet	15,94,250

Problem No. 26

The Authorised Capital of the Ideal Bank Ltd. is Rs. 10,00,000 in shares of Rs. 100 each. The following are the Balances extracted from the books of the Bank as on 31-12-1984 :

(1)	Issued Capital : 6000 Equity shares of Rs. 100 each	6,00,000
(2)	Reserve Fund	1,00,000
(3)	Deposits	40,00,000
(4)	Investment Fluctuation Reserve	30,000
(5)	Directors fees	12,000
(6)	Auditors fees	10,000
(7)	Premises *Less* Depreciation	1,50,000
(8)	Furnitures *Less* Depreciation	40,000
(9)	Interest and Discount	3,54,000
(10)	Stamps in hand	4,000
(11)	Cash with Reserve Bank	2,00,000
(12)	Bills discounted and purchased	3,00,000
(13)	Salaries and allowances	83,000
(14)	Depreciation	11,000
(15)	Profit and Loss A/c (Cr.)	15,000
(16)	Loans, cash credit etc.	27,90,000
(17)	Commission and Exchange	16,000
(18)	Branch Adjustment (Dr.)	20,000
(19)	Rent and Insurance	24,000
(20)	Investments	8,50,000
(21)	Cash in hand	2,50,000
(23)	Law charges	5,000
(24)	Unexpired Insurance	1,000
(25)	Contingency Account	25,000
(26)	Interest paid	45,000
(27)	Rebate on Bills Discounted	5,000

Adjustments :

(1) Bills for collection amounted to Rs. 1,50,000.

(2) Acceptances, Endorsement etc. on behalf of customers amounted to Rs. 1,00,000.

(3) Make provision for taxation Rs. 25,000 and for bad debts Rs. 15,000.

(4) Market value of Investments on 31-12-1984 was Rs. 8,00,000 and they are to be written down to this amount.

Prepare the Profit and Loss Account for the year ended 31-12-1984, and the Balance Sheet as at that date.

(K.U.D., April 1985)

Solution :

Working Note

(1) Interest and Discount			3,54,000
Less : Provisions :			
For taxation		25,000	
For R.D.D.		15,000	
		40,000	
Loss on Revaluate of Investment uncovered balance		20,000	
		60,000	60,000
			2,94,000
(2) Investments			8,50,000
(a) Market value			8,00,000
Loss on valuate			50,000
(b) Investment fluctuation			
Less : Loss as above uncovered balance adjusted			30,000
			20,000

Profit and Loss A/c for the year ended 31-12-84

Expenditure	Rs.	Income (*Less* Provisions)	Rs.
To Interest paid	45,000	By Interest & Discount	2,94,000
To Salaries & Allowances	83,000	By Commission & Exchange	16,000
To Directors fees	12,000	By Rent	—
To Rent, Taxes, Insurance	24,000	By Net Profit on sale or Revaluation of non-Banking property	—
To Law charges	5,000		
To Audit fees	10,000		
To Depreciation	11,000	By Income from non-Banking Assets	—
To Stationery & Printing	—	By Other Receipts	—
To Loss on sale on non-Banking Assets	—	By Loss (if any)	—
To Other Expenditures	—		
To Balance of Profit	—		
To Net Profit	1,20,000		
	3,10,000		3,10,000

Ideal Bank Ltd.

Balance Sheet as at 31-12-1984

Capital & Liabilities	Rs.	Rs.	Property & Assets	Rs.	Rs.
Share Capital			Cash in Hand		2,50,000
Authorised Capital			With Reserve Bank		2,00,000
10000 Equity shares of Rs. 100 each		10,00,000	With other Banks		3,50,000
6000 Equity shares of Rs. 100 each		6,00,000	Money at call and short notice		—
Reserve Fund & Other Reserves			Investment	8,50,000	8,00,000
Reserve Fund	1,00,000		Loans & Advance	27,90,000	
Statutory Reserve	24,000	1,24,000	*Less* R.D.D.	15,000	
Investment Fluctuation Reserve	30,000			27,75,000	
Less : Written off	30,000	—	Bills Discounted & purchased	3,00,000	30,75,000
Deposits		40,00,000	Bills Receivable being Bills for collection (per contra)		1,50,000
(a) Fixed Deposit					
(b) Saving Bank					
(c) Current A/c contingency provision for tax		25,000	Constituent Liabilities for acceptances, endorsement etc. (per contra)		1,00,000
Borrowings from other Banks		25,000			
Bills payable		—	Premises *Less* Depr.		1,50,000
Bills for collection being Bills receivable (per contra)		1,50,000	Furnitures *Less* Depr.		40,000
Other Liabilities			*Other Assets*		
			Stamps in Hand		4,000
			Branch Adjustment		20,000
Rebate on Bills discounted		5,000	Unexpired Insurance		1,000
Acceptances, Endorsement (per contra)		1,00,000	Non-Banking Assets		—
Profit & Loss A/c		1,11,000	Loss (if any)		—
Balance	15,000				
Profit for the year	1,20,000				
	1,35,000				
Less : Statutory Reserve 20% of 1,20,000	24,000				
		51,40,000			51,40,000

Problem No. 27

Karnataka Bank Ltd. had an Authorised Capital Rs. 10,00,000. The following are the Balance extracted from the books of the Bank as on 31-12-1978 :

(1)	Issued and Paid up Capital : share of Rs. 10 each	5,00,000
(2)	Reserve Fund	3,50,000
(3)	Fixed Deposit	9,50,000
(4)	Savings Banks deposits	30,00,000
(5)	Current Accounts	80,00,000
(6)	Money at call and short notice	3,00,000
(7)	Interest paid	2,00,000
(8)	Salaries and Allowances	80,000
(9)	Depreciation written off	20,000
(10)	Postage and Telegrams	500
(11)	Printing and Stationery	2,000
(12)	Audit fees	1,500
(13)	Directors fees	6,000
(14)	Profit and Loss A/c 1-1-78 (Cr.)	2,40,000
(15)	Dividend for 1977 paid	50,000
(16)	Premises *less* depreciation	12,00,000
(17)	Cash on hand with RBI	15,60,000
(18)	Deposits with Bharat Banks	13,00,000
(19)	Borrowings from other Bank	7,00,000
(20)	Interest and Discounts (Cr)	6,50,000
(21)	Bills payable	8,00,000
(22)	Loans overdrafts, cash credit etc.	75,00,000
(23)	Unclaimed Dividend	30,000
(24)	Bills for collection	1,40,000
(25)	Acceptances, Endorsement on behalf of customers	2,30,000

Adjustments :

(a) Provide for rebate on Bill discounted Rs. 5,000.

(b) Make provident for doubtful debts Rs. 30,000.

Prepare Profit and Loss A/c for the year ending 31-12-1978 and the Balance Sheet as on that date.

(K.U.D., October 1979)

Solution :

Profit and Loss Account for the year ended 31-12-1978

Expenditure	Rs.	Income (*Less* Provisions)	Rs.
Interest paid		Interest & Discount	6,15,000
On deposit borrowings	2,00,000	Commission & Brokerage	—
Salaries and allowances	80,000	Rent	—
Directors fees	6,000	Net Profit on sales or	
Rent, taxes, insurances	—	Revaluation of Interest	—
Law charges	—	Income from other sources	—
Postage & Telegrams	500	Other receipts	—
Audit fees	1,500	Loss, if any	—
Depreciation	20,000		
Printing & Stationery	2,000		
Loss on sale of Non-banking assets	—		
Other expenses	—		
Profit	3,05,000		
	6,15,000		6,15,000

Note : Interest and Discounts 6,50,000

Less : Rebate on Bills discount	5,000	
RDD	30,000	35,000
		6,15,000

Karnataka Bank Ltd.

Balance Sheet as at 31-12-1978

Capital & Liability		Rs.	Property & Assets		Rs.
Share Capital : Authorised			Cash in Hand & with RBI		15,60,000
10000 Shares of			With other Banks		13,00,000
Rs. 100 each		10,00,000	Money at call & short		
Issued & Paid up			notice		3,00,000
5000 shares of Rs. 100 each		5,00,000	Investments		30,00,000
Reserve Fund & Other			Loans, Advance	75,00,000	
Reserve Fund	3,50,000		Cash credit etc.	30,000	
Statutory	61,000	4,11,000			74,70,000
Deposits & Other A/c			Bills receivable being		
Fixed Deposits	9,50,000		bills for collection		1,40,000
Savings Banks	30,00,000		Constituent liability		
Current A/c	80,00,000	1,19,50,000	for acceptance,		
Borrowing from other			endorsement		2,30,000
Banks		7,00,000	Premises *less* depreciation		12,00,000
Bills payable		8,00,000	Furniture *less* depreciation		—
Bills for collection			Other Assets :		
being RBR per contra		1,40,000	Non-banking Assets		—
Other Liabilities			Profit & Loss A/c		—
Unclaim dividend	30,000				
Rebate on Bills	5,000	35,000			
Acceptance, endorsement					
and other obligation		2,30,000			
Profit & Loss A/c					
on 1-1-1978	24,000				
Less : Dividend 1977	50,000				
	1,90,000				
Add : Profit & loss					
A/c	3,05,000				
	4,95,000				
Less : Statutory					
Reserve 20%	61,000	4,34,000			
		1,52,00,000			1,52,00,000

Problem No. 28

The Krishna Bank Ltd. has an Authorised Capital of Rs. 10,00,000 divided into shares of Rs. 10 each. The following is the Trial Balance as on 31-12-1984 :

Trial Balance

(1)	Share Capital : Subscribed and Paid up	5,00,000
(2)	Statutory Reserve	1,25,000
(3)	Capital Reserve	25,000
(4)	Profit and Loss A/c on 1-1-84	62,500
(5)	Deposits	25,00,000
(6)	Interest and Discount	3,12,500
(7)	Commission and Exchange	30,000
(8)	Borrowing from State Banks	75,000
(9)	Rent	37,500.
(10)	Salaries and Allowances	1,25,000
(11)	Directors fees	30,000
(12)	Taxes and Insurance	20,000
(13)	Audit fees	25,000
(14)	Money at call and short notice	32,500
(15)	Balance with other banks	45,000
(16)	Investments in Govt. securities	4,50,000
(17)	Premises *less* depreciation	90,000
(18)	Furniture *less* depreciation	20,000
(19)	Cash in hand	50,000
(20)	Interim dividend paid	17,500
(21)	Loans and Advances	26,50,000
(22)	Income tax paid	12,500
(23)	Printing and Stationery	8,000
(24)	Postage and Telegram	7,000
(25)	Depreciation	5,000
(26)	Interest paid on deposits	80,000

The following information is to be considered :

(1) Interest accrued on Investment Rs. 35,000

(2) Provision for Doubtful debts to be made Rs. 15,000

(3) Interim Dividend declared was at Rs. 50 on the paid up capital.

(4) Bills for collection amounted to Rs. 1,00,000

(5) Acceptances, endorsement etc. on behalf of customers amounted to Rs. 1,50,000

(6) The market value of Investments was Rs. 4,25,000 and the Investment fluctuation reserve is to be credited for the fall in value of investments.

Prepare the Profit and Loss Account for the year ending 31-12-1984 and the Balance Sheet as on that date.

(K.U.D., April 1986)

Profit and Loss Account for the year ended 31-12-1984

Expenditure	Rs.	Income (*Less* Provisions)	Rs.
Interest paid on		Interest and Discount	3,07,500
Deposits	80,000		
Borrowings		Commission & Brokerage	30,000
Salaries & Allowances	1,25,000	Rent	37,500
Directors fees	30,000	Net profit on sales or	
Rent, Taxes, Insurance	20,000	Revaluation of Investment—	
Postage & Telegram	7,000	Income from other sources	—
Printing & Stationery	8,000	Other receipts	—
Audit fees	25,000	Loss, if any	—
Depreciation	5,000		
Loss on sale of Non-banking assets	—		
Loss, if any	—		
Net Profit	75,000		
	3,75,000		3,75,000

Note : (1) Interest and Discounts		3,12,500		
Less : Provision for doubtful debt	15,000			
Investment fluctuation	25,000	40,000	2,72,500	
Add : Interest accounted on Investment			35,000	3,07,500

(2) Interim Dividend paid	Rs. 17,500
Deducted at 5% on 5,00,000	25,000
Amount payable (Unclaimed dividend)	7,500
(3) Loans and Advances	26,50,000
Less : R.D.D.	15,000
	26,35,000

Krishna Bank Ltd.
Balance Sheet as at 31-12-1984

Capital & Liability		Rs.	Property & Assets		Rs.
Share Capital :			Cash in Hand		50,000
Authorised Capital		10,00,000	With Reserve Bank		—
Subscribed & Paid up			With other Banks		45,000
50000 equity share of 10 Rs.		5,00,000	Money at call & short notice		32,500
Reserve & Funds			Investments 4,25,000 MV		4,50,000
General Reserve		—	Loans advances	26,50,000	
Capital Reserve		25,000	Cash credits etc	15,000	26,35,000
Statutory Reserve	1,25,000		Bills receivable being		
Add for the year			bills for collection		1,00,000
Investment Fluctuation			per contra		
Reserve	15,000	1,40,000	Constituent Liablity		
Deposits & Other A/cs			for acceptance, endorsement		1,50,000
Fixed		—	Premises *less* depreciation		90,000
Savings Banks			Furniture *less* depreciation		20,000
Current A/c		25,00,000	Others receipts		
Borrowing from other Banks		75,000	Interest accrued		35,000
Bills payable		—	Non-banking assets		—
Bills for collection		1,00,000	Profit and Loss A/c		—
Audit fees		25,000			
Other Liabilities :					
Unclaimed dividend		7,500			
Acceptance, Endorsement		1,50,000			
Profit & Loss A/c					
Balance 1-1-1984	62,500				
Less: Interim dividend	25,000				
	37,500				
Less : Income tax	12,500				
	25,000				
Profit for the year	75,000				
	1,00,000				
Less Statutory					
Reserve of 20%	15,000	85,000			
Total		36,07,500			36,07,500

6

Insolvency Accounts

Insolvency

A businessman or a firm sole trading or a Partnership firm finds it difficult to meet the outside liabilities due to the increasing losses in business. That is his liabilities exceed his assets. The businessman or firm is not in a position to pay off the claims of outside liabilities. In such a situation he is called as insolvent.

In India there are two acts governing Insolvency cases.

(1) The Presidency Towns Insolvency Act, 1909 : Applicable to presidency Towns :

(a) Bombay (b) Calcutta (c) Madras.

(2) Provincial Insolvency Act, 1920 : Applicable to the rest of India.

Under these Acts, Insolvency proceedings are made only against :

(a) Individual; (b) Hindu joint family; (c) Partnership firm debt amount exceeding of Rs. 500.

Insolvency Proceedings

(1) Adjudication of debtor as Insolvent — When a Debtor is unable to pay his debt or unsatisfied creditors may file a petition in the Insolvency court to declare the debtor as Insolvent.

(2) Once the Debtor is adjudicated as Insolvent, the Court receiver is appointed to carry out the proceedings. Realisation of Assets and distribution of amount realised among the creditors.

(3) Official receiver takes the charge of all assets and realise for Payment of outside debt. The official Receiver, prepares the list of :

(a) Assets at Book value and Estimated Realisable value

(b) List of liabilities showing the amount of liabilities.

The list of liabilities are classified as :

List A — Unsecured Creditors

(1) Trade creditors, sundry creditor or creditor on open accounts.

(2) Bank Overdraft (Unsecured).

(3) Bills payable.

(4) Bills discounted likely to be dishonoured.

(5) Loans from friends or other loans from his wife (from Stree Dhan i.e. amount paid by the parents of wife).

(6) Creditors for taxes, salary wages and rent etc., in excess of preferential limit.

List B — Fully Secured Creditors

The security offered to such creditors is of more realisable value than the amount payable.

List C — Partly Secured Creditors

The realisable value of security offered is less than the amount payable. The unsatisfied amount would be claimed along with unsecured creditors.

List D — Preferential Creditors

Creditors for taxes due to Govt. etc., salary of clerks, wages of workers and rent to the landlord payable are treated as preferential payments under the Insolvency Act and their provision regarding this amount is deducted from the assets realised before any payment is made.

Preferential Creditors under :

(a) Presidency Town Insolvency Act, 1909 :

Applicable to Bombay, Calcutta and Madras

(b) Provincial Insolvency Act, 1920 : Applicable to Govt. of India.

Preferential Creditors

The following are the preferential payments under :

(a) Presidency Town Insolvency Act, 1909.

(b) Provincial Insolvency Act, 1920.

Particulars	Presidency Towns Insolvency Act, 1909	Provincial Insolvency Act, 1920
(1) Debts due to Govt. : Centre/State/Local Bodies etc. and also Taxes due to them.	Full Payment is to be made	Full payment is to be made.
(2) Salaries due to Clerks.	4 months' salary or Rs. 300 each whichever is less.	4 months' salary or Rs. 20 each whichever is less.
(3) Wages to works/ Servants.	4 months' wages or Rs. 100 each whichever is less.	4 months' wages or Rs. 20 each whichever is less.
(4) Rent payable to Landlord.	One month rent only.	No rent payable is preferential.

(a) Presidency Towns Insolvency Act, 1909, is made applicable to presidency Towns namely, Bombay, Calcutta and Madras only.

(b) Provincial Insolvency Act, 1920 is made applicable to the rest of India, other than presidency Towns as above.

Problem No. 1

Mr. Reckless an Insolvent filed his Insolvency petition on 31-12-1995 on which date his position was as follows :

He owed Rs. 70,000 to his creditors of which :

(a) Creditors amounting to Rs. 9,000 held on pledge stock of goods of the estimated value of Rs. 12,000.

(b) Creditors amounting to Rs. 38,000 held on pledge the stock of goods of the estimated value Rs. 21,000 and a mortgage on Building valued at Rs. 12,000.

(c) Taxes, Rent payable (of which preferential are Rs. 2,000) Rs. 2,000.

Bills Discounted amounted to Rs. 4,000 in respect of which it was estimated that he would be liable for Rs. 2,300.

The Assets consisted of

Books Debts	Rs.
Goods	3,000
Doubtful (estimated to produce Rs. 1,000)	2,000
Bad	1,000
Fixtures (estimated to produce Rs. 1,000)	1,800
Cash	2,000
BR	1,000
Stock of goods (estimated to Produce Rs. 5,000)	7,000

Mr. Reckless commenced his business with a Capital of Rs. 40,000 on 1-1-1992, after charging Interest on capital of Rs. 3,000 per year, he earned a profit of Rs. 16,800 in the first year but in the succeeding three years — he incurred losses of Rs. 12,000, Rs. 13,000 and Rs. 14,000 respectively. His personal drawings per year amounted to Rs. 4,000. The Buildings cost of acquisition was Rs. 22,000 and stock was subject to a discount of 25%.

Prepare Statement of Affairs as on 31-12-1995 and also Deficiency Account.

Solution :

Note : Ascertainment of stock of goods in the Firm. Prepare Balance Sheet as on 31-12-1995 date.

Balance Sheet as at 31-12-1995

Liabilities	Rs.	Assets		Rs.
Capital on 1-1-1992	40,000	Cash		2,000
Interest on Capital		Fixtures		1,800
Rs. 3,000 per year for 4 years		Building		22,000
(3,000 × 4)	12,000	Debtors		6,000
Profit for 1st year	16,800	Bill Receivable		1,000
Creditors	70,000	Drawings		
		Rs. 4,000 pa × 4 years		16,000
		Profit & Loss A/c		39,000
		2nd year	12,000	
		3rd year	13,000	
		4th year	14,000	
		Stock of Goods		51,000
	1,38,800	(Being Balancing figure)		1,38,800

Statement of Affairs

Liabilities		Expected to Rank	Property & Assets	Book value	Estimated to realise
	Rs.	Rs.		Rs.	Rs.
I. *Unsecured Creditors*			*Property List E*		
List A —	21,000		Cash	2,000	2,000
Bills discounted likely			Fixtures	1,800	1,000
to be dishonoured	2,300	23,300	Stock	7,000	5,000
II. *Fully Secured*			Total		8,000
creditors	9,000		Books Debts — F		
Value of securities			Good	3,000	3,000
List B			Doubtful	2,000	1,000
Stock-P	12,000		Bad	1,000	—
Surplus (per contra)	3,000				12,000
III. *Partly Secured*			Bills of Exchange — G		1000
Creditors — List C	38,00		Total Estimated		13,000
Value of securities			*Add* Surplus (per contra)		3,000
Stock — 21,000			Total Estimated Amount		16,000
Building 12,000	33,000	5,000	*Deduct* preferential creditors (per contra)		2,000

Liabilities	Rs.	Expected to Rank	Property & Assets	Book Value Rs.	Expected to produce Rs.
IV. *Preferential Creditors*			Total Estimated Amount		14,000
List D	2,000		Deficiency as per list H		14,300
Taxes, Rent payable					
deducted per contra	2,000	—			
		28,300			28,300

Note : Creditors		70,000	Books value of stock		51,000
Less Fully secured	9,000		*Less* : Value of stock	12,000	
Less Partly secured	38,000		Securities to fully		
Less Preferentials			secured	21,000	
Creditors	2,000		Value of stock		
		49,000	Partly secured	5,000	38,000
Unsecured Creditors		21,000	Stock in hand		13,000

Deficiency A/c as per List H

	Rs.				Rs.
Capital on 1-1-92	40,000	Business Loss			
Interest on Capital		II Year		12,000	
Rs. 3,000 per year for		III year		13,000	
4 years		IV year		14,000	39,000
(3,000 × 4)	12,000	Drawings			
Profit Ist year	16,800	Rs. 4,000 per year fro 4 year			
Deficiency as per		(4,000 × 4)			16,000
Statement of Affair	14,300	*Less on Realisation*			
		Book Debts	6,000		
		Less realise	4,000	2,000	
		Fixtures	1,800		
		Less realise	1,000	800	
		Building	22,000		
		Less	12,000	10,000	
		Stock	51,000		
		Less	38,000	13,000	25,800
		B.R. discounted likely to be dishonoured			2,300
	83,100				83,100

Problem No. 2

Mr. Govind an insolvent filed his insolvency petition on 30-6-1995. On that date his position was as follows :

	Rs.
Trade creditors	1,40,000
Bills payable	20,000
Bills discounted (estimated to Rank Rs. 8,000)	16,000
Creditors for taxes, rent, wages etc.	
(of which Rs. 6,000 are preferential)	8,000
Creditors holding first charge on Building	60,000
Creditors holding second charge on Building	30,000
Buildings (estimated to Produce Rs. 80,000)	1,00,000
Cash in hand	200
Cash at Bank	1,800
Stock in Trade (estimated to Produce Rs. 32,000)	40,000
Shares in X Ltd. (estimated to produce Rs. 9,000)	10,000
Furniture (estimated to produce Rs. 11,000)	14,000
Machinery (estimated to Realise Rs. 36,000)	50,000
Book Debts :	
Good	24,000
Doubtful (estimated) to produce Rs. 2,000	5,000
Bad	6,000
Bills Receivable	4,000

He commenced business with a capital of Rs. 90,000 on 1-7-1992 and the resulted in profit of Rs. 16,000, and Rs. 13,000 in the first two years respectively and in a loss of Rs. 57,000 in the third year after allowing Rs. 5,000 as interest on capital each year. His drawings for the whole period amounted to Rs. 80,000.

Prepared his Statement of Affairs and Deficiency Accounts.

[K.U.D., October 1996(O) & October 1987]

Statement of Affairs

Liabilities	Rs.	Expected to Rank Rs.	Property & Assets	Book Value Rs.	Expected to produce Rs.
I. *Unsecured Creditors*			*Property — List-E*		
List-A			Cash in hand	200	200
Trade Creditors	1,40,000		Cash at Bank	1,800	1,800
Bills payable	20,000		Stock	40,000	32,000
Bills discounted likely			Shares in X Ltd.	10,000	9,000
to be dishonoured	8,000		Furniture	14,000	11,000
Excess of preferential			Machinery	50,000	36,000
limit	2,000	1,70,000	Total List-E		90,000
II. *Fully Secured Creditors*			*Book Debts List-F*		
List-B	60,000		Good	24,000	24,000
Security — Building	80,000		Doubtful	5,000	2,000
Surplus transferred			Bad	6,000	—
to List-C	20,000				1,16,000
III. *Partly Secured Creditors*			Bills of exchange List-G	4,000	4,000
List-C	30,000		Total Estimated Amount		1,20,000
Security transferred			*Deduct* Preferential Creditors		
from List-B	20,000	10,000	per contra		6,000
IV. *Preferential Creditors*			Estimated Amount		1,14,000
List-D			Deficiency as per List-H		66,000
Taxes, rent, wages	6,000				
Deducted per contra	6,000	—			
		1,80,000			1,80,000

Deficiency A/c List-H

Capital on 1-7-1992	90,000	90,000	Business Loss		57,000
Interest of Capital			III-Year		80,000
Rs. 5,000 × 3 years	15,000	15,000	Drawings for 3 years		
Profit			*Loss on Realisation*		
I-year 16,000	80,000	20,000	Building 1,00,000		
II-year 13,000	29,000	29,000	80,000	20,000	
Statement of Affairs			Stock	8,000	
Deficiency	66,000	66,000	Shares	1,000	
			Furniture	3,000	
			Machinery	14,000	
			Debtors	9,000	55,000
			Bills discounted likely		
			to be dishonoured		8,000
		2,00,000			2,00,000

Problem No. 3

A has been adjudged insolvent on January 1982; his Creditors are as follows :

Trade Creditors — Rs. 50,000; Income Tax — Rs. 600; Municipal Tax — Rs. 500; Salary for 4 clerks for 4 months Rs. 2,000; wages for 3 workers for 4 months Rs. 350. Rent due to landlord for 3 months Rs. 1,500; Private Loan Rs. 5,000; Loan from his wife (Streedhan) Rs. 2,500.

Find out the amount due to unsecured creditors and preferential creditors under the provisions of Presidency Town Insolvency Act and Provincial Insolvency Act.

Solution :

	Presidency Towns Insolvency Act, 1909		Provincial Insolvency Act, 1920	
	Preferential	Unsecured	Preferential	Unsecured
(1) Trade Creditors	—	50,000	—	50,000
(2) Private Loan	—	5,000	—	5,000
(3) Loan from his wife (Streedhan)	—	2,500	—	2,500
(4) Taxes due to Govt. : Central/ State/Local bodies etc. :				
Income Tax	600	—	600	—
Municipal Taxes	500	—	500	—
(5) Salaries to 4 Clerks for 4 months	1,200	800	80	1,920
(Preferential Max. : Rs. 300 Rs. 20 each)				
(6) Wages for 3 workers	300	50	60	290
(Maximum : Rs. 100 each Rs. 20 each)				
(7) Rent due to Landlord for 3 months Preferential 1 month	500	1,000	—	1,500
	3,100	61,350	1,240	61,210

Problem No. 4

From the following particulars of Mr. Abdul, prepare the Statement of Affairs and his Deficiency Account as on 31-12-1994 :

1.	Creditors for goods	75,000
2.	Bills payable	6,000
3.	Creditors secured by shares	40,000
4.	Creditors secured by stock	15,000
5.	Liability on bills discounted (expected to rank Rs. 3,000)	7,000
6.	Mortgage on Mill	10,000
7.	Creditors payable in full	3,000
8.	Book Debts : Good	20,000
9.	Doubtful (estimated to produce Rs. 2,000)	10,000
10.	Consignment stock	5,000
11.	Shares (estimated at Rs. 16,000)	15,000
12.	Stock (estimated at Rs. 40,000)	60,000
13.	Cash	100
14.	Bills of exchange	1,400
15.	Mill (estimated at Rs. 11,000)	20,000
16.	Machinery (estimated at Rs. 12,000)	15,000
17.	Furniture (estimated at Rs. 4,500)	10,800

Mr. Abdul commenced his business on 1-1-1989 with a Capital of Rs. 50,000. His business resulted in a profit of Rs. 45,000 in the first four years and incurred a total loss of Rs. 25,000 in the last two years, after charging interest on capital at Rs. 2,500 every year. His drawings for all six years amounted to Rs. 77,200.

(K.U.D., October 1995)

Solution :

Working Note

I.	*Unsecured Creditors*			
	Creditors for goods	75,000		
	Bills payable	6,000		
	Liabilities on Bills Discounted	3,000		
		84,000		
II	*Fully Secured Creditors*	Amount	Security	Surplus
	Secured by stock	15,000	40,000	25,000
	Mortgage on Mill	10,000	11,000	1,000
		25,000	51,000	26,000
III.	*Partly Secured Creditors*			
	Creditors by shares	40,000	16,000	
IV.	Preferential Creditors	3,000		

Statement of Affairs as on 31-12-1994

Liabilities		Expected to Rank	Property & Assets	Book value	Expected to produce
I. *Unsecured Creditors*			*Property List-E*		
List-A			Cash	100	100
Creditors for goods	75,000		Consignment stock		5,000
Bills payable	6,000		Machinery	15,000	12,000
Liabilities on			Furnitures	10,800	4,500
Bills discounted	3,000	84,000			21,600
II. *Fully Secured Creditors*			*Book Debts List-F*		
List-B			Good	20,000	20,000
(15,000 + 10,000)	25,000		Doubtful	10,000	2,000
					43,600
Securities					
(40,000 + 11,000)	51,000		*Bills of Exchanges*		
Surplus (per contra)	26,000		*List-G*	1,400	1,400
			Total amount		45,000
III. *Partly Secured Creditors*			Surplus (per contra)		26,000
List-C	40,000		Estimated amount		71,000
Securities — shares	16,000	24,000	*Deducted* Pref. Creditors		3,000
IV. *Preferential Creditors*			(per contra)		
List-D	3,000		Estimated amount		68,000
(*Deducted* per contra)			Estimated to Deficiency as per List-H		40,000
		1,08,000			1,08,000

Deficiency Account List-H

Capital on 1-1-1989	50,000	Business Loss		25,000
Interest on Capital (2,500 × 6)	15,000	Drawings		77,200
		Loss on Realisation		
Net Profit	45,500	Stock	20,000	
Income from other source :		Mill	9,000	
Shares	1,000	Machinery	3,000	
Deficiency as per Statement		Furnitures	6,300	
of affairs	40,000	Book Debts	8,000	46,300
		Bills Discounted likely to be dishonoured		3,000
	1,51,500			1,51,500

Problem No. 5

Avinash commenced business on 1st January 1985 with a Capital of Rs. 1,34,000. His Profits for the year 1985 to 1989 were Rs. 16,000, 12,800, Rs. 7,200, Rs. 5,600 and Rs. 1,600 respectively and his drawings averaged Rs. 8,800 per annum. On 31st December 1989 Avinash became bankrupt and his affairs were as follows :

		Rs.
(1)	Unsecured creditors	80,000
(2)	Mortgage on freehold property	16,000
(3)	Creditors partly secured (Secured by life policy, estimated to Rs. 16,000)	48,000
(4)	Mrs. Avinash's loan from her own property	4,000
(5)	Creditors for salaries and wages	1,920
(6)	Bills receivable discounted and expected to rank	12,800
(7)	Freehold property costing Rs. 1,64,000 estimated to realise	80,000
(8)	Plant and Machinery cost Rs. 32,000 estimated to realise	8,000
(9)	Books debts — Good Rs. 24,000 Doubtful Rs. 8,000 estimated to realise Rs. 2,400, bad Rs. 20,000	
(10)	Furniture and fitting cost Rs. 3,200 estimated to realise	1,400
(11)	Cash in hand	320
(12)	Stock in trade cost Rs. 32,000 estimated to realise	22,200

Prepare : (a) Statement of Affairs

(b) Deficiency Account.

(K.U.D., April 1995)

Solution :

Statement of Affairs

Liabilities	Rs.	Expected to Rank Rs.	Property & Assets	Book value Rs.	Expected to realise Rs.
I. *Unsecured Creditors List-A*			*Property List-E*		
			Cash	320	320
Creditors	80,000		Stock	32,000	22,200
Mrs. Avinash loan	4,000		Furniture & Fitting	3,200	1,400
Bills receivable discounted likely to be dishonoured	12,800	96,800	Plant & Machinery	32,000	8,000
					31,920
II. *Fully Secured Creditors List-B*	16,000		*Book Debts-F*		
			Good	24,000	24,000
			Doubtful	8,000	2,400
Securities : Freehold property	80,000		Bad	20,000	—
Surplus (per contra)	64,000				58,320
III. *Partly Secured Creditors List-C*	48,000		*Bills of Exchange-G*		
			Total amount		58,320
Securities life policy	16,000	32,000	Surplus per contra		64,000
IV. Preferentials Creditors List-D			Amount available		1,22,320
Salaries & Wages			Deduct Preference Creditors per contra		1,920
deducted per contra	1,920	—	Total Amount available		1,20,400
			Deficiency as per List-H		8,400
		1,28,800			1,28,800

Deficiency Account

Liabilities	Rs.	Rs.	Property & Assets	Rs.	Rs.
Capital		1,34,400	Net loss		
Interest on Capital			Drawings 8,800 × 5		44,000
Income from business			Loss on realisation		
Profit 1985	16,000		Plant & Machinery	24,000	
1986	12,800		Debts	25,600	
1987	7,200		Freehold property	84,000	
1988	5,600		Furniture & Fitting	1,800	
1989	1,600	43,200	Stock	9,800	1,45,200
Income from other sources :			BR dishonoured		12,800
Life policy		16,000			
Deficiency as per Statement of affairs		8,400			
		2,02,000			2,02,000

Problem No. 6

Mr. Virendra Prabhu filed a petition of insolvency on 1st January 1992 on which date his books showed the following balance :

		Dr. (Rs.)	Cr. (Rs.)
Cash at Bank		1,500	
Furniture (estimated to produce Rs. 13,125)		17,500	
Stock in trade (estimated to produce Rs. 7,500)		12,500	
Trade creditors			28,500
Bills payable			4,000
Bank Overdraft			4,000
Sundry debtors :			
Good	5,000		
Doubtful	10,000		
Bad debt	2,000	17,000	
Creditors for rent, rates, and taxes			1,500
Capital			10,500
		48,500	48,500

Doubtful debts are estimated to realise 25%. Liabilities on bill discounted was Rs. 2,000 expected to rank Rs. 800. Trade creditors include Mr. Anand who held furniture of Rs. 5,000 for the loan given by him — Rs. 5,000, Mr. Prabhu's bicycle and which were valued at Rs. 400 and Rs. 300 respectively. He owns a house valued at Rs. 16,000 having a mortgage on it for Rs. 11,000. Prepare Deficiency Account and Statement of Affairs.

(K.U.D., October-1994)

Solution :

Statement of Affairs

Liabilities	Rs.	Expected to Rank Rs.	Assets		Book value	Estimated to produce Rs.
I. *Unsecured Creditors*			*Property List E*			
List A			Cash at Bank		1,500	1,500
Trade creditors	23,500		Furnitures	17,500		
Bills payable	4,000		*Less* : Partly			
Bank overdraft	4,000		secured	5,000	12,500	9,375
Bills discounted			Stocks		12,500	7,500
liability to be						18,375
dishonoured	800	32,300				
II. *Fully Secured*			Private property :			
Creditors List B			Bicycle	400		
Security		—	Watch	300		700
			Surplus from House property			5,000
			Total property			24,075
III. *Partly Secured*			*Books Debts List F*			
Creditors List C	5,000		Good		5,000	5,000
Security furnish			Doubtful		10,000	2,500
to 5,000	3,750	1,250	Bad		2,000	—
IV. *Preferential*						
Creditors List D			*Bills Exchange List G*			—
Rent, taxes etc.						31,575
deducted per contra	1,500		*Add* : Surplus per contra			—
						31,575
			Deducted from creditors			
			per contra			1,500
			Amount available			30,075
			Deficiency List H			3,475
		33,550				33,550

Deficiency Account

Liabilities	Rs.	Rs.	Assets	Rs.	Rs.
Capital		10,500	Premium loss		
Net profit			withdrawns		
Income from others			Loss on Realised		
sources private :			Furniture	4,375	
Bicycle	400		Stocks	5,000	
Watch	300		Deficiency	9,500	18,875
Surplus House			Bills discounted likely		
Property	5,000	5,700	to be dishonoured		800
Deficiency as per					
Statement of affairs		3,475			
		19,675			19,675

Problem No. 7

Shri Shetty of Bombay filed his petition in Insolvency on 31st March 1991. When his position was as under :

Cash		1,500
Trade Creditors		45,000
Mortgage on freehold property		15,000
Book Debts — Good		13,500
	Doubtful (Estimated to reduce Rs. 3,000)	6,750
	Bad	1,500
Creditors secured by Life Policy on Shetty		22,500
Surrender value of Shetty life policy		7,500
Rent to Landlord for 3 months		750
Salary to clerk for 2 months		450
Loan from Mrs. Shetty		6,000
Amount belong to her inherited property		
Stock (Estimated to produce Rs. 16,500)		19,500
Furniture (Estimated at Rs. 1,950)		3,000
Second Mortgage on Freehold property		5,250
Machinery (Estimated valued is Rs. 21,000)		30,000
Freehold property (Estimated to produce Rs. 18,000)		24,000
Bills Receivable discounted Rs. 7,000 of which likely to be dishonoured		3,000

Shetty started Business on 1-4-1987 with a capital of Rs. 67,500. His Profit for the first two years amounted to Rs. 7,500 and Loss during the last year amounted to Rs. 28,200. He had withdrawn Rs. 42,000 during this period. His private Liabilities were Rs. 6,000 and the private Assets including his life policy and household furniture of Rs. 2,000.

You are required to prepare :

(i) Statement of Affairs and

(ii) Deficiency Account.

(K.U.D., April 1994)

Solution :

Statement of Affairs as on 31-3-1991

Liabilities		Rs.	Estimated to Rank Rs.	Property & Assets	Book value Rs.	Estimated to Rank Rs.
I. *Unsecured Creditors*				*Property* List-E		
List-A				Cash	1,500	1,500
Trade Creditors		45,000		Stock	19,500	16,500
List A : 2 months Rent		500		Furniture	3,000	1,950
Salary		150		Machinery	30,000	21,000
Mrs Shetty Loan		6,000				40,950
Bills Receivable				Private Assets		2,000
discounted likely						42,950
to be dishonoured		3,000	54,650	*Books Debts List-F*		
Private liabilities			6,000	Good	13,500	13,000
			60,650	Doubtful	6,750	3,000
II. *Fully Secured Creditors*				Bad	1,500	1,500
List-B		15,000				
Securities Mortgage in freehold				*Bills of Exchange-G*		
				Total Estimated Amount		59,450
properties		18,000		*Add* Surplus per contra		—
Surplus transferred						59,450
to List-C		3,000		Total Deducted preferential		
III. *Partly Secured Creditors*				Credit per contra		550
List-C		5,250				58,900
Securities		22,500		Deficiency as per Statement-H		19,000
		27,750				
Surplus						
List-B	3,000					
Life Policy	7,500	10,500	17,250			
IV. *Preferential Creditors*						
List-D						
Rent (1 month)		250				
Salary-1 Clerk	450					
Excess	150	300				
Transfer deducted						
per contra		550				
			77,900			77,900

Deficiency A/c List-H

Excess of Assets over Liabilities		Rs.	Excess of Liabilities over Assets		Rs.
Capital 1-4-87		67,500	Business Loan		28,200
Interest on Capital :			Withdrawals		42,000
Net Profit		7,500	*Loss on Realisation of Assets*		
Income from other sources					
Private Assets	9,500		Freehold property	24,000	
Life Policy	6,000	3,500		18,000	
Deficiency as per Statement of Affairs		19,000		6,000	
			Stock	3,000	
			Furniture 3,000		
			1,450	1,050	
			Book Debts	5,250	
			Machinery	9,000	
					24,300
			Bills Discount likely to be dishonoured		3,000
		97,500			97,500

Problem No. 8

Shri Dhanapati filed his Insolvency petition on 1-1-1990. The following was in position :

(1)	Cash at Bank	1,200
(2)	Stock in trade (estimated to produce Rs. 19,200)	24,000
(3)	Shares in X Y Co. (estimated to realise Rs. 5,400)	6,000
(4)	Furniture (Estimated realise Rs. 6,600)	8,400
(5)	Machinery (estimated to produce Rs. 21,600)	30,000
(6)	Books Debts : Good	14,400
	Doubtful (estimated to to Rs. 1,200)	3,000
	Bad	3,600
(7)	Bills receivable	2,400
(8)	Building (estimated to produce Rs. 48,000)	60,000
(9)	Sundry Creditors	84,000
(10)	Bills payable	12,000
(11)	Bills discounted (likely to be dishonoured Rs. 4,800)	9,600
(12)	Creditors for taxes, rent, wages etc. (of which Rs. 3,600 are preferential)	4,800

(13) Creditors holding first charge on Building 36,000

(14) Creditors holding second charge on Building 18,000

He commenced business with a Capital of Rs. 54,000 on 1-1-1987 and earned a profit of Rs. 9,600 and Rs. 7,800 for the first two years and during the third year there was a Loss of Rs. 34,200 after allowing interest on Capital Rs. 3,000 each year. His drawings were Rs. 48,000 for the entire period.

Prepare : (a) Statement of Affairs and

(b) Deficiency Account.

(K.U.D., October 1993)

Solution :

Statement of Affairs

Liabilities	Rs.	Expected to Rank Rs.	Property & Assets	Book value Rs.	Estimated to Rank Rs.
I. *Unsecured Creditors*			*Property List-E*		
List-A		1,02,000	Cash at Bank	1,200	1,200
Sundry Creditors	84,000		Stock in Trade	24,000	19,200
Bills payable	12,000		Shares in XY Co.	6,000	5,400
Bills discounted likely to be dishonoured	4,800		Furnitures	8,400	6,600
			Machinery	30,000	21,600
Excess of Pref. Shares Limit			Total Property		54,000
			Book Debts List-F		
Taxes, Rent, Wages	1,200		Good	14,400	14,400
II. *Fully Secured Creditors*			Doubtful	3,000	1,200
List-B	36,000		Bad	3,600	—
Securities Building	48,000				69,600
Surplus Transferred to List-C	12,000		*Bills of Exchange-G*		
			Bills Receivable	2,400	2,400
III. *Partly Secured Creditors*			Total Amount		72,000
List-C	18,000		*Add* : Surplus per contra		—
Securities transferred to List-B	12,000	6,000	Total Estimated Amount		72,000
IV. *Preferential Creditors*			*Deduct* Preferential Creditors (per contra)		–3,600
Rent, Taxes & Wages	3,600				68,400
Deducted (per contra)	3,600	—	Deficiency as per List-H		39,600
		1,08,000			1,08,000

Deficiency Account

Excess of Assets over Liabilities	Rs.	Rs.	Excess of Liabilities over Assets	Rs.	Rs.
Capital		54,000	Net Loss III Year		34,200
Net Profit :			Drawings		48,000
I Year	9,600		*Loss on Realisation*		
II year	7,800	17,400	Stock in trade	4,800	
Interest on Capital			Share in XY Co.	600	
3,000 × 3		9,000	Furniture	1,800	
Statement of Affairs		39,600	Machinery	8,400	
			Building	12,000	
			Book Debts	5,400	33,000
			Bills Discounted likely to be dishonoured		4,800
		1,20,000			1,20,000

Problem No. 9

Shri Laxmi Narayan a resident of Bombay filed his petition in Insolvency on 31-12-90. On that date his Assets and Liabilities were as per his books of Accounts Rs. 1,20,000 and Rs. 77,500 respectively and he has estimated his difficiency at Rs. 22,500.

He found subsequently that the following had not taken in to account :

(i) Interest on Capital Rs. 70,000 @ 6% p.a. for one year.

(ii) Liabilities in Bills discounted amounted to Rs. 15,000 which bills worth Rs. 5,500 are likely to be dishonoured.

(iii) The following were outstanding dues :

(a) Salaries and wages to employees :

Rs. 11,500 of which Rs. 4,500 were preferential.

(b) Rent to the Landlord for 3 months Rs. 4,800.

(iv) Type-writing Machinery previously written off now found worth Rs. 2,000.

Prepare from the above information :

(a) Statement of Affairs

(b) Deficiency Account.

(K.U.D., April 1993)

Solution :

Laxmi Narayan resident of Bombay Investment
Statement of Affairs as on 31-12-1990

Liabilities		Rs.	Rs.	Property & Assets	Rs.	Rs.
I. *Unsecured Creditor*				*Property List-E*		
List-A		77,500		Sundry Assets	1,20,000	55,000
Liabilities on Bills Discounted		5,500		Typewriter		2,000
Excess of preference :				Total Property		57,000
Salaries,				*Books Debts List-F*		
wages etc.	11,500			Good		—
Less : Pref.	4,500	7,000		Doubtful		—
Rent	4,800			Bills of Exchange		—
Less : Pref.	1,600	3,200	93,200	Total Amount		57,000
II. *Fully Secured Creditors*				Surplus per contra		—
List-B				Total Amount available		57,000
Securities		—		*Deducted* Pref. Creditors		6,100
Surplus per contra		—	—	Total Amount available		50,900
III. *Partly Securities Creditors*				Deficiency as per List-H		42,300
List-C						
Securities		—				
IV. *Preferential Creditors*						
List-D						
Salaries		4,500				
Rent		1,600				
Deducted per contra		6,100	—			
			93,200			93,200

Deficiency A/c (List-H)

Excess of Assets over Liabilities	Rs.	Excess of Liabilities over Assets	Rs.	Rs.
Capital	70,000	Business Loss		27,500
Interest on Capital	4,200	Loss on Realisation		
Income from other sources :		Assets	1,20,000	
Typewriter	2,000	*Less* : Returns	55,000	65,000
Deficiency as per Statement of Affairs	42,300	*Outstanding Liabilities*		
		Salaries & Wages	11,500	
		Rent	4,800	16,300
		Interest on Capital		4,200
		Liabilities on Bills Discounted		5,500
	1,18,500			1,18,500

Balance Sheet as at 31-3-1990

Liabilities	Rs.	Assets	Rs.
Sundry Liabilities	77,500	Sundry Assets	1,20,000
Capital	70,000	Business Loss (Being Balancing figure)	27,500
	1,47,500		1,47,500

Problem No. 10

Shri Umashankar of Madras has filed his petition in Insolvency on 1-1-1991 when his Assets and Liabilities were as per books of accounts amounted to Rs. 1,20,000 and Rs. 82,000 respectively and estimated his deficiency at Rs. 22,000. He found the following had not been then into account; write estimatory of the above deficiency.

(a) Interest on capital of Rs. 50,000 at 10% p.a. for one year.

(b) Salaries to 3 clerks Rs. 1,500

(c) Wages of 6 workers due Rs. 950

(d) Rent due to Landlord for 5 months Rs. 4,000

(e) Taxes due to Government Rs. 2,500

(f) Liabilities on Bill discounted amounted to Rs. 10,500 out of which Bills worth Rs. 4,200 are likely to be dishonoured.

(g) He has taken a loan of Rs. 25,000 from a friend for his daughter's marriage by mortgaging his private property having realisable value of Rs. 40,000.

Prepare revised Statement of Affair and Deficiency Account.

(K.U.D., October 1992)

Solution :

(1) Ascertaiment of Business
Profit or Loss

Balance as at

Liabilities	Rs.	Assets	Rs.	Ascertainment of Assets Realised		Rs.
Capital	50,000	Assets	1,20,000	Total Assets		1,20,000
Liabilities	82,500	Loss		Liabilities	82,500	
		Being Balancing Figure	12,500	Estimated Deficiency	22,000	
				Assets Realised		60,500
	1,32,500		1,32,500	Loss on Realisation		59,500

Revised Statement of Affairs

Liabilities	Rs.	Expected to Rank Rs.	Assets	Book value Rs.	Estimated to produce Rs.
I. *Unsecured Creditors*			*Property List-E*		
List-A			Assets	1,20,000	60,500
Liabilities	82,500	90,850	Surplus from House property	—	15,000
Outstanding Liabilities			Total Assets		75,500
Excess of preferential limit :			*Books Debtors List-F*	—	—
Salary	600		Bills of Exchange List-G	—	—
Wages	350				
Rent	3,200		Total Estimated Assets	—	75,500
Bills Discounted likely to be dishonoured	4,200		Surplus per contra		—
					75,500
II. *Fully Secured Creditors*			*Deduct* Pref. Creditors per contra		4,800
List-B					
Securities	—		Estimated amount available		70,700
Surplus Purchase	—				

Liabilities	Rs.	Expected to Rank Rs.	Assets	Book value Rs.	Estimated to produce Rs.
III. *Partly Secured Creditors*			Deficiency as per List-H		20,150
List-C					
Securities	—				
IV. *Preferentials Creditors*					
List-D					
Salary 3 × 300	900				
Wages 6 × 100	600				
Rent 4,000 × 1/5	800				
Taxes to Govt.	2,500				
Deducted Percentage	4,800				
		90,850			90,850

Deficiency Account List H

	Rs.			Rs.
Capital	50,000	Business loss		12,500
Interest on Capital @ 10%	5,000	Loss on Realisation		59,500
		Outstanding Liabilities :		
Profit	—	Interest on Capital	5,000	
Surplus from		Salary	1,500	
other sources :		Wages	950	
House property	15,000	Rent	4,000	
Deficiency as per		Tax	2,500	13,950
Statement of Affairs	20,150	Bills Dishonours		4,200
	90,150			90,150

Problem No. 11

Shri Dhanapati of Kailas filed his petition of Insolvency on 31-3-1991; on that date his Assets and Liabilities were : Rs. 1,25,000 and Rs. 95,000 respectively. He estimated his deficiency to be Rs. 45,650 be taking into account of the following items which were omitted to be recorded in the Books of Accounts :

(1) Interest on Capital @ 10% on Rs. 55,000 for one year.

(2) Liabilities on Bills discounted Rs. 10,000 likely to be dishonoured Rs. 3,500.

(3) Amounts outstanding :

Wages	Rs. 450
Salary	Rs. 900
Taxes	Rs. 1,250
Rent	Rs. 600

(4) A Loan taken for the marriage of daughter from his friend Rs. 30,000 and from his wife Rs. 15,000 money given by her father.

(5) His life policy surrender value was Rs. 45,000.

Prepare : (a) Statement of Affairs

(b) Deficiency Account

(K.U.D., April 1992)

Note : It is assumed that he is a resident of other than Presidency towns.

Solution :

Opening Balance Sheet as at 31-3-1991

Liabilities	Rs.	Assets	Rs.
Capital A/c	55,000	Sundry Assets	1,25,000
Liabilities	95,000	Business Loss (Being Balancing figure)	25,000
	1,50,000		1,50,000

Statement of Affairs as on 31-3-1991

Liabilities	Rs.	Expected to Rank Rs.	Property & Assets	Book value Rs.	Estimated to produce Rs.
I. *Unsecured Creditors*			*Property List-E*		
List-A			Sundry Assets	1,25,000	49,350
Creditors	95,000		Life policy surrender		
Liabilities on			value		45,000
Bills dislikely			Books Debts List-F		94,350
to be dishonoured	3,500		*Bills of Exchange List-G*		—
Loan from Friend	30,000		Total Estimated Assets		94,350
Loan from wife	15,000	1,43,500	*Add* : Surplus (per contra)		—
Rent		600	Total estimated Amount		94,350
		1,44,100	*Deducted* Preferential		
II. *Fully Secured Creditors*			Creditors		2,600
List-B			Estimated Amount		
Securities	—		available for payment		91,750
			Deficiency as per		
Surplus	—		List-H		52,350
					1,44,100
III. *Partly Secured Creditors*					
List-C	—				
Securities	—				
IV. *Preferential Creditors*					
List-D					
Wages	450				
Salary	900				
Taxes	1,250				
	2,600				
Deducted per contra	2,600				
		1,44,100			1,44,100

Note : Preferential Creditors — Amounts outstanding : wages, salary, taxes and rent is taken as full since no limitations were mentioned in the problem.

Deficiency Account List-H

Excess of Assets over Liabilities	Rs.	Excess of Liabilities over Assets	Rs.	Rs.
Capital	55,000	Business Loss		25,000
Interest on Capital	—	Loan from Friend		30,000
Income from Business Profit :		Loan from Wife		15,000
Income from other sources :		*Loss on Realisation*		
Life Policy	45,000	Sundry Assets	1,25,000	
Deficiency as per Statement of Affairs	52,350	*Less :*	49,350	75,650
		Outstanding Liabilities		
		Wages	450	
		Salary	900	
		Taxes	1,250	
		Rent	600	3,200
		Liabilities on Bills Discounted		3,500
Total	1,52,350	Total		1,52,350

Problem No. 12

Shri Laxmipathi, a resident of Madras after difficulties in payment of outside liabilities filed a petition in insolvency. From the following information prepare his Statement of Affairs and Deficiency Account as on 31-3-1990 :

	Dr. Rs.	Cr. Rs.
Capital		85,500
Liabilities		
Sundry Creditors		1,06,500
Bills payable		81,000
Bank overdraft		33,000
Smt. Laxmipathi		13,500
Book Debts		
Good	45,000	
Doubtful (50% realisable)	54,000	
Bad	51,000	
Stock (Estimated to realise Rs. 78,000)	1,35,000	
Investments (Estimated to realise Rs. 26,000)	25,500	
Cash	9,000	
	3,19,500	3,19,500

Other Informations :

(a) Liabilities on Bills discounted Rs. 13,500 of which likely to be dishonoured Rs. 5,400.

(b) The amount due to Smt. Laxmipathi was a loan out of money given to her by Shri Laxmipathi.

(c) Preferential creditors (included in the Sundry creditors) amounted to Rs. 2,550 towards taxes, Rs. 750 towards salary, Rs. 360 towards Rent.

(d) The household Furniture valued at Rs. 6,000. He owned a House property valued at Rs. 75,000 and had taken a loan by mortgaging House property to Rs. 60,000.

(K.U.D., April 1991)

Solution :

Working Note

I. Unsecured Creditors List-A		
Sundry Creditors		1,06,500
Less : Preferential Creditors :		
Taxes	2,550	
Salary	750	
Rent	360	
		3,660
		1,02,840
Add :		
Bills Payable	81,000	
Bank Overdraft	33,000	
Bills Discounted likely to be dishonoured	5,400	1,19,400
Total List-H		2,22,240
II. Preferential Creditors List-D		
Taxes	2,550	
Salary	750	
Rent	360	
	3,660	

III. Smt. Laxmipathi's Loan amount was not Streedhan it was out of Money given by her husband.

This item should not be included in the list of liabilities but it should be shown on left-hand side of Deficiency Account as Income from other sources.

Statement of Affairs as at

Liabilities	Rs.	Expected to Rank Rs.	Assets	Book value Rs.	Estimated to produce Rs.
I. Unsecured Creditors			*Property List-E*		
List-A		2,22,240	Cash	9,000	9,000
II. Fully Secured			Stock	1,35,000	78,000
Creditors List-B			Investments	25,500	26,000
Securities	—		Household Furnitures		6,000
Surplus per contra	—		Surplus from Private		
III. Partly Secured			Property		15,000
Creditors List-C	—		Total		1,34,000
Securities	—		*Book Debts List-F*		
IV. Preferential Creditors			Good	45,000	45,000
List-D	3,660		Doubtful	54,000	27,000
Deducted per			Bad	51,000	—
contra	—				2,06,000
			Bills of Exchange		
			List-G	—	—
			Surplus per contra		2,06,000
			Deducted preferential		
			creditors per contra		3,660
			Estimated Amount		
			available		2,02,340
			Deficiency as		
			List-H		19,900
		2,22,240			2,22,240

Deficiency Account List-H

Excess of Assets over Liabilities	Rs.	Rs.	Excess of Liabilities over Assets		Rs.	Rs.
Capital		85,500	Business Loss			—
Income from Business :			Withdrawals			—
Net Profit		—	*Loss on Realisation*			
Interest on Capital		—	Stock	1,35,000		
Income from Other Source		—		78,000		
Profit on Realisation					57,000	
of Investment		500	Book Debt	1,50,000		
Surplus from House				72,000		
property	15,000				78,000	
Household						1,35,000
Furniture	6,000	21,000	Bills Discounted			
Smt. Laxmipathi Loan		13,500	likely to be			
Deficiency as per			dishonoured			5,400
Statement of Affairs		19,900				
		1,40,400				1,40,400

Problem No. 13

Shri Subray of Karvar has become bankrupt on 31st March 1991. He did not keep proper Books of Account and unable to tell Profit or Loss made by him. However he could give the following information as on the above date :

(1)	Due to suppliers		80,000
(2)	Bills Payable		10,000
(3)	Salary to 2 Clerks due to 6 months		1,200
(4)	Taxes owing		3,600
(5)	Banks Loan (Security of stock of Book value of Rs. 60,000)		30,000
(6)	Cash		300
(7)	Loan from Smt. Subray (from her salary)		30,000
(8)	Bills Endorsed (of which Rs. 6,000 bad)		12,000
(9)	Bills receivable (of which Rs. 6,000 bad)		15,000
(10)	Furniture (Realisable Rs. 6,000)		12,000
(11)	Stock (60% realisable)		90,000
(12)	Debtors :		
	Good	12,000	
	Doubtful (40% realisable)	20,000	
	Bad	10,000	42,000

He had started his business on 1st April 1985 with Rs. 75,000. He has been withdrawing Rs. 15,000 per annum for personal purpose. Smt. Subray gave her Jewellery worth Rs. 12,000 (Gift from her husband) to the receiver.

Prepare :

(a) Statement of Affairs

(b) Deficiency Account

(c) Working Note.

(K.U.D., October 1991)

Solution :

Statement Affairs

Liabilities	Rs.	Expected to Rank Rs.	Assets	Book value Rs.	Estimated to produce Rs.
I. *Unsecured Creditors*			*Property List-B*		
List-A			Cash	300	300
Bills Payable	10,000		Furniture	12,000	6,000
Sundry Creditors	80,000		Stock 60% 90,000		
Bills endorsed			Securities 60,000	30,000	18,000
likely to be Bad	6,000		Jewellery		12,000
Loan from			Total Property		36,300
Smt. Subray	30,000		*Book Debts List-F*		
Excess of pref.			Good	12,000	12,000
Limit — Salary	1,160	1,27,160	Doubtful 40%	20,000	8,000
II. *Fully Secured Creditors*			Bad	10,000	—
List-B	30,000		Bills of Exchange		
Securities stock			*List-G*	15,000	9,000
(60,000 @ 60%)	36,000				65,300
Surplus (per contra)	6,000		*Add* : Surplus per contra		6,000
III. *Partly Secured Creditors*			Total Estimated Amount		71,300
List-C	—		*Deduct* Pref. Creditors		3,640
Securities	—		Total Estimated Amount		
IV. *Preferential Creditors*			available		67,660
List-D			Estimated Deficiency		
Salary	40		as per List-H		59,500
Taxes due	3,600				
Deducted per contra	3,640				
		1,27,160			1,27,160

Deficiency A/c

Excess of Assets over Liabilities	Rs.	Excess of Liabilities over Assets		Rs.
Capital	75,000	Drawings (15,000 × 6)		90,000
Net Profit being Balancing figure	19,500	Loss on Realisation :		
Income from other source : Jewellery	12,000	Furniture	6,000	
		Stock	36,000	
		Debtors	22,000	
Statement of Affairs Deficiency	59,500	Bills Receivable	6,000	70,000
		Bills Endorsed — Bad		6,000
	1,66,000			1,66,000

Balance Sheet as at 31-3-1991

Liabilities	Rs.	Assets	Rs.
Capital	75,000	Cash	300
Due to Suppliers	80,000	Bills Receivable	15,000
Bills payable	10,000	Furniture	12,000
Outstanding dues		Stock	90,000
Salary to 2 Clerks for 6 months	1,200	Debtors	42,000
		Drawings (15,000 × 6)	90,000
Tax owing	3,600		
Bank Loan on security of stock of Books value Rs. 60,000	30,000		
Loan from Smt. Subray (from her Salary income)	30,000		
Profit (being Balancing figure)	19,500		
	2,49,300		2,49,300

Problem No. 14

M & N of Nagpur carried on business in partnership sharing Profits and Losses in the ratio of 3 : 2. They filed their petition in insolvency on 31st March 1990 when their Balance Sheet was as follows :

Balance Sheet as on 31-3-1990

Liabilities	Rs.	Assets	Rs.
Sundry Creditors	38,000	Plants & Machinery	10,000
Four months' Rent outstanding	1,200	Furniture	6,000
Two months' salary outstanding	1,800	Investments	4,000
Bank overdraft (secured on plant and machinery)	8,000	Stock	12,000
Capital : M	10,000	Debtors	23,000
N	7,000	Cash	1,000
		Profit & Loss A/c (Dr)	10,000
Total	66,000	Total	66,000

(a) There was deficiency of Rs. 3,200 in M's Private account; a surplus in N's private account to the extent of Rs. 500.

(b) The assets of the firm are estimated to realise as under :

Plant and Machinery	7,000
Furniture	3,000
Investments	2,500
Stock	9,000
Debtors (Doubtful) (Estimated to realise 70%)	13,000
Bad	3,000
Good	7,000

Prepare Statement of Affairs and Deficiency Account of the firm of M & N.

(K.U.D., October 1990)

Statement of Affairs as on 31-3-1990

Liabilities	Rs.	Expected to Rank Rs.	Property & Assets	Book value Rs.	Estimated to produce Rs.
I. *Unsecured Creditors*			*Property List-E*		
List-A			Cash	1,000	1,000
Sundry Creditors	38,000		Investments	4,000	2,500
4 month's Rent outstanding	1,200	39,200	Stock	12,000	9,000
II. *Fully Secured Creditors*			Furniture	6,000	3,000
List-B	—		Private Property of N		500
III. *Partly Secured Creditors*					16,000
Security	8,000		*Book Debt List-F*		
Plant & Machinery	7,000	1,000	Good	7,000	7,000
IV. *Preferential Creditors*			Doubtful (70%)	13,000	9,100
List-D			Bad	3,000	—
2 month's Salary *deducted* per contra	1,800				32,100
			Bills of Exchange List-G		—
			Total Estimated A/c		32,100
			Add : Surplus per contra		—
			Total Estimated amount		32,100
			Pref. Creditors *deducted* per contra		1,800
			Total Estimated Amount available		30,300
			Deficiency as per List-H		9,900
		40,200			40,200

Deficiency Account

Excess of Assets over Liabilities	Rs.	Rs.	Excess of Liabilities over Assets		Rs.	Rs.
Capital : M	10,000		Business Loss			10,000
N	7,000	17,000	*Loss on Realisation of Assets*			
Income from other sources		—	Plant & Machinery		3,000	
Surplus from			Furniture		3,000	
Private of N		500	Investments		1,500	
Deficiency as per			Stock		3,000	
			Debtors	23,000		
Statement of Affairs		9,900		16,100	6,900	17,400
		27,400				27,400

Problem No. 15

P and Q of Bombay carried on Business in partnership sharing profit and losses in proportion of 2/3 and 1/3 respectively. They filed their petition in Insolvency on 31-12-1988 when their Balance Sheet was as under :

Balance Sheet as at

Liabilities	Rs.	Assets	Rs.
Sundry Creditors	54,300	Plant & Machinery	18,000
Bills Payable	5,000	Furniture	2,500
Bank overdraft	30,000	Stock	15,000
6 months' salary to employees	9,000	Debtors	29,500
P's Capital	12,000	Investments	12,000
Q's Capital	4,600	Drawings : P	6,000
One year Rent	1,200	Q	3,200
		Loss Through building	20,000
		Cash at Bank	1,400
		Profit & Loss A/c	8,500
	1,16,100		1,16,100

(a) Included in the item of Sundry creditors was one creditor of Rs. 10,800 who had a charge on Plant & Machinery.

(b) Sundry creditors also included a sum of Rs. 5,200 in respect of claim against the firm not expected to Rank for payment.

(c) Bank overdraft was secured by a charge on Q's Private House.

(d) The assets of the firm are estimated to realise as under :

Plant & Machinery	12,000
Furniture	2,000
Investments	16,500
Stock	12,000

of the Debtors Rs. 15,000 were doubtful and are estimated to realise .50 Paise per Rupee and Rs. 2,500 bad.

It is expected that on P's Private Account there was a deficiency of Rs. 4,100 while Q had no personal property other than a house which was expected to produce Rs. 8,000. Q had no Private Liabilities.

Prepare : (1) Statement of Affairs and
(2) Deficiency Account.

(K.U.D., October 1990)

Working Note

Sundry Creditors	54,300	*Preferential Creditors*		
Less Fully Secured Crs.	10,800	(a) Salary to Employees 6 months		9,000
	43,500	Preferential 4 months	1,500	6,000
Less Claims not expected to Bank	5,200	Excess of preferential limit		3,000
Net Sundry Creditors	38,300	Rent one year		1,200
Add Bills payable	5,000	Preferential one month		100
	43,300	Excess of preferential		1,100
		Now preferential creditors :		
Add Excess of preferential limit salary	3,000	Salary		6,000
Rent	1,100	Rent		100
Total Credit	47,400			6,100
Fully Secured Crs.	10,800			
Security	12,000			
Plant & Machinery	1,200			
Surplus	30,000			
Partly Secured Bank Debt	8,000			
	22,000			

Solution :

Statement of Affairs

Liabilities	Rs.	Expected to Rank Rs.	Property & Assets	Book value Rs.	Estimated to produce Rs.
I. *Unsecured Creditors*			*Property List-E*		
List-A			Cash at Bank	1,400	1,400
Sundry Credit	38,300		Furniture	2,500	2,000
Bills payable	5,000		Stock	15,000	12,000
Excess of preferential			Instalments	12,000	16,500
Salary	3,000				31,900
Rent	1,100	47,400	Books Debts :		
II. *Fully Secured*			Good	12,000	12,000
Creditors			Doubtful	15,000	7,500
List-B			Bad	2,500	—
Security	10,800		Bills of		—
Plant & Machinery	12,000		Total		51,400
Surplus per contra	1,200		Surplus per contra		1,200
III. *Partly Secured*					52,600
Creditors			Deduct Pref.		
List-C			Credit per contra		6,100
Bank Overdraft	30,000				46,500
Less Security	8,000	22,000	Estimated Deficiency		
IV. *Preferential*			as per List-H		22,900
Creditors					
List-D					
Salary 4 × 15	6,000				
Rent one month	100				
Deducted per contra	6,100				
		69,400			69,400

Deficiency Account List-H

Excess of Assets over Liabilities	Rs.	Excess of Liabilities over Assets	Rs.	Rs.
Capital : P	12,000	Business Loss		8,500
Q	4,600	Drawings : P	6,000	
Interest on Capital	—	Q	3,200	9,200
Income from Other source		Loss through Building		20,000
Q's Private House	8,000	*Loss on Realisation*		
Claim not expected to rank	5,200	Plant and Machinery	6,000	
Surplus on sale of Investment	4,500	Furniture	500	
Deficiency as per		Stock	3,000	
Statement of Affairs	22,900	Book Debts	10,000	19,500
	57,200			57,200

Problem No. 16

Mohan of Hubli commence business on 1-1-1985 with a Capital of Rs. 15,000.

His annual withdrawals amounted to Rs. 1,300. The profits for the first three years amounted in all Rs. 4,000. No accounts were prepared by him for the next two years on 31-12-1989 and order of Adjudication was made against him.

He submits the following information for preparation of his Statement of Affairs and Deficiency Account :

(1)	Sundry Creditors	9,500
(2)	Mortgage on Building	2,000
(3)	Creditors Secured by Life policy estimated worth Rs. 2,000	6,000
(4)	Landlord's two months Rent	100
(5)	Clerks Salary for two months	100
(6)	Corporation Taxes owing	90
(7)	Mrs. Mohan's Loan	1,500
(8)	Bills Receivable discounted and expected to Rank	1,600
(9)	Building (Estimated to realise Rs. 10,000)	20,000
(10)	Plant & Machinery cost — Rs. 10,000	
	Less : Depreciation written off Rs. 3,000	
	Estimated to realise Rs. 1,000	
(11)	Second Mortgage on Building	6,000
(12)	Book Debts : Good	3,000
	Doubtful (Estimated to realise Rs. 300)	1,000
	Bad	250

(13) Furniture (Estimated to realise Rs. 175)	400
(14) Stock (Estimated to realise Rs. 2,775)	4,000
(15) Cash	40

The Loan by Mrs. Mohan is out of money given to her by Mr. Mohan about 5 years ago.

(K.U.D., April 1990)

Solution :

Statement of Affairs

Liabilities	Rs.	Expected to Rank Rs.	Property & Assets	Book value Rs.	Estimated to realise Rs.
I. *Unsecured Creditors List-A*			*Property List-E*		
			Cash	40	40
Sundry Creditors	9,500		Stock	4,000	2,775
Bills Discount likely to dishonour	1,600		Furniture	400	175
Landlord's two months 180			Plant & Machinery (10,000 — 3,000)	7,000	1,000
Rent 100			Total Property		3,990
Clerk Salary excess of 80		11,280	*Book Debts List-F*		
II. *Fully Secured Creditor List-B*			Good	3,000	3,000
Mortgage on Building	2,000		Doubtful	1,000	300
Securities Building	10,000		Bad	250	—
	8,000				7,290
Surplus			*Bills of Exchange*		
Second charge on Building	6,000		*List-G*		—
Surplus per contra	2,000		Total Estimated Amount		7,290
III. *Partly Secured Creditors List-C*	6,000		*Add* : Surplus per contra		2,000
Securities Life policy	2,000	4,000	Total Estimated Amount		9,290
IV. *Preferential Creditors* List-D			*Deduct* pref. Creditors		110
Rent 100			Total Estimated amount available		9,180
Not Preferential			Deficiency as per		
Clerks Salary 100			List-H		6,100
Excess paid 80	20				
Corporation Taxes	90				
Deducted per contra	110				
		15,280			15,280

Note : Mr. Mohan-Insolvent resides at Hubli. Provision of Provincial Insolvency Act of 1920 be applied in respect of preferential Creditors — regarding salaries, wages per person. Landlord's Rent is not preferential.

Deficiency Account List-H

Excess of Assets over Liabilities	Rs.	Rs.	Excess of Liabilities over Assets	Rs.	Rs.
Capital	15,000	15,000	Business Loss for last two years (as per Balance Sheet balancing figure)		2,100
Income from Business	4,000	4,000			
Profit for 3 years		—			
Income from other sources			Withdrawals (1,300 × 5)		6,500
Mrs. Mohan's Loan	1,500	1,500	*Loss on Realisation*		
Amount given by Mr. Mohan 5 years ago Life Policy		2,000	Stock	1,225	
			Furniture	225	
Deficiency A/c as per Statement of Affairs		6,100	Machinery	6,000	
			Book Debtors 4,250—3,300	950	
			Building (20,000 — 10,000)	10,000	18,400
			Bills Discounted likely to be dishonoured		1,600
		28,600			28,600

Note : (1) Private Life Insurance policy taken as Income from other source.

(2) Mrs. Mohan Loan A/c is not Streedhan and taken as Income from other source.

Balance Sheet as at 31-12-1989

Liabilities	Rs.	Rs.	Assets	Rs.	Rs.
Sundry Creditors		9,500	Building		20,000
Mortgage on Building		2,000	Plant & Machinery		
Creditors Secured by			Cost	10,000	
Life policy		6,000	*Less* : Depr.	3,000	7,000
Creditors second mortgage			Furniture		400
Building		6,000	Book Debts 3,000+1,000+250		4,250
Creditors for Rent		100	Stock		4,000
(Two months)			Cash		40
Clerk Salary 2 months		100	Profit & Loss A/c (Loss)		2,100
Corporation Tax		90	(Balancing Figure Loss		
		23,790	from last 2 years)		
Mrs. Mohan Loan		1,500			
		25,290			
Capital 1-1-85	15,000				
Add : Profit	4,000				
	19,000				
Less : Drawing	6,500	12,500			
		37,790			37,790

Problem No. 17

Mr. Dinesh finds himself insolvent on 31-12-1988. His position was as follows :

(1)	Sundry Debtors :	
	Good	10,000
	Doubtful Debts (estimated to produce Rs. 50,000)	60,000
	Bad	30,000
(2)	2000 Shares in Grasim Ltd. (Estimated to realise 30,000)	50,000
(3)	Shares in Oswal Agro Ltd. (Estimated to produce Rs. 1,50,000)	1,83,000
(4)	Loss through battery	4,000
(5)	Creditors on open accounts	1,71,200
(6)	Creditors holding second charge on shares of Oswal Agro Ltd. (to the extent of Rs. 50,000)	60,000
(7)	Creditors holding first charge on shares of Oswal Agro Ltd.	80,000
(8)	Bills Payable	8,000
(9)	Creditors for Rent, Rates, Taxes etc. (of which Rs. 9,000 Preferential)	10,000

(10) Furniture (Estimated to realise Rs. 6,000) 30,000
(11) Cash in hand and at Bank 1,100
(12) Stock (Estimated to realise Rs. 60,900) 71,900
(13) Bills Receivable (Estimated to realise Rs. 14,000) 18,000

Mr. Dinesh started Business with a Capital of Rs. 1,40,000 on 1-1-1986, and the business resulted in a profit of Rs. 17,600 and Rs. 20,000 for the first two years respectively and a Loss of Rs. 10,000 for the Third year other allowing Rs. 7,000 as interest on capital each year. Drawings for the whole period was Rs. 60,000.

Prepare Statement of Affairs and Deficiency A/c.

(K.U.D., April 1989)

Solution :

Statement of Affairs as on 31-12-1988

Liabilities	Rs.	Expected to Rank Rs.	Property & Assets	Book value Rs.	Estimated to realise Rs.
I. *Unsecured Creditors*			*Property List-E*		
List-A			Cash in hand & Book	1,100	1,100
Creditors on open A/c	1,71,200		Stock	71,900	60,000
Bills payable	8,000		Furniture	30,000	6,000
Excess of Pref. Creditors Rent,			2000 Shares in Grasim Ltd.	50,000	30,000
Rates, Tax etc.	1,000	1,80,200	Property Total		98,000
II. *Fully Secured Creditors*			*Book Debts List-F*		
List-B	80,000		Good	10,000	10,000
(Creditors hold first charge on Oswal Agro Ltd.)			Doubtful	60,000	50,000
			Bad	30,000	—
Securities (Oswal Shares)	1,50,000				1,58,000
Surplus	70,000		*Bills of Exchange*		
			List-G	18,000	14,000
Transferred to List-C	50,000		Total Estimated Amount		1,72,000
Surplus per contra	20,000		*Add* : Surplus per contra		20,000

Liabilities	Rs.	Expected to Rank Rs.	Property & Assets	Book Value Rs.	Estimated to realise Rs.
III. *Partly Secured Creditors* List-C			Total Estimated amount		1,92,000
Creditors holding second charge on			*Deducted* Pref. Creditors per contra		9,000
Oswal shares	60,000		Total Estimated Amount available for distribution		1,83,000
Transferred from List-B	50,000	10,000	Deficiency as per List-H		7,200
IV. *Preferential Creditors List-D*					
Rent, Rates, Taxes 10,000					
Excess of Pref. Limit 1,000	9,000				
Transfer to Unsecured Crs. *deducted* per contra	—				
		1,90,200			1,90,200

Deficiency Account List-H

Excess of Assets over Liabilities		Rs.	Excess of Liabilities over Assets	Rs.	Rs.
Capital		1,40,000	Business Loss		10,000
Income from Busines			Loss through Battery		4,000
Net Profit :			Withdrawals		60,000
					74,000
I Year	17,600		*Loss on Realisation*		
II Year	20,200	37,800	Stock (71,900–60,900)	11,000	
Interest on Capital 7,000 × 3		21,000	Furniture (30,000–6,000)	24,000	
Income from other Source			Shares in Grasim (50,000–30,000)	20,000	
Deficiency as per Statement of Affairs		7,200	Book Debts (1,00,000–60,000)	40,000	
			Shares in Oswal Agro Ltd. 1,83,000–1,50,000	33,000	
			Bills Receivable 18,000 – 14,000	4,000	1,32,000
		2,06,000			2,06,000

Problem No. 18

Shri Govind having failed to pay his Liabilities filed his petition in Bankruptcy on 31-12-1988. From the following particulars, prepare (a) Statement of Affairs and (b) Deficiency Account.

(1)	Furniture (Expected to produce Rs. 800)	1,400
(2)	Stock (Estimated to realise 75%)	16,000
(3)	Building (Estimated at Rs. 12,000)	11,000
(4)	Cash on hand	200
(5)	Debtors : Good	680
	Doubtful (Expected to realise Rs. 400)	600
	Bad	200
(6)	Bills of Exchange	780
(7)	Motor Car (Expected to be sold for Rs. 6,000)	12,000
(8)	The car is pledged with a Creditor for Loan	13,400
(9)	The Unsecured Creditors amounted to	18,060
(10)	Creditors for Rent, Taxes are but only Rs. 600 of this can rank as preferential	1,000
(11)	There is a contingent liabilities for Bills Discounted of which the sum of Rs. 2,000 excepted to Rank	5,000
(12)	Fully Secured Creditors have a charge of mortgage on Building	4,000
(13)	He had a surplus Assets of Rs. 11,600 on 1-1-1985. He had been withdrawing for his private expenses Rs. 2,000 a year.	

It appears from his books that he made a Profit of Rs. 5,800 in the first year, and Rs. 3,600 in the second year and losses of Rs. 4,000 in the third year and Rs. 4,200 in the fourth year after allowing Rs. 400 a year by way of Interest on Capital. Surplus of Rs. 400 is available from his private estate.

(K.U.D., October 1989)

Solution :

Working Note

Unsecured Creditors		Fully Secured Creditors	4,000
List-A	18,060	Security Building (Rs. 11,000)	12,000
Liability for Bills		Surplus	8,000
Receivable	2,000	Partly Secured Creditors	
Rent, Tax etc.	400	List	13,400
Excess of Pref. limit	20,400	Securities Motor Car	6,000
			7,400
Creditors Preferential	600		

Note : Surplus private property should be included in Assets.

Statement of Affairs as on 31-12-1988

Liabilities	Rs.	Expected to Rank Rs.	Property & Assets	Book value Rs.	Estimated to realise Rs.
I. *Unsecured Creditors*			*Property List-E*		
List-A			Cash in hand	200	200
Unsecured	18,060		Furniture	1,400	800
Liabilities for			Stock 75%	16,000	12,000
Bills Receivable discounted	2,000		Private Estate surplus		400
Excess of Pref. limit for Rent Rate, Tax (1,000 — 600)	400	20,460	Total Property		13,400
			Book Debts List-F		
II. *Fully Secured Creditors*			Good	680	680
List-B	4,000		Doubtful	600	400
Securities Building	12,000		Bad	200	—
Surplus (per contra)	8,000		Bills of Exchange List-G		14,480
					780
III. *Partly Secured Crs.*			Total Estimated amount		15,260
List-C	13,400		Surplus per contra		8,000
Security Motor	6,000	7,400	Total Estimated amount		23,260
IV. *Preferential Creditors*			*Deduct* Preferential Crs.		
List-C			per contra		600
Rent, Tax etc.			Total Estimated amount		
Deducted per contra	600		available		22,680
			Deficiency as per List-H		5,200
		27,860			27,860

Deficiency Account List-H

Excess of Assets over Liabilities	Rs.	Rs.	Excess of Liabilities over Assets	Rs.	Rs.
Surplus of Assets			Withdrawals (2,000 × 4)		8,000
Capital		11,600	Losses 3rd Year	4,000	
Net Profit :			4th Year	4,200	8,200
I Year	5,800		*Loss on Realisation*		
II Year	3,600	9,400	Furniture	600	
Interest on Capital		1,600	Stock	4,000	
(400 × 4)			Book Debts (200 + 200)	400	
Income from other Source			Motor Car (2,000 – 6,000)	6,000	11,000
Surplus from private Estate		400	Liabilities on		
Income from Building (Sale)			Bills Discounted		2,000
Profit on Realisation		1,000			
Deficiency as per Statement of Affairs		5,200			
		29,200			29,200

Problem No. 19

Shri Mane of Bangalore has filed a petition in the Court to adjudicate him as Insolvent. His financial position on 31-12-1987 was as under :

(1)	Trade Creditors	20,000
(2)	Bills payable	5,000
(3)	Overdraft	5,000
(4)	Salary due to 2 (two) Clerks	400
(5)	Taxes due	1,200
(6)	Bank Loan secured by stock	10,000
(7)	Cash	100
(8)	Furniture (50% realisable)	4,000
(9)	Stock (60% realisable)	30,000
(10)	Book Debts : Good	4,000
	Doubtful (realisable 40%)	10,000
(11)	Bills Receivable (of which Rs. 3,000 Bad)	5,000
(12)	Bills discounted (Rs. 2,000 bad)	6,000
(13)	Loan from Mrs. Mane (From her inherited property funds)	10,000

Shri Mane started his business on 1-1-1982 with a Capital of Rs. 25,000.

He does not maintain proper Books of Accounts and he is unable to give figure of Profit or Loss made my him. He tells that he has withdrawals Rs. 5,000 per year for his domestic purposes.

Mr. Mane gave her necklace worth of Rs. 4,000 to the court Receiver, which was presented to her by Shri Mane.

Prepare : (1) Statement of Affairs

(2) Deficiency Account

(3) Working Notes.

(K.U.D., April 1988)

Solution :

Note : Shri Mane resides at Bangalore. Provincial Insolvency Act, 1920 applied in respect of Preferential Creditors.

Statement of Affairs as on 31-12-1987

Liabilities	Rs.	Expected to Rank Rs.	Property & Assets	Book value Rs.	Estimated to produce Rs.
I. *Unsecured Creditors*			*Property List-E*		
List-A		42,360	Cash	100	100
Trade Creditors	20,000		Furniture 50%	4,000	2,000
Bills payable	5,000		Mrs. Mane's Necklace		4,000
Overdraft	5,000		Total Property		6,100
Bills discount likely to be dishonoured	2,000		Book Debts List-F		
Loan from Mrs. Mane	10,000		Good	4,000	4,000
Add : Salary—Excess of preferential Limit	360		Doubtful 40%	10,000	4,000
			Bad	—	—
					14,100
II. *Fully Secured Creditors* List-B	10,000		*Bills of Exchange* List-G	5,000	2,000
Bank Loan	18,000		Estimated Amount		16,100
Security stock surplus per contra	8,000		*Add* : Surplus per contra		8,000
III. *Partly Secured Creditors* List-C	—		Estimated amount available		24,100
IV. *Preferential Creditors* List-D			*Deduct* preferential creditors per contra		1,240
Salary	40				22,860
Taxes	1,200		Deficiency as per List-H		19,500
Deducted per contra	1,240				
		42,360			42,360

Deficiency Account

Excess of Assets over Liabilities	Rs.	Excess of Liabilities over Assets	Rs.	Rs.
Capital	25,000	Drawings		30,000
Net Profit	6,500	(5,000 × 6)		
(Balancing figure)		*Loss on Realisation*		
Income from other source		Stock (30,000 — 18,000)		
Mrs. Mane's Necklace	4,000		12,000	
Deficiency as per		Furniture		
Statement of Affairs	19,500	4,000—2,000	2,000	
		Bad Debts	6,000	
		Bills Receivable	3,000	23,000
		Bills Discounted likely		
		to be dishonoured		2,000
	55,000			55,000

Problem No. 20

Shri Gopal filed his petition in Insolvency on 31-12-1987 on which date his Trial Balance was as under :

Trial Balance as on 31-12-1987

Particulars		Dr. Rs.	Cr. Rs.
(1) Capital			50,000
(2) Trading Loss		29,400	
(3) Drawings		10,000	
(4) Creditors (including Rs. 15,000 secured against Private House estimated to produce Rs. 10,000)			41,000
(5) Bills payable			8,000
(6) Bank Loan (Secured by a charge on Stock)			30,000
(7) Taxes payable to Govt.			2,400
(8) Salary to clerk (for 4 months)			400
(9) Wages to worker (for 3 workers) for 4 months at Rs. 50 each			600
(10) Sundry Debtors : Good	12,000		
Doubtful (50% rebate)	8,000		
Bad	5,000	25,000	

(11)	Furniture (Estimated at Rs. 10,000)	9,000	
(12)	Stock (Estimated at Rs. 30,000)	45,000	
(13)	Bills Receivable (all Good)	4,000	
(14)	Loss on Race Course	6,000	
(15)	Loss on Guarantee	3,000	
(16)	Cash in Hand	1,000	
		1,32,400	1,32,400

He had discounted Bills of Rs. 7,000 of which bills worth Rs. 2,000 are estimated to be dishonoured.

Prepare : (1) Statement of Affairs and
(2) Deficiency Account.

(Gulbarga, October 1988)

Statement of Affairs

Liabilities	Rs.	Expected to Rank Rs.	Property & Assets	Book value Rs.	Estimated to produce Rs.
I. *Unsecured Creditors*			*Property List-E*		
List-A			Cash	1,000	1,000
Creditors	26,000		Furnitures	9,000	10,000
Bills payable	8,000		Total		11,000
Excess of preferential limit : Salary	100		*Book Debts List-F*		
Wages	300		Good	12,000	12,000
Bills Discounted likely to be dishonoured	2,000	36,400	Doubtful Debts	8,000	4,000
			Bad	5,000	—
II. *Fully Secured Creditors*			*Bills of Receivable*		
List-B	30,000		*List-G*	4,000	4,000
Security	30,000		Total estimated amount		31,000
Surplus	—		Surplus per contra		—
III. *Partly Secured Creditors*			Total estimated amount		31,000
List-C	15,000		*Deducted* preferential creditors		3,000
Securities	10,000	5,000	Amount available		28,000
IV. *Preferential Creditors*			Deficiency as per List-H		13,400
List-D					
Salary	300				
Wages	300				
Taxes	2,400				
Deducted per contra	3,000				
		41,400			41,400

Deficiency Account

Excess of Assets over Liabilities	Rs.	Excess of Liabilities over Assets	Rs.
Capital	50,000	Trade Loss	29,400
Interest on Capital	—	Drawings	10,000
Income from Business	—	Loss on Race Course	6,000
Income from other sources :		*Loss on Realisation*	
Surplus from Furniture	1,000	Stock	15,000
Private House	10,000	Book Debts	9,000
Deficiency as per Statement of Affairs	13,400	Bills Discounted likely to be dishonoured	2,000
		Loss on Guarantee	3,000
	74,400		74,400

Problem No. 21

Mr. Prakesh of Bombay has filed his petition in Insolvency on 31st March 1986. When his Assets and Liabilities as per Books of Accounts amounted to Rs. 80,000 and Rs. 55,000 respectively and estimated his deficiency at Rs. 12,000.

He found that the following had not be taken into A/c :

(a) Interest on Capital of Rs. 30,000 @ 5% p.a. for one year.

(b) Liabilities on Bills discounted amounted to Rs. 7,000 out of which Rs. 2,500 worth Bills were expected to be dishonoured.

(c) Salaries of three clerks Rs. 1,100.

(d) Wages of five Labourers Rs. 600.

(e) Rent to the Landlord for 3 months Rs. 300.

Prepare required Statement of Affairs and Deficiency A/c.

(K.U.D., October 1988)

Revised Statement of Affairs as on 31-3-86

Liabilities		Rs.	Expected to Rank Rs.	Property & Assets	Book value Rs.	Estimated to produce Rs.
I. *Unsecured Crs.*				Property List-E	80,000	43,000
List-A		55,000		Book Debts List-F	—	—
Liabilities on Bills				Good	—	
Discounted to likely to be dishonoured		2,500		Doubtful	—	
Excess of Pref. limit				Bad	—	
Salary	1,100			Bills of Exchange List-G		—
Less : Pref.	900	200		Estimated Total Amount		43,000
Wages	600			Surplus per contra		—
Less : Pref.	500	100		Estimated Total Amount		43,000
Rent	300			*Deducted* Preferential Crs. per contra		1,500
Less : Pref.	100	200	58,000	Estimated Total Amount available		41,500
II. *Fully Secured Creditors*				Deficiency as per List-H		16,500
List-B		—				
Security		—				
Surplus per contra		—				
III. *Partly Secured Creditors List-C*						
Securities		—				
IV. *Preferential Creditors*						
List-D						
Salary		900				
Wages		500				
Rent		100				
Deducted per contra		1,500				
			58,000			58,000

Deficiency A/c List-H

Excess of Assets over Liabilities	Rs.	Excess of Liabilities over Assets	Rs.	Rs.
Capital	30,000	Business Loss		5,000
Interest on Capital on 30,000 @ 5%	1,500	Loss on Realisation (80,000 — 43,000)		37,000
Income from other Source	—	*Outstanding Liabilities*		
		Salaries	1,100	
Statement of Affairs	16,500	Wages	600	
		Rent	300	2,000
		Liabilities on Bills discounted likely to be dishonoured		2,500
		Interest on Capital		1,500
	48,000			48,000

Problem No. 22

From the following information prepare a Statement of Affairs and Deficiency Account in respect of Mr. Bankrupt who filed his petition on 31-12-1986 :

(1)	Trade Creditors	65,000
(2)	Creditors Partly Secured by lien on shares	30,000
(3)	Mortgage on Building	10,000
(4)	Preferential Creditors for salaries, taxes etc.	2,000
(5)	Bills Discounted (Estimated to be dishonoured Rs. 3,000)	70,000
(6)	Book Debts : Good	20,000
	Doubtful (Estimated to produce Rs. 4,500)	3,500
	Bad	4,500
(7)	Bills of exchanges (Estimated to produce Rs. 4,500)	5,000
(8)	Stock (Estimated to realise Rs. 30,000)	38,000
(9)	Shares (Estimated to produce Rs. 12,000)	17,000
(10)	Cash at Bank	1,000
(11)	Building (Estimated to realise Rs. 16,000)	18,000
(12)	Machinery (Estimated to produce Rs. 4,000)	6,000
(13)	Furniture (Estimated at Rs. 1,500)	4,000
(14)	Loss on speculation	12,000

On 1-1-1982 he had a Capital of Rs. 40,000

The business resulted in a Profit of Rs. 25,000 in the first three years and a Loss of Rs. 14,000 in the last two years after allowing Rs. 2,000 for interest on Capital each year. The Total withdrawals amounted to Rs. 39,000 during the above period.

(K.U.D., April 1987)

Solution :

Working Note

I. *Unsecured Creditors* List-A		II. *Fully Secured Creditors* List-B	
Trade Creditors	65,000	Mortage on Building	10,000
Bills Discounted likely to be dishonoured	3,000	Securities	16,000
	68,000	Surplus	6,000
Pref. Creditors	2,000	Security Bank value	18,000
		Estimated to Realise	16,000
		Loss	2,000

III. *Partly Secured Creditors*

Shares	17,000	
	12,000	
	5,000	Loss

Statement of Affairs

Liabilities	Rs.	Expected to Rank Rs.	Property & Assets	Book value Rs.	Estimated to produce Rs.
I. *Unsecured Creditors*			Property List-E		
List-A			Cash at Bank	1,000	1,000
Trade Creditors	65,000		Stock	38,000	30,000
Bills Discounted likely			Machinery	6,000	4,000
to be dishonoured	3,000	68,000	Furniture	4,000	1,500
II. *Fully Secured Creditors*					36,500
List-B	10,000		*Book Debts List-F*		
(Mortage on Building)			Good	20,000	20,000
Securities	16,000		Doubtful	3,500	1,000
			Bad	4.500	—
Surplus per contra	6,000			28,000	57,500
III. *Partly Secured Creditors*					
List-C	30,000		Bills of Exchange-G	5,000	4,500
			Total Amount		62,000
Lien on shares	12,000	18,000	Surplus per contra		6,000
IV. *Preferential Creditors*			Total Amount		68,000
			Pref. Creditors		
List-D	2,000		*deducted* per contra		2,000
Salaries and wages			Total Estimated		
deducted per contra	—		amount available		66,000
			Deficiency as per List-H		20,000
		86,000			86,000

Deficiency A/c List-H

Excess of Assets over Liabilities	Rs.	Excess of Liabilities over Assets	Rs.	Rs.
Capital	40,000	Business Loss		14,000
Income from Business (Profit)	25,000	Loss in Speculation		12,000
		Withdrawals		39,000
Interest on Capital 2,000 × 5	10,000	*Loss on Realisation*		
Income from other source		Stock (38,000–30,000)	8,000	
		Machinery (6,000–4,000)	2,000	
		Furniture (4,000–1,500)	2,500	
Deficiency as per Statement of Affairs	20,000	Book Debts (28,000–21,000)	7,000	
		Bills of exchange (5,000—4,500)	500	
		Building (18,000–16,000)	2,000	
		Shares (17,000–12,000)	5,000	27,000
		Bills Discounted likely to be dishonoured		3,000
	95,000			95,000

Problem No. 23

From the following particulars of Mr. Prabha, who filed a petition of Bankruptcy, request you to prepare a Statement of Affairs and Diffciency A/c as on 31-12-1984 :

(1)	Cash	550
(2)	Stock (Estimated to produce Rs. 20,450)	30,950
(3)	Bills Receivable (Estimated to produce Rs. 7,000)	9,000
(4)	Sundry Debtors :	
	Good	5,000
	Doubtful Debts (Estimated to realise Rs. 18,000)	30,000
	Bad	15,000
(5)	Shares in 'X Ltd.' (Estimated to produce Rs. 15,000)	25,000
(6)	Creditors holding first charge on the shares of R Ltd.	35,000
(7)	Creditors holding second charge on the shares of R Ltd. (to the extent of Rs. 25,000)	30,000
(8)	Shares in R Ltd. (Estimated to produce Rs. 70,000)	86,500
(9)	Creditors for Rent, taxes etc. (of which Rs. 4,600 were preferential)	5,000
(10)	Furniture (Estimated to produce Rs. 3,000)	15,000
(11)	Bills payable	4,000
(12)	Loss in Horse Race	2,000
(13)	Creditors — Unsecured	80,600

Mr. Prabhu started business with Capital of Rs. 70,000 and the business showed a Profit of Rs. 8,000 and Rs. 10,900 for the first two years and a Loss of Rs. 5,000 for the Third year after allowing Rs. 3,500 as interest on Capital each year.

Drawings during 3 years period amounted for Rs. 30,000.

(K.U.D., April 1986)

Solution :

Statement of Affairs as on 31-12-1985

Liabilities	Rs.	Expected to Rank Rs.	Property & Assets	Book value Rs.	Estimated to realise Rs.
I. *Unsecured Creditors*			*Property List-E*		
List-A			Cash	550	550
Creditors Unsecured	80,600		Stock	30,950	20,450
Bills Payable	4,000		Shares in X Ltd.	25,000	15,000
Creditors for Rent,			Furnitures	15,000	3,000
Tax etc. 5,000			Total Property		39,000
Less : Pref. 4,600	400		*Book Debts List-F*		
Excess of Pref. Limit		85,000	Good	5,000	5,000
II. *Fully Secured Creditors*			Doubtful	30,000	18,000
List-B	35,000		Bad	15,000	—
Securities Shares					62,000
in R Ltd.	70,000		Bills of Exchange		
Surplus	35,000		List-G	9,000	7,000
Transfer to List-C	25,000		Total Estimated Amount		69,000
Surplus per contra	10,000		*Add* : Surplus per contra		10,000
III. *Partly Secured Creditors*			Total Estimated amount available		79,000
List-C	30,000		*Deduct* Preferential creditors per contra		4,600
Security transfer from List-B	25,000	5,000	Total Estimated Amount available for distribution		74,400
IV. *Preferential Creditors*			Deficiency as per		
List-D	4,600		List-H		15,600
(5,000—4,600)					
Deducted per contra	—				
		90,000			90,000

Deficiency Account List-H

Excess of Assets over Liabilities	Rs.	Rs.	Excess of Liabilities over Assets	Rs.	Rs.
Capital		70,000	Business Loss		5,000
Net Profit			Loss in Horse Race		2,000
I Year	8,000		Withdrawals		30,000
II Year	10,900	18,900	*Loss on Realisation*		
Interest on Capital		10,500	Stock	10,500	
3,500 × 3			Shares in 'X' Ltd.	10,000	
Deficiency as per			Furniture	12,000	
Statement of Affairs		15,600	Shares in 'R' Ltd.	15,000	
			Book Debts	27,000	
			Bills Receivable	2,000	76,500
		1,15,000			1,15,000

Problem No. 24

Mr. Mohan who facing financial difficulties in payment of outside liabilities, files a petition of Insolvency from the following particulars :

Prepare :

(a) Statement of Affairs and (b) Deficiency Account as on 30-6-1985.

(1)	Capital		28,500
(2)	Liabilities — Trade Creditors		35,500
(3)	Bills payable		27,000
(4)	Mrs. Shaila Mohan		4,500
(5)	Bank Overdraft		11,000
(6)	Book Debts : Good	15,000	
	Doubtful (50% Realisable)	18,000	
	Bad	17,000	
(7)	Duplication Machinery (Estimated to realise Rs. 2,200)	8,500	
(8)	Stock (Estimated to realise Rs. 20,500)	45,000	
(9)	Cash	3,000	
		1,06,500	1,06,500

Other Information

(1) Liabilities on Bills discounted Rs. 4,500 of which it is likely to be dishonoured Rs. 1,800.

(2) The amount due to Mrs. Shaila Mohan was a Loan out of money given to her by Mr. Mohan.

(3) The Household furniture valued @ Rs. 4,250. He owned a House

property valued @ Rs. 25,000 and had taken loan by mortgaging the House for Rs. 20,000.

(4) Preferential Creditors (Included in trade Creditors) amount to Rs. 850 towards taxes, Rs. 250 towards salary and Rs. 120 towards Rent.

(K.U.D., October 1986)

Working Note

Secured Creditors			*Preferential Creditors List D*		
List-A			Taxes	850	
Trade Creditors		35,500	Salaries	250	
Less Preferential Credit			Rent	120	1,220
for Taxes	850		*Private Assets*		
Salaries	250		House Property		25,000
Rent	120	1,220	Private loan		20,000
		34,280	Surplus from Home property		5,000
Bills Payable		27,000	Household furniture		4,250
Bills discounted		1,800			
Bank Overdraft		11,000			
		74,080			

Note : Mrs. Shaila Mohan loan amount is not Streedhan it was given by her husband and taken on Defficiency account left-side.

Solution :

Statement of Affairs

Liabilities	Rs.	Expected to Rank Rs.	Property & Assets	Book value Rs.	Estimated to realise Rs.
I. *Unsecured Creditors*			*Property List-E*		
List-A		74,080	Cash	3,000	3,000
II. *Fully Secured Creditors*			Stock	45,000	20,500
List-B	—		Duplication Machine	8,500	2,200
Securities	—		Household furniture	—	4,250
Surplus	—		Surplus from House property		5,000
III. *Partly Secured Creditors*			Total Property		34,950
List-C	—		*Book Debts List-F*		
Securities	—	—	Good	15,000	15,000
			Doubtful 50%	18,000	9,000
IV. *Preferential Creditors*			Bad	17,000	—
List-D	1,220				58,950
Deducted per contra	—		Bills of Exchange List-G		—
			Total Amount		58,950
			Surplus per contra		—
			Total Estimated amount		58,950
			Deducted Preferential Creditors (per contra)		1,220
					57,730
			Deficiency per contra		16,350
		74,080			74,080

Deficiency Account List-H

Excess of Assets over Liabilities	Rs.	Rs.	Excess of Liabilities over Assets	Rs.	Rs.
Capital		28,500	Business Loss		—
Income from Business		—	Withdrawals		—
Net Profit			*Loss on Realisation*		
Interest on Capital		—	Stock	24,500	
Income from Other source			Duplicating machine	6,300	
Household Furniture	4,250		Book Debts	26,000	
Surplus from Private			(9,000 + 17,000)		
House property	5,000	9,250		56,800	
Mrs. Shaila Loan A/c		4,500	Bills Discounted	1,800	58,600
Deficiency as per					
Statement of Affairs		16,350			
		58,600			58,600

Problem No. 25

Mr. Desai has become Insolvent on 31-12-1984. He supplies the following information as on the above date :

(1)	Sundry Creditors	60,000
(2)	Salary due to a Clerk	800
(3)	Taxes owing to Govt.	2,400
(4)	Bank Loans secured on stock of the books value of Rs. 40,000	20,000
(5)	Cash in hand	200
(6)	Furniture (Estimated to realise Rs. 4,000)	8,000
(7)	Stock (Expected to realise @ 60%)	60,000
(8)	Book Debts : Good	8,000
	Doubtful (Expected to realise 40%)	20,000
(9)	Bills Receivable (of which Rs. 6,000 bad)	10,000
(10)	Bills Discounted (of which Rs. 4,000 bad)	12,000
(11)	Loan from Smt. Desai	20,000

Mr. Desai commenced business on 1-1-1979 with a Capital of Rs. 50,000.

His drawings per year amounted to Rs. 10,000.

He did not maintain proper books of account.

Smt. Desai gave her Jewellery valued @ Rs. 8,000 to the receiver.

Prepare Statement of Affairs and Deficiency A/c.

(K.U.D., April 1980 & Gulbarga, April 1985)

Solution :

Balance Sheet as at 31-12-1984

Liabilities		Rs.	Assets	Rs.
Sundry Creditors		60,000	Cash in Hand	200
Outstanding Liabilities			Furniture	8,000
Salary	800		Stock	60,000
Taxes due to Govt.	2,400	3,200	Book Debts (8,000 + 20,000)	28,000
Bank Loan (secured on stock of Bank value of Rs. 40,000)		20,000	Bills Receivable	10,000
Loan from Smt. Desai		20,000	Drawings (6 years @ Rs. 10,000 per annum 6 × 10,000)	60,000
Capital		50,000		
Net Profit (Balancing figure)		13,000		
		1,66,200		1,66,200

Note : To Ascertain Business Profit or Loss. Balance Sheet is prepared now. Business Net Profit being Balancing figure.

Statement of Affairs as on 31-12-1984

Liabilities	Rs.	Expected to Rank Rs.	Property & Assets		Book value Rs.	Estimated to realise Rs.
I. *Unsecured Creditors*			*Property List-E*			
List-A			Cash		200	200
Sundry Creditors	60,000		Furniture		8,000	4,000
Bills Discounted likely to be dishonoured	4,000		Stock	60,000		
			Less : Transfer to secured crs. @ 60%	40,000	20,000	12,000
Loan from Smt. Desai	20,000		Jewellery			8,000
Excess of Pref. limit Salary to clerk (800—300)	500	84,500				24,200

Liabilities	Rs.	Expected to Rank Rs.	Property & Assets	Book value Rs.	Estimated to realise Rs.
II. *Fully Secured Creditors*			*Book Debts List-F*		
List-B	20,000		Good	8,000	8,000
Bank Loan			Doubtful	20,000	8,000
Security stock			Bad	—	—
40,000 @ 60%	24,000				40,200
Surplus per contra	4,000				
III. *Partly Secured Creditors*			Bills of Exchange		
			List-G	10,000	4,000
List-C	—		Total Estimated amount		44,200
Securities	—		*Add* : Surplus per contra		4,000
IV. *Preferential Creditors*			Total Estimated amount available for distribution		48,200
List-D			*Deducted* Preferential Crs.		2,700
Salary 800					45,500
Less : Transfer to Cr. 500	300		Deficiency as per List-H		39,000
Taxes to Govt.	2,400				
Deducted per contra	2,700				
		84,500			84,500

Deficiency A/c List-H

Excess of Assets over Liabilities	Rs.	Excess of Liabilities over Assets	Rs.	Rs.
Capital	50,000	Drawings		60,000
Net Profit	13,000	(10,000 × 6)		
Income from other source		*Loss on Realisation*		
Jewellery	8,000	Stock 60,000 @ 40%		24,000
Deficiency as per Statement		Furniture		4,000
of Affairs	39,000	Book Debts		12,000
		Bills Receivable		6,000
		Bills Discounted likely to be dishonoured		4,000
	1,10,000			1,10,000

Problem No. 26

Mr. A filed his petition in Bankruptcy on 31-12-1978. The information as to his position was as follows :

Creditors :	Unsecured	75,000
	Partly Secured by lien on shares	40,000
	Secured by lien as stock	100
Liability on Bills discounted (Estimated to Rank Rs. 3,500)		7,000
Mortgage on Building		10,000
Creditors Payable in full		3,000
Book Debts : Good		20,000
	Doubtful & bad (Estimated to produce Rs. 2,000)	10,000
Shares at Cost		16,000
Stock (Estimated to produce realise Rs. 40,000)		60,000
Cash at Bank		100
Bills Receivable		1,400
Machinery (Estimated to produce Rs. 17,000)		20,000
Building		17,000
Furniture (Estimated to realise Rs. 4,500)		6,500

On 1-1-1973 Mr. A had a Capital of Rs. 50,000. Profit were made in six years Rs. 20,500. After allowing interest on Capital of Rs. 10,000 and his total withdrawals amounted to Rs. 63,600.

Prepare Statement of Affairs & Deficiency A/c.

(K.U.D.)

Working Note

Unsecured Creditors		*List-B Fully Secured Creditors*	Amount	Security
List-A	75,000			
Liabilities on Bills discounted	3,500	Secured by Lien on stock	100	40,000
	78,500	Mortgage on Building	10,000	17,000
			10,100	57,000
		List-C Partly Secured		
		by lien on shares	40,000	—
		Shares at cost	—	16,000
			40,000	16,000
		List-D Preferential Creditors		
		Creditors payable in full		3,000

Solution :

Statement of Affairs as on 31-12-1978

Liabilities	Rs.	Expected to Rank Rs.	Property & Assets	Book value Rs.	Estimated to produce Rs.
I. *Unsecured Creditors*			*Property List-E*		
List-A			Cash at Bank	100	100
Unsecured Creditors	75,000		Furniture	6,500	4,500
Liabilities on			Machinery	20,000	17,000
Bills discounted	3,500	78,500	Total Property	26,600	21,600
II. *Fully Secured Creditors*			*Book Debts List-F*		
			Good	20,000	20,000
List-B	10,100		Doubtful & Bad	10,000	2,000
Securities	57,000		*Bills of Exchange*		
Surplus per contra	46,900		*List-G*		1,400
III. *Partly Secured Creditors*			Total estimated amount		45,000
List-C	40,000		*Add* : Surplus per contra		46,900
Securities	16,000	24,000			91,900
IV. *Preferential Creditors*			*Deducted* preferential		
List-B	3,000		creditors per contra		3,000
Deducted per contra	3,000	—			89,900
			Deficiency as per List-H		12,600
		1,02,500			1,02,500

Deficiency A/c as per List II

Liabilities	Rs.	Assets	Rs.	Rs.
Capital	50,000	Net Loss	—	—
Interest on Capital	10,000	Withdrawals		63,600
Profit in six years	20,500	Loss on Realisation		
Deficiency as per Statement		Machinery	3,000	
of Affairs	19,600	Furniture	2,000	
		Book Debts	8,000	
		Stock	20,000	33,000
		Bills discounted		
		likely to be dishonoured		3,500
	1,00,100			1,00,100

Problem No. 27

From the following information prepare the (1) Statement of Affairs and (2) Deficiency Accounts in respect of Mr. Insolvent who filed his petition on 31-12-1983 :

Sundry Creditors	60,000
Bills payable	15,000
Shares in Cotton Co. Ltd. (Estimated to produce of Rs. 12,000)	15,000
Shares in Sugar Co. Ltd. (Estimated to produce of Rs. 55,000)	70,000
Creditors holding first charge on Sugar Co. shares	32,000
Creditors holding second charge on Sugar Co. shares (to the extent of Rs. 8,000)	18,000
Book Debts : Good	8,000
Doubtful (Estimated to produce of Rs. 10,000)	20,000
Bad	4,000
Bills Receivable discounted (of which Rs. 4,000 likely to be dishonoured)	6,000
Creditors for salary Rent, Taxes etc. (of which Rs. 1,000 are preferential)	3,000
Furniture (Valued @ Rs. 3,000)	4,500
Cash in Hand	1,000
Stock on Trade (Estimated to produce Rs. 22,000)	32,000
Bills of Exchange (Estimated to realise Rs. 8,000)	10,000

He commenced business with a Capital of Rs. 60,000 on 1-1-1981. He made a profit of Rs. 27,000 in the first two years and incurred loss of Rs. 25,500 in the third year. His total drawings amounted of Rs. 25,000 during the period.

(K.U.D., April 1984)

Working Note

Calculations		II. *Fully Secured Creditors*	
I. *Unsecured Creditors*		Creditors holding	
List-A		first charge on Sugar Co.	
Sundry Creditors	60,000	share Security	32,000
Bills payable	15,000	Security Sugar Co. shares	
Bills receivable		(70,000 Estimated to produce)	55,000
discounted likely			23,000
to be dishonoured	4,000	Surplus Transferred	8,000
Creditors for salary, rent,		Surplus per contra	15,000
taxes etc., in excess of		III. *Party Secured Creditors*	
preferential limit		Creditors holding second	
(3,000—1,000)	2,000	charge on Sugar	
	81,000	Co. share	18,000
		Security shares	8,000
		Uncovered Balance	10,000

Solution :

Statement of Affairs as on 31-12-1983

Liabilities	Rs.	Expected to Rank Rs.	Property & Assets	Book value Rs.	Estimated to realise Rs.
I. *Unsecured Creditors*			*Property as per*		
List-A		81,000	*List-E*		
Sundry Creditors	60,000		Cash in Hand	1,000	1,000
Bills payable	15,000		Cash at Bank	—	—
Bills Receivable discounted likely to be dishonoured	4,000		Shares in Cotton Co Ltd.	15,000	12,000
Creditors for Salary taxable excess of Pref. limit	2,000		Stock in Trade	32,000	22,000
II. *Fully Secured Creditors*			Furniture	4,500	3,000
List-B	32,000		Total Property		38,000
Securities (Co. shares)	55,000		*Book Debt List-F*		
Excess	23,000		Good	8,000	8,000
Transfer to List-C	8,000		Doubtful	20,000	10,000
Surplus per contra	15,000		Bad	4,000	—
III. *Partly Secured Creditors*			*Bills of Exchange*		
List-C	18,000		*List-G*	10,000	8,000
Securities Transfer from List-B	8,000	10,000	Total Estimated amount		64,000
IV. *Preferential Creditors*			*Add* : Surplus per contra		15,000
List-D			Estimated Amount		79,000
Salary, Rent, Tax etc. (Preferential)	1,000		Preferential Creditors *Deducted* per contra		1,000
Deducted per contra	—		Estimated Amount available for distribution		78,000
			Deficiency as per List-H		13,000
		91,000			91,000

Deficiency Account

Excess of Assets over Liabilities	Rs.	Excess of Liabilities over Assets	Rs.	Rs.
Capital	60,000	Net Loss (during 1983)		25,500
Net Profit in 1981 & 1982	27,000	Drawings		25,000
Deficiency as per Statment of Affairs	13,000	*Loss on Realisation of Assets*		
		Shares in Cotton Co. (15,000–12,000)	3,000	
		Shares in Sugar Co. Ltd. (70,000–55,000)	15,000	
		Stock : 32,000–22,000	10,000	
		Furniture (4,500–3,000)	1,500	
		Bad Debts	14,000	
		Bills of Exchange (10,000–8,000)	2,000	45,500
		Bills Discounted likely to be dishonoured		4,000
	1,00,000			1,00,000

Problem No. 28

Mr. Reckless of Bangalore filed his petition for insolvency on 1-1-1981 when his Assets & Liabilities, as per Books of Account amounted to Rs. 45,000 and Rs. 33,500 respectively.

He estimated his deficiency to be Rs. 10,000. Subsequently he found that the following had not taken into account while estimating the deficiency :

(1) Interest on Capital @ 6% on Rs. 20,000.

(2) Liabilities on Bills discounted amounting to Rs. 5,000 of which Rs. 1,500 worth bills were expected to be dishonoured.

(3) Salaries of four clerks Rs. 700 and wages of Ten Labourers of Rs. 250 and Rent of three months amounting to Rs. 225 were due to the landlord.

Prepare revised Statement of Affairs and Deficiency A/c.

(K.U.D., April 1982)

Solution :

Balance Sheet as on 31-12-1981

Liabilities	Rs.	Assets	Rs.
Sundry Liabilities	33,500	Sundry Assets	45,000
Capital	20,000	Profit & Loss (Debit Balance) (Balancing figure)	8,500
	53,500		53,500

Unsecured Creditors

Sundry Creditors			33,500
Liabilities on Bills discounted			1,500
Creditors for			895
Salaries (4 × 20)	700	80	
Wages 10 × 20	250	200	
Rent	225	—	
	1,175	280	
Less : Pref. limit	280		
	895		

Excess of Pref.	700
	250
	225
Total	1,175
Less : Pref. Excess of Pref. Limit	280
Treat Unsecured	895

Preferential Creditors List-D

Business place at Bangalore

∴ Provincial Insolvency Act of 1920 applies.

Preferential Limit

Salaries & Wages Rs. 20 each or 3 months whichever is less.

Rent to Landlord Not Preferential

Now Preferential Creditors List-D

Salaries (4 × 20)	80
Wages (10 × 20)	200
Rent	—
	280

Revised Statement of Affairs as on 31-12-81

Liabilities	Rs.	Expected to Rank Rs.	Property & Assets	Book value Rs.	Estimated to realise Rs.
I. *Unsecured Creditors*			*Property List-E*		
List-A	33,500		Sundry Assets	45,000	23,500
Bills Discounted			*Book Debts List-F*		—
likely to be			Bills of Exchange		
dishonoured	1,500		List-G		—
Excess of Preferential	895	35,895	Total Estimated amount		23,500
Salaries 620			Surplus per contra		—
Wages 50			Total Estimated amount		23,500
Rent 225			*Deducted* Preferential Creditor		
			per contra		280
II. *Fully Secured Creditors*			Total Estimated Amount		
List-B	—		available		23,220
Securities	—		Deficiency as per		
Surplus	—		List-H		12,675
III. *Partly Secured*					
List-C	—				
Securities	—				
IV. *Preferential Creditors*					
List-D					
Salaries (4 × 20)	80				
Wages 10 × 20	200				
Rent	—				
Deducted per contra	280				
		35,895			38,895

Deficiency Account List-H

Excess of Assets over Liabilities	Rs.	Excess of Liabilities over Assets		Rs.
Capital	20,000	Business Loss		8,500
Investment on Capital @ 6% 20,000	1,200	*Loss on Realisation* (45,000 — 23,500)		21,500
Deficiency as per Statement of Affairs	12,675	Liabilities on Bills Discounted		1,500
		Interest on Capital		
		Salaries	700	
		Wages	250	
		Rent	225	1,175
	33,875			33,875

Problem No. 29

Mr. Ashok a businessman, become insolvent on 1-1-1982 on which date his total Assets were Rs. 75,000 and the Liabilities Rs. 65,000 and he estimated his deficiency of Rs. 20,000 before taking the following items into consideration which were not passed through his books of Accounts :

(1) Interest on Captital of Rs. 25,000 @ 6% for one year.

(2) A contingent Liability for Rs. 3,000 on Bills Discounted by him Rs. 8,000.

(3) Amount due as wages Rs. 300, as salaries Rs. 600, as rent Rs. 500, as rates & taxes Rs. 1,000.

(4) A loan of Rs. 5,000 taken from a friend for the marriage of his daughter and Rs. 2,000 from his wife.

Prepare a Statement of Affairs and Deficiency A/c.

Solution :

I. *Unsecured Creditors List-A*		Total Liabilities	65,000
Liabilities	65,000	*Less* : Deficiency	20,000
Liabilities on Bills Discounted	3,000	Assets Realised	45,000
Loan from Friend	5,000	Total Assets	75,000
Loan from his wife	2,000	*Less* : Assets realised	45,000
	75,000	Loss on Realisation of Assets	30,000
II. *Preferential Creditors*			
Wages	300		
Salaries	600		
Rent	500		
Rates & Taxes	1,000		
	2,400		

Balance Sheet as at 1-1-1982

Liabilities	Rs.	Assets	Rs.
Liabilities	65,000	Sundry Assets	75,000
Capital	25,000	Business Loss (Balancing figure)	15,000
	90,000		90,000

Revised Statement of Affairs as on 1-1-1982

Liabilities	Rs.	Expected to Rank Rs.	Property & Assets	Book value Rs.	Estimated to realise Rs.
I. *Unsecured Creditors List-A*			*Property List-E*		
			Sundry Assets	75,000	45,000
Liabilities	65,000				45,000
Liabilities on bills discounted	3,000		Book Debts List-F		—
Friend's Loan	5,000				45,000
Mrs. Loan	2,000	75,000	*Bills of Exchange List-G*		—
II. *Fully Secured Creditors*			Total Estimated Amount		45,000
List-B	—		*Add* : Surplus		—
Securities	—		Total Estimated Amount		45,000
Surplus	—				

Liabilities	Rs.	Expected to Rank Rs.	Property & Assets	Book value Rs.	Estimated to realise Rs.
III. *Partly Secured Creditors*					45,000
List-C	—		*Deducted* Preferential creditors per contra		2,400
Securities	—		Total Estimated Amount available		42,600
IV. *Preferential Creditors*			Deficiency as per List-H		32,400
List-D					
Wages 300					
Salary 600					
Rent 500					
Rate & Tax 1,000	2,400				
		75,000			75,000

Deficiency Account List-H

Excess of Assets over Liabilities	Rs.	Excess of Liabilities over Assets		Rs.
Capital	25,000	Business		15,000
Interest on Capital @ 6% on 25,000	1,500	Loss on realisation of Assets		30,000
Deficiency as per Statement of Affairs	32,400	Interest on Capital	1,500	
		Liabilities on Bills discounted	3,000	
		Wages, salary, rent, rates, taxes etc.	2,400	
		Private Loan (5,000 + 2,000)	7,000	13,900
	58,900			58,900

Problem No. 30

Mr. A filed his petition in Insolvency on 31-12-1978. The information as to his position was as follows :

1.	Creditors — Unsecured	75,000
2.	Creditors partly secured by lien on shares	40,000
3.	Fully secured creditors by lien on stock	100
4.	Liabilities on Bills discounted (Estimated to rank 3,500)	7,000
5.	Mortgage on Building	10,000
6.	Creditors payable in full	3,000
7.	Book Debts : Good	20,000
	Doubtful (Estimated to produce Rs. 2,000)	10,000
8.	Stock (Estimated to produce Rs. 40,000)	65,000
9.	Shares at Cost	16,000
10.	Cash at Bank	100
11.	Bills Receivable	1,400
12.	Building	11,000
13.	Machinery (Estimated to produce Rs. 12,000)	15,000
14.	Furnitures (Estimated to produce Rs. 4,500)	6,500

On 1-1-1973 Mr. A had a Capital of Rs. 50,000 his Profit for Six years were Rs. 20,500 after allowing interest on Capital Rs. 10,000 and withdrawals during the period were Rs. 63,600.

Prepare : (a) Statement of Affairs

(b) Deficiency Account.

(K.U.D., October 1979)

Solution :

Note : Unsecured Creditors

List-A	75,000	Fully Secured Creditors		
Bills discounted		List-B		Amount Secured
likely to be dishonoured	3,500	Secured by lien		
	78,500	on stock	100	40,000
		Mortgage on Building	10,000	11,000
			10,100	51,000
		Surplus	40,900	
		Partly Secured Creditors :		
		Partly Secured on shares	40,000	16,000
		Estimated to Rank		24,000

Statement of Affairs

Liabilities	Rs.	Expected to Rank Rs.	Property & Assets	Book value Rs.	Estimated to Rank Rs.
I. *Unsecured Creditors*			*Property List-E*		
List-A		78,500	Cash at Bank	100	100
II. *Fully Secured Crs.*			Furnitures	6,500	4,500
List-B	10,100		Machinery	15,000	12,000
					16,600
Securities	51,000		*Book Debts List-F*		
Surplus (per contra)	40,900		Good	20,000	20,000
III. *Partly Secured Creditors*			Doubtful	10,000	2,000
			Bills of Exchange List-G	1,400	1,400
List-C	40,000				
Securities	16,000	24,000	Total Estimated Amount		40,000
IV. *Preferential Creditors*			*Add* : Surplus per contra		40,900
List-D	3,000		Total Estimated amount		80,900
(*deducted* per contra)			Deducted per contra		3,000
			Total Estimated Amount		77,900
			Deficiency List-H		24,600
		1,02,500			1,02,500

Deficiency A/c List-H

Excess of Assets over Liabilities	Rs.	Excess of Liabilities over Assets	Rs.	Rs.
Capital	50,000	Net Loss		
Interest on Capital	10,000	Withdrawals		63,600
Income from Business		*Loss on Realisation*		
Profit for 6 years	20,500	Furniture	2,000	
		Machinery	3,000	
		Stock	25,000	
Deficiency as per Statement of Affairs	24,600	Book Debts	8,000	38,000
		Liabilities on Bills Discounted		3,500
Total	1,05,100	Total		1,05,100

7

Self Balancing Ledger

In a large scale business organisation where large number of credit sales and credit purchase transactions are done. Accordingly number of Debtors Accounts and Creditors Accounts are opened. The Trial Balance prepared. In such cases to identify the errors in trial balance becomes difficult and time consuming. So, the origination prefers to maintain Self Balancing Ledger.

Self Balancing Ledgers. Under this system periodical say quarterly or half yearly Trial Balance is prepared. This helps to locate errors existing and are immediately corrected.

Under Self Balancing ledger systems three Ledgers are maintained namely :

(1) Debtors ledger

(2) Creditors ledger

(3) General ledger or Nominal ledger.

Further to complete the double entry principle in each of the ledger, the adjustment ledger Accounts are opened that is :

(a) In Debtors Ledger — General Ledger Adjustment A/c

(b) In Creditors Ledger — General Ledger Adjustment A/c

(c) In General Ledger :

(i) Debtors Ledger Adjustment A/c

(ii) Creditors Ledger Adjustment A/c

Now let us observe the operations of various ledger Adjustment Accounts in respective ledger maintained as above under Self Balancing system.

Example No. 1

Recording of transactions of credit sales and credit purchases under balancing system.

(1)	Sales (Only Credit)	2,50,000
(2)	Purchase (Only Credit)	1,50,000
(3)	Sales Returns	1,250
(4)	Purchase Returns	875
(5)	Cash received from customer (Debtors)	1,50,000
(6)	Bills receivable received	50,000

(7)	Discount allowed to customers	1,500
(8)	Bills receivable received endorsed to creditors	10,000
(9)	Bills receivable discounted	15,000
(10)	Bills receivable endorsed dishonoured	4,500
(11)	Bills receivable discounted dishonoured	6,500
(12)	Noting charges debtors to debtors	125
(13)	Bank charges debited to debtors	85
(14)	Cash paid to creditors	85,000
(15)	Bills payable accepted	20,000
(16)	Discount received from creditors	1,250
(17)	Bad debts written off	2,000
(18)	Provision for doubtful debts	2,750
(19)	Bad debts previously written off now recovered	950
(20)	Transfers from debtors ledger to creditors ledger	3,000
(21)	Transfer from creditors ledger to debtors ledger	2,500

The Journal entries of the above transactions in original form as usual and the entries under Self Balancing system are given below :

Journal Entries

			Dr. Rs.	Cr. Rs.
(1) Original	Debtors Accounts	Dr.	2,50,000	
	To Sales A/c			2,50,000
	(Credit sales to customers)			
Under Self Balancing	(a) Debtors Ledger A/c	Dr.	2,50,000	
	To General Ledger			2,50,000
	(Transfer entry to ledger)			
	(b) Debtors Ledger Adjustment A/c	Dr.	2,50,000	
	(in General Ledger)			
	To General Ledger Adjustment A/c Dr.			2,50,000
	(in Debtors Ledger)			
	(Being entry for Self Balancing)			
(2) Original	Purchases A/c	Dr.	1,50,000	
	To Creditors A/c			1,50,000
	(Credit purchases made)			
Under Self Balancing	(a) General Ledger A/c	Dr.	1,50,000	
	To Creditors Ledger A/c			1,50,000
	(Transfer entry to ledger)			
	(b) General Ledger Adjustment A/c	Dr.	1,50,000	
	(in Creditors Ledger)			
	To Creditors Ledger Adjustment A/c			
	(in General Ledger)			1,50,000
	(Being entry Self Balancing)			

		Dr. Rs.	Cr. Rs.
(3) Original	Sales Returns A/c Dr.	1,250	
	To Debtors A/c		1,250
	(Being sales returns)		
Under Self Balancing	(a) General Ledger A/c Dr.	1,250	
	To Debtors Ledger A/c		1,250
	(Transfer entry to Ledger)		
	(b) General Ledger Adjustment A/c Dr. (in debtors Ledger)	1,250	
	To Debtors Adjustment A/c (in General Ledger)		1,250
	(Being entry for Self Balancing)		
(4) Original	Creditors A/c Dr	875	
	To Purchase Return A/c		875
	(Being purchase return)		
Under Self Balancing	(a) Creditors Ledger A/c Dr	875	
	To General Ledger		875
	(Transfer entry to ledger)		
	(b) Creditors Ledger Adjustment A/c Dr. (in General Ledger)	875	
	To General Ledger Adjustment A/c		875
	(Entry for Self Balancing)		
(5) Original	Cash A/c Dr	1,50,000	
	To Debtors A/c		1,50,000
	(Being cash received)		
Under Self Balancing	(a) General Ledger A/c Dr	1,50,000	
	To Debtors Ledger A/c		1,50,000
	(Transfer entry to ledgers)		
	(b) General Ledger Adjustment A/c Dr (in Debtors Ledger)	1,50,000	
	To Debtors Ledger Adjustment A/c (in General Ledger)		1,50,000
	(Entry for Self Balancing)		
(6) Original	Bills Receivable A/c Dr	50,000	
	To Debtors A/c	50,000	
	(Being Bills receivable received)		
Under Self Balancing	(a) General Ledger Adjustment A/c Dr (in Debtors Ledger)	50,000	
	To Debtors Ledger Adjustment A/c (in General Ledger)		50,000
	(Being entry Self Balancing)		

		Dr. Rs.	Cr. Rs.
	(b) General Ledger A/c Dr	50,000	
	(in Debtors Ledger)		
	To Debtors Ledger A/c		50,000
	(Transfer entry to ledger)		
(7) Original	Discount Allowed A/c Dr	1,500	
	To Debtors A/c		1,500
	(Being discount allowed to customers)		
Under Self Balancing	(a) General Ledger A/c Dr	1,500	
	To Debtors Ledger A/c		1,500
	(Transfer entry to ledger)		
	(b) General Ledger Adjustment A/c Dr	1,500	
	(in Debtors Ledger)		
	To Debtors Ledger Adjustment A/c		1,500
	(in General Ledger)		
	(Entry for Self Balancing)		
(8) Original	Creditors A/c Dr	10,000	
	To Bills Receivable A/c		10,000
	(Bills Receivable endorsed to creditors)		
Under Self Balancing	(a) Creditors Ledger A/c Dr	10,000	
	To General Ledger A/c		10,000
	(Transfer entry to ledger)		
	(b) Creditors Ledger Adjustment A/c Dr	10,000	
	(in General Ledger)		
	To General Ledger Adjustment A/c		10,000
	(Entry for Self Balancing)		
(9) Original	(a) Cash (Bank) A/c Dr	1,500	
	To Bills Receivable A/c		1,500
	(Bills Receivable discounted and Cash received)		
	(b) The above entry does not affect to Debtors. Therefore it is omitted in Self Balancing system.		
(10) Original	(a) Bills Receivable A/c Dr	4,500	
	To Creditors A/c		4,500
	(Bills Receivable endorsed to creditors dishonoured)		
	(b) Debtors A/c Dr	4,500	
	To Bills Receivable A/c		4,500
	(Bills receivable endorsed to creditor dishonoured and reverse entry passed)		
Under Self Balancing	The above entry (A) affects the Creditors Ledger and entry (B) affects the Debtors Ledger.		
(A)	(a) General Ledger A/c Dr	4,500	
	To Creditors Ledger		4,500
	(Transfer entry to Ledger)		

			Dr. Rs.	Cr. Rs.
	(b) General Ledger Adjustment (in Creditors Ledger)	A/c Dr	4,500	
	To Creditors Ledger Adjustment (in General Ledger)	A/c		4,500
	(Being entry for Self Balancing)			
(B)	(a) Debtors Ledger	A/c Dr	4,500	
	To Bills Receivable	A/c		4,500
	(Transfere entry to ledger)			
	(b) Debtors Ledger Adjustment (in General Ledger)	A/c Dr	4,500	
	To General Ledger Adjustment (in Debtors Ledger)	A/c		4,500
	(Being entry for Self Balancing)			
(11) Original	Debtors	A/c Dr	6,500	
	To Bills Receivable	A/c		6,500
	(Bills Receivable discounted dishonoured now original entry on Bills Receivable-reversed)			
Under Self Balancing	(a) Debtors Ledger	A/c Dr	6,500	
	To General Ledger	A/c		6,500
	(Transfer entry to ledger)			
	(b) Debtors Ledger Adjustment (in General Ledger)	A/c Dr	6,500	
	To General Ledger Adjustment (in Debtors Ledger A/c)	A/c		6,500
	(Being entry for Self Balancing)			
(12) Original	Debtors	A/c Dr	125	
	To Noting Charges	A/c		125
	(Noting Charges paid debited to Debtors)			
Under Self Balancing	(a) Debtors Ledger	A/c Dr	125	
	To General Ledger	A/c		125
	(Transfer entry to ledger)			
	(b) Debtors Ledger Adjustment (in General Ledger)	A/c Dr	125	
	To General Ledger Adjustment (in Debtors Ledger A/c)	A/c		125
	(Being entry for Self Balancing)			
(13) Original	Debtors	A/c Dr	85	
	To Bank Charges	A/c		85
	(Bank Charges debited to Debtors A/c)			
Under Self Balancing	(a) Debtors Ledger	A/c Dr	85	
	To General Ledger	A/c		85
	(Transfer entry to ledger)			

			Dr. Rs.	Cr. Rs.
	(b) Debtors Ledger Adjustment (in General Ledger)	A/c Dr	85	
	To General Ledger Adjustment (in Debtors Ledger)	A/c		85
	(Being entry for Self Balancing)			
(14) Original	Creditors	A/c Dr	85,000	
	To Bank	A/c		85,000
	(Cash paid to Creditors)			
Under Self Balancing	(a) Creditors Ledger	A/c Dr	85,000	
	To General Ledger	A/c		85,000
	(Transfer entry to ledger)			
	(b) Creditors Ledger Adjustment (in General Ledger)	A/c Dr	85,000	
	To General Ledger Adjustment	A/c		85,000
	(Being entry for Self Balancing)			
(15) Original	Creditors	A/c Dr	20,000	
	To Bills Payable	A/c		20,000
	(Bills Payable accepted in favour of Creditor)			
Under Self Balancing	(a) Creditors Ledger	A/c Dr	20,000	
	To General Ledger	A/c		20,000
	(Transfer entry to ledger)			
	(b) Creditors Ledger Adjustment (in General Ledger)	A/c Dr	20,000	
	To General Ledger Adjustment (in Creditors Ledger)	A/c		20,000
	(Being entry for Self Balancing)			
(16) Original	Creditor	A/c Dr	1,250	
	To Discount Received	A/c		1,250
	(Being Discount received from Creditors)			
Under Self Balancing	(a) Creditors Ledger	A/c Dr	1,250	
	To General Ledger	A/c		1,250
	(Being transfer entry to ledger)			
	(b) Creditors Ledger Adjustment	A/c	1,250	
	To General Ledger Adjustment (in Creditors Ledger)	A/c		1,250
	(Being entry for Self Balancing)			
(17)	Bad Debts	A/c Dr	2,000	
	To Debtors	A/c		2,000
	(Bad Debts written off)			

			Dr. Rs.	Cr. Rs.
Under Self Balancing	(a) General Ledger	A/c Dr	2,000	
	To Debtors Ledger	A/c		2,000
	(Being transfer entry to ledger)			
	(b) General Ledger Adjustment (in Debtors Ledger)	A/c Dr	2,000	
	To Debtors Ledger Adjustment (in General Ledger)	A/c		2,000
	(Being entry for Self Balancing)			
(18) Original	Profit & Loss	A/c Dr	2,000	
	To Provision for Doubtful debtors	A/c		2,000
	(Being Provision for Doubtful Debts)			
(*Note* :	The above entry does not affect Debtors Account. Therefore their item should not be considered in Self Balancing system and therefore it is omitted.)			
(19) Original	Cash	A/c Dr	950	
	To Bad debts previously	A/c		950
	(Being bad debts previously written off now recovered)			
(*Note* :	The above entry does not affect Debtors Account. Therefore this item should not be considered in Self Balancing system and therefore it is omitted.)			
(20) Original	(i) Creditors	A/c Dr	3,000	
	To Debtors	A/c		3,000
	(Transfer of Balances from Creditors A/c to Debtors A/c)			
	(ii) Creditors	A/c Dr	2,500	
	To Debtors	A/c		2,500
	(Transfer of Balances from Creditors A/c to Debtors A/c)			
Under Self Balancing	(a) Creditors Ledger	A/c Dr	5,500	
	To Debtors Ledger	A/c		5,500
	[The Combined entry of transfer to ledger (3,000 + 2,500 = 5,500)]			
	(b) Creditors Ledger Adjustment (in General Ledger)	A/c	5,500	
	To General Ledger Adjustment (in Creditors Ledger)	A/c		5,500
	(Being entry for Self Balancing)			

		Dr. Rs.	Cr. Rs.
(c) General Ledger Adjustment (in Debtors Ledger)	A/c Dr	5,500	
To Debtors Ledger Adjustment (in General Ledger)	A/c		5,500
(Being entry for Self Balancing)			

Posting of the above entries into Ledger Accounts (Original Ledger A/c)

Debtors A/c

Particulars	Amount Rs.	Particulars	Amount Rs.
To Sales Creditors	2,50,000	By Sales Returns	1,250
To Bills Receivable endorsed		By Cash Receivable	1,50,000
to creditors honoured	4,500	By Bills Receivable	50,000
To Bills Receivable discounted		By Discount allowed	1,500
dishonoured	6,500	By Bad Debts written off	2,000
To Noting Charges	125	By Transfer (3,000 + 2,500)	5,500
To Bank Charges	85	By Balance c/d	50,960
	2,61,210		2,61,210

Creditors A/c

To Purchase Returns	875	By Purchase (Credit)	1,50,000
To Bills Receivable endorsed	10,000	By Bills Receivable endorsed dishonoured	4,500
To Cash paid	85,000		
To Bills payable	20,000		
To Discount Received	2,500		
To Transfers	5,500		
To Balance c/d	30,625		
	1,54,500		1,54,500

Under Self Balancing system the main ledgers are :

(1) Debtors Ledger (2) Creditors Ledger (3) General Ledger.

Debtors Ledger

Particulars	Amount Rs.	Particulars	Amount Rs.
To General Ledger		*By General Ledger*	
Sales	2,50,000	Sales Returns	1,250
Bills Receivable endorsed creditors dishonoured	4,500	Cash Received	1,50,000
		Bills Receivable	50,000
Bills Receivable Dishonoured	6,500	Discount allowed	1,500
Noting Charges	125	Bad Debts written off	2,000
Bank Charges	85	Transfers (3,000 + 2,500)	5,500
		By Balance c/d	50,960
	2,61,210		2,61,210

Creditors Ledger

Particulars	Amount Rs.	Particulars	Amount Rs.
To General Ledger A/c		*By General Ledger*	
Purchase Returns	875	Purchase	1,50,000
Bills Receivable endorsed	10,000	Bills Receivable endorsed dishonoured	4,500
Cash paid	85,000		
Bills payable accepted	20,000		
Discount received	2,500		
Transfer (3,000 + 2,500)	5,500		
To Balance c/d	30,625		
	1,54,500		1,54,500

General Ledger

Particulars	Amount Rs.	Particulars	Amount Rs.
To Debtors Ledger		*By Debtors Ledger*	
Sales Returns	1,250	Sales	2,50,000
Cash Received	1,50,000	Bills Receivable endorsed to Creditors dishonoured	4,500
Bills Receivable	50,000		
Discount allowed	1,500	Bills Receivable dishonoured	6,500
Bad Debts written off	2,000	Noting Charges	125
Transfers (3,000 + 2,500)	5,500	Bank Charges	85
To Balance c/d	50,960		
	2,61,210		2,61,210

General Ledger

Particulars	Amount Rs.	Particulars	Amount Rs.
To Creditors Ledger A/c		*By Creditors Ledger A/c*	
Purchases	1,50,000	Purchase Returns	875
Bills Receivable endorsed dishonoured	4,500	Bills Receivable endorsed to Creditors	10,000
		Cash paid to Creditors	85,000
		Bills payable	20,000
		Discount received	2,500
		Transfer (3,000 + 2,500)	5,500
		By Balance c/d	30,625
	1,54,500		1,54,500

Under Self Balancing system necessary Adjustment Accounts are :

(1) In General Ledger — (a) Debtors Ledger Adjustment A/c
(b) Creditors Ledger Adjustment A/c

(2) In Debtors Ledger — General Ledger Adjustment A/c

(3) In Creditors Ledger — General Ledger Adjustment A/c

In General Ledger

Debtors Ledger Adjustment A/c

To Balance b/d		By Balance b/d	
To *General Adjustment A/c*		By *General Ledger Adjustment A/c*	
Sales (Credit)	2,50,000	Sales Returns	1,250
Bills receivable endorsed to creditors dishonoured	4,500	Cash received	1,50,000
Bills Receivable discounted dishonoured	6,500	Bills Receivable	50,000
Noting Charges	125	Discount allowed	1,500
Bank charges	85	Bad Debts written off	2,000
		Transfers (3,000 + 2,500)	5,500
		Balance c/d	50,960
	2,61,210		2,61,210

Creditors Ledger Adjustment A/c

Particulars	Amount Rs.	Particulars	Amount Rs.
To Balance b/d		By Balance b/d	
To *General Ledger Adjustment A/c*		By *General Ledger Adjustment A/c*	
Purchase Returns	875	Purchase (Credit)	1,50,000
Bills Receivable endorsed transferred	10,000	Bills Receivable endorsed dishonoured	4,500
Cash paid	85,000		
Bills payable	20,000		
Discount Received	2,500		
Transfers (3,000 + 2,500)	5,500		
Balance c/d	30,625		
	1,54,500		1,54,500

In Debtors Ledger

General Ledger Adjustment A/c

To Balance b/d		By Balance b/d	
To *Debtors Ledger Adjustment A/c*		By *Debtors Ledger Adjustment A/c*	
Sales Returns	1,250	Sales Creditors	2,50,000
Cash Received	1,50,000	Bills Receivable endorsed to Creditors dishonoured	4,500
Bills Receivable	50,000	Bills Receivable dishonoured	6,500
Discount allowed	1,500	Noting Charges	125
Bad Debts written off	2,000	Bank Charges	85
Transfers (3,000 + 2,500)	5,500		
By Balance c/d	50,960		
	2,61,210		2,61,210

In Creditors Ledger

General Ledger Adjustment A/c

To Balance b/d		By Balance b/d	
To *Creditors Ledger Adjustment A/c*		By *Creditors Ledger Adjustment A/c*	
Purchases	1,50,000	Purchase returns	875
Bills Receivable endorsed dishonoured	4,500	Bills Receivable endorsed to Creditors	10,000
		Cash paid	85,000
		Bills payable	20,000
		Discount received	2,000
		Transfer (3,000 + 2,500)	5,500
		Balance c/d	30,625
	1,54,500		1,54,500

Problem No. 10

Problem No. 1

Pass Self Balancing Journal Entires for the following :

(a) Sold goods to customers on Credit worth Rs. 1,00,000 subject to a Trade discount @ 5%.

(b) Cheques received from Customers Rs. 49,000 in full settlement of Rs. 49,500.

(c) Bills Receivable (received) Rs. 8,000 returned unpaid and noting charges due thereon Rs. 500.

(d) Bad Debts written off Rs. 1,000.

(e) Cash received from customers.

(f) Bills (Receivable) received from Debtors Rs. 2,000.

[K.U.D., April 1998 (N)]

Solution :

Self Balancing Journal Entries		Dr. Rs.	Cr. Rs.
(a) (i) Original Entry			
Customers A/c (Debtors) A/c	Dr	95,000	
Trade Discount allowed A/c	Dr	5,000	
To Sales A/c (Goods)			1,00,000
(Goods sold on credit and trade discount @ 5% allowed)			
(ii) Self Balancing Entry			
Debtors Ledger Adjustment A/c in GL	Dr	95,000	
General Ledger Adjustment A/c in DL	Dr	5,000	
To General Ledger Adjustment A/c in DL			1,00,000
(Good sold on credit @ 5% Trade Discount)			
(b) (i) Original Entry			
Bank A/c	Dr	49,000	
Discount allowed A/c	Dr	500	
To Customers A/c			49,500
(Cheques received from customers for Rs. 49,000 in full settlement of A/c of Rs. 49,500)			

Self Balancing Journal Entries		Dr. Rs.	Cr. Rs.
(ii) Self Balancing Entry			
General Ledger Adjustment A/c in DL	Dr	49,000 + 500	
To Debtors Ledger Adjustment A/c in G.L.			49,500
[Cheques received Rs. 49,000 and discount allowed — one is real A/c another is Nominal A/c and therefore transferred to General Ledger and debited to that A/c and the Customers A/c (Personal A/c Debtors credit)]			
(c) (i) Original Entry			
Debtors A/c	Dr	8,500	
To Bills Receivable A/c			8,000
To Noting Charges recoverable A/c			500
(Bills Receivable - returned unpaid and Noting charges due recoverable)			
(ii) Self Balancing Entry			
Debtors Ledger Adjustment A/c in G.L.		8,500	
To General Ledger Adjustment A/c in G.L.			8,000 + 500
(Bills receivable unpaid & Noting charges recoverable item of General Ledger credited and Customers A/c debited)			
(d) (i) Original Entry			
Bad Debts A/c	Dr	1,000	
To Customers A/c or Debtors A/c			1,000
(Bad Debts written off)			
(ii) Self Balancing Entry			
General Ledger Adjustment A/c in G.L.	Dr	1,000	
To Debtors Ledger Adjustment A/c in G.L.			1,000
(Bad Debts written off. Normal A/c G.L. Customers A/c Debtors Ledger Adj. in G.L.)			

Self Balancing Journal Entries		Dr. Rs.	Cr. Rs.
(e) (i) Original Entry			
Cash / or Bank A/c	Dr	50,000	
To Customers A/c (or Debtors A/c)			50,000
(Cash received from customers)			
(ii) Self Balancing Entry			
General Ledger Adjustment A/c in G.L.	Dr	50,000	
To Debtors Ledger Adjustment A/c in G.L.			50,000
(Cash received Real A/c General Ledger, Customers A/c & Debtors Ledger A/c)			
(f) (i) Original Entry			
Bills Receivable A/c	Dr	2,000	
To Debtors A/c			2,000
(Bills Receivable received from customers)			
(ii) Self Balancing Entry			
General Ledger Adjustment A/c in D.L.	Dr	2,000	
To Debtors Ledger Adjustment A/c in G.L.			2,000
(BR Real A/c & General Ledger Debtors)			

Problem No. 2

From the following transactions, prepare Creditors Ledger Adjustment Account in General Ledger as on 31-12-1997 which are kept on Self Balancing System :

	Rs.
(1) Creditors Balance on 1-1-1997 Cr.	40,000
(2) Creditors Balance on 1-1-1997 Dr.	4,000
(3) Credit purchases during the year	1,20,000
(4) Cash purchases during the year	60,000
(5) Cash paid to creditors during the year	80,000

(6)	Bills payable accepted of creditors	43,000
(7)	Bills payable dishonoured during the year	3,000
(8)	Discount received during the year	5,000
(9)	Purchase Returns during the year	4,800
(10)	Creditors Balance on 31-12-1997 (Dr)	2,000

[K.U.D., April 1998 (N)]

Solution :

In General Ledger

Creditors Ledger Adjustment A/c

		Rs.			Rs.
1-1-97	To Balance b/d	4,000	1-1-97	By Balance b/d	40,000
31-12-97	To *General Ledger Adjustment A/c*		31-12-97	By *General Ledger Adjustment A/c*	
	Bank A/c (Cash paid)	80,000		Purchases (Credit)	1,20,000
	Bills payable accepted	43,000		Bills payable dishonoured	3,000
	Discount Received	5,000		By Balance c/d	2,000
	Purchase Returned	4,800			
	To Balance c/d	28,200			
		1,65,000			1,65,000
1-1-98	To Balance b/d	2,000	1-1-98	By Balance b/d	28,200

Note : Item No. 4 — Cash purchases during the year Rs. 60,000 not considered here.

Problem No. 3

Pass Journal Entries under Self Balancing System.

		Rs.
(1)	Credit sales	1,00,000
(2)	Cash sales	25,000
(3)	Cash received from Debtors	50,000
(4)	Discount allowed	3,000
(5)	Bills Receivable received	30,000
(6)	Bills Receivable dishonoured	1,000
(7)	Provision for Doubtful Debts	5,000
(8)	Returns from Debtors	4,000
(9)	Bad Debts written off	500
(10)	Noting charges	100

[K.U.D., October 1997(N)]

Solution :

Journal Entries under Self Balancing System

		Dr. Rs.	Cr. Rs.
(1)	Debtors Ledger Adjustment A/c (in Gen. Ledger)	1,00,000	
	To General Ledger Adjustment A/c (in D.L.)		1,00,000
	[Credit sales made or (being credit sales)]		
(3)	General Ledger Adjustment A/c Dr. (in D.L.)	50,000	
	To Debtors Ledger Adjustment A/c. (in G.L.)		50,000
	(Being cash received from Debtors)		
(4)	General Ledger Adjustment A/c Dr. (in D.L.)	3,000	
	To Debtors Ledger Adjustment A/c (in G.L.)		3,000
	(Being discount allowed to Debtors)		
(5)	General Ledger Adjustment A/c Dr. (in D.L.)	30,000	
	To Debtors Ledger Adjustment A/c (in G.L.)		30,000
	(Being Bills Receivable received)		
(6)	Debtors Ledger Adjustment A/c Dr. (in G.L.)	1,000	
	To General Ledger Adjustment A/c (in D.L.)		1,000
	(Bills Receivable received dishonoured)		
(8)	General Ledger Adjustment A/c Dr. (in D.L.)	4,000	
	To Debtors Ledger Adjustment A/c (in G.L.)		4,000
	(Being sales Return from Debtors)		
(9)	General Ledger Adjustment A/c Dr. (in D.L.)	500	
	To Debtors Ledger Adjustment A/c (in G.L.)		500
	(Being Bad Debts written off)		
(10)	Debtors Ledger Adjustment A/c Dr. (in G.L.)	100	
	To General Ledger Adjustment A/c (in D.L.)		100
	(Being Noting charges Debted to Debtors)		

Note : Item No. 2 Cash sales and item No. 7 Provision for Bad Debts not concerned. Therefore no entry.

Problem No. 4

Prepare Sales Ledger Adjustment Account in General Ledger with the following items :

		Rs.
1-1-96	Balance of Debtors Account (Dr.)	35,500
	(Cr.)	1,000
31-12-96	Total Sales	2,00,000
	Cash Sales	10,000
	Sales Returns	2,500
	Cash and cheques received	1,00,000
	Discount allowed	3,000
	Transfer Debtors Balance to Creditor A/c	5,000
	Interest charges on overdue accounts	500
	Provision for bad debts	975
	Bad debts written off	1,250
	Bills drawn on customers	35,000
	Bad debts previously written off now recovered	900
	B.R. endorsed	10,000
	Dishonour of endorsed Bills	2,500
	Debtors cheques returned unpaid	1,000
	Noting charges on unpaid Bill	100
	Balance of Debtors (Cr.)	1,500

[K.U.D., October 1997(N)]

Solution :

In General Ledger

Debtors Ledger Adjustment A/c (Sales Ledger Adjustment)

		Rs.			Rs.
1-1-96	To Balance b/d	35,500	1-1-96	By Balance b/d	1,000
31-12-96			31-12-96		
	To *Gen. Ledger Adjustment A/c*			By *Gen. Ledge. Adjust. A/c*	
	Sales Credit	1,90,000		Sale Returns	2,500
	Total Sales 2,00,000			Cash & Cheques received	1,00,000
	Less Cash sales 10,000			Discount allowed	3,00
	Interest charges on			Transfer to creditors	5,000
	overdue A/c	5,000		Bad Debts Ledger A/c	
	Dishonour of Bills endorsed	2,500		written off	1,250
	Debtors cheques returned	1,000		Bills Receivable	25,000
	Noting charges unpaid	100		By Balance c/d	83,350
	To Balance c/d	1,500			
		2,31,100			2,31,100
1-2-96	To Balance b/d	83,350	1-2-96	By Balance b/d	1,500

Note : (1) Provision for Bad debts (2) Bad debts previously written off now recovered and (3) BR endorsed items are omitted as they are not concerned to Debtors.

Problem No. 5

Prepare : (a) Debtors Ledger Adjustment Account and (b) Creditors Ledger Adjustment Account in General Ledger of Mr. Sona from the following details :

		Rs.
Balance as on 1-1-1994 :		
Debtors	(Dr.)	36,000
Creditors	(Cr.)	26,000
Transactions for the year ending 31-12-1994 :		
Credit purchases		80,000
Credit sales		1,40,000
Returns outward		3,000
Returns inward		6,000
Cash received rom Debtors		1,00,000
Cash paid to Creditors		70,000
Discount allowed to Debtors		4,000
Discount earned from Creditors		2,000
Bills Receivable received from Debtors		26,000
Bills of Creditors accepted		10,000
Bad debts written off		1,000
Bills Receivable dishonoured		600
Bills payable dishonoured		500
Cash refunded to Debtors		1,900
Discount allowed to Debtors later disallowed		200

[K.U.D., October 1997(O)]

Solution :

In General Ledger

Debtors Ledger Adjustment A/c

		Rs.			Rs.
1-1-94	To Balance b/d	36,000	31-12-94		
31-12-94				By *Gen. Ledger Adjustment A/c*	
	To *Gen. Ledger Adjustment A/c*			Returns Inward	6,000
	Sales (Credit)	1,40,000		Cash received	1,00,000
	B.R. Dishonoured	600		Discount allowed	4,000
	Cash Refunded to Drs.	1,900		Bills Receivable	26,000
	Discount allowed later			Bad Debts written off	1,000
	disallowed	200		By Balance c/d	67,700
		2,04,700			2,04,700

Creditors Ledger Adjustment A/c

31-12-94			1-1-94	By Balance b/d	26,000
	To *Gen. Ledger Adjustment A/c*		31-12-94		
	Return outward	3,000		By *Gen. Ledger Adjustment A/c*	
	Cash paid	70,000		Purchases (Credit)	80,000
	Discount earned	2,000		Bills payable dishonoured	500
	Bills payable	10,000			
	To Balance c/d	21,500			
		1,06,500			1,06,500

Problem No. 6

From the following particulars prepare :

Creditors Ledger Adjustment Account in General Ledger on 31-12-1995.

		Rs.
Creditors Balance on 1-1-1995 : Cr.		30,000
	Dr	600
Total purchases		2,55,000
Cash purchases		75,000
Return outwards		3,500
Cash paid to Creditors		45,500
Cheques issued to Creditors		1,00,000
Discount received		3,000
Goods received as samples		1,000
Bills payable issued to Creditors		25,000
Bills payable unpaid		1,500

Noting charges due on unpaid Bills	200
Excess cash refunded by Creditors	300
Bills payable discounted by Creditors	10,000
Creditors balance on 31-12-95 (Dr.)	400

[K.U.D., April 1997(N)]

Solution :

In General Ledger

Creditors Ledger Adjustment A/c

		Rs.			Rs.
1-1-95			1-1-95		
	To Balance b/d	600		By Balance b/d	30,000
	To *Gen. Ledger Adj. A/c*			By *Gen. Ledger Adj. A/c*	
	Return outward	3,500		Credit purchases	1,80,000
	Cash paid	45,500		Total purchases 2,55,000	
	Cheques issued	1,00,000		*Less* Cash purchases 75,000	
	Discount received	3,000		By Bills payable unpaid	1,500
	Bills payable issued	25,000		Noting charges due on	
31-12-95				Bills unpaid	200
	To Balance c/d	34,800		Cash received (excess cash)	300
			31-12-95		
				By Balance c/d	400
		2,12,400			2,12,400

Note : (1) Goods received as sample Rs. 1000 — Free Supply-Not considered in this A/c.

(2) B.P. discounted by Creditors (BR discounted by creditors) not concerned to this A/c. No Entry.

Problem No. 7

From the following particulars prepare in General Ledger :

(a) Debtors Ledger Adjustment Account and

(b) Creditors Ledger Adjustment Account.

Opening Balances on 1-1-1995:		Rs.
(1) Debtors Ledger Balance	(Dr.)	45,200
(2) Debtors Ledger Balance	(Cr.)	750
(3) Creditors Ledger Balance	(Cr.)	36,500
(4) Creditors Ledger Balance	(Dr.)	2,500

Transactions and during the year :		Rs.
(5)	Purchases	2,05,000
(6)	Purchase Returns	7,500
(7)	Sales	2,75,000
(8)	Sale Returns	4,000
(9)	Cash received from Debtors	2,35,000
(10)	Discount allowed	9,500
(11)	Cash paid to Creditors	1,80,000
(12)	Discount received	5,600
(13)	Cash refunded to Debtors	500
(14)	Bills Receivable received	18,500
(15)	Bills Payable accepted	12,500
(16)	Bills Receivable dishonoured	2,500
(17)	Transfer from Debtors Ledger to Creditors Ledger	250
(18)	Transfer from Creditor Ledger to Debtors Ledger	150
(19)	Provision for Doubtful Debts	1,250
(20)	Bad Debts written off	4,500
(21)	Bad Debts written off recovered	2,750
Closing Balances on 31-12-1995 :		
(22)	Debtors Ledger Balance (Cr.)	1,500
(23)	Creditors Ledger Balance (Dr.)	2,500

[K.U.D., October 1996(O)]

Solution :

In General Ledger

Debtors Ledger Adjustment A/c

1-1-95	To Balance b/d	45,200	1-1-95	By Balance b/d	750
31-12-95			31-12-95		
	To Gen. Ledger Adj. A/c			By *Gen. Ledger Adj. A/c*	
	Sales (Credit)	2,75,000		Sales Returns	4,000
	Cash refunded	500		Cash received	2,35,000
	Bills Receivable Dishonoured	2,500		Discount allowed	9,500
31-12-95	To Balance c/d	1,500		Bills Receivable	18,500
				Transferred to Creditors	250
				Transferred from Creditors Ledger	150
				Bad Debts written off	4,500
				By Balance c/d	52,050
		3,24,700			3,24,700

Creditors Ledger Adjustment A/c

1-1-95 To Balance b/d	2,500	1-1-95 By Balance b/d	36,500
31-12-95 To *General Ledger Adj. A/c*		31-12-95 By *General Ledger. Adj. A/c*	
To Purchase Returns	7,500	Purchases (Credit)	2,05,000
To Cash paid	1,80,000	31-12-95	
Discount Received	5,600	By Balance c/d	2,500
To Bills Payable	12,500		
To Transferred from Debtors Ledger	250		
To Transferred to Debtors Ledger	150		
To Balance c/d	35,500		
	2,44,000		2,44,000
1-1-96 To Balance b/d	2,500	1-1-96 By Balance b/d	35,500

Note : Item No. 19 and 21, provision for Doubtful Debts and Bad Debts written off recovered respectively were not considered in above Ledger Adjustment Account.

Problem No. 8

Pass Self Balancing Journal Entries for the following :

(i) Goods sold to customers on credit worth Rs. 2,500 subject to trade discount at 10%.

(ii) Cheques received from customers Rs. 14,700 in full settlement of Rs. 15,000.

(iii) Rs. 5,000, balance on customers account is adjusted to Creditors Account.

(iv) Bills Receivable Rs. 10,000 returned unpaid and Noting charges due thereon Rs. 1,000.

[K.U.D., April 1996(N)]

Solution :

Self Balancing Ledger Journal Entries

		Dr. Rs.	Cr. Rs.
Original Entry :			
(i) (a) Customers or Debtors A/c	Dr.	22,500	
Trade Discount A/c	Dr.	2,500	
To Sales A/c			25,000
(Goods sold on credit at a Trade discount 10% on sales)			

			Dr. Rs.	Cr. Rs.
Under Self Balancing Ledger				
(b) Debtors Ledger A/c		Dr	22,500	
To General Ledger A/c				22,500
(Credit sales made Net Amount after deducting Trade discount)				
Entry for Self Balancing Ledger				
(c) Debtors Ledger Adjustment A/c (in G.L.)		Dr	22,500	
To General Ledger Adjustment				22,500
(Entry for Self Balancing Ledger System)				
Original Entry				
(ii) (a) Cash A/c or Bank A/c		Dr	14,700	
Discount allowed A/c		Dr	300	
To Debtors A/c				15,000
(Cheques for Rs. 14,700 received in full settlement of Rs. 15,000 due from customer)				
Under Self Balancing Ledger				
(b) General Ledger A/c		Dr	15,000	
Cash A/c	14,700			
Discount allowed A/c	300			
To Debtors Ledger A/c				15,000
(Entry for cash Cheques received & Discount allowed to customers in full settlement of A/c)				
(c) General Ledger Adjustment A/c (in D.L.)		Dr	15,000	
Cash received A/c	14,700			
Discount allowed A/c	300			
To Debtors Ledger Adjustment A/c (in G.L.)				15,000
(Entry for Self-Balancing Ledger System)				
Original Entry				
(iii) (a) Creditors A/c		Dr	5,000	
To Debtors Ledger A/c				5,000
(Transfer of Debtors Balance to Creditors A/c)				
Under Self Balancing Ledger				
(b) Creditors Ledger		Dr	5,000	
To Debtors Ledger A/c				5,000
(Transfer of Debtors Ledger Balance to Creditors Ledger Balance)				
(c) (i) Creditors Ledger Adjustment A/c (in G.L.)		Dr	5,000	
To General Ledger Adjustment A/c (in C.L.)				5,000
(Being transfer entry)				
(ii) General Ledger Adjustment in (D.L.)		Dr	5,000	
To Debtors Ledger Adjustment (in G.L.)				5,000
(Being transfer entry)				

		Dr. Rs.	Cr. Rs.
Original Entry			
(iv) (a) Debtors A/c	Dr	11,000	
To Bills Receivable A/c			10,000
To Noting charges A/c			1,000
(Being entry for Bills receivable unpaid or dishonoured and noting charges recoverable)			
Self Balancing			
(b) Debtors Ledger A/c.	Dr	11,000	
To General Ledger A/c			11,000
BR 10,000			
Noting charges 1,000			
(Entry for transfer to ledger under Self Balancing system)			
(c) Debtors Ledger Adjustment A/c in G.L.	Dr	11,000	
To General Ledger Adjustment A/c (D.L.)			11,000
BR 10,000			
Noting charges 1,000			
(Entry for Self Balancing Ledger System)			

Or Direct entries may be passed under Self Balancing Ledger system as under

		Dr. Rs.	Cr. Rs.
Entry (i)	Debtors Ledger Adjustment A/c Dr. (in G.L.)	22,500	
	To General Ledger Adjustment A/c (in D.L.)		22,500
	(Being Entry under Self Balancing Ledger)		
(ii)	General Ledger Adjustment A/c Dr. (in D.L.)	15,000	
	To Debtors Ledger Adjustment A/c (in G.L.)		15,000
	(Cheques/cash received Rs. 14,700 Discount allowed Rs. 300)		
(iii)	(a) Creditors Ledger Adjustment A/c Dr. (in G.L.)	5,000	
	To General Ledger Adjustment A/c (in C.L.)		5,000
	(Being transfer entry from Debtors Balance to Creditors Ledger A/c)		
	(b) General Ledger Adjustment A/c Dr. (in D.L.)	5,000	
	To Debtors Ledger Adjustment A/c (in G.L.)		5,000
	(Being transfer entry of Debtors Ledger Balance to Creditors Ledger Balance)		
OR	Creditors Ledger Adjustment A/c Dr. (in GL)	5,000	
	To Debtors Ledger Adjustment (in GL)		5,000
	(Being direct entry of transfer of Debtors Ledger balance to Creditors Ledger A/c)		
(iv)	Debtors Ledger Adjustment A/c Dr (in GL)	11,000	
	To General Ledger Adjustment A/c (in DL)		11,000
	(Being entry for BR dishonoured and Noting charges recoverable. B.R. dishonoured Rs. 10,000 Noting Charges 1,000)		

Problem No. 9

Prepare Adjustment Accounts maintained under Self Balancing Ledger System.

			Rs.
(1)	Customers Balance on 1-4-95 :	Dr.	40,000
		Cr.	500
(2)	Suppliers Balances on 1-4-95 :	Cr.	20,000
		Dr.	3,000
	Transactions during the year 1995-96 :		
(3)	Credit sales		82,000
(4)	Cash sales		14,000
(5)	Total purchases		38,000
(6)	Cash purchases		6,000
(7)	Payments of cash to suppliers		12,000
(8)	Collections from customers		62,000
(9)	Provisions for doubtful debts		3,520
(10)	Bad debts written off now		480
(11)	Discounts allowed to customers		4,000
(13)	Return Inward		5,000
(14)	Return Outward		500
(15)	B.R. received		8,000
(16)	B.P. accepted		3,000
(17)	Freight paid on purchases		1,000
(18)	B.R. Endosed to suppliers		3,000
(19)	B.R. unpaid (dishonoured)		2,000
(20)	B.R. endorsed (dishonoured)		1,000
(21)	Interest and Noting charges on dishonoured Bills		500
(22)	Transfer of Balances from Debtors Ledger to Creditors Ledger		1,000
(23)	Balance due to a supplier adjusted against another supplier with mutual consent		2,000
(24)	Irrecoverable Debts		500
(25)	Refund of excess cash paid to suppliers		1,000
	Balances on 31-3-1996 :		
	Customers Accounts	(Cr.)	500
	Suppliers Accounts	(Dr.)	200

[K.U.D., April 1996(N)]

Solution :

In General Ledger

Debtors Ledger Adjustment A/c

Date	Particulars	Rs.	Date	Particulars	Rs.
1-4-1995	To Balance b/d	40,000	1-4-95	By Balance b/d	500
31-3-96			31-3-96		
	To *Gen. Ledger Adjustment A/c*			By *Gen. Ledger Adjustment A/c*	
	Sales (Credit)	82,000		Cash received	62,000
	B.R. dishonoured	2,000		Bad debts written off now	480
	B.R. endorsed			Dis. allowed to customers	4,000
	dishonoured	1,000		Return inward	5,000
	Interest & Noting charges on			B.R. received	8,000
	dishonoured Bill	500		Transfer from Debtors Ledger	
31-3-96	To Balance c/d	500		to Creditor Ledger	1,000
				Bad Debt (Irrecoverable)	500
			31-3-96	By Balance c/d	44,520
		1,26,000			1,26,000
1-4-96	To Balance b/d	44,520	1-4-96	By Balance b/d	500

Creditors Ledger Adjustment A/c

Date	Particulars	Rs.	Date	Particulars	Rs.
1-4-95	To Balance b/d	300	1-4-95	By Balance b/d	20,000
31-3-96			31-3-96		
	To *Gen. Ledger Adjustment A/c* :			By *Gen. Ledger Adjustment A/c* :	
	Cash paid	12,000		Purchases (Credit)	32,000
	Discount allowed by Suppliers	1,000		Total Purchases 38,000	
	Return outward	500		*Less* Cash purchases 6,000	
	B.P. accepted	3,000		Cash refunded excess paid	1,000
	B.R. endorsed	3,000		B.R. endorsed dishonoured	1,000
	Transfer-from Debtors Ledger	1,000	31-3-96	By Balance c/d	200
	To Balance c/d	33,400			
		54,200			54,200
1-4-96	To Balance b/d	200	1-4-96	By Balance b/d	33,400

Note : Item Nos.

(4) Cash sales

(6) Cash purchases

(9) Provisions for Doubtful Debt

(17) Freight paid on purchases

(24) Balances due to supplier

All these above mentioned transactions do not affect either customers or suppliers A/cs therefore, are not considered.

In Debtors Ledger

General Ledger Adjustment A/c

	Rs.		Rs.
1-4-95 To Balance b/d	500	1-4-95 By Balance b/d	20,000
31-3-96		31-3-96	
To *Debtors Ledger Adjustment A/c*		By *Debtors Ledger Adjustment A/c*	
Cash received	62,000	Sales (Credit)	82,000
Bad debt written off	480	B.R. unpaid dishonoured	2,000
Discount allowed	4,000	B.R. endorsed dishonoured	1,000
Return Inward	5,000	Interest & Noting charges	500
B.R. received	8,000	31-3-96 By Balance c/d	500
Transfer to Crs. Ledger	1,000		
Bad Debts (irrecoverable)	500		
31-3-96 To Balance c/d	44,520		
	1,26,000		1,26,000

In Creditors Ledger

General Ledger Adjustment A/c

	Rs.		Rs.
1-4-95 To Balance b/d	20,000	1-4-95 By Balance b/d	300
31-3-96		31-3-96	
To *Gen. Ledger Adjustment A/c*		By *Gen. Ledger Adjustment A/c*	
Purchases (Credit)	32,000	Cash paid	
Total Purchases	38,000	Cash paid	12,000
Less Cash purchases	6,000	Discount received	1,000
Cash Refunded by Suppliers	1,000	Return outward	500
BR endorsed dishonoured	1,000	BP accepted	3,000
31-3-96 To Balance c/d	200	BR endorsed	3,000
		Transfer from Drs. Ledger	1,000
		31-3-96 By Balance c/d	33,400
	54,200		54,200

Problem No. 10

Prepare Sales Ledger Ajustment Account in General Ledger.

		Rs.
1-1-96	Balance of Debtors Account (Dr)	71,000
	(Cr)	2,000
31-1-96	Total Sales	4,00,000
	Cash Sales	20,000
	Sales return	5,000
	Cash and Cheques received	2,00,000
	Discount allowed	6,000
	Transfer Debtors balance to a Creditor A/c	10,000
	Transfer of a debtor's balance to another customer's account under the instructions from both parties	15,000
	Interest charged on overdue accounts	1,000
	Provision for bad debts	1,950
	Bad debts written off	2,500
	Bad debt previously written off now recovered	1,800
	Excess cash received refunded	2,000
	Bills drawn on customers	70,000
	B.R. endorsed	20,000
	Dishonour of endorsed bills	5,000
	Debtors cheques returned unpaid	2,000
	Noting charges on unpaid bills	200
	Balance of debtors (Cr)	3,000

(October 1996)

Solution :

In General Ledger
Debtors Ledger Adjustment A/c

		Rs.			Rs.
1-1-96 To Balance b/d		71,000	1-1-96 By Balance b/d		2,000
31-12-96			3-12-96		
To *Gen. Ledger Adjustment A/c*			By *Gen Ledger Adj. A/c*		
Credit Sales		3,80,000	Sales Return		5,000
Total Sales	4,00,000		Cash & Cheques received		2,00,000
Less : Cash Sales	20,000		Discount allowed		6,000
Interest		1,000	Transfer of Balance to Creditors A/c		10,000
Excess Cash refunded		2,000	Bad Debts written off		2,500
Bills endorsed dishonoured		5,000	Bills drawn		70,000
Cheques Unpaid		2,000	31-12-86 By Balance c/d		1,68,700
Noting Charges		200			
31-12-96 To Balance c/d		3,000			
		4,64,200			4,64,200

Note : (1) Total sales Rs. 4,00,000 included Cash sales of Rs. 20,000. It should be deducted from total sales you will get credit sales.

(2) Transfer of a debtor's balance to another customer Account under instruction from both the parties. It is the item of debtors and therefore will not have any effect under Self Balancing system.

(3) Provision for Bad Debt not considered.

(4) Bad Debts written off previously now recovered is not considered.

(5) Bills endorsed this item does not affect Debtors.

In Debtors Ledger
General Ledger Adjustment A/c

1-1-96 To Balance b/d		2,000	1-1-96 By Balance b/d		71,000
3-12-96			31-12-96		
To *Debtors Ledger Adjustment A/c* :			By *Debtors Ledger Adjustment A/c* :		
Sales Return		5,000	Total Sales	4,00,000	
Cash & Cheques received		2,00,000	*Less* : Cash Sales	20,000	3,80,000
Discount allowed		6,000	Interest		1,000
Transfer Balance to Creditors Ledger		10,000	Excess Cash refunded		2,000
Bad Debts written off		2,500	Bills endorsed dishonoured		5,000
Bills drawn		70,000	Cheques Unpaid		2,000
			Noting Charges		200
31-12-86 Balance c/d		1,68,700	31-12-96 By Balance c/d		3,000
		4,64,200			4,64,200
1-1-97 To Balance b/d		3,000	1-1-97 By Balance b/d		1,68,700

Problem No. 11

Pass Self Balancing Journal entries for the following information :

(i) Goods sold to customers on credit worth Rs. 25,000 subject to trade discount @ 10%.

(ii) Cheque received from customers Rs. 14,700 in full settlement of Rs. 15,000.

(iii) Rs. 5,000 Balance on customers account is adjusted to Creditors A/c.

(iv) Bill Receivable Rs. 10,000 returned unpaid and noting charges due thereon Rs. 1,000.

(K.U.D., April 1996)

Solution :

Journal Entries Self Balancing System

		Dr. Rs.	Cr. Rs.
Original :			
(i) (a) Debtors A/c	Dr	22,500	
Discount A/c	Dr	2,500	
To Sales			25,000
(Goods sold to customer subject to 10% Discount)			
Self Balancing :			
(b) Debtors Ledger A/c	Dr	22,500	
General Ledger A/c	Dr	2,500	
To General Ledger A/c			25,000
(Entry for transfer to ledgers)			
For Adjustment :			
(c) Debtors Ledger Adjustment A/c (in General Ledger)	Dr	22,500	
General Ledger Adjustment A/c	Dr	2,500	
To General Ledger Adjustment A/c (Debtors Ledger)	Dr		25,000
(Entry for transfer to adjustment A/c in respective ledger)			
(ii) (a) Cash A/c	Dr	14,700	
Discount A/c	Dr.	300	
To Debtors A/c			15,000
(Cash received in full settlement A/c)			
For Self Balancing :			
(b) General Ledger A/c	Dr	14,700	
General Ledger A/c	Dr	300	
To Debtors Ledger A/c			15,000
(Entry for transfer to ledger A/c)			

		Dr. Rs.	Cr. Rs.
For Adjustment A/c			
(c) General Ledger Adjustment A/c	Dr	14,700	
General Ledger Adjustment A/c	Dr	300	
To Debtors Ledger A/c			15,000
(Entry for transfer to ledger A/c)			
(iii) (a) Creditors A/c	Dr	5,000	
To Debtors A/c			5,000
(Balance on customer A/c transfer to Creditors A/c)			
(b) Creditors Ledger A/c	Dr	5,000	
To Debtors Ledger A/c			5,000
(Entry for transfer to ledger A/c)			
(c) Creditors Ledger Adjustment A/c (in G.L.)	Dr	5,000	
To General Ledger Adjustment A/c (in C.L.)			5,000
General Ledger Adjustment (in D.L.)	Dr	5,000	
To Debtors Ledger Adjustment A/c (in G.L.)			5,000
(iv) (a) Debtors A/c	Dr	11,000	
To Bills Receivable A/c			10,000
To Noting Charges A/c			1,000
(Bills receivable dishonoured and Noting charges thereon)			
(b) Debtors Ledger A/c	Dr	11,000	
To General Ledger A/c			11,000
(Being Bills receivable noting charges)			
For Adjustment A/c			
(c) Debtors Ledger Adjustment A/c (in G.L.)	Dr	11,000	
To General Ledger Adjustment A/c (in D.L.)			11,000
(Bills Receivable 10,000 + 1,000 dishonoured noting charges entry for adjustment A/c)			

Problem No. 12

From the following particulars as extracted from the books of a trader, prepare the necessary Ledger Adjustment accounts in the respective Ledgers :

		Rs.
Debtors Balance (on 1-1-90)	Dr	80,000
Debtors Balance (on 1-1-90)	Cr	4,000
Credit Sales		2,00,000
Cash Sales		50,000
Cash received from Debtors		1,00,000
Discount allowed		6,000
Bills receivable received		60,000
Bills receivable dishonoured		2,000
Bad debts written off		1,000
Provision for Doubtful debts		10,000

Return from debtors		8,000
Debtors Balance (on 31-12-90)	Cr	3,000

[K.U.D., April 1996 (a)]

Solution :

In General Ledger

Debtors Ledger Adjustment A/c

	Rs.		Rs.
1-1-90		1-1-90	
To Balance c/d	80,000	By Balance b/d	4,000
To *Gen. Ledger Adjustment A/c*		By *Gen. Ledger Adjustment A/c*	
To Sales (Credit)	2,00,000	Cash received	1,00,000
To Bills receivable		Disallowed	6,000
dishonoured	2,000	Bill Receivable received	60,000
31-12-90		Bad Debts written off	1,000
To Balance c/d	3,000	Return from debtors	8,000
		31-12-90	
		By Balance c/d	1,06,000
Total	2,85,000		2,85,000

In Debtors Ledger

General Ledger Adjustment A/c

1-1-90		1-1-90	
To Balance b/d	4,000	By Balance b/d	80,000
To *Debtors Ledger Adj. A/c*		By *Debtors Ledger Adj. A/c*	
Cash received	1,00,000	Sales (Cr)	2,00,000
Discount allowed	6,000	Bills Receivable	
Bills received	60,000	dishonoured	2,000
Bad debts written off	1,000	31-12-90	
Returns from debtors	8,000	By Balance c/d	3,000
31-12-90			
To Balance c/d	1,06,000		
Total	2,85,000	Total	2,85,000

Note : (1) Cash Sales and (2) Provision for doubtful debts are omitted.

Problem No. 13

Prepare Adjustment Account maintained under Self Balancing ledger sysem.

		Rs.
Customer Balance 1-4-95	Dr	40,000
	Cr	500
Suppliers Balance on 1-4-95	Cr	20,000
	Dr	300
Transactions during the year 1995-96 :		
Credit sales		82,000
Cash sales		14,000
Total purchases		38,000
Cash purchases		6,000
Payments of cash to suppliers		12,000
Collection from customers		62,000
Provision of doubtful debts		3,520
Bad Debts written off		480
Discount allowed by suppliers		1,000
Discount allowed to customers		4,000
Return Inward		5,000
Return Outward		500
Bills Receivable received		8,000
Bills payable accepted		3,000
Freight paid to purchases		1,000
Bills receivable endorsed to suppliers		3,000
Bills Receivable unpaid		2,000
Bills endorsed dishonoured		1,000
Interview and noting charges on Bills dishonoured		500
Transfer of Balance from Debtors Ledger to Creditors Ledger		1,000
Balance due to suppliers adjusted against another supplier with mutual consent		2,000
Irrecoverable debts		500
Refund of excess cash paid to suppliers		1,000
Customers Account (Cr)		500
Suppliers Account (Dr)		200

[K.U.D., April 1996 (N)]

Solution :

In General Ledger

Debtors Ledger Adjustment Account

	Rs.		Rs.
1-4-95		1-4-95	
To Balance b/d	40,000	By Balance b/d	500
To *Gen. Ledger Adj. A/c*		By *Gen. Ledger Adj. A/c*	
Credit Sales	82,000	Collection from customer	62,000
B.R. unpaid	2,000	Bad debts written off	480
B.R. Endorsed dishonoured	1,000	Discount allowed	4,000
Interest & Noting charges		Return Inward	5,000
on dishonoured	500	B.R. received	8,000
31-3-96		Transfers to creditors	
To Balance c/d	500	Ledger A/c	1,000
		Bad debts	500
		By Balance c/d	44,520
	1,26,000		1,26,000

Creditors Ledger Adjustment Account

1-4-95		1-4-95		
To Balance b/d	300	By Balance b/d		20,000
To *General Ledger Adj. A/c*		By *Gen. Ledger Adj. A/c*		
Cash paid	12,000	Credit purchases		32,000
Discount Allowed	1,000	Total purchases	38,000	
Return outward	500	*Less* : Cash purchases	6,000	
Bills payable accepted	3,000	Freight on purchases		1,000
Bills Receivable endorsed	3,000	B.R. endorsed dishonour		1,000
Transfer from Drs. Ledger	1,000	Cash Refunded		1,000
To Balance c/d	34,400	31-3-96		
		By Balance c/d		200
Total	55,200	Total		55,200

In Debtors Ledger
General Ledger Adjustment Account

	Rs.		Rs.
1-4-95		1-4-95	
To Balance b/d	500	By Balance b/d	40,000
To *Debtors Ledger Adj. A/c*		By *Debtors Ledger Adj. A/c*	
Collection from customer	62,000	Credit sales	82,000
Bad debts written off	480	B.R. unpaid	2,000
Discount allowed	4,000	B.R. endorsed dishonoured	1,000
Return Inward	5,000	Interest and Noting charges on dishonoured Bill	500
B.R. Received	8,000	31-3-96	
Transfer to credit Ledger A/c	1,000	By Balance c/d	500
Bad debts	500		
31-3-96			
To Balance c/d	44,520		
Total	1,26,000	Total	1,26,000

In Creditors Ledger
General Ledger Adjustment A/c

1-4-95		1-4-95	
To Balance b/d	20,000	By Balance b/d	300
To *Creditors Ledger Adj. A/c*		By *Creditors Ledger Adj. A/c*	
Credit purchases	32,000	Cash paid	12,000
Total purchase 38,000		Discount allowed	1,000
Less : Cash purchases 6,000		Return outward	500
Freight on purchases	1,000	B.P. accepted	3,000
B.R. endorsed dishonoured	1,000	B.R. endorsed	3,000
Cash refunded	1,000	Transfer from Debt Ledger	1,000
31-3-96		31-3-96	
To Balance c/d	200	By Balance c/d	34,400
	55,200		55,200

Note : (1) Provision for doubtful debts, and

(2) Balance due to supplier adjusted against another supplier with mutual consent omitted as the item do not affect.

Problem No. 14

From the following information prepare the necessary Ledger Adjustment account as on 31-12-1994 in the respective Ledgers which are kept on Self Balancing system :

			Rs.
1.	Balance of debtors on 1-1-1994	(Dr)	12,000
2.	Balance of debtors on 1-1-1994	(Cr)	600
3.	Credit sales		37,400
4.	Cash received from debtors		30,000
5.	Returns from debtors		3,000
6.	Discount allowed		300
7.	Bad debts written off		700
8.	Cash sales		8,000
9.	Bills Receivable received		1,400
10.	Bills Receivable dishonoured		500
11.	Sundry charges debited to debtors		400
12.	Balance of Debtors on 31-12-1994	(Cr)	700

(K.U.D., October 1995)

Solution :

In General Ledger

Debtors Ledger Adjustment A/c

		Rs.			Rs.
1-1-94			1-1-94		
	To Balance b/d	12,000		By Balance b/d	600
	To *General Ledger Adjustment A/c*			By *General Ledger Adjustment A/c*	
	Credit sales	37,400		Cash received	30,000
	Bills Receivable dishonoured	500		Return Inward	3,000
				Discount allowed	300
	Sundry charge	400		Bad Debts written off	700
31-12-94	To Balance c/d	700		Bills Receivable received	1,400
			31-12-94	By Balance c/d	15,000
		51,000			51,000
1-1-95	To Balance b/d	15,000	1-1-95	By Balance b/d	700

In Debtors Ledger
General Ledger Adjustment A/c

Date	Particulars	Rs.	Date	Particulars	Rs.
1-1-94			1-1-94		
	To Balance b/d	600		By Balance b/d	12,000
	To *Debtors Ledger Adjustment A/c*			By *Debtors Ledger Adjustment A/c*	
	Cash received	30,000		Credit sales	37,400
	Return Inward	3,000		Bills Receivable dishonoured	500
	Discount allowed	300		Sundry charges	400
	Bad Debts written off	700	31-12-94	By Balance c/d	700
	Bills Receivable received	1,400			
31-12-94	To Balance c/d	15,000			
		51,000			51,000
1-1-95	To Balance b/d	700	1-1-95	By Balance b/d	15,000

Note : Item No. 8 Cash sales — omitted.

Problem No. 15

From the following information prepare Sales Ledger Adjustment Account and Bought Ledger Adjustment Account in the General Ledger.

		Rs.	Rs.
Bought Ledger Balance on 1-1-1993	(Dr)	2,500	
	(Cr)	24,000	
Sales Ledger Balance on 1-1-1993	(Dr)	35,470	
	(Cr)	560	
31st January 1993			1,35,000
Purchase			5,000
Purchase Returns			1,92,000
Total Sales			10,000
Total Cash sales			10,000
Sales Returns			2,500
Cash Received from Customers			1,56,000
Discounts allowed			2,800
Cash paid to suppliers			1,20,000
Transfer from sales ledger to bought ledger			5,200
Reserve for Doubtful Debts			2,290
Cash paid to customers			460
Discount received from Creditors			1,800

		Rs.
Bills Receivable received		10,000
Bills payable issued		5,600
Bills Receivable dishonoured		1,500
Bought Ledger Balance	(Dr)	2,600
Sales Ledger Balance	(Dr)	45,800

(K.U.D., April 1995)

Solution :

In General Ledger

Sales Ledger Adjustment A/c

			Rs.			Rs.
1-1-93			Rs.	1-1-93		Rs.
	To Balance b/d		35,470		By Balance b/d	560
31-12-93					By *General Ledger Adjustment A/c*	
	To *General Ledger Adjustment A/c*				Sales Return	2,500
	Credit Sales		1,82,000		Cash received	1,56,000
	Total Sales	192,000			Discount allowed	2,800
	Less Cash Sales	20,000			Transfer to bought Ledger	5,200
	Cash paid to Customers		460		Bills Receivable received	10,000
	Bills Receivable dishonours		1,500	31-1-93		
31-1-95					By Balance c/d	45,800
	To Balance c/d		3,430			
			2,22,860			2,22,860
1-2-93	To Balance b/d		45,800	1-2-93	By Balance b/d	3,430

Bought Ledger Adjustment A/c

					Rs.
1-1-93		Rs.	1-1-93		Rs.
	To Balance b/d	2,500		By Balance b/d	24,000
31-1-93			31-1-93		
	To *General Ledger Adjustment A/c*			By *General Ledger Adjustment A/c*	
	Cash paid to supplier	1,20,000		Purchases	1,35,000
	Purchase Returns	5,000		By Balance c/d	2,600
	Transfer from sales Ledger	5,200			
	Discount received from customers	1,800			
	Bills payable	5,600			
	To Balance c/d	21,500			
		1,61,600			1,61,600
1-2-93	To Balance b/d	2,600	1-2-93	By Balance b/d	21,500

In Sales Ledger
General Ledger Adjustment Account

		Rs.			Rs.
1-1-93	To Balance b/d	560	1-1-93	By Balance b/d	35,470
31-1-93			31-12-93		
	To *Sales Ledger Adjustment A/c*			By *Sales Ledger Adjustment A/c*	
	Sales Return	2,500		Total Salesales 1,92,000	
	Cash received	1,56,000		*Less* Cash sales 20,000	
	Discount allowed	2,800		Credit sales	1,82,000
	Transfer to bought Ledger	5,200		Cash paid to Customers	460
	Bills Reeivable received	10,000		Bills Receivable dishonours	1,500
31-1-93	By Balance c/d	45,800	31-1-93	To Balance c/d	3,430
		2,22,860			2,22,860
1-2-93	By Balance b/d	3,430	1-2-93	To Balance b/d	45,800

In Bought Ledger Account
General Ledger Adjustment A/c

		Rs.			Rs.
1-1-93	To Balance b/d	24,000	1-1-93	By Balance b/d	2,500
31-1-93			31-1-93		
	To *Bought Ledger Adjustment A/c*			By *Bought Ledger Adjustment A/c*	
	Purchases	1,35,000		Purchase Returns	5,000
	To Balance c/d	2,600		Cash paid to suppliers	1,20,000
				Transfer from sales Ledger	5,200
				Discount received from customers	1,800
				Bills payable	5,600
				By Balance c/d	21,500
		1,61,600			1,61,600
1-2-93	To Balance b/d	21,500	1-2-93	By Balance b/d	2,600

Problem No. 16

Prepare necessary Ledger Accounts in the ledger of Ramanath, who keeps his ledger on self balancing system.

Debtors balance on 1-1-1993 (Dr) 38,000; (Cr) 400	Rs.
Creditors balance on 1-1-1993 (Cr) 47,000; (Dr) 700	
Credit sales	1,50,000
Credit purchases	1,20,000
Cash received from Debtors	1,23,000
Cash paid to Creditors	97,000
Allowance to Customers	1,000
Bad Debt written off	20,000
Bills received	5,000
Bills accepted	6,000
Discount received from Creditors	700
Return outward	12,500
Return inward	9,600
Cash sales	40,000
Cash paid to Customers	12,000
Bills Receivable endorsed to Creditors	2,000
Bills Receivable endorsed dishonoured	800
Bad debt written off recovered	1,300
Sundry charges charged to Debtors	50

(K.U.D., October 1994)

Solution :

In the General Ledger
Debtors Ledger Adjustment A/c

		Rs.			Rs.
1-1-93	To Balance b/d	38,000	1-1-93	By Balance b/d	400
	To *General Ledger Adjustment A/c*			By *General Ledger Adjustment A/c*	
	Credit Sales	1,50,000		Cash received	1,23,000
	Cash paid to customer	12,000		Allowances to customers	1,000
	Sundry charges	50		Bad debts written off	20,000
				Bill Receivable received	5,000
				Return Inward	9,600
				By Balance c/d	41,050
		2,00,050			2,00,050
	To Balance b/d	41,050			

Creditors Ledger Adjustment Account

		Rs.			Rs.
1-1-93	To Balance b/d	7,000	1-1-93	By Balance b/d	47,000
	To *General Ledger Adjustment A/c*			By *General Ledger Adjustment A/c*	
	Bills payable accepted	6,000		Purchases	1,20,000
	Cash paid	97,000		BR endorsed dishonoured	800
	Discount received	700			
	BR endorsed to Creditors	2,000			
	Return outward	12,500			
	To Balance c/d	48,900			
		1,67,800			1,67,800
				By Balance b/d	48,900

In the Debtors Ledger
General Ledger Adjustment A/c

1-1-93	To Balance b/d	400	1-1-93	By Balance b/d	38,000
	To *Debtors Ledger Adjustment A/c*			By *Debtors Ledger Adjustment A/c*	
	Cash received	1,23,000		Creditors sales	1,50,000
	Allowances to Customers	1,000		Cash paid to Customers	12,000
	Bad debts written off	20,000		Sundry charges	50
	Bills receivable received	5,000			
	Return inward	9,600			
	To Balance c/d	41,050			
		2,00,050			2,00,050
				By Balance b/d	41,050

In the Creditors Ledger
General Ledger Adjustment Account

1-1-93	To Balance b/d	47,000	1-1-93	By Balance b/d	700
	To *Creditors Ledger Adjustment A/c*			By *Creditors Ledger Adjustment A/c*	
	BR endorsed	800		Cash paid	97,000
	Credit purchases	1,20,000		BP accepted	6,000
				Discount received	700
				Return outward	12,500
				BR endorsed to Creditors	2,000
				By Balance c/d	48,900
		1,67,800			1,67,800
	To Balance b/d	48,900			

Problem No. 17

From the following particulars prepare necessary adjustment accounts in the respective ledgers which are kept on self-balancing system :

		Rs.
Jan. 1st, 1990	Balance on purchase ledger	15,000
Jan. 31st, 1990	Credit purchase	60,000
	Returns outwards	3,000
	Cash paid to suppliers	25,000
	Cheques issued to suppliers	20,000
	Cash purchases	10,000
	Bills accepted in favour of Creditors	4,000
	Discounts allowed by Creditors	1,000
	Cheques dishonoured	500
	Noting charges on dishonoured Bill	50
	Bills Unpaid	1,000
	Rebate allowed by suppliers	400
	Interest charged by Creditors	100
	Excess amount paid to Creditors refunded	200
	Transfer from Debtors Ledger	600
	Purchase ledger Balance (Dr)	200

(K.U.D., April 1994)

Solution :

In General Ledger

Creditors Ledger Adjustment A/c

	Rs.		Rs.
To *General Ledger Adjustment A/c*		1-1-90	
		By Balance b/d	15,000
Return outward	3,000	By *General Ledger Adjustment A/c*	
Cash paid	25,000		
Cheques issued	20,000	Credit purchases	60,000
Bills payable	4,000	Cheques dishonoured	500
Discounts allowed	1,000	Noting charges on Dishonoured Bills	50
Rebate allowed	400	Bills Unpaid	1,000
Transfer from Drs. Ledger	600	Excess amount paid refunded	200
31-3-90 To Balance c/d	23,050	31-1-90 By Balance c/d	200
	77,050		77,050
Feb. 1 To Balance b/d	200	By Balance b/d	23,050

In Creditors Ledger

General Ledger Adjustment A/c

		Rs.			Rs.
1-1-90			1-1-90		
	To Balance b/d	15,000		By *Creditors Ledger Adjustment A/c*	
	To *Creditors Ledger Adjustment A/c*			Return outward	3,000
	Credit Purchases	60,000		Cash paid	25,000
	Cheques dishonoured	500		Cheques issued	20,000
	Noting charges on dishonoured Bill	50		Bills payable	4,000
	Bills unpaid	1,000		Discount allowed	1,000
	Interest charges	100		Rebate allowed	400
	Excess Amount paid refunded	200		Transfer from Debtors Ledger	600
31-1-90	To Balance c/d	200	31-1-90	By Balance c/d	23,050
		77,050			77,050
Feb. 1.	To Balance b/d	23,050		By Balance b/d	200

Note : Cash purchases — omitted.

Problem No. 18

Prepare necessary Ledger Accounts in the Ledger of Mr. P.M. Parvatikar, who keeps his Ledger on Self Balancing System.

		Rs.
(1)	Debtors Balance on 1-1-1990 (Dr)	20,000
(2)	Debtors Balance on 1-1-1990 (Cr)	100
(3)	Total Sales	1,37,000
(4)	Cash sales	7,000
(5)	Cash Purchases	8,000
(6)	Received from Debtors	60,000
(7)	Discount allowed	900
(8)	Bills Receivable debited	11,500
(9)	Sundry Charges debited	550
(10)	Interest Debited to Debtors	300
(11)	Bills Dishonoured	2,000
(12)	Transfer from Creditors Ledger	900
(13)	Reserve for Doubtful Debts	600
(14)	Bad Debts	450
(15)	Debtors Balance on 31-12-1990 (Cr)	200
(16)	Receipts by Cheque	40,000

(K.U.D., April 1993)

Solution :

In General Ledger
Debtors Ledger Adjustment A/c

	Rs.		Rs.
1-1-90 To Balance b/d	20,000	1-1-90 By Balance b/d	100
To *General Ledger Adjustment A/c*		By *General Ledger Adjustment A/c*	
Total Sales 1,37,000		Cash received	60,000
Less : Cash Sales 7,000		Discount allowed	900
Sales (Credit)	1,30,000	Bills Receivable	11,500
Sundry Charges	550	Transfers	900
Interest	300	Bad Debts	450
Bill dishonoured	2,000	Receipt by Cheque	40,000
31-12-90 To Balance c/d	200	31-12-90 By Balance c/d	39,200
	1,53,050		1,53,050
1-1-91 To Balance b/d	39,200	1-1-91 By Balance b/d	200

In Debtors Ledger
General Ledger Adjustment A/c

1-1-90 To Balance b/d	100	1-1-90 By Balance b/d	20,000
To *Debtors Ledger Adjustment A/c*		By *Debtors Ledger Adjustment A/c*	
Cash received	60,000	Sales (Credit) (1,37,000–7,000)	1,30,000
Discount allowed	900	Sundry Charges	550
Bills Receivable	11,500	Interest	300
Transfers	900	Bills dishonoured	2,000
Bad Debts	450	31-12-90 By Balance c/d	200
Receipts by cheque	40,000		
31-12-90 To Balance c/d	39,200		
	1,53,050		1,53,050

Note : (1) Cash Purchases not concerned — omitted.

(2) R.D.D. not concerned — omitted.

Problem No. 19

From the following particulars prepare necessary Ledger Adjustment Account in the respective Ledgers under Self Balancing system :

(1)	Creditors Balance on 1-1-91	Dr	4,000
		Cr	80,000

Transaction during the period :

(2)	Credit purchases	2,00,000
(3)	Cash purchases	40,000
(4)	Returns (Out of credit purchases)	15,000
(5)	Cash paid to suppliers	1,20,000
(6)	Discount received	12,000
(7)	Bills payable accepted	60,000
(8)	Bills payable accepted and cancelled	15,000
(9)	Interest on Bills cancelled	150
(10)	Transfer Debtors Ledger to Creditors Ledger	4,000
(11)	Creditors Debts Balance on 31-12-1991	4,500

(K.U.D., October 1993)

Solution :

Self Balancing Ledger (In General Ledger)
Creditors Ledger Adjustment A/c

1-1-91	To Balance b/d	4,000	1-1-91	By Balance b/d	80,000
	To *General Ledger Adjustment A/c*			By *General Ledger Adjustment A/c*	
	Returns (Credit Purchase)	15,000		Purchase (Credit)	2,00,000
	Cash paid	1,20,000		Bills payable cancelled	15,000
	Discount received	12,000		Interest on Bills cancelled	150
	Bills payable (accepted)	60,000	31-12-91	By Balance c/d	4,500
	Transfer from Drs. Ledger to Creditors Ledger	4,000			
31-12-91	To Balance c/d	84,650			
		2,99,650			2,99,650

In Creditor's Ledger
General Ledger Adjustment A/c

		Rs.			Rs.
1-1-91			1-1-91		
	To Balance b/d	80,000		By Balance b/d	4,000
	To *General Ledger Adjustment A/c*			By *General Ledger Adjustment A/c*	
	Purchases (Credit)	2,00,000		Returns	15,000
	Bills payable cancelled	15,000		Cash paid	1,20,000
	Interest on Bills cancelled	150		Bills payable (accepted)	60,000
1-12-91				Transfers from Debtors Ledger to Crs. Ledger	4,000
	To Balance c/d	4,500	31-12-91		
				By Balance c/d	84,650
		2,99,650			2,99,650

Problem No. 20

From the following particulars, prepare necessary Ledger Adjustment Accounts in the respective Ledgers kept under Self Balancing system :

		Rs.
Creditors Ledger Balances on 1-3-1992	Dr	600
	Cr	45,250
Transactions during the month of March 1992		
Purchases (including Cash Rs. 1,070)		62,570
Returns to suppliers		4,950
Cash paid to suppliers		49,500
Discount allowed by them		1,500
Cheques issued to suppliers		22,000
Bills payable accepted		14,500
Bills payable withdrawn		5,600
Cheques issued withdrawn		9,500
Interest paid on withdrawn cheque and Bills payable		950
Transfers from Debtors Ledger		2,000
Creditors Balance on 31-3-1991	Dr	1,475

(K.U.D., April 1992)

Solution :

In General Ledger
Creditors Ledger Adjustment A/c

		Rs.			Rs.
To Balance b/d		600	By Balance b/d		45,250
To *General Ledger Adjustment A/c*			By *General Ledger Adjustment A/c*		
Returns		4,950	Purchases	62,570	
Cash paid		49,500	*Less* : Cash	1,070	61,500
Discount allowed		1,500	Bills payable withdrawn		5,600
Cheque issued		22,000	Cheque withdrawn		9,500
Bills payable accepted		14,500	Interest paid		950
Transfers		2,000	By Balance c/d		1,475
To Balance c/d		29,225			
		1,24,275			1,24,275

In Creditors Ledger
General Ledger Adjustment A/c

To Balance b/d		45,250	By Balance b/d		600
To *Creditors Ledger Adjustment A/c*			By *Creditors Ledger Adjustment A/c*		
Purchases	62,570		Returns		4,950
Less : Cash	1,070	61,500	Cash paid		49,500
Bills payable withdrawn		5,600	Discount allowed		1,500
Cheque withdrawn		9,500	Cheque issued		22,000
Interest paid		950	Bills payable accepted		14,500
To Balance c/d		1,475	Transfer		2,000
			By Balance c/d		29,225
		1,24,275			1,24,275
1-4-91 To Balance b/d		29,225	By Balance b/d		1,475

Problem No. 21

Pass Self Balancing entries for the following :

(1) Sold Goods on credit worth Rs. 30,000 and allowed Trade discount @ 10%.

(2) Received Rs. 19,200 from customers and allowed them discount Rs. 800.

(3) Acceptances in favour of suppliers Rs. 10,000

(4) Bills Receivable unpaid Rs. 3,000

(5) Transferred 2,500 from Creditors A/c to Debtors A/c.

(6) Credit purchases of goods Rs. 8,900 and for cash Rs. 1,100.

(K.U.D., October 1992)

Solution :

Journal Entries for Self Balancing

			Dr. Rs.	Cr. Rs.
Original	(1) (a) Debtors A/c	Dr	27,000	
	To Sales A/c			27,000
	(Goods sold on credit Rs. 30,000 *Less* : Trade Discount @ 10% 3,000 = 27,000)			
OR	Debtors A/c	Dr	27,000	
	Trade Discount A/c	Dr	3,000	
	To Sales A/c			30,000
	(Goods sold on credit Rs. 30,000 and Trade discount allowed @ 10%)			
Self Balancing	(b) Debtors Ledger Adjustment A/c (in General Ledger)	Dr	27,000	
	To General Ledger Adjustment A/c (in Debtors Ledger)			27,000
	(Being entry for Self Balancing ledger)			
Original	(2) (a) Cash A/c	Dr	19,200	
	Discount A/c	Dr	800	
	To Debtors A/c			20,000
	(Cash received and discount allowed)			
Self Balancing	(b) General Ledger Adjustment A/c (in Debtors Ledger)		20,000	
	To Debtors Ledger Adjustment A/c (in General Ledger)			20,000
	(Being entry for Self Balancing Ledger)			

				Dr. Rs.	Cr. Rs.
Original	(3) (a)	Creditors A/c	Dr	10,000	
		To Bills Payable A/c			10,000
		(Bills accepted)			
Self Balancing	(b)	Creditors Ledger Adjustment A/c (in General Ledger)	Dr	10,000	
		To General Ledger Adjustment A/c			10,000
		(Being entry for Self Balancing)			
Original	(4) (a)	Debtors A/c	Dr	3,000	
		To Bills Receivable A/c			3,000
		[Bills Receivable unpaid (Dishonoured)]			
Self Balancing	(b)	Debtors Ledger Adjustment A/c (in General Ledger)	Dr	3,000	
		To General Ledger Adjustment A/c (In Debtors Ledger)			3,000
		(Being entry for Self Balancing Ledger)			
Original	(5) (a)	Creditors A/c	Dr	2,500	
		To Debtors A/c			2,500
		(Transfer from Creditor A/c to Debtor A/c)			
Self Balancing	(b)	Creditor Ledger Adjustment A/c (in General Ledger)	Dr	2,500	
		To General Ledger Adjustment A/c (in Creditors Ledger)			2,500
		(Being entry for transfer from Creditors Ledger)			
	(c)	Debtors Ledger Adjustment A/c (in General Ledger)	Dr	2,500	
		To General Ledger Adjustment A/c (in Debtors Ledger)			2,500
		(Being entry for transfer to Debtors Ledger)			
Original	(6) (a)	Purchase A/c	Dr	8,900	
		To Creditors A/c			8,900
		(Goods purchased on credit)			
Self Balancing	(b)	General Ledger Adjustment A/c (in Creditors Ledger)	Dr	8,900	
		To Creditors Adjustment A/c (in General Ledger)			8,900
		(Being entry for Self Balancing Ledger)			

Note : For cash purchases Rs. 1,100 no entry.

Problem No. 22

From the following particulars prepare the necessary Ledger Adjustment Accounts in the respective Ledgers kept under Self Balancing system :

			Rs.
(a)	Debtors Balance on 1-1-1990	(Dr)	65,000
(b)	Debtors Balance on 1-1-1990	(Cr)	3,750
	Transactions during the month :		
(c)	Sales : Credit		1,85,000
	Cash		35,750
(d)	Returns inward (of Credit sales)		9,750
(e)	Cash received from Debtors		1,69,000
(f)	Cheque received from Debtors		12,500
(g)	Discount allowed to customers		1,850
(h)	Bills Receivable received from Debtors		18,000
(i)	Bills Receivable endorsed		6,000
(j)	Bills Receivable discounted		9,000
(k)	Bills Receivable endorsed dishonoured		1,500
(l)	Bills Receivable discounted dishonoured		4,500
(m)	Noting charges debted to customers		625
(n)	Allowances to customers		125
(o)	Bad Debts written off		1,200
(p)	Reserve for Doubtful Debts		3,500
(q)	Bad Debts previously written off now recovered		2,750
(r)	Bank Charges debted to customers A/c		75
(s)	Transfer from Debtors Ledger to Creditors Ledger		1,000
(t)	Debtors Balance on 31-1-90		2,450

(K.U.D., April 1991)

Solution :

In General Ledger
Debtors Ledger Adjustment A/c

Date	Particulars	Rs.	Date	Particulars	Rs.
1-1-90			1-1-90		
	To Balance b/d	65,000		By Balance b/d	3,750
	To *General Ledger Adjustment A/c*			By *General Ledger Adjustment A/c*	
	Sales (Credit only)	1,85,000		Return Inward	9,750
	Bills Receivable endorsed dishonoured	1,500		Cash received	1,69,000
	Bills Receivable discounted dishonoured	4,500		Cheque received	12,500
	Noting Charges	625		Discount allowed	1,850
	Bank Charges	75		Bills Receivable received	18,000
31-1-90	To Balance c/d	2,450		Allowances to customers	125
				Bad Debts written off	1,200
				Transfers	1,000
			31-1-90	By Balance c/d	41,975
		2,59,150			2,59,150
1-2-90	To Balance b/d	41,975	1-2-90	By Balance b/d	2,450

In Debtors Ledger
General Ledger Adjustment A/c

Date	Particulars	Rs.	Date	Particulars	Rs.
1-1-90			1-1-90		
	To Balance b/d	3,750		By Balance b/d	65,000
	To *Debtors Ledger Adjustment A/c*			By *Debtors Ledger Adjustment A/c*	
	Return	9,750		Sales (Credit)	1,85,000
	Cash received	1,69,000		Bills Receivable endorsed dishonoured	1,500
	Cheques received	12,500		Bills discounted dishonoured	450
	Discount allowed	1,850		Noting Charges	625
	Bills Receivable recovered	18,000		Bank Charges	75
	Allowances to customers	125	31-1-90	By Balance c/d	2,450
				Bad Debts written off	1,200
				Transfers	1,000
31-1-90	To Balance c/d	41,975			
		2,59,150			2,59,150
1-2-90	To Balance b/d	2,450	1-2-90	By Balance b/d	41,975

Note : Items : (1) Cash sales (2) Bills Receivable endorsed (3) Bills Receivable Discounted (4) Bad Debts previously written off now recovered these are not concerned to debtors. Therefore omitted in above Ledger.

Problem No. 23

Prepare Self Balancing Account in the General Ledger for the following transactions :

			Rs.
(1)	Customer Balance on 1-4-1990	(Dr)	60,000
		(Cr)	1,000
(2)	Suppliers Balance on 1-4-90	(Cr)	30,000
		(Dr)	600
	Transactions during the year :		
(3)	Credit sales		42,000
(4)	Cash sales		9,000
(5)	Total Purchases		36,000
(6)	Cash Purchases		10,000
(7)	Payments to suppliers		31,000
(8)	Collections from customers		62,000
(9)	Reserve for Doubtful Debts		4,000
(10)	Bad Debts written off now recovered		1,500
(11)	Discount allowed to customers		1,200
(12)	Discount allowed by suppliers		1,300
(13)	Returns Inward		2,000
(14)	Carriages Inward		2,500
(15)	Purchase Returns		5,000
(16)	Bills Payable issued		8,000
(17)	Bills drawn on Debtors		6,000
(18)	Bills Receivable unpaid		3,000
(19)	Interest and Noting charges on Unpaid Bills		2,000
(20)	Bills Receivable endorsed in favour of Creditors		1,000
(21)	Balances transfers from Customers Accounts to Suppliers Account		500
(22)	Bad Debts written off		1,000
(23)	Balance of customer (Cr) on 31-3-1991		1,500
(24)	Balances of suppliers (Dr) on 31-3-1991		1,200

(K.U.D., October 1991)

Solution :

In General Ledger

Debtors (Customer) Ledger Adjustment A/c

	Rs.		Rs.
1-4-90 To Balance b/d	60,000	1-4-90 By Balance b/d	1,000
To *General Ledger Adjustment A/c*		By *General Ledger Adjustment A/c*	
Credit sales	42,000	Cash received	62,000
Bills receivable unpaid	3,000	Discount allowed	1,200
Interest and Noting charges on unpaid bill	200	Return Inward	2,000
31-3-91 To Balance c/d	1,500	Bills drawn on Debtors	6,000
		Balances transferred from Customers A/c to Suppliers A/c	500
		Bad debts written off	1,000
		31-3-91 By Balance c/d	33,000
	1,06,700		1,06,700
1-4-91 To Balance b/d	33,000	1-4-91 By Balance b/d	1,500

Creditors (Suppliers) Ledger Adjustment A/c

1-4-90 To Balance b/d	600	1-4-90 By Balance b/d		30,000
31-3-91 To *General Ledger Adjustment A/c*		By *General Ledger Adjustment A/c*		
Cash paid	31,000	Total Purchases	36,000	
Discount allowed	1,300	*Less* : Cash Purchases	10,000	
Purchase returns	5,000	Credit purchases		26,000
Bills payable issued	8,000	31-3-91 By Balances c/d		1,200
Bills Receivable endorsed in favour of credit	1,000			
Balances transferred from Customer A/c to Suppliers A/c	500			
To Balance c/d	9,800			
	57,200			57,200
1-4-91 To Balance b/d	1,200	1-4-91 By Balance b/d		9,800

In Debtors Ledger
General Ledger Adjustment A/c

		Rs.			Rs.
1-4-90	To Balance b/d	1,000	1-4-90	By Balance b/d	60,000
	To *Debtors Ledger Adjustment A/c*			By *Debtors Ledger Adjustment A/c*	
	Cash received	62,000		Credit sales	42,000
	Discount allowed	1,200		Bills receivable unpaid	3,000
	Return Inward	2,000		Interest and Noting	
	Bills drawn on Debtors	6,000		charges on unpaid bill	200
	Balances transferred	500	31-3-91	By Balance c/d	1,500
	Bad debts written off	1,000			
30-6-91	To Balance c/d	33,000			
		1,06,700			1,06,700
1-7-91	To Balance b/d	1,500	1-7-91	By Balance b/d	33,000

In Creditors Ledger
General Ledger Adjustment A/c

1-4-90	To Balance b/d		30,000	1-4-90	By Balance b/d	600
	To *Creditors Ledger Adjustment A/c*				By *Creditors Ledger Adjustment A/c*	
	Total Purchases	36,000			Cash paid	31,000
	Less : Cash				Discount received	1,300
	Purchases	10,000			Purchase returns	5,000
	Credit purchases		26,000		Bills payable issued	8,000
30-6-91	To Balance c/d		1,200		Bills Receivable endorsed in favour of credit	1,000
					Balances transferred	500
				30-6-91	By Balance c/d	9,800
			57,200			57,200
1-7-91	To Balance b/d		9,800	1-7-91	By Balance b/d	1,200

Problem No. 24

From the following particulars as extracted from the Books of Madhu prepare Debtors Ledger Adjustment Account and Creditors Ledger Adjustment Account in General Ledger kept under Self Balancing Ledger :

			Rs.
January 1, 1988			
(1)	Balance on Bought Ledger	(Dr)	1,750
	Balance on Bought Ledger	(Cr)	23,880
	Balance on Sold Ledger	(Dr)	29,240
	Balance on Sold Ledger	(Cr)	480
January 31, 1988			
(2)	Purchases		1,32,360
(3)	Purchases Returns		5,120
(4)	Sales		1,74,980
(5)	Sales Returns		2,340
(6)	Cash received from customer		1,52,420
(7)	Discount allowed thereon		5,640
(8)	Cash paid to creditors		1,16,860
(9)	Discount earned thereon		3,320
(10)	Cash paid to customer		260
(11)	Bills Receivable		8,240
(12)	Bills payable		4,500
(13)	Bills Receivable dishonoured		500
(14)	Bills Receivable discounted		1,000
(15)	Bills Receivable endorsed to Creditors		1,000
(16)	Bills Receivable endorsed dishonoured		500
(17)	Bought Ledger Balance	(Dr)	1,540
(18)	Sold Ledger Balance	(Dr)	36,700

(K.U.D., April 1990)

Solution :

In General Ledger

Sold Ledger Adjustment A/c

Or

Debtors Ledger Adjustment A/c

		Rs.			Rs.
1-1-88	To Balance b/d	29,240	1-1-88	By Balance b/d	480
	To *General Ledger Adjustment A/c*			By *General Ledger Adjustment A/c*	
	Sales	1,74,980		Sales returns	2,340
	Cash paid to customer	260		Cash received	1,52,420
	Bills Receivable dishonoured	500		Discount allowed	5,640
	Bills Receivable endorsed dishonoured	500		Bills Receivable	8,240
			31-1-88	By Balance c/d	36,700
31-1-88	To Balance c/d	340			
		2,05,820			2,05,820
1-2-88	To Balance b/d	36,700	1-2-88	By Balance c/d	340

Bought Ledger Adjustment A/c

Or

Creditors Ledger Adjustment A/c

1-1-88	To Balance b/d	1,750	1-1-88	By Balance b/d	23,880
	To *General Ledger Adjustment A/c*			By *General Ledger Adjustment A/c*	
	Purchases return	5,120		Purchases	1,32,360
	Cash paid to Creditors	1,16,860		Bills receivable endorsed dishonoured	500
	Bills payable	4,500			
	Discount earned	3,3203	1-1-88	By Balance c/d	1,540
	Bills Receivable endorsed	1,000			
31-1-88	To Balance c/d	25,730			
		1,58,280			1,58,280
1-2-88	To Balance b/d	1,540	1-2-88	By Balance b/d	25,730

Note : Bills Receivable discounted — omitted.

In Sold Ledger

Or

In Debtors Ledger A/c

General Ledger Adjustment A/c

		Rs.			Rs.
1-1-88	To Balance b/d	480	1-1-88	By Balance b/d	29,240
	To *Debtors Ledger Adjustment A/c*			By *Debtors Ledger Adjustment A/c*	
	Sales returns	2,340		Sales	1,74,980
	Cash received	1,52,420		Cash paid to customer	260
	Discount allowed	5,640		Bills Receivable discounted	500
	Bills Receivable	8,240		Bills Receivable endorsed dishonoured	500
31-1-88	To Balance c/d	36,700	31-1-88	By Balance c/d	340
		2,05,820			2,05,820
1-2-88	To Balance b/d	340	1-2-88	By Balance b/d	36,700

In Bought Ledger

In Creditors Ledger

General Ledger Adjustment A/c

1-1-88	To Balance b/d	23,880	1-1-88	By Balance b/d	1,750
	To *Creditors Ledger Adjustment A/c*			By *Creditors Ledger Adjustment A/c*	
	Purchases	1,32,360		Purchase Returns	5,120
	Bills Receivable endorsed dishonoured	500		Cash paid to Creditors	1,16,860
31-1-88	To Balance c/d	1,540		Discount earned	3,320
				Bills payable	4,500
				Bills Receivable endorsed to Creditors	1,000
			31-1-88	By Balance c/d	25,730
		1,58,280			1,58,280

Problem No. 25

From the following transactions prepare the necessary Ledger Adjustment Accounts in the respective Ledgers maintained under Self Balancing system :

		Rs.
(1)	Balance of Debtors on 1-1-1989 (Dr)	32,000
(2)	Balance of Debtors on 1-1-1989 (Cr)	500
(3)	Sales (including cash sales Rs. 15,000)	1,90,000
(4)	Sales Returns	2,500
(5)	Received from Debtors (including by Cheque of Rs. 30,000)	1,50,000
(6)	Discount allowed to Debtors	4,500
(7)	Sundry Charges Debtors to Debtors	125
(8)	Interest charged to customer for overdue	75
(9)	Bills endorsed to Creditors	1,200
(10)	Bills accepted by Debtors	10,000
(11)	Transfers from Creditors Ledger	4,000
(12)	Cheques recovered from Debtors dishonoured	500
(13)	Bills Receivable dishonoured	2,000
(14)	Bad Debts written off after deducting bad debts written off previously now recovered Rs. 200	800
(15)	Bills receivable endorsed dishonoured	600
(16)	Provision for doubtful debts	1,500
(17)	Balance of Debtors on 31-12-89	700

(K.U.D., October 1990)

Solution :

In General Ledger

Debtors Ledger Adjustment A/c

1-1-89	To Balance b/d		32,000	1-1-89	By Balance b/d		500
	To *General Ledger Adjustment A/c*				By *General Ledger Adjustment A/c*		
	Sales	1,90,000			Sales Return		2,500
	Less : Cash sales	15,000			Received from Debtors :		
	Credit Sales		1,75,000		Cash	1,20,000	
	Sundry charges		125		Cheque	30,000	1,50,000
	Interest on overdue amount		75		Discount allowed		4,500
	Cheques dishonoured		500		Bills receivable		10,000
	Bills Receivable endorsed dishonoured		600		Transfer from Credit Ledger		4,000
31-12-89	To Balance c/d		700		Bad Debtors written off (800 + 200)		1,000
				31-12-89	By Balance c/d		36,500
			2,09,000				2,09,000

In Debtors Ledger
General Ledger Adjustment A/c

			Rs.				Rs.
1-1-89	To Balance b/d		500	1-1-89	By Balance b/d		32,000
	To *Debtors Ledger Adjustment A/c*				By *Debtors Ledger Adjustment A/c*		
	Sales Returns		2,500		Sales	1,90,000	
	Received from Debtors :				*Less* : Cash Sales	15,000	
	Cash	1,20,000			Credit Sales		1,75,000
	By Cheque	30,000	1,50,000		Sundry Charges		125
	Discount allowed		4,500		Interest on overdue amount		75
	Bills Receivable		10,000		Cheques Dishonoured		500
	Transfer from Cr. Ledger		4,000		Bills Receivable endorsed dishonoured		600
	Bad debts written off (800 + 200)		1,000	31-12-89	By Balance c/d		700
31-12-89	To Balance c/d		36,500				
			2,09,000				2,09,000

Note : (1) Bills Receivable endorsed and R.D.D. omitted.

(2) Bad Debts written off will be (800 + 200) Rs. 1,000.

Problem No. 26

From the following prepare necessary Ledger Adjustment Accounts in the Books of Mr. Bhaskar Rao who keeps his books under Self Balancing system :

			Rs.
(1)	Balance of Debtors on 1-1-1989	Dr	40,000
(2)	Balance of Debtors on 1-1-1989	Cr	200
	Transactions for the year 1989 :		
(3)	Credit Sales		2,60,000
(4)	Cash Sales		10,000
(5)	Sales Returns (out of credit sales)		2,000
(6)	Cash Received from Debtors		1,15,000
(7)	Discount allowed		1,800
(8)	Bills Receivable received from Debtors		21,000
(9)	Sundry Charges debited to Customer A/c		1,100
(10)	Bills dishonoured by Debtors		4,000
(11)	Bills Receivable discounted		8,000
(12)	Interest debited to Customer A/c		600
(13)	Bills Receivable endorsed to Creditors		2,000
(14)	Transfers from Creditors Ledger to Debtors Ledger		1,800

		Rs.
(15)	Provision for Doubtful Debts	1,200
(16)	Bad Debts written off	900
(17)	Balance of Debtors 31-12-1989 (Cr)	400

(K.U.D., October 1990)

Note : Self Balancing Ledger.

Solution :

In General Ledger

Debtors Ledger Adjustment A/c

		Rs.			Rs.
1-1-89	To Balance b/d	40,000	1-1-89	By Balance b/d	200
	To *General Ledger Adjustment A/c*			By *General Ledger Adjustment A/c*	
	Sales (Credit)	2,60,000		Sales returns	2,000
	Sundry Charges	1,100		Cash received	1,15,000
	Interest Debited	600		Discount allowed	1,800
	Bills Receivable dishonoured	4,000		Bills Receivable	21,000
				Transfers from Creditors Ledger	1,800
31-12-89	To Balance c/d	400		Bad Debts written off	900
			31-12-89	By Balance c/d	1,63,400
		3,06,100			3,06,100

In Debtors Ledger

General Ledger Adjustment A/c

1-1-89	To Balance b/d	200	1-1-89	By Balance b/d	40,000
	To *Debtors Ledger Adjustment A/c*			By *Debtors Ledger Adjustment A/c*	
	Sales return	2,000		Sales (Credit)	2,60,000
	Cash received	1,15,000		Sundry Charges	1,100
	Discount allowed	1,800		Interest Debited	600
	Bills Receivable	21,000		Bills Receivable dishonoured	4,000
	Transfer	1,800			
	Bad Debts written off	900	31-12-89	By Balance c/d	400
31-12-89	To Balance c/d	1,63,400			
		3,06,000			3,06,000

Note : Bills Receivable discounted and provision for Doubtful Debts omitted.

Problem No. 27

From the following transactions extracted from three Ledger namely Debtors Ledger, Creditors Ledger and General Ledger which are kept in Self Balancing system. Prepare the concerned Adjustment Accounts as they would appear in each of their Ledger :

1-1-1984		Rs.
(1)	Balance of Debtors	5,00,000
(2)	Balance of Creditors	3,50,000
31-12-1984		
(3)	Credit Purchases	1,20,000
(4)	Cash Purchases	1,50,000
(5)	Credit Sales	3,00,000
(6)	Cash Sales	1,80,000
(7)	Cash paid to Creditors	2,00,000
(8)	Received from Debtors	5,00,000
(9)	Discount allowed	12,000
(10)	Discount earned	8,000
(11)	Bills payable accepted	1,20,000
(12)	Bills Receivable received	1,00,000
(13)	Bills Receivable dishonoured	40,000
(14)	Returns from Debtors	18,000
(15)	Returns to Creditors	14,000
(16)	Bad Debts	6,000
(17)	Provision for Bad Debts	10,000

(Gulbarga, 1990)

Solution :

In General Ledger

Debtors Ledger Adjustment A/c

		Rs.			Rs.
1-1-84	To Balance b/d	5,00,000		By *General Ledger Adjustment A/c*	
	To *General Ledger Adjustment A/c*			Cash Received	5,00,000
	Sales (Credit)	3,00,000		Discount allowed	12,000
	Bills Receivable dishonoured	40,000		Bills Receivable received	1,00,000
				Returns from Debtors	18,000
				Bad Debts	6,000
			31-12-84	By Balance c/d	2,04,000
		8,40,000			8,40,000
1-1-85	To Balance b/d	2,04,000			

Creditors Ledger Adjustment A/c

		Rs.			Rs.
			1-1-84	By Balance b/d	3,50,000
	To *General Ledger Adjustment A/c*			By *General Ledger Adjustment A/c*	
	Cash paid to Creditors	2,00,000		Credit Purchases	1,20,000
	Discount earned	8,000			
	Bills payable accepted	1,20,000			
	Returns from Creditors	14,000			
31-12-84	To Balance c/d	1,28,000			
		4,70,000			4,70,000
			1-1-85	By Balance b/d	1,28,000

Note : (1) Cash Sales,

(2) Cash Purchased and

(3) Provision for Bad Debts — omitted.

Extra Solution :

In Debtors Ledger

General Ledger Adjustment A/c

			1-1-84	By Balance b/d	5,00,000
	To *Debtors Ledger Adjustment A/c*			By *Debtors Ledger Adjustment A/c*	
	Cash Received	5,00,000		Credit Sales	3,00,000
	Discount allowed	12,000		Bills Receivable dishonoured	40,000
	Bills Receivable received	1,00,000			
	Returns from Debtors	18,000			
	Bad Debts	6,000			
31-12-84	To Balance c/d	2,04,000			
		8,40,000			8,40,000

In Creditors Ledger
General Ledger Adjustment A/c

		Rs.			Rs.
1-1-84	To Balance b/d	3,50,000			
	To *Creditors Ledger Adjustment A/c*			By *Creditors Ledger Adjustment A/c*	
	Credit Purchases	1,20,000		Cash paid to Creditors	2,00,000
				Discount earned	8,000
				Bills payable accepted	1,20,000
				Returns to Creditors	14,000
			31-12-84	By Balance c/d	1,28,000
		4,70,000			4,70,000

Problem No. 28

From the following transactions prepare the necessary Ledger Adjustment Accounts in the respective Ledgers as on 31-12-1988 :

			Rs.
(1)	Balance of Debtors on 1-1-1988	(Dr)	30,000
(2)	Balance of Debtors on 1-1-1988	(Cr)	1,500
(3)	Credit Sales		75,000
(4)	Cash received from Debtors		40,000
(5)	Cash Sales		35,000
(6)	Discount allowed		2,500
(7)	Bills Receivable received		25,000
(8)	Bad Debts written off		750
(9)	Returns from Debtors		3,000
(10)	Bills Receivable dishonoured		1,250
(11)	Bad Debts previously written off now recovered		1,000
(12)	Transfer from Creditors Ledger		3,000
(13)	Bills Receivable discounted		3,000
(14)	Provision for doubtful debts		2,000
(15)	Balance of Debtors on 31-12-1988	(Cr)	1,000

(K.U.D., April 1989)

Solution :

In General Ledger
Debtors Ledger Adjustment A/c

		Rs.			Rs.
1-1-88	To Balance b/d	30,000	1-1-88	By Balance b/d	1,500
	To *General Ledger Adjustment A/c*			By *General Ledger Adjustment A/c*	
	Credit Sales	75,000		Cash received	40,000
	Bills Receivable dishonoured	1,250		Discount allowed	2,500
31-12-88	To Balance c/d	1,000		Bills Receivable	25,000
				Bad Debts written off	750
				Returns from Debtors	3,000
				Transfer from Creditors Ledger	3,000
			31-12-88	By Balance c/d	31,500
		1,07,250			1,07,250
1-1-88	To Balance b/d	31,500	1-1-89	By Balance b/d	1,000

In Debtors Ledger
General Ledger Adjustment A/c

1-1-88	To Balance b/d	1,500	1-1-88	By Balance b/d	30,000
	To *Debtors Ledger Adjustment A/c*			By *Debtors Ledger Adjustment A/c*	
	Cash received	40,000		Creditors	75,000
	Discount allowed	2,500		Bills Receivable dishonoured	1,250
	Bills Receivable	25,000	31-12-88	By Balance c/d	1,000
	Bad Debts written off	750			
	Returns from Debtors	3,000			
	Transfer to Drs. Ledger	3,000			
31-12-88	To Balance c/d	31,500			
		1,07,250			1,07,250
1-1-88	To Balance b/d	1,000	1-1-89	By Balance b/d	31,500

Note : (1) Cash Sales,

(2) Bills Receivable Discounted,

(3) Bad Debts previously written off now recovered and

(4) Provision for Bad Debts — omitted.

Problem No. 29

From the following particulars prepare the Debtors Ledger Adjustment Account and Creditors Ledger Adjustment Account as they would appear in the General Ledger :

		Rs.
(1)	Debit Balance of Trade Debtors on 1st March	28,500
(2)	Credit Balance of Trade Debtors on 1st March	650
(3)	Credit Balance of Trade Creditors on 1st March	47,800
(4)	Debit Balance of Trade Creditors on 1st March	380
Transactions during the month :		
(5)	Creditors Sales	43,800
(6)	Cash Sales	36,000
(7)	Cash received from Trade Debtors	30,750
(8)	Discount allowed	2,600
(9)	Bills Receivable received	5,000
(10)	Bad Debts	200
(11)	Credit Purchases	68,800
(12)	Cash paid to Trade Creditors	59,000
(13)	Purchase return	2,000
(14)	Credit Balance of Trade Debtors on 31st March	750
(15)	Debt Balance of Trade Creditors on 31st March	500

(K.U.D., October 1989)

Solution :

In General Ledger

Debtors Ledger Adjustment A/c

	Rs.		Rs.
March 1 To Balance b/d	28,500	March 1 By Balance b/d	650
To *General Ledger Adjustment A/c*		By *General Ledger Adjustment A/c*	
Credit Sales	43,800	Cash Received	30,750
March 31 To Balance c/d	750	Discount allowed	2,600
		Bills Receivable received	5,000
		Bad Debts	200
		March 31 By Balance c/d	33,850
	73,850		73,850
April 1 To Balance b/d	33,850	April 1 By Balance b/d	750

Creditors Ledger Adjustment A/c

	Rs.		Rs.
March 1		March 1	
To Balance b/d	380	By Balance b/d	47,000
To *General Ledger Adjustment A/c*		By *General Ledger Adjustment A/c*	
Cash paid to Creditors	59,000	Credit purchases	68,800
Purchase Return	2,000	March 31	
March 31		By Balance c/d	500
To Balance c/d	55,720		
	1,17,100		1,17,100
April 1 To Balance b/d	500	April 1 By Balance b/d	55,720

Note : Cash sale omitted.

Extra Solution :

In Debtors Ledger

General Ledger Adjustment A/c

Mar. 1 To Balance b/d	650	Mar. 1 By Balance	28,500
To *Debtors Ledger Adjustment A/c*		By *Debtors Ledger Adjustment A/c*	
Cash received	30,750	Credit Sales	43,800
Discount allowed	2,600	March 31	
Bills receivable	5,000	By Balance c/d	750
Bad debts	200		
Mar. 31 To Balance c/d	33,850		
	73,050		73,050
April 1 To Balance b/d	750	April 1 By Balance b/d	33,850

In Creditors Ledger

General Ledger Adjustment A/c

Mar. 1 To Balance b/d	47,800	Mar. 1 By Balance b/d	380
To *Creditors Ledger Adjustment A/c*		By *Creditors Ledger Adjustment A/c*	
Credit Purchase	68,800	Cash paid to Creditors	59,000
Mar. 31 To Balance c/d	500	Purchase return	2,000
		Mar. 31 By Balance c/d	55,720
	1,17,100		1,17,100
April 1 To Balance b/d	55,720	April 1 By Balance b/d	500

Problem No. 30

From the following particulars as extracted from the books of Basavaraj of Hubli prepare necessary Ledger Adjustment Accounts in the respective Ledgers :

			Rs.
(1)	Creditors Balance on 1-1-1988	(Cr)	26,000
(2)	Creditors Balance on 1-1-1988	(Dr)	3,000
(3)	Credit Purchases during the month		65,000
(4)	Cash purchase during the month		24,000
(5)	Cash paid to Creditors		36,000
(6)	Discount allowed by them		2,500
(7)	Bills payable accepted		21,000
(8)	Bills payable dishonoured		1,500
(9)	Purchase return		2,400
(10)	Creditors Balance on 31-1-1988	(Dr)	1,000

(K.U.D., April 1988)

Solution :

In General Ledger

Creditors Ledger Adjustment A/c

		Rs.			Rs.
1-1-88	To Balance b/d	3,000	1-1-88	By Balance b/d	26,000
	To *General Ledger Adjustment A/c*			By *General Ledger Adjustment A/c*	
	Cash paid to Creditors	36,000		Purchases (Credit)	65,000
	Discount received	2,500		Bills payable dishonoured	1,500
	Bills payable accepted	21,000	31-1-88	By Balance c/d	1,000
	Purchase return	2,400			
31-1-88	To Balance c/d	28,600			
		93,500			93,500
1-2-88	To Balance b/d	1,000	1-2-88	By Balance b/d	28,600

In Creditors Ledger

General Ledger Adjustment A/c

1-1-88	To Balance b/d	26,000	1-1-88	By Balance b/d	3,000
	To *Creditors Ledger Adjustment A/c*			By *Creditors Ledger Adjustment A/c*	
	Purchase (Credit)	65,000		Cash paid to Creditors	36,000
	Bills payable dishonoured	1,500		Discount received	2,500
31-12-88	To Balance c/d	1,000		Bills payable accepted	21,000
				Purchase Return	2,400
			31-12-88	By Balance c/d	28,600
		93,500			93,500

Problem No. 31

Pass the Self Balancing entries for the following transactions :

(1) Credit sales amounted to Rs. 30,000

(2) Payment to suppliers Rs. 42,500 and discount allowed by them Rs. 2,500

(3) Bills Receivable received from customers Rs. 10,000

(4) Bad Debts written off Rs. 2,000

(5) Bills Receivable discounted Rs. 5,000

(6) Transfer of Rs. 2,000 from Debtors Ledger to Creditors Ledger.

(K.U.D., October 1988)

Solution :

Self Balancing Entries

			Dr. Rs.	Cr. Rs.
Original	(1) (a) Debtors A/c	Dr	30,000	
	To Sales A/c			30,000
	(Goods sold on credit)			
For Self Balancing	(b) Debtors Ledger A/c	Dr	30,000	
	To General Ledger A/c			30,000
	(Entry on Self Balancing)			
Original	(2)(a) Creditors A/c	Dr	45,000	
	To Cash A/c			42,500
	To Discount allowed A/c			2,500
	(Cash pay and discount received)			
	(b) Creditors Ledger A/c	Dr	45,000	
	To General Ledger A/c			45,000
	(Transfer to Ledger)			
	(c) Creditors Ledger Adjustment A/c (in General Ledger)		45,000	
	To General Ledger Adjustment A/c (in Creditors Ledger)			45,000
	(Self Balancing entry)			
	(3) (a) Bills Receivable A/c	Dr	10,000	
	To Debtors A/c			10,000
	(Bills receivable to receive)			
	(b) General Ledger A/c	Dr	10,000	
	To Debtors Ledger A/c			10,000
	(Transfer entry)			

			Dr. Rs.	Cr. Rs.
(c)	General Ledger Adjustment A/c (in Debtors Ledger)	Dr	10,000	
	To Debtors Ledger Adjustment A/c (in General Ledger) (Self Balancing entry)			10,000
(4) (a)	Bad Debtors A/c	Dr	2,000	
	To Debtors A/c (Bad Debts written off)			2,000
(b)	General Ledger A/c	Dr	2,000	
	T. Debtors Ledger A/c (Transfer entry)			2,000
(c)	General Ledger Adjustment A/c (in Debtors Ledger)		2,000	
	To Debtors Ledger Adjustment A/c (in General Ledger) (Self Balancing entry)			2,000

Problem No. 32

Ramesh of Gulbarga maintains three Ledgers i.e., Debtors Ledger, Creditors Ledger and General Ledger. From the following particulars prepare : Debtors Ledger Adjustment Account, Creditors Ledger Account as they would appear in General Ledger.

			Rs.		Rs.
(1)	Debtors Balance on 1-1-1987	Dr	2,00,000	Cr	1,000
(2)	Creditors Balance on 1-1-1987	Dr	2,500	Cr	1,50,000

Transactions during month of January 1987 :

(3)	Total Sales	3,50,000
(4)	Total Purchases	2,00,000
(5)	Cash Purchases	50,000
(6)	Cash received from Debtors	2,35,000
(7)	Cash paid to Creditors	1,80,000
(8)	Cash Sales	50,000
(9)	Sales Returns	10,000
(10)	Purchase Returns	5,000
(11)	Discount allowed	16,000
(12)	Discount earned	8,000
(13)	Sundry charges debited to Debtors	1,500
(14)	Bills Receivable Received	20,000
(15)	Accepted Bills payable	25,000

		Rs.
(16)	Bad Debts	15,000
(17)	Provisions for Doubtful Debts	10,000
(18)	Bills Receivable dishonoured	4,000
(19)	Bad Debts previously written off recovered	3,000
(20)	Transfers from Debtors Ledger to Creditors Ledger	10,000
(21)	Balance of Creditors on 31-1-1987 (Dr)	500
(22)	Balance of Debtors on 31-1-1987 (Cr)	1,500

(Gulbarga, April 1987)

Solution :

In General Ledger

Debtors Ledger Adjustment A/c

			Rs.				Rs.
1-1-87	To Balance b/d		2,00,000	1-1-87	By Balance b/d		1,000
	To *General Ledger Adjustment A/c*				By *General Ledger Adjustment A/c*		
	Sales	3,50,000			Cash received		2,35,000
	Less : Cash sales	50,000	3,00,000		Sales Returns		10,000
	Sundry charges		1,500		Discount allowed		16,000
	Bills Receivable				Bills Receivable received		20,000
	dishonoured		4,000		Bad Debts		15,000
31-1-87	To Balance c/d		1,500		Transfer to Creditor Ledger		10,000
			31-1-87		By Balance c/d		2,00,000
			5,07,000				5,07,000
1-2-87	To Balance b/d		2,00,000	1-2-87	By Balance b/d		1,500

Creditors Ledger Adjustment A/c

			Rs.				Rs.
1-1-87	To Balance b/d		2,500	1-1-87	By Balance b/d		1,50,000
	To *General Ledger Adjustment A/c*				By *General Ledger Adjustment A/c*		
	Cash paid		1,80,000		Purchases	2,00,000	
	Purchase return		5,000		*Less* : Cash		
	Discount earned		8,000		Purchases	50,000	
	Bills payable		25,000				1,50,000
	Transfer from Debtors			31-1-87	By Balance c/d		500
	Ledger		10,000				
31-1-87	To Balance c/d		70,000				
			3,00,500				3,00,500

Note : (1) Cash Sales, (2) Cash purchases, (3) Provision for Doubtful debts, and (4) Bad debts previously written off now recovered — omitted.

Solution :

In Debtors Ledger
General Ledger Adjustment A/c

			Rs.				Rs.
1-1-87	To Balance b/d		1,000	1-1-87	By Balance b/d		2,00,000
	To *Debtors Ledger Adjustment A/c*				By *Debtors Ledger Adjustment A/c*		
	Cash received		2,35,000		Sales	3,50,000	
	Cash return		10,000		*Less* : Cash Sales	50,000	3,00,000
	Discount allowed		16,000		Sundry Charges		1,500
	Bills Receivable received		20,000		Bills Receivable dishonoured		4,000
	Bad Debts		15,000	31-1-87	By Balance c/d		15,000
	Transfer to Creditors Ledger		10,000				
31-1-87	To Balance c/d		2,00,000				
			5,07,000				5,07,000

In Creditors Ledger
General Ledger Adjustment A/c

1-1-87	To Balance b/d		1,50,000	1-1-87	By Balance b/d	2,500
	To *Creditors Ledger Adjustment A/c*				By *Creditors Ledger Adjustment A/c*	
	Purchases	2,00,000			Cash paid	1,80,000
	Less : Cash				Discount earned	8,000
	Purchase	50,000	1,50,000		Purchases return	5,000
31-1-87	To Balance c/d		500		Bills payable	25,000
					Transfer from Debtors Ledger	10,000
				31-1-87	By Balance c/d	70,000
			3,00,500			3,00,500

Problem No. 33

Mr. Avinash of Raichur maintains three Ledgers viz., Debtors Ledger, Creditors and General Ledger on Self Balancing system. From the following particulars prepare General Ledger Adjustment Accounts as they would appear in Debtors Ledger and Creditors Ledger :

		Rs.	Rs.
(1)	Debtors Balance on 1-1-89	Dr. 60,000	Cr. 1,000
(2)	Creditors Balance on 1-1-89	Dr. 500	Cr. 40,000
	Transactions during the month of January 1987 :		
(3)	Collections from Debtors : by Cheques		10,000
	in Cash		30,000
(4)	Bills receivable received from Debtors		10,000
(5)	Total Purchases (including Cash purchase Rs. 7,000)		20,000
(6)	Total Sales (including Cash sales Rs. 5,000)		40,000
(7)	Bills accepted to Creditors		8,000
(8)	Cash paid to Creditors		30,000
(9)	Discount allowed to Debtors		500
(10)	Discount allowed by Creditors		200
(11)	Provisions for Bad Doubtful Debts		2,000
(12)	Bad Debts		4,000
(13)	Sales Returns		1,000
(14)	Purchase Returns		600
(15)	Transfers		5,000
(16)	Bad Debts recovered		2,000
(17)	Sundry Expenses charged to Debtors		1,000
(18)	Sundry Expenses charged by Creditors		300
(19)	Bills receivable dishonoured		1,000
(20)	Debtors Credit Balance 31-1-87		1,500
(21)	Creditors Debit Balance 31-1-87		950

(Gulbarga, October 1987)

Solution :

In Debtors Ledger
General Ledger Adjustment A/c

			Rs.				Rs.
1-1-87	To Balance b/d		1,000	1-1-87	By Balance b/d		60,000
	To *Debtors Ledger Adjustment A/c*				By *Debtors Ledger Adjustment A/c*		
	Collection from Debtors :				Sales	40,000	
	by Cheque	10,000			*Less* : Cash		
	in Cash	30,000	40,000		Sales	5,000	
	Bills Receivable received		10,000		Credit Sales		35,000
	Discount allowed		500		Sundry Expenses		1,000
	Bad Debts		4,000		Bills Receivable dishonoured		1,000
	Sales Return		1,000				
	Transfers		5,000	31-1-87	By Balance c/d		1,500
31-1-87	To Balance c/d		37,000				
			98,500				98,500
1-2-87	To Balance b/d		1,500	1-2-87	By Balance b/d		37,000

In Creditors Ledger
General Ledger Adjustment A/c

1-1-87	To Balance b/d		40,000	1-1-87	By Balance b/d		500
	To *General Ledger Adjustment A/c*				By *General Ledger Adjustment A/c*		
	Purchase	20,000			Bills Payable accepted		8,000
	Less : Cash				Cash paid		30,000
	Purchase	7,000			Discount received		200
	Credit Purchases		13,000		Purchases return		600
	Sundry Expenses		300		Transfer		5,000
31-1-87	To Balance c/d		950	31-1-87	By Balance c/d		9,950
			54,250				54,250

Note : (1) Cash Sales, (2) Cash Purchases,

(3) Provision for Doubtful debts, and (4) Bad debts recovered - omitted.

Extra Solution :

In General Ledger
Debtors Ledger Adjustment A/c

			Rs.				Rs.
1-1-87	To Balance b/d		60,000	1-1-87	By Balance b/d		1,000
	To *General Ledger Adjustment A/c*				By *General Ledger Adjustment A/c*		
	Sales	40,000			Collection from Debtors :		
	Less : Cash Sales	5,000	35,000		by Cheque	10,000	
	Sundry Expenses Debtors		1,000		in Cash	30,000	40,000
	Bills Receivable dishonoured		1,000		Bills Receivable received		10,000
31-1-87	To Balance c/d		1,500		Discount allowed		500
					Bad Debts		4,000
					Sales Return		1,000
					Transfers		5,000
				31-1-87	By Balance c/d		37,000
			98,500				98,500
1-2-87	To Balance b/d		37,000	1-1-87	By Balance b/d		1,500

In Creditors Ledger
General Ledger Adjustment A/c

1-1 87	To Balance b/d		500	1-1-87	By Balance b/d		40,000
	To *General Ledger Adjustment A/c*				By *General Ledger Adjustment A/c*		
	Bills Payable accepted		8,000		Purchase	20,000	
	Cash paid to Creditors		30,000		*Less* : Cash Purchase	7,000	
	Discount received		200		Credit Purchases		13,000
	Purchases return		600		Sundry Expenses		300
	Transfer		5,000				
31-1-87	To Balance c/d		9,950	31-1-87	By Balance c/d		950
			54,250				54,250
1-2-87	To Balance b/d		950	1-2-87	By Balance b/d		9,950

Problem No. 34

Manmohan Traders Ltd. provided the following particular for the year ending 30-6-1985. You are required to prepare the necessary Ledger Adjustment Accounts in the respective Ledgers which are maintained under Self Balancing system.

1-7-1984

		Rs.
(1)	Sales Ledger Balance	38,500
(2)	Provision for Doubtful debts	2,500
30-6-1985	*Transactions during the year :*	
(3)	Sales (including Cash sales Rs. 20,000)	1,25,000
(4)	Sales Return	6,500
(5)	Received from customers (including Rs. 10,000 by cheques)	95,000
(6)	Cheques dishonoured	4,250
(7)	Bills accepted by customers	8,750
(8)	Bills dishonoured	950
(9)	Bad debts written off	1,600
(10)	Interest on Customers overdue Accounts	100
(11)	Carriages charged to customers	200
(12)	Cash discount allowed to customers	1,800
(13)	Bad debts previously written off now recovered	400
(14)	Sales Ledger Closing Balance (Cr)	1,500

(K.U.D., April 1986)

Solution :

In General Ledger
Sales Ledger Adjustment A/c
OR, Debtors Ledger Adjustment A/c

1-7-84	To Balance b/d		38,500			
	To *General Ledger Adjustment A/c*				By *General Ledger Adjustment A/c*	
	Sales	1,25,000			Sales Return	6,500
	Less : Cash sales	20,000			Cash received (including cheques 10,000)	95,000
	Credit Sales		1,05,000		Bills Receivable received	8,750
	Cheque dishonoured		4,250		Bad debts	1,600
	Bills Receivable dishonoured		950		Discount allowed	1,800
	Interest on overdue		100			
	Carriage charged		200	30-6-85	By Balance c/d	36,850
30-6-85	To Balance c/d		1,500			
			1,50,500			1,50,500
1-7-85	To Balance b/d		36,850	1-7-85	By Balance b/d	1,500

In Debtors Ledger
(Sales Ledger)
General Ledger Adjustment A/c

			Rs.				Rs.
1-7-84	To Balance b/d		—	1-7-84	By Balance b/d		38,500
	To *Debtors Ledger Adjustment A/c*				By *Debtors Ledger Adjustment A/c*		
	Sales Return		6,500		Sales	1,25,000	
	Cash received (including cheques 10,000)		95,000		*Less* : Cash sales	20,000	
					Credit Sales		1,05,000
	Bills Receivable received		8,750		Cheque dishonoured		4,250
	Bad Debts		1,600		Bills Receivable dishonoured		950
	Discount allowed		1,800		Interest on overdue		100
30-6-85	To Balance c/d		36,850		Carriage charges		200
				30-6-85	By Balance c/d		1,500
			1,50,500				1,50,500
1-7-85	To Balance b/d		1,500	1-7-85	By Balance b/d		36,850

Note : (1) Cash sales, (2) Cash purchase, (3) Provision for doubtful debts — omitted.

Problem No. 35

From the following transactions prepare the necessary Ledger Adjustment Accounts as on 31-12-1978 in the respective Ledgers which are maintained on Self Balancing System :

			Rs.
(1)	Balance of Debtors on 1-1-1978	(Dr)	52,500
(2)	Balance of Debtors on 1-1-1978	(Cr)	4,500
(3)	Collected from Debtors by cheque		20,000
(4)	Credit Sales		2,50,000
(5)	Sundry charges debited to Debtors		100
(6)	Cash received from Debtors		1,21,300
(7)	Bills Receivable received		84,000
(8)	Goods returned from Debtors		2,500
(9)	Discount allowed to Debtors		900
(10)	Bad Debts written off		2,400
(11)	Debtors cheques dishonoured		4,000
(12)	Transfer from Creditors Ledger		5,940
(13)	Balance of Debtors on 31-12-1978	(Cr)	4,550

(K.U.D., October 1979)

Solution :

Self Balancing Ledger
In the Books of General Ledger
Debtors Ledger Adjustment Account

		Rs.			Rs.
1978			1978		
Jan. 1	To Balance b/d	52,500	Jan. 1	By Balance b/d	4,500
	To *General Ledger Adjustment A/c*			By *General Ledger Adjustment A/c*	
	Sales (Credit only)	2,50,000		Cheques received	20,000
	Sundry charges	100		Cash received	1,21,300
	Cheques dishonoured	4,000		Bills receivable	84,000
31-12-78	By Balance c/d	4,550		Return inward	2,500
				Disallowed	900
				Bad Debts written off	2,400
				Transfer from Creditor	5,940
			31-12-78	By Balance c/d	60,610
		3,11,150			3,11,150
1-1-79	To Balance b/d	69,610	1-1-79	By Balanced b/d	4,550

In the Books of Debtors Ledger
General Ledger Adjustment Account

1-1-78	To Balance b/d	4,500	1-1-78	By Balance b/d	52,500
	To *Debtors Ledger Adjustment A/c*			By *Debtors Ledger Adjustment A/c*	
	Cheques received	20,000		Sales (Credit)	2,50,000
	Bills Receivable received	84,000		Sundry charges	100
	Cash received	1,21,300		Cheques dishonoured	4,000
	Return Inward	2,500	31-12-78	By Balance b/d	4,550
	Disallowed	900			
	Bad Debts written off	2,400			
	Transfer from Creditors Ledger	5,940			
31-12-78	To Balance c/d	69,610			
		3,11,150			3,11,150

Problem No. 36

Prepare the Bought Ledger Adjustment A/c and Sales Ledger Adjustment Account as would appear in General Ledger of M/s Hindustan Traders for the year 31-12-1985 from the following information :

			Rs.
(1)	Bought Ledger Balance on 1-1-1985	(Dr)	3,920
		(Cr)	54,500
(2)	Sales Ledger Balance on 1-1-1985	(Dr)	66,300
		(Cr)	1,250
	Transactions during the year :		
(3)	Purchases		2,97,800
(4)	Purchases return		11,500
(5)	Sales		3,93,700
(6)	Sales return		5,400
(7)	Cash received from Debtors		3,42,950
(8)	Discount allowed		12,700
(9)	Cash paid to Creditors		2,50,000
(10)	Discount received		5,000
(11)	Cash refunded to Debtors		1,050
(12)	Bills receivable received		24,500
(13)	Bills payable accepted		14,000
(14)	Bills receivable dishonoured		2,500
(15)	Bad Debts written off		4,500
(16)	Provision for Doubtful debts		6,500
(17)	Transferred from Debtors Ledger to Creditors Ledger		1,500
(18)	Transferred from Creditors Ledger to Debtors Ledger		3,500
(19)	Closing Balance 31-12-1985 :		
	Bought Ledger	(Dr)	4,500
	Sales Ledger	(Cr)	2,500

Solution :

In General Ledger

Sales Ledger Adjustment A/c

Or

Debtors Ledger Adjustment A/c

			Rs.				Rs.
1-1-85	To Balance b/d		66,300	1-1-85	By Balance b/d		1,250
	To *General Ledger Adjustment A/c*				By *General Ledger Adjustment A/c*		
	Sales		3,93,700		Sales Return		5,400
	Cash refunded		1,050		Cash received		3,42,950
	Bills Receivable dishonoured		2,500		Discount allowed		12,700
31-12-85	To Balance c/d		2,500		Bills Receivable		24,500
					Bad Debts written off		4,500
					Transfers from Debtors to Creditors	1,500	
					Creditors to Debtors	3,500	5,000
				31-12-85	By Balance c/d		69,750
			4,66,050				4,66,050

Bought Ledger Adjustment A/c

Or

Creditors Ledger Adjustment A/c

1-1-85	To Balance b/d		3,920	1-1-85	By Balance b/d	54,500
	To *General Ledger Adjustment A/c*				By *General Ledger Adjustment A/c*	
	Purchase Return		11,500		Purchases	2,97,800
	Cash paid		2,50,500	31-12-85	By Balance c/d	4,500
	Discount received		5,000			
	Transfer from Drs to Crs	1,500				
	Crs to Drs	3,500	5,000			
31-12-85	To Balance c/d		66,880			
			3,56,800			3,56,800

Note : Provision for Doubtful debt omitted.

In Sales Ledger *OR* In Debtors Ledger
General Ledger Adjustment A/c

			Rs.				Rs.
1-1-85	To Balance b/d		1,250	1-1-85	By Balance b/d		66,300
	To *Debtors Ledger Adjustment A/c*				By *Debtors Ledger Adjustment A/c*		
	Sales Return		5,400		Sales		3,93,700
	Cash received		3,42,950		Cash refunded		1,050
	Discount allowed		12,700		Bills Receivable dishonoured		2,500
	Bill Receivable		24,500				
	Bad Debts written off		4,500	31-12-85	By Balance c/d		2,500
	Transfer from :						
	Drs to Crs	1,500					
	Crs to Drs	3,500	5,000				
31-12-85	To Balance c/d		69,750				
			4,66,050				4,66,050

In Bought Ledger *OR* In Creditors Ledger
General Ledger Adjustment A/c

			Rs.				Rs.
1-1-85	To Balance b/d		54,500	1-1-85	By Balance b/d		3,920
	To *Creditors Ledger Adjustment A/c*				By *Creditors Ledger Adjustment A/c*		
	Purchases		2,97,800		Purchases returns		11,500
31-12-85	To Balance c/d		4,500		Cash paid		2,50,500
					Discount received		5,000
					Bills payable		14,000
					Transfers from :		
					Drs to Crs	1,500	
					Crs to Drs	3,500	5,000
				31-12-85	By Balance c/d		66,880
			3,56,800				3,56,800

Problem No. 37

From the following transactions of Business concern for the month of January 1990 prepare necessary Ledger Accounts in the respective Ledgers kept under Self Balancing system :

		Dr. Rs.	Cr. Rs.
(1)	Debtors Balance on 1-1-1990	38,000	1,250
(2)	Creditors Balance 1-1-1990	950	25,000
(3)	Provision for Bad debts		1,800
(4)	Sales (including Cash sales Rs. 15,000)		1,40,000
(5)	Purchases (including Cash purchases Rs. 2,000)		1,20,000
(6)	Return Inward		3,000
(7)	Return Outward		2,500
(8)	Cash received from Debtors (including Rs. 6,000 against Bad debts previously written off)		1,15,000
(9)	Cash paid to Creditors (in full settlement of Rs. 74,600)		72,000
(10)	Discount allowed to Debtors		1,800
(11)	Bills Receivable received from Debtors		10,500
(12)	Bills payable accepted		4,500
(13)	Bills receivable endorsed to Creditors		1,000
(14)	Provision for discount on Debtors		900
(15)	Provision for discount on Creditors		850
(16)	Endorsed Bills receivable dishonoured		500
(17)	Noting charges debited to Debtors		60
(18)	Bills Receivable discounted		6,000
(19)	Bills Receivable discounted dishonoured		4,500
(20)	Interest charges debited to Debtors		650
(21)	Allowance to Debtors		1,250
(22)	Bad debts written off		2,500
(23)	Balance of Debts on 31-1-90 (Cr)		2,570
(24)	Balance of Creditors on 31-1-90 (Dr)		3,750

Solution :

In General Ledger

Debtors Ledger Adjustment Account

Date	Particulars		Rs.	Date	Particulars		Rs.
1-1-90	To Balance b/d		38,000	1-1-90	By Balance b/d		1,250
	To *General Ledger Adjustment A/c*				By *General Ledger Adjustment A/c*		
	Sales	1,40,000			Return Inward		3,000
	Less Cash Sales	15,000	1,25,000		Cash received	1,15,000	
	Bills Receivable endorsed dishonoured		500		*Less* previously written off	6,000	1,09,000
	Noting charges		60		Discount allowed		1,800
	Bills Receivable discount dishonoured		4,500		Bills Receivable received		10,500
	Interest charges		650		Allowances		1,250
					Bad Debts written off		2,500
31-1-90	To Balance c/d		2,570	31-1-90	By Balance c/d		41,980
			1,71,280				1,71,280
1-2-90	To Balance c/d		41,980	1-2-90	By Balance c/d		2,570

Creditors Ledger Adjustment A/c

Date	Particulars		Rs.	Date	Particulars		Rs.
1-1-90	To Balance b/d		950	1-1-90	By Balance b/d		25,000
	To *General Ledger Adjustment A/c*				By *General Ledger Adjustment A/c*		
	Return outward		2,500		Purchases	1,20,000	
	Cash paid to creditors		72,000		*Less* Cash Purchase	2,000	1,18,000
	Discount received		2,600		Bills Receivable endorsed dishonoured		500
	Bills payable		4,500				
	Bills Receivable endorsed to Creditors		1,000	31-1-90	By Balance c/d		3,750
31-1-90	To Balance c/d		63,700				
			1,47,250				1,47,250
1-2-90	To Balance c/d		3,750	1-2-90	By Balance c/d		63,700

Note : (1) Provision for Doubtful Debts,

(2) Provision for discount on Debtors & Creditors, and

(3) Bills Receivable Discount — omitted.

(4) Cash sales & purchases deducted.

In Debtors Ledger
General Ledger Adjustment A/c

			Rs.				Rs.
1-1-90	To Balance b/d		1,250	1-1-90	By Balance b/d		38,000
	To *Debtors Ledger Adjustment A/c*				By *Creditors Ledger Adjustment A/c*		
	Return Inward		3,000		Sales	1,40,000	
	Cash paid	1,15,000			*Less* : Cash Sales	15,000	
	Less : Previously written off	6,000			Credit Sales		1,25,000
			1,09,000		Bills Receivable endorsed dishonoured		500
	Discount allowed		1,800		Noting charges		60
	Bills Receivable		10,500		Bills Receivable discounted dishonoured		4,500
	Allowance		1,250		Interest charges		650
	Bad Debts written off		2,500				
31-1-90	To Balance c/d		41,980	31-1-90	By Balance c/d		2,570
			1,71,280				1,71,280
1-2-90	To Balance b/d		2,570	1-2-90	By Balance b/d		41,980

In Creditors Ledger
General Ledger Adjustment A/c

1-1-90	To Balance b/d		25,000	1-1-90	By Balance b/d		950
	To *Creditors Ledger Adjustment A/c*				By *Creditors Ledger Adjustment A/c*		
	Purchases	1,20,000			Return outward		2,500
	Less : Cash Purchase	2,000			Cash paid		72,000
	Credit Purchases		1,18,000		Discount received		2,600
	Bills Receivable endorsed dishonoured		500		Bills payable		4,500
					Bills receivable endorsed to Creditors		1,000
31-1-90	By Balance c/d		3,750	31-1-90	By Balance c/d		63,700
			1,47,250				1,47,250
1-2-90	To Balance c/d		63,700	1-2-90	By Balance b/d		3,750

Problem No. 38

From the following information you are required to prepare the necessary Ledger Adjustment Account in the respective Ledgers under Self Balancing System :

		Rs.
(1)	Debtors Ledger Balance on 1-1-1988	54,200
(2)	Creditors Ledger Balance on 1-1-1988	40,350
(3)	Sales (including Cash sales Rs. 27,800)	4,52,400
(4)	Sales Return	3,300
(5)	Purchases (including Cash purchases 10,000)	3,36,700
(6)	Purchase Return	7,500
(7)	Cash received from Debtors (including Rs. 4,000 against Debts previously written off)	3,74,500
(8)	Discount allowed to Debtors	6,100
(9)	Bills Receivable received from Debtors	63,000
(10)	Cash paid to Creditors	2,16,900
(11)	Transfer from Bought Ledger to Sales Ledger	4,800
(12)	Bad Debts	3,800
(13)	Bills Receivable endorsed to Creditors	37,000
(14)	Discount received from Creditors	16,500
(15)	Bills payable accepted in favour of Creditors	72,000
(16)	Bills Receivable endorsed dishonoured	8,000
(17)	Credit Balance in Sales Ledger on 31-12-1988	3,100
(18)	Debts Balance in Bought Ledger on 31-12-1988	2,400

Solution :

In General Ledger

Sales Ledger Adjustment A/c

Date	Particulars		Rs.	Date	Particulars		Rs.
1-1-88	To Balance b/d		54,200				
	To *General Ledger Adjustment A/c*				By *General Ledger Adjustment A/c*		
	Sales	4,52,400			Sales Return		3,300
	Less : Cash Sales	27,800			Cash received	3,74,500	
	Credit Sales		4,24,600		*Less* : Cash received previously written off	4,000	
	Bills Receivable endorsed dishonoured		8,000				3,70,500
31-12-88	To Balance c/d		3,100		Discount allowed		6,100
					Bills Receivable received		63,000
					Transfer from Bought Ledger		4,800
					Bad Debts		3,800
				31-12-88	By Balance c/d		38,400
			4,89,900				4,89,900
1-1-89	To Balance b/d		35,400	1-1-89	By Balance b/d		3,100

Bought Ledger Adjustment A/c

Or

Creditors Ledger Adjustment A/c

			Rs.				Rs.
	To *General Ledger Adjustment A/c*			1-1-88	By Balance b/d		40,350
	Purchase Return		7,500		By *General Ledger Adjustment A/c*		
	Cash paid		2,16,900		Purchases	3,36,700	
	Transfer to Sales Ledger		4,800		*Less* : Cash		
	Discount Received		16,500		Purchases	10,000	3,26,700
	Bills Receivable endorsed		37,000		Bills Receivable endorsed		
	Bills payable accepted		72,000		dishonoured		8,000
31-12-88	To Balance c/d		22,750	31-12-88	By Balance c/d		2,400
			3,77,450				3,77,450

In Sales Ledger *Or* Debtors Ledger

General Ledger Adjustment A/c

				1-1-88	By Balance b/d		54,200
	To *Debtors Ledger Adjustment A/c*				By *Debtors Ledger Adjustment A/c*		
	Sales Return		3,300		Sales	4,52,400	
	Cash recd.	3,74,500			*Less* Cash		
	Less : Cash received previously				sales	27,800	4,24,600
	written off	4,000	3,70,500		Bills Receivable endorsed dishonoured		8,000
	Discount allowed		6,100	31-12-88			
	Bills Receivable		63,000		By Balance c/d		3,100
	Transfer from Bought Ledger		4,800				
	Bad Debts		3,800				
31-12-88	To Balance c/d		38,400				
			4,89,900				4,89,900
1-1-89	To Balance b/d		3,100	1-1-89	By Balance b/d		38,400

In Bought Ledger

General Ledger Adjustment A/c

		Rs.			Rs.
1-1-88	To Balance b/d	40,350		By *Creditors Ledger Adjustment A/c*	
	To *Creditors Ledger Adjustment A/c*			Purchase Return	7,500
	Purchases 3,36,700			Cash paid	2,16,900
	Less : Cash Purchases 10,000	3,26,700		Transfer to Sales Ledger	4,800
	Bills Receivable endorsed			Discount Received	16,500
	dishonoured	8,000		Bills Receivable endorsed	37,000
31-12-88	To Balance c/d	2,400		Bills payable accepted	72,000
			31-12-88	By Balance c/d	22,750
		3,,77,450			3,77,450

Problem No. 39

Prepare necessary Ledger Adjustment Accounts in the Ledger of Mr. Bhaskar who keeps his ledger on Self Balancing system.

		Rs.
Balance as on 31-12-1990		40,000
Balance of Debt on 1-1-1990	(Dr)	200
Credit Sales		2,60,000
Cash Sales		10,000
Sales Returns		2,000
Received from Debtors		1,15,000
Discount allowed to Debtors		1,800
Bills Receivable received from Debtors		21,000
Sundry charges debited to Customer accounts		1,100
Interest debited to Customer accounts		600
Bills dishonoured by Debtors		4,000
Bills Receivable discounted		8,000
Bills Receivable endorsed to Creditors		2,000
Transfers from Creditors ledgers		1,800
Provision for doubtful debts		1,200
Bad debts written off		900
Balance Debtors on 31-12-1990	(Cr)	400

(K.U.D., October 1990)

Solution :

Self Balancing Ledger

In General Ledger (Debtors Ledger Adjustment A/c)

		Rs.			Rs.
1-1-90	To Balance b/d	40,000	1-1-90	By Balance b/d	200
	To *General Ledger Adjustment A/c*			By *General Ledger Adjustment A/c*	
	Credit Sales	2,60,000		Sales Return	2,000
	Sundry charges	1,100		Cash received from Debtors	1,15,000
	Interest	600		Discount allowed	1,800
	Bills Receivable dishonoured	4,000		Bills Receivable received	21,000
31-12-90	To Balance c/d	400		Transfer from Creditors Ledger	1,800
				Bad Debts written off	900
			31-12-90	By Balance c/d	1,63,400
		3,06,100			3,06,100
1-1-91	To Balance b/d	1,63,400	1-1-91	By Balance b/d	400

In Debtors Ledger

General Ledger Adjustment A/c

1-1-90	To Balance b/d	200	1-1-90	By Balance b/d	40,000
	To *Debtors Ledger Adjustment A/c*			By *Debtors Ledger Adjustment A/c*	
	Sales Return	2,000		Credit Sales	2,60,000
	Cash received	1,15,000		Sundry Charge	1,100
	Discount allowed	1,800		Interest	600
	Bills Receivable	21,000		Bills Receivable dishonoured	4,000
	Transfer from credit	1,800	31-12-90	By Balance c/d	400
	Bad Debts written off	900			
	To Balance c/d	1,63,400			
		3,06,400			3,06,400

8

Royalty Accounts

The nature has provided abundant natural resources on the surface as well as beneath the surface of the earth. Particularly valuable mineral deposits like Coal, Iron-ore, Manganese, Boxite, Copper, Bronze, Silver, Gold and even Stones like granite, Diamond etc. The quantity of deposits can not be correctly assessed. Further the ownership of the land in which these deposits are found may be with private individuals or Government Authorities. They do not want to part with such lands containing the Minerals to the Mining Company for price or *vice-versa*. The practice followed in such situations is the offer made by the owner of the land on lease of land for particular period at a certain price for the output raised in a period of one year.

Similarly, the invention of Machinery or a new design or a product by the individual may not possess the required financial resources to produce commercially and market it. However the individual inventor of the new machinery or design or product may register with the Government established authorities under the Patent Rights Act. The manufacturing company may come forward to manufacture the product commercially on largescale and market the same. The manufacturing company agrees to pay certain price for acquiring of patent Rights to produce and sell the product.

In the same way the author of a Book normally offer the publishing company to publish the Book and sales of the same for consideration to pay certain amount on the number of copies sold or on the total sales. The author retains the copy right of the Book.

Now let us understand about the meaning of various terms used in Royalty Accounts.

(I) *Royalty*

(a) Is the amount payable by the Mining Company or miners (individual) to the owner of the land per ton (called as landlord).

(b) Is the amount payable by the Manufacturing to the owner of the patent called patentee.

(c) Is the amount payable by the Publishing House to the author of a Book.

(II) Minimum Rent is the minimum amount payable by the :

(a) Mining Company to the landlord.

(b) Manufacturing Company to the patentee.

(c) Publishing House to the Author of a Book annually where the Royalty earned is less than the Minimum amount as fixed and agreed by both the parties.

(III) *Shortworkings*

Is the amount of difference resulting out of Royalties earned is less than the Minimum rent.

Minimum Rent – Royalty earned = Shortworking.

However, the terms of lease provide the recoupment of shortworking of the previous year/s during the subsequent period, when the actual Royalties earned are more than the minimum Rent. The period of recoupment/recovery of shortworkings during the period of surplus, is generally fixed as next two years or next three years period. After the expiry of the period of recovery of the irrecovered amount is treated as loss and written off to the Profit and Loss Account in that period.

Pro-forma Journal Entries in the Books of :

(a) Mining Company (b) Manufacturing Company

(c) Publishing Company.

(I) *Where Royalties earned are less than Minimum Rent*

	Particulars		Rs.	Rs.
1.	Royalty A/c	Dr	—	
	Shortworkings A/c	Dr	—	
	To Landlord A/c			—
	(Royalties earned and shortworking payable)			
2.	Landlord A/c	Dr	—	
	To Bank A/c			—
	(Cash paid to Landlord)			
3.	Profit & Loss A/c	Dr	—	
	To Royalties A/c			—
	(Royalty A/c transferred)			

The above three entries are to be repeated till the Royalties exceed Minimum Rent.

(II) *Where Royalties earned are more than the Minimum Rent*

1.	Royalty A/c	Dr	—	
	To Landlord A/c			—
	(Royalties earned and payable)			
2.	Landlord A/c	Dr	—	
	To Shortworking A/c			—
	(Shortworkings recovered out of surplus)			
3.	Landlord A/c	Dr	—	
	To Bank A/c			—
	(Cash paid to Landlord)			
4.	Profit & Loss A/c	Dr	—	
	To Shortworking A/c			—
	(Shortworking irrecoverable written off to Profit & Loss A/c)			

Particulars		Rs.	Rs.
5. Profit & Loss A/c	Dr	—	
To Royalty A/c			—
(Royalty A/c transferred)			
(*Or* 4 & 5)			
Profit & Loss A/c	Dr	—	
To Shortworking A/c			—
To Royalty A/c			—
(Shortworking irrecoverable written off and Royalty A/c transferred to Profit & Loss A/c)			
Where Minimum Rent Account is maintained			
(I) *Royalties earned are less than Minimum Rent*			
1. Minimum Rent A/c	Dr	—	
To Landlord A/c		—	
(Minimum Rent Payable)			
2. Royalty A/c	Dr	—	
Shortworking A/c	Dr	—	
To Minimum Rent A/c			—
(Royalties earned and shortworking payable)			
3. Landlord A/c	Dr	—	
To Bank A/c			—
(Cash paid to Landlord)			
4. Profit & Loss A/c	Dr	—	
To Royalties A/c			—
(Royalty A/c transferred)			
The above entries are to be repeated till Royalties earned are less than the Minimum Rent.			
(II) *Where Royalties earned are more than the Minimum Rent*			
1. Royalty A/c	Dr	—	
To Landlord A/c			—
(Royalties earned and payable)			
2. Landlord A/c	Dr	—	
To Shortworking A/c			—
(Shortworking recovered out of surplus)			
3. Landlord A/c	Dr	—	
To Bank A/c			—
(Cash paid to Landlord)			
4. Profit & Loss A/c	Dr	—	
To Shortworking A/c			—
(Shortworking irrecoverable after the period written off is Profit & Loss A/c)			
5. Profit & Loss A/c	Dr	—	
To Royalty A/c			—
(Royalty A/c transferred)			

Problem No. 1

A Coal company took a Mine from a Landlord at a Royalty of Rs. 5 per ton of coal raised with a Minimum Rent 8 Rs. 25,000 per year. Shortworkings are recoverable out of excess royalties of the next two years only. In the event of strike, Minimum Rent is to be reduced proportionately. The results of working are as under :

Year	Output in Tons	Year	Output in Tons
1991	4000	1994	7000
1992	4500	1995	3000 (Strike for 3 months)
1993	6000		

Prepare Royalty Chart.

[K.U.D., October 1997(N)]

Solution :

Working Table — Royalty Chart

Year	Output in Tons	Royalty Rs. 5 per Ton	Minimum Rent	Short-working	Surplus	Shortworkings Recovered	Shortworkings Not recovered	Landlord Amount Payable
1991	4000	20,000	25,000	5,000	—	—	—	25,000
1992	4500	22,500	25,000	2,500	—	—	—	25,000
1993	6000	30,000	25,000	—	5,000	5,000 1991	—	25,000
1994	7000	35,000	25,000	—	10,000	2,500 1992	—	32,500
1995	3000 strike for 3 months	15,000	18,750	3,750	—			18,750

Minimum Rent per annum Rs. 25,000

In the year of strike Minimum Rent reduced proportionate to the period of strike

25,000 × 3/12 = 6,250 reduced by

Minimum Rent pa	Rs. 25,000
Less Strike period 3 months	6,250
Minimum Rent during strike period	18750

Royalty A/c

1991	To Landlord A/c	20,000	1991	By Profit & Loss A/c	20,000
1992	To Landlord A/c	22,500	1992	By Profit & Loss A/c	22,500
1993	To landlord A/c	30,000	1993	By Profit & Loss A/c	30,000
1994	To Landlord A/c	35,000	1994	By Profit & Loss A/c	35,000
1995	To Landlord	15,000	1995	By Profit & Loss A/c	15,000

Shortworkings A/c

1991	To Landlord A/c	5,000	1991	By Balance c/d	5,000
1992	To Balance b/d	5,000	1992	By Balance c/d	7,500
	To Landlord	2,500			
		7,500			7,500
1993	To Balance b/d	7,500	1993	By Landlord A/c (1991 recovered)	5,000
				By Balance c/d	2,500
		7,500			7,500
1994	To Balance b/d	2,500	1994	By Landlord A/c (1992 recovered)	2,500
1995	To Landlord	3,750	1995	By Balance c/d	3,750

Landlord A/c

1991	To Bank A/c	25,000	1991	By Royalty A/c	20,000
				By Shortworkings A/c	5,000
		25,000			25,000
1992	To Bank A/c	25,000	1992	By Royalty A/c	22,500
				By Shortworkings A/c	2,500
		25,000			25,000
1993	To Shortworkings A/c (1991 recovered)	5,000	1993	By Royalty A/c	30,000
	To Bank A/c	25,000			
		30,000			30,000
1994	To Shortworkings A/c (1992 recovered)	2,500	1994	By Royalty A/c	35,000
	To Bank A/c	32,500			
		35,000			35,000
1995	To Bank A/c	18,750	1995	By Royalty A/c	15,000
				By Shortworkings A/c	3,750
		18,750			18,750

Journal Entries

			Dr Rs.	Cr Rs.
1991				
(1)	Royalty A/c	Dr.	20,000	
	Shortworkings A/c	Dr.	5,000	
	To Landlord A/c			25,000
	(Royalty earned & shortworkings payable)			
(2)	Landlord A/c	Dr.	25,000	
	To Bank A/c			25,000
	(Cash paid)			
(3)	Profit & Loss A/c	Dr.	20,000	
	To Royalty A/c			20,000
	(Royalty A/c closed by transfer)			
1992				
(1)	Royalty A/c	Dr.	22,500	
	Shortworkings A/c	Dr.	2,500	
	To Landlord A/c			25,000
	(Royalty earned and shortworkings payable)			
(2)	Landlord A/c	Dr.	25,000	
	To Bank A/c			25,000
	(Cash paid)			
(3)	Profit & Loss A/c	Dr.	22,500	
	To Royalty A/c			22,500
	(Royalty A/c closed by transfer)			
1993				
(1)	Royalty A/c	Dr.	30,000	
	To Landlord A/c			30,000
	(Royalty earned and payable)			
(2)	Landlord A/c	Dr.	5,000	
	To Shortworking A/c			5,000
	(Shortworking of 1991 recovered)			
(3)	Landlord A/c	Dr.	25,000	
	To Bank A/c			25,000
	(Cash Paid)			
(4)	Profit & Loss A/c	Dr.	30,000	
	To Royalty A/c			30,000
	(Royalty A/c closed by Transfer)			

Journal Entries

			Dr Rs.	Cr Rs.
1994				
(1)	Royalty A/c	Dr.	35,000	
	To Landlord A/c			35,000
	(Royalty earned and payable)			
(2)	Landlord A/c	Dr.	2,500	
	To Shortworkings A/c			2,500
	(Shortworking of 1992 recovered)			
(3)	Landlord A/c	Dr.	32,500	
	To Bank A/c			32,500
	(Cash paid)			
(4)	Profit & Loss A/c	Dr.	35,000	
	To Royalty A/c			35,000
	(Royalty A/c closed by transfer)			
1995				
(1)	Royalty A/c	Dr.	15,000	
	Shortworkings A/c	Dr.	3,750	
	To Landlord A/c			18,750
	(Royalty earned & Shortworking payable. Minimum rent reduced proportionate to the period of strike — 3 months)			
(2)	Landlord A/c	Dr.	18,750	
	To Bank A/c			18,750
	(Cash paid)			
(3)	Profit & Loss A/c	Dr.	15,000	
	To Royalty A/c			15,000
	(Royalty A/c closed by transfer)			

Problem No. 2

On 1st January 1992, Ilkal Co. leased a piece of land for a Minimum Rent of Rs. 5,000, in the first year, Rs. 10,000 in the second year and thereafter Rs. 15,000 per annum merging into a Royalty of Rs. 2.50 per ton with a power to recouped the shortworkings over first 3 years only. The annual output for the four years ending on 31-12-1992 was — 500 tons, 3000 tons 8000 tons and 12000 tons respectively.

Show the accounts that would appear in the Books of company.

[K.U.D., April 1997(N)]

Solution :

Working Table — Royalty Chart

Year	Output in Tons	Royalty per ton Rs. 2.50	Minimum Rent	Short-working	Surplus	Shortworkings Recovered	Shortworkings Not recovered	Landlord Amount Payable
1992	500	1,250	5,000	3,750	—	—	—	5,000
1993	3000	7,500	10,000	2,500	—	—	—	10,000
1994	8000	20,000	15,000	—	5,000	3,750 92 + 1250 93 + 1250	—	15,000
1995	12000	30,000	15,000	—	15,000	—		30,000

In the Books of the Company

Royalty A/c

Date	Particulars	Rs.	Date	Particulars	Rs.
31-12-92	To Landlord A/c	1,250	31-12-92	By Profit & Loss A/c	1,250
31-12-93	To Landlord A/c	7,500	31-12-93	By Profit & Loss A/c	7,500
31-12-94	To Landlord A/c	20,000	31-12-94	By Profit & Loss A/c	20,000
31-12-95	To Landlord A/c	30,000	31-12-95	By Profit Loss A/c	30,000

Shortworkings A/c

Date	Particulars	Rs.	Date	Particulars	Rs.
31-12-92	To Landlord A/c	3,750	31-12-92	By Balance c/d	3,750
31-12-93	To Balance b/d	3,750	31-12-93	By Balanced c/d	6,250
	To Landlord A/c	2,500			
		6,250			6,250
31-12-94	To Balance b/d	6,250	31-12-94	By Landlord A/c 1992-3,750 } Recovered 1993-1,250 }	5,000
				By Profit & Loss A/c	1,250
		6,250			6,250

Landlord A/c

Date	Particulars	Rs.	Date	Particulars	Rs.
31-12-92	To Bank A/c	5,000	31-12-92	By Royalty A/c	1,250
				By Shortworkings A/c	3,750
		5,000			5,000
31-12-93	To Bank A/c	10,000	31-12-93	By Royalty A/c	7,500
				By Shortworking A/c	2,500
		10,000			10,000
31-12-94	To Shortworkings A/c 1992-3,750 } Recovered 1993-1,250 }	5,000	31-12-94	By Royalty A/c	20,000
	To Bank A/c	15,000			
		20,000			20,000
31-12-95	To Bank A/c	30,000	31-12-95	By Royalty A/c	30,000
		30,000			30,000

Problem No. 3

Sumo Minerals company Ltd. is the lessee of an iron ore mine. The terms agreed upon between the lessee and the landlord are as below :

(a) A minimum Rent of Rs. 12,000 be paid per year. It shall merge into a Royalty payable at the rate of Rs. 5 per tonne of ore extracted.

(b) Each year's excess of Minimum Rent over actual royalties is recoverable out of the excess Royalties of the next three years.

(c) Proportionate reduction in the Minimum Rent is to made in event of strike or lock out in any year.

The quantities of the iron ore extracted for the period of five years are as follows :

Year	Output in tonnes	Year	Output in tonnes
1992	240	1995	4560
1993	1680	1996	1920
1994	2640		

During the year 1996, because of unrest among the local people, the company had declared "lock out" for 3 months and hence the work was stopped during the said three months.

Prepare : (a) Landlord A/c (b) Shortworkings Account in the Books of the company

(K.U.D., October 1997)

Solution :

Working Table — Royalty Chart

Year	Output in Tons	Royalty per ton Rs. 5	Minimum Rent	Short-working	Surplus	Shortworkings Recovered	Shortworkings Not recovered	Landlord Amount Payable
1992	240	1,200	12,000	10,800				12,000
1993	1680	8,400	12,000	3,600				12,000
1994	2640	13,200	12,000	—	1,200	1,200	—	12,000
1995	4560	22,800	12,000	—	10,800	92-9,600 93-1,200	—	12,000
1996	1920	9,600	9,000	—	600	600	1,800	9,000

Note : Minimum Rent per year Rs. 12,000

Lock out 3 months — M.R. reduced proportionately

$12,000 \times 3/12 = 3,000$ 12,000

− 3,000

9,000

In the Books of Sumo-Minerals Co. Ltd.

Royalty A/c

1992	To Landlord A/c	1,200	1992	By Profit & Loss A/c	1,200
1993	To Landlord A/c	8,400	1993	By Profit & Loss A/c	8,400
1994	To Landlord A/c	13,200	1994	By Profit & Loss A/c	13,200
1995	To Landlord A/c	22,800	1995	By Profit & Loss A/c	22,800
1996	To Landlord A/c	9,600	1996	By Profit & Loss A/c	9,600

Shortworkings A/c

1992	To Landlord A/c	10,800	1992	By Balance c/d	10,800
1993	To Balance b/d	10,800	1993	By Balance c/d	14,400
	To Landlord A/c	3,600			
		14,400			14,400
1994	To Balance b/d	14,400	1994	By Landlord A/c 1992-recovered Rs. 1,200	1,200
					13,200
		14,400		By Balance c/d	14,400
1995	To Balance b/d	13,200	1995	By Landlord A/c 1992-9,600 } 1993-1,200 } 10,800 Recovered	10,800
				By Balance c/d	2,400
		13,200			13,200
1996	To Balance c/d	2,400	1996	By Landlord A/c (1993-600 recovered)	600
		2,400		By profit Loss A/c (1993 Not recovered written off)	1,800
					2,400

Landlord A/c

1992	To Bank A/c	12,000	1992	By Royalty A/c	1,200
				By Shortworkings A/c	10,800
		12,000			12,000
1993	To Bank A/c	12,000	1993	By Royalty A/c	8,400
				By Shortworkings A/c	3,600
		12,000			12,000
1994	To Shortworkings A/c 1992- Rs. 1200 recovered	1,200	1994	By Royalty A/c	13,200
	To Bank A/c	12,000			
		13,200			13,200

1995	To Shortworking A/c 1992-9,600 } Recovered 1993-1,200 }	10,800	1995	By Royalty A/c	22,800
	To Bank A/c	12,000			
		22,800			22,800
1996	To Shortworking A/c 93-600 recovered	600	1996	By Royalty A/c	9,600
	To Bank A/c	9,000			
		9,600			9,600

Problem No. 4

On 1-1-1991, the Chittapur Collieries Ltd. leased a land for a Minimum Rent of Rs. 5,000 in the First year, Rs. 10,000 in the second year and thereafter Rs. 15,000 per annum merging into a Royalty of Rs. 2.50 per tonne of coal raised with a power to recoup shortworkings over the first three years only. The annual output for the four years ending with 31-12-1994 was 500, 3000, 8000 and 12000 tonnes respectively.

Prepare : Royalty Chart and Royalty Account in the Books of Lessees.

[K.U.D., April 1996(N)]

Solution :

Working Table — Royalty Chart

Year	Output in Tons	Royalty Rs. 2.50 per ton	Minimum Rent	Short-workings	Surplus	Shortworkings Recovered	Shortworkings Not recovered	Landlord Amount Payable
I Year 91	500	1,250	5,000	3,750	—	—	—	5,000
II Year 91	3000	7,500	10,000	2,500		—	—	10,000
III Year 93	8000	20,000	15,000	—	5,000	5,000 (91-3,750 + 92-1,250)	—	15,000
IV Year 94	12000	30,000	15,000	—	15,000	1,250 (92)	—	30,000

In the Books of Collieries Ltd.

Royalty A/c

1991	To Landlord A/c	1,250	1991	By Profit & Loss A/c	1,250
1992	To Landlord A/c	7,500	1992	By Profit & Loss A/c	7,500
1993	To Landlord A/c	20,000	1993	By Profit & Loss A/c	20,000
1994	To Landlord A/c	30,000	1994	By Profit & Loss A/c	30,000

Shortworking A/c

1991	To Landlord A/c	3,750	1991	By Balance c/d	3,750
1992	To Balance b/d	3,750	1992	By Balance c/d	6,250
	To Landlord A/c	2,500			
		6,250			6,250
1993	To Balance b/d	6,250	1993	By Landlord A/c 1991- Rs. 3,750 + 1992 Rs. 1,250 5,000 (Shortworking recovered)	5,000
				By Profit & Loss A/c written off	1,250
		6,250			6,250

Landlord A/c

1991	To Bank A/c	5,000	1991	By Royalty A/c	1,250
				By Shortworking A/c	3,750
		5,000			5,000
1992	To Bank A/c	10,000	1992	By Royalty A/c	7,500
				By Shortworking A/c	2,500
		10,000			10,000
1993	To Shortworking A/c 1991-Rs. 3750 } recovered 1992 Rs. 1250 }	5,000	1993	By Royalty A/c	20,000
	To Bank A/c	15,000			
		20,000			20,000
1994	To Bank A/c	30,000	1994	By Royalty A/c	30,000
		30,000			30,000

Journal Entries

			Dr Rs.	Cr Rs.
1991				
(1)	Royalty A/c	Dr.	1,250	
	Shortworkings A/c	Dr.	3,750	
	To Landlord A/c			5,000
	(Royalty earned & shortworkings payable)			
(2)	Landlord A/c	Dr.	5,000	
	To Bank A/c			5,000
	(Cash paid)			
(3)	Profit & Loss A/c	Dr.	1,250	
	To Royalty A/c			1,250
	(Royalty A/c closed by transfer to Profit & Loss A/c)			
1992				
(1)	Royalty A/c	Dr	7,500	
	Shortworkings A/c	Dr.	2,750	
	To Landlord A/c			10,000
	(Royalty earned and shortworkings payable)			
(2)	Landlord A/c	Dr.	10,000	
	To Bank			10,000
	(Cash paid)			
(3)	Profit & Loss A/c	Dr.	7,500	
	To Royalty A/c			7,500
	(Royalty A/c closed by transfer to Profit Loss A/c)			
1993				
(1)	Royalty A/c	Dr.	20,000	
	To Landlord A/c			20,000
	(Royalty earned are more than Minimum Rent and therefore Actual Royalty earned payable)			
(2)	Landlord A/c	Dr.	5,000	
	To Shortworkings A/c			5,000
	(Shortworking of 1991-Rs. 3,750 + 1992 Rs. 1,250 recovered out of surplus over M.R.)			
(3)	Landlord A/c	Dr.	15,000	
	To Bank A/c			15,000
	(Cash paid)			

			Dr Rs.	Cr Rs.
(4)	Profit & Loss A/c	Dr.	20,000	
	To Royalty A/c			20,000
	(Royalty A/c closed by transfer to Profit & Loss A/c)			
(5)	Profit & Loss A/c	Dr.	1,250	
	To Shortworkings A/c			1,250
	(Unrecovered shortworkings in 1993 written off as the period of recovery is over)			
1994				
(1)	Royalty A/c	Dr.	30,000	
	To Landlord A/c			30,000
	(Actual Royalty earned are more than MR and payable)			
(2)	Landlord A/c	Dr.	30,000	
	To Bank A/c			30,000
	(Cash paid)			
(3)	Profit & Loss A/c	Dr.	30,000	
	To Royalty A/c			30,000
	(Royalty A/c closed by transfer to Profit & Loss A/c)			

Problem No. 5

A Coal company took a Mine from a Landlord at a Royalty of Re per tonne of coal raised with a Minimum Rent of Rs. 10,000 per year. Each year's excess of Minimum Rent over actual Royalty is recoupable out of excess Royalties of the next two years. In the event of strike and the Minimum Rent is not reached. The Lease provided that the actual Royalties earned for that year will discharge all the rental obligations of that year.

Year	Output in tons	Year	Output in tons
1990	7000	1992	11000
1991	9000	1993	8000 (strike year)

Pass the necessary Journal Entries in the Books of Coal company for the above period.

[K.U.D., October 1996(N)]

Solution :

Working Table — Royalty Chart

Year	Output in Tons	Royalty per ton Re. 1	Minimum Rent	Short-working	Surplus	Shortworkings Recovered	Shortworkings Not recovered	Landlord Amount Payable
1990	7000	7,000	10,000	3,000	—			10,000
1991	9000	9,000	10,000	1,000	—			10,000
1992	11000	11,000	10,000	—	1,000	1,000	2,000	10,000
1993	8000 (Strike)	8,000	8,000	—	—	—		8,000

Minimum Rent per year Rs. 10,000.

In the year of strike Minimum Rent is the amount of Actual Royalties earned will discharge the rental obligation.

In the Books of Coal Company

Journal Entries

			Dr Rs.	Cr Rs.
1990				
(1)	Royalty A/c	Dr.	7,000	
	Shortworkings A/c	Dr.	3,000	
	To Landlord A/c			10,000
	(Royalty earned and shortworkings payable)			
(2)	Landlord A/c	Dr.	10,000	
	To Bank A/c			10,000
	(Cash paid)			
(3)	Profit & Loss A/c	Dr.	7,000	
	To Royalty A/c			7,000
	(Royalty A/c closed by transfer)			
1991				
(1)	Royalty A/c	Dr.	9,000	
	Shortworkings A/c	Dr.	1,000	
	To Landlord A/c			1,000
	(Royalty earned and shortworkings payable)			
(2)	Landlord A/c	Dr.	10,000	
	To Bank A/c			10,000
	(Cash paid)			
(3)	Profit & Loss A/c	Dr.	9,000	
	To Royalty A/c			9,000
	(Royalty A/c closed by transfer)			

Journal Entries

			Dr Rs.	Cr Rs.
1992				
(1)	Royalty A/c	Dr.	11,000	
	To Landlord A/c			11,000
	(Royalty earned and payable)			
(2)	Landlord A/c		1,000	
	To Shortworkings A/c			1,000
	(Shortworking of 1990 recovered)			
(3)	Profit & Loss A/c	Dr.	2,000	
	To Shortworkings			2,000
	(Shortworkings of 1990 not recoverd written off to Profit & Loss A/c)			
(4)	Landlord A/c	Dr.	10,000	
	To Bank A/c			10,000
	(Cash paid)			
(5)	Profit & Loss A/c		11,000	
	To Royalty A/c			11,000
	(Royalty A/c closed by transfer)			
1993				
(1)	Royalty A/c	Dr.	8,000	
	To Landlord A/c			8,000
	(Royalty earned and payable, as the year of strike. Minimum Rent is the actual Royalties earned will discharge all the rental obligation)			
(2)	Landlord A/c	Dr.	8,000	
	To Bank A/c			8,000
	(Cash paid)			
(3)	Profit & Loss A/c	Dr.	1,000	
	To Shortworkings			1,000
	(Shortworking of 1991 not recovered written off)			
(4)	Profit & Loss A/c	Dr.	8,000	
	To Royalty A/c			8,000
	(Royalty A/c closed by transfer)			

Additional Solution :

Royalty A/c

1990	To Landlord A/c	7,000	1990	By Profit & Loss A/c	7,000
1990	To Landlord A/c	9,000	1991	By Profit & Loss A/c	9,000
1992	To Landlord A/c	11,000	1992	By profit & Loss A/c	11,000
1993	To Landlord A/c	8,000	1993	By Profit & Loss A/c	8,000

Shortworking A/c

1990	To Landlord A/c	3,000	1990	By Balance c/d	3,000
1991	To Balance b/d	3,000	1991	By Balance c/d	4,000
	To Landlord	1,000			
		4,000			4,000
1992	To Balance b/d	4,000	1992	By Landlord A/c (1990 recovered)	1,000
				By Profit & Loss A/c (1990 not recovered written off)	2,000
				By Balance c/d	1,000
		4,000			4,000
1993	To Balance b/d	1,000	1993	By Profit & Loss A/c (1991 Not recovered written off to P & L A/c)	1,000
		1,000			1,000

Landlord A/c

1990	To Bank A/c	10,000	1990	By Royalty A/c	7,000
				By Shortworkings	3,000
		10,000			10,000
1991	To Bank A/c	10,000	1991	By Royalty A/c	9,000
				By Shortworkings A/c	1,000
		10,000			10,000
1992	To Shortworkings (1990 recovered)	1,000	1992	By Royalty A/c	11,000
	To Bank A/c	10,000			
		11,000			11,000
1993	To Bank A/c	8,000	1993	By Royalty A/c	8,000
		8,000			8,000

Problem No. 6

A Coal company took a lease from Mr. Kumar of a Coal Mine for a period of 25 years from 1988 on a Royalty of Rs. 2.50 per tonne of coal raised with a Minimum Rent of Rs. 25,000 per annum and power to recoup the shortworkings during first 5 years of lease. The annual output in tonnes was as follows :

Year	Out-put	Year	Out-put
1988	600 tonnes	1991	12,000
1989	900 tonnes	1992	15,000
1990	11,000		

Prepare : (a) Royalty Account

(b) Shortworking Account and

(c) Kumar's Account

in the Books of Coal company.

(Gulbarga, April 1996)

Solution :

Working Table

Year	Output in Tonnes	Royalty Rs. 2.50 per tonne	Minimum Rent	Short-working	Surplus	Shortworkings Recovered	Shortworkings Not recovered	Landlord Amount Payable
1988	6000	15,000	25,000	10,000			—	25,000
1989	9000	22,500	25,000	2,500			—	25,000
1990	11000	27,500	25,000		2,500	2,500 (1988)	—	25,000
1991	12000	30,000	25,000		5,000	5,000 (1988)	—	25,000
1992	15000	37,500	25,000		12,500	2,500 (1988) +2,500 (1989)	—	32,500

In the Books of Coal Company

Journal Entries

			Dr. Rs.	Cr. Rs.
1988				
(1)	Royalty A/c	Dr.	15,000	
	Shortworkings A/c	Dr.	10,000	
	To Landlord A/c			25,000
	(Royalties earned and shortworking payable)			

Journal Entries

			Dr Rs.	Cr Rs.
(2)	Landlord A/c	Dr.	25,000	
	To Bank A/c			25,000
	(Cash paid Minimum Rent)			
(3)	Profit & Loss A/c	Dr.	15,000	
	To Royalty A/c			15,000
	(Royalty A/c closed by transfer to Profit & Loss A/c)			
1989				
(1)	Royalty A/c	Dr.	22,500	
	Shortworking A/c	Dr.	2,500	
	To Landlord A/c			25,000
	(Royalities earned and shortworking & payable)			
(2)	Landlord A/c	Dr.	25,000	
	To Bank A/c			25,000
	(Cash paid Minimum Rent)			
(3)	Profit & Loss A/c	Dr.	22,500	
	To Royalty A/c			22,500
	(Royalty A/c closed by transfer to Profit & Loss A/c)			
1990				
(1)	Royalty A/c	Dr.	27,500	
	To Landlord A/c			27,500
	(Actual Royalty earned in more than Minimum Rent therefore Royalty earned payabale)			
(2)	Landlord A/c	Dr.	2,500	
	To Shortworkings A/c			2,500
	(Shortworking of 1988 recovered out of surplus)			
(3)	Landlord A/c	Dr.	25,000	
	To Bank A/c			25,000
	(Cash paid)			
(4)	Profit & Loss A/c	Dr.	27,500	
	To Royalty A/c			27,500
	(Royalty A/c closed by transfer to Profit & Loss A/c)			
1991				
(1)	Royalty A/c	Dr.	30,000	
	To Landlord A/c			30,000
	(Royalty earned are more than M.R. and actual Royalty payable)			

			Dr Rs.	Cr Rs.
(2)	Landlord A/c	Dr.	5,000	
	To Shortworkings			5,000
	(Shortworkings of 1988 recovered out of surplus)			
(3)	Landlord A/c	Dr.	25,000	
	To Bank A/c			25,000
	(Cash paid)			
(4)	Profit & Loss A/c	Dr.	30,000	
	To Royalty A/c			30,000
	(Royalty A/c closed by transfer to Profit & Loss A/c)			
1992				
(1)	Royalty A/c	Dr.	37,500	
	To Landlord A/c			37,500
	(Royalty earned are more than M.R. and therefore actual Royalty earned payable)			
(2)	Landlord A/c	Dr.	5,000	
	To Shortworking A/c			5,000
	(Shortworkings of 1988 Rs. 2,500 + of 1989 Rs. 2,500 recovered out of surplus)			
(3)	Landlord A/c	Dr.	32,500	
	To Bank A/c			32,500
	(Cash paid)			
(4)	Profit & Loss A/c	Dr.	37,500	
	To Royalty A/c			37,500
	(Royalty A/c closed by transfer to Profit & Loss A/c)			

Royalty A/c

1998	To Landlord A/c	15,000	1988	By Profit & Loss A/c	15,000
1989	To Landlord A/c	22,500	1989	By Profit & Loss A/c	22,500
1990	To Landlord A/c	27,500	1990	By Profit & Loss A/c	27,500
1991	To Landlord A/c	30,000	1991	By Profit & Loss	30,000
1992	To Landlord A/c	37,500	1992	By Profit & Loss A/c	37,500

Shortworkings A/c

1988	To Landlord A/c	10,000		By Balance c/d	10,000
1989	To Balance b/d	10,000	1989	By Balance c/d	12,500
	To Landlord	2,500			
		12,500			12,500

1990	To Balance b/d	12,500	1990	By Landlord A/c Shortworking of 1988 recovered	2,500
				By Balance c/d	10,000
		12,500			12,500
1991	To Balance b/d	10,000	1991	By Landlord A/c Shortworking of 1988 recovered	5,000
				By Balance c/d	5,000
		10,000			10,000
1992	To Balance b/d	5,000	1991	By Landlord A/c 1988-2,500 + 89-2,500 Shortworking recovered	5,000
		5,000			5,000

Landlord A/c (Mr. Kumar)

1988	To Bank A/c	25,000	1988	By Royalty A/c	15,000
				By Shortworking A/c	10,000
		25,000			25,000
1989	To Bank A/c	25,000	1989	By Royalty A/c	22,500
			1990	By Shortworking A/c	2,500
		25,000			25,000
1990	To Shortworking 1988 recovered	2,500	1990	By Royalty A/c	27,500
	To Bank A/c	25,000			
		27,500			27,500
1991	To Shortworking A/c	5,000	1991	To Royalty	30,000
	To Bank A/c	25,000			
		30,000			30,000
1992	To Shortworking A/c (1988-2,500 + 1989-2,500)	5,000	1992	By Royalty A/c	37,500
	To Bank A/c	32,500			
		37,500			37,500

Problem No. 7

Gadag Publications agreed to take up Printing and sales of Books from the Author, Prof. Anand on 1-1-1990. Following are the terms of agreement :

(i) Royalty payable 20% on the price of a Book. The Book is priced at Rs. 25 per copy.

(ii) The Author is to be paid a Minimum amount of Rs. 10,000 per annum.

(iii) Each year's excess of Minimum Amount over the actual Royalties is recoverable out of excess Royalty of next three years.

Following are the sales for the first five years :

Year ending	No. of copies sold
1	400
2	750
3	1600
4	3000
5	4500

Show in the Books of Gadag Publication :

(a) Royalty A/c (b) Author A/c

(c) Minimum Rent A/c (d) Shortworking A/c.

(K.U.D., October 1996)

Solution :

Working Table — Royalty Chart

(Royalty 20% of Rs. 25 = Rs. 5 per copy)

Year	Copies sold	Royalty Rs. 5 per copy	Minimum Amount	Short-working	Surplus	Shortworkings Recovered	Shortworkings Not recovered	Landlord Amount Payable
1	400	2,000	10,000	8,000				10,000
2	750	3,750	10,000	6,250				10,000
3	1600	8,000	10,000	2,000				10,000
4	3000	15,000	10,000	—	5,000	5,000 I Year	3,000	10,000
5	4500	22,500	10,000	—	12,500	II Yr. 6,250 III Yr. 2,000	—	14,250

In the Books of Godag Publications

Minimum Rent A/c

I	To Anand A/c (Author)	10,000	I	By Royalty A/c	2,000
				By Shortworking A/c	8,000
		10,000			10,000
II	To Anand	10,000	II	By Royalty A/c	3,750
				By Shortworking A/c	6,250
		10,000			10,000
III	To Anand A/c	10,000	III	By Royalty A/c	8,000
				By Shortworking A/c	2,000
		10,000			10,000

Royalty A/c

I	To Minimum Rent A/c	2,000	I	By Profit & Loss A/c	2,000
II	To Minimum Renet A/c	3,750	II	By Profit & Loss A/c	3,750
III	To Minimum Rent A/c	8,000	III	By Profit & Loss A/c	8,000
IV	To Anand A/c Author	15,000	IV	By Profit & Loss A/c	15,000
V	To Anand A/c Author	22,500	V	By Profit & Loss A/c	22,500

Shortworkings A/c

I	To Minimum Rent A/c	8,000	I	By Balance c/d	8,000
II	To Balance b/d	8,000	II	By Balance c/d	14,250
	To Minimum Rent A/c	6,250			
		14,250			14,250
III	To Balance b/d	14,250	III	By Balance c/d	16,250
	To Minimum Rent A/c	2,000			
		16,250			16,250
IV	To Balance b/d	16,250	IV	By Author A/c I year Rs. 5,000 recovered	5,000
				By Profit & Loss A/c (I Year (8,000–5,000) 3,000 Not recovered written off)	3,000
				By balance c/d	8,250
		16,250			16,250
V	To Balance b/d	8,250	V	By Author A/c II Year - 6,250 } Recovered III Year - 2,000 }	8,250
		8,250			8,250

Anand A/c (Author)

I Year	To Bank A/c	10,000	I Year	By Minimum Rent A/c	10,000
II	To Bank A/c	10,000	II	By Minimum Rent A/c	10,000
III	To Bank A/c	10,000	III	By Minimum Rent A/c	10,000
IV	To Shortworking A/c (I Year-Rs. 5,000 recovered)	5,000	IV	By Royalty A/c	15,000
	To Bank A/c	10,000			
		15,000			15,000
	To Shortworking A/c (II Year 6,250, III 2,000 } Recovered)	8,250	V	By Royalty A/c	22,500
	To Bank A/c	14,250			
		22,500			22,500

Problem No. 8

Record the following in the Journal of Mining Company (Lessees) :

(a) Minimum Rent Rs. 10,000 p.a.

(b) Recoupment period is next one year only.

(c) Royalty earned : 1st Year Rs. 6,000 and in the second year Rs. 12,000.

[K.U.D., April 1995(N)]

Solution :

In the Books of Mining Co.

Journal Entries

		Dr Rs.	Cr Rs.
Ist Year			
1. Royalty A/c	Dr.	6,000	
Shortworkings A/c	Dr.	4,000	
To Landlord A/c			10,000
(Royalty earned and shortworking payable)			
2. Landlord A/c	Dr.	10,000	
To Bank A/c			10,000
(Cash paid)			
3. Profit & Loss A/c	Dr.	6,000	
To Royalty A/c			6,000
(Royalty A/c closed by transferred to Profit & Loss A/c)			

		Dr Rs.	Cr Rs.
II Year			
1. Royalty A/c	Dr.	12,000	
To Landlord A/c			12,000
(Royalty earned are more and therefore actual Royalty earned payable)			
2. Landlord A/c	Dr.	2,000	
To Shortworkings			2,000
(Shortworkings of Ist Year recovered)			
3. Profit & Loss A/c	Dr.	2,000	
To Shortworkings			2,000
(Being period of recouping is over and the shortworking not recovered be written off to Profit & Loss A/c)			
4. Landlord A/c	Dr.	10,000	
To Bank A/c			10,000
(Cash paid)			
5. Profit of Loss A/c	Dr.	12,000	
To Royalty A/c			12,000
(Royalty A/c closing by transfer to Profit & Loss A/c)			

Additional Solution :

Royalty A/c

Ist Year To Landlord A/c	6,000	Ist Year By Profit & Loss A/c	6,000
II Year To Landlord A/c	12,000	II Year By Profit & Loss A/c	12,000

Shortworkings A/c

I Year To Landlord A/c	4,000	Ist Year By Balance c/d	4,000
II Year To Balance b/d	4,000	II Year By Landlord A/c (Shortworking recovered)	2,000
		By Profit & Loss A/c (Shortworking not recovered written off)	2,000
	4,000		4,000

Landlord A/c

I Year To Bank A/c	10,000	I Year By Royalty A/c	6,000
		By Shortworking A/c	4,000
	10,000		10,000
II Year To Shortworking (Ist Year shortworking recovered)	2,000	II Year By Royalty A/c	12,000
To Bank A/c	10,000		
	12,000		12,000

Problem No. 9

Mr. Kamal wrote a Book on "Management" and entered into an agreement with, "Novman" Publishers for the publication on 1-1-1989. The following were the terms of agreement :

(a) Royalty be payable @ 25% of the sales price of the Books sold. The book is priced @ Rs. 80 per copy.

(b) Minimum rent be Rs. 30,000 per annum.

(c) Each year's excess of Minimum amount over the actual Royalties be recoverable out of the Royalties of the next three years period. The other details are :

Year	No. of Copies Printed	No. of copies in closing stock
1989	1000	600
1990	1300	200
1991	2100	300
1992	1600	350

Prepare : (a) Royalty Account (b) Shortworking Account
(c) Author's Account in the Books of Novman Publishers.

[K.U.D., April 1995(N)]

Solution :

Calculation of No. of copies sold :

Year	Opening stock	+	Copies printed	=	Copies	–	Closing Stock	=	No. of copies sold
1989	Nil	+	1000	=	1000	–	600	=	400
1990	600	+	1300	=	1900	–	200	=	1700
1991	200	+	2100	=	2300	–	300	=	2000
1992	300	+	1600	=	1900	–	350	=	1550

Working Table

Royalty 25% on sales price Rs. 80 × 25% = Rs. 20 per Copy

Year	No. of Copies sold	Royalty Rs. 20 per copy	Minimum Rent	Short-working	Surplus	Shortworkings Recovered	Shortworkings Not recovered	Author Payable
1989	400	8,000	30,000	22,000	—	—	—	30,000
1990	1700	34,000	30,000	—	4,000	4,000	—	30,000
1991	2000	40,000	30,000	—	10,000	10,000	—	30,000
1992	1550	31,000	30,000	—	1,000	1,000	7,000	30,000

In the Books of Novman Publishers

Royalty A/c

1989	To Author A/c Dr.	8,000	1989	By Profit & Loss A/c	8,000
1990	To Author A/c Dr.	34,000	1990	By Profit & Loss A/c	34,000
1991	To Author A/c	40,000	1991	By Profit & Loss A/c	40,000
1992	To Author A/c	31,000	1992	By Profit & Loss A/c	31,000

Shortworking A/c

1989	To Author A/c	22,000	1989	By Balance c/d	22,000
1990	To Balance b/d	22,000	1990	By Author A/c (Shortworkings recovered)	4,000
				By Balance c/d	18,000
		22,000			22,000
1991	To Balance b/d	18,000	1991	By Author A/c (Shortworking recovered)	10,000
				By Balance c/d	8,000
		18,000			18,000
1992	To Balance c/d	8,000	1992	By Author A/c (Shortworking recovered)	1,000
				By Profit & Loss A/c (Short not-recovered written off to Profit & Loss A/c)	7,000
		8,000			8,000

Author A/c

1989	To Bank A/c	30,000	1989	By Royalty A/c	8,000
				By Shortworking A/c	22,000
		30,000			30,000
1990	To Shortworking A/c (recovered)	4,000	1990	By Royalty A/c	34,000
	To Bank A/c	30,000			
		34,000			34,000
1991	To Shortworking A/c (recovered)	10,000	1991	By Royalty	40,000
	To Bank A/c	30,000			
		40,000			40,000
1992	To Shortworking A/c (recovered)	1,000	1992	By Royalty A/c	31,000
	To Bank A/c	30,000			
		31,000			31,000

Problem No. 10

A Coal Company leased a property from P on a Royalty of 0.50 paise per tonne with a Dead Rent (Minimum Rent) of Rs. 10,000 p.a. and power to recoup shortworkings within next two years only in the event of strike, the lease provided for proportionate reduction in the Dead Rent to its working period. The output was as follows :

Year	Output in tonnes	Year	Output in tonnes
31-12-90	10000	31-12-93	30000
31-12-91	16000	31-12-94	12000 (3 months strike)
31-12-92	25000		

Prepare : (a) Minimum Rent Account

(b) Royalty Account

(c) Shortworkings Account and

(d) P's Account (Landlord A/c).

[K.U.D., October 1995(N)]

Solution :

Woorking Table — Royalty Chart

Year	Output in tonnes	Royalty 0.50 paise per tonnes	Minimum Rent	Short-working	Surplus	Shortworkings Recovered	Shortworkings Not recovered	P.S. A/c Payment Landlord
31-12-90	10000	5,000	10,000	5,000	—	—	—	10,000
31-12-91	16000	8,000	10,000	2,000	—	—	—	10,000
31-12-92	25000	12,500	10,000	—	2,500	2,500 (90)	2,500 (90)	10,000
31-12-93	30000	15,000	10,000	—	5,000	2,000 (1991)	—	13,000
31-12-94	12000 strike 3 months	6,000	7,500	1,500	—	—	—	7,500

Minimum Rent pa - Rs. 10,000 (strike 3 months) reduced proportionately to the period of working
(12-3) 9 months working 10,000 × 9/12 = Rs. 7,500 Minimum Rent during period of strike.

Minimum Rent A/c

31-12-90	To Landlord A/c	10,000	31-12-90	By Royalty A/c	5,000
				By Shortworking A/c	5,000
		10,000			10,000
31-12-91	To Landlord A/c	10,000	31-12-91	By Royalty A/c	8,000
				By Shortworking A/c	2,000
		10,000			10,000
31-12-94	To Landlord A/c	7,500	31-12-94	By Royalty A/c	6,000
				By Shortworking A/c	1,500
		7,500			7,500

Royalty A/c

31-12-90	To Minimum Rent A/c	5,000	31-12-90	By Profit & Loss A/c	5,000
31-12-91	To Minimum Rent A/c	8,000	31-12-91	By Profit & Loss A/c	8,000
31-12-92	To Landlord A/c	12,500	31-12-92	By Profit & Loss A/c	12,500
31-12-93	To Landlord A/c	15,000	31-12-93	By Profit & Loss A/c	15,000
31-12-94	To Minimum Rent	6,000	31-12-94	By Profit & Loss A/c	6,000

Shortworking A/c

31-12-90	To Minimum Rent A/c	5,000	31-12-90	By Balance c/d	5,000
		5,000			5,000
31-12-91	To Balance b/d	5,000	31-12-91	By Balance c/d	7,000
	To Minimum Rent	2,000			
		7,000			7,000
31-12-92	To Balance b/d	7,000	31-12-92	By Landlord A/c (1990 recovered)	2,500
				By Profit & Loss A/c (1990 Not recovered written off)	2,500
				By Balance c/d	2,000
		7,000			7,000
31-12-93	To Balance b/d	2,000	31-12-93	By Landlord A/c (1991 recovered)	2,000
31-12-94	To Minimum Rent	1,500	31-12-94	By Balance c/d	1,500

P's A/c (Landlord)

31-12-90	To Bank A/c	10,000	31-12-90	By Min. Rent A/c	10,000
31-12-91	To Bank A/c	10,000	31-12-91	By Min. Rent A/c	10,000
31-12-92	To Shortworking A/c (1990 recovered)	2,500	31-12-92	By Royalty	12,500
	To Bank A/c	10,000			
		12,500			12,500
31-12-93	To Shortworking A/c (1991 recovered)	2,000	31-12-93	By Royalty A/c	15,000
	To Bank A/c	13,000			
		15,000			15,000
31-12-94	To Bank A/c	7,500	31-12-94	By Min. Rent A/c	7,500

Additional Solution :

Journal Entries

			Dr Rs.	Cr Rs.
31-12-90				
(1)	Minimum Rent A/c	Dr.	10,000	
	To Landlord A/c			10,000
	(Minimum Rent payable where actual Royalties earned are less than M.R.)			
(2)	Landlord A/c	Dr.	10,000	
	To Bank A/c			10,000
	(Cash paid)			
(3)	Royalty A/c	Dr.	5,000	
	Shortworking A/c	Dr.	5,000	
	To Minimum Rent A/c			10,000
	(Royalties earned & shortworking payable)			
(4)	Profit & Loss A/c	Dr.	5,000	
	To Royalty A/c			5,000
	(Royalty A/c closed by transfer)			
31-12-91				
(1)	Minimum Rent A/c	Dr.	10,000	
	To Landlord A/c			10,000
	(M.R. Payable where Royalties earned are less than M.R.)			
(2)	Landlord A/c	Dr.	10,000	
	To Bank A/c			10,000
	(Cash paid)			
(3)	Royalty A/c	Dr.	8,000	
	Shortworkings A/c	Dr.	2,000	
	To Minimum Rent A/c			10,000
	(Royalties earned & Shortworking payable A/c)			
(4)	Profit & Loss A/c	Dr.	8,000	
	To Royalty A/c			8,000
	(Royalty A/c closed by transfer)			
31-12-92				
(1)	Royalty A/c	Dr.	12,500	
	To Landlord A/c			12,500
	(Royalty earned and payable)			
(2)	Landlord A/c	Dr.	2,500	
	To Shortworkings A/c			2,500
	(1990 shortworking recovered)			

Journal Entries			Dr Rs.	Cr Rs.
(3)	Landlord A/c	Dr.	10,000	
	To Bank A/c			10,000
	(Cash paid)			
(4)	Profit & Loss A/c	Dr.	2,500	
	To Shortworkings A/c			2,500
	(1990 shortworkings not recovered written off to Profit & Loss A/c)			
(5)	Profit & Loss A/c	Dr.	12,500	
	To Royalty A/c			12,500
	(Royalty A/c closed by transfer)			
31-12-93				
(1)	Royalty A/c	Dr.	15,000	
	To Landlord A/c			15,000
	(Royalty A/c earned and payable)			
(2)	Landlord A/c	Dr.	2,000	
	To Shortworking A/c			2,000
	(1991 Shortworking A/c recovered)			
(3)	Landlord A/c	Dr.	13,000	
	To Bank A/c			13,000
	(Cash paid)			
(4)	Profit & Loss A/c	Dr.	15,000	
	To Royalty A/c			15,000
	(Royalty A/c closed by transfer)			
31-12-94				
(1)	Minimum Rent A/c	7,500		
	To Landlord A/c			7,500
	(Minimum Rent payable where Royalties earned less than MR)			
(2)	Landlord A/c	Dr.	7,500	
	To Bank A/c			7,500
	(Cash paid)			
(3)	Royalty A/c	Dr.	6,000	
	Shortworking A/c		1,500	
	To Minimum Rent			7,500
	(Royalties earned & shortworking payable)			
(4)	Profit & Loss A/c		6,000	
	To Royalty A/c			6,000
	(Royalty A/c closed by transfer)			

Problem No. 11

The Ideal Minerals Ltd. has taken on lease a Mine on a Royalty of 0.50 paise per tonne of iron ore raised with a Minimum Rent of Rs. 20,000 per year and power to recoup shortworkings during the first 4 years. The output was as under :

Year	Output in tonnes	Year	Output in tonnes
I	10000	III	40000
II	24000	IV	90000

Prepare : (a) Royalty payable chart

(b) Royalty Account in the Books of Lessees.

[K.U.D., April 1995(N)]

Solution :

Working Table — Royalty Chart

Year	Output in tonnes	Royalty per tonne 0.50 paise	Minimum Rent	Short-working	Surplus	Shortworkings Recovered	Shortworkings Not recovered	Landlord Amount payable
I	10000	5,000	20,000	15,000	—	—	—	20,000
II	24000	12,000	20,000	8,000	—	—	—	20,000
III	40000	20,000	20,000	—	—	—	—	20,000
IV	90000	45,000	20,000	—	25,000	15,000 (I Year) 8,000 (II Year)		22,000

Royalty A/c

I Year	To Landlord A/c	5,000	I Yr.	By Profit & Loss A/c	5,000
II	To Landlord A/c	12,000	II	By Profit & Loss A/c	12,000
III	To Landlord A/c	20,000	III	By Profit & Loss A/c	20,000
IV	To Landlord A/c	45,000	IV	By Profit & Loss A/c	45,000

Shortworkings A/c

I Yr.	To Landlord A/c	15,000	I Yr.	By Balance c/d	15,000
II	To Balance b/d	15,000	II	By Balance c/d	23,000
	To Landlord A/c	8,000			
		23,000			23,000
III	To Balance b/d	23,000	III	By Balance b/d	23,000
IV	To Balance b/d	23,000	IV	By Landlord A/c I year - 15,000 II year - 8,000 (shortworking recovered)	23,000
		23,000			23,000

Landlord A/c

I Year	To Banks A/c	20,000	I Year	By Royalty A/c	5,000
				By Shortworking A/c	15,000
		20,000			20,000
II	To Bank A/c	20,000	II	By Royalty A/c	12,000
				By Shortworking A/c	8,000
		20,000			20,000
III	To Bank A/c	20,000	III	By Royalty A/c	20,000
IV	To Shortworking A/c I - 15,000 II - 8,000 } 23,000	23,000	IV	By Royalty A/c	45,000
	To Bank A/c	22,000			
		45,000			45,000

Problem No. 12

Mysore Soaps Ltd. entered into agreement with Mr. Vinayak who have developed Ayurvedic Soap to acquire the patent right for manufacture and sale of the soaps. The soap was priced at Rs. 10 each. The terms of agreement were :

(a) The period of Lease shall be for 10 years from 1-1-1988.

(b) The Company shall pay a Minimum amount of Rs. 20,000 per annum merging into a Royalty of 10% on sales payable on 31st December every year.

(c) The shortworkings can be recovered from the excess of Royalty earned over the Minimum Rent during the first four years of the lease.

The other details were :

Year	Output (in numbers)	Closing stock in Numbers
1988	10000	200
1989	16000	100
1990	19000	—
1991	22000	1000
1992	32000	4000

Prepare : (a) Royalty Account
(b) Shortworkings Account and
(c) Vinayak A/c (patentee)
in the Books of the Company.

(K.U.D., October 1994)

Solution :

Working Table — Calculation of Sales and Royalty

Year	Opening Stock	+ Output	– Closing stock	=	Sales Rs.
1988	Nil	10000	– 200	=	9,800 × 10 = 98,000
1989	200	+ 16000	– 100	=	16,100 × 10 = 1,61,000
1990	100	+ 19000	– —	=	19,100 × 10 = 1,91,000
1991	Nil	+ 22000	– 1000	=	21,000 × 10 = 2,10,000
1992	1000	+ 32000	– 4000	=	29,000 × 10 = 2,90,000

Working Table — Royalty Chart

Year	Sales Price Rs.	Royalty 10% on sales price	Minimum Amount	Short-working	Surplus	Shortworkings Recovered	Shortworkings Not recovered	Vinayak Patentec Amount Payable
1988	98,000	9,800	20,000	10,200	—	—	—	20,000
1989	1,61,000	16,100	20,000	3,900	—	—	—	20,000
1990	1,91,000	19,100	20,000	900	—	—	—	20,000
1991	2,10,000	21,000	20,000	—	1,000	1,000	14,000 9,200 + 3,900 + 900	20,000
1992	2,90,000	29,000	20,000	—	9,000			29,000

Note : The Period of recovery of Shortworkings is over in 1991 i.e. First 4 years 1988-1991 and therefore unrecovered Balance of Shortworkings is written off in 1991 only.

Royalty A/c

31-12-88	To Vinayak A/c	9,800	31-12-88	By Profit & Loss A/c	9,800
1989	To Vinayak A/c	16,100	1989	By Profit & Loss A/c	16,100
1990	To Vinayak A/c	19,100	1990	By Profit & Loss A/c	19,100
1991	To Vinayak A/c	21,000	1991	By Profit & Loss A/c	21,000
1992	To Vinayak A/c	29,000	1992	By Profit & Loss A/c	29,000

Shortworking A/c

End of 1988	To Vinayak A/c	10,200	End of 1988	By Balance c/d	10,200
1989	To Balance b/d	10,200	1989	By Balance c/d	14,100
	To Vinayak A/c	3,900			
		14,100			14,100
1990	To Balance b/d	14,100	1990	By Balance c/d	15,000
	To Vinayak A/c	900			
		15,000			15,000
1991	To Balance b/d	15,000	1991	By Vinayak A/c 1988-Rs. 1,000 recovered	1,000
				By Profit & Loss A/c Shortworking of 1988 - 9,200 1989 - 3,900 } Not recovered 1990 - 900 } written off 14,000	14,000
		15,000			15,000

Vinayak A/c (Patentee)

End of 1988	To Bank A/c	20,000	End of 1988	By Royalty A/c	9,800
				By Shortworkings A/c	10,200
		20,000			20,000
1989	To Bank A/c	20,000	1989	By Royalty A/c	16,100
				By Shortworkings A/c	3,900
		20,000			20,000
1990	To Bank A/c	20,000	1990	By Royalty A/c	19,100
				By Shortworkings A/c	900
		20,000			20,000
1991	To Shortworkings A/c (1988-1,000 recovered)	1,000	1991	By Royalty A/c	21,000
	To Bank A/c	20,000			
		21,000			21,000
1992	To Bank A/c	29,000	1992	By Royalties A/c	29,000

Note : The Period of recovery of Short-workings is over in 1991 *i.e.* First 4 years 1988-1991 and therefore unrecovered Balance of Short-workings is written off in 1991 only.

Problem No. 13

Goa Steel Ltd. leased a mine from P at a Royalty of Rs. 2 per ton of ore raised with a Minimum Rent of Rs. 20,000 p.a. Each year's excess of minimum Rent over royalty was recoverable out of the royalty of the next three years. The working of the lease for the first five years is as follows :

Year ending	Output in tons
31-12-1985	4000
31-12-1986	6000
31-12-1987	9000
31-12-1988	15000
31-12-1989	25000

You are required to prepare :

(a) Royalty Account

(b) Minimum Rent Account

(c) Shortworking Account

(d) Landlord Account in the books of Goa Steel Ltd.

[K.U.D., April 1996 (a)]

Solution :

Working Note
(Royalty Rs. 2 per ton)

Year ending	Output	Royalty	Short-working	Surplus	Shortworkings		Land-lord
					Recover	Not-Recover	
31-12-85	4000	8,000	12,000	—	—	—	20,000
31-12-86	6000	12,000	8,000	—	—	—	20,000
31-12-87	9000	18,000	2,000	—	—	—	20,000
31-12-88	15000	30,000	—	10,000	10,000	2,000 (1985)	20,000
31-12-89	25000	50,000	—	30,000	8,000 2,000		40,000

Note : Minimum Rent is 20,000.

In the Book Goa Steel Ltd.

Minimum Rent A/c

1985	To Landlord A/c	20,000	By Royalty A/c	8,000
			By Shortworking A/c	12,000
		20,000		20,000
1986	To Landlord A/c	20,000	By Royalty A/c	12,000
			By Shortworking A/c	8,000
		20,000		20,000
1987	To Landlord a/c	20,000	By Royalty A/c	18,000
			By Shortworking A/c	2,000
		20,000		20,000

Royalty A/c

1985	To Minimum Rent A/c	8,000	By Profit & Loss A/c	8,000
1986	To Minimum Rent A/c	12,000	By Profit & Loss A/c	12,000
1987	To Minimum Rent A/c	18,000	By Profit & Loss A/c	18,000
1988	To Landlord A/c	30,000	By Profit & Loss A/c	30,000
1989	To Landlord A/c	50,000	By Profit & Loss A/c	50,000

Shortworking A/c

1985	To Minimum Rent A/c	12,000	By Balance c/d	12,000
1986	To Balance b/d	12,000	By Balance c/d	20,000
	To Minimum Rent A/c	8,000		
		20,000		20,000
1987	To Balance b/d	20,000	By Balance c/d	22,000
	To Minimum Rent A/c	2,000		
		22,000		22,000
1988	To Balance b/d	22,000	By Landlord A/c 1985 recovered	10,000
			By Profit & Loss A/c Not recovered written off	2,000
			By Balance c/d	10,000
		22,000		22,000
1989	To Balance b/d	10,000	By Landlord A/c 1986 & 87 8,000 recovered + 2,000	10,000
		10,000		10,000

Landlord A/c

1985	To Bank A/c	20,000	1985	By Minimum Rent A/c	20,000
1986	To Bank A/c	20,000	1986	By Minimum Rent A/c	20,000
1987	To Bank A/c	20,000	1987	By Minimum Rent A/c	20,000
1988	To Shortworking A/c (1985 recovered)	10,000	1985	By Royalty A/c	30,000
	To Bank A/c	20,000			
		30,000			30,000
1989	To Shortworking A/c (1986 & 87 recovered)	10,000	1989	By Royalty A/c	50,000
	To Bank A/c	40,000			
		50,000			50,000

Problem No. 14

X Co. Ltd. took a mine on lease at a royalty of 50 paise per tonne of coal raised with a minimum rent of Rs. 40,000 per year. Each year excess of minimum rent over royalties is recoverable out of the royalties of the next two years. In the event of strike the lease provides for the proportionate reduction in the miminum rent. The output for the first five years is given below :

Year ending		Output in tonnes
31-12-1990		40000
31-12-1991		64000
31-12-1992		100000
31-12-1993		120000
31-12-1994	(Strike for 3 months)	48000

Your are required to prepare :

(1) Minimum Rent Account

(2) Shortworking Account

(3) Landlord Account in the books of X Co. Ltd.

(K.U.D., October 1995 & 1985)

Solution :

Working Note

(Royalty Re. 0.50 P. Tonne)

Year ending	Output	Royalty	Short-working	Surplus	Shortworking Recover	Shortworking Not-Recover	Amount Payable
31-12-90	40000	20,000	20,000	—	—	—	40,000
31-12-91	64000	32,000	8,000	—	—	—	40,000
31-12-92	100000	50,000	—	10,000	10,000 (1990)	10,000 (1990)	40,000
31-12-93	120000	60,000	—	20,000	8,000	—	52,000
31-12-94	48,000	24,000	6,000	—	—	—	30,000

Note : (1) Minimum Rent is 40,000.

(2) Strike for 3 months

Minimum Rent is for One Year	40,000
Less Strike for 3 months	10,000
3/12 × 40,000 = 10,000	
	Rs. 30,000 MR

In the Books of X Co. Ltd.

Minimum Rent A/c

31-12-90	To Landlord A/c	40,000	By Royalty A/c	20,000
			By Shortworking A/c	20,000
		40,000		40,000
31-12-91	To Landlord A/c	40,000	By Royalty A/c	32,000
			By Shortworking A/c	8,000
		40,000		40,000
31-12-94	To Landlord A/c	30,000	By Royalty A/c	24,000
			By Shortworking A/c	6,000
		30,000		30,000

Royalty A/c

31-12-90	To Minimum Rent A/c	20,000	By Profit and Loss A/c	20,000
31-12-91	To Minimum Rent A/c	32,000	By Profit and Loss A/c	32,000
31-12-92	To Minimum Rent A/c	50,000	By Profit and Loss A/c	50,000
31-12-93	To Minimum Rent A/c	60,000	By Profit and Loss A/c	60,000

X Co. Ltd. A/c

Date	Particulars	Amount	Date	Particulars	Amount
31-12-90	To Bank A/c	40,000	31-12-90	By Minimum Rent A/c	40,000
		40,000			40,000
31-12-91	To Bank A/c	40,000	31-12-91	By Minimum Rent A/c	40,000
		40,000			40,000
31-12-92	To Shortworking A/c (1990 recovered)	10,000	31-12-92	By Royalty A/c	50,000
	To Bank A/c	40,000			
		50,000			50,000
31-12-93	To Shortworking A/c	8,000	31-12-93	By Royalty A/c	60,000
	To Bank A/c	52,000			
		60,000			60,000
31-12-94	To Bank A/c	30,000	31-12-94	By Minimum Rent A/c	30,000

Shortworking A/c

Date	Particulars	Amount	Particulars	Amount
31-12-90	To Minimum Rent A/c	20,000	By Balance c/d	20,000
01-01-91	To Balance b/d	20,000	By Balance c/d	28,000
31-12-91	To Minimum Rent A/c	8,000		
		28,000		28,000
01-01-92	To Balance b/d	28,000	By Landlord A/c (1990 recovered)	10,000
			By Profit & Loss A/c (not recovered written off)	10,000
			By Balance c/d	8,000
		28,000		28,000
31-12-93	To Balance b/d	8,000	By Landlord A/c	8,000
1994	To Minimum Rent A/c	6,000	By Balance c/d	6,000

Problem No. 15

Mr. Bhairav Kamat wrote a Book on Business Management and entered into an agreement with Navaman Publishers, Gadag for its publications on 1-1-1989. The following were the terms of agreement :

(a) Royalty payable 25% of the sales price of the books sold. The book is priced at Rs. 80 per copy.

(b) Minimum amount was Rs. 30,000 per annum.

(c) Each year's excess of minimum amount over the actual Royalties is recoverable out of the Royalties of the next three years period.

The other details are :

Year	No. of copies printed	No. of copies closing stock
1989	1000	600
1990	1300	200
1991	2100	300
1992	1600	350

Prepare :

(a) Royalty account

(b) Shortworking account

(c) Author's account in the books of Navaman Publishers.

(K.U.D., April 1995)

Solution :

Year	No. of copies printed	No. of copies closing stock	No. of Books sold
1989	1000	600	400
1990	1300	200	1700
Add : Opening Stock	600		
	1900		
1991	2100		
Add : Opening Stock	200		
	2300	300	2000
1992	1600		
Add : Opening Stock	300		
	1900	350	1550

Royalty 25% of sales price

Sales price per copy – Rs. 80

Royalty per copy – Rs. 80 × $\frac{25}{100}$ = Rs. 20 per copy.

Year	No. of Books sold	Royalty Rs. 20 per copy	Minimum amount	Short-working	Surplus	Shortworkings Recovered	Shortworkings Not recovered	Amount Payable to Author
1989	400	8,000	30,000	22,000	—	—	—	30,000
1990	1700	34,000	30,000		4,000	4,000	—	30,000
1991	2000	40,000	30,000	—	10,000	10,000	—	30,000
1992	1550	31,000	30,000	—	1,000	1,000	7,000	30,000

In the Books of Navaman Publishers

Royalty A/c

1989 To Author A/c	8,000	By Profit & Loss A/c	8,000
1990 To Author A/c	34,000	By Profit & Loss A/c	34,000
1991 To Author A/c	40,000	By Profit & Loss A/c	40,000
1992 To Author A/c	31,000	By Profit & Loss A/c	31,000

Author A/c

1989 To Bank A/c	30,000	1989 By Royalty A/c	8,000
		By Shortworking A/c	22,000
	30,000		30,000
1990 To Shortworking A/c	4,000	1990 By Royalty A/c	34,000
To Bank A/c	30,000		
	34,000		34,000
1991 To Shortworking A/c	10,000	1991 By Royalty A/c	40,000
To Bank A/c	30,000		
	40,000		40,000
1992 To Shortworking A/c	1,000	1992 By Royalty A/c	31,000
To Bank A/c	30,000		
	31,000		31,000

Shortworking Account

1989 To Author A/c	22,000	By Balance c/d	22,000
1990 To Balance b/d	22,000	By Author A/c (1989 recovered)	4,000
		By Balance c/d	18,000
	22,000		22,000
1991 To Balance b/d	18,000	By Author A/c (1989 recovered)	10,000
		By Balance c/d	8,000
	18,000		18,000
1992 To Balance b/d	8,000	By Author A/c (1989 recovered)	1,000
		By Profit & Loss A/c	7,000
	8,000		8,000

Problem No. 16

Mrs. Parvati Amar Tandel took a lease of land from Fish Federation of Karnataka for Prawn culturing in Tadadi Aghanashine Belt.

The Royalty is agreed to be Rs. 500 per ton of Prawns subject to a minimum amount of Rs. 5,00,000 and shortworking recoupment period extending to two succeeding years only.

31st March 1987	500 Tons
31st March 1988	800 Tons
31st March 1989	1100 Tons
31st March 1990	1300 Tons
31st March 1991	1500 Tons

Pass Journal Entries in the Books of Mrs Parvati Amar Tandel.

(K.U.D., April 1994)

Solution :

Working Table

Year ending 31st March	Output in tons	Royalty Rs. 500 per ton	Minimum Amount	Shortworking	Surplus	Shortworking Recovered	Shortworking Not recovered	Paid to Landlord
1987	500	2,50,000	5,00,000	2,50,000				5,00,000
1988	800	4,00,000	5,00,000	1,00,000				5,00,000
1989	1100	5,50,000	5,00,000	—	50,000	50,000	2,00,000	5,00,000
1990	1300	6,50,000	5,00,000	—	1,50,000	1,00,000	—	5,50,000
1991	1500	7,50,000		—	2,50,000		—	7,50,000

In the Books of Parvati Amar Tandel

Journal Entries

Particulars			Amount	Amount
31-3-1987				
1.	Royalty A/c	Dr	2,50,000	
	Shortworking A/c	Dr	2,50,000	
	To Landlord A/c			5,00,000
	(Royalties earned and shortworking payable)			
2.	Landlord A/c	Dr	5,00,000	
	To Bank A/c			5,00,000
	(Cash paid)			
3.	Profit & Loss A/c	Dr	2,50,000	
	To Royalty A/c			2,50,000
	(Royalty A/c transferred)			
1988				
1.	Royalty A/c	Dr	4,00,000	
	Shortworking A/c	Dr	1,00,000	
	To Landlord A/c			5,00,000
	(Royalty earned and shortworking payable)			
2.	Landlord A/c	Dr	5,00,000	
	To Bank A/c			5,00,000
	(Cash paid)			
3.	Profit & Loss A/c	Dr	4,00,000	
	To Royalty A/c			4,00,000
	(Royalty A/c transferred)			
1989				
1.	Royalty A/c	Dr	5,50,000	
	To Landlord A/c			5,50,000
	(Royalty earned & shortworking payable)			
2.	Landlord A/c	Dr	50,000	
	To Shortworking A/c			50,000
	(Shortworking recovered out of surplus)			
3.	Landlord A/c	Dr	5,00,000	
	To Bank A/c			5,00,000
	(Cash paid)			
4.	Profit & Loss A/c	Dr	2,00,000	
	To Shortworking A/c			2,00,000
	(Shortworking of 1989 not recovered written off)			

Particulars		Amount	Amount
5. Profit & Loss A/c	Dr	5,50,000	
To Royalty A/c			5,50,000
(Royalty transfer)			
1990			
1. Royalty A/c	Dr	6,50,000	
To Landlord A/c			6,50,000
(Royalties earned shortworking payable)			
2. Landlord A/c	Dr	1,00,000	
To Shortworking A/c			1,00,000
(Shortworking of 1988 recovered out of surplus)			
3. Landlord A/c	Dr	5,50,000	
To Bank A/c			5,50,000
(Cash paid)			
4. Profit & Loss A/c	Dr	6,50,000	
To Royalty A/c			6,50,000
(Royalty A/c transferred)			
1991			
1. Royalty A/c	Dr	7,50,000	
To Landlord A/c			7,50,000
(Royalties earned & payable)			
2. Landlord A/c	Dr	7,50,000	
To Bank A/c			7,50,000
(Cash paid)			
3. Profit & Loss A/c	Dr	7,50,000	
To Royalty A/c			7,50,000
(Royalty Account transferred)			

In the of Books Mrs Parvati Amar Tandel

Royalty A/c

31-3-1987 To Landlord A/c	2,50,000	By Profit & Loss A/c	2,50,000
31-3-1988 To Landlord A/c	4,00,000	By Profit & Loss A/c	4,00,000
31-3-1989 To Landlord A/c	5,50,000	By Profit & Loss A/c	5,50,000
31-3-1990 To Landlord A/c	6,50,000	By Profit & Loss A/c	6,50,000
31-3-1991 To Landlord A/c	7,50,000	By Profit & Loss A/c	7,50,000

Shortworking A/c

31-3-87	To Landlord A/c	2,50,000	By Profit & Loss A/c	2,50,000
		2,50,000		2,50,000
1988	To Balance b/d	2,50,000	By Balance c/d	3,50,000
31-3-88	To Landlord A/c	1,00,000		
		3,50,000		3,50,000
1989	To Balance b/d	3,50,000	By Landlord A/c (1987 shortworking recovered)	50,000
			By Profit & Loss A/c (1987 received written off)	2,00,000
			By Balance c/d	1,00,000
		3,50,000		3,50,000
1990	To Balance b/d	1,00,000	By Landlord A/c	1,00,000

Landlord A/c

March					
1987	To Bank A/c	5,00,000	1987	By Royalty A/c	2,50,000
				By Shortworking A/c	2,50,000
		5,00,000			5,00,000
1988	To Bank A/c	5,00,000	1988	By Royalty A/c	4,00,000
				By Shortworking A/c	1,00,000
		5,00,000			5,00,000
1989	To Bank A/c	5,00,000	1989	By Royalty A/c	5,50,000
	To Shortworking	50,000			
		5,50,000			5,50,000
1990	To Shortworking A/c	1,00,000	1990	By Royalty A/c	6,50,000
	To Bank A/c	5,50,000			
		6,50,000			6,50,000
1991	To Bank A/c	7,50,000	1991	By Royalty A/c	7,50,000
		7,50,000			7,50,000

Problem No. 17

The 'Stone Traders' Co. took a Mine on lease from Government of Karnataka at a Royalty of Rs. 200 per ton of stone raised with a minimum Rent of Rs. 80,000 per annum. Each year excess of Minimum Rent over Royalties is recoverable out of the Royalties of the next two years. In the event of strike and the minimum Rent is not reached, the lease provided that the actual Royalties earned during the year will discharge all the rental obligations for that year.

The following are the figures of the mine working for the period of five years :

Year	Output (in tons)
1987	250
1988	360
1989	500
1990	350 (Strike)
1991	800

Prepare : (a) Royalty Account
(b) Shortworkings Account
(c) Government of Karnataka (Landlord)
in the Books of 'Stone Trader' Co.

(K.U.D., October 1993)

Solution :

Working Chart

Year	Output	Royalty Rs. 200 per ton	Minimum Rent	Short working	Surplus	Shortworking Recovered	Shortworking Not recovered	Govt. of Karnataka Landlord
1987	250	50,000	80,000	30,000	—	—	—	80,000
1988	360	72,000	80,000	8,000	—	—	—	80,000
1989	500	1,00,000	80,000	—	20,000	20,000	10,000 (P & L)	80,000
1990 (strike)	350	70,000	70,000	—	—	—	8,000 (P & L)	70,000
1991	800	1,60,000	80,000	—	—	—		1,60,000

Government of Karnataka A/c
(Landlord)

Particulars	Amount	Year	Particulars	Amount
To Bank A/c	80,000	1987	By Royalty A/c	50,000
			By Shortworking A/c	30,000
	80,000			80,000
To Bank A/c	80,000	1988	By Royalty A/c	72,000
			By Shortworking A/c	8,000
	80,000			80,000
To Shortworking A/c	20,000	1989	By Royalty A/c	1,00,000
To Bank A/c	80,000			
	1,00,000			1,00,000
To Bank A/c	70,000	1990	By Royalty A/c	70,000
	70,000			70,000
To Bank A/c	1,60,000	1991	By Royalty A/c	1,60,000
	1,60,000			1,60,000

Shortworking A/c

1987	To Landlord A/c	30,000		By Balance c/d	30,000
		30,000			30,000
1988	To Balance b/d	30,000		By Balance c/d	38,000
	To Landlord A/c	8,000			
		38,000			38,000
1989	To Balance b/d	38,000	1989	By Landlord A/c (1987 shortworking recovered)	20,000
				By Profit & Loss A/c (1987 shortworking not received)	10,000
				By Balance c/d	8,000
		38,000			38,000
1990	To Balance B/d	8,000	1990	By Profit & Loss A/c (1988 shortworking not recovered written off)	8,000
		8,000			8,000

Problem No. 18

Kaveri Limited obtained on 1st January 1986 the use of patent of "Komal Mixi", from Krishna Limited under the following terms :

(a) A Royalty of 2% on sales subject to a Minimum Amount of Rs. 20,000 per payable at the end of each year.

(b) Kaveri Limited will have the right of recouping shortworkings in the next two years period only.

Sales during the first Five years period :

Year	Sales
	Rs.
1986	4,00,000
1987	7,00,000
1988	10,00,000
1989	12,00,000
1990	19,00,000

Prepare the following ledger Accounts in the Books of Kaveri Limited :

(1) Royalty A/c

(2) Shortworking A/c

(3) Landlord A/c.

(K.U.D., April 1993)

Solution :

Working Table

Year	Sales	Royalty 2%	Minimum Amount	Short-working	Surplus	Shortworkings Recovered	Shortworkings Not recovered	Amount Payable
1986	4,00,000	8,000	20,000	12,000	—	—		20,000
1987	7,00,000	14,000	20,000	6,000	—	—	—	20,000
1988	10,00,000	20,000	20,000	—	—	—	12,000 P & L	20,000
1989	12,00,000	24,000	20,000	—	4,000	—	2,000 1987	20,000
1990	19,00,000	38,000	20,000	—	18,000	—		38,000

Royalty A/c

Year	Particulars	Amount	Particulars	Amount
1986	To Krishna Ltd. A/c	8,000	By Profit & Loss A/c	8,000
1987	To Krishna Ltd. A/c	14,000	By Profit & Loss A/c	14,000
1988	To Krishna Ltd. A/c	20,000	By Profit & Loss A/c	20,000
1989	To Krishna Ltd. A/c	24,000	By Profit & Loss A/c	24000
1990	To Krishna Ltd. A/c	38,000	By Profit & Loss A/c	38,000

Shortworking A/c

Year	Particulars	Amount	Particulars	Amount
1986	To Krishna Ltd. A/c	12,000	By Balance c/d	12,000
1987	To Balance b/d	12,000	By Balance c/d	18,000
	To Krishna Ltd.	6,000		
		18,000		18,000
1988	To Balance b/d	18,000	By Profit & Loss A/c (1986 shortworking not received written off to Profit & Loss)	12,000
			By Balance c/d	6,000
		18,000		18,000
1989	To Balance b/d	6,000	By Krishna Ltd. A/c (1987 recovered)	4,000
			By Profit & Loss A/c (1987 not recovered written off)	2,000
		6,000		6,000

Krishna Ltd. A/c

1986	To Bank A/c	20,000	1986	By Royalty A/c	8,000
				By Shortworking A/c	12,000
		20,000			20,000
1987	To Bank A/c	20,000	1987	By Royalty A/c	14,000
				By Shortworking A/c	6,000
		20,000			20,000
1988	To Bank A/c	20,000	1988	By Royalty A/c	20,000
		20,000			20,000
1989	To Shortworking A/c	4,000	1989	By Royalty A/c	24,000
	To Bank A/c	20,000			
		24,000			24,000
1990	To Bank A/c	38,000	1990	By Royalty A/c	38,000
		38,000			38,000

Problem No. 19

X Ltd. took a coal mine on lease at a Royalty of Rs. 2 per tonne of coal raised with a Dead Rent of Rs. 40,000 per annum, subject to the right of recoupment of shortworking in the next two years only. The lease provided that in the event of strike the Dead Rent be reduced proportionately to the period of working.

The Output during five years was :

Year ending	Output
On 31 March 1987	10000 tonnes
On 31 March 1988	18000 tonnes
On 31 March 1989	25000 tonnes
On 31 March 1990	12000 tonnes (Strike for 3 months)
On 31 March 1991	30000 tonnes

Prepare :

(1) Royalty A/c (2) Dead Rent A/c

(3) Shortworking A/c (4) Landlord A/c

in the Books of X Co. Ltd. (the assessee).

(K.U.D., October 1992)

Solution :

Working Table

(Royalty = Rs. 2 per tonne)

Year	Output (in tonne)	Royalty Rs. 2 per tonne	Minimum Amount	Short-working	Surplus	Shortworkings Recover	Shortworkings Not recover	Amount paid
31-3-87	10,000	20000	40,000	20,000	—	—	—	40,000
31-3-88	18,000	36000	40,000	4,000	—	—		40,000
31-3-89	25,000	50000	40,000	—	10,000	10,000 (1987)	10,000 (P&L)	40,000
31-3-90 (3 months strike)	12,000	24000	30,000	6,000	—	—	4,000 (1988)	30,000
31-3-91	20000	60,000	40,000	—	20,000	6,000 (1990)	—	54,000

Minimum Rent A/c

31-3-87	To Landlord A/c	40,000	By Royalty A/c	20,000
			By Shortworking A/c	20,000
		40,000		40,000
1988	To Landlord A/c	40,000	By Royalty A/c	36,000
			By Shortworking A/c	4,000
		40,000		40,000
1990	To Landlord A/c	30,000	By Royalty A/c	24,000
			By Shortworking A/c	6,000
		30,000		30,000

Royalty A/c

31-3-87	To Minimum Rent A/c	20,000	By Profit and Loss A/c	20,000
1988	To Minimum Rent A/c	36,000	By Profit and Loss A/c	36,000
1989	To Landlord A/c	50,000	By Profit and Loss A/c	50,000
1990	To Minimum Rent A/c	24,000	By Profit and Loss A/c	24,000
1991	To Landlord A/c	60,000	By Profit and Loss A/c	60,000

Shortworking A/c

31-3-87	To Minimum Rent A/c	20,000	By Balance c/d	20,000
1988	To Balance b/d	20,000	By Balance c/d	24,000
	To Minimum Rent A/c	4,000		
		24,000		24,000
1989	To Balance b/d	24,000	By Landlord A/c (1987 recovered)	10,000
			By Profit and Loss A/c (Not recovered)	10,000
			By Balance c/d	4,000
		24,000		24,000
1990	To Balance b/d	4,000	By Profit and Loss A/c (1988 not recovered)	4,000
	To Minimum Rent A/c	6,000	By Balance c/d	6,000
		10,000		10,000
1991	To Balance b/d	6,000	By Landlord A/c (1990 recovered)	6,000
		6,000		6,000

Landlord A/c

31-3-87	To Bank	40,000	31-3-87	By Minimum Rent A/c	40,000
1988	To Bank	40,000	1988	By Minimum Rent A/c	40,000
1989	To Shortworking Recover A/c	10,000	1989	By Royalty A/c	50,000
	To Bank A/c	40,000			
		50,000			50,000
1990	To Bank A/c	30,000	1990	By Minimum Rent A/c	30,000
1991	To Shortworking Recover A/c	6,000	1991	By Royalty A/c	60,000
	To Bank A/c	54,000			
		60,000			60,000

Problem No. 20

Mr. Ishwar of Belgaum a professional Author of Managerial technique has entered into an agreement with India Publishing House, Delhi on 1st January 1986, for publication and sale of Book. The term agreed were as follows :

1. Royalty payable is 20% on sales price of Book; the book is priced at Rs. 75 per copy.
2. The Author is to be paid the minimum amount of Rs. 50,000 pa.

3. Each year's excess of minimum amount over Royalties earned is recoverable out of surplus royalties, during the next three years period subject to a maximum amount of Rs. 6,000 in that particular year of recovery. Following are the particulars of sales :

Year ending	No. of Books sold
1986	2000 Copies
1987	2800 Copies
1988	4500 Copies
1989	6000 Copies
1990	4000 Copies

Prepare : (1) Royalty A/c (2) Author A/c (3) Shortworking A/c in the Books of India Publishing House.

(K.U.D., April 1992)

Solution :

Working Table

Year	No. of Copy Sold	Royalty 2% per copy	Minimum Amount	Short-working	Surplus	Shortworkings Recovered	Shortworkings Not recovered	Amount payable
1986	2000	30,000	50,000	20,000	—	—	—	50,000
1987	2800	42,000	50,000	8,000	—	—	—	50,000
1988	4500	67,500	50,000	—	17,500	6,000	—	61,500
1989	6000	90,000	50,000	—	40,000	6,000	8,000	84,000
1990	4000	60,000	50,000	—	10,000	6,000	2,000	54,000

Royalty A/c

1986 To Author A/c	30,000	By Profit & Loss A/c	30,000
1987 To Author A/c	42,000	By Profit & Loss A/c	42,000
1988 To Author A/c	67,500	By Profit & Loss A/c	67,500
1989 To Author A/c	90,000	By Profit & Loss A/c	90,000
1990 To Author A/c	60,000	By Profit & Loss A/c	60,000

Author A/c (Ishwar A/c)

1986	To Bank A/c	50,000	1986	By Royalty A/c	30,000
				By Shortworking A/c	20,000
		50,000			50,000
1987	To Bank A/c	50,000	1987	By Royalty A/c	42,000
				By Shortworking A/c	8,000
		50,000			50,000
1988	To Shortworking	6,000	1988	By Royalty A/c	67,500
	To Bank A/c	61,500			
		67,500			67,500
1989	To Shortworking	6,000	1989	By Royalty A/c	90,000
	To Bank A/c	84,000			
		90,000			90,000
1990	To Shortworking	6,000	1990	By Royalty A/c	60,000
	To Bank A/c	54,000			
		60,000			60,000

Shortworking A/c

1986	To Author A/c	20,000	By Balance c/d	20,000
1987	To Balance b/d	20,000	By Balance c/d	28,000
	To Author A/c	8,000		
		28,000		28,000
1988	To Balance b/d	28,000	By Author A/c (1986 recovered)	6,000
			By Balance c/d	22,000
		28,000		28,000
1989	To Balance b/d	22,000	By Author A/c (1986 recovered)	6,000
			By Profit & Loss A/c	8,000
			By Balance c/d	8,000
		22,000		22,000
1990	To Balance b/d	8,000	By Author A/c (1987 recovered)	6,000
			By Profit & Loss A/c (1987 not recovered)	2,000
		8,000		8,000

Problem No. 21

Shri Anand had developed a Kitchen appliance item. Kitchen Appliance Manufacturing Co. Ltd. has entered into agreement on 1st January 1985 with Shri Anand to acquire patent right for the manufacture and sale of appliance.

The terms of agreement were :

1. The period of lease shall be Seven years from 1-1-1985.
2. The Company shall pay minimum amount of Rs. 60,000 p.a. Merging into a Royalty of 20% of sales Price payable on 31st December every year.
3. The shortworking loss of a year can be recovered from excess of Royalty earned over the minimum amount during the next two years.

The production and sales of the article during 5 years are as follows :

Year	Sales Rs.
1985	2,00,000
1986	2,80,000
1987	3,90,000
1988	4,10,000
1989	4,60,000

Write in the Books of Kitchen Manufacture Company Limited.

(K.U.D., October 1991)

Solution :

Working Chart

Year	Sales Rs.	Royalty 20%	Minimum Amount	Short-working	Surplus	Shortworkings Recovered	Shortworkings Not recovered	Amount payable to patentee
1985	2,00,000	40,000	60,000	20,000	—	—	—	60,000
1986	2,80,000	56,000	60,000	4,000	—	—	—	60,000
1987	3,90,000	78,000	60,000	—	18,000	18,000 (1985)	2,000 (1985)	60,000
1988	4,10,000	82,000	60,000	—	22,000	4,000 (1986)	—	78,000
1989	4,60,000	92,000	60,000	—	32,000	—	—	92,000

Royalty A/c

1985	To Patentee A/c	40,000	31-12	By Profit & Loss A/c	40,000
1986	To Patentee A/c	56,000		By Profit & Loss A/c	56,000
1987	To Patentee A/c	78,000		By Profit & Loss A/c	78,000
1988	To Patentee A/c	82,000		By Profit & Loss A/c	82,000
1989	To Patentee A/c	92,000		By Profit & Loss A/c	92,000

Patentee A/c

1985	To Bank A/c	60,000	1985	By Royalty A/c	40,000
				By Shortworking A/c	20,000
		60,000			60,000
1986	To Bank A/c	60,000	1986	By Royalty A/c	56,000
				By Shortworking A/c	4,000
		60,000			60,000
1987	To Shortworking	18,000	1987	Royalty A/c	78,000
	To Bank A/c	60,000			
		78,000			78,000
1988	To Shortworking	4,000	1988	By Royalty A/c	82,000
	To Bank A/c	78,000			
		82,000			82,000
1989	To Bank A/c	92,000	1989	By Royalty A/c	92,000

Shortworking A/c

1985	To Patentee A/c	20,000	By Balance c/d	20,000
1986	To Balance c/d	20,000	By Balance c/d	24,000
	To Patentee A/c	4,000		
		24,000		24,000
1987	To Balance b/d	24,000	By Patentee 1985	18,000
			By Profit & Loss A/c 1985 (Not recovered)	2,000
			By Balance c/d	4,000
		24,000		24,000
1988	To Balance b/d	4,000	By Patentee	4,000

Problem No. 22

Karnataka Company took a mine on lease at a Royalty of Rs. 4 per tonne of iron ore raised with a Minimum Rent of Rs. 50,000 per annum. Each year's. excess of Minimum Rent over Royalties is recoverable out of the Royalties of the next two years.

In the event of strike the lease provided that the actual Royalties earned would discharge all the rental obligations for that year. The output for the first six years is as follows :

Year ending	Output in tonnes
1985	8000
1986	12000
1987	16000
1988	20000
1989 (Strike)	9000
1990	14000

Prepare : (a) Royalty Account (b) Shortworkings Account

(c) Landlords Account

in the Books of Karnataka Company.

(K.U.D., April 1991)

Solution :

Working Table

Year	Output in ton	Royalty Rs. 4 per ton	Minimum Rent	Short-working	Surplus	Shortworkings Recover	Shortworkings Not recover	Amount Payable
1985	8000	32,000	50,000	18,000	—	—	—	50,000
1986	12000	48,000	50,000	2,000	—	—	—	50,000
1987	16000	64,000	50,000	—	14,000	14,000 (1985)	4,000 (1985)	50,000
1988	20000	80,000	50,000	—	30,000	2,000 (1986)	—	78,000
1989 (Strike)	9000	36,000	36,000	—	—	—	—	36,000
1990	14000	56,000	50,000	—	6,000	—	—	56,000

In the Books of Karnataka (Mining Co.)

Royalty A/c

1985	To Landlord A/c	32,000	By Profit & Loss A/c	32,000
1986	To Landlord A/c	48,000	By Profit & Loss A/c	48,000
1987	To Landlord A/c	64,000	By Profit & Loss A/c	64,000
1988	To Landlord A/c	80,000	By Profit & Loss A/c	80,000
1989	To Landlord A/c	36,000	By Profit & Loss A/c	36,000
1990	To Landlord A/c	56,000	By Profit & Loss A/c	56,000

Shortworking A/c

1985	To Landlord A/c	18,000	1985	By Balance c/d	18,000
1986	To Balance b/d	18,000	1986	By Balance c/d	20,000
	To Landlord A/c	2,000			
		20,000			20,000
1987	To Balance b/d	20,000	1987	By Landlord A/c (1985 recovered)	14,000
			1988	By Profit & Loss A/c (1985 not recovered written off)	4,000
				By Balance c/d	2,000
		20,000			20,000
1988	To Balance b/d	2,000	1988	By Landlord A/c (recovered)	2,000

Landlord A/c

1985	To Bank A/c	50,000	1985	By Royalty A/c	32,000
				By Shortworking A/c	18,000
		50,000			50,000
1986	To Bank A/c	50,000	1986	By Royalty A/c	48,000
				By Shortworking A/c	2,000
		50,000			50,000
1987	To Shortworking (1985 recovered)	14,000	1987	By Royalty A/c	64,000
	To Bank A/c	50,000			
		64,000			64,000
1988	To Shortworking (1986 recovered)	2,000	1988	By Royalty A/c	80,000
	To Bank A/c	78,000			
		80,000			80,000
1989	To Bank A/c	36,000	1989	By Royalty A/c	36,000
1990	To Bank A/c	56,000	1990	By Royalty A/c	56,000

Problem No. 23

Merchant Mining Company took a mine on lease for five years for a royalty of Rs. 20 per tonne of coal raised subject to a minimum rent of Rs. 6,000. The excess of minimum rent over the Royalty can be recovered out of the surplus of the next year immediately after the year of shortfall. The actual royalty itself is payable in the year of strike. Following is the output for the said period of five years :

1st Year	150 tonnes
2nd Year	400 tonnes
3rd Year	450 tonnes
4th Year (Strike)	200 tonnes
5th Year	400 tonnes

Give : Royalty A/c
Minimum Rent A/c
Shortworking A/c
Landlord's A/c

in the Books of Merchant Mining Co.

(K.U.D., October 1990)

Solution :

Working Chart

Year	Output in tonne	Royalty Rs. 20	Minimum Rent	Short-working	Surplus	Shortworkings Recovered	Shortworkings Not recovered	Amount payable to Landlord
1st Year	150	3,000	6,000	3,000	—	—	—	6,000
2nd Year	400	8,000	6,000	—	2,000	2,000	1,000 (P&L)	6,000
3rd Year	450	9,000	6,000	—	3,000	—	—	9,000
4th Year (Strike)	200	4,000	4,000	—	—	—	—	4,000
5th Year	400	8,000	6,000	—	2,000	—	—	8,000

Minimum Rent A/c

I Year	To Landlord A/c	6,000	I Year	By Royalty A/c	3,000
				By Shortworking A/c	3,000
		6,000			6,000

Royalty A/c

I Year	To Minimum Rent A/c	3,000	I Year	By Profit & Loss A/c	3,000
II	To Landlord A/c	8,000	II	By Profit & Loss A/c	8,000
III	To Landlord A/c	9,000	III	By Profit & Loss A/c	9,000
IV	To Landlord A/c	4,000	IV	By Profit & Loss A/c	4,000
V	To Landlord A/c	8,000	V	By Profit & Loss A/c	8,000

Landlord A/c

I Year	To Bank A/c	6,000	I Year	By Minimum Rent A/c	6,000
II	To Shortworking A/c	2,000	II	By Royalty A/c	8,000
III	To Bank A/c	6,000			
		8,000			8,000
IV	To Bank A/c	9,000	III	By Royalty A/c	9,000
V	To Bank A/c	4,000	IV	By Royalty A/c	4,000
VI	To Bank A/c	8,000	V	By Royalty A/c	8,000

Shortworking A/c

I Year	To Minimum Rent A/c	3,000	I Year	By Landlord A/c	2,000
				By Profit & Loss A/c (Written off)	1,000
		3,000			3,000

Problem No. 24

Daneshwari Publishers agreed to take up printing and sales of Book from the Author Somanath on 1-1-1986. The following are the terms of agreement :

(1) Royalty payable @ 20% on sales of Books. The Book is priced at Rs. 30 per copy.

(2) The Author is to be paid minimum amount of Rs. 20,000 p.a.

(3) Each year's excess of minimum amount over the actual Royalties is recoverable out of the Royalties of the next two years.

Year ending	No. of Copies Printed	No. of Copies of Closing stock
31-12-1986	3000	250
31-12-1987	3200	300
31-12-1988	3500	100
31-12-1989	3650	200

Record the Journal Entries in the Books of Daneshwari Publishers.

(K.U.D., October 1990)

Solution :

Ascertainment of No. Copies Sold

Year	Opening Stock	Printed during the year	Closing Stock	No. of Copies sold
1986	Nil	+3,000	– 250	2750
1987	250	+3,200	– 300	3150
1988	300	+3,500	– 100	3700
1989	100	+3,650	– 200	3550

Note : Royalty 20% of Selling Price = 20% of Rs. 30 = Rs. 6 per copy.

Working Table

Year	No. of copy sold	Royalty Rs. 6 per Copy	Minimum Amount	Short-working	Surplus	Shortworkings Recovered	Shortworkings Not recovered	Amount Paid
1986	2750	16,500	20,000	3,500	—	—	—	20,000
1987	3150	18,900	20,000	1,100	—	—	—	20,000
1988	3700	22,200	20,000	--	2,200	2,200	1,300	20,000
1989	3550	21,300	20,000	—	1,300	1,100	—	20,200

In the Books of Daneshwari Publishers

Royalty A/c

1986	To Author Somanath	16500	1986	By Profit & Loss A/c	16,500
1987	To Author Somanath	18900	1987	By Profit & Loss A/c	18,900
1988	To Author Somanath	22200	1988	By Profit & Loss A/c	22,200
1989	To Author Somanath	21300	1989	By Profit & Loss A/c	21,300

Shortworking A/c

1986	To Author Somanath A/c	3,500	By Balance c/d	3,500
1987	To Balance b/d	3,500	By Balance c/d	4,600
	To Author Somanath	1,100		
		4,600		4,600
1988	To Balance b/d	4,600	By Author Somanath A/c (1986 recovered)	2,200
			By Profit & Loss A/c (1986 not recovered written off)	1,300
			By Balance c/d	1,100
		4,600		4,600
1989	To Balance b/d	1,100	By Author Somanath A/c (1987 recovered)	1,100
		1,100		1,100

Author Somanath A/c

1986	To Bank A/c	20,000	1986	By Royalty A/c	16,500
				By Shortworking A/c	3,500
		20,000			20,000
1987	To Bank A/c	20,000	1987	By Royalty A/c	18,900
				By Shortworking A/c	1,100
		20,000			20,000
1988	To Shortworking A/c (1986 recovered)	2,200	1988	By Royalty A/c	22,200
	To Bank A/c	20,000			
		22,200			22,200
1989	To Shortworking A/c (1987 recovered)	1,100	1989	By Royalty A/c	21,300
	To Bank A/c	20,200			
		21,300			21,300

In the Books of Daneshwari Publishers

Journal Entries

	Particulars		Rs.	Rs.
1986				
(1)	Royalty A/c	Dr	16,500	
	Shortworking A/c	Dr	3,500	
	To Author Somanath A/c			20,000
	(Royalties earned and shortworking payable)			
(2)	Author Somanath A/c	Dr	20,000	
	To Bank A/c			20,000
	(Cash paid)			
(3)	Profit & Loss A/c	Dr	16,500	
	To Royalty A/c			16,500
	(Royalty A/c transferred)			
1987				
(1)	Royalty A/c	Dr	18,900	
	Shortworking A/c	Dr	1,100	
	To Author Somanath A/c			20,000
	(Royalty earned and shortworking payable)			
(2)	Author Somanath A/c	Dr	20,000	
	To Bank A/c			20,000
	(Cash paid)			

	Particulars		Rs.	Rs.
(3)	Profit & Loss A/c	Dr	18,900	
	To Royalty A/c			18,900
	(Royalty A/c transferred)			
1988				
(1)	Royalty A/c	Dr	22,200	
	To Author Somanath A/c			22,200
	(Royalty earned & payable)			
(2)	Author Somanath A/c	Dr	2,200	
	To Shortworking A/c			2,200
	(Shortworking of 1986 recovered out of surplus)			
(3)	Author Somanath A/c	Dr	20,000	
	To Bank A/c			20,000
	(Cash paid)			
(4)	Profit & Loss A/c	Dr	23,500	
	To Shortworking A/c			1,300
	To Royalty A/c			22,200
	(Shortworking of 1986 not recovered written off and Royalty A/c transferred)			
1989				
(1)	Royalty A/c	Dr	21,300	
	To Author Somanath A/c			21,300
	(Royalty earned and payable)			
(2)	Author Somanath A/c	Dr	1,100	
	To Shortworking A/c			1,100
	(Shortworking of 1987 recovered)			
(3)	Author Somanath A/c	Dr	20,200	
	To Bank A/c			20,200
	(Cash paid)			
(4)	Profit & Loss A/c	Dr	21,300	
	To Royalty A/c			21,300

Problem No. 25

Dharwar Colliery Co. Ltd., lease a Mine at a Royalty of Re. 0.50 Paise per ton with a minimum rent of Rs. 10,000 p.a. Each year's excess of minimum rent over royalty is recoverable out of the royalties of next three years. In the event of strike and the minimum rent is not reached, the lease provided that the actual royalty earned for the year discharged all the rental obligations for that year.

The results of the working was as follows :

Year	Output in ton
1985	15000
1986	21000
1987 (Strike)	12000
1988	16000
1989	22000

Write up the (1) Royalties A/c (2) Shortworking A/c (3) Landlord A/c.

(K.U.D., April 1990)

Solution :

Working Chart

Year	Output in ton	Royalty 0.50 per ton	Minimum Rent	Short-working	Surplus	Shortworkings Recovered	Shortworkings Not recovered	Amount Payable
1985	15000	7,500	10,000	2,500	—	—	—	10,000
1986	21000	10,500	10,000	—	500	500 (1985)	—	10,000
1987 (Strike)	12000	6,000	6,000	—	—	—	—	6,000
1988	16000	8,000	10,000	2,000	—	—	2,000 (1985)	10,000
1989	22000	11,000	10,000	—	1,000	1,000 (1988)	—	10,000

Note : Right to recoup shortworking next three years unrecovered shortworking within the period written off to Profit & Loss A/c.

Books of Dharwar Colliery Company

Royalty A/c

1985	To Landlord A/c	7,500	1985	By Profit & Loss A/c	7,500
1986	To Landlord A/c	10,500	1986	By Profit & Loss A/c	10,500
1987	To Landlord A/c	6,000	1987	By Profit & Loss A/c	6,000
1988	To Landlord A/c	8,000	1988	By Profit & Loss A/c	8,000
1989	To Landlord A/c	11,000	1989	By Profit & Loss A/c	11,000

Shortworking A/c

1985	To Landlord A/c	2,500	1985	By Balance c/d	2,500
1986	To Balance b/d	2,500	1986	By Landlord A/c (1985 recovered)	500
				By Balance c/d	2,000
		2,500			2,500
1987	To Balance b/d	2,000	1987	By Balance c/d	2,000
		2,000			2,000
1988	To Balance b/d	2,000	1988	By Profit & Loss A/c (1985 not recovered written off)	2,000
	To Landlord A/c	2,000			
				By Balance c/d	2,000
		4,000			4,000
1989	To Balance b/d	2,000	1989	By Landlord A/c (1988 recovered)	1,000
				By Balance c/d	1,000
		2,000			2,000

Landlord A/c

1985	To Bank	10,000	1985	By Royalty A/c	7,500
				By Shortworking A/c	2,500
		10,000			10,000
1986	To Shortworking A/c	500	1986	By Royalty A/c (1985 recovered)	10,500
	To Bank	10,000			
		10,500			10,500
1987	To Bank A/c	6,000	1987	By Royalty A/c	6,000
1988	To Bank A/c	10,000	1988	By Royalty A/c	8,000
				By Shortworking A/c	2,000
		10,000			10,000
1989	To Shortworking A/c (1988 recovered)	1,000	1989	By Royalty A/c	11,000
	To Bank	10,000			
		11,000			11,000

Problem No. 26

The Ashok Engineering Co. Ltd. took a lease of Coal Mine, the rate of Royalty is 0.50 paise per ton of Coal raised. The Minimum Rent is Rs. 20,000 per year. Each year's excess of Minimum Rent over Royalties is recoverable out of the Royalties of the next two years. In the event of strike, the lease provides for the proportionate reduction in the minimum Rent.

The Output for the first Five years is as follows :

Year ending	Output (in tons)
31-12-1984	20000
31-12-1985	32000
31-12-1986	50000
31-12-1987	60000
31-12-1988	24000

There was a strike for 3 months in the year 1988.

Prepare the : (1) Minimum Rent A/c (2) Royalty A/c
(3) Shortworking A/c (4) Landlord A/c.

(K.U.D., October 1989)

Solution :

In the Books of Mining Co.

Working Chart

Year ending	Output in ton	Royalty 0.50 Ps per ton	Minimum Rent	Short-working	Surplus	Shortworkings Recovered	Shortworkings Not recovered	Amount
31-12-84	20000	10,000	20,000	10,000	—	—	—	20,000
31-12-85	32000	16,000	20,000	4,000	—	—	—	20,000
31-12-86	50000	25,000	20,000	—	5,000	5,000 (1984)	5,000 (1984)	20,000
31-12-87	60000	30,000	20,000	—	10,000	4,000	—	26,000
31-12-88	24000	12,000	15,000	3,000	—	—	—	15,000

Note : Strike for 3 months in the year 1988.

Minimum Rent reduced proportionately

= 20,000 × 9/12 = 15,000 Minimum Rent for 1988.

Minimum Rent A/c

31-12-84	To Landlord A/c	20,000	31-12-84	By Royalty A/c	10,000
				By Shortworking A/c	10,000
		20,000			20,000
31-12-85	To Landlord A/c	20,000	31-12-85	By Royalty A/c	16,000
				By Shortworking A/c	4,000
		20,000			20,000
31-12-88	To Landlord A/c	15,000	31-12-88	By Royalty A/c	12,000
				By Shortworking A/c	3,000
		15,000			15,000

Royalty A/c

31-12-84	To Minimum Rent A/c	10,000	31-12-84	By Profit & Loss A/c	10,000
31-12-85	To Minimum Rent A/c	16,000	31-12-85	By Profit & Loss A/c	16,000
31-12-86	To Landlord A/c	25,000	31-12-86	By Profit & Loss A/c	25,000
31-12-87	To Landlord A/c	30,000	31-12-87	By Profit & Loss A/c	30,000
31-12-88	To Minimum Rent	12,000	31-12-88	By Profit & Loss A/c	12,000

Shortworking A/c

31-12-84	To Minimum Rent	10,000	31-12-84	By Balance c/d	10,000
01-01-85	To Balance b/d	10,000	31-12-85	By Balance c/d	14,000
31-12-85	To Minimum rent	4,000			
		14,000			14,000
01-01-86	To Balance c/d	14,000	31-12-86	By Landlord A/c (1984 recovered)	5,000
				By Profit & Loss A/c (1984 not recovered written off)	5,000
				By Balance c/d	4,000
		14,000			14,000
01-01-87	To Balance b/d	4,000	31-12-87	By Landlord A/c	4,000
		4,000			4,000
31-12-88	To Minimum Rent	3,000	31-12-88	By Balance c/d	3,000

Landlord A/c

31-12-84	To Bank A/c	20,000	31-12-84	By Minimum Rent A/c	20,000
31-12-85	To Bank A/c	20,000	31-12-85	By Minimum Rent A/c	20,000
31-12-86	To Shortworking A/c (1984 recovered)	5,000	31-12-86	By Royalty A/c	25,000
	To Bank A/c	20,000			
		25,000			25,000
31-12-87	To Shortworking A/c (1985 recovered)	4,000	31-12-87	By Royalty A/c	30,000
		26,000			
		30,000			30,000
31-12-88	To Bank A/c	15,000	31-12-88	By Minimum Rent A/c	15,000

Problem No. 27

On 1st January 1985 the Mysore Collieries Ltd. leased a piece of land for a Minimum rent of Rs. 20,000 in the First year, Rs. 4,000 in the second year and thereafter Rs. 6,000 per annum. Merging into a Royalty of Re. 0.25 paise per ton, with power to recoup shortworking over the first three years ending the annual output for the four-year ending with 31st December 1988 was 2000, 12000, 32000 and 48000 tons respectively.

Write up : (1) Minimum Rent A/c (2) Shortworking (3) Landlord A/c (4) Royalty A/c

in the books of Mysore Collieries Ltd.

(K.U.D., April 1989)

Solution :

Working Table

Year	Output in ton	Royalty Re. 0.25 per ton	Minimum Rent	Short-working	Surplus	Shortworkings Recovered	Shortworkings Not recovered	Amount Paid
1985	2000	500	2,000	1,500	—	—	—	2,000
1986	12000	3,000	4,000	1,000	—	—	—	4,000
1987	32000	8,000	6,000	—	2,000	1,500 500	5,000	6,000
1988	48000	12,000	6,000	—	6,000	—	—	12,000

Minimum Rent A/c

31-12-85	To Landlord A/c	2,000	31-12-85	By Royalty A/c	500
				By Shortworking	1,500
		2,000			2,000
1986	To Landlord A/c	4,000	1986	By Royalty A/c	3,000
				By Shortworking A/c	1,000
		4,000			4,000

Royalty A/c

1985	To Minimum Rent A/c	500	1985	By Profit & Loss A/c	500
1986	To Minimum Rent A/c	3,000	1986	By Profit & Loss A/c	3,000
1987	To Landlord A/c	8,000	1987	By Profit & Loss A/c	8,000
1988	To Landlord A/c	12,000	1988	By Profit & Loss A/c	12,000

Landlord A/c

31-12-85	To Bank A/c	2,000	31-12-85	By Minimum Rent A/c	2,000
1986	To Bank A/c	4,000	1986	By Minimum Rent A/c	4,000
1987	To Shortworking A/c Recovered 1985 – 1,500 1986 – 500	2,000	1987	By Royalty A/c	8,000
	To Bank A/c	6,000			
		8,000			8,000
1988	To Bank A/c	12,000	1988	By Royalty A/c	12,000
		12,000			12,000

Shortworking A/c

31-12-85	To Minimum Rent A/c	1,500	1985	By Balance c/d	1,500
01-01-86	To Balance b/d	1,500	1986	By Balance c/d	2,500
31-12-86	To Minimum Rent A/c	1,000			
		2,500			2,500
1-1-1987	To Balance b/d	2,500	1987	By Landlord A/c Recovered 1985 – 1,500 1986 – 500	2,000
				By Profit & Loss A/c (Not recovered)	500
		2,500			2,500

Problem No. 28

Prakash Ltd. took a Coal mine on a lease at Royalty of Re. 1 per ton of Coal received with a minimum Rent of Rs. 40,000 subject to recoupment of shortworking during the first four years of the lease.

In the event of strike the Minimum Rent in reduced proportionately to the working period the output was as under :

Year	Output in tons
1983	20000
1984	32000
1985	45000
1986	60000
1987	25000

There was a strike for 3 months in 1987.

Prepare : (a) Minimum Rent A/c (b) Landlord A/c
(c) Royalty A/c (d) Shortworking A/c.

(K.U.D., October 1988)

Solution :

Working Chart

Year	Output in ton	Royalty Re. 1 per ton	Minimum Rent	Short-working	Surplus	Shortworkings Recovered	Shortworkings Not recovered	Amount Paid to the landlord
1983	20000	20,000	40,000	20,000	—	—	—	40,000
1984	32000	32,000	40,000	8,000	—			40,000
1985	45000	45,000	40,000	—	5,000	5,000 (1983)	—	40,000
1986	60000	60,000	40,000	—	20,000	15,000	3,000	40,000
1987 (Strike for 3 months)	25000	25,000	30,000	5,000	—	—	—	30,000

Note : In the event of strike minimum rent recovered to the working period.

Strike – 3 months

Actual working period 9 months.

Minimum rent for 12 months – Rs. 40,000

For 9 months = 40,000 × 9/12 = Rs. 30,000 M. Rent.

Ledger A/c in the Books of Prakesh Ltd.

Minimum Rent a/c

1983	To Landlord A/c	40,000	1983	By Royalty A/c	20,000
				By Shortworking A/c	20,000
		40,000			40,000
1984	To Landlord A/c	40,000	1984	By Royalty A/c	32,000
				By Shortworking A/c	8,000
		40,000			40,000
1987	To Landlord A/c	30,000	1987	By Royalty A/c	25,000
				By Shortworking A/c	5,000
		30,000			30,000

Royalty A/c

1983	To Minimum Rent A/c	20,000	1983	By Profit & Loss A/c	20,000
1984	To Minimum Rent A/c	32,000	1984	By Profit & Loss A/c	32,000
1985	To Landlord A/c	45,000	1985	By Profit & Loss A/c	45,000
1986	To Landlord A/c	60,000	1986	By Profit & Loss A/c	60,000
1987	To Minimum Rent A/c	25,000	1987	By Profit & Loss A/c	25,000

Shortworking A/c

1983	To Minimum Rent A/c	20,000	1983	By Balance c/d	20,000
1984	To Balance b/d	20,000	1984	By Balance c/d	28,000
	To Minimum Rent A/c	8,000			
		28,000			28,000
1985	To Balance b/d	28,000	1985	By Landlord A/c (1983 recovered)	5,000
				By Balance c/d	23,000
		28,000			28,000
1986	To Balance b/d	23,000	1986	By Landlord A/c 1983 — 15,000 } Recovered 1984 — 5,000 }	20,000
				By Profit & Loss A/c (Not Recovered)	3,000
		23,000			23,000
1987	To Minimum Rent	5,000	1987	By Balance c/d	5,000
		5,000			5,000

Landlord A/c

1983	To Bank A/c	40,000	1983	By Minimum Rent A/c	40,000
1984	To Bank A/c	40,000	1984	By Minimum Rent A/c	40,000
1985	To Shortworking A/c (1983 recovered)	5,000	1985	By Royalty A/c	45,000
	To Bank A/c	40,000			
		45,000			45,000
1986	To Shortworking A/c 1983 — 15,000 1984 — 5,000	20,000	1986	By Royalty A/c	60,000
	To Bank	40,000			
		60,000			60,000
1987	To Bank A/c	30,000	1987	By Minimum Rent A/c	30,000

Problem No. 29

Bharat Publishers took the publication of Accountancy Book at a Royalty of 20% payable to the Author on the Books sold, with a minimum Annual payment of Rs. 5,000. Accounts are to be settled on 31st December every year.

If in any year the Royalty calculated on Books sold does not reach the minimum amount of Rs. 5,000 Bharat Publishers has a right to deduct the deficiency from the Royalty payable in excess of that sum in the two following years :

No. of Books sold was as follows :

1981	800 Copies	@ Rs. 20 each
1982	1000 Copies	@ Rs. 20 each
1983	1600 Copies	@ Rs. 20 each
1984	2000 Copies	@ Rs. 20 each

Pass the Journal Entries in the Books of Bharat Publishers.

(K.U.D., April 1988)

Solution :

Working Table

Year	No. of Copies sold	Sales Price Rs. 20 per Copy	Royalty 20% on Sales	Minimum Amount	Short-working	Surplus	Shortworkings Recovered	Shortworkings Not recovered	Amount Paid
1981	800	16,000	3,200	5,000	1,800	—	—	—	5,000
1982	1000	20,000	4,000	5,000	1,000	—	—	—	5,000
1983	1600	32,000	6,400	5,000	—	1,400	1,400 (1981)	400 (1981) (P & L)	5,000
1984	2000	40,000	8,000	5,000	—	3,000	1,000	—	7,000

In the Books of Bharat Publishers Ltd.

Journal Entries

	Particulars		Rs.	Rs.
1981				
(1)	Royalty A/c	Dr	3,200	
	Shortworking A/c	Dr	1,800	
	To Author A/c			5,000
	(Royalties earned & shortworking payable)			
(2)	Author A/c	Dr	5,000	
	To Bank A/c			5,000
	(Cash paid)			
(3)	Profit & Loss A/c	Dr	3,200	
	To Royalty A/c			3,200
	(Royalty A/c transferred)			
1982				
(1)	Royalty A/c	Dr	4,000	
	Shortworking A/c	Dr	1,000	
	To Author A/c			5,000
	(Royalties earned and shortworking payable)			
(2)	Author A/c	Dr	5,000	
	To Bank A/c			5,000
	(Cash paid)			
(3)	Profit & Loss A/c	Dr	4,000	
	To Royalty A/c			4,000
	(Royalty A/c transfer)			
1983				
(1)	Royalty A/c	Dr	6,400	
	To Author A/c			6,400
	(Royalties earned & payable)			
(2)	Author A/c	Dr	1,400	
	To Shortworking A/c			1,400
	(1981 shortworking recovered)			
(3)	Author A/c	Dr	5,000	
	To Bank A/c			5,000
	(Cash paid)			
(4)	Profit & Loss A/c	Dr	6,800	
	To Shortworking A/c			400
	To Royalty A/c			6,400
	(1981 shortworking not recovered written off Royalty A/c)			

Particulars			Rs.	Rs.
1984				
(1)	Royalty A/c	Dr	8,000	
	To Author A/c			8,000
	(Royalties earned and payable)			
(2)	Author A/c	Dr	1,000	
	To Shortworking A/c			1,000
	(1982 shortworking recovered)			
(3)	Author A/c	Dr	7,000	
	To Bank A/c			7,000
	(Cash paid)			
(4)	Profit & Loss A/c	Dr	8,000	
	To Royalties A/c			8,000
	(Royalty A/c transfer)			

In the Ledger A/c

Royalty A/c

1981	To Author A/c	3,200	1981	By Profit & Loss A/c	3,200
1982	To Author A/c	4,000	1982	By Profit & Loss A/c	4,000
1983	To Author A/c	6,400	1983	By Profit & Loss A/c	6,400
1984	To Author A/c	8,000	1984	By Profit & Loss A/c	8,000

Shortworking A/c

1981	To Author A/c	1,800	1981	By Balance c/d	1,800
1982	To Balance b/d	1,800	1982	By Balance c/d	2,800
	To Author A/c	1,000			
		2,800			2,800
1983	To Balance b/d	2,800	1983	By Author A/c (1981 recovered)	1,400
				By Profit & Loss A/c (1981 not recovered)	400
				By Balance c/d	1,000
		2,800			2,800
1984	To Balance b/d	1,000	1984	By Author A/c (1982 recovered)	1,000
		1,000			1,000

Author A/c

1981	To Bank A/c	5,000	1981	By Royalty A/c	3,200
				By Shortworking A/c	1,800
		5,000			5,000
1982	To Bank A/c	5,000	1982	By Royalty A/c	4,000
				By Shortworking A/c	1,000
		5,000			5,000
1983	To Shortworking (1981 recovered)	1,400	1983	By Royalty A/c	6,400
	To Bank A/c	5,000			
		6,400			6,400
1984	To Shortworking A/c	1,000	1984	By Royalty A/c	8,000
	To Bank A/c	7,000			
		8,000			8,000

Problem No. 30

Minerals Ltd. leased a property from Mr. Shankar at a Royalty of Rs. 1.50 per ton raised with a minimum rent of Rs. 10,000 p.a. Each year's excess of minimum rent over a Royalties is recoverable out of Royalties of next three years.

In the event of strike in any year the lease provides for the proportionate reduction of minimum rent for that year. Accounts are to be settled every year on 31st December.

The Actual output for the First five years is as follows :

Year ending 31st December	Output in tons
1981	4000
1982	5000
1983	6000
1984	10000
1985 (Strike for 3 months)	4000

Prepare : (a) Royalty A/c (b) Shortworking A/c (c) Mr. Shankar A/c in the Books of Minerals Ltd.

(Gulbarga, October 1987)

Solution :

Working Table

Year	Output in tons	Royalty Rs. 1.50 per ton	Minimum Rent	Short-working	Surplus	Shortworkings Recovered	Shortworkings Not recovered	Amount payable
1981	4000	6,000	10,000	4,000	—	—	—	10,000
1982	5000	7,500	10,000	2,500	—	—	—	10,000
1983	6000	9,000	10,000	1,000	—	—	—	10,000
1984	10000	15,000	10,000	—	5,000	5,000	—	10,000
1985	4000	6,000	7,500	1,500	—	–	1,500 (1982)	7,500

Note (1) : During 1985 strike for 3 months.

Minimum Rent - reduced proportionately.

i.e. 10,000 × 3/12 = 2,500

Minimum rent p.a.	Rs. 10,000
reducedly	2,500
	7,500

(2) : 1984 surplus recovered as follows : 1981 - 4,000

1982 - 1,000

Total recovered amount Rs. 5,000

In the Books of Mineral Ltd.
Royalty A/c

1981	To Landlord A/c (Shankar)	6,000	1981	By Profit and Loss A/c	6,000
1982	To Landlord A/c	7,500	1982	By Profit and Loss A/c	7,500
1983	To Landlord A/c	9,000	1983	By Profit and Loss A/c	9,000
1984	To Landlord A/c	15,000	1984	By Profit and Loss A/c	15,000
1985	To Landlord A/c	6,000	1985	By Profit and Loss A/c	6,000

Shortworking A/c

1981	To Landlord A/c	4,000	1981	By Balance c/d	4,000
1982	To Balance b/d	4,000	1982	By Balance c/d	6,500
	To Landlord A/c	2,500			
		6,500			6,500
1983	To Balance b/d	6,500	1983	By Balance c/d	7,500
	To Landlord A/c	1,000			
		7,500			7,500
1984	To Balance b/d	7,500	1984	By Landlord A/c 1981-4,000 1982-1,000	5,000
				By Balance c/d	2,500
		7,500			7,500
1985	To Balance b/d	2,500	1985	By Profit and Loss A/c (1982 Not recovered Written off)	1,500
	To Landlord A/c	1,500		By Balance c/d	2,500
		4,000			4,000
1986	To Balance b/d	2,500	1986	By Balance c/d	2,500

Landlord A/c

1981	To Bank A/c	10,000	1981	By Royalty A/c	6,000
				By Shortworking	4,000
		10,000			10,000
1982	To Bank A/c	10,000	1982	By Royalty A/c	7,500
				By Shortworking	2,500
		10,000			10,000
1983	To Bank A/c	10,000	1983	By Royalty A/c	9,000
				By Shortworking	1,000
		10,000			10,000
1984	To Bank A/c (1981—4,000 1982—1,000)	5,000	1984	By Royalty A/c	15,000
	To Bank A/c	10,000			
		15,000			15,000
1985	To Bank	7,500	1985	By Royalty A/c	6,000
				By Shortworking	1,500
		7,500			7,500

Problem No. 31

The Coal India Ltd. took from P a lease of Mine for a period of 25 years from 1-1-1982 on Royalty of Rs. 5 per ton of Coal raised with a dead Rent of Rs. 20,000 and power to recoup shortworking during first 5 years of the lease.

The Annual output was as follows :

Year	Output in ton
1982	2000
1983	3000
1984	4000
1985	4500
1986	5000

Pass the Journal entries in the Books of Coal India Ltd. for the above period.

(K.U.D., April 1987)

Solution :

Working Table

Year	Output in ton	Royalty Rs. 5 per ton	Minimum Rent	Short-working	Surplus	Shortworkings Recovered	Shortworkings Not recovered	Amount payable
1982	2000	10,000	20,000	10,000	—	—	—	20,000
1983	3000	15,000	20,000	5,000	—	—	—	20,000
1984	4000	20,000	20,000	—	—	—	—	20,000
1985	4500	22,500	20,000	—	2,500	2,500 (1982)	—	20,000
1986	5000	25,000	20,000	—	5,000	5,000 (1982)	2,500 (1982) 5,000 (1983)	20,000

In the Books of Coal India Ltd.

Journal Entries

	Particulars		Rs.	Rs.
1982				
(1)	Royalty A/c	Dr	10,000	
	Shortworking A/c	Dr	10,000	
	To Landlord A/c			20,000
	(Royalty earned and shortworking payable)			
(2)	Landlord A/c	Dr	20,000	
	To Bank A/c			20,000
	(Cash paid)			
(3)	Profit & Loss A/c	Dr	10,000	
	To Royalty A/c			10,000
	(Royalty A/c transfer)			

	Particulars		Rs.	Rs.
1983				
(1)	Royalty A/c	Dr	15,000	
	Shortworking A/c	Dr	5,000	
	To Landlord A/c			20,000
	(Royalties earned & shortworkings payable)			
(2)	Landlord A/c	Dr	20,000	
	To Bank A/c			20,000
	(Cash paid)			
(3)	Profit & Loss A/c	Dr	15,000	
	To Royalty A/c			15,000
	(Royalty A/c transferred)			
1984				
(1)	Royalty A/c	Dr	20,000	
	To Landlord A/c			20,000
	(Royalty earned & payable)			
(2)	Landlord A/c	Dr	20,000	
	To Bank A/c			20,000
	(Cash paid)			
(3)	Profit & Loss A/c	Dr	20,000	
	To Royalty A/c			20,000
	(Royalty A/c transferred)			
1985				
(1)	Royalty A/c	Dr	22,500	
	To Landlord A/c			22,500
	(Royalty earned & payable)			
(2)	Landlord A/c	Dr	2,500	
	To Shortworking A/c			2,500
	(1982 Shortworking recovered)			
(3)	Landlord A/c	Dr	20,000	
	To Bank A/c			20,000
	(Cash paid)			
(4)	Profit & Loss A/c	Dr	22,500	
	To Royalty A/c			22,500
	(Royalty A/c transferred)			
1986				
(1)	Royalty A/c	Dr	25,000	
	To Landlord A/c			25,000
	(Royalty earned & payable)			

	Particulars		Rs.	Rs.
(2)	Landlord A/c	Dr	5,000	
	To Shortworking A/c			5,000
	(Shortworking 1982 recovered)			
(3)	Landlord A/c	Dr	20,000	
	To Bank A/c			20,000
	(Cash paid)			
(4)	Profit & Loss A/c	Dr	7,500	
	To Shortworking A/c			7,500
	[1982 - Rs. 2,500 and 1983 - Rs. 5,000]			
	(Shortworking not recovered written off)			
(5)	Profit & Loss A/c	Dr	25,000	
	To Royalty A/c			25,000
	(Royalty A/c transferred)			

Royalty A/c

1982	To Landlord A/c	10,000	1982	By Profit & Loss A/c	10,000
1983	To Landlord A/c	15,000	1983	By Profit & Loss A/c	15,000
1984	To Landlord A/c	20,000	1984	By Profit & Loss A/c	20,000
1985	To Landlord A/c	22,500	1985	By Profit & Loss A/c	22,500
1986	To Landlord A/c	25,000	1986	By Profit & Loss A/c	25,000

Shortworking A/c

1982	To Landlord A/c	10,000	1982	By Balance c/d	10,000
1983	To Balance b/d	10,000	1983	By Balance c/d	15,000
	To Landlord A/c	5,000			
		15,000			15,000
1984	To Balance b/d	15,000	1984	By Balance c/d	15,000
1985	To Balance b/d	15,000	1985	By Landlord A/c (1982 recovered)	2,500
				By Balance c/d	12,500
		15,000			15,000
1986	To Balance b/d	12,500	1986	By Landlord A/c (1982 recovered)	5,000
				By Profit & Loss A/c (1982 not recovered written off)	2,500
				By Balance c/d	5,000
		12,500			12,500

Landlord A/c

1982	To Bank A/c	20,000	1982	By Royalty A/c	10,000
				By Shortworking A/c	10,000
		20,000			20,000
1983	To Bank A/c	20,000	1983	By Royalty A/c	15,000
				By Shortworking A/c	5,000
		20,000			20,000
1984	To Bank A/c	20,000	1984	By Royalty A/c	20,000
1985	To Shortworking A/c (1982 recovered)	2,500	1985	By Royalty A/c	22,500
	To Bank A/c	20,000			
		22,500			22,500
1986	To Shortworking A/c (1982 recovered)	5,000	1986	By Royalty A/c	25,000
	To Bank A/c	20,000			
		25,000			25,000

Problem No. 32

Saraswati Publications, agreed to take up printing and sale of a Book from the Author Sadanand on 1-7-1980. Following are the terms of agreement :

(1) Royalty payable is 20% on the sales price of the Book. The Book is priced at Rs. 25 per copy.

(2) The Author is to be paid Minimum Amount of Rs. 10,000 per annum.

(3) Each year's excess of Minimum Amount over the actual Royalties is recoverable out of the Royalties during the *next three* years period.

The following are the particulars of sales :

Year	No. of Copies sold
I	400
II	750
III	1600
IV	3000
V	4000

Show the necessary Ledger A/c in the Books of Saraswati Publications for the above period.

(K.U.D., October 1986)

Solution :

Working Chart

Year	No. of Copies sold	Royalty Rs. 5 per copy	Minimum Amount	Deficiency	Surplus	Deficiency Recovered	Deficiency Not recovered	Amount payable to Author
I	400	2,000	10,000	8,000	—	—	—	10,000
II	750	3,750	10,000	6,250	—	—	—	10,000
III	1600	8,000	10,000	2,000	—	—	—	10,000
IV	3000	15,000	10,000	—	5,000	5,000 I Year	3,000 I Not recovered P & L	10,000
V	4500	22,500	10,000		12,500	6,250 (II) 2,000 (III)	—	14,250

Books of Saraswati Publications — Publishing Company

Royalty A/c

I Year	To Author A/c	2,000	I Year	By Profit & Loss A/c	2,000
II Year	To Author A/c	3,750	II Year	By Profit & Loss A/c	3,750
III Year	To Author A/c	8,000	III Year	By Profit & Loss A/c	8,000
IV Year	To Author A/c	15,000	IV Year	By Profit & Loss A/c	15,000
V Year	To Author A/c	22,500	V Year	By Profit & Loss A/c	22,000

Shortworking A/c

I Year	To Author A/c	8,000	I Year	By Balance c/d	8,000
II Year	To Balance b/d	8,000	II Year	By Balance c/d	14,250
	To Author A/c	6,250			
		14,250			14,250
III Year	To Balance b/d	14,250	III Year	By Balance c/d	16,250
	To Author A/c	2,000			
		16,250			16,250
IV Year	To Balance b/d	16,250	IV Year	By Author A/c (I Year Recovered)	5,000
				By Profit & Loss A/c (I Year Not recovered written off-8,000-5,000)	3,000
				By Balance c/d	8,250
		16,250			16,250
V Year	To Balance b/d	8,250	V Year	By Author A/c (II Year — 6,250 III Year — 2,000 recover	8,250
		8,250			8,250

Author A/c

I Year	To Bank A/c	10,000	I Year	By Royalty A/c	2,000
				By Shortworking A/c	8,000
		10,000			10,000
II Year	To Bank A/c	10,000	II Year	By Royalty A/c	3,750
				By Shortworking A/c	6,250
		10,000			10,000
III Year	To Bank A/c	10,000	III Year	By Royalty A/c	8,000
				By Shortworking A/c	2,000
		10,000			10,000
IV Year	To Shortworking A/c (I Year Recovered)	5,000	IV Year	By Royalty A/c	15,000
	To Bank A/c	10,000			
		15,000			15,000
V Year	To Shortworking II — 6,250, III — 2,000 Recovered	8,250	V Year	By Royalty A/c	22,500
	To Bank A/c	14,250			
		22,500			22,500

Problem No. 33

Vasavi Ltd. took a 20 years lease of Gold Mine from Vasant on a Royalty of Rs. 2 per ton with a minimum rent of Rs. 20,000 per annum. Each year excess of minimum Rent over Royalties is recoverable out of the Royalty of the next two years only. The output of the first six years was as follows :

Years	Output in tons
I	4000
II	7000
III	8000
IV	12000
V	19000
VI	20000

Prepare the necessary Ledger Accounts in the books of Vasavi Ltd. for the above period.

(K.U.D., April 1986)

Solution :

Working Table

Year	Output in tons	Royalty Rs. 2 per ton	Minimum Rent	Short-working	Surplus	Shortworkings Recovered	Shortworkings Not recovered	Amount paid to Landlord
I	4000	8,000	20,000	12,000	—	—	—	20,000
II	7000	14,000	20,000	6,000	—	—	—	20,000
III	8000	16,000	20,000	4,000	—	—	12,000 (P&L)	20,000
IV	12000	24,000	20,000	—	4,000	4,000	2,000 (P&L)	20,000
V	19000	38,000	20,000	—	18,000	4,000	—	34,000
VI	20000	40,000	20,000	—	20,000	—	—	40,000

Royalty A/c

Year			Year		
I	To Minimum Rent A/c	8,000	I	By Profit & Loss A/c	8,000
II	To Minimum Rent A/c	14,000	II	By Profit & Loss A/c	14,000
III	To Minimum Rent A/c	16,000	III	By Profit & Loss A/c	16,000
IV	To Landlord A/c	24,000	IV	By Profit & Loss A/c	24,000
V	To Landlord A/c	38,000	V	By Profit & Loss A/c	38,000
VI	To Landlord A/c	40,000	VI	By Profit & Loss A/c	40,000

Minimum Rent A/c

Year			Year		
I	To Landlord A/c	20,000	I	By Royalty A/c	8,000
				By Shortworking A/c	12,000
		20,000			20,000
II	To Landlord A/c	20,000	II	By Royalty A/c	14,000
				By Shortworking A/c	6,000
		20,000			20,000
III	To Landlord A/c	20,000	III	By Royalty A/c	16,000
				By Shortworking A/c	4,000
		20,000			20,000

Landlord A/c

Year			Year		
I	To Bank A/c	20,000	I	By Minimum Rent A/c	20,000
II	To Bank A/c	20,000	II	By Minimum Rent A/c	20,000
III	To Bank A/c	20,000	III	By Minimum Rent A/c	20,000
IV	To Shortworking A/c (II year)	4,000	IV	By Royalty A/c	24,000
	To Bank A/c	20,000			
		24,000			24,000
V	To Shortworking A/c (III Year)	4,000	V	By Royalty A/c	38,000
	To Bank A/c	34,000			
		38,000			38,000
VI	To Bank A/c	40,000	VI	By Royalty A/c	40,000

Shortworking A/c

Year			Year		
I	To Minimum Rent A/c	12,000	I	By Balance c/d	12,000
II	To Balance b/d	12,000	II	By Balance c/d	18,000
	To Minimum Rent A/c	6,000			
		18,000			18,000
III	To Balance b/d	18,000	III	By Profit & Loss A/c (Amount not recovered transfer I year)	12,000
	To Minimum Rent A/c	4,000		By Balance c/d	10,000
		22,000			22,000
IV	To Balance b/d	10,000	IV	By Landlord A/c (II year shortwork recovered)	4,000
				By Profit & Loss A/c (Not recover & transfer)	2,000
				By Balance c/d	4,000
		10,000			10,000
V	To Balance b/d	4,000	V	By Landlord A/c (Shortworking recovered)	4,000

Problem No. 34

A Coal Company took a mine on lease from D at a Royalty of Rs. 4 per ton of coal raised with a Minimum Rent of Rs. 20,000 per year.

Each year's excess of Minimum Rent over the Royalties is recoverable out of the Royalties in the next two years.

In the event of Strike and the Minimum Rent is not reached, the lease provided that the *Actual Royalties earned* for the year discharge all the *Rental* obligations for that year.

The Quantity of Coal raised were as under :

First Year	3500 tons
Second Year	4500 tons
Third Year	5500 tons
Fourth Year (Strike)	4000 tons (Strike year)

Pass the Journal Entries in the Books of Coal Company for the above period.

(K.U.D., October 1985)

Solution :

Working Table

Year	Output in tons	Royalty Rs. 4 per ton	Minimum Rent	Short-working	Surplus	Shortworkings Recovered	Shortworkings Not recovered	Amount payable to Landlord
First	3500	14,000	20,000	6,000	—	—	—	20,000
Second	4500	18,000	20,000	2,000	—	—	—	20,000
Third	5500	22,000	20,000	—	2,000	2,000 I Year	4,000 I Year	20,000
Fourth (Strike)	4000	16,000	16,000	—	—	—	2,000 II Year	16,000

Note : Strike Period : Fourth Year.
Minimum Rent : The Actual Royalties earned.
: Discharge all Rental obligations.

In the Books of Coal Company

Journal Entries

	Particulars		Rs.	Rs.
	First Year			
1.	Royalty A/c	Dr	14,000	
	Shortworking A/c	Dr	6,000	
	To Landlord A/c			20,000
	(Royalties considered & shortworking payable)			
2.	Landlord A/c	Dr	20,000	
	To Bank A/c			20,000
	(Cash paid)			

Particulars		Rs.	Rs.
3. Profit & Loss A/c	Dr	14,000	
To Royalty A/c			14,000
(Royalty A/c transferred)			
Second Year			
1. Royalty A/c	Dr	18,000	
Shortworking A/c	Dr	2,000	
To Landlord A/c			20,000
(Royalty earned & shortworking payable)			
2. Landlord A/c	Dr	20,000	
To Bank A/c			20,000
(Cash paid)			
3. Profit & Loss A/c	Dr	18,000	
To Royalty A/c			18,000
(Royalty A/c transferred)			
Third Year			
1. Royalty A/c	Dr	22,000	
To Landlord A/c			22,000
(Royalty earned & Payable)			
2. Landlord A/c	Dr	2,000	
To Shortworking A/c			2,000
(Cash paid)			
4. Profit & Loss A/c		4,000	
To Shortworking A/c			4,000
(First year shortworking not recovered written off)			
5. Profit & Loss A/c	Dr	22,000	
To Royalty A/c			22,000
(Royalty A/c transferred)			
Fourth Year			
1. Royalty A/c	Dr	16,000	
To Landlord A/c			16,000
(Royalty earned & payable)			
2. Landlord A/c	Dr	16,000	
To Bank A/c			16,000
(Cash paid)			

	Particulars		Rs.	Rs.
3.	Profit and Loss A/c	Dr	2,000	
	To Shortworking A/c			2,000
	(Second year shortworking not recovered written off)			
4.	Profit and Loss A/c	Dr	16,000	
	To Royalty A/c			16,000
	(Royalty A/c transferred)			

Problem No. 35

A Colliery Company leased a land from B at a Royalty of Re. 1 per ton of Iron ore raised with a Minimum Rent of Rs. 20,000 per annum.

Each year's excess of Minimum Rent over actual Royalties was recoverable out of the Royalties of the next two years. The working of the lease for the first four years was as follows :

Year ending	Output in tons
31-12-1980	8000
31-12-1981	16000
31-12-1982	18000
31-12-1983	30000

Pass the necessary Journal entries in the Books of the Colliery Company for the above period.

(K.U.D., October 1984)

Solution :

Working Table

Year ending	Output in tons	Royalty Re. 1 per ton	Minimum Rent	Short-working	Surplus	Shortworkings Recovered	Shortworkings Not recovered	Amount payable to Landlord
31-12-80	8000	8,000	20,000	12,000	—	—	—	20,000
31-12-81	16000	16,000	20,000	4,000	—	—	—	20,000
31-12-82	18000	18,000	20,000	2,000	—	—	12,000 (1980 P & L)	20,000
31-12-83	30000	30,000	20,000	—	10,000	4,000 (1981) 2,000 (1982) 6,000	—	24,000

In the Book of Colliery Company

Ledger A/c

Journal Entries

		Particulars		Rs.	Rs.
Year ending					
1980	1.	Royalty A/c	Dr	8,000	
		Shortworking A/c	Dr	12,000	
		To Landlord A/c			20,000
		(Royalties earned & shortworking payable)			
	2.	Landlord A/c	Dr	20,000	
		To Bank A/c			20,000
		(Cash paid)			
	3.	Profit & Loss A/c	Dr	8,000	
		To Royalty A/c			8,000
		(Royalty A/c transferred)			
1981	1.	Royalty A/c	Dr	16,000	
		Shortworking A/c	Dr	4,000	
		To Landlord A/c			20,000
		(Royalties earned and shortworking payable)			
	2.	Landlord A/c	Dr	20,000	
		To Bank A/c			20,000
		(Cash paid)			
	3.	Profit & Loss A/c		16,000	
		To Royalty A/c			16,000
		(Royalty A/c transferred)			
1982	1.	Royalty A/c	Dr	18,000	
		Shortworking A/c	Dr	2,000	
		To Landlord A/c			20,000
		(Royalties earned & shortworking payable)			
	2.	Landlord A/c	Dr	20,000	
		To Bank A/c			20,000
		(Cash paid)			
	3.	Profit & Loss A/c	Dr	18,000	
		To Royalty A/c			18,000
		(Royalty A/c transferred)			

		Particulars		Rs.	Rs.
	4.	Profit & Loss A/c	Dr	12,000	
		To Shortworking A/c			12,000
		(1980 Shortworking not recovered written off)			
1983	1.	Royalty A/c	Dr	30,000	
		To Landlord A/c			30,000
		(Royalties earned & payable)			
	2.	Landlord A/c	Dr	6,000	
		To shortworking A/c			6,000
		(Recovered out of excess of Royalty)			
	3.	Landlord A/c	Dr	24,000	
		To Bank A/c			24,000
		(Cash paid)			
	4.	Profit & Loss A/c	Dr	30,000	
		To Royalty A/c			30,000
		(Royalty account transfer)			

Royalty A/c

Year			Year		
1980	To Landlord A/c	8,000	1980	By Profit & Loss A/c	8,000
1981	To Landlord A/c	16,000	1981	By Profit & Loss A/c	16,000
1982	To Landlord A/c	18,000	1982	By Profit & Loss A/c	18,000
1983	To Landlord A/c	30,000	1983	By Profit & Loss A/c	30,000

Shortworking A/c

1980	To Landlord A/c	12,000	1980	By Balance c/d	12,000
1981	To Balance b/d	12,000	1981	By Balance c/d	16,000
	To Shortworking A/c	4,000			
		16,000			16,000
1982	To Balance b/d	16,000	1982	By Profit & Loss A/c (1980 Shortworking not recovered & written off)	12,000
				By Balance c/d	6,000
		18,000			18,000
1983	To Balance b/d	6,000	1983	By Landlord A/c (1981 — 4,000 1982 — 2,000) Shortworking recovered	6,000
		6,000			6,000

Landlord A/c

1980	To Bank A/c	20,000	1980	By Royalty A/c	8,000
				By Shortworking A/c	12,000
		20,000			20,000
1981	To Bank A/c	20,000	1981	By Royalty A/c	16,000
				By Shortworking A/c	4,000
		20,000			20,000
1982	To Bank A/c	20,000	1982	By Royalty A/c	18,000
				By Shortworking A/c	2,000
		20,000			20,000
1983	To Shortworking A/c (1981—4,000 1982—2,000)	6,000	1983	By Royalty A/c	30,000
	To Bank A/c	24,000			
		30,000			30,000

Problem No. 36

M Co. Ltd. took a lease of mine from Kumar at a Royalty of Rs. 1.50 per ton of Coal raised with minimum rent of Rs. 10,000 p.a. each year's excess of minimum rent over Royalties is recoverable out of royalties of the next five years.

In the event of strike and the minimum rental not being reached the lease provided the actual royalties earned for the year discharged all rental obligations for the year.

The result of the working of the Mine were given as below :

Year ending	Actual Royalties
1972	Nil
1973	3,300
1974	9,000
1975	11,100
1976	14,000
1977	15,000
1978 (Strike)	8,000

Prepare the following accounts in the books of M Co. Ltd. for the above period (a) Royalty A/c (b) Shortworking A/c.

(K.U.D., October 1979)

Solution :

Working Table

Year ending	Output in tons	Actual Royalty	Minimum Rent	Short-working	Surplus	Shortworkings Recovered	Shortworkings Not recovered	Amount payable to Landlord
1972		Nil	10,000	10,000	—	—	—	10,000
1973		3,300	10,000	6,700	—	—	—	10,000
1974		9,000	10,000	1,000	—	—	—	10,000
1975		11,100	10,000	—	1,100	1,100	—	10,000
1976		14,000	10,000	—	4,000	4,000	—	10,000
1977		15,000	10,000	—	5,000	4,900 (1972) 100 (1973)	—	10,000
1978 (Strike)		8,000	8,000	—	—	—	7,600	8,000

Royalty A/c

1972	To Landlord A/c	Nil	1972	By Profit & Loss A/c	Nil
1973	To Landlord A/c	3,300	1973	By Profit & Loss A/c	3,300
1974	To Landlord A/c	9,000	1974	By Profit & Loss A/c	9,000
1975	To Landlord A/c	11,100	1975	By Profit & Loss A/c	11,100
1976	To Landlord A/c	14,000	1976	By Profit & Loss A/c	14,000
1977	To Landlord A/c	15,000	1977	By Profit & Loss A/c	15,000
1978	To Landlord A/c	8,000	1978	By Profit & Loss A/c	8,000

Shortworking A/c

1972	To Landlord A/c	10,000	1972	By Balance c/d	10,000
1973	To Balance b/d	10,000	1973	By Balance c/d	16,700
	To Landlord A/c	6,700			
		16,700			16,700
1974	To Balance b/d	16,700	1974	By Balance c/d	17,700
	To Landlord A/c	1,000			
		17,700			17,700
1975	To Balance b/d	17,700	1975	By Landlord A/c (1972 recovered)	1,100
				By Balance c/d	16,600
		17,700			17,700

1976	To Balance b/d	16,600	1976	By Landlord A/c	4,000
				By Balance c/d	12,600
		16,600			16,600
1977	To Balance b/d	12,600	1977	By Landlord A/c (4,900 + 100)	5,000
				By Balance c/d	7,600
		12,600			12,600
1978	To Balance b/d	7,600	1978	By Profit & Loss A/c (1973 not recovered)	6,600
				By Balance c/d	1,000
		7,600			7,600

Landlord A/c

1972	To Bank A/c	10,000	1972	By Royalty A/c	Nil
				By Shortworking A/c	10,000
		10,000			10,000
1973	To Bank A/c	10,000	1973	By Royalty A/c	3,300
				By Shortworking A/c	6,700
		10,000			10,000
1974	To Bank A/c	10,000	1974	By Royalty A/c	9,000
				By Shortworking A/c	1,000
		10,000			10,000
1975	To Shortworking A/c	1,100	1975	By Royalty A/c	11,100
	To Bank A/c	10,000			
		11,100			11,100
1976	To Shortworking A/c	4,000	1976	By Royalty A/c	14,000
	To Bank A/c	10,000			
		14,000			14,000
1977	To Shortworking A/c (4,900 + 100)	5,000	1977	By Royalty A/c	15,000
	To Bank A/c	10,000			
		15,000			15,000
1978	To Bank A/c	8,000	1978	By Royalty A/c	8,000

Problem No. 37

Mr. Anand owned the patent of a folding chair on 1st January 1987, he granted a licence to Karnataka Furnitures' firm for a period of 5 years to manufacture and sell the chairs on the following terms :

(a) Royalty of Rs. 20 per chair sold.

(b) Minimum amount of Rs. 36,000 p.a.

(c) Shortworkings could be recouped in the next two years following the year in which shortworkings occur, subject to a maximum amount of Rs. 5,000 p.a. If in any year normal sales was not reached due to strike the minimum amount was to be regarded as having been reduced proportionately to be period of stoppage.

Following are the particulars of sales during the period :

Year ending	No. of Chairs sold
1987	1200
1988	1500
1989	2900
1990	1400
1991	1700

During the 1990 there was a stoppage of work due to strike lasting 4 months.

You are required to prepare : (1) Royalty A/c (2) Shortworking A/c (3) Mr. Anand A/c in the books of Karnataka Furnitures.

Solution :

Working Table

Year	No. of Chair sold	Royalty Rs. 20 per chair	Minimum Rent	Short-working	Surplus	Shortworking Recovered	Shortworking Not recovered	Amount payable
1987	1200	24,000	36,000	12,000	—	—	—	36,000
1988	1500	30,000	36,000	6,000	—	—	—	36,000
1989	2900	58,000	36,000	—	22,000	5,000	7,000	53,000
1990	1400	28,000	24,000	—	4,000	4,000	7,000	24,000
1991	1700	34,000	36,000	2,000	—	—	2,000 (Last year)	36.000

Note : (1) Minimum Rent of Rs. 36,000 p.a. reduced proportionate during period of strike 4 months work stopped. Rs. 24,000 (4/12 × 36.000 = 12,000)

(2) Shortworking recouped maximum of Rs. 5,000 out the balance unrecovered transferred to Profit & Loss A/c.

(3) Shortworking of the last year unrecovered transfer to Profit & Loss A/c.

In the Book of Karnataka Furniture

Royalty A/c

1987	To Mr. Anand A/c	24,000	1987	By Profit & Loss A/c	24,000
1988	To Mr. Anand A/c	30,000	1988	By Profit & Loss A/c	30,000
1989	To Mr. Anand A/c	58,000	1989	By Profit & Loss A/c	58,000
1990	To Mr. Anand A/c	28,000	1990	By Profit & Loss A/c	28,000
1991	To Mr. Anand A/c	34,000	1991	By Profit & Loss A/c	34,000

Shortworking A/c

1987	To Mr. Anand A/c	12,000	1987	By Balance c/d	12,000
1988	To Balance b/d	12,000	1988	By Balance c/d	18,000
	To Mr. Anand A/c	6,000			
		18,000			18,000
1989	To Balance b/d	18,000	1989	By Mr. Anand A/c (1987 recovered)	5,000
				Profit & Loss A/c (1987 not recovered written off)	7,000
				By Balance c/d	6,000
		18,000			18,000
1990	To Balance b/d	6,000	1990	By Mr. Anand A/c	4,000
				By Profit & Loss A/c	2,000
		6,000			6,000
1991	To Mr. Anand A/c	2,000	1991	By Profit & Loss A/c (Last year not recovered)	2,000

Mr. Anand Account

1987	To Bank A/c	36,000	1987	By Royalty A/c	24,000
				By Shortworking A/c	12,000
		36,000			36,000
1988	To Bank A/c	36,000	1988	By Royalty A/c	30,000
				By Shortworking A/c	6,000
		36,000			36,000
1989	To Shortworking A/c (1987 Max. Recovered)	5,000	1989	By Royalty A/c	58,000
	To Bank A/c	53,000			
		58,000			58,000
1990	To Shortworking A/c (1988 recovered)	4,000	1990	By Royalty A/c (Minimum Rent reduce to 24,000)	28,000
	To Bank A/c	24,000			
		28,000			28,000
1991	To Bank A/c	36,000	1991	By Royalty A/c	34,000
				By Shortworking A/c	2,000
		36,000			36,000

Problem No. 38 (Extra)

Bengol Mining Co. acquired a land on lease from Sundarlal on a Royalty of Rs. 8 per ton of coal raised subject is to minimum Rent of Rs. 50,000 p.a. with a right is recoup the shortworking over the next three years' period. Following are the particulars :

Year	Sales in ton	Closing stock in ton
1985	3000	400
1986	4200	600
1987	5800	700
1988	8200	500
1989	9000	800

Prepare : (a) Royalty A/c (b) Shortworking A/c (c) Landlord A/c in the books of Bengol Mining Co.

Solution :

Note : The Royalty is payable on output during the period. Therefore total during the period is Sales + Closing stock – Opening stock.

Now = Sales + Closing Stock – Opening stock = Total output

1985	3,000 + 400 = 3,400 – Nil = 3,400
1986	4,200 + 600 = 4,800 – 400 = 4,400
1987	5,800 + 700 = 6,500 – 600 = 5,900
1988	8,200 + 500 = 8,700 – 700 = 8,000
1989	9,000 + 800 = 9,800 – 500 = 9,300

Solution :

Working Table

Year	Output in ton	Royalty Rs. 8 per ton	Minimum Rent	Short-working	Surplus	Shortworking Recovered	Shortworking Not recovered	Amount payable
1985	3400	28,200	50,000	21,800	—	-	—	50,000
1986	4400	35,200	50,000	14,800	—	—	—	50,000
1987	5900	47,200	50,000	2,800	—	—	—	50.000
1988	8000	64,000	50,000	—	14,000	14.000 (1985)	7,800 (1985)	50.000
1989	9300	74,400	50,000	—	24,400	14,800 2,800	—	56,800

In the Books of Bengol Mining Co.

Royalty A/c

1985	To Landlord A/c	28,200	1985	By Profit & Loss A/c	28,200
1986	To Landlord A/c	35,200	1986	By Profit & Loss A/c	35,200
1987	To Landlord A/c	47,200	1987	By Profit & Loss A/c	47,200
1988	To Landlord A/c	64,000	1988	By Profit & Loss A/c	64,000
1989	To Landlord A/c	74,400	1989	By Profit & Loss A/c	74,400

Shortworking A/c

1985	To Landlord A/c	21,800	1985	By Balance c/d	21,800
1986	To Balance b/d	21,800	1986	By Balance c/d	36,600
	To Landlord A/c	14,800			
		36,600			36,600
1987	To Balance b/d	36,600	1987	By Balance c/d	39,400
	To Landlord A/c	2,800			
		39,400			39,400
1988	To Balance b/d	39,400	1988	By Landlord A/c (1985 recovered)	14,000
				By Profit & Loss A/c (1985 not recovered written off)	7,800
				By Balance c/d	17,600
		39,400			39,400
1989	To Balance b/d	17,600	1989	By Landlord A/c (1986 & 1987 — 14,800 & 2,800 recovered respectively)	17,600
		17,600			17,600

Landlord A/c

1985	To Bank A/c	50,000	1985	By Royalty A/c	28,200
				By Shortworking A/c	21,800
		50,000			50,000
1986	To Bank A/c	50,000	1986	By Royalty A/c	35,200
				By Shortworking A/c	14,800
		50,000			50,000
1987	To Bank A/c	50,000	1987	By Royalty	47,200
				By Shortworking A/c	2,800
		50,000			50,000
1988	To Shortworking A/c	14,000	1988	By Royalty A/c	64,000
	To Bank A/c	50,000			
		64,000			64,000
1989	To Shortworking A/c (1986 – 14,800 1987 – 2,800 recovered)	17,600	1989	By Royalty A/c	74,400
	To Bank A/c	56,800			
		74,400			74,400

Problem No. 39

Mr. M owned the patent of a Folding Chair on 1st January 1987, he granted finance to a Karnataka Furniture Firm for a period of 5 years to manufacutre and sell the chairs on the following terms :

(a) Royalty of Rs. 10 per chair sold.

(b) Minimum Rent of Rs. 15,000 per annum.

(c) Shortworking could be recovered within two years in which short-working occur, subject to a Maximum of Rs. 3,500 per annum and,

(d) if in any year normal sale was not attained due to strike, the minimum Rent was to be regarded as having been reduced proportionately having regard to the length of the stoppage.

The No. of chairs sold during the period was as follows :

Year ended	No. of chairs sold
1987	900
1988	1300
1989	2000
1990	1100
1991	1400

During the year 1990 there was a stoppage due to strike lasting 4 months. You are required to show :

(1) Royalty A/c (2) Shortworking A/c (3) Mr. M A/c (Patentee A/c) in the books of Karnataka Furniture.

Solution :

Working Table

Year	No. of Chair sold	Royalty Rs. 10 per chair	Minimum Rent	Short-working	Surplus	Shortworking Recovered	Shortworking Not recovered	Amount payable
1987	900	9,000	15,000	6,000	—	—	—	15,000
1988	1300	13,000	15,000	2,000	—	—	—	15,000
1989	2000	20,000	15,000	—	5,000	3,500 (1987)	2,500 (1987)	16,500
1990	1100	11,000	10,000	—	1,000	1,000	1,000 (1988)	10,000
1991	1400	14,000	15,000	1,000	—	—	1,000 (1991)	15,000

Note : (1) Minimum Rent for 1990 Strike period works stoppage for 4 months. Therefore reduced to 15,000 × 4/12 = 5,000

Rs. 15,000 – 5,000 = 10,000.

(2) Maximum Recovery of Shortworking in a year of Surplus-fixed at Rs. 3,500 only.

Royalty A/c

1987	To Mr. M A/c	9,000	1987	By Profit and Loss A/c	9,000
1988	To Mr. M A/c	13,000	1988	By Profit and Loss A/c	13,000
1989	To Mr. M A/c	20,000	1989	By Profit and Loss A/c	20,000
1990	To Mr. M A/c	11,000	1990	By Profit and Loss A/c	11,000
1991	To Mr. M A/c	14,000	1991	By Profit and Loss A/c	14,000

Shortworking A/c

1987	To Mr. M A/c	6,000	1987	By Balance c/d	6,000
1988	To Balance b/d	6,000	1988	By Balance c/d	8,000
	To Mr. M A/c	2,000			
		8,000			8,000
1989	To Balance b/d	8,000	1989	By Mr. M A/c (Shortworking 1987 recovered)	3,500
				By Profit & Loss A/c (1987 not recovered)	2,500
				By Balance c/d	2,000
		8,000			8,000
1990	To Balance b/d	2,000	1990	By Mr. M A/c (1988 Shortworking recovered)	1,000
				By Profit & Loss A/c (1988 Shortworking not recovered)	1,000
		2,000			2,000
1991	To Mr. M A/c	1,000	1991	By Profit & Loss A/c	1,000

Mr. M A/c (Owner of Patent)

1987	To Bank A/c	15,000	1987	By Royalty A/c	9,000
				By Shortworking A/c	6,000
		15,000			15,000
1988	To Bank A/c	15,000	1988	By Royalty A/c	13,000
				By Shortworking A/c	2,000
		15,000			15,000
1989	To Shortworking A/c	3,500	1989	By Royalty A/c	20,000
	To Bank A/c	16,500			
		20,000			20,000
1990	To Shortworking A/c	1,000	1990	By Royalty A/c	11,000
	To Bank A/c	10,000			
		11,000			11,000
1991	To Bank A/c	15,000	1991	By Royalty A/c	14,000
				By Shortworking A/c	1,000
		15,000			15,000

9

Hire Purchase and Instalments Account

HIRE PURCHASE AND INSTALMENTS SYSTEM

Hire Purchase

The assets are purchased under Hire Purchase system wherein on signing the agreement, Hire Purchaser takes the possession of goods and agree to pay Cash Price of the Assets purchased, in instalments. The agreement provides that the interest on unpaid balance is to be paid along with instalments. For Non-payment of any of the instalments by the Hire purchaser the seller takes back the Assets sold and settle the accounts.

Main Features

(1) Assets sold under this system (Hire Purchase system) the seller (or Hire vendor) retains the right of ownership in the goods till the last instalment is paid.

(2) Hire purchase price is paid in instalments.

(3) Interest on unpaid balance is charged by the hire vendor and payable along with instalments.

(4) For Non-payment of any instalments by the Hire Purchaser, Hire vendor takes back the possession of goods sold.

(5) The amount already paid by the Hire-Purchaser is to be treated as the Hire charges for the use of Assets and that settles the accounts.

(6) The assets account is debited with cash price.

Instalments System

Assets are purchased and payment is made in agreed instalments. Ownership in the goods sold is immediately transferred in the name of the purchaser.

For Non-payment of any instalments, the seller may file a suit against purchaser in the court of Law for the recovery of dues. Interest on unpaid balance is charged by the seller. It is paid by the purchaser along with instalments.

Types of Problems

(1) *Cash price given, Instalment given, Rate of interest given*

Solution becomes easy. The amount of cash price of Assets purchased is debited to Assets A/c and credited to Hire Vendor A/c. If down payment on signing of the agreement is made, this amount is deducted from total Cash price and the balance remaining is taken for calculation of interest at the end of the year or when next instalment falls due. In the subsequent period, when instalments fall due first calculate interest on unpaid balance and credit to the Vendor Account and then entry for payment of instalment amount plus interest paid. If the instalment amount includes interest, after crediting the interest on unpaid balance, such instalment amount paid is debited to Vendor A/c. This procedure is followed for the period stated in the problem.

(2) *Instalments given, Rate of Interest given, Cash price not given*

In this case it is necessary to ascertain first cash price of Assets purchased, since the Assets A/c is to be debited with cash price only. The instalments include the amount of interest on unpaid balance of cash price. It means in each instalments : Cash Price + Interest on Unpaid balance included.

In such cases the ascertainment interest and cash price included in instalments the procedure followed is,

$$\text{Instalment Amount} \times \frac{\text{Rate of Interest}}{100 + \text{Rate of Interest}}$$

You get = Interest – Amount included in instalment

This interest amount is deducted from the instalment and then

you get = Cash price.

i.e., Instalment – Interest = Cash price.

The procedure mentioned above should start from last instalment amount.

e.g. : There are four instalments. In each instalment interest is included.

The calculation of interest and cash price

$$\text{start from Fourth Instalment} \times \frac{\text{\% of Interest}}{100 + \text{\% of Interest}} = \text{Interest amount.}$$

i.e.,

			Interest Amount	Cash Price	Instalment
IV Instalment ×		$\frac{\text{Interest}}{\frac{\%}{100 + \%}}$ =			
Less : Interest	—		—	—	—
Amount due					
Add : III Instalment	— ×	$\frac{\%}{100 + \%}$	—	—	—
Total	—				
Less : Interest	—				
Add : II Instalment	— ×	$\frac{\%}{100 + \%}$	—	—	—
Total	—				

Less : Interest —

Add : I Instalment — × — — —

Total $\frac{\%}{100 + \%}$ Interest + Cash Price = Instalment

(3) *Cash Price given, Instalments given, Rate of Interest not given*

In this case in each of the Instalment how much amount of interest included is not known. Therefore, we are to ascertain the total amount of interest payable i.e., Total amount of Instalment. Total cash price of Assets purchased = Total amount of interest payable. This total amount of interest payable is distributed among instalments in the ratio of Total instalment amount due at the end of the year.

E.g. : Total Amount of Instalment Rs. 20,000

There are four instalments each of Rs. 5,000

and the Total interest is Rs. 6,000

Distribution of interest in each instalment is as follows :

Year	Instalment due at the end	Total Amount Outstanding in the beginning	Ratio	Interest	Cash Price
Ist Year	5,000	20,000	4	6,000 × 4/10 = 2,400	2,600
II Year	5,000	15,000	3	6,000 × 3/10 = 1,800	3,200
III Year	5,000	10,000	2	6,000 × 2/10 = 1,200	3,800
IV Year	5,000	5,000	1	6,000 × 1/10 = 600	4,400
	20,000		10		14,000

Note : Cash Price = Instalment due at the end – Interest.

Total Cash Price + Interest = Total Amount.

Proforma Entries in the Books of Hire Purchaser

	Particulars		Dr Rs.	Cr Rs.
I Year	(1) Assets A/c	Dr	—	
	To Hire Vendor A/c			—
	(Cash price of the Assets Purchased)			
Down Payment or payment on signing the agreement	(2) Hire Vendor A/c	Dr	—	
	To Bank A/c			—
	(Cash paid on signing the agreement)			

		Particulars		Dr Rs.	Cr Rs.
At the end of the year or on instalment due	(3)	Interest A/c	Dr	—	
		To Hire Vendor A/c			—
		(Interest on unpaid Balance)			
On Payment	(4)	Hire Vendor A/c	Dr	—	
		To Bank A/c			—
		[Cash paid due on Instalment (includes interest) or Cash paid due on Instalment + Interest]			
End of the year	(5)	Depreciation A/c	Dr	—	
		To Assets A/c			—
		(Being annual Depreciation A/c)			
	(6)	Profit and Loss A/c	Dr	—	
		To Interest A/c			—
		To Depreciation A/c			—
		(Depreciation A/c transferred)			

In the second year and successive period till final Instalment is paid II year, III year, IV year etc., the above entries : No. 3, 4, 5 & 6 are to be repeated with changes in amounts.

Entries in the Books of Hire Vendor (Or Seller)

		Particulars		Dr Rs.	Cr Rs.
I Year	(1)	Hire Purchaser A/c	Dr	—	
		To Sales A/c			—
		(Goods sold on Hire Purchase at Cash price)			
On receipt of cash on signing agreement	(2)	Bank A/c	Dr	—	
		To Hire Purchaser A/c			—
		(Cash received on signing the agreement)			
	(3)	Hire Purchaser A/c	Dr	—	
		To Interest A/c			—
		(Being interest on unpaid balance)			
	(4)	Bank A/c	Dr	—	
		To Hire Purchaser A/c			—
		(Cash received on instalment due)			
	(5)	Interest A/c	Dr	—	
		To Profit & Loss A/c			—
		(Interest A/c transferred)			

In the Second year and the successive period till Final instalment is paid i.e., II year, III, IV year the above entries : No. 3, 4, & 5 are to be repeated.

Problem No. 1

Raja Purchased a van from Tata Ltd., on Hire Purchase system on 1-1-1994 and agreed to pay interest @ 20% per annum on unpaid Balance of cash price.

Raja decided to Depreciate van @ 10% pa on reducing Balance Method.

He paid Rs. 20,000 on signing the contract and the Balance in following four yearly instalment at the end of each year :

Year ending	Instalment Amount
	Rs.
31-12-94	36,000
31-12-95	32,000
31-12-96	28,000
31-12-97	24,000

Prepare Van Account.

(K.U.D., April 1998 IV)

Solution

Working Note

(1) Instaments given (2) Rate & Interest given. Ascertain Cash price of van purchased. (3) Each instalment include interest

Instalment = Cash Price + Interest

Instalment = 120 = If 100 + 20

$$\text{Calculation of Interest} = \frac{\%\text{ of Interest}}{100+20} \times \text{Instalment}$$

Procedure — Start from last Instalment

Start from	Total amount due		Interest	Cash Price
31-12-97	24,000	× 20/120	= 4,000	20,000
Less Interest	4,000			
	20,000			
Add 31-12-96	28,600	× 20/120	= 8,000	2,000
	48,000			
Less Interest	8,000			
	40,000			
Add 31-12-95	32,000	× 20/120	= 12,000	20,000
	72,000			
Less Interest	12,000			
	60,000			
Add 31-12-94	36,000	96,000 × 20/120	16,000	20,000
			40,000	Rs. 80,000
			Cash price	80,000
			+ Cash paid	20,000
			On signing contract	1,00,000
			Interest	40,000

In the Books of Raja
Van A/c

Date	Particulars	Amount	Date	Particulars	Amount
1-1-94	To Tata Ltd. (Cash Price)	1,00,000	31-12-94	By Depreciation @ 10%	10,000
				By Balance c/d	90,000
		1,00,000			1,00,000
1-1-95	To Balance b/d	90,000	31-12-95	By Depreciation @ 10% on 90,000	9,000
				By Balance c/d	81,000
		90,000			90,000
1-1-96	To Balance b/d	81,000	31-12-96	By Depreciation @ 10% on 81,000	8,100
				By Balance c/d	72,900
		81,000			81,000
1-1-97	To Balance b/d	72,900	31-12-97	By Depreciation A/c 10% on 72,900	7,290
				By Balance c/d	65,610
		72,900			72,900

Additional Answer

Tata Ltd. (Vendor) A/c

1-1-94	To Bank A/c (Cash paid on signing contract)	20,000	1-1-94	By Van A/c Cash Price	1,00,000
31-12-94	To Bank A/c (Instalment paid)	36,000	31-12-94	By Interest A/c @ 20% on 80,000	16,000
	To Balance c/d	60,000			
		1,16,000			1,16,000
31-12-95	To Bank A/c (Instalment paid)	32,000	1-1-95	By Balance b/d	60,000
	To Balance b/d	40,000	31-12-95	By Interest A/c @ 20% on 60,000	12,000
		72,000			72,000
31-12-96	To Bank A/c (Instalment paid)	28,000	1-1-96	By Balance b/d	40,000
	To Balance c/d	20,000	31-12-96	By Interest A/c 20% on 40,000	8,000
		48,000			48,000
31-12-97	To Bank A/c (Last Instalment paid)	24,000	1-1-97	By Balance b/d	20,000
			31-12-97	By Interest A/c 20% on 20,000	4,000
		24,000			24,000

Problem No. 2

Shri Shivanand purchased a Machinery on Hire purchase system on 1-1-1995. The total cash price of the Machinery is Rs. 31,950 payable Rs. 8,000 on signing the agreement and the Balance Rs. 12,000 at the end of first year, Rs. 10,000 at the end of second year, and Rs. 4,000 at the end of third year. Interest is charged @ 5% p.a.

He provided depreciation @ 10% p.a. on diminishing Balance Method.

Prepare : (a) Machinery Account,
(b) Vendors Account,
(c) Interest Account and
(d) Depreciation Account.

(K.U.D., April 1998)

Solution :

In the Books of Shivanand

Machinery A/c

Date	Particulars	Amount	Date	Particulars	Amount
1-1-95	To Vendor A/c (Cash Price)	31,950	31-12-95	By Depreciation 10% on 31,950	3,195
				By Balance c/d	28,755
		31,950			31,950
1-1-96	To Balance b/d	28,755	31-12-96	By Depreciation @ 10% on 28,755	2,876
				By Balance c/d	25,879
		28,755			28,755
1-1-97	To Balance b/d	25,879	31-12-97	By Depreciation 10% on 25,879	2,588
				By Balance c/d	23,291
		25,879			25,879

Depreciation A/c

31-12-95	To Machinery A/c	3,195	31-12-95	By Profit & Loss A/c	3,195
31-12-96	To Machinery A/c	2,876	31-12-96	By Profit & Loss A/c	2,876
31-12-97	To Machinery A/c	2,588	31-12-97	By Profit & Loss A/c	2,588

Vendor A/c

Date	Particulars	Rs.	Date	Particulars	Rs.
1-1-95	To Bank A/c	8,000	1-1-95	By Machinery A/c	31,950
	(Cash paid on signing the agreement)		31-12-95	By Interest A/c @ 5% on 23,950 (1,197.5)	1,198
31-12-95	To Bank A/c	12,000			
	To Balance c/d	13,148			
		33,148			33,148
31-12-96	To Bank A/c	10,000	1-1-96	By Balance b/d	13,148
	To Balance c/d	3,806	31-12-96	By Interest @ 5% on 13,148	658
		13,806			13,806
31-12-97	To Bank A/c	4,000	1-1-97	By Balance b/d	3,806
	(Last instalment paid)		31-12-97	By Interest (being balancing figure)	194
		4,000			4,000

Interest A/c

31-12-95	To Vendor A/c Interest @ 5% on 23,950	1,198	31-12-95	By Profit & Loss A/c	1,198
31-12-96	To Vendor A/c @ 5% 12,148	658	31-12-96	By Profit & Loss A/c	658
31-12-97	To Vendor A/c @ 5% 3,806 = 190.3 (or Balancing figure)	194	31-12-97	By Profit & Loss A/c	194

Problem No. 3

Mr. Ashok purchased a Tractor from HMT Ltd. on 1-1-1993 and agreed to pay 10% interest on the unpaid Balance of cash price. Ashok provides depreciation @ 10% p.a. on diminishing balance method.

He paid Rs. 10,000 on signing the contract and the Balance in the following instalments :

Date of Payment	Rs.
on 31-12-1993	14,000
on 31-12-1994	13,000
on 31-12-1995	12,000
on 31-12-1996	11,000

Ascertain cash price of the tractor and prepare : (1) Tractor Account, (2) Interest Suspense Account and (3) H.M.T. Account in the Books of Ashok under Instalment System.

[K.U.D., October 1997(N)]

Solution :

Ascertainment of Cash Price

Procedure :

Start from last instalment. Each instalment include interest @10% on unpaid Balance. Calculation of Interest included in each of the instalments.

If cash price is Rs. 100 interest @ 10% i.e. Rs. 10 = Instalment Rs. 110

$$\text{Interest} = \frac{\text{\% of interest}}{100 + \%} \times \text{Instalment} = \frac{10}{110} \times \text{Instalment}$$

Start from last Instalment due			Interest	Cash Price	
31-12-96	11,000	× 10/110	= 1,000	10,000	
Less Interest	1,000				
	10,000				
31-12-95 *Add*	12,000				
	22,000	× 10/110	= 2,000	10,000	
Less Interest	2,000				
	20,000				
31-12-94 *Add*	13,000				
	33,000	× 10/110	= 3,000	10,000	
Less Interest	3,000				
	30,000				
31-12-93 *Add*	14,000				
	44,000	× 10/110	= 4,000	10,000	
			10,000	40,000	Cash price
Less Interest	4,000		Interest	10,000	down payment
	40,000				
				50,000	Cash price

In the Books of Ashok

Tractor A/c

1-1-93	To H.M.T. A/c (Vendor) (Cash price)	50,000	31-12-93	By Depreciation A/c 10% on 50,000	5,000
				By Balance c/d	45,000
		50,000			50,000
1-1-94	To Balance b/d	45,000	31-12-94	By Depreciation A/c	4,500
				By Balance c/d	40,500
		45,000			45,000
1-1-95	To Balance b/d	40,500	31-12-95	By Depreciation	4,050
				By Balance c/d	36,450
		40,500			40,500
1-1-96	To Balance b/d	36,450	31-12-96	By Depreciation A/c	3,645
					32,805
		36,450			36,450
1-1-97	To Balance b/d	32,805			

H.M.T. A/c (Vendor)

1-1-93	To Bank A/c down payment	10,000	1-1-93	By Tractor A/c	50,000
				Interest Suspense A/c	10,000
	To Bank A/c	14,000			
	To Balance c/d	36,000			
		60,000			60,000
31-12-94	To Bank A/c	13,000	1-1-94	By Balance b/d	36,000
	To Balance c/d	23,000			
		36,000			36,000
31-12-94	To Bank A/c	12,000	1-1-95	To Balance b/d	23,000
	To Balance c/d	11,000			
		23,000			23,000
31-12-96	To Bank A/c Last instalment	11,000	1-1-96	By Balance b/d	11,000

Interest Suspense A/c

1-1-93	To H.M.T. A/c (Interest payable)	10,000	31-12-93	By Interest A/c	4,000
				By Balance c/d	6,000
		10,000			10,000
1-1-94	To Balance b/d	6,000	31-12-94	By Interest A/c	3,000
				By Balance	3,000
		6,000			6,000
1-1-95	To Balance b/d	3,000	31-12-95	By Interest A/c	2,000
				By Balance c/d	1,000
		3,000			3,000
1-1-96	To Balance b/d	1,000	31-12-96	By Interest	1,000

Note : Every year Interest A/c is closed by transferred to Profit & Loss A/c Debit side entry is

Profit & Loss A/c	Dr	—	
To Interest A/c			—

Problem No. 4

Shri Kantupriya purchased a scooter on hire purchase system from Solar Scooter Ltd. on 1-1-1992 with an agreement to pay Rs. 2,500 cash down and Balance in three instalments as shown below :

Rs. 3,250 at the end of first year

Rs. 3,000 at the end of second year

Rs. 2,750 at the end of third year

Interest is charged at the rate of 10% p.a. Write off depreciation @ 10% on written down value method. Calculate the cash price of the scooter and prepare :

(1) Scooter Account and

(2) Solar Scooter Ltd. A/c in the Books of Shri Kantupriya.

[K.U.D., October 1997(O)]

Solution :

Working Note

Calculation of interest included in each instalment and the cash price of scooter.

Procedure :

Start from Last Instalment. Each instalment include interest @ 10% on unpaid Balance. Calculation of Interest included in each of the instalment.

If cash price is Rs. 100 interest at 10% is = Rs. 10 and therefore instalment will Rs. 110.

$$\text{Now Interest} = \frac{\%}{100 + \%} \times \text{Instalment} - \text{i.e. instalment} \times \frac{10}{110}$$

Start from last	Instalment due	= × 10/110	= Interest	– Cash Price
Third Year	2,750	× 10/110	= 250	2,500
Less Interest	250			
	2,500			
II *Add* Instalment	3,000			
	5,500	× 10/110	500	2,500
Less Interest	500			
	5,000			
I *Add* Instalment	3,250	× 10/110	= 750	2,500
	8,250		1,500	7,500 Cash Price
			Interest	+ 2,500 down payment
			Rs. 1,500	Rs. 10,000 Cash Price

In the Books of Shri Kantupriya

Scooter A/c

1-1-92	To Solar Scooter Ltd. (Cash price)	10,000	31-12-92	By Depreciation A/c 10% p.a.	1,000
				By Balance c/d	9,000
		10,000			10,000
1-1-93	To Balance b/d	9,000	31-12-93	By Depreciation A/c 10% on 9,000	900
				By Balance cld	8,100
		9,000			9,000
1-1-94	To Balance b/d	8,100	31-12-94	By Depreciation 10% on 8,100	810
				By Balance c/d	7,290
		8,100			81,000
1-1-95	To Balance b/d	7,290			

Solar Scooters Ltd. A/c

1-1-92	To Bank A/c down payment	2,500	1-1-92	By Scooter A/c Cash price	10,000
			31-12-92	By Interest A/c Interest on (10,000-2,500) 7,500 × 10%	750
31-12-92	To Bank A/c	3,250			
	To Balance c/d	5,000			
		10,750			10,750
31-12-93	To Bank A/c	3,000	1-1-93	By Balance b/d	5,000
	To Balance c/d	2,500	31-12-93	By Interest A/c 10% on 5,000	500
		5,500			5,500
31-12-94	To Bank A/c (Last instalment)	2,750	1-1-94	By Balance b/d	2,500
			31-12-94	By Interest A/c 10% on 2,500	250
		2,750			2,750

Problem No. 5

Shivanand bought a Taxi vehicle on Hire Purchase basis from M/s. Y Co. Ltd. on 1-4-1992, paying Rs. 20,000 advance. It was decided to pay the balance amount at 10% interest p.a. as under :

on 31-3-1993	Rs. 28,000
on 31-3-1994	Rs. 26,000
on 31-3-1995	Rs. 24,000
on 31-3-1996	Rs. 22,000

He charges Depreciation @ 20% p.a. on written down value basis.

Ascertain cash price and prepare necessary ledger accounts in the Books of Shivanand.

[K.U.D., April 1997(N)]

Solution :

Ascertainment of cash price

Procedure :

Start from last instalment

Each instalment include interest @ 10% along with cash price

Calculation of interest included in instalment. If cash price is Rs. 100 interest @ 10% will be the Instalment amount Rs. 100 + 10% = Rs. 110.

For Rs. 110 instalment for 2200 Rs. 10 will be interest.

From last instalment	Instalment		Interest	Cash Price
On 31-3-96	22,000	× 10/110	= 2,000	20,000
Less Interest	2,000			
	20,000			
Add 31-3-95	24,000			
	44,000	× 10/110	= 4,000	40,000
Less Interest	4,000			
	40,000			
On 31-3-1994	26,000			
	66,000	× 10/110	= 6,000	60,000
Less Interest	6,000			
	60,000			
On 31-3-93	28,000			
	88,000	× 10/110	= 8,000	80,000
Less Interest	8,000		20,000	80,000 Cash Price
	80,000			20,000 *Add* Advance
				1,00,000 Cash Price

In the Books of Shivanand

Taxi A/c

1-4-92	To M/s. Y Co. Ltd. (Vendor) (Cash price)	1,00,000	31-3-93	By Depreciation A/c 20% on 1,00,000	20,000
				By Balance c/d	80,000
		1,00,000			1,00,000
1-4-93	To Balance b/d	80,000	31-3-94	By Depreciation A/c 20% on 80,000	16,000
				By Balance c/d	64,000
		80,000			80,000
1-4-94	To Balance b/d	64,000	31-3-95	By Depreciation A/c 20% on 64,000	12,800
				By Balance c/d	51,200
		64,000			64,000
1-4-95	To Balance b/d	51,200	31-3-96	By Depreciation A/c 20% on 51,200	10,240
				By Balance c/d	40,960
		51,200			51,200
1-4-96	To Balance b/d	40,960			

M/s. Y Co. Ltd. A/c (Vendor A/c)

1-4-92	To Bank A/c Advance paid	20,000	1-4-92	By Taxi A/c (Cash price)	1,00,000
31-3-93	To Bank A/c (Instalment paid)	28,000	31-3-93	By Interest A/c 10% on 80,000	8,000
	To Balance c/d	60,000			
		1,08,000			1,08,000
31-3-94	To Bank A/c (Instalment paid)	26,000	1-4-93	By Balance b/d	60,000
	To Balance c/d	40,000	31-3-94	By Interest A/c 10% on 60,000	6,000
		66,000			66,000
31-3-95	To Bank A/c (Instalment paid)	24,000	1-4-94	By Balance b/d	40,000
	To Balance c/d	20,000	31-3-95	By Interest A/c 10% on 40,000	4,000
		44,000			44,000
31-3-96	To Bank A/c Last Instalment paid	22,000	1-4-95	By Balance b/d	20,000
			31-3-96	By Interest A/c 10% on 20,000	2,000
		22,000			22,000

Problem No. 6

Prashant purchased a scooter on 1-1-93 on instalment basis costing Rs. 36,000. The terms of payment are as follows :

(a) Rs. 6,000 on signing the agreement and

(b) The balance in four half yearly instalments of Rs. 9,000 each over two years.

He provides depreciation @ 20% p.a. on reducing balance method on 31st December every year. Ascertain interest included in each instalment and prepare : (a) Scooters A/c for two years in the books of Prashant.

[K.U.D., April 1997(N)]

Solution :

Working Note

Ascertainment of Interest included in each of the instalments :

Cash price – of scooter – Rs. 36,000 is given :

Cash payment

Payment on signing the agreement	Rs. 6,000
Balance in 4 half yearly instalments of Rs. 9,000 × 4	36,000
Total payment	42,000
Excess payment made toward interest	6,000

Rate of Interest Not Given. It is be ascertain on Ratio Basis

Year	Amount of Instalment outstanding		Ratio Interest Rs. 6,000	Interest	Cash Price
1-1-93	42,000 – 6,000 down Payment	36,000	4/10 × 6,000	2,400	6,600
1-7-93	36,000 – 9,000 Instalment	27,000	3/10 × 6,000	1,800	7,200
31-12-93	27,000 – 9,000 "	18,000	2/10 × 6,000	1,200	7,800
30-6-94	18,000 – 9,000 "	9,000	1/10 × 6,000	600	8,400
31-12-94	9,000 – 9,000	—	10	6,000	30,000

Cash price paid	
On-1-93 down payment	6,000
On payment of 4 half yearly instalment	30,000
Total Cash price	36,000

In the Books of Prashant

Scooter A/c

Date	Particulars	Amount	Date	Particulars	Amount
1-1-93	To Vendor A/c (Cash Prakash)	36,000	31-12-93	By Depreciation A/c	7,200
				By Balance b/d	28,800
		36,000			36,000
1-1-94	To Balance b/d	28,800	31-12-94	By Depreciation A/c	5,760
				By Balance c/d	23,040
		28,800			28,800
1-1-95	To Balance b/d	23,040			

Vendor A/c

1-1-93	To Bank A/c (down payment)	6,000	1-1-1993	By Scooter A/c (Cash price)	36,000
30-6-93	To Bank A/c (Instalment paid)	9,000	30-6-93	By Interest	2,400
	To Balance c/d	23,400			
		38,400			38,400
31-12-93	To Bank A/c (Instalment paid)	9,000	1-7-93	By Balance b/d	23,400
	To Balance b/d	16,200	31-12-93	By Interest	1,800
		25,200			25,200
30-6-94	To Bank A/c (Instalment paid)	9,000	1-1-94	By Balance b/d	16,200
	To Balance c/d	8,400	30-6-94	By Interest	1,200
		17,400			17,400
31-12-94	To Bank A/c (Instalment paid) (Last)	9,000	1-7-94	By Balance b/d	8,400
			31-12-94	By Interest	600
		9,000			9,000

Problem No. 7

Mr. Suresh purchased a Machine from H.M.T. Ltd. on 1-1-1990 on Hire-Purchase System. The agreement provides that Rs. 6,000 be paid on signing the agreement and the balance in four annual instalments with 10% interest as follows :

Year ending	Rs.
31-12-1990	8,400
31-12-1991	7,800
31-12-1992	7,200
31-12-1993	6,600

Mr. Suresh writes off depreciation @ 10% per annum on diminishing balance method.

Your are required to ascertain the cash price of the Machine.

Prepare : (a) Machine Account
(b) H.M.T. Ltd. and
(c) Interest Account (Suspense A/c)
in the Books of Suresh.

[K.U.D., October 1996(O)]

Solution :

Ascertainment of cash price of Machine each of the instalments include interest. The calculation of interest included in each of the instalments. The procedure is to start from last instalment.

Instalment = Cash Price + Interest

110 = 100 + 10%

Calculation of Interest = 10/110 × Instalment

	Instalment	× 10/110	= Interest	Cash Price
Start from Last Instalment				
31-12-93	6,600	× 10/110	= 600	6,000
Less Interest	600			
	6,000			
Add Instalment - 92	7,200			
	13,200	× 10/110	= 1,200	6,000
Less Interest	1,200			
	12,000			
Add Instalment 91	7,800			
	19,800	× 10/110	= 1,800	6,000
Less Interest	1,800			
	18,000		= 2,400	6,000
Add Instalment 90	8,400	26,400×10/110	= 6,000	24,000
			Add	6,000 on 1-1-90
				30,000
				Rs. 30,000 Cash Price
				6,000 Interest

In the Books of Suresh

Machine A/c

1-1-90	To H.M.T. Ltd. A/c (Cash price)	30,000	31-12-90	By Depreciation A/c 10% on 30,000	3,000
				By Balance c/d	27,000
		30,000			30,000
1-1-91	To Balance b/d	27,000	31-12-91	By Depreciation A/c 10% on 27,000	2,700
				By Balance c/d	24,300
		27,000			27,000
1-1-92	To Balance b/d	24,300	31-12-92	By Depreciation A/c	2,430
				By Balance c/d	21,870
		24,300			24,300
1-1-93	To Balance b/d	21,870	31-12-93	By Depreciation A/c	2,187
				By Balance c/d	19,683
		21,870			21,870
1-1-94	To Balance b/d	19,683			

H.M.T. Ltd. A/c

1-1-90	To Bank A/c down payment	6,000	1-1-90	By Machine A/c Cash Price	30,000
31-12-90	To Bank A/c (Instalment paid)	8,400		Interest Suspense A/c	6,000
	To Balance c/d	21,600			
		36,000			36,000
31-12-91	To Bank A/c	7,800	1-1-91	By Balance b/d	21,600
	To Balance c/d	13,800			
		21,600			21,600
31-12-92	To Bank A/c	7,200	1-1-92	By Balance b/d	13,800
	To Balance c/d	6,600			
		13,800			13,800
31-12-93	To Bank A/c *Less* Instalment	6,600	1-1-93	By Balance b/d	6,600
		6,600			6,600

Interest Suspense A/c

1-1-90	To H.M.T. Ltd. A/c (Total Interest payable)	6,000	31-12-90	By Interest A/c	2,400
				By Balance c/d	3,600
		6,000			6,000
1-1-91	To Balance b/d	3,600	31-12-91	By Interest	1,800
				By Balance c/d	1,800
		3,600			3,600
1-1-92	To Balance b/d	1,800	31-12-92	By Interest A/c	1,200
				By Balance c/d	600
		1,800			1,800
1-1-93	To Balance b/d	600	31-12-93	By Interest	600
		600			600

Problem No. 8

Santosh Transport Ltd., Hubli purchased a vehicle on Hire Purchase System. The terms of payment are as follows :

		Rs.
1-1-1992	On signing Contract	16,000
31-12-92	Ist Instalment	22,400
31-12-93	2nd Instalment	20,800
31-12-94	3rd Instalment	19,200
31-12-95	Last Instalment	17,600

Depreciation is charged @ 20% p.a. on reducing Balance method. Interest is to be calculated @ 10% p.a. Ascertain cash price and

Prepare : (1) Vehicle Account and

(2) Vendor Account in the Books of Santosh Transport Ltd.

[K.U.D., April 1996(N)]

Solution :

Working Note

Ascertainment of Cash price of vehicle. Each of the instalments included interest @ 10% on unpaid cash price Balance.

Instalment = Cash Price + 10% Interest

110 = 100 + 10

Calculation of Interest = 10/110 × Instalment

Procedure start from last instalment

	Instalment × 10/110		= Interest	Cash Price	
Last Instalment	17,600	× 10/110	= 1,600	16,000	
Less Interest	1,600				
	16,000				
Add 3rd Instalment	19,200	× 10/110	= 3,200	16,000	
	35,200				
Less Interest	3,200				
	32,000				
Add 2nd Instalment	20,800				
	52,800	× 10/110	= 4,800	16,000	
Less Interest	4,800				
	48,000				
Add 1st Instalment	22,400		6,400	16,000	
	70,400		16,000	64,000	Cash
				16,000	down payment
				80,000	
			Cash-Price	Rs. 80,000	
			Intrest	16,000	

In the Books of Santosh Transport Ltd.

Vehicle A/c

1-1-92	The Vendor A/c (Cash price)	80,000	31-12-92	By Depreciation A/c 20% on 80,000	16,000
				By Balance c/d	64,000
		80,000			80,000
1-1-93	To Balance b/d	64,000	31-12-93	By Depreciation A/c 20% on 64,000	12,800
				By Balance c/d	51,200
		64,000			64,000
1-1-94	To Balance b/d	51,200	31-12-94	By Depreciation A/c 20% on 51,200	10,240
				By Balance c/d	40,960
		51,200			51,200
1-1-95	To Balance b/d	40,960	31-12-95	By Depreciation A/c 20% on 40,960	8,192
				By Balance c/d	32,768
		40,960			40,960
1-1-96	To Balance b/d	32,768			

Vendor Co. A/c

1-1-92	To Bank A/c (down payment)	16,000	1-1-92	By Vehicle A/c Cash price	80,000
31-12-92	To Bank A/c	22,400	31-12-92	By Interest A/c 10% on 64,000	
	To Balance c/d	48,000			
		86,400			86,400
31-12-93	To Bank A/c	20,800	1-1-93	By Balance b/d	48,000
	To Balance c/d	32,000	31-12-93	By Interest A/c 10% on 48,000	4,800
		52,800			52,800
31-12-94	To Bank A/c	19,200	1-1-94	By Balance b/d	32,000
	To Balance c/d	16,000	31-12-94	By Interest A/c 10% on 3,200	3,200
		35,200			35,200
31-12-95	To Bank A/c (Last instalment)	17,600	1-1-95	By Balance b/d	16,000
			31-12-95	By Interest A/c 10% on 16,000	1,600
		17,600			17,600

Problem No. 9

A firm purchased an equipment costing Rs. 15,000 on 1-1-1993 from M/s. M.V. Ltd. on instalment basis. It paid Rs. 5,000 on signing of the contract and the balance in three equal instalments of Rs. 4,000 each due on 31st December every year. The firm depreciates the equipment at 20% on written down value basis. The vendors charged interest at 10% p.a. on unpaid balance of cash price. Prepare relevant Ledger Account in the books of the firm. Also show computation of interest in each instalment.

(October 1996)

Solution :

Working Table

Date	Instalment + Interest	Computation		Interest	Cash Price
01-01-93	5,000		Cash Price	—	5,000
31-12-93	4,000	15,000	– 5,000 = 10,000 × 10%	1,000	3,000
31-12-94	4,000	10,000	– 3,000 = 7,000 × 10%	700	3,300
31-12-95	4,000	7,000	– 3,300 = 3,700 – 4,000	300	3,700
	17,000			2,000	15,000

In the Books of Firm

Machinery (Equipment) A/c

1-1-93	To M/s. M.V. Ltd. (Vendor Co.)	15,000	31-12-93	By Depreciation A/c @ 20%	3,000
				By Balance c/d	12,000
		15,000			15,000
1-1-94	To Balance b/d	12,000	31-12-94	By Depreciation A/c @ 20%	2,400
				By Balance c/d	9,600
		12,000			12,000
1-1-95	To Balance b/d	9,600	31-12-95	By Depreciation A/c @ 20%	1,920
				By Balance c/d	7,680
		9,600			9,600
1-1-96	To Balance b/d	7,680			

M/s. H.V. Ltd. (Vendor Co.)

1-1-93	To Bank A/c	5,000	1-1-93	By Machinery A/c	15,000
31-12-93	To Bank A/c	4,000	31-12-93	By Interest 10% (15,000 – 5,000 =10,000 · 10%)	1,000
	To Balance c/d	7,000			
		16,000			16,000
31-12-94	To Bank A/c	4,000	1-1-94	By Balance b/d	7,000
	To Balance c/d	3,700	31-12-94	By Interest A/c	700
		7,700			7,700
31-12-95	To Bank A/c	4,000	1-1-95	By Balance b/d	3,700
			31-12-95	By Interest (being balancing figure)	300
		4,000			4,000

Problem No. 10

Prakash purchased a scooter from Bajaj Ltd. on 1-1-1989 and agreed to pay interest @ 20% p.a. on unpaid balance of cash price. Prakash decided to depreciate scooter @ 10% p.a. on reducing balance method. He paid Rs. 2,000 on signing the contract and the Balance in the following four yearly instalments at the end of each year :

Year ending	Instalment (in Rs.)
31-12-1989	3,600
31-12-1990	3,200
31-12-1991	2,800
31-12-1992	2,400

Prepare : (a) Scooter Account (b) Interest Suspense Account, and
(c) Bajaj Ltd. Account in the Books of Prakash.

[K.U.D., April 1996 (a)]

Solution :

Note : (a) Instalment given (b) Rate of Interest given @ 20% p.a. now it is necessary to ascertain cash price and the interest included in each instalment.

Ascertainment of cash price and the Interest included in each of the instalment

Start from Last	Instalment due	Interest 20/120	Cash Price
31-12-1992	2,400 × 20/120	400	2,000
Less : Interest	400		
	2,000		
31-12-1993 *Add*	2,800		
	4,800 × 20/120	800	2,000
Less : Interest	800		
	4,000		
31-12-1990 *Add*	3,200		
	7,200 × 20/120	1,200	2,000
Less : Interest	1,200		
	6,000		
31-12-1989 *Add*	3,600		
	9,600 × 20/120	1,600	2,000
		4,000	8,000
	∴ Paid on 1-1-89	—	2,000
		4,000	10,000

In the Books of Prakash

Scooter A/c

1-1-89	To Bajaj Co. Ltd. A/c	10,000	31-12-98	By Depr. 10%	1,000
				By Balance c/d	9,000
		10,000			10,000
1-1-90	To Balance b/d	9,000	31-12-90	By Depr. 10%	900
				By Balance c/d	8,100
		9,000			9,000
1-1-91	To Balance b/d	8,100	31-12-92	By Depr. 10%	810
				By Balance c/d	7,290
		8,100			8,100
1-1-92	To Balance b/d	7,290	31-12-92	By Depr. 10%	729
				By Balance c/d	6,561
		7,290			7,290

Interest Suspense A/c

1-1-89	To Bajaj Ltd.	4,000	31-12-89	By Interest A/c	1,600
				By Balance c/d	2,400
		4,000			4,000
1-1-90	To Balance b/d	2,400	31-12-90	By Interest A/c	1,200
				By Balance c/d	1,200
		2,400			2,400
1-1-91	To Balance b/d	1,200	31-12-91	By Interest A/c	800
				By Balance c/d	400
		1,200			1,200
1-1-92	To Balance b/d	400	31-12-92	By Interest	400

Bajaj Co. Ltd. A/c

1-1-89	To Cash	2,000	1-1-89	By Scooter A/c	10,000
31-12-89	To Cash	3,600		By Interest Suspense	4,000
	To Balance c/d	8,400			
		14,000			14,000
31-12-90	To Cash A/c	3,200	1-1-90	By Balance b/d	8,400
	To Balance c/d	5,200			
		8,400			8,400
31-12-91	To Cash	2,800	1-1-91	By Balance b/d	5,200
	To Balance c/d	2,400			
		5,200			5,200
31-12-92	To Cash A/c	2,400	1-1-92	By Balance b/d	2,400

Problem No. 11

Ravi purchased a Tractor H.M.T. Ltd. on 1-1-1991 and agreed to pay 10% interest on the unpaid balance of cash price. Ravi provides depreciation at 10% p.a. on diminishing balance method. He paid Rs. 20,000; on signing the contract and balance in the following instalments :

On 31-12-1991	28,000
On 31-12-1992	26,000
On 31-12-1993	24,000
On 31-12-1994	22,000

Ascertain the cash price of the Tractor and prepare Tractor account, Interest Suspense account and H.M.T. Ltd. account in the books of Ravi, under Instalment system.

(K.U.D., October 1995)

Solution :

Total Payments made :

On 1-1-1991	on signing the agreement	20,000
On 31-12-91	Instalment	28,000
On 31-12-92	Instalment	26,000
On 31-12-93	Instalment	24,000
On 31-12-94	Instalment	22,000
	Total Payments	1,20,000

In each of the instalments paid Interest is included in such situation Interest and Cash Price are separated from the Instalments.

	Amount Outstanding			Interest 10%	Cash Price
Start from Last Instalment :					
31-12-1994	22,000	× 10/110	=	2,000	20,000
Less : Interest	2,000				
	20,000				
Add : Instalment '93	24,000				
	44,000	× 10/10	=	4,000	20,000
Less : Interest	4,000				
	40,000				
Add : Instalment '92	26,000				
	66,000	× 10/10	=	6,000	20,000
Less : Interest	6,000				
	60,000				
Add : Instalment	28,000				
	88,000	× 10/10	=	8,000	20,000
		Total		20,000	80,000
		Add : Cash paid signing the Contract			20,000
					1,00,000
Now Total Payment :		Cash Price		1,00,000	
		Interest		20,000	Total Rs. 1,20,000

In the Books of Ravi

Tractor A/c

1-1-91	To H.M.T. A/c (Cash Price)	1,00,000	31-12-91	By Depreciation @ 10%	10,000
				By Balance c/d	90,000
		1,00,000			1,00,000
1-1-92	To Balance b/d	90,000	31-12-92	By Depreciation @ 10%	9,000
				By Balance c/d	81,000
		90,000			90,000
1-1-93	To Balance	81,000	31-12-93	By Depreciation @ 10%	8,100
				By Balance c/d	72,900
		81,000			81,000
1-1-94	To Balance b/d	72,900	31-12-94	By Depreciation @ 10%	7,290
				By Balance c/d	65,610
		72,900			72,900
1-1-95	To Balance b/d	65,610			

H.M.T. A/c

1-1-91	To Bank A/c	20,000	1-1-91	By Tractor A/c	1,00,000
31-12-91	To Bank A/c	28,000		By Interest Suspense A/c	20,000
	To Balance c/d	72,000			
		1,20,000			1,20,000
31-12-92	To Bank	26,000	1-1-92	By Balance b/d	72,000
	To Balance c/d	46,000			
		72,000			72,000
31-12-93	To Bank A/c	24,000	1-1-93	By Balance b/d	46,000
	To Balance c/d	22,000			
		46,000			46,000
31-12-94	To Bank A/c	22,000	1-1-94	By Balance b/d	22,000
		22,000			22,000

Interest Suspense A/c

1-1-91	To H.M.T. A/c	20,000	31-12-91	By Interest A/c	8,000
				By Balance c/d	12,000
		20,000			20,000
1-1-92	To Balance b/d	12,000	31-12-92	By Interest A/c	6,000
				By Balance c/d	6,000
		12,000			12,000
1-1-93	To Balance b/d	6,000	31-12-93	By Interest A/c	4,000
				By Balance c/d	2,000
		6,000			6,000
1-1-94	To Balance b/d	2,000	31-12-94	By Interest A/c	2,000
		2,000			2,000

Problem No. 12

Shailesh purchases a Motor Car from Bagi Motors Co., on a Hire-purchase agreement on 1st January 1988. Paying cash Rs. 20,000, and agreeing to pay further three instalments of Rs. 20,000 each on 31st December each year. The cash price of the Car is Rs. 74,500 and Bagi Motors Co. charges interest @ 5% p.a. Shailesh write off 10% p.a. as depreciation on reducing balance method. Show Motor Car Account and Bagi Motor Co. Account in the Book of Mr. Shailesh.

(K.U.D., April 1995)

Solution :

In the Books of Shailesh

Motor Car A/c

1-1-88	To Bagi Motor Co. (Cash price)	74,500	31-12-88	By Depreciation	7,450
				By Balance c/d	67,050
		74,500			74,500
1-1-89	To Balance b/d	67,050	31-12-89	By Depreciation	6,705
				By Balance c/d	60,345
		67,050			67,050
1-1-90	To Balance b/d	60,345	31-12-90	By Depreciation	6,035
				By Balance c/d	54,310
		60,345			60,345
1-1-91	To Balance b/d	54,310			

Bagi Motor Company A/c

1-1-88	To Bank A/c	20,000	1-1-88	By Motor Car A/c	74,500
31-12-88	To Bank	20,000	31-12-88	By Interest A/c	2,725
	To Balance c/d	37,225		@ 5% on 54,500	
		77,225			77,225
31-12-90	To Bank A/c	20,000	1-1-89	By Balance b/d	37,225
	To Balance c/d	19,086	31-12-90	To Interest A/c	
				on 37,225 @ 5%	1,861
		39,086			39,086
31-12-91	To Bank A/c	20,000	1-1-91	By Balance b/d	19,086
				By Interest A/c	914
				(Being balance figure)	
		20,000			20,000

Problem No. 13

Mr. Rakesh Prabhu purchased a truck on hire-purchase system on 1st January 1988 from Tata Ltd. He paid Rs. 48,000 on signing the agreement, Rs. 50,600 at the end of first year, Rs. 61,000 at the end of second year, and Rs. 66,000 at the end of the third year. Interest at 10% p.a. on cash price of the truck is included in the above instalments. Mr. Rakesh Prabhu charges depreciation at 10% p.a. on diminishing balance method. Show Truck Account and Tata Ltd. Account in the books of Mr. Rakesh Prabhu.

(K.U.D., October 1994)

Solution :

	Rs.
I. Payment made on the agreement	48,000
End of 1st year	50,600
End of IInd year	61,000
End of IIIrd year	66,000
	Rs. 2,25,600

II. Ascertainment of cash price and interest.

	Amount Outstanding	Interest	Cash Price
III. Start from last instalment =	Rs. 66,000 × 10/110 =	6,000	60,000
Less : Interest	6,000		
	60,000		
Add : II year instalment	61,000		
	1,21,000 × 10/110 =	11,000	50,000
Less : Interest	11,000		
	1,10,000		
Add : Ist year instalment	50,600		
	1,60,600 × 10/110 =	14,600	36,000
		31,600	1,46,000
Add : Down payment			48,000
Cash price			1,94,000
Add : Interest			31,600
Total payment			2,25,600

In the Books of Prakash Prabhu

Truck A/c

1988	To Tata Ltd. A/c (Cash price)	1,94,000	31-12-88	By Depreciation	19,400
				By Balance A/c	1,74,600
		1,94,000			1,94,000
1-1-89	To Balance b/d	1,74,600	31-12-89	By Depreciation A/c	17,460
				By Balance c/d	1,37,140
		1,74,600			1,74,600
1-1-90	To Balance b/d	1,57,140	31-12-90	By Depreciation A/c	15,714
				By Balance c/d	1,41,426
		1,57,140			1,57,140
1-1-91	To Balance b/d	1,41,426			

Tata Ltd. A/c (Vendor)

1-1-88	To Banks A/c	48,000	1-1-88	By Truck A/c	1,94,000
31-12-88	To Banks A/c	50,600	31-12-88	By Interest A/c on 1,46,000 @ 10%	14,600
	To Balance c/d	1,10,000			
		2,08,600			2,08,600
31-12-89	To Banks A/c	61,000	1-1-89	By Balance b/d	1,10,000
	To Balance c/d	60,000	31-12-89	By Interest A/c	11,000
		1,21,000			1,21,000
31-12-90	To Banks A/c	66,000	1-1-90	By Balance b/d	60,000
			31-12-90	By Interest A/c	6,000
		66,000			66,000

Problem No. 14

Sri Sai Prasad brought a Hero-Honda scooter on 1-4-1987 on instalment basis. The cash price was Rs. 17,000 and the instalment were paid as Rs. 5,000 down and the three annual instalment payments of Rs. 5,000 each. He charges depreciation at 20% p.a. on reducing balance system. You are required to prepare :

(i) Scooter A/c

(ii) Interest Suspense A/c

(iii) Vendor A/c.

(K.U.D., April 1994)

Solution :

Cash price – Rs. 17,000 given

Instalments		Total payment =	20,000
Amount down payment	5,000	Cash price	17,000
Balance 3 × 5,000	15,000	Balance being Interest	3,000
Total payment	20,000		

Rate of Interest not given.

Now Ascertainment of interest included in instalment on Ratio method.

Year	Amount of Instalment outstanding		Ratio	Interest Rs. 3,000
1987	20,000 – 5,000 = downpay	15,000	3	3/6 × 3,000 = 1,500
1987	15,000 – 5,000 = Instalment	10,000	2	2/6 × 3,000 = 1,000
1988	10,000 – 5,000 = Instalment	5,000	1	1/6 × 3,000 = 500
1989	5,000 – 5,000 = Instalment	—	6	— — —

Solution : Extra

In the Books of Purchaser

Journal Entries

Particulars		Dr Rs.	Cr Rs.
1-4-87			
(1) Scooter A/c	Dr	17,000	
Interest Suspense A/c	Dr	3,000	
To Vendor A/c			20,000
(Cash price of the scooter & Interest payable)			
(2) Vendor A/c	Dr	5,000	
To Bank A/c			5,000
(Down payment)			
31-3-88			
(1) Interest A/c	Dr	1,500	
To Interest Suspense A/c			1,500
(Annual interest transferred)			
(2) Vendor A/c	Dr	5,000	
To Bank A/c			5,000
(Annual instalment paid)			
(3) Depreciation A/c	Dr	3,400	
To Scooter A/c			3,400
(Depreciation at 20%)			
(4) Profit & Loss A/c	Dr	4,900	
To Interest A/c			1,500
To Depreciation A/c			3,400
(Interest & Depreciation transferred to Profit and Loss A/c)			
31-3-1989			
(1) Interest A/c	Dr	1,000	
To Interest Suspense A/c			1,000
(Annual Interest transfer)			
(2) Vendor A/c	Dr	5,000	
To Bank A/c			5,000
(Annual Instalment paid)			
(3) Depreciation A/c	Dr	2,720	
To Scooter A/c			2,720
(Annual Depreciation)			
(4) Profit and Loss A/c	Dr	3,720	
To Interest A/c			1,000
To Depreciation A/c			2,720
(Interest and Depreciation transferred)			

Particulars		Dr Rs.	Cr Rs.
31-3-90			
(1) Interest A/c	Dr	500	
To Interest Suspense A/c			500
(Annual interest transfer)			
(2) Vendor A/c	Dr	5,000	
To Bank A/c			5,000
(Annual Instalment paid)			
(3) Depreciation A/c	Dr	2,176	
To Scooter A/c			2,176
(Annual depreciation)			
(4) Profit & Loss A/c	Dr	2,676	
To Interest A/c			500
To Depreciation A/c			2,176
(Interest and depreciation transferred)			

In the Books of Purchaser

Scooter A/c

1-4-87	To Vendor A/c (Cash price)	17,000	31-3-88	By Depreciation A/c (20% on 17,000)	3,400
				By Balance c/d	13,600
		17,000			17,000
1-4-88	To Balance b/d	13,600	31-3-89	By Depreciation A/c (20% on 13,600)	2,720
				By Balance c/d	10,880
		13,600			13,600
1-4-89	To Balance b/d	10,880	31-3-90	By Depreciation A/c (20% on 10,880)	2,176
				By Balance c/d	8,704
		10,880			10,880
1-4-90	To Balance b/d	8,704			

Vendor A/c

1-4-87	To Bank A/c	5,000	1-4-87	By Scooter A/c	17,000
31-3-88	To Bank A/c (Instalment)	5,000		By Interest Suspense A/c	3,000
	To Balance c/d	10,000			
		20,000			20,000
31-3-89	To Bank A/c	5,000	1-4-88	By Balance b/d	10,000
	To Balance c/d	5,000			
		10,000			10,000
31-3-90	To Bank A/c	5,000	1-4-89	By Balance b/d	5,000

Interest Suspense A/c

1-4-87	To Vendor A/c	3,000	31-3-88	By Interest A/c	1,500
				By Balance c/d	1,500
		3,000			3,000
1-4-88	To Balance b/d	1,500	31-3-89	By Interest A/c	1,000
				By Balance c/d	500
		1,500			1,500
1-4-89	To Balance b/d	500	31-3-90	By Interest A/c	500

Problem No. 15

Mr. Vinaya purchased a Car on Instalment system on 1-1-1985 from "Tata Ltd." and paid Rs. 20,000 down and the balance amount in the following instalment are payable :

31-12-1985	Rs. 36,000
31-12-1986	Rs. 32,000
31-12-1987	Rs. 28,000
31-12-1988	Rs. 24,000

Prepare Car A/c and Tata Ltd. A/c in the Books of Mr. Vinaya providing depreciation at 10% on reducing Balance method. Interest charged at 10% per annum.

(K.U.D., April 1993)

Solution :

Calculation of Interest included in each of the Instalment and Ascertainment of Cash price

Start from	Instalment			Interest @ 20%	Cash Price
31-12-1988	24,000	× 20/120	=	4,000	20,000
Less : Interest	4,000				
	20,000				
Add : 31-12-1987	28,000				
	48,000	× 20/120	=	8,000	20,000
Less : Interest	8,000				
	40,000				
Add : 31-12-1986	32,000				
	72,000	× 20/120	=	12,000	20,000
Less : Interest	12,000				
	60,000				
Add : Instalment	36,000				
31-12-1985	96,000	× 20/120	=	16,000	20,000
Less : Interest	16,000			Total Cash Price	80,000
	80,000			*Add* : Down payment	20,000
				Total Cash price	1,00,000

Instalment System in the Books of Purchaser

Car A/c

Date	Particulars	Amount	Date	Particulars	Amount
1-1-85	To Vendor A/c (Tata Ltd.)	1,00,000	31-1-85	By Depreciation A/c (@ 10%)	10,000
				By Balance c/d	90,000
		1,00,000			1,00,000
1-1-86	To Balance b/d	90,000	31-12-86	By Depreciation A/c	9,000
				By Balance c/d	81,000
		90,000			90,000
1-1-87	To Balance b/d	81,000	31-12-87	By Depreciation A/c	8,100
				By Balance c/d	72,900
		81,000			81,000
1-1-88	To Balance b/d	72,900	31-12-88	By Depreciation A/c	7,290
				By Balance c/d	65,610
		72,900			72,900
1-1-89	To Balance b/d	65,610			

Vendor A/c (Tata Ltd.)

1-1-85	To Bank A/c	20,000	1-1-85	By Car A/c	1,00,000
31-12-85	To Bank A/c	36,000	31-12-85	By Interest @ 20% on 80,000	16,000
	To Balance c/d	60,000			
		1,16,000			1,16,000
31-12-86	To Bank A/c	32,000	1-1-86	By Balance b/d	60,000
	To Bank c/d	40,000	31-12-86	By Interest @ 20% on 60,000	12,000
		72,000			72,000
31-12-87	To Bank A/c	28,000	1-1-87	By Balance b/d	40,000
	To Bank c/d	20,000	31-12-87	By Interest A/c	8,000
		48,000			48,000
31-12-88	To Bank A/c	24,000	1-1-88	By Balance b/d	20,000
				By Interest A/c	4,000
		24,000			24,000

Problem No. 16

Shri Prasanna purchased a Machinery on 1-1-1988 from Electronics Co. under Hire purchase system at a cost price of Rs. 42,000. The terms provided that (1) Rs. 11,250 be paid on signing the agreement (2) The balance in three equal instalments of Rs. 11,250 each at the end of each year. The vendor company charges interest @ 5% p.a. on unpaid Balance. Machinery was depreciated @ 20% p.a. on diminishing Balance method. The Accounts are closed on 31-12-(31st December) each year.

Prepare : (1) Machinery A/c (2) Electronics Co. (Vendor) A/c.

(K.U.D., October 1993)

Solution :

In the Books of Prasanna (Hire Purchaser)

Machinery A/c

1-1-88	To Electronics Co. A/c	42,000	31-12-88	By Depreciation A/c	8,400
				By Balance c/d	33,600
		42,000			42,000
1-1-89	To Balance b/d	33,600	31-12-89	By Depreciation A/c	6,720
				By Balance c/d	26,880
		33,600			33,600
1-1-90	To Balance b/d	26,880	31-12-90	By Depreciation A/c	5,376
				By Balance c/d	21,504
		26,880			26,880
1-1-91	To Balance b/d	21,504			

Electronics Co. (Vendor) A/c

1-1-88	To Bank A/c	11,250	1-1-88	By Machinery A/c	42,000
31-12-88	To Bank A/c	11,250	31-12-88	By Interest @ 5% on 30,750	1,537.50
	To Balance c/d	21,037			
		43,537			43,537.50
31-12-89	To Bank A/c	11,250	01-12-89	By Balance b/d	21,037
	To Balance c/d	10,839	31-12-89	By Interest @ 5%	1,052
		22,089			22,089
31-12-90	To Bank A/c	11,250	1-1-90	By Balance b/d	10,839
			31-12-90	By Interest	411
		11,250		Last year being balance	11,250

Problem No. 17

Mr. Ramesh, handicapped person a technical graduate under self-employment scheme purchased a machinery costing Rs. 60,000 on 1-1-1986, on Instalment basis from H.M.T. Bangalore.

The terms of payments were :

(1) Down payment of Rs. 15,000 on signing the agreement.

(2) The balance in three equal instalments of Rs. 15,000 each with interest @ 10% p.a. on unpaid Balance, payable at end of each year. The Machinery was depreciated @ 20% p.a. on reducing balance method. The accounts are closed on 31st December each year.

Show in the Ledger Accounts : (1) Machinery A/c (2) H.M.T. A/c.

(K.U.D., April 1992)

Solution :

In the Books of Ramesh

Machinery A/c

1-1-86	To H.M.T. A/c	60,000	31-12-86	By Depreciation A/c @ 20% on 60,000	12,000
				By Balance c/d	48,000
		60,000			60,000
1-1-87	To Balance b/d	48,000	31-12-87	By Depreciation A/c	9,600
				By Balance c/d	38,400
		48,000			48,000
1-1-88	To Balance b/d	38,400	31-12-88	By Depreciation A/c	7,680
				By Balance c/d	30,720
		38,400			38,400
1-1-89	To Balance b/d	30,720			

H.M.T. Co. A/c

1-1-86	To Bank A/c	15,000	1-01-86	By Machinery A/c	60,000
31-12-86	To Bank A/c (15,000 + 4,500)	19,500	31-12-86	By Interest 10% on 45,000	4,500
	To Balance c/d	30,000			
		64,500			64,500
31-12-87	To Bank A/c (15,000 + 3,000)	18,000	1-01-87	To Balance b/d	30,000
			31-12-87	To Balance 10% on 30,000	3,000
	To Balance c/d	15,000			
		33,000			33,000
31-12-88	To Bank A/c (15,000 + 1,500)	16,500	1-01-88	By Balance b/d	15,000
			31-12-88	By Interest 10% on 15,000	1,500
		16,500			16,500

Problem No. 18

Shri. Ram purchased on 1st April 1989 a Kinetic Honda scooter costing Rs. 19,000 on instalment basis from Shri Sai Agencies, Karwar. He paid Rs. 5,000 immediately and the balance of price is payable in (4) four equal instalments of Rs. 5,000 each at the end of half yearly interest. He decided to write off the vechcle @ 20% p.a. on written down value on 31st March every year.

Pass the Journal Entries in the books of Shri Ram.

(K.U.D., October 1992)

Solution :

Cash Price-given, Instalment given, but Rate of Interest is not given. Total Interest is first ascertained.

Total amount payable :

Down payment on 1-4-1989	5,000
First Half Yearly instalment on 30-9-89	5,000
Second Half Yearly instalment on 31-3-90	5,000
Third Half Yearly instalment on 30-9-90	5,000
Fourth Half Yearly instalment on 31-3-91	5,000
Total Amount payable	25,000
Less : Cash Price	19,000
Difference is Interest payable	6,000

Total amount of interest payable Rs. 6,000 is distributed in half yearly instalment by a adopting ratio basis.

Date	Instalment	Amount Outstanding	Ratio	Interest	Cash Price
01-04-1989	5,000 Down payment	—	—	—	6,000
30-09-1989	5,000	20,000	4	6,000 × 4/10 = 2,400	2,600
31-03-1990	5,000	15,000	3	6,000 × 3/10 = 1,800	3,200
30-09-1990	5,000	10,000	2	6,000 × 2/10 = 1,200	3,800
31-03-1991	5,000	5,000	1	6,000 × 1/10 = 600	4,400
		25,000		6,000	19,000

Calculation : of Depreciation on Assets – Scooters

		Depreciation
Date of purchase – 1-4-89 — Cash price Rs.	19,000	
31-3-90 *Less* Depreciation @ 20%	3,800	3,800
Balance on 1-4-90	15,200	
31-3-1991 *Less* Depreciation @ 20%	3,040	3,040
Balance on 1-4-91	12,160	

In the Books of Shri Ram

Journal Entries

Date	Particulars		1989-90 Dr	1989-90 Cr	1990-91 Dr	1990-91 Cr
1-4-1989	(1) Scooter A/c	Dr	19,000			
	To Shri Sai Agency A/c			19,000		
	(Being Cash price of Assets purchased)					
	(2) Shri Sai Agency A/c	Dr	5,000			
	To Bank A/c			5,000		
	(Cash paid on signing the agreement)					
30-9-89	(3) Interest A/c	Dr	2,400		1,200	
	To Shri Sai Agency A/c			2,400		1,200
	(Being interest on unpaid balance)					
	(4) Shri Sai Agency A/c	Dr	5,000			
	To Bank A/c			5,000		
	(Half yearly instalment paid)					
	(5) Interest A/c	Dr	1,800		600	
	To Shri Sai Agency A/c			1,800		600
	(Being half yearly interest on unpaid Balance)					

Date	Particulars		1989-90 Dr	1989-90 Cr	1990-91 Dr	1990-91 Cr
31-3-89	(6) Depreciation A/c	Dr	3,800		3,040	
	To Scooter A/c			3,800		3,040
	(Being Annual Depreciation)					
31-3-89	(7) Profit and Loss A/c	Dr	8,000		4,840	
	To Depreciation A/c			3,800		3,040
	To Interest A/c			4,200		1,800
	(Being Annual Depreciation and interest transferred)					

In the Books of Ram

Ledger Accounts

Scooter A/c

Date	Particulars	Amount	Date	Particulars	Amount
1-4-89	To Shri Sai Agency	19,000	31-3-90	By Depreciation @ 20%	3,800
				By Balance c/d	15,200
		19,000			19,000
1-4-90	To Balance b/d	15,200	31-3-91	By Depreciation @ 20%	3,040
				By Balance c/d	12,160
		15,200			15,200
1-4-91	To Balance b/d	12,160			

Shri Sai Agency A/c (Vendor A/c)

Date	Particulars	Amount	Date	Particulars	Amount
1-4-89	To Bank A/c	5,000	1-4-89	By Scooter A/c	19,000
30-9-89	To Bank A/c	5,000	30-9-89	By Interest A/c	2,400
31-3-90	To Bank A/c	5,000	31-3-91	By Interest A/c	1,800
	To Balance c/d	8,200			
		23,200			23,200
30-9-90	To Bank A/c	5,000	1-4-90	By Balance b/d	8,200
31-3-91	To Bank A/c	5,000	30-9-90	By Interest A/c	1,200
			31-3-91	By Interest A/c	600
		10,000			10,000

Problem No. 19

Dr. Ashok purchased under self-employment scheme a Delivery Van from Tata Co. Ltd. on 1-1-86 under Hire Purchase system and the total payment was agreed upto at Rs. 60,000 to be made as under on signing of the agreement :

	Rs.
on 1-1-86	9,600
on 31-12-86	16,200
on 31-12-87	21,000
on 31-12-88	13,200

Interest was charged at 10% p.a. by vendors on unpaid Balance. The vehicle was written off @ 20% p.a. on diminishing balance method.

Ascertain the cash price of the van and show the Van Account and Vendor Account in the Books of Ashok who closes his accounts on 31st December every year.

(K.U.D., October 1991)

Solution :

(a) Instalments given (b) Rate of Interest given

(c) Required to ascertain Cash price of Delivery van.

Calculation of Cash price and interest included in each of the Instalment

Particulars	Instalment		Interest 10%	Cash Price	Instalment
Start from last Instalment					
on 31-12-1988	13,200	× 10/110	1,200	12,000	13,200
Less : Interest	1,200				
	12,000				
Add : Instalment (31-12-87)	21,000				
	33,000	× 10/110	3,000	18,000	21,000
Less : Interest	3,000				
	30,000				
1-1-87 Balance					
Add : 31-12-86	16,200				
	46,200	× 10/110	4,200	12,000	16,200
1-1-1986 on signing agreement			—	9,600	9,600
	Total		8,400	51,600	60,000
			Interest +	Cash Price =	Total Amount

In the Books of Mr. Ashok

Machinery A/c

1-1-86	To Tata Co. Ltd. A/c (Cash Price)	51,600	31-12-86	By Depreciation A/c @ 20%	10,320
				By Balance c/d	41,280
		51,600			51,600
1-1-87	To Balance b/d	41,280	31-12-87	By Depreciation A/c @ 20%	8,256
				By Balance c/d	33,024
		41,280			41,280
1-1-88	To Balance b/d	33,024	31-12-88	By Depreciation @ 20%	6,605
				By Balance c/d	26,419
		33,024			33,024
1-1-89	To Balance b/d	26,419			

Tata Co. Ltd. A/c (Vendor A/c)

1-1-86	To Bank A/c	9,600	1-1-86	By Machinery A/c	51,600
31-12-86	To Bank A/c	16,200	31-12-86	By Interest A/c @ 10% on 42,000	4,200
	To Balance c/d	30,000			
		55,800			55,800
31-12-87	To Bank A/c	21,000	1-1-87	By Balance b/d	30,000
	To Balance c/d	12,000	31-12-87	By Interest A/c (@ 10%)	3,000
		33,000			33,000
31-12-88	To Bank A/c	13,200	1-1-88	By Balance b/d	12,000
			31-12-88	By Interest A/c (@ 10%)	1,200
		13,200			13,200

Problem No. 20

A New Firm purchased a printing machine on 1-1-1987 on Instalment system.

The cash price was Rs. 15,000 payment was to be made in four half yearly instalments of Rs. 40,000 each the First payment to be made on 30-6-87. Interest is to be charged by vendor @ 5% p.a. The Machine is to depreciated @ 15% p.a. in the diminishing value.

Record the transactions in the books of the purchaser assuming that the accounts are closed on 31st December every year.

(K.U.D., April 1990)

Solution :

Date	Cash price due	Interest @ 5% one year	Interest @ 5% 1/2 year	Instalment	Cash Price		Balance cash price
1-1-1987	15,000	—	—	—	—		—
30-6-1987	15,000	750	375	4,000	3,625	15,000 − 3,625	11,375
31-12-1987	11,375	568	284	4,000	3,716	11,375 − 3,716	7,659
30-6-1988	7,659	383	191	4,000	3,809	7,659 − 3,809	3,850
31-12-1988	3,850	Being balancing figure	150	4,000	3,850	3,850 − 3,850	—
			1,000	16,000	15,000		

Vendor (Seller) A/c

30-6-87	To Bank A/c	4,000	1-1-87	By Sales (Machine)	15,000
31-12-87	To Bank A/c	4,000	30-6-87	By Interest @ 5% for 1/2 year (750 × 1/2)	375
	To Balance c/d	7,659	31-12-87	By Interest A/c	284
		15,659			15,659
30-6-88	To Bank A/c	4,000	1-1-88	By Balance b/d	7,659
31-12-88	To Bank A/c	4,000	30-6-88	By Interest @ 5% for 1/2 year (382.95 × 1/2)	191
			31-12-88	By Interest (Being balancing figure)	150
		8,000			8,000

In the Books of Hire Purchaser
Machinery A/c

1-1-87	To Vendor A/c (Cash Price)	15,000	31-12-87	By Depreciation @ 15% on 15,000	2,250
				By Balance c/d	12,750
		15,000			15,000
1-1-88	To Balance b/d	12,750	31-12-88	By Depreciation @ 15% on 12,750	1,912
				By Balance c/d	10,838
		12,750			12,750
1-1-89	To Balance b/d	10,838			

Problem No. 21

Govardhandas took a Machinery on hire purchase basis on 1st January 1986. The Cash price of the Machinery is Rs. 20,000. The terms of purchase were as follows :

(a) Rs. 2,000 to be paid on signing the agreement.

(b) The balance amount is payable in three equal instalments of Rs. 6,000 each alongwith interest @ 6% per annum on 31st December every year starting from December 1986.

(c) Govardhan and Co., closes his books on 31st December every year and he provides depreciation on the said machinery at the sale of 20% per annum on Deducing Balance method.

Give journal entries in the books of Govardhandas for three years to second the above transactions.

(K.U.D., October 1990)

Solution :

I. Calculations of interest and Cash price and instalments amount

	Total amount of cash price	Interest @ 6%	Cash price	Instalment amount
On 1-1-86 Cash price	20,000	—	—	—
Less 1-1-86 down payment	2,000	—	2,000	—
On 1-1-1986	18,000	1,080	6,000	7,080
31-12-1986 interest @ 6%				
less cash price paid	6,000			
1-1-1987 Cash price balance	12,000	720	6,000	6,720
31-12-1987 *less* Cash price paid	6,000			
1-1-1988 Cash price Balance	6,000	360	6,000	6,360

II. Calculation of Depreciation

	Cash price of Machine	Depreciation
1-1-1986 Cash price	20,000	
31-12-1986 *Less* : Depreciation @ 20%	4,000	4,000
	16,000	
31-12-1987 *Less* Depreciation 20%	3,200	3,200
On 1-1-1988 Balance	12,800	
On 31-12-1988 *Less* : Depreciation	2,560	2,560
On 1-1-1989 Balance	10,240	

In the Books of Govardhandas

Journal Entries

			1986 Dr	1986 Cr	1987 Dr	1987 Cr	1988 Dr	1988 Cr
01-01-86	Machinery A/c	Dr	20,000	—	—		—	
	To Govardhandas A/c			20,000		—		—
	(Being Cash price of Machinery)							
01-01-86	Govardhandas A/c	Dr	2,000		—		—	
	To Bank A/c			2,000		—		—
	(Cash paid on signing the contract)							
31-12-	Govardhandas A/c	Dr	7,080		6,720		6,360	
	To Bank A/c			7,080		6,720		6,360
	(Cash Price + Interest 6,000 + 1080 6,000 + 720 6,000 + 360)							
31-12-	Depreciation A/c	Dr	4,000		3,200		2,560	
	To Machinery A/c			4,000		3,200		2,560
	(Being annual Depreciation @ 20% on Reducing Balance method)							
31-12-	Profit & Loss A/c	Dr	4,000		3,200		2,560	
	To Depreciation A/c			4,000		3,200		2,560
	(Depreciation transferred)							

In the Books of Govardhandas (Hire Purchaser)

Machinery A/c

Date	Particulars	Amount	Date	Particulars	Amount
1-1-86	To Hire Vendor A/c (Cash Price)	20,000	31-12-86	By Depreciation (@ 20% on 20,000)	4,000
				By Balance c/d	16,000
		20,000			20,000
1-1-87	To Balance b/d	16,000	31-12-87	By Depreciation (@ 20% on 16,000)	3,200
				By Balance c/d	12,800
		16,000			16,000
1-1-88	To Balance b/d	12,800	31-12-88	By Depreciation (@ 20% on 12,800)	2,560
				By Balance c/d	10,240
		12,800			12,800
1-1-89	To Balance b/d	10,240			

Hire Vendor A/c

Date	Particulars	Amount	Date	Particulars	Amount
1-1-86	To Bank A/c (Down payment)	2,000	1-1-86	By Machinery A/c (Cash Price)	20,000
31-12-86	To Bank A/c (6,000 + 1,080)	7,080	31-12-86	By Interest A/c (@ 6% on 18,000)	1,080
	To Balance c/d	12,000			
		21,080			21,080
31-12-87	To Bank A/c (6,000 + 720)	6,720	1-1-87	By Balance b/d	12,000
			31-12-87	By Interest A/c	720
	To Balance c/d	6,000			
		12,720			12,720
31-12-88	To Bank A/c (6,000 + 360)	6,360	1-1-88	By Balance b/d	6,000
			31-12-88	By Interest A/c @ 6%	360
		6,360			6,360

Problem No. 22

The following are the particulars relating to Hire purchaser.

Purchaser — X & Co., Seller — Y & Co., Date of Purchase-1-1-1986,

Asset purchased — Delivery Van, Cash Price of Assets — 12,894

Payments Made : Rs. 2,000 on signing the contract and the Balance in three instalments of Rs. 4,000 each due on 31st December each year. Rate of Interest 5% per annum. Depreciation @ 20% on written down value each year.

Pass the Journal entries in the Books of Hire Purchaser.

(K.U.D., October 1990)

Solution :

I. Calculation of Interest and Cash price included in each Instalments

	Total Amount of Cash Price	Interest @ 5%	Cash Price	Instalments
On 1-1-1986	12,894		2,000	2,000
Less : Down Payment	2,000			
	10,894	545	3,455	4,000
Less Paid on 31-12-86	3,455			
	7,439	372	3,628	4,000
Less Paid on 31-12-89	3,628			
	3,811	189	3,811	4,000
Total		1,106	12,894	14,000

Note : Interest being Balancing figure in the last instalment.

II. Calculation of Depreciation on Assets Delivery Van

Delivery Van purchased on 1-1-1986 Cash price	12,894
Less : Depreciation on 31-12-1986 @ 20%	2,579
Balance on 1-1-1987	10,315
Less : Depreciation on 31-12-1987 @ 20%	2,063
Balance on 1-1-1988	8,252
Less : Depreciation on 31-12-88	1,650
Balance on 1-1-1989	6,602

In the Books of Hire Purchaser X & Co.

Journal Entries

Date	Particulars		1986 Dr	1986 Cr	1987 Dr	1987 Cr	1988 Dr	1988 Cr
1-1-86	Delivery Van A/c	Dr	12,894		—		—	
	To Y & Co.			12,894		—		—
	(Cash Price of Assets purchased on hire purchase)							

Date	Particulars		1986 Dr	1986 Cr	1987 Dr	1987 Cr	1988 Dr	1988 Cr
1-1-86	Y & Co. A/c	Dr	2,000		—		—	
	To Bank A/c			2,000		—		—
	(Down payment)							
31-12-	Interest A/c	Dr	545		372		189	
	To Y & Co. A/c			545		372		189
	(Being Interest unpaid balance)							
31-12-	Y & Co. A/c	Dr	4,000		4,000		4,000	
	To Bank A/c			4,000		4,000		4,000
	(Annual Instalment paid including interest)							
31-12-	Depreciation A/c	Dr	2,579		2,063		1,650	
	To Delivery Van A/c			2,579		2,063		1,650
	(Being Annual Depreciation)							
31-12-	Profit & Loss A/c	Dr	2,579		2,063		1,650	
	To Depreciation A/c			2,579		2,063		1,650
	(Being Depreciation transferred)							

Delivery Van A/c

1-1-86	To Y & Co.	12,894	31-12-86	By Depreciation A/c @ 20%	2,579
				By Balance c/d	10,315
		12,894			12,894
1-1-87	To Balance b/d	10,315	31-12-87	By Depreciation @ 20%	2,063
				By Balance c/d	8,252
		10,315			10,315
1-1-88	To Balance b/d	8,252	31-12-88	By Depreciation @ 20%	1,650
				By Balance c/d	6,602
		8,252			8,252
1-1-89	To Balance b/d	6,602			

Y & Co. A/c (Hire Vendor A/c)

1-1-86	To Bank A/c (Down payment)	2,000	1-1-86	By Delivery Van A/c	12,894
31-12-86	To Bank A/c	4,000	31-12-86	By Interest A/c (@ 5% on 10,894)	545
	To Balance c/d	7,439			
		13,439			13,439
31-12-87	To Bank A/c	4,000	1-1-87	By Balance b/d	7,439
	To Balance c/d	3,811	31-12-88	By Interest A/c @ 5%	372
		7,811			7,811
31-12-88	To Bank A/c	4,000	1-1-88	By Balance b/d	3,811
			31-12-88	By Interest A/c (Being balancing figure)	189
		4,000			4,000

Problem No. 23

Bhavani Collieries Ltd. purchased on 1st Jan. 1985, Machinery on Instalment system. A sum of Rs. 6,000 was to be paid on delivery and the balance was paid in four annual instalments of Rs. 6,000 each payable on 31st December, each year. The cash price of the Machinery was Rs. 27,300. The Vendor charged interest @ 5% p.a. Depreciation at 10% is to be written off on the Machinery on reducing Balance method.

You are required to write up the (1) Machinery Account (2) Interest Suspense A/c in the Books of Bhavani Collieries Ltd. for the four years.

(K.U.D., April 1989)

Solution :

In the Books of Bhavani Collieries Ltd.

Machinery A/c

1-1-85	To Vendor A/c (Cash Price)	27,300	31-12-85	By Depreciation A/c (@ 15%)	4,095
				By Balance c/d	23,205
		27,300			27,300
1-1-86	To Balance b/d	23,205	31-12-86	By Depreciation A/c (@ 15%)	3,481
				By Balance c/d	19,724
		23,205			23,205
1-1-87	To Balance b/d	19,724	31-12-87	By Depreciation A/c	2,959
				By Balance c/d	16,765
		19,274			19,274
1-1-88	To Balance b/d	16,765	31-12-88	By Depreciation A/c	2,515
				By Balance c/d	14,250
		16,765			16,765
1-1-89	To Balance b/d	14,250			

Calculation of Interest

Cash Price	27,300			
Less : Cash paid	6,000			
1-1-1985	21,300	@ 5% Interest	1,065	4,935
31-12- *Less* Paid	4,935			
1-1-1986	16,365	@ 5% Interest	818.25	5,182
31-12- *Less* : Paid	5,182			
1-1-1987	11,183	@ 5% Interest	559.15	5,441
31-12- *Less* : Paid	5,441			
	5,742	Balancing figure	258.00	5,742
			2,700	21,300
		Add Down Payment		6,000
		Total Cash Price		27,300
		Add Interest		2,700
		Total Amount		30,000

Interest Suspense A/c

31-12-85	To Interest	1,065	1-1-85	By Bhavani Collieries Co. A/c (Purchaser)	2,700
	To Balance c/d	1,635			
		2,700			2,700
31-12-86	To Interest	818	1-1-86	By Balance b/d	1,635
	To Balance c/d	817			
		1,635			1,635
31-12-87	To Interest	559	1-1-87	By Balance b/d	817
	To Balance c/d	258			
		817			817
31-12-88	To Interest	258	1-1-88	By Balance b/d	258

Vendor A/c

1-1-85	To Bank A/c	6,000	1-1-85	By Machinery A/c	27,300
31-12-85	To Bank A/c	6,000	31-12-85	By Interest A/c (@ 5% on 21,300)	1,065
	To Balance c/d	16,365			
		28,365			28,365
31-12-86	To Bank A/c	6,000	1-1-86	By Balance b/d	16,365
	To Balance c/d	11,183	31-12-86	By Interest A/c (@ 5% on 16,365)	818
		17,183			17,183

31-12-86	To Bank A/c	6,000	1-1-87	By Balance b/d	11,183
	To Balance c/d	5,742	31-12-86	By Interest A/c	559
		11,742			11,742
31-12-88	To Bank A/c	6,000	1-1-88	By Balance b/d	5,742
				By Interest A/c (Balancing figure)	258
		6,000			6,000

Interest A/c

31-12-85	To Vendor A/c	1,065	By Profit & Loss A/c	1,065
31-12-86	To Vendor A/c	818	By Profit & Loss A/c	818
31-12-87	To Vendor A/c	559	By Profit & Loss A/c	559
31-12-88	To Vendor A/c	258	By Profit & Loss A/c	258

In the Books of Vendor

Bhavani Collieries Co. Ltd. A/c

1-1-85	To Sales	27,300	1-1-85	By Bank A/c	6,000
	To Interest	2,700	31-12-85	By Bank A/c	6,000
				By Balance c/d	18,000
		30,000			30,000
1-1-86	To Balance b/d	18,000	31-12-87	By Bank A/c	6,000
				By Balance c/d	12,000
		18,000			18,000
1-1-87	To Balance b/d	12,000	31-12-87	By Bank A/c	6,000
				By Balance c/d	6,000
		12,000			12,000
1-1-88	To Balance b/d	6,000	31-12-88	By Bank A/c	6,000

Interest Received A/c

To Profit & Loss A/c	1,065	31-12-85	By Interest Suspense A/c	1,065
	1,065			1,065
To Profit & Loss A/c	818	31-12-86	By Interest Suspense A/c	818
	818			818
To Profit & Loss A/c	559	31-12-87	By Interest Suspense A/c	559
	559			559
To Profit & Loss A/c	258	31-12-88	By Interest Suspense A/c	258
	258			258

Problem No. 24

Mr. Mehta purchased a scooter from Bajaj Ltd. on Hire Purchases system.

The total Cash price of the scooter is Rs. 15,980 payable Rs. 4,000 down and the balance in three instalments of Rs. 6,000, Rs. 5,000 and Rs. 2,000 payable at the end of First year, Second year and Third year respectively.

Interest is charged @ 5% p.a.

You are required to give Journal Entries in the Books of Mehta. Depreciation is charged 10% p.a. on Straight Line Method.

(K.U.D., October 1989)

Solution :

Scooter purchased Cash Price		Rs. 15,980	
Payment :			
Down payment	4,000		
Balance in 3 (Three)			
Instalments :			
at Ist Year	6,000		
at IInd Year	5,000		
at IIIrd Year	2,000	Rs. 17,000	Total payment.
Excess Payment of		Rs. 1,020	Being Interest on Unpaid Balance.

Working Chart

Year	Instalment	Interest @ 5%	Cash Value	Balance of Cash Value	
Beginning of the year	—	—	15,980	15,980	
Down Payment	4,000	—	4,000	15,980 – 4,000 =	11,980 @ 5% 599
I Year	6,000	599	5,401	11,980 – 5,401	12,579
					6,000
					6,579 @ 5% 329
II Year	5,000	329	4,571	6,579 – 4,671	329
					6,908
III Year	2,000	92	1,908	1,908 – 1,908	5,000
	17,000	1,020	15,980		1,908 @ 5% 92
			1,020		92
			17,000		2,000

In the Books of Purchaser

Journal Entries

Particulars		Dr	Cr
I Year being			
(1) Scooter A/c	Dr	15,980	
To Vendor A/c			15,980
(Purchased in Hire purchase system Cash Price)			
(2) Vendor A/c	Dr	4,000	
To Bank A/c			4,000
(Down payment)			
(3) Interest A/c	Dr	599	
To Vendor A/c			599
(Interest @ 5% on 11,980)			
(4) Vendor A/c	Dr	6,000	
To Bank A/c			6,000
(Instalment paid)			
(5) Depreciation A/c	Dr	1,598	
To Scooter A/c			1,598
(@ 10% on original Cost)			
(6) Profit & Loss A/c	Dr	2,197	
To Interest A/c			599
To Depreciation A/c			1,598
(Interest and Depreciation transfer)			
II Year			
(1) Interest A/c	Dr	329	
To Vendor A/c			329
(Interest @ 5% on 6,579)			
(2) Vendor A/c	Dr	5,000	
To Bank A/c			5,000
(Instalment paid)			
(3) Depreciation A/c	Dr	1,598	
To Scooter A/c			1,598
(Annual Depreciation)			
(4) Profit & Loss A/c	Dr	1,927	
To Interest A/c			329
To Depreciation A/c			1,598
(Interest & Depreciation transfer)			

Particulars		Dr	Cr
III Year			
(1) Interest A/c	Dr	92	
To Vendor A/c			92
(Interest @ 5% on 1908 or Being balancing figure)			
(2) Vendor A/c	Dr	2,000	
To Bank A/c			2,000
(Instalment paid)			
(3) Depreciation A/c	Dr	1,598	
To Scooter A/c			1,598
(Annual Depreciation)			
(4) Profit & Loss A/c	Dr	1,690	
To Instalment A/c			92
To Depreciation A/c			1,598
(Interest & Depreciation A/c Transferred)			

Scooter A/c

I Year	To Vendor A/c	15,980	By Depreciation A/c (@ 10%)	1,598
			By Balance c/d	14,382
		15,980		15,980
II Year	To Balance b/d	14,382	By Depreciation A/c	1,598
			By Balance c/d	12,784
		14,382		14,382
III Year	To Balance b/d	12,784	By Depreciation A/c	1,598
			By Balance c/d	11,186
		12,784		12,784
IV Year	To Balance b/d	11,186		

Vendor A/c

I Year	To Bank A/c	4,000	I Year	By Scooter A/c	15,980
	To Bank A/c	6,000		By Interest A/c (@ 5% on 11,980)	599
	To Balance c/d	6,579			
		16,579			16,579
II Year	To Bank A/c	5,000	II Year	By Balance b/d	6,579
	To Balance c/d	1,908		By Interest A/c	329
		6,908			6,908
III Year	To Bank A/c	2,000	III Year	By Balance b/d	1,908
				By Interest A/c (Balancing Figure)	92
		2,000			2,000

Problem No. 25

Mahesh Industries Ltd. purchased a Machinery on Hire Purchase system on 1st January 1981, from Tata Co., Bombay to pay in five Instalments and agreed to pay interest @ 10% p.a. on the unpaid Balance of Cash Price.

Mahesh Industries Ltd. decided to depreciate the Machinery by 10% on Reducing Balance Method.

The Instalments agreed are as follows :

	Rs.
31-12-1981	2,250
31-12-1982	2,100
31-12-1983	1,950
31-12-1984	1,800
31-12-1985	1,650

Ascertain Cash price and prepare Machinery A/c for the period of five years in the Books of Mahesh Industries Ltd.

(K.U.D., April 1988)

Solution :

Ascertainment of Cash Price and Interest

Date end of the year	Net Amount due at the end of the year	Instalment Paid	Total Amount due at the end of the year	Interest @ 10% 10/110	Cash Price Balance at the beginning	Beginning of
Start from last year						
31-12-85	Nil	1,650	1,650 × 10/110 =	150	1,000	1-1-85
31-12-84	1,500	1,800	3,300 × 10/110 =	300	3,000	1-1-84
31-12-83	3,000	1,950	4,950 × 10/110 =	450	4,500	1-1-83
31-12-82	4,500	2,100	6,600 × 10/110 =	600	6,000	1-1-82
31-12-81	6,000	2,250	8,250 × 10/110 =	750	7,500	1-1-81
		9,750		2,250		

Note :

	Rs.
Total Amount paid	9,750
Less : Interest paid	2,250
Cash Price	7,500

In the Books of Mahesh Industries Ltd.

Machinery A/c

1-1-81	To Tata Co., Bombay (Vendor A/c) Cash Price	7,500	31-12-81	By Depreciation A/c (@ 10% on 7,500)	750
				By Balance c/d	6,750
		7,500			7,500
1-1-82	To Balance b/d	6,750	31-12-82	By Depreciation (@ 10% on 6,750)	675
				By Balance c/d	6,075
		6,750			6,750
1-1-83	To Balance b/d	6,075	31-12-83	By Depreciation (@ 10% on 6,075)	608
				By Balance c/d	5,467
		6,075			6,075
1-1-84	To Balance b/d	5,467	31-12-84	By Depreciation (@ 10% on 5,467)	547
				By Balance c/d	4,920
		5,467			5,467
1-1-85	To Balance b/d	4,920	31-12-85	By Depreciation (@ 10% on 4,920)	492
				By Balance c/d	4,428
		4,920			4,920
1-1-86	To Balance c/d	4,428			

Tata Co., Bombay A/c (Vendor Co.)

31-12-81	To Bank A/c	2,250	1-1-81	By Machinery A/c	7,500
	To Balance c/d	6,000		By Interest A/c	750
		8,250			8,250
31-12-82	To Bank A/c	2,100	1-1-82	By Balance b/d	6,000
	To Balance c/d	4,500		By Interest A/c @ 10% on 6,000	600
		6,600			6,600
31-12-83	To Bank A/c	1,950	1-1-83	By Balance b/d	4,500
	To Balance c/d	3,000		By Interest A/c @ 10% on 4,500	450
		4,950			4,950
31-12-84	To Bank A/c	1,800	1-1-84	By Balance b/d	3,000
	To Balance c/d	1,500		By Interest A/c @ 10% on 3,000	300
		3,300			3,300
31-12-85	To Bank A/c	1,650	1-1-85	By Balance b/d	1,500
				By Interest A/c @ 10% on 1,500	150
		1,650			1,650

Problem No. 26

Prasad purchased a Scooter on 1-1-1985 costing Rs. 12,000 on instalment basis, the terms being payment of Rs. 2,000 down and the Balance in four half yearly instalments of Rs. 3,000 each over two years. He provides depreciation @ 20% p.a. on original cost on 31st December every year. Pass necessary entries in the books of Prasad.

(K.U.D., October 1988)

Solution :

Working Notes

		Rs.
Cash price of the scooter		12,000
Total instalment amount paid on 1-1-85 down payment Rs. 2,000		2,000
		10,000
Balance	on 30-6-85 I instalment	3,000
	on 31-12-85 II instalment	3,000
	on 30-6-86 III instalment	3,000
	on 31-12-86 IV instalment	3,000
	Total	12,000
	Less Balance of Cash price	10,000
	Difference being interest	2,000

Ascertainment of interest and cash price included in each instalment Amount

Date	Instalment	Amount Outstanding	Ratio	Interest	Cash Price
1-1-85	2,000	—	—	—	—
30-6-85	3,000	12,000	4	4/10 × 2,000 = 800	3,000 – 800 = 2,200
31-12-85	3,000	9,000	3	3/10 × 2,000 = 600	3,000 – 600 = 2,400
30-6-86	3,000	6,000	2	2/10 × 2,000 = 400	3,000 – 400 = 2,600
31-12-86	3,000	3,000	1	1/10 × 2,000 = 200	3,000 – 200 = 2,800
			10	Total 2,000	10,000
					+ 2,000
					12,000

In the Books of Prasad (Purchaser)

Journal Entries

	Particulars		Dr	Cr
1-1-85				
(1)	Scooter A/c	Dr	12,000	
	To Vendor A/c			12,000
	(Cash price of the scooter purchased on Instalment)			

	Particulars		Dr	Cr
(2)	Vendor A/c	Dr	2,000	
	To Bank A/c			2,000
	(Cash paid on 1-1-1985)			
30-6-85				
(3)	Interest A/c	Dr	800	
	To Vendor A/c			800
	(Being Interest on unpaid balance)			
(4)	Vendor A/c	Dr	3,000	
	To Bank A/c			3,000
	(Instalment paid)			
31-12-1985				
(5)	Interest A/c	Dr	600	
	To Vendor A/c		600	
	(Interest on unpaid Balance)			
(6)	Vendor A/c	Dr	3,000	
	To Bank A/c			3,000
	(Instalment paid)			
(7)	Depreciation A/c	Dr	2,400	
	To Scooter A/c			2,400
	(Depreciation @ 20% on original cost)			
(8)	Profit & Loss A/c	Dr	3,800	
	To Interest A/c			1,400
	To Depreciation A/c			2,400
	(Interest and Depreciation transferred)			
30-6-86				
(9)	Interest A/c	Dr	400	
	To Vendor A/c			400
	(Interest on unpaid balance)			
(10)	Vendor A/c	Dr	3,000	
	To Bank A/c			3,000
	(Instalment paid)			
31-12-86				
(11)	Interest A/c	Dr	200	
	To Vendor A/c			200
	(Interest on unpaid Balance)			
(12)	Vendor A/c	Dr	3,000	
	To Bank A/c			3,000
	(Instalment paid)			

	Particulars		Dr	Cr
(13)	Depreciation A/c	Dr	1,200	
	To Scooter A/c			1,200
	(Annual Depreciation @ 20% on original cost)			
(14)	Profit and Loss A/c	Dr	3,000	
	To Interest A/c			600
	To Depreciation A/c			2,400
	(Interest and Depreciation transferred)			

Ledger Accounts

Scooter A/c

1-1-85	To Vendor (Cash price)	12,000	31-12-85	By Depreciation (@ 20% on 12,000)	2,400
				By Balance c/d	9,600
		12,000			12,000
1-1-86	To Balance b/d	9,600	31-12-86	By Depreciation (@ 20% on 12,000)	2,400
				By Balance c/d	7,200
		9,600			9,600
1-1-87	To Balance b/d	7,200			

Vendor A/c

1-1-85	To Bank A/c	2,000	1-1-85	By Scooter A/c	12,000
30-6-85	To Bank A/c	3,000	30-6-85	By Interest A/c	800
	To Balance c/d	7,800			
		12,800			12,800
31-12-85	To Bank A/c	3,000	1-7-85	By Balance c/d	7,800
	To Balance c/d	5,400	30-12-85	By Interest A/c	600
		8,400			8,400
30-6-86	To Bank A/c	3,000	1-7-86	By Balance b/d	5,400
	To Balance c/d	2,800	30-6-86	By Interest A/c	400
		5,800			5,800
31-12-86	To Bank A/c	3,000	1-7-86	By Balance b/d	2,800
			31-12-86	By Interest A/c	200
		3,000			3,000

Problem No. 27

X Co. Ltd. purchased a Machinery on instalment system on 1-1-1983 from Bharat Ltd. and agreed to pay 20% interest on unpaid balance of Cash price X Co. Ltd. decided to depreciate Machinery @ 10% p.a. on reducing balance method.

It paid Rs. 4,000 on signing the contract and the balance in the following four instalments :

31-12-1983	7,200
31-12-1984	6,400
31-12-1985	5,600
31-12-1986	4,800

Prepare Machinery A/c and Bharat Ltd. A/c in the Books of X Co. Ltd.

(K.U.D., April 1987)

Solution :

Ascertainment of Cash price and Interest included in Instalment

Date	Net Amount due at the end of the year	Instalment paid	Total Amount due at the end of the year	Interest 20%	Cash Price Balance at the beginning	Beginning of the year
Start from last year						
31-12-86	Nil	4,800	4,800 × 20/120	800	4,000	1-1-1986
31-12-85	4,000	5,600	9,660 × 20/120	1,600	8,000	1-1-1985
31-12-84	8,000	6,400	1,440 × 20/120	2,400	12,000	1-1-1984
31-12-83	12,000	7,200	19,200 × 20/120	3,200	16,000	1-1-1983
		24,000		8,000		

Total Instalment paid	24,000	Cash Price	16,000
Less : Interest	8,000	*Add* : Interest	8,000
Total Cash Price	16,000	Total	24,000

Chart Redrafted

Date	Cash Price due at the beginning	Interest on unpaid balance at 31-12	Instalment due at the end of the year	Cash Price paid in Instalment	Total Cash Price due at the end of year	Date (End of year)
1-1-83	16,000	3,200	7,200	4,000	12,000	31-12-83
1-1-84	12,000	2,400	6,400	4,000	8,000	31-12-84
1-1-85	8,000	1,600	5,600	4,000	4,000	31-12-85
1-1-86	4,000	800	4,800	4,000	Nil	31-12-86
Total Amount		8,000	24,000	16,000		
		Interest	Instalment paid.	Cash Price		

Machinery A/c

1-1-83	To Bharat Ltd.	16,000	31-12-83	By Depreciation (@ 10% on 16,000)	1,600
				By Balance c/d	14,400
		16,000			16,000
1-1-84	To Balance b/d	14,400	31-12-84	By Depreciation (@ 10% on 14,400)	1,440
				By Balance c/d	12,960
		14,400			14,400
1-1-85	To Balance b/d	12,960	31-12-85	By Depreciation (@10% on 12,960)	1,296
				By Balance c/d	11,664
		12,960			12,960
1-1-86	To Balance b/d	11,664	31-12-86	By Depreciation (@10% on 11,664)	1,166
				By Balance c/d	10,498
		11,664			11,664
1-1-87	To Balance b/d	10,498			

Bharat Ltd. (Vendor) A/c

31-12-83	To Bank A/c	7,200	1-1-83	By Machinery A/c	16,000
	To Balance c/d	12,000	31-12-83	By Interest A/c (@10% on 6,000)	3,200
		19,200			19,200
31-12-84	To Bank A/c	6,400	1-1-84	By Balance b/d	12,000
	To Balance c/d	8,000	31-12-84	By Interest A/c (@ 20% on 12,000)	2,400
		14,400			14,400
31-12-85	To Bank A/c	5,600	1-1-85	By Balance b/d	8,000
	To Balance c/d	4,000	31-12-85	By Interest A/c (@ 20% on 8,000)	1,600
		9,600			9,600
31-12-86	To Bank A/c	4,800	1-1-86	By Balance b/d	4,000
				By Interest A/c (@ 20% on 4,000)	800
		4,800			4,800

Problem No. 28

Mr. Ashok an unemployed graduate under the scheme of self-employment purchased a Taxi for a cash price of 55,860 under Hire purchase system from Hindustan Motor Ltd. on 1st January 1982. The terms provided that Rs. 15,000 be paid on signing the agreement and the balance in three equal instalments of Rs. 15,000 at the end of each year. The interest @ 5% on unpaid balance is charged from the above transactions.

Show the necessary Ledger Accounts in the Books of Mr. Ashok for the above period. The Car (Taxi) was depreciated @ 20% p.a. on Reducing Balance Method.

(K.U.D., April 1986)

Working Table

Date	Particulars	Instalment paid	Interest paid	Cash Price paid	Unpaid balance of cash	Interest @ 5% on Unpaid Balance
1-1-82	Cash Price due	—	—	—	55,860	
	Cash paid on			15,000	15,000	
					40,860 @ 5%	= 2,043
31-12	Cash Price due					
	Instalment	15,000	2,043	12,957	12,957	
1-1-83	Cash Price due				27,903 @ 5%	1,395
31-12-83	Instalment	15,000	1,395	13,605	13,605	
1-1-84	Cash Price due				14,298 @ 5%	714.90
31-12-84	Instalment	15,000	702	14,298	14,298	
		45,000	4,140	55,860		
	Add :	15,000		4,140		
		60,000		60,000		

In the Books of Mr. Ashok

Taxi A/c

Date	Particulars	Amount	Date	Particulars	Amount
1-1-82	To Hire Vendor (Hindustan Motors Cash Price)	55,860	31-12-82	By Depreciation A/c @ 20%	11,172
				By Balance c/d	44,688
		55,860			55,860
1-1-83	To Balance b/d	44,688	31-12-83	By Depreciation A/c @ 20%	8,938
				By Balance c/d	35,750
		44,688			44,688
1-1-84	To Balance b/d	35,750	31-12-84	By Depreciation A/c	7,150
				By Balance c/d	28,600
		35,750			35,750
1-1-85	To Balance b/d	28,600			

Hindustan Motors (Hire Vendor) A/c

1-1-82	To Bank A/c	15,000	1-1-82	By Taxi A/c	55,860
31-12-82	To Bank A/c	15,000	31-12-82	By Interest A/c	2,043
	To Balance c/d	27,903		(@ 5% on 40,860)	
		57,903			57,903
31-12-83	To Bank A/c	15,000	1-1-83	By Balance b/d	27,903
	To Balance c/d	14,298	31-12-83	By Interest A/c (@ 5%)	1,395
		29,298			29,298
31-12-84	To Bank A/c	15,000	1-1-84	By Balance b/d	14,298
				By Interest A/c (Balancing figure)	702
		15,000			15,000

In the Books of Hire Vendor (Hindustan Motor Ltd.)

Mr. Ashok A/c

1-1-82	To Sales	55,860	1-1-82	By Bank A/c	15,000
31-12-82	To Interest A/c (@ 5% on 40,860)	2,043	31-12-82	By Bank A/c	15,000
				By Balance c/d	27,903
		57,903			57,903
1-1-83	To Balance b/d	27,903	31-12-83	By Bank A/c	15,000
31-12-83	To Interest A/c	1,395		By Balance c/d	14,298
		29,298			29,298
1-1-84	To Balance b/d	14,298	31-12-84	By Bank A/c	15,000
31-12-84	To Interest A/c (Balancing figure)	702			
		15,000			15,000

Problem No. 29

Sri Rajshekhar B.E. (Mech.) Engineer started his own workshop at Hubli and purchased a Machinery on 1-1-1981 at a Cash Price of Rs. 28,000 under Hire purchase system from H.M.T. Bangalore.

The Payment was to be as under :

Rs. 7,500 down payment on signing the agreement and Balance in three equal instalments of Rs. 7,500 each payable at the end of each year. The H.M.T. charges interest at 5% p.a. on unpaid Balance.

Sri Rajshekhar provides depreciation @ 10% p.a. on the Diminishing Balance Method.

Write up the necessary account of Rajshekhar for the above period.

(K.U.D., October 1986)

Solution :

Working Table

Year	Unpaid Balance of Cash Price	Interest @ 5%	Instalment paid	Cash Price	Cash Price Balance at end of the year	
1-1-1981	28,000	—	7,500	7,500	—	—
Less : Down Payment	7,500	1,025	7,500	6,475	20,500 – 6,475 =	14,025
31-12-81	20,500					
1-1-82	14,025	701	7,500	6,799	14,025 – 6,799 =	7,226
1-1-83	7,226	274	7,500	7,226	7,226 – 7,226 =	Nil
		2,000	30,000	28,000		

Total Amount paid	Rs. 30,000
Less : Interest	2,000
Total Cash Price	28,000

Note : 1983 last Interest is being Balancing figure.

In the Books of Rajshekhar
Machinery A/c

Date	Particulars	Amount	Date	Particulars	Amount
1-1-81	To H.M.T. Bangalore (Vendor A/c) Cash Price	28,000	31-12-81	By Depreciation A/c @ 10% on 28,000	2,800
				By Balance c/d	25,200
		28,000			28,000
1-1-82	To Balance b/d	25,200	31-12-82	By Depreciation A/c (@ 10% on 25,200)	2,520
				By Balance c/d	25,680
		25,200			25,200
1-1-83	To Balance b/d	22,680	31-12-83	By Depreciation A/c (@ 10% on 22,680)	2,268
				By Balance c/d	20,412
		22,680			22,680
1-1-84	To Balance b/d	20,412			

H.M.T. Bangalore (Vendor) A/c

1-1-81	To Bank A/c (Down Payment)	7,500	1-1-81	By Machinery A/c	28,000
	To Bank A/c	7,500		By Interest A/c (@ 5% on 20,500)	1,025
	To Balance c/d	14,025			
		29,025			29,025
31-12-82	To Bank A/c	7,500	1-1-82	By Balance b/d	14,025
	To Balance c/d	7,226		By Interest A/c (@ 5% on 14,025)	701
		14,226			14,726
31-12-83	To Bank A/c	7,500	1-1-83	By Balance b/d	7,226
				By Interest A/c (Being balancing figure)	274
		7,500			7,500

Problem No. 30

Ravi Ltd. purchased a Tractor on Instalment system on 1-1-81 from Geeta Ltd. and agreed to pay 10% interest on unpaid Balance of Cash price. Ravi Ltd. provides depreciation @ 10% p.a. on Diminishing Balance Method. It paid Rs. 2,000 on signing the contract and the Balance in the following four instalments :

On 31-12-1981	2,800
On 31-12-1982	2,600
On 31-12-1983	2,400
On 31-12-1984	2,200

Ascertain cash price of the Tractor and prepare : (1) Tractor A/c (2) Interest Suspense A/c (3) Geeta Ltd. A/c (Vendor) in the Books of Ravi Ltd.

(K.U.D., April 1985)

Solution :

Ascertainment of Cash Price

				Interest	Cash Price
Start from last Instalment :					
On 31-12-1984	Instalment	2,200	× 10/110 =	200	2,000
	Less : Interest	200			
1-1-1984		2,000			
31-12-1983	*Add* : Instalment	2,400			
		4,400	× 10/110 =	400	2,000
	Less : Interest	400			
		4,000			
31-12-1982	*Add* : Instalment	2,600			
		6,600	× 10/110 =	600	2,000
	Less : Interest	600			
		6,000			
31-12-1981	*Add* : Instalment	2,800			
		8,800	× 10/110 =	800	2,000
				2,000	8,000
Cash Price 8,000			Total Amount paid		12,000
Add : 2,000					10,000
10,000 Total Cash Price			Total Interest		2,000

Year	Unpaid Balance	Interest @ 10%	Instalment	Cash Price paid	Balance of Cash Price		
1-1-81		—	2,000	2,000	10,000		
31-12-81	8,000	800	2,800	2,000	2,000	(Less)	1-1-81
					8,000		
31-12-82	6,000	600	2,600	2,000	2,000	(Less)	1982
					6,000		
31-12-83	4,000	400	2,400	2,000	2,000	(Less)	1983
					4,000		
31-12-84	2,000	200	2,200	2,000	2,000	(Less)	1984
		2,000	10,000	10,000			

In the Books of Ravi Ltd. (Purchaser)

Tractor A/c

1-1-1981	To Vendor A/c (Geeta Ltd. Cash Price)	10,000	31-12-81	By Depreciation A/c (@ 10% on 10,000)	1,000
				By Balance c/d	9,000
		10,000			10,000
1-1-82	To Balance b/d	9,000	31-12-82	By Depreciation A/c (@ 10% on 9,000)	900
				By Balance c/d	8,100
		9,000			9,000
1-1-83	Balance b/d	8,100	31-12-83	By Depreciation A/c (@ 10% on 8,100)	810
				By Balance c/d	7,290
		8,100			8,100
1-1-84	To Balance b/d	7,290	31-12-84	By Depreciation A/c (@ 10% on 7,290)	729
				By Balance c/d	6,561
		7,290			7,290
1-1-85	To Balance b/d	6,561			

Vendor (Geeta) A/c

1-1-81	To Bank A/c	2,000	1-1-81	By Tractor A/c	10,000
31-12-81	To Bank A/c	2,800		By Interest Suspense A/c	2,000
	To Balance c/d	7,200			
		12,000			12,000
31-12-82	To Bank A/c	2,600	1-1-82	By Balance b/d	7,200
	To Balance c/d	4,600			
		7,200			7,200
31-12-83	To Bank A/c	2,400	1-1-83	By Balance b/d	4,600
	To Balance c/d	2,200			
		4,600			4,600
31-12-84	To Balance A/c	2,200	1-1-84	By Balance b/d	2,200

Interest Suspense A/c

1-1-81	To Vendor A/c	2,000	31-12-81	By Interest A/c	800
				By Balance c/d	1,200
		2,000			2,000
1-1-82	To Balance b/d	1,200	31-12-82	By Interest A/c	600
				By Balance c/d	600
		1,200			1,200
1-1-83	To Balance b/d	600	31-12-83	By Interest A/c	400
				By Balance c/d	200
		600			600
1-1-84	To Balance b/d	200	31-12-84	By Interest A/c	200

Problem No. 31

Y Co. Ltd. purchased a Motor Car on Hire purchase system from Ashok Motors Ltd. on 1-1-81 and agreed to pay interest at 20% p.a. on unpaid Balance of Cash price. Y Co. Ltd. decided to depreciate the car by 20% p.a. on reducing balance method. Y Co. Ltd. paid Rs. 5,000 on signing the contract and the balance in the following instalments at the end of each year :

First Instalment	Rs. 9,000
Second Instalment	Rs. 8,000
Third Instalment	Rs. 7,000
Fourth Instalment	Rs. 6,000

Prepare Motor Car Account and Ashok Motors Ltd. Account in the books Y Co. Ltd.

(K.U.D., October 1985)

Solution :

Calculation of Interest and Cash Price included in Instalments

Instalments	Total Amount due at the end of the year	Interest 20/120	Cash Price	Instalment
Down Payment	—	—	5,000	5,000
IVth Instalment	6,000 × 20/120 =	1,000	5,000	6,000
Less : Interest	1,000			
	5,000			
Add : III Instalment	7,000			
	12,000 × 20/120 =	2,000	5,000	7,000
Less : Interest	2,000			
	10,000			

Instalments	Total Amount due at the end of the year		Interest 20/120	Cash Price	Instalment
Add : II Instalment	8,000				
	18,000	× 20/120 =	3,000	5,000	8,000
Less : Interest	3,000				
	15,000				
Add : Ist Instalment	9,000				
	24,000	× 20/120 =	4,000	5,000	9,000
			10,000	25,000	35,000
			Interest	Cash Price	Total Amount

In the Books of Y Co. Ltd.

Motor Car A/c

1-1-81	To Ashok Motor A/c	25,000	31-12-81	By Depreciation A/c @ 20% on 25,000	5,000
				By Balance c/d	20,000
		25,000			25,000
1-1-82	To Balance b/d	20,000	31-12-82	By Depreciation A/c @ 20%	4,000
				By Balance c/d	16,000
		20,000			20,000
1-1-83	To Balance b/d	16,000	31-12-83	By Depreciation A/c @ 20%	3,200
				By Balance c/d	12,800
		16,000			16,000
1-1-84	To Balance b/d	12,800	31-12-84	By Depreciation A/c @ 20%	2,560
				By Balance c/d	10,240
		12,800			12,800
1-1-85	To Balance b/d	10,240			

Ashok Motors Ltd. A/c

1-1-81	To Bank A/c (Down payment)	5,000	1-1-81	By Motor Car A/c (Cash Price)	25,000
31-12-81	To Bank A/c	9,000		By Interest A/c @ 20% on 20,000	4,000
	To Balance c/d	15,000			
		29,000			29,000
1-1-82	To Bank A/c	8,000	1-1-82	By Balance c/d	15,000
31-12-82	To Balance c/d	10,000	31-12-82	By Interest A/c	3,000
		18,000			18,000
1-1-83	To Bank A/c	7,000	1-1-83	By Balance c/d	10,000
31-12-83	To Balance c/d	5,000	31-12-83	By Interest A/c	2,000
		12,000			12,000
31-12-84	To Bank A/c	6,000	1-1-84	By Balance b/d	5,000
				By Interest A/c	1,000
		6,000			6,000

Problem No. 32

Mr. Ramesh purchased a Machinery on Hire Purchase system on 1-1-1980 of the Cash price of Rs. 27,300. Rs. 6,000 was payable as advance and the Balance in four yearly instalments of Rs. 6,000 each at the end of each year.

The Vendors charged interest @ 5% on outstanding balances.

Depreciation at the rate of 10% was written off each year on Diminishing Balance Method.

Show Machinery Accounts and Vendors Accounts in the Books of Mr. Ramesh.

(K.U.D., October 1984)

Solution :

Working Table showing amount of Interest included in each instalment

Date	Particulars	Instalment paid	Interest paid	Cash Price paid	Unpaid balance of Cash Price	Interest @ 5% on Unpaid Balance
1-1-80	Cash Price Due	—	—	—	27,300	
	Advance					
31-12-80	Cash Price due			6,000	6,000	
					21,300 @ 5%	1,065
	Instalment	6,000	1,065	4,935	4,935	
1-1-81	Cash Price due				16,365 @ 5%	818
31-12-81	Cash Instalment	6,000	818	5,182	5,182	
1-1-81	Cash Price due				11,183 @ 5%	559
31-12-82	Instalment	6,000	559	5,441	5,441	
1-1-83	Cash Price due				5,742 @ 5%	287
31-12-83	Instalment	6,000	258	5,742	5,742	
		24,000	2,700	27,300		
	Add : Advance	6,000				
		30,000				

Total Payment = Cash Price	27,300
Add : Interest	2,700
	30,000

Note : Last Instalment Interest being the difference between Instalment and cost price 6,000 – 5,742 = 258

In the Books of Mr. Ramesh

Machinery A/c

1-1-80	To Vendor A/c	27,300	31-12-80	By Depreciation A/c	2,730
				By Balance c/d	24,570
		27,300			27,300
1-1-81	To Balance b/d	24,570	31-12-81	By Depreciation	2,457
				By Balance c/d	22,113
		24,570			24,570
1-1-82	To Balance b/d	22,113	31-12-82	By Depreciation	2,211
				By Balance c/d	19,902
		22,113			22,113
1-1-83	To Balance b/d	19,902	31-12-83	By Depreciation	1,990
				By Balance c/d	17,912
		19,902			19,902
1-1-84	To Balance b/d	17,912			

Vendor A/c

1-1-80	To Bank A/c	6,000	1-1-80	By Machinery A/c	27,300
31-12-80	To Bank A/c	6,000	31-12-80	By Interest A/c	1,065
	To Balance c/d	16,365			
		28,365			28,365
31-12-81	To Bank A/c	6,000	1-1-81	By Balance b/d	16,365
	To Balance c/d	11,183	31-12-81	By Interest A/c	818
		17,183			17,183
31-12-82	To Bank A/c	6,000	1-1-82	By Balance b/d	11,183
	To Balance c/d	5,742	31-12-82	By Interest A/c	559
		11,742			11,742
31-12-83	To Bank A/c	6,000	1-1-83	By Balance b/d	5,742
				By Interest A/c (Being balance)	258
		6,000			6,000

In the Books of Vendor

(Vendor) Mr. Ramesh A/c

1-1-80	To Sales A/c	27,300	1-1-80	By Bank A/c	6,000
31-12-80	To Interest A/c	1,065	31-12-80	By Bank A/c	6,000
				By Balance c/d	16,365
		28,365			28,365
1-1-81	To Balance b/d	16,365	31-12-81	By Bank A/c	6,000
31-12-81	To Interest A/c	818		By Balance c/d	11,183
		17,183			17,183
1-1-82	To Balance b/d	11,183	31-12-82	By Bank A/c	6,000
31-12-82	To Interest A/c	559		By Balance c/d	5,742
		11,742			11,742
1-1-83	To Balance b/d	5,472	31-12-83	By Bank	6,000
31-12-82	To Interest A/c Being Balancing figure	258			
		6,000			6,000

In the Books of Mr. Ramesh Hire Purchaser

Journal Entries

Date		Particulars		Dr	Cr
1-1-80	(1)	Machinery A/c	Dr	27,300	
		To Hire Vendor A/c			27,300
		(Cash Price of Machinery purchased)			
	(2)	Hire Vendor A/c	Dr	6,000	
		To Bank A/c			6,000
		(Advance paid)			
31-12-80	(3)	Interest A/c	Dr	1,065	
		To Hire Vendor A/c			1,065
		(Being Interest @ 5% on 21,300 unpaid balance)			
	(4)	Hire Vendor A/c	Dr	6,000	
		To Bank A/c			6,000
		(Instalment due paid)			
	(5)	Depreciation A/c	Dr	2,730	
		To Machinery A/c			2,730
		(Being annual Depreciation @ 10%)			
	(6)	Profit & Loss A/c	Dr	3,795	
		To Interest A/c			1,065
		To Depreciation A/c			2,730
		(Interest and Depreciation A/c transferred)			
31-12-81	(1)	Interest A/c	Dr	818	
		To Hire Vendor A/c			818
		(Interest @ 5% on unpaid balance 16,365)			
	(2)	Hire Vendor A/c	Dr	6,000	
		To Bank A/c			6,000
		(Instalment paid)			
	(3)	Depreciation A/c	Dr	2,457	
		To Machinery A/c			2,457
		(Annual Depreciation @ 10% on 24,570)			
	(4)	Profit & Loss A/c	Dr	3,275	
		To Interest A/c			818
		To Depreciation A/c			2,457
		(Interest and Depreciation transferred)			
31-12-82	(1)	Interest A/c	Dr	559	
		To Hire Vendor A/c			559
		(Interest @ 5% on 11,183 Unpaid balance)			

Date		Particulars		Dr	Cr
	(2)	Hire Vendor A/c	Dr	6,000	
		To Bank A/c			6,000
		(Instalment paid)			
	(3)	Depreciation A/c	Dr	2,211	
		To Machinery A/c			2,211
		(Depreciation @ 10% on 21,113)			
	(4)	Profit & Loss A/c	Dr	2,770	
		To Interest A/c			559
		To Depreciation A/c			2,211
		(Interest and Depreciation A/c transferred)			
31-12-83	(1)	Interest A/c	Dr	258	
		To Hire Vendor A/c			258
		(Interest balancing figures)			
	(2)	Hire Vendor A/c	Dr	6,000	
		To Bank A/c			6,000
		(Instalment paid)			
	(3)	Depreciation A/c	Dr	1,990	
		To Machinery A/c			1,990
		(Depreciation 10% on 19,902)			
	(4)	Profit and Loss A/c	Dr	2,248	
		To Interest A/c			258
		To Depreciation A/c			1,990
		(Interest and Depreciation A/c transferred)			

Problem No. 33

Mr. Shrikant B.E. Mechanical Engineer decided to start workshop under self-employment scheme. He purchased on 1st January 1978 a machine on Hire purchase system. The total payment being Rs. 1,00,000 and the payment was to be made as under :

On signing the agreement on 1-1-1978	16,000
at the end of 1978	27,000
at the end of 1979	35,000
at the end of 1980	22,000

Interest was charged by the Vendor Co. @ 10% p.a. on unpaid Balance. Depreciation on machine was written off @ 10% p.a. on Diminishing Balance Ascertain cash price of the Machine and also show (a) Machine A/c and (b) Vendors A/c in the Books of purchaser.

(K.U.D., April 1982)

Solution :

Ascertainment of Cost Price

Start from last Instalment - Rate of Interest 10% p.a.

Last Instalment include interest.

$$\text{Formula} = \frac{\text{\% of include}}{100 + \%} \times \text{Amount}$$

End of + 1980	22,000	× 10/110	= 2,000	= 20,000
Less : Interest	2,000			
1-1-1980 Cost Price	20,000			
Add : 1979	35,000			
	55,000	× 10/110	= 5,000	= 30,000
Less : Interest	5,000			
1-1-79 Cost Price	50,000			
Add : 1978	27,000			
	77,000	× 10/110	= 7,000	= 20,000
Total Amount			14,000	70,000 + 16,000
				= 86,000 Cash Price
				14,000 Interest
Total Amount paid				1,00,000

In the Books of Purchaser

Machinery A/c

1-1-78	To Vendor A/c	86,000	31-12-78	By Depreciation A/c (@ 10% on 85,000)	8,600
				By Balance c/d	77,400
		86,000			86,000
1-1-79	To Balance b/d	77,400	31-12-79	By Depreciation (@ 10% on 77,400)	7,400
				By Balance c/d	69,660
		77,400			77,400
1-1-80	To Balance b/d	69,660	31-12-80	By Depreciation (@ 10% on 69,660)	6,966
				By Balance c/d	62,694
		69,660			69,660
1-1-81	To Balance b/d	62,694			

Vendor A/c

1-1-78	To Bank A/c	16,000	1-1-78	By Machinery A/c	86,000
	To Bank A/c	27,000		By Interest A/c	7,000
	To Balance A/c	50,000			
		93,000			93,000
31-12-79	To Bank A/c	35,000	1-1-79	By Balance b/d	50,000
	To Balance c/d	20,000		By Interest A/c	5,000
		55,000			55,000
31-12-80	To Bank A/c	22,000	1-1-80	By Balance b/d	20,000
				By Interest A/c (@ 10% on 20,000)	2,000
		22,000			22,000

Problem No. 34

On 1-1-1974 X Co. Ltd. bought from Machinery Co. Ltd. a machinery on instalment system and the cash price was Rs. 10,000 and the instalment price was Rs. 11,190 payable as to Rs. 2,120 on delivery, the balance being payable in five equal instalments. The books are closed on 31st December. X Co. Ltd. writes off depreciation @ 10% p.a. on diminishing balance method. The vendors charged interest at 4% p.a. on the unpaid Balance of cash price. Prepare the following accounts in the Books of X Co. Ltd. :

(a) Machinery Account.
(b) Vendor Account.

(K.U.D., October 1979)

In the Books of X Co. Ltd.

Machinery A/c

1-1-74	To Vendor A/c	10,200	31-12-74	By Depreciation A/c	1,020
				By Balance c/d	9,180
		10,200			10,200
1-1-75	To Balance b/d	9,180	31-12-75	By Depreciation A/c	918
				By Balance c/d	8,262
		9,180			9,180
1-1-76	To Balance b/d	8,262	31-12-76	Depreciation A/c	826
				By Balance c/d	7,436
		8,262			8,262
1-1-77	To Balance b/d	7,436	31-12-77	By Depreciation A/c	744
				By Balance c/d	6,692
		7,436			7,436
1-1-78	To Balance b/d	6,692	31-12-78	By Depreciation A/c	670
				By Balance c/d	6,022
		6,692			6,692

Vendor A/c

1-1-74	To Cash A/c Down Payment	2,190	1-1-74	By Machinery A/c Cash Price	10,200
31-12-74	To Cash A/c	1,800	31-12-74	By Interest (on 8,010 @ 4% p.a.)	320
	To Balance c/d	6,530			
		10,520			10,520
31-12-75	To Cash A/c	1,800	1-1-75	By Balance b/d	6,530
	To Balance c/d	4,991	31-12-75	By Interest A/c (@ 4% on 6,530)	261
		6,791			6,791
31-12-76	To Cash A/c	1,800	1-1-76	By Balance b/d	4,991
	To Balance c/d	3,391	31-12-76	By Interest A/c (@ 4% p.a.)	200
		5,191			5,191
31-12-77	To Cash A/c	1,800	1-1-77	By Balance b/d	3,391
	To Balance c/d	1,727	31-12-77	By Interest A/c	136
		3,527			3,527
31-12-78	To Cash	1,800	1-1-78	By Balance b/d	1,727
			31-12-78	By Interest A/c	73
		1,800			1,800

PROBLEMS ON REPOSSESSED STOCKS

Problem No. 35

Shri Prakash purchased 5 (five) Delivery vans from Tata Automobiles on 1-7-1985 under Hire purchase scheme. The cash price of each van is Rs. 70,000. The terms of agreement were as under : Payment of 20% of cash price at the time of delivery on 1-7-1985 and the balance in five half yearly instalments starting from 31-12-1985 along with interest at 5% per annum, Depreciation was written off @ 20% per annum on reducing balance method. The accounts were closed on 30th June each year.

Shri Prakash after having paid down payment and the first instalment on 31-12-1985 failed to pay, the second intalment was due on 30-6-1986. The vans were seized by the vendor. After negotiations the purchaser could return two vans to the vendor on the condition that the total amount paid upto this day less 25% would settle the amount due on the two vans taken in possession. The remaining three vans could be retained by the purchaser.

The vendor after taking in possession of the vans, spent Rs. 5,500 on repairs and sold them for Rs. 1,22,000 on 10-7-1986. Show the necessary Ledger Accounts in the books of both the parties.

(K.U.D., April 1991)

Solution :

Working Notes

I. Cash price of Vans purchased :

Cash price Rs. 70,000 × 5 =	3,50,000			
Less : Down payment on 1-7-85 @ 20% of 3,50,000	70,000			
Balance is five instalment	2,80,000			
Starting from 31-12-1985		I Instalment	56,000	
30-6-1986		II Instalment	56,000	Not paid
30-12-1986		III Instalment	56,000	
30-06-1987		IV Instalment	56,000	
31-12-1987		V Instalment	56,000	
			2,80,000	

II. Payment made :

On 1-7-1985		70,000
On 31-12-85 I Instalment :	56,000	
Add : Interest	7,000	63,000
Payment up to 31-12-1985		1,33,000

Value of Vans Left

No. of Vans	3	
Cash price	70,000	2,10,000
Less : Depreciation @ 20% on	2,10,000	
From 1-7-85 to 30-6-86 upto date of seizer of vans		42,000
On 30-6-1986 Balance on Vans Account		1,68,000

Value of Vans taken by Vendor

No. of Vans	2	
Cash Pride	70,000	1,40,000
Less Payments made		
on 1-7-85	70,000	
on 31-12-85	63,000	
Total Payment for 5 Vans	1,33,000	
Now for 2 Vans = 1,33,000 × 2/5	= 53,200	
Less : 25% of 53,200	= 13,300	39,900
Value of vans taken in possession by Vendor		1,00,100

In the books of Hire Purchaser

Delivery Vans A/c

1-7-85	To Tata Automobiles (Vendor A/c) (Cash price of vans)	3,50,000	30-6-86	By Depreciation (20% on 3,50,000)	70,000
				By Balance c/d	2,80,000
		3,50,000			3,50,000
1-7-86	To Balance b/d	2,80,000	30-6-86	By Tata Automobiles A/c	1,00,100
				By Profit & Loss A/c	11,900
				By Balance c/d	1,68,000
		2,80,000			2,80,000
1-7-86	To Balance b/d	1,68,000			

Tata Automobiles A/c (Vendor A/c)

1-7-85	To Bank A/c	70,000	1-7-85	By Delivery Vans A/c (Cash price)	3,50,000
31-12-85	To Bank A/c (56,000 + 7,000)	63,000	31-12-85	By Interest A/c @ 5% on 2,80,000 for one year 14,000 for 1/2 year 7,000	7,000
30-6-86	To Delivery Vans A/c Value of 2 Vans taken	1,00,100	30-6-86	By Interest @ 5% on 2,24,000 for 1/2 year	5,600
	To Balance	1,29,500			
		3,62,600			3,62,600

In the Books of Tata Auto Mobiles (Vendor)

Sri Prakash A/c (Hire Purchaser A/c)

1-7-85	To Sales A/c (5 × 70,000)	3,50,000	1-7-85	By Bank A/c	70,000
				By Bank A/c (56,000 + 7,000)	63,000
31-12-85	To Interest A/c @ 5% for 1/2 year on 2,80,000	7,000	30-6-86	By Re-possessed Stock	1,00,100
				By Balance c/d	1,29,500
30-6-86	To Interest A/c @ 5% for 1/2 year on 2.24,000	5,600			
		3,62,600			3,62,600

Re-possessed Stock A/c

30-6-86	To Hire purchaser A/c	1,00,100	1-7-86	By Bank A/c (Sales)	1,22,000
	To Bank Expenses on repairs	5,500			
	To Profit & Loss A/c Profit on Sale	16,400			
		1,22,000			1,22,000

Problem No. 36

The Delhi Transport Ltd. acquired 5 Tempos on Hire purchase system on 1-1-1984 from Bajaj Ltd. The cashdown price for each Tempo being Rs. 20,000. The price was payable in 5 instalments of Rs. 4,400 each every year the first being paid on signing the contract and the instalment including interest charged at 5% p.a. The Delhi Transport Ltd. decided to provide depreciation @ 10% p.a. calculated on the diminishing balance method. It paid the instalment due at the end of the first year but could not pay the next.

Give the necessary Ledger Account in the books of both parties for two years if the Bajaj Ltd. agreed to leave 3 Tempos with Hire purchaser adjusting the value of other 2 Tempos against the amount due. The Tempos were valued by Bajaj Ltd. on the basis of 20% depreciation on diminishing balance method annually. The Hire vendor spent Rs. 1,600 on getting these Tempos thoroughly overhauled and sold them for Rs. 35,200.

(Gulbarga, April 1987)

Solution :

On 1-1-1984 No. of Tempos purchased - 5		
Cash price of each Tempo	20,000	
Total for 5 Tempos	1,00,000	
Payments in instalments - 5 × 4,400	22,000	
On 1-1-1984 First instalment signing the agreement	22,000	
On 31-12-1984 Second instalment	22,000	
On 31-12-1985 Third instalment	22,000	not paid

For non payment of instalment due on 31-12-1985 vendor take back 2 Tempos valued @ cost *Less* 20% on diminishing balance method.

Value of Tempos Left		Value of Tempos taken	
Cost Price 20,000 × 3 =	60,000	Cost Price 20,000 × 2 =	40,000
1-1-1984		1-1-1984	
31-12-1984 *Less* Depreciation		31-12-1984 *Less* Depreciation	
@ 10%	6,000	@ 20%	8,000
	54,000		32,000
31-12-1985 *Less* Depreciation		31-12-1985 *Less* Depreciation	
@ 10%	5,400	@ 20%	6,400
Value of 3 Tempos	48,600	Value of 2 Tempos taken by vendor on 31-12-1985	25,600

In the Books of Delhi Transports Ltd.

Tempo A/c

1-1-84	To Bajaj Ltd. (Cost Price 20,000 × 5)	1,00,000	31-12-84	By Depreciation A/c @ 10%	10,000
				By Balance c/d	90,000
		1,00,000			1,00,000
1-1-85	To Balance b/d	90,000	31-12-85	By Depreciation A/c @ 10%	9,000
				By Bajaj Ltd. A/c (value of 2 Tempos taken back)	25,600
				By Profit & Loss A/c (Balancing figures being loss)	6,800
			31-12-85	By Balance c/d	48,600
		90,000			90,000

Bajaj Ltd. A/c (Hire Vendor A/c)

1-1-84	To Bank A/c (Down payment)	22,000	1-1-84	By Tempo A/c (Cost Price)	1,00,000
31-12-84	To Bank A/c	22,000	31-12-84	By Interest A/c	
	To Balance c/d	59,900		@ 5% on 78,000	3,900
		1,03,900			1,03,900
31-12-85	To Tempo A/c (2 Tempos value)	25,600	1-1-85	By Balance c/d	59,900
			31-12-85	By Interest A/c	2,995
	To Balance c/d	37,295		@ 5% on 59,900	
		62,895			62,895

In the Books of Bajaj Ltd. (Hire Vendor)

Delhi Transport Ltd. A/c (Hire Purchaser)

1-1-84	To Sales A/c (Cost of 5 × 20,000)	1,00,000	1-1-84	By Bank A/c (Down payment)	22,000
				By Bank A/c	22,000
31-12-84	To Interest A/c @ 5% on 78,000	3,900		By Balance c/d	59,900
		1,03,900			1,03,900
1-1-85	To Balance b/d	59,900	31-12-85	By Re-possessed Stock	25,600
	To Interest A/c @ 5% on 59,900	2,995		By Balance c/d	37,295
		62,895			62,895

Re-possessed Stock A/c

1-1-86	To Delhi Transport Ltd. (Hire purchaser)	25,600	1-1-86	By Bank A/c	35,200
	To Bank A/c (Expenses)	1,600			
	To Profit & Loss A/c (Profit on Sales)	8,000			
		35,200			35,200

Problem No. 37 (Extra-1)

Mr. Amar purchased a truck on Hire Purchaser system for Rs. 2,24,000. The payment to be made Rs. 60,000 down and 3 (Three) Instalments of Rs. 60,000 each at the end of each year. Rate of interest is charged at 5% p.a. Amar depreciated (Truck) Assets at 10% p.a. on written down value.

Because of financial difficulties Amar after having paid down payment and first instalment at the end of the year, could not pay second instalment and took possession of the truck. Seller after spending Rs. 1,400 on repairs of the truck sold it away for Rs. 1,26,440.

Open the Ledger Accounts in the books of both the parties.

Solution :

Working Table

(1) Cash Price of the Truck		2,24,000
Payments :		
Down Payment (paid)	60,000	
End of the Year I (paid)	60,000	
End of the Year II (paid)	60,000	
End of the Year III (paid)	60,000	2,40,000
Difference is interest payment		16,000

In the Books of Hire Purchaser

Truck A/c

Beginning			End of		
Ist Year	To Hire Vendor A/c (Cash Price)	2,24,000	Ist Year	By Depreciation A/c (10% on 2,24,000)	22,400
				By Balance c/d	2,01,600
		2,24,000			2,24,000
II Year	To Balance b/d	2,01,600	II Year	By Depreciation A/c 10% on 2,01,600	20,160
				By Hire Vendor A/c Assets taken back	1,17,810
				By Profit & Loss A/c Loss being balancing figure	63,630
		2,01,600			2,01,600

Hire Vendor A/c

Year ending			Year beginning		
I Year	To Bank A/c	60,000	I Year	By Truck A/c	2,24,000
	To Bank A/c	60,000		By Interest A/c (@ 5% on 1,64,000)	8,200
	To Balance c/d	1,12,200			
		2,32,000			2,32,000
	To Truck A/c (Assets taken back)	1,17,810	II Year Beginning	By Balance b/d	1,12,200
			End of Year	By Interest A/c (@ 5% on 1,12,200)	5,610
		1,17,810			1,17,810

Note : For non payment of II Instalment due at the end of II year. The Truck was taken by the Hire vendor and the Account of Hire purchaser is settled to balance due to Hire vendor.

In the Books of Hire Vendor

Hire Purchaser A/c (Mr. Amar)

I Year beginning			I Year Beginning		
	To Sales A/c	2,24,000		By Bank A/c (Down payment)	60,000
End of the Year	To Interest (@ 5% 1,64,000)	8,200	End of the Year	By Bank A/c	60,000
				By Balance c/d	1,12,200
		2,32,200			2,32,200
II Year beginning			End of the year		
	To Balance b/d	1,12,200		By Re-possessed Stock A/c	1,17,810
End of the year	To Interest A/c (@ 5% on 1,12,000)	5,610			
		1,17,810			1,17,810

Re-possessed Stock A/c

To Hire Purchaser A/c (Amar)	1,17,810	By Sales	1,26,440
To Repair Expenses A/c	1,400		
To Profit & Loss A/c (Profit on Sale)	7,230		
	1,26,440		1,26,440

Problem No. 38

The Belgaum Passenger Transport Company purchased on 1-1-1988 five Mini Passenger Buses on hire purchaser system. The Cash price of each of Rs. 1,75,000. The terms of payment are :

(a) Payment of 20% of the Cash Price at the time of delivery and the Balance in five half yearly instalments from 1-7-1988 with interest at 5% p.a.

The Belgaum Transport Company failed to pay the instalment due on 30-6-89 and it was agreed that the Hire Purchaser could retain three buses and return two buses to the vendor. The Vendor agreed to allow him a credit for the amount paid against these returned buses *less* 25% on original cost.

Show the necessary Accounts in the books of Belgaum Transport Co. assuming that the accounts are closed every year on 31st December. The Company (Purchaser) depreciates vehicles @ 20% on written down value.

The Vendor after taking possession of the two buses spent Rs. 13,750 on repairs and sold them Rs. 3,07,500.

Show the necessary Ledger Accounts in the books of Vendor also.

Solution :

Working Note

	Rs.		Date of Purchase
(1) Cash price			
Of no. of buses 5 × 1,75,000	8,75,000		1-1-1988
Payments :			
on 1-1-1988 20% of 8,75,000	1,75,000		
Half yearly instalment			
(1) 30-6-1988 — 20% 7,00,000	1,40,000	+ 35,000	interest at 5%
(2) 31-12-1988 — 20% 7,00,000	1,40,000	+ 28,000	interest 5% on 5,60,000
(3) 30-6-1989 — 20% 7,00,000	1,40,000	+ 21,000	on 4,20,000
(4) 31-12-1989 — 20% 7,00,000	1,40,000	+ 14,000	on 2,80,000
(5) 30-6-90 — 20% 7,00,000	1,40,000	+ 7,000	on 1,40,000
Total Cash price	7,00,000	1,05,000	
+ Down payment	1,75,000		
	8,75,000	1,05,000	
	Cash price	Interest	

Value of Buses retained		Value of Buses taken		
No. of Buses – 3		No. of Buses – 2		
Cash Price	1,75,00	Cash Price		1,75,000
Total Cash Price	5,25,000	Total Cash Price		3,50,000
Less : Depreciate @ 20%	1,05,000	*Less* : Depreciate @ 25% (87,500 for one Year)	87,500	
	4,20,000	On 30-6-89	43,750	1,31,250
Less : Depr. @ 20% = 84,000				
For 1/2 year	42,000			
Value of Buses retained :	3,78,000	Value of Buses taken :		2,18,750

In the Books of Hire Purchaser
Belgaum Passenger Transport A/c (Bus A/c)

1-1-88	To Hire Vendor A/c	8,75,000	31-12-88	By Depreciation A/c @ 20%	1,75,000
				By Balance c/d	7,00,000
		8,75,000			8,75,000
1-1-89	To Balance b/d	7,00,000	30-6-89	By Depreciation A/c 20% 1/2 Year	70,000
				By Hire Vendor A/c (Cost of 2 Buses taken back)	2,18,750
				By Profit & Loss A/c (Loss being balancing figure)	33,250
				By Balance c/d	3,78,000
		7,00,000			7,00,000

Hire Vendor A/c

1-1-88	To Bank A/c (Down Payment)	1,75,000	1-1-88	By Bus A/c	8,75,000
30-6-88	To Bank A/c (1,40,000 + 17,500)	1,57,500	30-6-88	By Interest A/c @ 5% on 7,00,000 for 1/2 year	17,500
31-12-88	To Bank A/c	1,54,000	31-12-88	By Interest A/c @ 5% on 5,60,000 for six months	14,000
	To Balance c/d	4,20,000			
		9,06,500			9,06,500
30-6-88	To Buses A/c (Value bus transfer)	2,18,750	1-1-89	By Balance b/d	4,20,000
To Balance c/d		2,11,750	30-6-89	By Interest A/c (@ 5% on 4,20,000)	10,500
		4,30,500			4,30,500
			1-7-89	By Balance b/d	2,11,750

In the Books of Hire Vendor
Hire Purchaser A/c
(Belgaum Passenger Transport Co.)

1-1-88	To Sales A/c Cash Price 5 × 1,75,000	8,75,000	1-1-88	By Bank A/c (Down payment)	1,75,000
30-6-88	To Interest A/c @ 5% on 7,00,000 for six months	17,500	30-6-88	By Bank A/c (1,40,000 + 17,500)	1,57,500
			30-12-88	By Bank A/c (14,000 + 14,000)	1,54,000
31-12-88	To Interest A/c @ 5% on 5,60,000 for six months	14,000		By Balance c/d	4,20,000
		9,06,500			9,06,500
1-1-89	To Balance b/d	4,20,000	30-6-89	By Repossessed Stock A/c	2,18,750
30-6-89	To Interest A/c @ 5% on 4,20,000 for 6 months	10,500		By Balance c/d	2,11,750
		4,30,500			4,30,500
1-7-89	To Balance b/d	2,11,750			

Re-possessed Stock A/c

To Hire Vendor A/c	2,18,750	By Sales A/c	3,07,500
To Bank A/c (Expenses on repairs)	13,750		
To Profit & Loss A/c (Profit on Sale)	75,000		
	3,07,500		3,07,500